P9-ASJ-162

DISPUTED PLAYS OF WILLIAM SHAKESPEARE

DISPUTED PLAYS OF WILLIAM SHAKESPEARE

Edited and with a commentary by William Kozlenko

HAWTHORN BOOKS, INC.
PUBLISHERS / NEW YORK

DISPUTED PLAYS OF WILLIAM SHAKESPEARE

Copyright © 1974 by William Kozlenko. Copyright under International and Pan-American Copyright Conventions. All rights reserved, including the right to reproduce this book or portions thereof in any form, except for the inclusion of brief quotations in a review. All inquiries should be addressed to Hawthorn Books, Inc., 260 Madison Avenue, New York, New York 10016. This book was manufactured in the United States of America and published simultaneously in Canada by Prentice-Hall of Canada, Limited, 1870 Birchmount Road, Scarborough, Ontario.

Library of Congress Catalog Card Number: 73-18898
ISBN: 0-8015-2142-4
1 2 3 4 5 6 7 8 9 10

This book is dedicated
to the memory
of my son Paul

Contents

Preface

The scope of this collection is deliberately restricted. I have attempted to deal, as the title of the book indicates, only with those plays written by or in part ascribed to Shakespeare, which, though excluded from the First Folio, nevertheless reveal traces of his authorship or of his revision.

The classical demonstration of the presence of Shakespeare's hand in a disputed play is the essay by R. W. Chambers in his *Man's Unconquerable Mind* (1939) identifying at least one scene in the banned play *Sir Thomas More* as Shakespeare's contribution. In this work Chambers has much to say about those apocryphal plays that some critics have questioned as having been written or revised by Shakespeare.

In this regard I have also leaned heavily on other well-known Shakespearean scholars—namely, Kenneth Muir, J. A. Symonds, Baldwin Maxwell, J. Q. Adams, Thomas Marc Parrott, J. M. Nosworthy, Ashley H. Thorndike, Hallett Smith, D. A. Traversi, and E. M. W. Tillyard, among others—whose arguments and comments I found indispensable in preparing my own exegesis of the disputed plays.

Finally, I cannot close without acknowledging my deep gratitude to James Neyland, senior editor of Hawthorn Books. This collection would never have materialized were it not for his help and advice. His patience and faith in this project were to me a constant encouragement.

Publisher's Note

The texts of the plays included here have been reproduced photographically from *The Doubtful Plays of Shakspere,* edited by Henry Tyrrell and published in 1860 by John Tallis and Company (London and New York) as a companion volume to *The Complete Works of Shakspere* (3 volumes), edited by J. O. Halliwell. Also included in that volume, but not included here, are *Titus Andronicus; Pericles, Prince of Tyre; Fair Em, The Miller's Daughter of Manchester;* and *The Two Noble Kinsmen.*

For the student, Tyrrell's notes to each play have also been reproduced from the original volume. It should also be noted that the act and scene division of *Arden, of Feversham, The Merry Devil of Edmonton, Mucedorus,* and *The Birth of Merlin* are Tyrrell's own contribution, these distinctions not having been made previously for these plays.

Introduction

As editor of this collection of disputed plays by William Shakespeare, I find myself in the anomalous position of attempting not only to defend an apparent inconsistency but to offer, at the same time, critical and historical evidence that, despite the dubious question of authorship, Shakespeare did in fact have a hand either in writing some of these plays or, at least, revising them for use by his own acting company or other acting companies during his years as a practicing dramatist.

Between 1586 and 1592, we lose all traces of Shakespeare. We know only that he must have been an active member of a company of players, that of the Earl of Leicester's owned the Blackfriars' and afterwards the Globe theatre. It has also been proved by several passages in contemporary writings that, partly as actor, partly as adapter of older plays, he had, at the age of twenty-eight, made a certain name for himself and had therefore become the object of envy and hatred.

While in his youth Shakespeare had to adapt or retouch the plays of other dramatists, in later life he sometimes collaborated with younger men; and the company to which Shakespeare had attached himself and in which he had already attracted notice as a promising poet would most likely have employed him to revise and refurbish the older pieces of the repertory. The theatrical announcements of the period, according to Georg Brandes, (7)*

---

* A parenthetical number following an author's name corresponds to a numbered entry in the Bibliography; it will be supplied for the first reference to a work, here and in the introduction to each individual play (or for each reference when the Bibliography lists more than one work by the author).

would show us, even if we had no other evidence, that it was a constant practice to rewrite old plays in order to heighten their powers of attraction. It is announced, for instance, that such and such a play will be acted as it was last presented before Her Majesty or before this or that nobleman. Playwrights sold their works outright to the theatre for such sums as five or ten pounds, or for a share in the receipts. As the interests of the theatre demanded that plays should not at first be printed, in order that rival companies might not obtain possession of them, they remained in manuscript (unless pirated), and the players or printers could accordingly do what they pleased with the text.

As an example of how Shakespeare's fame as a "play doctor" had grown by 1592, Hallett Smith (42) cites Robert Greene's bitter complaint in his *Groats Worth of Wit* that Sakespeare had almost a monopoly of dramatic production in London and that he had made himself necessary not to one stage company but to players in general. During that time he was probably writing not only for his own acting company but for those of the Earl of Pembroke and the Earl of Sussex. It may further be shown, according to Richard Simpson, (41) that some of the so-called "doubtful plays" attributed to Shakespeare by some historians are in fact early productions of his pen, written at the demand of various companies. When the plays of other dramatists were acted by these companies, for which Shakespeare was, in Greene's mocking phrase, *Iohannes factotum*, they were often altered or rewritten by Shakespeare. This was a task he would naturally be called upon to undertake, and, when he had completed it, the style of the plays would often have been transformed into his own.

In presenting this collection of disputed plays by Shakespeare, we are brought face to face with the problem of whether works have been falsely or correctly attributed to this poet. In dealing with these so-called "doubtful plays," we are "wandering about in worlds not realized," tantalized by suspicious tradition. It seems likely that before Shakespeare began writing his mature work, he spent some years of strenuous activity as an apprentice playwright for the company of players he had joined. In this inchoate period, he was probably employed in revising earlier compositions or writing new ones for the stage, and at the same time he also collaborated with other dramatists—among them John Fletcher and William Rowley, to name only two—in the preparation of old and new plays for his acting company. Shakespeare, moreover, as is clearly proved by the gradual emergence of his final style, by his slow self-disentanglement from rhyme, and by his lingering fondness for prettiness and conceits, did not begin as so fixed and unmistakable a playwright as Christopher Marlow.

When, therefore, there is any scintilla of evidence, external or internal, in favor of his influence or authorship, we are, as J. A. Symonds (44) insists, bound to weigh the question and not to discard a work because it may seem to us palpably dubious or, measured against his more mature work, unworthy.

Hence, if we wish to find traces of true individuality in the plays of Shakespeare's youth, we must look, as D. A. Traversi (48) suggests, not to the complete work, which is still derivative and artificial in conception, but primarily to individual turns of phrase, the occasional striking choice of a word or image to be discerned in otherwise commonplace passages of verse.

Furthermore, according to the same writer, the development of Shakespeare's art took place at first within dramatic conventions established by less gifted authors. The first plays from his hand show him mainly concerned with perfecting his mastery of the instruments of his craft—so much so that the earliest works connected with his name have sometimes been regarded as the reshaping for performance by his own company of plays originally written by other hands.

The significant question we have to ask ourselves, therefore, is, Is the play under consideration, even though a little or obscure work, a work of merit that is written by or retouched by Shakespeare's hand? Is it a play on which he engrafted fresh scenes of incontestable mastery and poetic beauty? If so, it finds its analogue in *Edward III* or in *Pericles.* Is it one in which he worked with a collaborator? If so, we may compare it with *The Two Noble Kinsmen.* The fine play *Arden, of Feversham* is another example of an early effort that is, for Symonds and other critics, the ripe production of a dramatic artist, even though it does not resemble in style or theme any of Shakespeare's canonical plays. What marks *Arden, of Feversham,* in the eyes of this writer and others, is considerable grasp of character, black humor, absence of fancy and euphuism, and baldness of blank verse, sparely relieved by decorative or impassioned rhetoric. But the domestic tragedy was a well-defined species aiming, as the Epilogue to *Arden* states, at nakedness and "simple truth" without "filed points" and "glozing stuff." Shakespeare may therefore have deliberately suppressed his own early manner when he was called upon to produce a domestic tragedy for the players of his own company.

Internal evidence has been adduced for the Shakespearean authorship of some of these apocryphal plays. According to careful investigation by Kenneth Muir (28) and other critics, the evidence includes resemblances in versification, in vocabulary, in treatment of similar themes, in imagery, and especially in the use of the same image clusters.

Although it had no immediate influence when it was published in 1794, in recent years Walter Whiter's *Specimen of a Commentary on Shakespeare* has acquired considerable importance as the first book in which Shakespeare's imagery was systematically studied. Its chief merit is in its demonstration that the imagery is often connected by unconscious puns or other innate links. Whiter was the first, incidentally, to point out iterative imagery and image clusters such as the famous one of "flatterers, dogs and melting sweets" (as quoted by Muir), which was later rediscovered by E. E. Kellett and Caroline Spurgeon.

The presence of the same image clusters in the disputed plays and their absence in the work of rival dramatists would seem to go far toward establishing if not Shakespeare's sole authorship of a doubtful play or scene, at least his hand in writing it. The occurrence of these image clusters in such plays is apparently significant to Muir because an imitator is quite unlikely to have had the same imagistic associations.

In addition to image clusters, Kenneth Muir uses vocabulary tests to show that an apocryphal play or scene contains unusual words to be found also in Shakespeare's acknowledged works. These tests reveal that the incidence of coinages and of words not before used by Shakespeare corresponds to their incidence in his later plays.

Moreover, we know for a fact that, though John Heminges and Henry Condell's inclusions were in the main sound, there is considerable evidence that, for one reason or another, they did not include all the plays in which Shakespeare had a hand.

Francis Meres mentions, for example, in his *Palladis Tamia* a *Love's Labour's Won*, and some new evidence for the existence of a play of that title has recently been discovered by Professor Thomas W. Baldwin. It has not come down to us under that title, but it may be an alternative title to *All's Well That Ends Well,* as Baldwin and Muir postulate, or (if we are to believe Leslie Hotson) of *Troilus and Cressida.* Another instance is that of a play performed at court by Shakespeare's company in 1613, apparently entitled *The History of Cardenio* and based on an episode in Cervantes' *Don Quixote.* It was advertised by the publisher as being by Shakespeare and Fletcher, but Heminges and Condell did not include it in the First Folio either.

Perhaps, as Joseph Quincy Adams (1) theorizes, when Heminges and Condell instituted a search for Shakespeare's own manuscripts of these plays, it was discovered that they had been destroyed or mislaid; they may have perished in the printer's office or through accident, as, for example, in the burning of the Globe in 1613.

Whatever the cause, Heminges and Condell thought fit to omit those plays in which Shakespeare's task was merely that of reviser. On these grounds they excluded *Pericles*, despite the fact that it was published as Shakespeare's in his lifetime and contains scenes and passages that no one denies are his. Possibly they intended also to exclude *Timon of Athens*, which was set up and printed to fill the gap originally held open for *Troilus and Cressida.* By the same standard, they also excluded *The Two Noble Kinsmen*, ascribed by the publisher to Shakespeare and Fletcher; *A Yorkshire Tragedy*; and many other original and revised plays of which prompt copies were doubtless at their disposal, which were later attributed to Shakespeare by critics and scholars in various folios and quarto editions. There is reason to believe that Shakespeare also contributed at least one revised scene to the banned play *Sir Thomas More.* It has been forcefully argued, and, in fact, a reasoned case can be made out, that there are unmistakable traces of Shakespeare's authorship in the play *Edward III.*

In judging whether or not a disputed play is by Shakespeare, we may find, as Muir does, that the external evidence of his hand in plays not included in the First Folio by Heminges and Condell is unsubstantial. We are compelled to rely for the most part on internal evidence that, from the nature of things, is somewhat subjective but nevertheless still valid and difficult to disprove.

Finally, it has been estimated that about twenty of Shakespeare's plays were never issued in printed form, including *Edmund Ironside; The Second Maiden's Tragedy; The Birth of Hercules,* based on a play by Plautus, which was discovered recently in the British Museum by the German Shakespearean scholar Dr. Dieter Schamp; and several that are irretrievably lost, among them *The History of Cardenio,* mentioned above; *The History of King Stephen; Duke Humphrey, a tragedy;* and *Iphis and Iantha or a marriage without a man, a Comedy.*

King Edward the Third

It was in 1760 that the historical play *King Edward the Third,* after sedulous research, was first seriously and definitely ascribed to Shakespeare by Edward Capell. In the Introduction to his volume *Prolusions, or Select Pieces of Ancient Poetry,* he puts forth the argument of Shakespeare's authorship boldly and persuasively. In addition to Capell, the number of critics and scholars who concur that this play is a remarkable early work by Shakespeare includes Alfred Tennyson, J. P. Collier, A. F. Hopkinson, Ludwig Tieck, A. Teetgen, Kenneth Muir, Georg Brandes, F. W. Moorman, J. A. Symonds, and J. O. Halliwell-Phillips, to name only a few.

Moorman was of the opinion that Shakespeare revised *Edward III* between 1590 and 1596, after the piece had been "sundry times played about the city of London." Based on Bandello's story of the Countess of Salisbury and Holinshed's digest of Froissart's *Chronicles,* it was published in 1596, under the title *The Reign of King Edward the Third,* after it had already enjoyed considerable popularity upon the stage.

To Symonds (44) the play is not, like the three parts of *Henry VI,* a composite, conglomerated piece of patchwork, but a finished production. It displays unity of style sufficient to justify a belief that it was written as we possess it; and this style is of a high order. It is indeed so good that it makes us think of Shakespeare in one of his finest periods of lyricism, or of Shakespeare following the track of Christopher Marlowe. If, however, *Edward III* is by another author and revised by Shakespeare, Sir Edmund Chambers, (10) for one, supports the view that Shakespeare wrote not only the Countess and Warwick scenes but also Act IV, Scene iv. Several other English critics, among them Halliwell-Phillips (18) have attributed *Edward III* in part to Shakespeare, claiming that at least the better scenes must have been retouched by him. His individual touch may be recognized in several passages; and especially noteworthy are the following lines from a speech by **Warwick**:

> A spacious field of reasons could I urge,
> Between his glory, daughter, and thy shame:
> That poison shows worst in a golden cup;
> Dark night seems darker by the lightning flash;
> Lilies, that fester, smell far worse than weeds;
> And every glory that inclines to sin,
> The shame is treble by the opposite.
>
> [II. i]

The line "Lilies, that fester, smell far worse than weeds" reappears as the last line of Shakespeare's Sonnet XCIV.

More recently, Miss Mary Bell (in an unpublished thesis, Liverpool, 1959) has forcefully argued that an examination of the compounding of words, phrases, and image clusters provides substantial evidence of Shakespeare's authorship of *Edward III*. She further shows that a comparison of *Henry VI* and *Edward III* reveals a close affinity between the vocabularies of these plays.

The first group of images tabulated evokes a distinct contrast, as Kenneth Muir (28) also implies, between appearance and reality, between true beauty and false:

> These ragged walls no testimony are
> What is within. . . .
>
> [I. ii]

> And truth hath pull'd the vizard from his face. . . .
>
> [I. i]

> Thus have I, in his majesty's behalf,
> Apparel'd sin in virtuous sentences,
> And dwell upon thy answer in his suit.
>
> [II. i]

> . . . Deck an ape
> In tissue, and the beauty of the robe
> Adds but the greater scorn unto the beast.
>
> [Ibid.]

> Away, loose silks of wavering vanity!
>
> [II. ii]

> . . . my passion;
> Which he shall shadow with a vail of lawn. . . .
>
> [II. i]

And with a strumpet's artificial line
To paint thy vicious and deformed cause,
Be well assur'd, the counterfeit will fade,
And in the end thy foul defects be seen. . . .

[III. ii]

With the last passage we may compare the following one from *Antony and Cleopatra*:

And is become the bellows and the fan
To cool a gypsy's lust. . . .
Take but good note, and you shall see in him
The triple pillar of the world transform'd
Into a strumpet's fool.

[I. i. 12]

Clothing and disguise images are used in *Edward III* for much the same purpose as in *Much Ado About Nothing*—and indeed, as Muir points out, in much Elizabethan literature.

The images borrowed from the precious metals and treasure symbolize the value of love and the counterfeit nature of adultery (and also, as we shall note later, in the case of silver, as a metaphor to describe old age):

For she is all the treasure of our land. . . .

[II. i]

And be enriched by thy sovereign's love.

[Ibid.]

Why dost thou tip men's tongues with golden words,
And peize their deeds with weight of heavy lead . . . ?

[Ibid.]

But, soft, here comes the treasure of my spirit.

[Ibid.]

Of her, whose ransack'd treasury hath task'd
The vain endeavor of so many pens. . . .

[II. ii]

He, that doth clip, or counterfeit your stamp,
Shall die, my lord: And will your sacred self
Commit high treason 'gainst the king of heaven,
To stamp his image in forbidden metal,
Forgetting your allegiance and your oath?

[II. i]

The images of the sun, moon, and stars, as in Shakespeare's sonnets, are used by King Edward to symbolize love and beauty:

> What is she, when the sun lifts up his head,
> But like a fading taper, dim and dead?
> My love shall brave the eye of heaven at noon,
> And, being unmask'd, outshine the golden sun.
>
> [II. i]

> Say, she hath thrice more splendour than the sun,
> That her perfection emulates the sun,
> That she breeds sweets as plenteous as the sun,
> That she doth thaw cold winter like the sun,
> That she doth cheer fresh summer like the sun,
> That she doth dazzle gazers like the sun.
> And, in this application to the sun,
> Bid her be free and general as the sun;
> Who smiles upon the basest weed that grows,
> As lovingly as on the fragrant rose.
>
> [Ibid.]

> ... like an humble shadow,
> It haunts the sun-shine of my summer's life.
>
> [Ibid.]

> Now, in the sun alone it doth not lie,
> With light to take light from a mortal eye. . . .
>
> [I. ii]

> ... alas, she wins the sun of me,
> For that is she herself. . . .
>
> [II. ii]

> ... thy presence, like the April sun. . . .
>
> [I. ii]

> But love has eyes as judgment to his steps,
> 'Till too much loved glory dazzles them.
>
> [II. ii]

> For here two day stars, that mine eyes would see,
> More than the sun, steal mine own light from me.
>
> [I. ii]

Apart from the image clusters appearing in *Edward III* as well as in several plays by Shakespeare, many other passages in *Edward III* have multiple links with single passages in Shakespeare's works. The pun on "appar'd" and "suit" noted above reappears in *As You Like It* (IV.i.88–89), and in both contexts the pun is closely followed by mention of a solicitor or attorney. A few lines later in *Edward III* (II.i), a passage contains "blood," "leprous," "die," "envenometh," "dug," and "sin." This may be compared with the speech of the ghost in *Hamlet* (I.v.42–79) which contains "leperous distilment," "blood," "milk" (cf. "dug"), and "sin."

A few more examples are given by Miss Bell of less extended parallels. The pun on "habit," whether intentional or not, in the line:

> Whose habit rude, and manners blunt and plain
>
> [I. ii]

may be compared with a similar juxtaposition in the following:

> Or by some habit that too much o'er-leavens
> The form of plausive manners . . . .
>
> [*Hamlet* I. iv. 29–30]

> the manner how: . . . in the habit of some sir of note. . . .
>
> [*Twelfth Night* III. iv. 79–81]

The same wordplay occurs in *Love's Labour's Lost*:

> My lady (to the manner of the days)
> In courtesy gives undeserving praise.
> We four indeed confronted were with four
> In Russian habit.
>
> [V. ii. 365–68]

The comparison of a face to a book and the juxtaposition of "face," "matter," and "printed" are cited by Miss Bell in the following lines:

> . . . that very fear indeed,
> Which is ghastly printed in thy face:
> What is the matter?
>
> [IV. v]

This passage may also correspond to several in plays by Shakespeare, as, for example:

> Although the print be little, the whole matter
> And copy of the father—eye, nose, lip,
> The trick of 's frown . . .
>
> [*The Winter's Tale* II. iii. 98–100]

Your face, my Thane, is as a book where men
May read strange matters.

[*Macbeth* I. v. 63–64]

The lines of the Countess of Salisbury alluding to "ore":

. . . like a country swain,
Whose habit rude, and manners blunt and plain,
Presageth nought; yet inly beautify'd
With bounty's riches, and fair hidden pride:
For, where the golden ore doth bury'd lie,
The ground, undeck'd with nature's tapestry,
Seems barren, sere, unfertile, fruitless, dry. . . .

[I. ii]

may be compared with these of the queen in *Hamlet:*

To draw apart the body he hath kill'd;
O'er whom his very madness, like some ore
Among a mineral of metals base,
Shows itself pure. He weeps for what is done. . . .

[IV. i. 24–27]

Another speech in *Edward III,* which perhaps contains a quibble on "ore":

For I will stain my horse quite o'er with blood,
And double-gild my spurs . . .

[IV. iv]

may be compared, as Muir informs us, with "double gild his treble guilt" (2 *Henry IV* IV. v. 129), and with Lady Macbeth's determination to "gild the faces of the grooms" (*Macbeth* II. ii. 56).

A description in the same scene of *Edward III*:

. . . the banners, bannerets,
And new-replenish'd pendants, cuffs the air,
And beat the winds, that, for their gaudiness,
Struggles to kiss them.

[IV. iv]

looks forward to a passage in *Macbeth:*

Where the Norweyan banners flout the sky
And fan our people cold.

[I. ii. 49–50]

And, as Muir explains. it may also be compared to the famous description of Cleopatra's first meeting with Antony:

> Purple the sails, and so perfumed that
> The winds were lovesick with them; the oars were silver,
> Which to the tune of flutes kept stroke, and made
> The water which they beat to follow faster,
> As amorous of their strokes.
>
> [*Antony and Cleopatra* II. ii. 198–202]

Here, as in the last-quoted passage from *Edward III,* there is also a lavish use of "gold" and "silver." And a phrase in *Edward III,* "eyeless terror of all-ending night" (IV. iv), is paralleled by "eyeless night" in *King John* (V. vi. 12).

There now remains to be considered the relationship between *Edward III* and plays known to be by Shakespeare. According to Muir, the resemblances between the Countess scenes and the Lady Grey scene in *3 Henry VI* may be due to the fact that the author of *Edward III* was deliberately imitating Shakespeare's early play. The resemblances between the battle scenes of *Edward III* and those of *Henry V* may be explained as Shakespeare's imitation of a play he had seen, read, or performed. But Angelo's temptation of Isabella in *Measure for Measure* offers more substantial grounds for believing that Shakespeare wrote the Countess scenes in *Edward III.* In both plays a virtuous woman preserves her chastity against the assaults of a ruler, although Edward chides old Lodowick when the latter describes the Countess as "more fair, and chaste, than is the queen of shades" with a punning retort:

> I did not bid thee talk of chastity—
> To ransack so the treasure of her mind;
> For I had rather have her chas'd than chaste.
>
> [II. i]

In both plays the heroines attack the abuse of authority. And Warwick's lines about the ape, already quoted:

> An evil deed, done by authority,
> Is sin, and subornation: Deck an ape
> In tissue, and the beauty of the robe
> Adds but the greater scorn unto the beast
>
> [II. i]

appear, to Muir, to have suggested the following passages:

> ... proud man,
> Drest in a little brief authority,
> Most ignorant of what he's most assur'd
> (His glassy essence), like an angry ape,
> Plays such fantastic tricks before high heaven
> As make the angels weep. ...
>
> [*Measure for Measure* II. ii. 117–22]

> Foul subornation is predominant,
> And equity exil'd your highness' land.
>
> [*2 Henry VI* III. i. 145–46]

The same writer compares Warwick's admonition to his daughter:

> That sin doth ten times aggravate itself,
> That is committed in a holy place ...
>
> [II. i]

with Angelo's asking himself:

> Shall we desire to raze the sanctuary,
> And pitch our evils there?
>
> [*Measure for Measure* II. ii. 171–72]

Warwick declares:

> The freshest summer's day doth soonest taint
> The loathed carrion that it seems to kiss ...
>
> [II. i]

And Angelo cries:

> ... But it is I
> That, lying by the violet in the sun,
> Do as the carrion does, not as the flowr,
> Corrupt with virtuous season.
>
> [*Measure for Measure* II. ii. 165–68]

The Countess speaks of "the dangerous rein of liberty" (II. i.); Angelo tells Isabella:

> And now I give my sensual race the rein
>
> [*Measure for Measure* II. iv. 160]

and Claudio declares that his restraint comes from "too much liberty" (Ibid., I. ii. 129).

Finally, the Countess compares counterfeiting coins with adultery, in a passage quoted earlier:

> He, that doth clip, or counterfeit your stamp
> Shall die, my lord: And will your sacred self
> Commit high treason 'gainst the king of heaven,
> To stamp his image in forbidden metal,
> Forgetting your allegiance and your oath?
>
> [II. i]

Angelo similarly declares:

> It were as good
> To pardon him that hath from nature stol'n
> A man already made, as to remit
> Their saucy sweetness that do coin heaven's image
> In stamps that are forbid.
>
> [*Measure for Measure* II. iv. 42–46]

To E. M. W. Tillyard (46), *Edward III,* for all its brightness and glitter, is also one of the most intellectual and steadily thoughtful of the chronicle plays. Especially evident in this play, as in the sonnets and plays, is Shakespeare's brooding preoccupation with time and old age, using the metaphor to describe both. In *Edward III* the young Prince says:

> Now, Audley, sound those silver wings of thine,
> And let those milk-white messengers of time
> Show thy time's learning in this dangerous time. . . .
>
> [IV. iv]

Metellus in *Julius Caesar,* urging the inclusion of Cicero in the murder plot, declaims:

> O, let us have him! for his silver hairs
> Will purchase us a good opinion. . . .
>
> [II. i. 144–45]

The theme reoccurs consistently:

> O gentlemen, the time of life is short!
> To spend that shortness basely were too long
> If life did ride upon a dial's point,
> Still ending at the arrival of an hour.
>
> [*1 Henry IV* V. ii. 82–85]

But thoughts the slaves of life, and life time's fool,
And time, that takes survey of all the world,
Must have a stop.
                            [Ibid., V. iv. 81–83]

... To beguile the time,
Look like the time; bear welcome in your eye,
Your hand, your tongue; look like the innocent flower,
But be the serpent under't.
                            [*Macbeth* I. v. 64–67]

Love's not Time's fool, though rosy lips and cheeks
Within his bending sickle's compass come.
Love alters not with his brief hours and weeks,
But bears it out even to the edge of doom.
                            [Sonnet CXVI]

Enrich the time to come with smooth-fac'd peace,
With smiling plenty, and fair prosperous days!
                            [*Richard III* V. v. 33–34]

Well, Time is the old justice that examines all such offenders,
and let Time try again.
                            [*As You Like It* IV. i. 203–4]

And thus the whirligig of time brings in his revenges.
                            [*Twelfth Night* V. i. 384–85]

Misshapen Time, copesmate of ugly Night,
Swift subtle post, carrier of grisly care,
Eater of youth, false slave to false delight,
Base watch of woes, sin's packhorse, virtue's snare!
Thou nursest all, and murth'rest all that are.
  O, hear me then, injurious, shifting Time!
  Be guilty of my death, since of my crime.
                            [*The Rape of Lucrece* 925–31]

    D. A. Traversi suggests that a sense of the hostility of time is fundamental not only to the sonnets but to the plays of this period in Shakespeare's career. The theme was indeed a commonplace of the age; it was associated with the Platonizing philosophy of the court poets and with the religious "pessimism" of medieval tradition. Natural fear of the action of time was not balanced by any residue of Christian morality, still less by any sense of the significance or inevitability of death. Renaissance feeling regarded time as the enemy and solvent of personal experience, which it wears remorselessly into insensibility. Shakespeare gave this feeling magnificent expression in his line

> Devouring Time, blunt thou the lion's paws
> [Sonnet XIX]

where the epithet "devouring," which belongs naturally to the lion, is transferred to time, thus creating a very subtle balance of emotions. The lion as the king of beasts (as well as the symbol of English power, and therefore of the English monarch), naturally raises associations of splendid life and activity as well as menacing terror; but the transfer of "devouring" indicates that all this activity is self-consuming, a wearing down, a pure annihilation, of life. The verb "blunt" shows the typical sensing of the intangible in terms of the life of the fingertips; it simply makes more intense by contrast the life that is subdued by the blunting action of mutability. What is rooted in time, time itself destroys. If man, as a temporal unity of body and spirit, can perceive spiritual values only in the guise of time, it is equally true that his perceptions are, in time, fatally transient.

Traversi concludes that the whole of Shakespeare's tragic experience, in its personal, intimate aspect, can be described as reaction to his consciousness of the tragic implications of the temporal nature of man. The final ambiguity lies in the experience itself, in the simultaneous fulfillment and destruction of the values of human life by time.

Finally, so much has been written indicating Shakespeare's probable share in *Edward III* that Tillyard finds its Shakespearean affinities cannot be doubted. Likewise, Muir affirms that there are many parallels between scenes and passages in *Edward III* and genuine plays of Shakespeare. To the same writer, the strongest argument for Shakespeare's authorship of part of *Edward III* is the presence of close parallels with *Henry V* and *Measure for Measure*. One theory that would cover all the facts—and it is difficult to think of another that would—is that Shakespeare was hastily revising a play by another dramatist, entirely rewriting certain scenes, which contain some of Shakespeare's characteristic mannerisms, and leaving the remainder with comparatively few alterations.

PERSONS REPRESENTED.

EDWARD THE THIRD, *King of* England.
Appears, Act I. sc. 1; sc. 2. Act II. sc. 1; sc. 2. Act III. sc. 3; sc. 5. Act IV. sc. 2. Act V. sc. 1.

EDWARD, *Prince of* Wales, *his Son.*
Appears, Act I. sc. 1. Act II. sc. 2. Act III. sc. 3; sc. 4; sc. 5. Act IV. sc. 4; sc. 6; sc. 7. Act V. sc. 1.

EARL OF WARWICK.
Appears, Act I. sc. 1; sc. 2. Act II. sc. 1; sc. 2.

EARL OF DERBY.
Appears, Act I. sc. 1. Act II. sc. 2. Act III. sc. 3; sc. 5. Act IV. sc. 2. Act V. sc. 1.

EARL OF SALISBURY.
Appears, Act IV. sc. 1; sc. 5. Act V. sc. 1.

LORD AUDLEY.
Appears, Act I. sc. 1. Act II. sc. 2. Act III. sc. 3; sc. 5. Act IV. sc. 4; sc. 6; sc. 7. Act V. sc. 1.

LORD PERCY.
Appears, Act IV. sc. 2.

LODOWICK, *a Confident of* King Edward.
Appears, Act II. sc. 1; sc. 2.

SIR WILLIAM MOUNTAGUE
Appears, Act I. sc. 1; sc. 2.

COPLAND, *an Esquire, afterwards* Sir John Copland.
AN ENGLISH HERALD.
Appear, Act V. sc. 1.

ROBERT, *styling himself* Earl of Artois.
Appears, Act I. sc. 1; sc. 2. Act II. sc. 2. Act III. sc. 3; sc. 5. Act IV. sc. 6; sc. 7. Act V. sc. 1.

EARL OF MONTFORD.
Appears, Act IV. sc. 1.

GOBIN DE GREY, *a* Frenchman, *Prisoner to the* English.
Appears, Act III. sc. 3.

JOHN, *King of* France.
Appears, Act III. sc. 1; sc. 3; sc. 4. Act IV. sc. 3; sc. 5; sc. 6; sc. 7. Act V. sc. 1.

CHARLES, *Duke of* Normandy, *his Son.*
Appears, Act III. sc. 1; sc. 3. Act IV. sc. 3; sc. 5; sc. 6; sc. 7.

PHILIP, *Second Son of the* French King.
Appears, Act III. sc. 1; sc. 3. Act IV. sc. 5; sc. 6; sc. 7. Act. V. sc. 1.

DUKE OF LORRAIN.
Appears, Act I. sc. 2. Act III. sc. 1; sc. 3; sc. 4.

VILLIERS, *a* French *Lord.*
Appears, Act IV. sc. 1; sc. 3.

KING OF BOHEMIA, *an Ally of the* French King.
Appears, Act. III. sc. 1; sc. 3; sc. 5.

A FRENCH MARINER.
Appears, Act III. sc. 1.

THREE FRENCH HERALDS.
Appear, Act IV. sc. 4.

CITIZENS OF CALAIS.
Appears, Act V. sc. 1.

DAVID, *King of* Scotland.
Appears, Act I. sc. 2. Act V. sc. 1.

EARL DOUGLAS.
Appears, Act I. sc. 2.

PHILIPPA, *Queen to* King Edward.
Appears, Act V. sc. 1.

COUNTESS OF SALISBURY.
Appears, Act I. sc. 2. Act II. sc. 1; sc. 2.

A FRENCH WOMAN.
Appears, Act III. sc. 2.

Lords, Heralds, Officers, Soldiers, &c.

SCENE.—*Dispersed, in* ENGLAND, FLANDERS, *and* FRANCE.

King Edward the Third.

———◆———

ACT I.

SCENE I.—London. *A Room of State in the Palace.*

Flourish. Enter KING EDWARD, *attended;* PRINCE OF WALES, WARWICK, DERBY, AUDLEY, ARTOIS, *and* Others.

Edw. Robert of Artois, banish'd though thou be[1]
From France, thy native country, yet with us
Thou shalt retain as great a signiory;
For we create thee Earl of Richmond here.
And now go forwards with our pedigree;
Who next succeeded Philip le Beau?[2]
 Art. Three sons of his; which all, successively,
Did sit upon their father's regal throne;
Yet died, and left no issue of their loins.
 Edw. But was my mother sister unto those?
 Art. She was, my lord; and only Isabelle
Was all the daughters that this Philip had:
Whom afterward your father took to wife;
And, from the fragrant garden of her womb,
Your gracious self, the flower of Europe's hope,
Derived is inheritor to France.
But note the rancour of rebellious minds.
When thus the lineage of Le Beau was out,
The French obscured your mother's privilege;
And, though she were the next of blood, proclaim'd
John, of the house of Valois, now their king:
The reason was, They say, the realm of France,
Replete with princes of great parentage,
Ought not admit a governor to rule,
Except he be descended of the male:
And that's the special ground of their contempt,
Wherewith they study to exclude your grace:
But they shall find that forged ground of theirs
To be but dusty heaps of brittle sand.
Perhaps, it will be thought a heinous thing,
That I, a Frenchman, should discover this:
But heaven I call to record of my vows;
It is not hate, nor any private wrong,
But love unto my country, and the right,
Provokes my tongue thus lavish in report

You are the lineal watchman of our peace,
And John of Valois indirectly climbs:
What then should subjects, but embrace their king?
Ah, wherein may our duty more be seen,
Than, striving to rebate[3] a tyrant's pride,
Place the true shepherd of our commonwealth?
 Edw. This counsel, Artois, like to fruitful showers,
Hath added growth unto my dignity:
And, by the fiery vigour of thy words,
Hot courage is engender'd in my breast,
Which heretofore was rak'd in ignorance;
But now doth mount with golden wings of fame,
And will approve fair Isabelle's descent
Able to yoke their stubborn necks with steel
That spurn against my sov'reignty in France.—
 [Cornet within.
A messenger?—Lord Audley, know from whence.
 [Exit AUD. *and returns.*
 Aud. The duke of Lorrain, having cross'd the seas,
Intreats he may have conference with your highness.
 Edw. Admit him, lords, that we may hear the news.—
 [Exeunt Lords. KING *takes his State.*

Re-enter Lords; *with* LORRAIN, *attended.*

Say, duke of Lorrain, wherefore art thou come?
 Lor. The most renowned prince, King John of France,
Doth greet thee, Edward: and by me commands,
That, for so much as by his liberal gift
The Guyenne dukedom is entail'd to thee,
Thou do him lowly homage for the same:
And, for that purpose, here I summon thee
Repair to France within these forty days,
That there, according as the custom is,
Thou may'st be sworn true liege-man to the king;
Or, else, thy title in that province dies,
And he himself will repossess the place.
 Edw. See, how occasion laughs me in the face!

No sooner minded to prepare for France,
But, straight I am invited; nay, with threats,
Upon a penalty, enjoin'd to come:
'Twere but a foolish part, to say him nay,—
Lorrain, return this answer to thy lord:
I mean to visit him, as he requests;
But how? not servilely dispos'd to bend;
But like a conqueror, to make him bow:
His lame unpolish'd shifts are come to light;
And truth hath pull'd the vizard from his face,
That set a gloss upon his arrogance.
Dare he command a fealty in me?
Tell him, the crown, that he usurps, is mine;
And where he sets his foot, he ought to kneel:
'Tis not a petty dukedom that I claim,
But all the whole dominions of the realm:
Which if with grudging he refuse to yield,
I'll take away those borrowed plumes of his,
And send him naked to the wilderness.

Lor. Then, Edward, here, in spite of all thy
    lords,
I do pronounce defiance to thy face.

Prince. Defiance, Frenchman? we rebound it
    back,
Even to the bottom of thy master's throat:
And,—be it spoke with reverence of the king
My gracious father, and these other lords,
I hold thy message but as scurrilous;
And him that sent thee, like the lazy drone,
Crept up by stealth unto the eagle's nest;
From whence we'll shake him with so rough a
    storm,
As others shall be warned by his harm.

War. Bid him leave off the lion's case he wears;
Lest, meeting with the lion in the field,
He chance to tear him piece-meal for his pride.

Art. The soundest counsel I can give his grace,
Is, to surrender ere he be constrain'd:
A voluntary mischief hath less scorn,
Than when reproach with violence is born.

Lor. Regenerate traitor,[4] viper to the place
Where thou wast foster'd in thine infancy,
                    [*Drawing his Sword.*
Bear'st thou a part in this conspiracy?

Edw. Lorrain, behold the sharpness of this steel:
                    [*Drawing his.*
Fervent desire, that sits against my heart,
Is far more thorny-pricking than this blade;
That, with the nightingale, I shall be scar'd,
As oft as I dispose myself to rest,
Until my colours be display'd in France:
This is thy final answer, so be gone.

Lor. It is not that, nor any English brave,

Afflicts me so, as doth his poison'd view;
That is most false, should most of all be true.
                    [*Exeunt* Lor. *and Train.*

Edw. Now, lords, our fleeting bark is under sail:
Our gage is thrown; and war is soon begun,
But not so quickly brought unto an end.

Enter Sir William Mountague.

But wherefore comes Sir William Mountague?
How stands the league between the Scot and us?

Mount. Crack'd and dissever'd, my renowned
    lord,
The treacherous king no sooner was inform'd
Of your withdrawing of your army back,
But straight, forgetting of his former oath,
He made invasion on the bordering towns:
Berwick is won; Newcastle spoil'd and lost;
And now the tyrant hath begirt with siege
The castle of Roxborough, where enclos'd
The countess Salisbury is like to perish.

Edw. That is thy daughter, Warwick, is it not;
Whose husband hath in Bretagne serv'd so long,
About the planting of Lord Montfort there?

War. It is, my lord.

Edw. Ignoble David! hast thou none to grieve,
But silly ladies, with thy threat'ning arms?
But I will make you shrink your snaily horns.—
First, therefore, Audley, this shall be thy charge;
Go levy footmen for our wars in France:—[5]
And, Ned, take muster of our men at arms:
In every shire elect a several band;
Let them be soldiers of a lusty spirit,
Such as dread nothing but dishonour's blot:
Be wary therefore; since we do commence
A famous war, and with so mighty nation.
Derby, be thou ambassador for us
Unto our father-in-law, the Earl of Hainault:
Make him acquainted with our enterprise;
And likewise will him, with our own allies,
That are in Flanders, to solicit too
The Emperor of Almaigne in our name.—
Myself, whilst you are jointly thus employ'd,
Will, with these forces that I have at hand,
March, and once more repulse the trait'rous Scots.
But, sirs, be resolute; we shall have wars
On every side:—and, Ned, thou must begin
Now to forget thy study and thy books,
And ure thy shoulders to an armour's weight.

Prince. As cheerful sounding to my youthful
    spleen
This tumult is of war's increasing broils,
As, at the coronation of a king,
The joyful clamours of the people are,

When, *ave*, Cæsar! they pronounce aloud;
Within this school of honour I shall learn,
Either to sacrifice my foes to death,
Or in a rightful quarrel spend my breath.
Then cheerfully forward, each a several way;
In great affairs 'tis naught to use delay. [*Exeunt.*

SCENE II.---Roxborough. *Before the Castle.*

Enter COUNTESS OF SALISBURY, *and certain of her*
People *upon the Walls.*

Cou. Alas, how much in vain my poor eyes gaze
For succour that my sovereign should send!
Ah, cousin Mountague, I fear, thou want'st
The lively spirit, sharply to solicit
With vehement suit the king in my behalf:
Thou dost not tell him, what a grief it is
To be the scornful captive to a Scot;
Either to be woo'd with broad untuned oaths,
Or forc'd by rough insulting barbarism:
Thou dost not tell him, if he here prevail,
How much they will deride us in the north;
And, in their vile, uncivil, skipping jigs,
Bray forth their conquest, and our overthrow,
Even in the barren, bleak, and fruitless air.

Enter KING DAVID *and* Forces, *with* DOUGLAS,
LORRAIN, *and* Others.

I must withdraw; the everlasting foe
Comes to the wall: I'll closely step aside,
And list their babble; blunt, and full of pride.
[*Retiring behind the Works.*
Dav. My Lord of Lorrain, to our brother of
France
Commend us, as the man in Christendom
Whom we most reverence, and entirely love.
Touching your embassage, return, and say
That we with England will not enter parley,
Nor never make fair weather, or take truce;
But burn their neighbour towns, and so persist
With eager roads beyond their city York.
And never shall our bonny riders rest;
Nor rusting canker have the time to eat
Their light-born snaffles, nor their nimble spurs;
Nor lay aside their jacks of gymold mail;[6]
Nor hang their staves of grained Scottish ash,
In peaceful wise, upon their city walls;
Nor from their button'd tawny leathern belts
Dismiss their biting whinyards,[7] 'till your king
Cry out, " Enough; spare England now for pity."
Farewell: and tell him, that you leave us here
Before this castle; say, you came from us,
Even when we had that yielded to our hands.

Lor. I take my leave; and fairly will return
Your acceptable greeting to my king.
[*Exit.* LOR.
Dav. Now Douglas, to our former task again,
For the division of this certain spoil.
Dou. My liege, I crave the lady, and no more.
Dav. Nay, soft ye, sir, first I must make my
choice;
And first I do bespeak her for myself.
Dou. Why then, my liege, let me enjoy her
jewels.
Dav. Those are her own, still liable to her,
And, who inherits her, hath those withal.

Enter a Messenger, *hastily.*

Mes. My liege, as we were pricking on the hills,
To fetch in booty, marching hitherward
We might descry a mighty host of men:
The sun, reflecting on the armour, show'd
A field of plate, a wood of pikes advanc'd;
Bethink your highness speedily herein:
An easy march within four hours will bring
The hindmost rank unto this place, my liege.
Dav. Dislodge, dislodge, it is the king of Eng-
land.
Dou. Jemmy my man, saddle my bonny black.[8]
Dav. Mean'st thou to fight, Douglas? we are
too weak.
Dou. I know it well, my liege, and therefore flee.
Cou. My lords of Scotland, will ye stay and
drink? [*Rising from her concealment.*
Dav. She mocks at us; Douglas, I can't en-
dure it.
Cou. Say, my lord, which is he, must have the
lady;
And which, her jewels? I am sure, my lords,
Ye will not hence, 'till you have shar'd the spoils.
Dav. She heard the messenger, and heard our
talk;
And now that comfort makes her scorn at us.

Enter another Messenger.

Mes. Arm, my good lord; O, we are all sur-
pris'd!
Cou. After the French ambassador, my liege,
And tell him, that you dare not ride to York;
Excuse it, that your bonny horse is lame.
Dav. She heard that too; intolerable grief!—
Woman, farewell: although I do not stay,—
[*Alarums. Exeunt Scots.*
Cou. 'Tis not for fear,—and yet you run away.—
O happy comfort, welcome to our house!
The confident and boist'rous boasting Scot,—

That swore before my walls, they would not back
For all the armed power of this land,—
With faceless fear, that ever turns his back,
Turn'd hence again the blasting north-east wind,
Upon the bare report and name of arms.

Enter MOUNTAGUE, *and* Others.

O summer's day! see where my cousin comes.
 Mou. How fares my aunt? Why, aunt, we are
  not Scots;
Why do you shut your gates against your friends?
 Cou. Well may I give a welcome, cousin, to thee,
For thou com'st well to chase my foes from hence.
 Mou. The king himself is come in person hither;
Dear aunt, descend, and gratulate his highness.
 Cou. How may I entertain his majesty,
To show my duty, and his dignity? [*Exit from above.*

Flourish. *Enter* KING EDWARD, WARWICK,
  ARTOIS, *and* Others.

 Edw. What, are the stealing foxes fled and gone,
Before we could uncouple at their heels?
 War. They are, my liege; but, with a cheerful
  cry,
Hot hounds, and hardy, chase them at the heels.

Re-enter COUNTESS, *attended.*

 Edw. This is the countess, Warwick, is it not?
 War. Even she, my liege; whose beauty tyrants
  fear,
As a May blossom with pernicious winds,
Hath sully'd, wither'd, overcast, and done.
 Edw. Hath she been fairer, Warwick, than she is?
 War. My gracious king, fair is she not at all,
If that herself were by to stain herself,
As I have seen her when she was herself.
 Edw. What strange enchantment lurk'd in those
  her eyes,
When they excell'd this excellence they have,
That now her dim decline hath power to draw
My subject eyes from piercing majesty,
To gaze on her with doting admiration? [*Aside.*
 Cou. In duty lower than the ground I kneel,
And for my dull knees bow my feeling heart,
To witness my obedience to your highness;
With many millions of a subject's thanks
For this your royal presence, whose approach
Hath driven war and danger from my gate.
 Edw. Lady, stand up: I come to bring thee peace,
However thereby I have purchas'd war.
 Cou. No war to you, my liege; the Scots are gone,
And gallop home toward Scotland with their haste.
 Edw. Lest yielding here I pine in shameful love,

Come, we'll pursue the Scots [*Aside*];—Artois,
  away.
 Cou. A little while, my gracious sovereign, stay,
And let the power of a mighty king
Honour our roof; my husband in the wars,
When he shall hear it, will triumph for joy:
Then, dear my liege, now niggard not thy state;
Being at the wall, enter our homely gate.
 Edw. Pardon me, countess, I will come no near;
I dream'd to-night of treason, and I fear.
 Cou. Far from this place let ugly treason lie!
 Edw. No farther off, than her conspiring eye;
Which shoots infected poison in my heart,
Beyond repulse of wit, or cure of art.
Now in the sun alone it doth not lie,
With light to take light from a mortal eye;
For here two day stars, that mine eyes would see,
More than the sun, steal mine own light from me.
Contemplative desire! desire to be,
In contemplation, that may master thee! [*Aside.*
Warwick, Artois, to horse, and let's away.
 Cou. What might I speak, to make my sovereign
  stay?
 Edw. What needs a tongue to such a speaking
  eye,
That more persuades than winning oratory? [*Aside.*
 Cou. Let not thy presence, like the April sun,
Flatter our earth, and suddenly be done:
More happy do not make our outward wall,
Than thou wilt grace our inward house withal.
Our house, my liege, is like a country swain,
Whose habit rude, and manners blunt and plain,
Presageth nought; yet inly beautify'd
With bounty's riches, and fair hidden pride:
For, where the golden ore doth bury'd lie,
The ground, undeck'd with nature's tapestry,
Seems barren, sere, unfertile, fruitless, dry;
And where the upper turf of earth doth boast
His proud perfumes, and party-colour'd cost,
Delve there, and find this issue, and their pride,
To spring from ordure, and corruption's side.
But, to make up my all too long compare,—
These ragged walls no testimony are
What is within; but, like a cloak, doth hide,
From weather's west, the under garnish'd pride.
More gracious than my terms can let thee be,
Entreat thyself to stay a while with me.
 Edw. As wise as fair; What fond fit can be heard,
When wisdom keeps the gate as beauty's guard?—
           [*Aside.*
Countess, albeit my business urgeth me,
It shall attend, while I attend on thee.—
Come on, my lords, here will I host to-night.

ACT II.

SCENE I.—*The Same.   Gardens of the Castle.*

Enter LODOWICK.

Lod. I might perceive his eye in her eye lost,
His ear to drink her sweet tongue's utterance;
And changing passion, like inconstant clouds,—
That, rack'd upon the carriage of the winds,
Increasé, and die,—in his disturbed cheeks.
Lo, when she blush'd, even then did he look pale;
As if her cheeks, by some enchanted power,
Attracted had the cherry blood from his:
Anon, with reverent fear when she grew pale,
His cheeks put on their scarlet ornaments;
But no more like her oriental red,
Than brick to coral, or live things to dead.
Why did he then thus counterfeit her looks?
If she did blush, 'twas tender modest shame,
Being in the sacred presence of a king;
If he did blush, 'twas red immodest shame,
To vail his eyes amiss, being a king:
If she look'd pale, 'twas silly woman's fear,
To bear herself in presence of a king;
If he look'd pale, it was with guilty fear,
To dote amiss, being a mighty king:
Then, Scottish wars, farewell; I fear, 'twill prove
A ling'ring English siege of peevish love.[9]
Here comes his highness, walking all alone.

Enter KING EDWARD.

Edw. She is grown more fairer far since I came
      hither;
Her voice more silver every word than other,
Her wit more fluent: What a strange discourse
Unfolded she, of David, and his Scots?
" Even thus," quoth she, " he spake,"—and then
      spake broad,
With epithets and accents of the Scot;
But somewhat better than the Scot could speak:
" And thus," quoth she,—and answer'd then her-
      self;
For who could speak like her? but she herself
Breathes from the wall an angel's note from heaven
Of sweet defiance to her barbarous foes.
When she would talk of peace, methinks, her tongue
Commanded war to prison; when of war,
It waken'd Cæsar from his Roman grave,
To hear war beautify'd by her discourse.
Wisdom is foolishness, but in her tongue;
Beauty a slander, but in her fair face:

There is no summer, but in her cheerful looks;
Nor frosty winter, but in her disdain.
I cannot blame the Scots, that did besiege her,
For she is all the treasure of our land;
But call them cowards, that they ran away,
Having so rich and fair a cause to stay.—
Art thou there, Lodowick? give me ink and paper.
      Lod. I will, my sovereign.
      Edw. And bid the lords hold on their play at
            chess,
For we will walk and meditate alone.
      Lod. I will, my liege.   *Exit* LOD.
      Edw. This fellow is well read in poetry,
And hath a lusty and persuasive spirit:
I will acquaint him with my passion;
Which he shall shadow with a vail of lawn,
Through which the queen of beauty's queen shall
            see
Herself the ground of my infirmity.—

Re-enter LODOWICK.

Hast thou pen, ink, and paper ready, Lodowick?
      Lod. Ready, my liege.
      Edw. Then in the summer arbour sit by me,
Make it our council-house, or cabinet;
Since green our thoughts, green be the conventicle,
Where we will ease us by disburd'ning them.
Now, Lodowick, invocate some golden muse,
To bring thee hither an enchanted pen,
That may, for sighs, set down true sighs indeed;
Talking of grief, to make thee ready groan;
And, when thou writ'st of tears, encouch the word,
Before, and after, with such sweet laments,
That it may raise drops in a Tartar's eye,
And make a flint heart Scythian pitiful:
For so much moving hath a poet's pen;
Then, if thou be a poet, move thou so,
And be enriched by thy sovereign's love.
For, if the touch of sweet concordant strings
Could force attendance in the ears of hell;
How much more shall the strain of poet's wit
Beguile, and ravish, soft and humane minds?
      Lod. To whom, my lord, shall I direct my stile?
      Edw. To one that shames the fair, and sots the
            wise;
Whose body, as an abstract, or a brief,
Contains each general virtue in the world:
Better than beautiful,—thou must begin;
Devise for fair a fairer word than fair;

And every ornament, that thou would'st praise,
Fly it a pitch above the soar of praise:
For flattery fear thou not to be convicted;
For, were thy admiration ten times more,
Ten times ten thousand more the worth exceeds,
Of that thou art to praise, thy praise's worth.
Begin, I will to contemplate the while:
Forget not to set down, how passionate,
How heart-sick, and how full of languishment,
Her beauty makes me.

    Lod. Write I to a woman?

    Edw. What beauty else could triumph over me;
Or who, but women, do our love-lays greet?
What, think'st thou I did bid thee praise a horse?

    Lod. Of what condition or estate she is,
'Twere requisite that I should know, my lord.

    Edw. Of such estate, that hers is as a throne,
And my estate the footstool where she treads:
Then may'st thou judge what her condition is,
By the proportion of her mightiness.
Write on, while I peruse her in my thoughts.—
Her voice to music, or the nightingale:—
To music every summer-leaping swain
Compares his sun-burnt lover when she speaks:
And why should I speak of the nightingale?
The nightingale sings of adulterate wrong;
And that, compar'd, is too satirical:
For sin, though sin, would not be so esteem'd;
But, rather, virtue sin, sin virtue deem'd.
Her hair, far softer than the silk-worm's twist,
Like as a flattering glass, doth make more fair
The yellow amber: Like a flattering glass
Comes in too soon; for, writing of her eyes,
I'll say, that like a glass they catch the sun,
And thence the hot reflection doth rebound
Against my breast, and burns my heart within.
Ah, what a world of descant makes my soul
Upon this voluntary ground of love!—
Come, Lodowick, hast thou turn'd thy ink to gold?
If not, write but in letters capital
My mistress' name,
And it will gild thy paper: Read, lord, read,
Fill thou the empty hollows of mine ears
With the sweet hearing of thy poetry.

    Lod. I have not to a period brought her praise.

    Edw. Her praise is as my love, both infinite,
Which apprehend such violent extremes,
That they disdain an ending period.
Her beauty hath no match, but my affection;
Hers more than most, mine most, and more than
    more:
Hers more to praise, than tell the sea by drops;
Nay, more, than drop the massy earth by sands,

And, sand by sand,[10] print them in memory:
Then wherefore talk'st thou of a period,
To that which craves unended admiration?
Read, let us hear.

    Lod. "More fair, and chaste, than is the **queen**
    of shades,"

    Edw. That line hath two **faults, gross and**
    palpable:
Compar'st thou her to the pale queen of night,
Who, being set in dark, seems therefore light?
What is she, when the sun lifts up his head,
But like a fading taper, dim and dead?
My love shall brave the eye of heaven at noon,
And, being unmask'd, outshine the golden sun.

    Lod. What is the other fault, **my sovereign**
    lord?

    Edw. Read o'er the line again.

    Lod. "More fair, and chaste."

    Edw. I did not bid thee talk of chastity,—
To ransack so the treasure of her mind;
For I had rather have her chas'd than chaste,
Out with the moon-line, I will none of it,
And let me have her liken'd to the sun:
Say, she hath thrice more splendour than the sun,
That her perfection emulates the sun,
That she breeds sweets as plenteous as the sun,
That she doth thaw cold winter like the sun,
That she doth cheer fresh summer like the sun,
That she doth dazzle gazers like the sun:
And, in this application to the sun,
Bid her be free and general as the sun;
Who smiles upon the basest weed that grows,
As lovingly as on the fragrant rose.
Let's see what follows that same moon-light line.

    Lod. "More fair, and chaste, than is the queen of
    shades;
More bold in constancy,"—

    Edw. In constancy! than who?

    Lod. —"than Judith was."[11]

    Edw. O monstrous line! Put in the next a
    sword,
And I shall woo her to cut off my head.
Blot, blot, good Lodowick! Let us hear the next.

    Lod. There's all that yet is done.

    Edw. I thank thee then, thou hast done little
    ill;
But what is done, is passing passing ill.
No, let the captain talk of boist'rous war;
The prisoner, of immured dark constraint;
The sick man best sets down the pangs of death;
The man that starves, the sweetness of a feast;
The frozen soul, the benefit of fire;
And every grief, his happy opposite:

Love cannot sound well, but in lovers' tongues;
Give me the pen and paper, I will write.—

Enter COUNTESS.

But, soft, here comes the treasure of my spirit.—
Lodowick, thou know'st not how to draw a battle;
These wings, these flankers, and these squadrons
   here,
Argue in thee defective discipline:
Thou should'st have plac'd this here, this other
   here.
   Cou. Pardon my boldness, my thrice gracious
      lord;
Let my intrusion here be call'd my duty,
That comes to see my sovereign how he fares.
   Edw. Go, draw the same, I tell thee in what
      form.
   Lod. I go.   [*Exit.* Lod.
   Cou. Sorry I am, to see my liege so sad:
What may thy subject do, to drive from thee
This gloomy consort, sullen melancholy?
   Edw. Ah, lady, I am blunt, and cannot straw
The flowers of solace in a ground of shame:
Since I came hither, countess, I am wrong'd.
   Cou. Now, God forbid, that any in my house
Should think my sovereign wrong! Thrice gentle
      king,
Acquaint me with your cause of discontent.
   Edw. How near then shall I be to remedy?
   Cou. As near, my liege, as all my woman's
      power
Can pawn itself to buy thy remedy.
   Edw. If thou speak'st true, then have I my
      redress:
Engage thy power to redeem my joys,
And I am joyful, countess! else I die.
   Cou. I will, my liege.
   Edw.   Swear, countess, that thou wilt.
   Cou. By heaven, I will.
   Edw. Then take thyself a little way aside;
And tell thyself, a king doth dote on thee:
Say, that within thy power it doth lie,
To make him happy; and that thou hast sworn,
To give me all the joy within thy power:
Do this; and tell me, when I shall be happy.
   Cou. All this is done, my thrice dread sovereign:
That power of love, that I have power to give,
Thou hast with all devout obedience;
Employ me how thou wilt in proof thereof.
   Edw. Thou hear'st me say, that I do dote on
      thee.
   Cou. If on my beauty, take it if thou can'st;
Though little, I do prize it ten times less:

If on my virtue, take it if thou can'st;
For virtue's store by giving doth augment:
Be it on what it will, that I can give,
And thou can'st take away, inherit it.
   Edw. It is thy beauty that I would enjoy.
   Cou. O, were it painted, I would wipe it off,
And dispossess myself, to give it thee:
But, sovereign, it is solder'd to my life;
Take one, and both; for, like an humble shadow,
It haunts the sun-shine of my summer's life.
   Edw. But thou may'st lend it me, to sport
      withal.
   Cou. As easy may my intellectual soul
Be lent away, and yet my body live,
As lend my body, palace to my soul,
Away from her, and yet retain my soul.
My body is her bower, her court, her abbey,
And she an angel, pure, divine, unspotted;
If I should lend her house, my lord, to thee,
I kill my poor soul, and my poor soul me.
   Edw. Did'st thou not swear to give me what I
      would?
   Cou. I did, my liege; so, what you would, I
      could.
   Edw. I wish no more of thee, than thou may'st
      give:
Nor beg I do not, but I rather buy,
That is, thy love; and, for that love of thine,
In rich exchange, I tender to thee mine.
   Cou. But that your lips were sacred, O my lord,
You would profane the holy name of love.
That love, you offer me, you cannot give:
For Cæsar owes that tribute to his queen:
That love, you beg of me, I cannot give;
For Sarah owes that duty to her lord.
He, that doth clip, or counterfeit your stamp,
Shall die, my lord: And will your sacred self
Commit high treason 'gainst the king of heaven,
To stamp his image in forbidden metal,
Forgetting your allegiance and your oath?
In violating marriage sacred law,
You break a greater honour than yourself:
To be a king, is of a younger house
Than to be married; your progenitor,
Sole-reigning Adam on the universe,
By God was honour'd for a married man,
But not by him anointed for a king.
It is a penalty, to break your statutes,
Though not enacted by your highness' hand:
How much more, to infringe the holy act
Made by the mouth of God, seal'd with his hand?
I know, my sovereign—in my husband's love,
Who now doth loyal service in his wars—

Doth but to try the wife of Salisbury,
Whether she will hear a wanton's tale, or no;
Lest being therein guilty by my stay,
From that, not from my liege, I turn away.

                    [*Exit* Cou.

  Edw. Whether is her beauty by her words divine;
Or are her words sweet chaplains to her beauty?
Like as the wind doth beautify a sail,
And as a sail becomes the unseen wind,
So do her words her beauty, beauty words.
O, that I were a honey-gathering bee,
To bear the comb of virtue from this flower;
And not a poison-sucking envious spider,
To turn the vice I take to deadly venom!
Religion is austere, and beauty gentle;
Too strict a guardian for so fair a ward.
O that she were, as is the air, to me!
Why so she is; for, when I would embrace her,
This do I, and catch nothing but myself.
I must enjoy her; for I cannot beat,
With reason and reproof, fond love away.

          Enter WARWICK.

Here comes her father: I will work with him,
To bear my colours in this field of love.
  War. How is it, that my sovereign is so sad?
May I with pardon know your highness' grief,
And that my old endeavour will remove it,
It shall not cumber long your majesty.
  Edw. A kind and voluntary gift thou offer'st,
That I was forward to have begg'd of thee.
But, O thou world, great nurse of flattery,
Why dost thou tip men's tongues with golden
        words,
And peize their deeds with weight of heavy lead,
That fair performance cannot follow promise?
O, that a man might hold the heart's close book;
And choke the lavish tongue, when it doth utter
The breath of falsehood not character'd there!
  War. Far be it from the honour of my age,
That I should owe bright gold, and render lead!
Age is a cynic, not a flatterer:
I say again, that if I knew your grief,
And that by me it may be lessened,
My proper harm should buy your highness' good.
  Edw. These are the vulgar tenders of false men,
That never pay the duty of their words.
Thou wilt not stick to swear what thou hast said;
But, when thou know'st my grief's condition,
This rash disgorged vomit of thy word
Thou wilt eat up again, and leave me helpless.
  War. By heaven, I will not; though your majesty
Did bid me run upon your sword, and die.

  Edw. Say, that my grief is no way med'cinable,
But by the loss and bruising of thine honour?
  War. If nothing but that loss may vantage you,
I would account that loss my vantage too.
  Edw. Think'st, that thou can'st unswear thy
      oath again?
  War. I cannot; nor I would not, if I could.
  Edw. But, if thou dost, what shall I say to thee?
  War. What may be said to any perjur'd villain,
That breaks the sacred warrant of an oath.
  Edw. What wilt thou say to one that breaks an
      oath?
  War. That he hath broke his faith with God and
      man,
And from them both stands excommunicate.
  Edw. What office were it, to suggest a man
To break a lawful and religious vow?
  War. An office for the devil, not for man.
  Edw. That devil's office must thou do for me;
Or break thy oath, or cancel all the bonds
Of love and duty 'twixt thyself and me.
And therefore, Warwick, if thou art thyself,
The lord and master of thy word and oath,
Go to thy daughter: and, in my behalf,
Command her, woo her, win her any ways,
To be my mistress, and my secret love.
I will not stand to hear thee make reply;
Thy oath break hers, or let thy sovereign die.

                    [*Exit* EDW.

  War. O doting king! O detestable office!
Well may I tempt myself to wrong myself,
When he hath sworn me by the name of God,
To break a vow made by the name of God.
What if I swear by this right hand of mine,
To cut this right hand off? the better way
Were, to profane the idol, than confound it:
But neither will I do; I'll keep my oath,
And to my daughter make a recantation
Of all the virtue I have preach'd to her:
I'll say, she must forget her husband Salisbury,
If she remember to embrace the king;
I'll say, an oath may easily be broken,
But not so easily pardon'd, being broken
I'll say, it is true charity to love,
But not true love to be so charitable;
I'll say, his greatness may bear out the shame,
But not his kingdom can buy out the sin
I'll say, it is my duty to persuade,
But not her honesty to give consent.

         Enter COUNTESS.

See, where she comes: Was never father, had,
Against his child, an embassage so bad.

Cou. My lord and father, I have sought for you:
My mother and the peers importune you,
To keep in presence of his majesty,
And do your best to make his highness merry.

　War. How shall I enter in this graceless errand?
I must not call her child; for where's the father
That will, in such a suit, seduce his child?
Then, Wife of Salisbury,—shall I so begin?
No, he's my friend; and where is found the friend,
That will do friendship such endamagement?
Neither my daughter, nor my dear friend's wife,
I am not Warwick, as thou think'st I am,
But an attorney from the court of hell;
That thus have hous'd my spirit in his form,
To do a message to thee from the king.
The mighty king of England dotes on thee:
He, that hath power to take away thy life,
Hath power to take thine honour; then consent
To pawn thine honour, rather than thy life:
Honour is often lost, and got again;
But life, once gone, hath no recovery.
The sun, that withers hay, doth nourish grass;
The king, that would distain thee, will advance
　　thee.
The poets write, that great Achilles' spear
Could heal the wound it made: the moral is,
What mighty men misdo, they can amend.
The lion doth become his bloody jaws,
And grace his foragement, by being mild
When vassal fear lies trembling at his feet.
The king will in his glory hide thy shame;
And those, that gaze on him to find out thee,
Will lose their eye-sight, looking in the sun.
What can one drop of poison harm the sea,
Whose hugy vastures can digest the ill,
And make it lose his operation?
The king's great name will temper thy misdeeds,
And give the bitter potion of reproach
A sugar'd-sweet and most delicious taste:
Besides, it is no harm, to do the thing
Which without shame could not be left undone.
Thus have I, in his majesty's behalf,
Apparel'd sin in virtuous sentences,
And dwell upon thy answer in his suit.

　Cou. Unnatural besiege! Woe me unhappy,
To have escap'd the danger of my foes,
And to be ten times worse invir'd by friends!
Hath he no means to stain my honest blood,
But to corrupt the author of my blood,
To be his scandalous and vile solicitor?
No marvel, though the branches be infected,
When poison hath encompassed the root:
No marvel, though the leprous infant die,

When the stern dam envenometh the dug.
Why then, give sin a passport to offend,
And youth the dangerous rein of liberty:
Blot out the strict forbidding of the law;
And cancel every canon, that prescribes
A shame for shame, or penance for offence.
No, let me die, if his too boist'rous will
Will have it so, before I will consent
To be an actor in his graceless lust.

　War. Why, now thou speak'st as I would have
　　thee speak:
And mark how I unsay my words again.
An honourable grave is more esteem'd,
Than the polluted closet of a king:
The greater man, the greater is the thing,
Be it good, or bad, that he shall undertake:
An unreputed mote, flying in the sun,
Presents a greater substance than it is:
The freshest summer's day doth soonest taint
The loathed carrion that it seems to kiss:
Deep are the blows made with a mighty axe:
That sin doth ten times aggravate itself,
That is committed in a holy place:
An evil deed, done by authority,
Is sin, and subornation: Deck an ape
In tissue, and the beauty of the robe
Adds but the greater scorn unto the beast.
A spacious field of reasons could I urge,
Between his glory, daughter, and thy shame:
That poison shows worst in a golden cup;
Dark night seems darker by the lightning flash;
Lilies, that fester, smell far worse than weeds;[12]
And every glory that inclines to sin,
The shame is treble by the opposite.
So leave I, with my blessing in thy bosom;
Which then convert to a most heavy curse,
When thou convert'st from honour's golden name
To the black faction of bed-blotting shame! [*Exit.*

　Cou. I'll follow thee; And, when my mind
　　turns so,
My body sink my soul in endless woe! 　　[*Exit.*

SCENE II.—*The Same.　A Room in the Castle.*

　　Enter DERBY, *and* AUDLEY, *meeting.*

　Der. Thrice noble Audley, well encounter'd here:
How is it with our sovereign, and his peers?
　Aud. 'Tis full a fortnight, since I saw his high-
　　ness,
What time he sent me forth to muster men;
Which I accordingly have done, and bring them
In fair array before his majesty.
What news, my lord of Derby, from the emperor?

Der. As good as we desire: the emperor
Hath yielded to his highness friendly aid;
And makes our king lieutenant-general,
In all his lands and large dominions:
Then *via* for the spacious bounds of France![13]

Aud. What, doth his highness leap to hear this
      news?

Der. I have not yet found time to open them;
The king is in his closet, malcontent,
For what, I know not, but he gave in charge,
'Till after dinner, none should interrupt him:
The countess Salisbury, and her father Warwick,
Artois, and all, look underneath the brows.

Aud. Undoubtedly, then something is amiss.
                                    [*Trumpet within.*

Der. The trumpets sound; the king is now abroad.

Enter EDWARD.

Aud. Here comes his highness.

Der. Befall my sovereign all my sovereign's wish!

Edw. Ah, that thou wert a witch, to make it so!

Der. The emperor greeteth you:
                            [*Presenting Letters.*

Edw. 'Would it were the countess!

Der. And hath accorded to your highness' suit.

Edw. Thou ly'st, she hath not; But I would,
      she had!

Aud. All love, and duty, to my lord the king!

Edw. Well, all but one is none:—What news
      with you?

Aud. I have, my liege, levy'd those horse and foot,
According to your charge, and brought them hither.

Edw. Then let those foot trudge hence upon
      those horse,
According to our discharge, and be gone.—
Derby, I'll look upon the countess' mind
Anon.[14]

Der.   The countess' mind, my liege?

Edw. I mean, the emperor: Leave me alone.

Aud. What's in his mind?

Der.   Let's leave him to his humour.
                            [*Exeunt* DER., *and* AUD.

Edw. Thus from the heart's abundant speaks the
      tongue;
Countess for emperor: And, indeed, why not?
She is as imperator over me;
And I to her
Am as a kneeling vassal, that observes
The pleasure, or displeasure, of her eye.—

Enter LODOWICK.

What says the more than Cleopatra's match
To Cæsar now?

Lod. That yet, my liege, ere night
She will resolve your majesty.   [*Drum within.*

Edw. What drum is this, that thunders forth
      this march,
To start the tender Cupid in my bosom?
Poor sheep-skin, how it brawls with him that
      beateth it!
Go, break the thundering parchment bottom out,
And I will teach it to conduct sweet lines
Unto the bosom of a heavenly nymph:
For I will use it as my writing-paper;
And so reduce him, from a scolding drum,
To be the herald, and dear counsel-bearer,
Betwixt a goddess and a mighty king.
Go, bid the drummer learn to touch the lute,
Or hang him in the braces of his drum;
For now we think it an uncivil thing,
To trouble heaven with such harsh resounds:
Away.   [*Exit* LOD.
The quarrel, that I have, requires no arms,
But these of mine; and these shall meet my foe
In a deep march of penetrable groans:
My eyes shall be my arrows; and my sighs
Shall serve me as the vantage of the wind,
To whirl away my sweet'st artillery:
Ah but, alas, she wins the sun of me,
For that is she herself; and thence it comes
That·poets term the wanton warrior, blind;
But love hath eyes as judgment to his steps,
'Till too much loved glory dazzles them.—

Re-enter LODOWICK.

How now?

Lod. My liege, the drum, that strook the lusty
      march,
Stands with prince Edward, your thrice valiant son.

Enter PRINCE. LODOWICK *retires to the Door.*

Edw. I see the boy. O, how his mother's face,
Moulded in his, corrects my stray'd desire,
And rates my heart, and chides my thievish eye;
Who, being rich enough in seeing her,
Yet seeks elsewhere: and basest theft is that,
Which cannot check itself on poverty.—
Now, boy, what news?

Prince. I have assembl'd, my dear lord and fa-
      ther,
The choicest buds of all our English blood,
For our affairs in France; and here we come,
To take direction from your majesty.

Edw. Still do I see in him delineate
His mother's visage; those his eyes are hers,
Who, looking wistly on me, made me blush;

For faults against themselves give evidence:
Lust is a fire; and men, like lanterns, show
Light lust within themselves, even through them-
　　　selves.
Away, loose silks of wavering vanity!
Shall the large limit of fair Brittany
By me be overthrown? and shall I not
Master this little mansion of myself?
Give me an armour of eternal steel;
I go to conquer kings; And shall I then
Subdue myself, and be my enemy's friend?
It must not be.—Come, boy, forward, advance!
Let's with our colours sweep the air of France.
　　Lod. My liege, the countess, with a smiling
　　　cheer,
Desires access unto your majesty.
　　　[Advancing from the Door, and whispering him.
　　Edw. Why, there it goes! that very smile of
　　　hers
Hath ransom'd captive France; and set the king,
The dauphin, and the peers, at liberty.—
Go, leave me, Ned, and revel with thy friends.
　　　　　　　　　　　　　　[Exit PRINCE.
Thy mother is but black; and thou, like her,
Dost put into my mind how foul she is.—
Go, fetch the countess hither in thy hand,
And let her chase away those winter clouds;
For she gives beauty both to heaven and earth.
　　　　　　　　　　　　　　[Exit LOD.
The sin is more, to hack and hew poor men,
Than to embrace, in an unlawful bed,
The register of all rarieties
Since leathern Adam 'till this youngest hour.

　　　Re-enter LODOWICK, *with the* COUNTESS.

Go, Lodowick, put thy hand into my purse,
Play, spend, give, riot, waste; do what thou wilt,
So thou wilt hence awhile, and leave me here.
　　　　　　　　　　　　　　[Exit LOD.
Now, my soul's play-fellow! and art thou come,
To speak the more than heavenly word, of yea,
To my objection in thy beauteous love?
　　Cou. My father on his blessing hath com-
　　　manded—
　　Edw. That thou shalt yield to me.
　　Cou. Ay, dear my liege, your due.
　　Edw. And that, my dearest love, can be no less
Than right for right, and tender love for love.
　　Cou. Than wrong for wrong, and endless hate
　　　for hate.—
But,—sith I see your majesty so bent,
That my unwillingness, my husband's love,
Your high estate, nor no respect respected

Can be my help, but that your mightiness
Will overbear and awe these dear regards,—
I bind my discontent to my content,
And, what I would not, I'll compel I will;
Provided, that yourself remove those lets,[15]
That stand between your highness' love and mine.
　　Edw. Name them, fair countess, and, by heaven,
　　　I will;
　　Cou. It is their lives, that stand between our
　　　love,
That I would have chok'd up, my sovereign.
　　Edw. Whose lives, my lady?
　　Cou. My thrice loving liege,
Your queen, and Salisbury my wedded husband
Who living have that title in our love,
That we cannot bestow but by their death.
　　Edw. Thy opposition is beyond our law.
　　Cou. And so is your desire: If the law
Can hinder you to execute the one,
Let it forbid you to attempt the other:
I cannot think you love me as you say,
Unless you do make good what you have sworn.
　　Edw. No more; thy husband and the queen
　　　shall die.
Fairer thou art by far than Hero was;
Beardless Leander not so strong as I:
He swam an easy current for his love;
But I will, through a helly spout of blood,[16]
Arrive that Sestos where my Hero lies.
　　Cou. Nay, you'll do more; you'll make the river
　　　too,
With their heart-bloods that keep our love asunder,
Of which, my husband, and your wife, are twain.
　　Edw. Thy beauty makes them guilty of their
　　　death,
And gives in evidence, that they shall die:
Upon which verdict, I, their judge, condemn them.
　　Cou. O perjur'd beauty! more corrupted judge!
When, to the great star-chamber o'er our heads,
The universal sessions calls to count
This packing evil,[17] we both shall tremble for it.
　　Edw. What says my fair love? is she resolute?
　　Cou. Resolute to be dissolv'd; and, therefore,
　　　this,—
Keep but thy word, great king, and I am thine.
Stand where thou dost, I'll part a little from thee,
And see how I will yield me to thy hands.
　　　[Turning suddenly upon him, and showing two
　　　Daggers.
Here by my side do hang my wedding knives:
Take thou the one, and with it kill thy queen,
And learn by me to find her where she lies;
And with the other I'll dispatch my love,

Which now lies fast asleep within my heart :
When they are gone, then I'll consent to love.
Stir not, lascivious king, to hinder me ;
My resolution is more nimbler far,
Than thy prevention can be in my rescue,
And, if thou stir, I strike : therefore stand still,
And hear the choice that I will put thee to :
Either swear to leave thy most unholy suit,
And never henceforth to solicit me ;
Or else, by heaven, [*kneeling*] this sharp-pointed
    knife
Shall stain thy earth with that which thou would'st
    stain,
My poor chaste blood.   Swear, Edward, swear,
Or I will strike, and die, before thee here.
    Edw. Even by that Power I swear, that gives
    me now
The power to be ashaméd of myself
I never mean to part my lips again
In any word that tends to such a suit.

Arise, true English lady ; whom our isle
May better boast of, than e'er Roman might
Of her, whose ransack'd treasury hath task'd
The vain endeavour of so many pens :[18]
Arise ; And be my fault thy honour's fame,
Which after ages shall enrich thee with.
I am awaked from this idle dream ;—
Warwick, my son, Derby, Artois, and Audley,
Brave warriors all, where are you all this while ?

Enter PRINCE *and* Lords.

Warwick, I make thee warden of the north :—
You, prince of Wales, and Audley, straight to sea ;
Scour to Newhaven ; some there stay for me :—
Myself, Artois, and Derby, will through Flanders,
To greet our friends there, and to crave their aid :
This night will scarce suffice me, to discover
My folly's siege against a faithful lover ;
For, ere the sun shall gild the eastern sky,[19]
We'll wake him with our martial harmony. [*Exeunt.*

ACT III.

SCENE I.—Flanders.   *The* French *Camp.*

Enter KING JOHN of France ; *his two sons,* CHARLES
    Duke of Normandy, *and* PHILIP ; DUKE OF
    LORRAIN, *and* Others.

    John. Here, 'till our navy, of a thousand sail,
Have made a breakfast to our foe by sea,
Let us encamp, to wait their happy speed.—
Lorrain, what readiness is Edward in ?
How hast thou heard that he provided is
Of martial furniture for this exploit ?
    Lor. To lay aside unnecessary soothing,
And not to spend the time in circumstance,
'Tis bruited for a certainty, my lord,
That he's exceeding strongly fortify'd ;
His subjects flock as willingly to war,
As if unto a triumph they were led.
    Cha. England was wont to harbour malcontents,
Blood-thirsty and seditious Catalines,[20]
Spend-thrifts, and such as gape for nothing else
But change and alteration of the state ;
And is it possible, that they are now
So loyal in themselves ?
    Lor. All but the Scot ; who solemnly protests,
As heretofore I have inform'd his grace,
Never to sheath his sword, or take a truce.
    John. Ah, that's the anchorage of some better
    hope !

But, on the other side, to think what friends
King Edward hath retain'd in Netherland,
Among those ever-bibbing epicures,
Those frothy Dutchmen, puff'd with double beer,
That drink and swill in every place they come,
Doth not a little aggravate mine ire :
Besides, we hear, the emperor conjoins,
And stalls him in his own authority :
But, all the mightier that their number is,
The greater glory reaps the victory.
Some friends have we, beside domestic power ;
The stern Polonian, and the warlike Dane,
The king of Boheme, and of Sicily,
Are all become confederates with us,
And, as I think, are marching hitherward.
                 [*Drum within.*
But, soft, I hear the music of their drums,
By which I guess that their approach is near.

Enter BOHEMIA, *and* Forces ; *and Aid of* Danes,
    Poles, *and* Muscovites.

    Boh. King John of France, as league, and neigh-
    bourhood
Requires, when friends are any way distress'd,
I come to aid thee with my country's force.
    Pol. And from great Moscow, fearful to the
    Turk,
And lofty Poland, nurse of hardy men,

I bring these servitors to fight for thee,
Who willingly will venture in thy cause.

   John. Welcome, Bohemian king; and welcome,
     all:
This your great kindness I will not forget;
Beside your plentiful rewards in crowns,
That from our treasury ye shall receive:
There comes a hare-brain'd nation, deck'd in pride,
The spoil of whom will be a treble gain.—
And now my hope is full, my joy complete:
At sea, we are as puissant as the force
Of Agamemnon in the haven of Troy;[21]
By land, with Xerxes we compare of strength,[22]
Whose soldiers drank up rivers in their thirst:
Then, Bayard-like, blind over-weening Ned,
To reach at our imperial diadem,
Is, either to be swallow'd of the waves,
Or hack'd a-pieces when thou com'st ashore.

      Enter a Mariner.

   Mar. Near to the coast I have descried, my lord,
As I was busy in my watchful charge,
The proud armado of King Edward's ships;
Which, at the first, far off when I did ken
Seem'd as it were a grove of wither'd pines;
But, drawing near, their glorious bright aspect,
Their streaming ensigns wrought of colour'd silk,
Like to a meadow full of sundry flowers,
Adorns the naked bosom of the earth:
Majestical the order of their course,
Figuring the horned circle of the moon:
On the top-gallant of the admiral,
And likewise all the handmaids of his train,
The arms of England and of France unite
Are quarter'd equally by herald's art.[23]
Thus, tightly carried with a merry gale,
They plough the ocean hitherward amain.

   John. Dare he already crop the flower-de-luce?
I hope, the honey being gather'd thence,
He, with the spider, afterward approach'd,
Shall suck forth deadly venom from the leaves.—
But where's our navy? how are they prepar'd
To wing themselves against this flight of ravens?

   Mar. They, having knowledge brought them by
     the scouts,
Did break from anchor straight; and, puffed with
     rage,
No otherwise than were their sails with wind,
Made forth; as when the empty eagle flies,
To satisfy his hungry griping maw.

   John. There's for thy news. Return unto thy
     bark;
And, if thou 'scape the bloody stroke of war,

And do survive the conflict, come again,
And let us hear the manner of the fight.—
                 [*Exit* Mar.
Mean space, my lords, 'tis best we be dispers'd
To several places, lest they chance to land:
First, you, my lord, with your Bohemian troops,
Shall pitch your battles on the lower hand;
My eldest son, the duke of Normandy,
Together with this aid of Muscovites,
Shall climb the higher ground another way;
Here in the middle coast, betwixt you both,
Philip, my youngest boy, and I will lodge.
So, lords, be gone, and look unto your charge;
You stand for France, an empire fair and large.—
    [*Exeunt* CHA. LOR. BOH. *and* Forces.
Now tell me, Philip, what is thy conceit,
Touching the challenge that the English make?

   Phi. I say, my lord, claim Edward what he can,
And bring he ne'er so plain a pedigree,
'Tis you are in possession of the crown,
And that's the surest point of all the law:
But, were it not; yet, ere he should prevail,
I'll make a conduit of my dearest blood,
Or chase those straggling upstarts home again.

   John. Well said, young Philip! Call for bread
     and wine,
That we may cheer our stomachs with repast,
To look our foes more sternly in the face.
   [*A Table and Provisions brought in;* King
     and his Son *set down to it. Ordnance
     afar off.*
Now is begun the heavy day at sea.
Fight, Frenchmen, fight: be like the field of bears,
When they defend their younglings in their caves!
Steer, angry Nemesis, the happy helm;
That, with the sulphur'd battles of your rage,
The English fleet may be dispers'd, and sunk!
             [*Ordnance again.*
   Phi. O, father, how this echoing cannon shot,
Like sweetest harmony, digests my cates!

   John. Now, boy, thou hear'st what thundering
     terror 'tis,
To buckle for a kingdom's sovereignty:
The earth, with giddy trembling when it shakes,
Or when the exhalations of the air
Break in extremity of lightning flash,
Affrights not more, than kings, when they dis-
     pose
To shew the rancour of their high-swollen hearts.
               [*Retreat heard.*
Retreat is sounded; one side hath the worse:
O, if it be the French!—Sweet fortune, turn;
And, in thy turning, change the froward winds,

That, with advantage of a favouring sky,
Our men may vanquish, and the other fly!

Enter Mariner.

My heart misgives:—Say, mirror of pale death,
To whom belongs the honour of this day?
Relate, I pray thee, if thy breath will serve,
The sad discourse of this discomfiture.
   Mar. I will, my lord.
My gracious sovereign, France hath ta'en the
      foil,
And boasting Edward triumphs with success.
These iron-hearted navies,
When last I was reporter to your grace,
Both full of angry spleen, of hope, and fear,
Hasting to meet each other in the face,
At last conjoin'd; and by their admiral
Our admiral encounter'd many shot:
By this, the other, that beheld these twain
Give earnest penny of a further wreck,
Like fiery dragons took their haughty flight;
And, likewise meeting, from their smoky wombs
Sent many grim ambassadors of death.
Then 'gan the day to turn to gloomy night;
And darkness did as well enclose the quick,
As those that were but newly reft of life:
No leisure serv'd for friends to bid farewell;
And, if it had, the hideous noise was such,
As each to other seeméd deaf and dumb:
Purple the sea; whose channel fill'd as fast
With streaming gore, that from the maiméd fell,
As did her gushing moisture break into
The crannied cleftures of the through-shot planks:
Here flew a head, dissever'd from the trunk;
There mangl'd arms, and legs, were toss'd aloft;
As when a whirlwind takes the summer dust,
And scatters it in middle of the air:
Then might ye see the reeling vessels split,
And tottering sink into the ruthless flood,
Until their lofty tops were seen no more.
All shifts were tried, both for defence and hurt:
And now the effects of valour, and of fear,
Of resolution, and of cowardice,
Were lively pictur'd; how the one for fame,
The other by compulsion laid about:
Much did the Nonpareille, that brave ship;
So did the Black-Snake of Boulogne, than which
A bonnier vessel never yet spread sail:
But all in vain; both sun, the wind and tide,
Revolted all unto our foemen's side,
That we perforce were fain to give them way,
And they are landed: Thus my tale is done;
We have untimely lost, and they have won.

John. Then rests there nothing, but, with present
      speed,
To join our several forces all in one,
And bid them battle, ere they range too far.—
Come, gentle Philip, let us hence depart;
This soldier's words have pierc'd thy father's heart.

SCENE II.—Picardy.   *Fields near* Crecy.

Enter a Frenchman, *meeting certain* Others, *a*
Woman, *and two* Children, *laden with Household-
stuff, as removing.*

   1st Fr. Well met, my masters: How now?
      what's the news?
And wherefore are you laden thus with stuff?
What, is it quarter-day, that you remove,
And carry bag and baggage too?
   2nd Fr. Quarter-day? ay, and quartering day, I
      fear:
Have you not heard the news that flies abroad?
   1st Fr. What news?
   3rd Fr. How the French navy is destroy'd at
      sea,
And that the English army is arriv'd.
   1st Fr. What then?
   2nd Fr. What then, quoth you? why, is't not
      time to fly,
When envy and destruction is so nigh?
   1st Fr. Content thee, man; they are far enough
      from hence;
And will be met, I warrant you, to their cost,
Before they break so far into the realm.
   2nd Fr. Ay, so the grasshopper doth spend the
      time
In mirthful jollity, 'till winter come;
And then too late he would redeem his time,
When frozen cold hath nipped his careless head.
He, that no sooner will provide a cloak,
Than when he sees it doth begin to rain,
May, peradventure, for his negligence,
Be thoroughly wash'd when he suspects it not.
We, that have charge, and such a train as this,
Must look in time to look for them and us,
Lest, when we would, we cannot be reliev'd.
   1st Fr. Belike, you then despair of all success,
And think your country will be subjugate.
   3rd Fr. We cannot tell; 'tis good, to fear the
      worst.
   1st Fr. Yet rather fight, than, like unnatural
      sons,
Forsake your loving parents in distress.
   2nd Fr. Tush, they, that have already taken arms,
Are many fearful millions, in respect

Of that small handful of our enemies;
But 'tis a rightful quarrel must prevail;
Edward is son unto our late king's sister,
Where John Valois is three degrees remov'd.

Wom. Besides, there goes a prophecy abroad,
Publish'd by one that was a friar once,
Whose oracles have many times prov'd true;
And now he says, " The time will shortly come,
When as a lion, roused in the west,
Shall carry hence the flower-de-luce of France:"
These, I can tell ye, and such like surmises
Strike many Frenchmen cold unto the heart.

Enter another Frenchman, *hastily.*

4th Fr. Fly, countrymen, and citizens of France!
Sweet-flow'ring peace, the root of happy life,
Is quite abandon'd and expuls'd the land:
Instead of whom, ransack-constraining war
Sits like to ravens on your houses' tops;
Slaughter and mischief walk within your streets,
And, unrestrain'd, make havoc as they pass:
The form whereof even now myself beheld,
Now, upon this fair mountain, whence I came.
For so far as I did direct mine eyes,
I might perceive five cities all on fire,
Corn-fields, and vineyards, burning like an oven;
And, as the leaking vapour in the wind
Turned aside, I likewise might discern
The poor inhabitants, escap'd the flame,
Fall numberless upon the soldiers' pikes:
Three ways these dreadful ministers of wrath
Do tread the measures of their tragic march;
Upon the right hand comes the conquering king,
Upon the left his hot unbridl'd son,
And in the midst our nation's glittering host;
All which, though distant, yet conspire in one
To leave a desolation where they come.
Fly, therefore, citizens, if you be wise,
Seek out some habitation further off:
Here if you stay, your wives will be abus'd,
Your treasure shar'd before your weeping eyes;
Shelter yourselves, for now the storm doth rise;
Away, away! methinks, I hear their drums:—
Ah wretched France, I greatly fear thy fall;
Thy glory shaketh like a tottering wall.

                             [Exeunt.

SCENE III.—*The Same.*

Drums. *Enter* KING EDWARD, *marching;* DERBY,
  &c., and Forces, *and* GOBIN DE GREY.

Edw. Where is the Frenchman, by whose cunning guide

We found the shallow of this river Somme,
And had direction how to pass the sea?
  Gob. Here, my good lord.
  Edw.   How art thou call'd? thy name?
  Gob. Gobin de Grey, if please your excellence.
  Edw. Then, Gobin, for the service thou hast done,
We here enlarge and give thee liberty;
And, for a recompense, beside this good,
Thou shalt receive five hundred marks in gold.—
I know not how, we should have met our son;
Whom now in heart I wish I might behold.

Enter ARTOIS.

  Art. Good news, my lord; the prince is hard at
      hand,
And with him comes lord Audley, and the rest,
Whom since our landing we could never meet.

Drums. *Enter* PRINCE, AUDLEY, *and* Forces.

  Edw. Welcome, fair prince! How hast thou
      sped, my son,
Since thy arrival on the coast of France?
  Prince. Successfully, I thank the gracious hea-
      vens:
Some of their strongest cities we have won,
As Harfleur, Lo, Crotage, and Carentan;
And others wasted; leaving at our heels
A wide apparent field, and beaten path,
For solitariness to progress in:
Yet, those that would submit, we kindly pardon'd;
For who in scorn refus'd our proffer'd peace,
Endur'd the penalty of sharp revenge.
  Edw. Ah, France, why should'st thou be thus
      obstinate
Against the kind embracement of thy friends?
How gentle had we thought to touch thy breast,
And set our foot upon thy tender mould,
But that, in forward and disdainful pride,
Thou, like a skittish and untaméd colt,
Dost start aside, and strike us with thy heels?—
But tell me, Ned, in all thy warlike course
Hast thou not seen the usurping king of France?
  Prince. Yes, my good lord, and not two hours ago,
With full an hundred thousand fighting men,
Upon the one side o' the river's bank,
I on the other; with his multitudes
I fear'd he would have crop'd our smaller power:
But, happily, perceiving your approach,
He hath withdrawn himself to Crecy' plains;
Where, as it seemeth by his good array,
He means to bid us battle presently.
  Edw. He shall be welcome, that's the thing we
      crave.

Drums. Enter KING JOHN; CHARLES *and* PHILIP,
his Sons; BOHEMIA, LORRAIN, *&c., and* Forces.

John. Now, Edward, know, that John, true king
    of France,—
Musing thou should'st encroach upon his land,
And, in thy tyrannous proceeding, slay
His faithful subjects, and subvert his towns,—
Spits in thy face; and in this manner following
Upbraids thee with thine arrogant intrusion.
First, I condemn thee for a fugitive,
A thievish pirate, and a needy mate;
One, that hath either no abiding place,
Or else, inhabiting some barren soil,
Where neither herb or fruitful grain is had,
Dost altogether live by pilfering:
Next,—insomuch thou hast infring'd thy faith,
Broke league and solemn covenant made with
    me,—
I hold thee for a most pernicious wretch:
And last of all,—although I scorn to cope
With one so much inferior to myself;
Yet, in respect thy thirst is all for gold,
Thy labour rather to be fear'd than lov'd,—
To satisfy thy lust in either part,
Here am I come; and with me I have brought
Exceeding store of treasure, pearl, and coin.
Leave therefore now to persecute the weak;
And, armed ent'ring conflict with the arm'd,
Let it be seen, 'mongst other petty thefts,
How thou canst win this pillage manfully.
    Edw. If gall, or wormwood, have a pleasant
    taste,
Then is thy salutation honey-sweet:
But as the one hath no such property,
So is the other most satirical.
Yet wot how I regard thy worthless taunts;—
If thou have utter'd them to foil my fame,
Or dim the reputation of my birth,
Know, that thy wolfish barking cannot hurt:
If slily to insinuate with the world,
And with a strumpet's artificial line
To paint thy vicious and deformed cause,
Be well assur'd, the counterfeit will fade,
And in the end thy foul defects be seen:
But if thou did'st it to provoke me on,—
As who should say, I were but timorous,
Or, coldly negligent, did need a spur,—
Bethink thyself, how slack I was at sea;
How, since my landing, I have won no towns,
Enter'd no further but upon thy coast,
And there have ever since securely slept.
But if I have been otherways employ'd,

Imagine, Valois, whether I intend
To skirmish, not for pillage, but the crown
Which thou dost wear; and that I vow to have,
Or one of us shall fall into his grave.
    Prince. Look not for cross invectives at our
    hands,
Or railing execrations of despite:
Let creeping serpents, hid in hollow banks,
Sting with their tongues; we have remorseless
    swords,
And they shall plead for us, and our affairs.
Yet thus much, briefly, by my father's leave:
As all the immodest poison of thy throat
Is scandalous and most notorious lies,
And our pretended quarrel[24] truly just,
So end the battle when we meet to-day;
May either of us prosper and prevail,
Or, luckless curst, receive eternal shame!
    Edw. That needs no further question; and, I
    know,
His conscience witnesseth, it is my right.—
Therefore, Valois, say, wilt thou yet resign,
Before the sickle's thrust into the corn,
Or that enkindl'd fury turn'd to flame?
    John. Edward, I know what right thou hast in
    France:
And ere I basely will resign my crown,
This champion field shall be a pool of blood,
And all our prospect as a slaughter-house.
    Prince. Ay, that approves thee, tyrant, what
    thou art:
No father, king, or shepherd of thy realm;
But one, that tears her entrails with thy hands,
And, like a thirsty tiger, suck'st her blood.
    Aud. You peers of France, why do you follow
    him
That is so prodigal to spend your lives?
    Cha. Whom should they follow, agéd impotent,
But he that is their true-born sovereign?
    Edw. Upbraid'st thou him, because within his
    face
Time hath engrav'd deep characters of age?
Know, these grave scholars of experience,
Like stiff-grown oaks, will stand immovable,
When whirlwind quickly turns up younger trees.
    Der. Was ever any of thy father's house
King, but thyself, before this present time?
Edward's great lineage, by the mother's side,
Five hundred years hath held the sceptre up:—
Judge then, conspirators, by this descent,
Which is the true-born sovereign, this, or that.[25]
    Phi. Good father 'range your battles, prate no
    more;

These English fain would spend the time in words,
That, night approaching, they might 'scape unfought.
    John. Lords, and my loving subjects, now's the time,
That your intended force must 'bide the touch :
Therefore, my friends, consider this in brief,—
He, that you fight for, is your natural king ;
He, against whom you fight, a foreigner :
He, that you fight for, rules in clemency,
And reins you with a mild and gentle bit ;
He, against whom you fight, if he prevail,
Will straight enthrone himself in tyranny,
Make slaves of you, and, with a heavy hand,
Curtail and curb your sweetest liberty.
Then, to protect your country, and your king,
Let but the haughty courage of your hearts
Answer the number of your able hands,
And we shall quickly chase these fugitives.
For what's this Edward, but a belly-god,
A tender and lascivious wantonness,
That t'other day was almost dead for love ?
And what, I pray you, is his goodly guard ?
Such as, but scant them of their chines of beef,
And take away their downy feather-beds,
And, presently, they are as resty-stiff
As 'twere a many over-ridden jades.
Then, Frenchmen, scorn that such should be your
    lords,
And rather bind ye them in captive bands.
    Fr. Vive le roi ! God save King John of France !
    John. Now on this plain of Crecy spread your-
    selves,—
And, Edward, when thou dar'st, begin the fight.
    [*Exeunt* KING JOHN, CHA. PHI. LOR. BOH.
    and Forces.
    Edw. We presently will meet thee, John of
    France :—
And, English lords, let us resolve this day,
Either to clear us of that scandalous crime,
Or be entombed in our innocence.—
And, Ned, because this battle is the first
That ever yet thou fought'st in pitched field,
As ancient custom is of martialists,
To dub thee with the type of chivalry,
In solemn manner we will give thee arms :—
Come, therefore, heralds, orderly bring forth
A strong attirement for the prince my son.—

Flourish. Enter Four Heralds, *bringing a Coat-*
armour, a Helmet, a Lance, and a Shield: First
Herald *delivers the Armour to* KING EDWARD ;
who, putting it on his Son,

Edward Plantagenet, in the name of God,
As with this armour I impall thy breast,

So be thy noble unrelenting heart
Wall'd in with flint of matchless fortitude,
That never base affections enter there ;
Fight and be valiant, conquer where thou com'st !
Now follow, lords, and do him honour too.
    Der. [*Receiving the Helmet from the Second*
    Herald.
Edward Plantagenet, Prince of Wales,
As I do set this helmet on thy head,
Wherewith the chamber of thy brain is fenc'd,
So may thy temples, with Bellona's hand,
Be still adorn'd with laurel victory :
Fight and be valiant, conquer where thou com'st !
    Aud. [*Receiving the Lance from the Third*
    Herald.
Edward Plantagenet, Prince of Wales,
Receive this lance, into thy manlike hand ;
Use it in fashion of a brazen pen,
To draw forth bloody stratagems in France,
And print thy valiant deeds in honour's book :
Fight and be valiant, conquer where thou com'st !
    Art. [*Receiving the Shield from the Fourth*
    Herald.
Edward Plantagenet, Prince of Wales,
Hold, take this target, wear it on thy arm ;
And may the view thereof, like Perseus' shield,
Astonish and transform thy gazing foes
To senseless images of meagre death ;
Fight and be valiant, conquer where thou com'st !
    Edw. Now wants there nought but knighthood ;
    which, deferr'd,
We leave till thou hast won it in the field.
    Pri. My gracious father, and ye forward peers,
This honour, you have done me, animates
And cheers my green yet-scarce-appearing strength
With comfortable good-presaging signs ;
No otherwise than did old Jacob's words,
When as he breath'd his blessings on his sons :
These hallow'd gifts of yours when I profane,
Or use them not to glory of my God,
To patronage the fatherless, and poor,
Or for the benefit of England's peace,
Benumb my joints ! wax feeble both mine arms !
Wither my heart ! that, like a sapless tree,
I may remain the map of infamy.
    Edw. Then thus our steeled battles shall be
    rang'd ;—
The leading of the vaward,[26] Ned, is thine ;
To dignify whose lusty spirit the more,
We temper it with Audley's gravity ;
That, courage and experience join'd in one,
Your manage may be second unto none :
For the main battles, I will guide myself ;

And Derby, in the rearward march behind.
That orderly dispos'd, and set in 'ray,
Let us to horse; and God grant us the day!

SCENE IV.—*Near the Field of Battle.*

Alarums. Enter a many Frenchmen, *flying;* PRINCE,
and English *pursuing; and Exeunt: then Enter*
KING JOHN, *and* LORRAIN.

John. O Lorrain, say, what mean our men to fly?
Our number is far greater than our foes.
Lor. The garrison of Genoeses, my lord,
That came from Paris, weary with their march,
Grudging to be so suddenly employ'd,[27]
No sooner in the fore-front took their place,
But, straight retiring, so dismay'd the rest,
As likewise they betook themselves to flight;
In which, for haste to make a safe escape,
More in the clust'ring throng are press'd to death,
Than by the enemy, a thousand fold.
John. O hapless fortune! Let us yet assay
If we can counsel some of them to stay. [*Exeunt.*

SCENE V.—*A Hill near the Battle-field.*

Drums. Enter KING EDWARD *and* AUDLEY.

Edw. Lord Audley, whiles our son is in the chase,
Withdraw your powers unto this little hill,
And here a season let us breathe ourselves.
Aud. I will, my lord.   [*Exit* AUD. *Retreat.*
Edw. Just-dooming heaven, whose secret pro-
            vidence
To our gross judgment is inscrutable,
How are we bound to praise thy wondrous works,
That hast this day giv'n way unto the right,
And made the wicked stumble at themselves?

Enter ARTOIS, *hastily.*

Art. Rescue, King Edward! rescue for thy son!
Edw. Rescue, Artois? what, is he prisoner?
Or, else, by violence fell beside his horse?
Art. Neither, my lord; but narrowly beset
With turning Frenchmen, whom he did pursue,
As 'tis impossible that he should 'scape,
Except your highness presently descend.
Edw. Tut, let him fight; we gave him arms to-
            day,
And he is labouring for a knighthood, man.

Enter DERBY, *hastily.*

Der. The prince, my lord, the prince! O succour
            him;
He's close encompassed with a world of odds!

Edw. Then will he win a world of honour too.
If he by valour can redeem him thence:
If not, what remedy? we have more sons
Than one, to comfort our declining age.

Re-enter AUDLEY, *hastily.*

Aud. Renowned Edward, give me leave, I pray,
To lead my soldiers, where I may relieve
Your grace's son, in danger to be slain.
The snares of French, like emmets on a bank,
Muster about him; whilst he, lion-like,
Entangl'd in the net of their assaults,
Franticly rends, and bites the woven toil:
But all in vain, he cannot free himself.
Edw. Audley, content; I will not have a man,
On pain of death, sent forth to succour him:
This is the day ordain'd by destiny
To season his green courage with those thoughts,
That, if he break'th out Nestor's years on earth,
Will make him savour still of this exploit.
Der. Ah, but he shall not live to see those days.
Edw. Why, then his epitaph is lasting praise.
Aud. Yet, good my lord, 'tis too much wilfulness,
To let his blood be spilt, that may be sav'd,
Edw. Exclaim no more; for none of you can tell,
Whether a borrow'd aid will serve, or no;
Perhaps, he is already slain, or ta'en:
And dare a falcon when she's in her flight,
And ever after she'll be haggard-like:[28]
Let Edward be deliver'd by our hands,
And still, in danger, he'll expect the like;
But if himself himself redeem from thence,
He will have vanquish'd, cheerful, death, and fear,
And ever after dread their force no more,
Than if they were but babes, or captive slaves.
Aud. O cruel father!—Farewell, Edward, then!
Der. Farewell, sweet prince, the hope of chivalry!
Art. O, would my life might ransom him from
            death!
Edw. Forbear, my lords,—But, soft; methinks, I
            hear   [*Retreat sounded.*
The dismal charge of trumpets' loud retreat:
All are not slain, I hope, that went with him;
Some will return with tidings, good, or bad.

Flourish. Enter PRINCE EDWARD *in Triumph,
bearing in his Hand his shiver'd Lance; his
Sword, and batter'd Armour, borne before him,
and the Body of the* King of Bohemia, *wrapt in
the Colours:* Lords *run and embrace him.*

Aud. O joyful sight! victorious Edward lives!
Der. Welcome, brave prince!
Edw. Welcome, Plantagenet! [*Embracing him.*

35

Prince. First having done my duty, as beseem'd,
　　[*Kneels, and kisses his* Father's *Hand.*
Lords, I regreet you all with hearty thanks.
And now, behold,—after my winter's toil,
My painful voyage on the boist'rous sea
Of war's devouring gulfs and steely rocks,—
I bring my fraught unto the wished port,
My summer's hope, my travel's sweet reward:
And here, with humble duty, I present
This sacrifice, this first fruit of my sword,
Cropp'd and cut down even at the gate of death,
The king of Boheme, father, whom I slew;
Whose thousands had intrench'd me round about,
And lay as thick upon my batter'd crest,
As on an anvil, with their pond'rous glaives:
Yet marble courage still did underprop;
And when my weary arms, with often blows,—
Like the continual-lab'ring woodman's axe,
That is enjoin'd to fell a load of oaks,—
Began to falter, straight I would remember
My gifts you gave me, and my zealous vow,
And then new courage made me fresh again;
That, in despite, I carv'd my passage forth,
And put the multitude to speedy flight.
Lo, thus hath Edward's hand fill'd your request,
And done, I hope, the duty of a knight.
　　Edw. Ay, well thou hast descrv'd a knighthood,
　　　　Ned.
And, therefore, with thy sword, yet reeking warm
　　[*Receiving it from the* Soldier *who bore it, and
　　laying it on the kneeling* PRINCE.

With blood of those that sought to be thy bane,
Arise, prince Edward, trusty knight at arms:
This day thou hast confounded me with joy,
And prov'd thyself fit heir unto a king.
　　Prince. Here is a note, my gracious lord, of
　　　　those
That in this conflict of our foes were slain:
Eleven princes of esteem;[29] four score
Barons, and earls; and hundred twenty knights;
And thirty thousand private soldiers;
And, of our men, a thousand.
　　Edw. Our God be prais'd! Now, John of France,
　　　　I hope,
Thou know'st king Edward for no wantonness,
No love-sick cockney;[30] nor his soldiers, jades.—
But which way is the fearful king escap'd?
　　Prince. Towards Poitiers, noble father, and his
　　　　sons.
　　Edw. Ned, thou, and Audley, shall pursue them
　　　　still;
Myself, and Derby, will to Calais straight,
And there begirt that haven-town with siege:
Now lies it on an upshot; therefore strike,
And wistly follow while's the game's on foot.
What picture's this?　　[*Pointing to the Colours.*
　　Prince.　A pelican, my lord,
Wounding her bosom with her crooked beak,
That so her nest of young ones may be fed
With drops of blood that issue from her heart;
The motto, *Sic et vos,* "And so should you."
　　　　[*Flourish.　Exeunt in Triumph.*

---————◆———---

ACT IV.

SCENE I.—Bretagne. *Camp of the* English Forces
under the Earl of Salisbury; Salisbury's *Tent.*

Enter SALISBURY; *to him, the* EARL OF MONTFORT,
attended, a Coronet in his Hand.

　　Mon. My lord of Salisbury, since by your aid
Mine enemy sir Charles of Blois is slain,
And I again am quietly possest
In Bretagne's dukedom, know, that I resolve,
For this kind furtherance of your king, and you,
To swear allegiance to his majesty:
In sign whereof, receive this coronet,
Bear it unto him; and, withal, my oath,
Never to be but Edward's faithful friend.
　　Sal. I take it, Montfort: Thus, I hope, ere long
The whole dominions of the realm of France
Will be surrender'd to his conquering hand.
　　　　[*Exeunt* MON., *and* Train.

Now, if I knew but safely how to pass,
I would at Calais gladly meet his grace,
Whither, I am by letters certify'd,
That he intends to have his host remov'd.
It shall be so; this policy will serve:—
Ho, who's within? Bring Villiers to me.—

Enter VILLIERS.

Villiers, thou know'st, thou art my prisoner,
And that I might, for ransom, if I would,
Require of thee an hundred thousand franks,
Or else retain and keep thee captive still:
But so it is, that for a smaller charge
Thou may'st be quit, an if thou wilt thyself;
And this it is, Procure me but a passport
Of Charles the duke of Normandy, that I,
Without restraint, may have recourse to Calais
Through all the countries where he hath to do,

(Which thou may'st easily obtain, I think,
By reason I have often heard thee say,
He and thyself were students once together)
And then thou shalt be set at liberty.
How say'st thou? wilt thou undertake to do it?

    Vil. I will, my lord; but I must speak with him.

    Sal. Why, so thou shalt; take horse, and post
        from hence:
Only, before thou go'st, swear by thy faith,
That, if thou can'st not compass my desire,
Thou wilt return my prisoner back again;
And that shall be sufficient warrant for thee.

    Vil. To that condition I agree, my lord,
And will unfeignedly perform the same.

    Sal. Farewell, Villiers.—   [*Exit* VIL.
Thus, once I mean to try a Frenchman's faith.

SCENE II.—Picardy. *The* English *Camp before*
    Calais.

Enter KING EDWARD, *and* DERBY, *with* Soldiers.

    Edw. Since they refuse our proffer'd league, my
        lord,
And will not ope the gates, and let us in,
We will intrench ourselves on every side,
That neither victuals, nor supply of men,
May come to succour this accursed town;
Famine shall combat where our swords are stopt.

    Der. The promis'd aid, that made them stand
        aloof,
Is now retir'd, and gone another way;
It will repent them of their stubborn will.

Enter some poor Frenchmen.

But what are these poor ragged slaves, my lord?

    Edw. Ask what they are; it seems they come
        from Calais.

    Der. You wretched patterns of despair and woe,
What are ye? living men; or gliding ghosts,
Crept from your graves to walk upon the earth?

    1st Fr. No ghosts, my lord, but men that breathe
        a life
Far worse than is the quiet sleep of death:
We are distressèd poor inhabitants,
That long have been diseased, sick, and lame:
And now, because we are not fit to serve,
The captain of the town hath thrust us forth,
That so expense of victuals may be sav'd.[31]

    Edw. A charitable deed, and worthy praise.—
But how do you imagine then to speed?
We are your enemies; in such a case
We can no less but put you to the sword,
Since, when we proffer'd truce, it was refus'd.

    1st Fr. An if your grace no otherwise vouchsafe,
As welcome death is unto us as life.

    Edw. Poor silly men, much wrong'd, and more
        distress'd!—
Go, Derby, go, and see they be reliev'd;
Command that victuals be appointed them,
And give to every one five crowns apiece:—
                 [*Exeunt* DER. *and* Fr.
The lion scorns to touch the yielding prey;
And Edward's sword must fresh itself in such
As wilful stubbornness hath made perverse.—

Enter the LORD PERCY, *from England.*

Lord Percy! welcome: What's the news in Eng-
    land?

    Per. The queen, my lord, commends her to your
        grace;
And from her highness and the lord vicegerent,
I bring this happy tidings of success:
David of Scotland, lately up in arms,
(Thinking, belike, he soonest should prevail,
Your highness being absent from the realm)
Is, by the faithful service of your peers,
And painful travel of the queen herself,
That, big with child, was every day in arms,
Vanquish'd, subdu'd, and taken prisoner.

    Edw. Thanks, Percy, for thy news, with all my
        heart!
What was he, took him prisoner in the field?

    Per. A squire, my lord; John Copland is his
        name:
Who since, entreated by her majesty,
Denies to make surrender of his prize
To any but unto your grace alone;
Whereat the queen is grievously displeas'd.

    Edw. Well, then we'll have a pursuivant dis-
        patch'd,
To summon Copland hither out of hand,
And with him he shall bring his prisoner king.

    Per. The queen's, my lord, herself by this at
        sea;
And purposeth, as soon as wind will serve,
To land at Calais, and to visit you.

    Edw. She shall be welcome; and, to wait her
        coming,
I'll pitch my tent near to the sandy shore.

Enter a French Captain.

    Capt. The burgesses of Calais, mighty king,
Have, by a council, willingly decreed
To yield the town, and castle to your hands;
Upon condition, it will please your grace
To grant them benefit of life and goods.

Edw. They will so! then, belike, they may command,
Dispose, elect, and govern as they list.
No, sirrah, tell them, since they did refuse
Our princely clemency at first proclaim'd,
They shall not have it now, although they would ;
I will accept of nought but fire and sword,
Except, within these two days, six of them,
That are the wealthiest merchants in the town,
Come naked, all but for their linen shirts,
With each a halter hang'd about his neck,
And prostrate yield themselves, upon their knees,
To be afflict'd, hang'd, or what I please ;
And so you may inform their masterships.
                         [*Exeunt* EDW. *and* PER.
Cap. Why, this it is to trust a broken staff.
Had we not been persuaded, John our king
Would with his army have reliev'd the town,
We had not stood upon defiance so :
But now 'tis past that no man can recall ;
And better some do go to wreck, than all.   [*Exit.*

SCENE III.—Poitou.   *Fields near* Poitiers.

The French *Camp ; Tent of the* DUKE OF NOR-
MANDY.   *Enter* CHARLES, *and* VILLIERS.

Chas. I wonder, Villiers, thou should'st importune me
For one that is our deadly enemy.
Vil. Not for his sake, my gracious lord, so much
Am I become an earnest advocate,
As that thereby my ransom will be quit.
Chas. Thy ransom, man ! why, need'st thou talk of that ?
Art thou not free ? and are not all occasions,
That happen for advantage of our foes,
To be accepted of, and stood upon ?
Vil. No, good my lord, except the same be just ;
For profit must with honour be co-mixed,
Or else our actions are but scandalous :
But, letting pass these intricate objections,
Wilt please your highness to subscribe, or no ?
Chas. Villiers, I will not, nor I cannot do it ;
Salisbury shall not have his will so much,
To claim a passport how it pleas'th himself.
Vil. Why, then I know the extremity, my lord,
I must return to prison whence I came.
Chas. Return ! I hope thou wilt not, Villiers :
What bird, that hath escap'd the fowler's gin,
Will not beware how she's ensnared again ?
Or, what is he, so senseless, and secure,

That, having hardly passed a dangerous gulf,
Will put himself in peril there again ?
Vil. Ah, but it is my oath, my gracious lord,
Which I in conscience may not violate,
Or else a kingdom should not draw me hence.
Chas. Thine oath ! why, that doth bind thee to abide :
Hast thou not sworn obedience to thy prince ?
Vil. In all things that uprightly he commands :
But either to persuade or threaten me,
Not to perform the covenant of my word,
Is lawless, and I need not to obey.
Chas. Why, is it lawful for a man to kill,
And not, to break a promise with his foe ?
Vil. To kill, my lord, when war is once proclaim'd,
So that our quarrel be for wrongs receiv'd,
No doubt, is lawfully permitted us :
But, in an oath, we must be well advis'd
How we do swear ; and, when we once have sworn,
Not to infringe it, though we die therefore :
Therefore, my lord, as willing I return,
As if I were to fly to paradise.   [*Going.*
Chas. Stay, my Villiers ; thy honourable mind
Deserves to be eternally admir'd.
Thy suit shall be no longer thus deferr'd ;
Give me the paper, I'll subscribe to it :
                  [*Signs, and gives it back.*
And, wheretofore I loved thee as Villiers,
Hereafter I'll embrace thee as myself ;
Stay, and be still in favour with thy lord.
Vil. I humbly thank your grace : I must dispatch,
And send this passport first unto the earl,
And then I will attend your highness' pleasure.
                              [*Exit* VIL.
Chas. Do so, Villiers ;—and Charles, when he hath need,
Be such his soldiers, howsoe'er he speed !

Enter KING JOHN.

John. Come, Charles, and arm thee ; Edward is entrapp'd,
The prince of Wales is fall'n into our hands,
And we have compassed him, he cannot 'scape.
Chas. But will your highness fight to-day ?
John. What else, my son ? he's scarce eight thousand strong,
And we are threescore thousand at the least.
Chas. I have a prophecy, my gracious lord,
Wherein is written, what success is like
To happen us in this outrageous war ;

It was delivered me at Crecy' field,
By one that is an aged hermit there. [*Reads.*

When feather'd fowl shall make thine army tremble,
  And flint stones rise, and break the battle 'ray,
Then think on him that doth not now dissemble ;
  For that shall be the hapless dreadful day :
Yet, in the end, thy foot thou shalt advance
As far in England, as thy foe in France.

John. By this it seems we shall be fortunate :
For as it is impossible, that stones
Should ever rise, and break the battle 'ray ;
Or airy fowl make men in arms to quake ;
So is it like, we shall not be subdu'd :
Or, say this might be true, yet, in the end,
Since he doth promise, we shall drive him hence,
And forage their country, as they have done ours,
By this revenge that loss will seem the less.
But all are frivolous fancies, toys, and dreams :
Once, we are sure we have ensnar'd the son,
Catch we the father after how we can. [*Exeunt.*

SCENE IV.—*The Same.   The English Camp.*

Enter PRINCE EDWARD, AUDLEY, *and* Others.

Prince. Audley, the arms of death embrace us
      round,
And comfort have we none, save that to die,
To pay sour earnest for a sweeter life.
At Crecy field our clouds of warlike smoke
Chok'd up those French mouths, and dissever'd
      them,
But now their multitudes of millions hide,
Masking as 'twere, the beauteous burning sun ;
Leaving no hope to us, but sullen dark,
And eyeless terror of all-ending night.
  Aud. This sudden, mighty, and expedient head,
That they have made, fair prince, is wonderful.
Before us in the valley lies the king,
Vantag'd with all that heaven and earth can yield ;
His party stronger battl'd than our whole :
His son, the braving duke of Normandy,
Hath trimm'd the mountain on our right hand up
In shining plate, that now the aspiring hill
Shows like a silver quarry, or an orb ;
Aloft the which, the banners, bannerets,
And new-replenished pendants, cuff the air,
And beat the winds, that, for their gaudiness,
Struggles to kiss them : on our left hand lies
Philip, the younger issue of the king,
Coating the other hill in such array,
That all his gilded upright pikes do seem
Straight trees of gold, the pendant streamers,
      leaves ;

And their device of antique heraldry,
Quarter'd in colours seeming sundry fruits,
Makes it the orchard of the Hesperides :
Behind us too the hill doth bear his height,
(For, like a half-moon, op'ning but one way,
It rounds us in) there at our backs are lodg'd
The fatal cross-bows ; and the battle there
Is govern'd by the rough Chatillion.
Then thus it stands,—The valley for our flight
The king binds in ; the hills on either hand
Are proudly royalized by his sons ;
And on the hill behind stands certain death,
In pay and service with Chatillion.
  Prince. Death's name is much more mighty than
      his deeds ;—
Thy parcelling this power hath made it more.
As many sands as these my hands can hold,
Are but my handful of so many sands ;
Then, all the world,—and call it but a power,—
Is easily ta'en up, and quickly thrown away :
But, if I stand to count them sand by sand,
The number would confound my memory,
And make a thousand millions of a task,
Which briefly, is no more, indeed, than one.
These quarter'd squadrons, and these regiments,
Before, behind us, and on either hand,
Are but a power : When we name a man,
His hand, his foot, his head, have several strengths ;
And being all but one self instant strength,
Why, all this many, Audley, is but one,
And we can call it but one man's strength.
He, that hath far to go, tells it by miles ;
If he should tell the steps, it kills his heart :
The drops are infinite that make a flood ;
And yet, thou know'st, we call it but a rain.
There is but one France, and one king of France,
That France hath no more kings ; and that same
      king
Hath but the puissant legion of one king ;
And we have one : Then apprehend no odds ;
For one to one is fair equality.—

Enter a Herald.

What tidings, messenger ? be plain, and brief.
  Her. The king of France, my sovereign lord
      and master,
Greets thus by me his foe the Prince of Wales :
If thou call forth an hundred men of name,
Of lords, knights, 'squires, and English gentlemen,
And with thyself and those kneel at his feet,
He straight will fold his bloody colours up,
And ransom shall redeem lives forfeited :
If not, this day shall drink more English blood

Than e'er was buried in our British earth.
What is the answer to his proffer'd mercy?

Prince. This heaven, that covers France, con-
tains the mercy
That draws from me submissive orisons;
That such base breath should vanish from my lips,
To urge the plea of mercy to a man,
The Lord forbid! Return, and tell thy king,
My tongue is made of steel, and it shall beg
My mercy on his coward burgonet;
Tell him, my colours are as red as his,
My men as bold, our English arms as strong,
Return him my defiance in his face.

Her. I go.   [*Exit* Her.

Enter another Herald.

Prince.   What news with thee?

Her. The duke of Normandy, my lord and
master,
Pitying thy youth is so engirt with peril,
By me hath sent a nimble-jointed jennet,
As swift as ever yet thou did'st bestride,
And therewithal he counsels thee to fly;
Else, death himself hath sworn, that thou shalt die.

Prince. Back with the beast unto the beast that
sent him;
Tell him, I cannot sit a coward's horse:
Bid him to-day bestride the jade himself;
For I will stain my horse quite o'er with blood,
And double-gild my spurs, but I will catch him;
So tell the carping boy, and get thee gone.
          [*Exit* Her.

Enter another Herald.

Her. Edward of Wales, Philip, the second son
To the most mighty christian king of France,
Seeing thy body's living date expir'd,
All full of charity and christian love,
Commends this book, full fraught with holy
prayers,
To thy fair hand, and, for thy hour of life,
Intreats thee that thou meditate therein,
And arm thy soul for her long journey towards.
Thus have I done his bidding, and return.

Prince. Herald of Philip, greet thy lord from
me;
All good, that he can send, I can receive:
But think'st thou not, the unadvisèd boy
Hath wrong'd himself, in thus far tend'ring me?
Haply, he cannot pray without the book;
I think him no divine extemporal:
Then render back this common-place of prayer,
To do himself good in adversity:

Besides, he knows not my sin's quality,
And therefore knows no prayers for my avail;
Ere night his prayer may be, to pray to God
To put it in my heart to hear his prayer;
So tell the courtly wanton, and be gone.

Her. I go.   [*Exit* Her.

Prince. How confident their strength and num-
ber makes them!—
Now, Audley, sound those silver wings of thine,
And let those milk-white messengers of time[32]
Show thy time's learning in this dangerous time:
Thyself art bruis'd and bent with many broils,
And stratagems forepassed with iron pens
Are texed in thine honourable face;
Thou art a married man in this distress,
But danger woos me as a blushing maid;
Teach me an answer to this perilous time.

Aud. To die is all as common, as to live;
The one in choice, the other holds in chace:
For, from the instant we begin to live,
We do pursue and hunt the time to die:
First bud we, then we blow, and after seed;
Then, presently, we fall; and, as a shade
Follows the body, so we follow death.
If then we hunt for death, why do we fear it?
Or, if we fear it, why do we follow it?
If we do fear, with fear we do but aid
The thing we fear to seize on us the sooner:
If we fear not, then no resolved proffer
Can overthrow the limit of our fate:
For, whether ripe, or rotten, drop we shall,
As we do draw the lottery of our doom.

Prince. Ah, good old man, a thousand thousand
armours
These words of thine have buckl'd on my back:
Ah, what an idiot hast thou made of life,
To seek the thing it fears! and how disgrac'd
The imperial victory of murd'ring death!
Since all the lives, his conquering arrows strike,
Seek him, and he not them, to shame his glory.
I will not give a penny for a life,
Nor half a halfpenny to shun grim death;
Since for to live is but to seek to die,
And dying but beginning of new life:
Let come the hour when He that rules it will!
To live, or die, I hold indifferent.   [*Exeunt.*

SCENE V.—*The Same. The* French *Camp.*

Enter KING JOHN, *and* CHARLES.

John. A sudden darkness hath defac'd the sky,[33]
The winds are crept into their caves for fear,
The leaves move not, the world is hush'd and still,

The birds cease singing, and the wand'ring brooks
Murmur no wonted greeting to their shores :
Silence attends some wonder, and expecteth
That heaven should pronounce some prophecy :
Where, or from whom, proceeds this silence,
    Charles ?
    Chas. Our men, with open mouths, and staring
        eyes,
Look on each other, as they did attend
Each other's words, and yet no creature speaks ;
A tongue-tied fear hath made a midnight hour,
And speeches sleep through all the waking regions.
    John. But now the pompous sun, in all his pride,
Look'd through his golden coach upon the world,
And, on a sudden hath he hid himself ;
That now the under earth is as a grave,
Dark, deadly, silent, and uncomfortable.
            [*A Clamour of Ravens heard.*
Hark ! what a deadly outcry do I hear !
    Chas. Here comes my brother Philip.
    John.   All dismay'd :—

Enter PHILIP.

What fearful words are those thy looks presage ?
    Phi. A flight, a flight !
    John. Coward, what flight ? thou liest, there
        needs no flight.
    Phi. A flight !
    John. Awake thy craven powers, and tell on
The substance of that very fear indeed,
Which is so ghastly printed in thy face :
What is the matter ?
    Phi.   A flight of ugly ravens
Do croak and hover o'er our soldiers' heads,
And keep in triangles, and corner'd squares,
Right as our forces are embattled ;
With their approach there came this sudden fog,
Which now hath hid the airy floor of heaven,
And made at noon a night unnatural
Upon the quaking and dismayéd world :
In brief, our soldiers have let fall their arms,
And stand like metamorphos'd images,
Bloodless and pale, one gazing on another.
    John. Ay, now I call to mind the prophecy ;
But I must give no entrance to a fear.—
Return, and hearten up those yielding souls ;
Tell them, the ravens, seeing them in arms,—
So many fair against a famished few,—
Come but to dine upon their handiwork,
And prey upon the carrion that they kill :
For when we see a horse laid down to die,
Although he be not dead, the ravenous birds
Sit watching the departure of his life ;

Even so these ravens, for the carcases
Of those poor English, that are mark'd to die,
Hover about ; and, if they cry to us,
'Tis but for meat that we must kill for them.
Away, and comfort up my soldiers,
And sound the trumpets ; and at once dispatch
This little business of a silly fraud.   [*Exit* PHI.

    Noise within.   Enter a French Captain, *with*
        SALISBURY, *Prisoner.*

    Capt. Behold, my liege, this knight, and forty
        more,—
Of whom the better part are slain and fled,—
With all endeavour sought to break our ranks,
And make their way to the encompass'd prince ;
Dispose of him as please your majesty.
    John. Go, and the next bough, soldier, that thou
        see'st,
Disgrace it with his body presently :
For I do hold a tree in France too good
To be the gallows of an English thief.
    Sal. My lord of Normandy, I have your pass
And warrant for my safety through this land.
    Chas. Villiers procur'd it for thee, did he not ?
    Sal. He did.
    Chas. And it is current, thou shalt freely pass.
    John. Ay, freely to the gallows to be hang'd,
Without denial, or impediment :—
                    Away with him.
    Chas. I hope, your highness will not so disgrace
        me,
And dash the virtue of my seal at arms :
He hath my never-broken name to shew,
Character'd with this princely hand of mine ;
And rather let me leave to be a prince,
Than break the stable verdict of a prince :
I do beseech you, let him pass in quiet.
    John. Thou and thy word lie both in my com-
        mand ;
What can'st thou promise, that I cannot break ?
Which of these twain is greater infamy,
To disobey thy father, or thyself ?
Thy word, nor no man's, may exceed his power ;
Nor that same man doth never break his word,
That keeps it to the utmost of his power :
The breach of faith dwells in the soul's consent ;
Which if thyself without consent do break,
Thou art not charged with the breach of faith.—
Go, hang him ; for thy licence lies in me :—
And my constraint stands the excuse for thee.
    Chas. What, am I not a soldier in my word ?
Then, arms adieu, and let them fight that list :
Shall I not give my girdle from my waist,[34]

But with a guardian I shall be controul'd,
To say, I may not give my things away?
Upon my soul, had Edward prince of Wales,
Engag'd his word, writ down his noble hand,
For all your knights to pass his father's land,
The royal king, to grace his warlike son,
Would not alone safe conduct give to them,
But with all bounty feasted them and theirs.

    John. Dwell'st thou on precedents? Then be
      it so.—
Say, Englishman, of what degree thou art?

    Sal. An earl in England, though a prisoner here;
And those, that know me, call me Salisbury.[35]

    John. Then, Salisbury, say, whither thou art
      bound?

    Sal. To Calais, where my liege, king Edward,
      is.

    John. To Calais, Salisbury? Then to Calais
      pack;
And bid the king prepare a noble grave,
To put his princely son, black Edward, in.
And as thou travel'st westwards from this place,
Some two leagues hence there is a lofty hill,
Whose top seems topless, for the embracing sky
Doth hide his high head in her azure bosom;
Upon whose tall top when thy foot attains,
Look back upon the humble vale below,
(Humble of late, but now made proud with arms)
And thence behold the wretched prince of Wales,
Hoop'd with a band of iron round about.
After which sight, to Calais spur amain,
And say, the prince was smother'd, and not slain:
And tell the king, this is not all his ill;
For I will greet him, ere he thinks I will.
Away, be gone; the smoke but of our shot
Will choke our foes, though bullets hit them not.

SCENE VI.—*The Same. A part of the Field of
    Battle.*

*Alarums, as of a Battle joined; Skirmishings.
    Enter* PRINCE EDWARD *and* ARTOIS.

    Art. How fares your grace? are you not shot,
      my lord?

    Prince. No, dear Artois; but chok'd with dust
      and smoke,
And stepp'd aside for breath and fresher air.

    Art. Breathe then, and to 't again: the amazed
      French
Are quite distract with gazing on the crows:
And, were our quivers full of shafts again,
Your grace should see a glorious day of this:—
O, for more arrows, lord! that is our want.

    Prince. Courage, Artois! a fig for feather'd
      shafts,
When feather'd fowls do bandy on our side!
What need we fight, and sweat, and keep a coil,
When railing crows out-scold our adversaries?
Up, up, Artois! the ground itself is arm'd
With fire-containing flint; command our bows
To hurl away their pretty-colour'd yew,
And to 't with stones: Away, Artois, away;
My soul doth prophecy we win the day. [*Exeunt.*

Alarums, and Parties skirmishing. Enter KING
    JOHN.

    John. Our multitudes are in themselves con-
      founded,
Dismayed and distraught; swift-starting fear
Hath buzz'd a cold dismay through all our army,
And every petty disadvantage prompts
The fear-possess'd abject soul to fly:
Myself, whose spirit is steel to their dull lead,
(What with recalling of the prophecy,
And that our native stones from English arms
Rebel against us)[36] find myself attainted
With strong surprise of weak and yielding fear.

Enter CHARLES.

    Chas. Fly, father, fly! the French do kill the
      French;
Some, that would stand, let drive at some that fly:
Our drums strike nothing but discouragement,
Our trumpets sound dishonour and retire;
The spirit of fear, that feareth nought but death,
Cowardly works confusion on itself.

Enter PHILIP.

    Phi. Pluck out your eyes, and see not this day's
      shame!
An arm hath beat an army; one poor David
Hath with a stone foil'd twenty stout Goliahs:
Some twenty naked starvelings, with small flints,
Have driven back a puissant host of men,
Array'd and fenc'd in all accomplements.

    John. Mordieu, they quoit at us, and kill us
      up;
No less than forty thousand wicked elders
Have forty lean slaves this day ston'd to death.[37]

    Chas. O, that I were some other countryman!
This day hath set derision on the French;
And all the world will blurt and scorn at us.

    John. What, is there no hope left?

    Phi. No hope, but death, to bury up our shame.

    John. Make up once more with me; the twen
      tieth part

Of those that live, are men enough to quail
The feeble handful on the adverse part.

 Chas. Then charge again : if heaven be not op-
   pos'd,
We cannot lose the day

 John.   On, on; away. [*Exeunt.*

Alarums, &c. Enter AUDLEY, *wounded, and two*
 Esquires, *his Rescuers.*

 1st Esq. How fares my lord ?
 Aud.   E'en as a man may do,
That dines at such a bloody feast as this.

 2nd Esq. I hope, my lord, that is no mortal scar.

 Aud. No matter, if it be ; the count is cast,
And in the worst, ends but a mortal man.
Good friends, convey me to the princely Edward,
That, in the crimson bravery of my blood,
I may become him with saluting him :
I 'll smile, and tell him, that this open scar
Doth end the harvest of his Audley's war.

   [*Exeunt. Other Alarums ; afterwards, a*
   Retreat.

  SCENE VII.—*The Same. The* English *Camp.*

Flourish. Enter PRINCE EDWARD, *in Triumph,*
leading Prisoners, KING JOHN, *and his Son*
CHARLES ; *and* Officers, Soldiers, *&c., with En-*
signs spread.

 Prince. Now, John in France, and lately John
  of France,
Thy bloody ensigns are my captive colours :
And you, high-vaunting Charles of Normandy,
That once to-day sent me a horse to fly,
Are now the subjects of my clemency.
Fie, lords ! is 't not a shame,[38] that English boys,
Whose early days are yet not worth a beard,
Should in the bosom of your kingdom thus,
One against twenty, beat you up together ?

 John. Thy fortune, not thy force, hath conquer'd us.

 Prince. An argument, that heaven aids the right.—

   Enter ARTOIS, *with* PHILIP.

See, see, Artois doth bring along with him
The late good counsel-giver to my soul !—
Welcome, Artois ;—and welcome, Philip, too :
Who now, of you, or I, have need to pray ?
Now is the proverb verified in you,
Too bright a morning breeds a lowering day.—

   Enter AUDLEY, *led by the Two* Esquires.

But, say, what grim discouragement comes here !

Alas, what thousand arméd men of France
Have writ that note of death in Audley's face ?—
Speak, thou that woo'st death with thy careless
  smile,
And look'st so merrily upon thy grave
As if thou wert enamour'd on thy end,
What hungry sword hath so bereav'd thy face,
And lopp'd a true friend from my loving soul ?

 Aud. O prince, thy sweet bemoaning speech
  to me
Is as a mournful knell to one dead-sick.

 Prince. Dear Audley, if my tongue ring out thy
  end,
My arms shall be thy grave : What may I do,
To win thy life, or to revenge thy death ?
If thou wilt drink the blood of captive kings,—
Or, that it were restorative, command
A health of king's blood, and I 'll drink to thee :
If honour may dispense for thee with death,
The never-dying honour of this day
Share wholly, Audley, to thyself, and live.

 Aud. Victorious prince,—that thou art so, be-
  hold
A Cæsar's fame in kings' captivity,—
If I could hold dim death but at a bay,
'Till I did see my liege thy royal father,
My soul should yield this castle of my flesh,
This mangl'd tribute, with all willingness,
To darkness' consummation, dust, and worms.

 Prince. Cheerly, bold man ! thy soul is all too
  proud,
To yield her city, for one little breach,
Should be divorced from her earthly spouse
By the soft temper of a Frenchman's sword :
Lo, to repair thy life, I give to thee
Three thousand marks a year in English land.

 Aud. I take thy gift, to pay the debts I owe :
These two poor 'squires redeem'd me from the
  French,
With lusty and dear hazard of their lives ;
What thou hast given to me, I give to them ;
And, as thou lov'st me, prince, lay thy consent
To this bequeath in my last testament.

 Prince. Renown'd Audley, live, and have from
  me
This gift twice doubled, to these 'squires, and thee :
But, live, or die, what thou hast given away,
To these, and theirs, shall lasting freedom stay.—
Come, gentlemen, I 'll see my friend bestow'd
Within an easy litter : then we 'll march
Proudly towards Calais, with triumphant pace,
Unto my royal father, And there bring
The tribute of my wars, fair France's king.

ACT V.

SCENE — Picardy. *The* English *Camp before* Calais.

Enter EDWARD, *with* PHILIPPA *his* Queen, *and* DERBY; Officers, Soldiers, *&c.*

Edw. No more, queen Philippe, pacify yourself;
Copland, except he can excuse his fault,
Shall find displeasure written in our looks.—
And now unto this proud resisting town:
Soldiers, assault; I will no longer stay,
To be deluded by their false delays;
Put all to sword, and make the spoil your own.

[*Trumpets sound to Arms.*

Enter, from the Town, six Citizens, *in their Shirts, and bare-footed, with Halters about their Necks.*

Cit. Mercy, King Edward! mercy, gracious lord!
Edw. Contemptuous villains! call ye now for truce?
Mine ears are stopped against your bootless cries:—
Sound, drums; [*Alarum*] draw, threat'ning swords!
1st Cit. Ah, noble prince,
Take pity on this town, and hear us, mighty king!
We claim the promise that your highness made;
The two days' respit is not yet expir'd,
And we are come, with willingness, to bear
What torturing death, or punishment, you please,
So that the trembling multitude be sav'd.
Edw. My promise? well, I do confess as much:
But I require the chiefest citizens,
And men of most account, that should submit;
You, peradventure, are but servile grooms,
Or some felonious robbers on the sea,
Whom, apprehended, law would execute,
Albeit severity lay dead in us:
No, no, ye cannot over-reach us thus.
2nd Cit. The sun, dread lord, that in the western fall
Beholds us now low brought through misery,
Did in the orient purple of the morn
Salute our coming forth, when we were known;
Or may our portion be with damnéd fiends.
Edw. If it be so, then let our covenant stand,
We take possession of the town in peace:
But, for yourselves, look you for no remorse;
But, as imperial justice hath decreed,
Your bodies shall be dragg'd about these walls,
And after feel the stroke of quartering steel:
This is your doom;—Go, soldiers, see it done.

Queen. Ah, be more mild unto these yielding men!
It is a glorious thing, to 'stablish peace;
And kings approach the nearest unto God,
By giving life and safety unto men:
As thou intendest to be king of France,
So let her people live to call thee king;
For what the sword cuts down, or fire hath spoil'd,
Is held in reputation none of ours.
Edw. Although experience teach us this is true,
That peaceful quietness brings most delight
When most of all abuses are controul'd,
Yet, insomuch it shall be known, that we
As well can master our affections,
As conquer other by the dint of sword,
Philippe, prevail; we yield to thy request;
These men shall live to boast of clemency,—[39]
And, tyranny, strike terror to thyself.
Cit. Long live your highness! happy be your reign!
Edw. Go, get you hence, return unto the town;
And if this kindness hath deserv'd your love,
Learn then to reverence Edward as your king.—

[*Exeunt* Cit.

Now, might we hear of our affairs abroad,
We would, 'till gloomy winter were o'erspent,
Dispose our men in garrison a while.
But who comes here?

Enter COPLAND, *and* KING DAVID.

Der. Copland, my lord, and David king of Scots.
Edw. Is this the proud presumptuous squire o' the north,
That would not yield his prisoner to my queen?
Cop. I am, my liege, a northern 'squire, indeed,
But neither proud nor insolent, I trust.
Edw. What mov'd thee then, to be so obstinate
To contradict our royal queen's desire?
Cop. No wilful disobedience, mighty lord,
But my desert, and public law of arms:
I took the king myself in single fight;
And, like a soldier, would be loth to lose
The least pre-eminence that I had won:
And Copland, straight, upon your highness' charge,
Is come to France, and, with a lowly mind,
Doth vail the bonnet of his victory.[40]
Receive, dread lord, the custom of my fraught,
The wealthy tribute of my labouring hands;
Which should long since have been surrender'd up,
Had but your gracious self been there in place.

Queen. But, Copland, thou didst scorn the king's
    command,
Neglecting our commission in his name.

    Cop. His name I reverence, but his person
    more ;
His name shall keep me in allegiance still,
But to his person I will bend my knee.

    Edw. I pray thee, Philippe, let displeasure pass ;
This man doth please me, and I like his words :
For what is he, that will attempt high deeds,
And lose the glory that ensues the same ?
All rivers have recourse unto the sea ;
And Copland's faith, relation to his king.—
Kneel therefore down ; now rise, King Edward's
    knight :
And, to maintain thy state, I freely give
Five hundred marks a year to thee and thine.—

Enter SALISBURY.

Welcome, Lord Salisbury : What news from Bre-
    tagne ?

    Sal. This, mighty king : The country we have
    won ;
And John de Montfort, regent of that place,
Presents your highness with this coronet,
Protesting true allegiance to your grace.

    Edw. We thank thee for thy service, valiant
    earl ;
Challenge our favour, for we owe it thee.

    Sal. But now, my lord, as this is joyful news,
So must my voice be tragical again,
And I must sing of doleful accidents.

    Edw. What, have our men the overthrow at
    Poitiers ?
Or is my son beset with too much odds ?

    Sal. He was, my lord : and as my worthless self,
With forty other serviceable knights,
Under safe-conduct of the dauphin's seal
Did travel that way, finding him distressed,
A troop of lances met us on the way,
Surpris'd, and brought us prisoners to the king ;
Who, proud of this, and eager of revenge,
Commanded straight to cut off all our heads :
And surely we had dy'd, but that the duke,
More full of honour than his angry sire,
Procur'd our quick deliverance from thence :
But, ere we went, "Salute your king," quoth he,
" Bid him provide a funeral for his son,
To-day our sword shall cut his thread of life ;
And, sooner than he thinks, we'll be with him,
To quittance those displeasures he hath done :"
This said, we pass'd, not daring to reply ;
Our hearts were dead, our looks diffus'd and wan.

Wand'ring, at last we clim'd unto a hill ;
From whence, although our grief were much
    before,
Yet now to see the occasion with our eyes
Did thrice so much increase our heaviness :
For there, my lord, O, there we did descry
Down in a valley how both armies lay.
The French had cast their trenches like a ring ;
And every barricado's open front
Was thick imbost with brazen ordinance :
Here stood a battle of ten thousand horse ;
There twice as many pikes, in quadrant wise ;
Here cross-bows, arm'd with deadly-wounding
    darts :
And in the midst, like to a slender point
Within the compass of the horizon,—
As 'twere a rising bubble in the sea,
A hazel-wand amidst a wood of pines,—
Or as a bear fast chain'd unto a stake,
Stood famous Edward, still expecting when
Those dogs of France would fasten on his flesh.
Anon, the death-procuring knell begins :
Off go the cannons, that, with trembling noise,
Did shake the very mountain where they stood ;
Then sound the trumpets' clangors in the air,
The battles join : and, when we could no more
Discern the difference 'twixt the friend and foe,
(So intricate the dark confusion was)
Away we turn'd our watery eyes, with sighs
As black as powder fuming into smoke.
And thus, I fear, unhappy have I told
The most untimely tale of Edward's fall.

    Queen. Ah me ! is this my welcome into France ?
Is this the comfort, that I look'd to have,
When I should meet with my beloved son?
Sweet Ned, I would, thy mother in the sea
Had been prevented of this mortal grief ?

    Edw. Content thee, Philippe ; 'tis not tears, will
    serve
To call him back, if he be taken hence :
Comfort thyself, as I do, gentle queen,
With hope of sharp, unheard of, dire revenge.—
He bids me to provide his funeral ;
And so I will : but all the peers in France
Shall mourners be, and weep out bloody tears,
Until their empty veins be dry and sear :
The pillars of his hearse shall be his bones ;
The mould that covers him, their city' ashes ;
His knell, the groaning cries of dying men ;
And, in the stead of tapers on his tomb,
An hundred fifty towers shall burning blaze,
While we bewail our valiant son's decease.

                  [*Flourish of Trumpets within.*

Enter a Herald.

Her. Rejoice, my lord, ascend the imperial
    throne!
The mighty and redoubted prince of Wales,
Great servitor to bloody Mars in arms,
The Frenchman's terror, and his country's fame,
Triumphant rideth like a Roman peer:
And, lowly at his stirrup, comes afoot
King John of France, together with his son,
In captive bonds; whose diadem he brings,
To crown thee with, and to proclaim thee king.
    Edw. Away with mourning, Philippe, wipe thine
    eyes;—
Sound, trumpets, welcome in Plantagenet!
                       [A loud Flourish.

Enter PRINCE, AUDLEY, ARTOIS, *with* KING JOHN,
    and PHILIP.

As things, long lost, when they are found again,
So doth my son rejoice his father's heart,
For whom, even now, my soul was much perplex'd!
    [Running to the PRINCE, *and embracing him.*
    Queen. Be this a token to express my joy,
                       [Kissing him.
For inward passions will not let me speak.
    Prince. My gracious father, here receive the gift,
    [Presenting him with KING JOHN's *Crown.*
This wreath of conquest, and reward of war,
Got with as mickle peril of our lives,
As e'er was thing of price before this day;
Install your highness in your proper right:
And, herewithal, I render to your hands
These prisoners, chief occasion of our strife,
    Edw. So, John of France, I see, you keep your
    word;
You promis'd to be sooner with ourselt
Than we did think for, and 'tis so indeed:
But, had you done at first as now you do,
How many civil towns had stood untouch'd,
That now are turn'd to ragged heaps of stones?
How many people's lives might you have sav'd,
That are untimely sunk into their graves?

    John. Edward, recount not things irrevocable;
Tell me what ransom thou requir'st to have?
    Edw. Thy ransom, John, hereafter shall be
    known:
But first to England thou must cross the seas,
To see what entertainment it affords;
Howe'er it falls, it cannot be so bad
As ours hath been since we arriv'd in France.
    John. Accursèd man! of this I was foretold,
But did misconster what the prophet told.
    Prince. Now, father, this petition Edward
    makes,—
To Thee, [*kneels*] whose grace hath been his
    strongest shield,
That as thy pleasure chose me for the man,
To be the instrument to show thy power,
So thou wilt grant that many princes more,
Bred and brought up within that little isle,
May still be famous for like victories!—
And, for my part, the bloody scars I bear,
The weary nights that I have watch'd in field,
The dangerous conflicts I have often had,
The fearful menaces were proffer'd me,
The heat, and cold, and what else might displease,
I wish were now redoubl'd twenty fold;
So that hereafter ages, when they read
The painful traffic of my tender youth,
Might thereby be inflam'd with such resolve,
As not the territories of France alone,
But likewise Spain, Turkey, and what countries
    else
That justly would provoke fair England's ire,
Might, at their presence, tremble, and retire!
    Edw. Here, English lords, we do proclaim a
    rest,
An interceasing of our painful arms:
Sheath up your swords, refresh your weary limbs,
Peruse your spoils; and, after we have breath'd
A day or two within this haven town,
God willing, then for England we'll be shipp'd;
Where, in a happy hour, I trust, we shall
Arrive, three kings, two princes, and a queen.
            [Flourish. Exeunt omnes.

NOTES TO KING EDWARD THE THIRD.

¹ *Robert of Artois, banish'd though thou be.*

Robert of Artois was descended from the royal family of France; he had married the sister of the French king; and his talents were considered equal to his birth and connexions. He was deprived of the country of Artois, which he claimed as his birthright; and in consequence of some disgraceful conduct on his part, driven into exile. He was a man of violent passions, and so enraged against the French king, that he is said to have attempted the life of that monarch by witchcraft and assassination. These efforts failing, he endeavoured to raise up in Edward a rival claimant to the throne of France; and his sinister persuasions doubtless had some share in producing that series of wars which for so long desolated his native land.

² *Who next succeeded Philip le Beau?*

The old quartos erroneously read, *Philip of Bew.*

³ *Striving to rebate.*

To *rebate* is to blunt, to beat back, to deprive of power. From *rebattre*, French.

⁴ *Regenerate traitor.*

This does not convey any definite meaning; should we not read *degenerate?*

⁵ *Go levy footmen for our wars in France.*

Edward made the most extensive preparations for the war with France; he obtained subsidies, tallages, and forced loans, adopted many arbitrary and tyrannical means of raising money, and even pawned the jewels of his crown.

⁶ *Their jacks of gymold mail.*

Gymold mail is armour composed of a number of links, like small chains; it was flexible, and therefore fitted better to the body than any other description of defensive covering.

⁷ *Their biting whinyards.*

Their sharp broadswords. In Barry's comedy of *Ram Alley; or Merry Tricks:*

If you be pleased hold up your finger; if not,
By heaven I'll gar my *whyniard* through your womb.

⁸ *Jemmy, my man, saddle my bonny black.*

The Scots are treated very contemptuously in this drama; they were disliked both by Queen Elizabeth and by the English people; therefore, for an author to ridicule them, was frequently to gain the applause of his audiences. But the Scots, who were in reality, during the reign of Edward III., the terror of the English living near the borders, are very differently described by the chivalrous and romantic chronicler Froissart. The passage is of so interesting a character that I will extract it. "The Scots are bold, hardy, and much inured to war. When they make their invasions into England, they march from twenty to twenty-four leagues without halting, as well by night as day; for they are all on horseback, except the camp followers, who are on foot. The knights and esquires are well mounted on large bay horses, the common people on little galloways. They bring no carriages with them, on account of the mountains they have to pass in Northumberland; neither do they carry with them any provisions of bread or wine; for their habits of sobriety are such, in time of war, that they will live for a long time on flesh half-sodden, without bread, and drink the river water without wine. They have, therefore, no occasion for pots or pans; for they dress the food of their cattle in the skins, after they have taken them off: and, being sure to find plenty of them in the country which they invade, they carry none with them. Under the flaps of his saddle, each man carries a broad plate of metal; behind the saddle, a little bag of oatmeal: when they have eaten too much of the sodden flesh, and their stomach appears weak and empty, they place this plate over the fire, mix with water their oatmeal, and when the plate is heated, they put a little of the paste upon it, and make a thin cake, like a cracknel or biscuit, which they eat to warm their stomachs: it is therefore no wonder that they perform a longer day's march than other soldiers."

⁹ *Peevish love,* i.e. *silly love.*

¹⁰ *And sand by sand.*

The old copy reads erroneously—" and said by said."

¹¹ *Than Judith was.*

Judith the beautiful Hebrew widow, who by a stratagem destroyed Holofernes the captain of the Assyrian army. See the book of *Judith,* in the Apocrypha.

¹² *Lilies, that fester, smell far worse than weeds.*

This beautiful line is contained in the ninety-fourth of Shakspere's *Sonnets.* If play and poem are the production of different authors, one of them has unwittingly copied the other.

¹³ *Then via for the spacious bounds of France.*

That is, then away for France; away joyfully.

¹⁴ *Derby, I'll look upon the countess' mind anon.*

The dramatist here very skilfully shows how the powerful mind of Edward is completely filled and subdued by his admiration of the fascinating countess. Froissart speaks at some length of this traditionary amour, and his *Chronicles* quite justify the position taken by our poet. He says: " You have heard how passionately he (Edward) was smitten with the charms of the noble lady, Catherine, countess of Salisbury; insomuch that he could not put her out of his mind, for love reminded him of her day and night, and represented her beauties and lively behaviour in such bewitching points of view, that he could think of nothing else, notwithstanding that the earl of Salisbury was one of his most trusty counsellors, and one who in England had most loyally served him."

¹⁵ *Remove those lets,* i.e. hindrances.

¹⁶ *Through a helly spout of blood.*

I think we should read *Hellespont,* otherwise the comparison is incomplete.

¹⁷ *This packing evil.*

Packing evil is subtle, underhand, treacherous evil. In *King Lear* the word *packings* is used to express deceitful contrivances.

¹⁸ *Of her, whose ransacked treasury hath task'd*
   The vain endeavour of so many pens.

An allusion to Lucretia, the chaste and noble victim of the violence of Sextus Tarquin.

¹⁹ *Ere the sun shall gild the eastern sky.*

The old copy reads, " shall *guide* the," &c.

²⁰ *Blood-thirsty and seditious Catalines.*

Cataline was a Roman noble of infamous character. Having ruined himself by debauchery and extravagance, and been refused the consulship, he conspired, with other desperate men, to murder every member of the senate, seize the public treasure, and burn Rome to ashes. He is reported to have taken an oath to accomplish these savage objects, and together with the rest of the conspirators, confirmed it by a draught of human blood, warm from the veins of a slave whom they slew for the occasion. The conspiracy was discovered by Cicero, and Cataline fled to Gaul, where he assembled an army, and a battle took place, in which he was slain, sixty-three years before Christ. Besides many other great and revolting crimes, he was guilty of the murder of his own brother.

²¹ *Of Agamemnon in the haven of Troy.*

Agamemnon, the king of Mycenæ and Argos. He was the brother of Menelaus, and chosen king of the allied Grecian princes during the siege of Troy. He was married to Clytemnestra, the sister of the beautiful but voluptuous Helen. During the protracted war which the Greeks waged against the Trojans he behaved with great valour, but having taken away the mistress of Achilles, his quarrel with that hero was fatal to the Greeks. After the destruction of Troy, Cassandra, Priam's mad daughter, who was regarded as a prophetess, fell to the share of Agamemnon and foretold that his wife would murder him. He disregarded this prediction and returned to Argos, where it was verified.

Clytemnestra, assisted by her paramour Ægisthus, killed her husband with a hatchet as he was emerging from the bath. Cassandra, to whom he was greatly attached, shared his fate. Agamemnon was of a very noble and commanding appearance; Homer makes Priam, in allusion to him, ask :—

——— What Greek is he
(Far as from hence these aged orbs can see)
Around whose brow such awful graces shine,
So tall, so awful, and almost divine ?
Though some of larger stature tread the green,
None match his grandeur and exalted mien.

²² *With Xerxes we compare of strength.*

Xerxes was a monarch of Persia who terminated his career about 464 years before Christ. Having subdued Egypt he led an army against the Greeks; this army, with its retinue of servants, eunuchs, and women, is said to have amounted to the enormous and almost incredible number of nearly five millions and a quarter of people. So great was this concourse that they spread famine in the provinces through which they passed, and are metaphorically said to have drank up whole rivers. When Xerxes reviewed them he is reported to have burst into tears from the reflection that in one hundred years not one of that vast multitude would be left alive; all that mass of living breathing creatures would be cold and still; those millions of hearts would have ceased to beat, and grass and wild flowers be growing over their graves. Wonderful are the chances of war, and great the power of science and discipline; this gigantic army was stopped at Thermopylæ by the valour of three hundred Spartans, under King Leonidas; and the Persian monarch, although he burnt the deserted city of Athens, was compelled to return in disgrace to his own country. There he gave himself up to indolence and voluptuousness, and was in consequence murdered in his bed by Artabanus, the captain of his guards.

²³ *The arms of England and of France unite*
   Are quarter'd equally by herald's art.

Edward publicly assumed the title of King of France, and quartered the French lilies in his arms.

²⁴ *And our pretended quarrel.*

That is, our *in*tended or proposed quarrel. The word pretence is frequently used by Shakspere for design or purpose, and pretended as intended.

²⁵ *Which is the true-born sovereign, this or that ?*

Edward's claim to the French crown, if not ridiculous was manifestly unjust. It was as follows :—Philip the Fair, King of France, left three sons and one daughter. Isabella, the daughter, was married to Edward II. and was the mother of Edward III. Lewis Hutin, the eldest son, ascended the throne, but as he died without male children, and females being by an ancient custom of France, excluded from regal honours, the crown descended to his brother Philip. Edward's claim was through his mother, who, though he acknowledged that she, being a woman, could not legally claim the sovereignty of France, he urged that he, to whom her right descended, being a man, could. Thus the son insisted that he inherited, through his mother, a property which she herself had never possessed ; and the result of this wicked sophistry was, that many thousands of French and English mingled their blood upon the fields of France, and left their mangled bodies to the kites and crows.

[26] *The vaward,* i.e. the van, or advanced part of the army.

[27] *Grudging to be so suddenly employ'd.*

Froissart tells us, "As soon as the King of France came in sight of the English, his blood began to boil, and he cried out to his marshals, 'Order the Genoese forward, and begin the battle, in the name of God and St. Denis.' There were about fifteen thousand Genoese cross-bowmen ; but they were quite fatigued, having marched on foot that day six leagues, completely armed, and with their cross-bows. They told the constable they were not in a fit condition to do any great things that day in battle. The Earl of Alençon, hearing this, said, ' This is what one gets by employing such scoundrels, who fall off when there is any need for them.'" The Genoese, who were thus forced into action, fell back before the terrible flight of arrows with which they were saluted by the sturdy English archers ; when the French King, mad with passion, exclaimed : "Kill me those scoundrels ; for they stop up our road without any reason." His horsemen immediately attacked the Genoese, and such was the confusion which resulted from this foolish and vindictive proceeding, that it mainly contributed to the loss of the battle.

[28] *And dare a falcon when she's in her flight,*
And ever after she'll be haggard-like.

That is, check a falcon in her flight and afterwards she will be but a tame, spiritless bird. *Dare* was anciently sometimes used in the sense of *to check*, and a haggard was a species of worthless hawk. Edward compares his son to a falcon, and fears that if he checks or aids him in his first military exploit, he will be deficient in courage and self-reliance in future.

[29] *Eleven princes of esteem.*

Among those princes who were slain at the fatal battle of Crecy was John de Luxembourg, the blind old king of Bohemia. Fearing that his son was killed, and that the fortune of the day was against the side he had embraced, he begged to be placed between two knights, and carried into the battle, that he might strike a blow in revenge for his son, and expire with him. This was done, and the sightless and sorrowing old man soon lay cold and lifeless upon the ensanguined field. His crest was three ostrich feathers, and the motto of " ICH DIEN," (I serve) ; it was adopted by the Black Prince, and to this day is borne by the princes of Wales.

[30] *No love-sick cockney.*

Antiquarians have been unable to agree as to the exact meaning of this term of contempt. Mr. Steevens conjectures that a cockney was an ancient name for a cook. Thus, in *King Lear* the fool says ; "Cry to it, nuncle, as the *cockney* did to the eels, when she put them in the paste alive." In the ancient ballad of *The Tournament of Tottenham* it seems also to mean a cook :—

At that feast were they served in rich array ;
Every five and five had a *cokeney*.

Dr. Percy imagines the word to signify some common kind of food ; and Mr. Whalley, agreeing with him, quotes the following epigram from Davies :—

He that comes every day, shall have a *cock-nay*,
And he that comes but now and then, shall have a fat hen.

Chaucer, in his *Reve's Tale*, uses it in much the same sense in which it is employed in the present day :—

And when this jape is told another day,
I shall be halden a daffe or a *cokenay*.

[31] *The captain of the town hath thrust us forth,*
That so expense of victuals may be sav'd.

This cruel action is one of the many black spots which disgrace the pages of history. It is thus related by Froissart. "The king made no attacks upon the town, as he knew it would be only lost labour ; and he was sparing of his men and artillery ; but said, he would remain there so long that he would starve the town into a surrender, unless the king of France should come there to raise the siege. When the governor of Calais saw the preparations of the king of England, he collected together all the poor inhabitants, who had not laid in any store of provisions, and, one Wednesday morning, sent upwards of seventeen hundred men, women, and children out of the town. As they were passing through the English army, they asked them, why they had left the town? They replied, because they had nothing to eat. The king, upon this, allowed them to pass through in safety, ordered them a hearty dinner, and gave to each two sterlings as charity and alms, for which many of them prayed earnestly for the king."

[32] *Those milk-white messengers of time.*

A beautiful simile for his grey hairs.

[33] *A sudden darkness hath defaced the sky.*

On the morning of the battle of Crecy, there was an eclipse of the sun, accompanied by a heavy fall of rain, and frequent thunder. Before the rain a great flight of crows, the harbingers of the storm, hovered over the French army, but there is no mention of any of these things occurring at Poictiers.

[34] *Shall I not give my girdle from my waste.*

Waste and *waist* appear to have been used by our ancient writers as words of synonymous import.

[35] *And those, that know me, call me Salisbury.*

Froissart relates this incident, but makes the hero of it to be Sir Walter Manny, and not the Earl of Salisbury.

[36] *And that our native stones from English arms rebel against us.*

The English bowmen having shot away all their arrows, have been just commanded to continue the conflict with the flint stones with which the place abounded; the language of the prophecy was thus fulfilled:—

And flint stones rise, and break the battle 'ray.

Stones were also used as cannon-balls at this period. In Shakspere's *Henry the Fifth*, mention is made of gun-stones.

[37] *No less than forty thousand wicked elders*
Have forty lean slaves this day ston'd to death.

An allusion to the story of Susannah and the Elders. See the Apocrypha.

[38] *Fie lords! is't not a shame.*

The poet here deviates from historical truth, which, in most points, he has followed with a literal fidelity. Prince Edward, instead of galling the unfortunate French king with ungenerous taunts, behaved to him with great kindness and humanity. He consoled him in his adversity, praised his personal valour, invited him to supper, and waited upon him personally; saying, "Dear sir, do not make a poor meal, because the Almighty God has not gratified your wishes in the event of this day; for be assured that my lord and father will show you every honour and friendship in his power, and will arrange your ransom so reasonably, that you will henceforward always remain friends."

[39] *These men shall live to boast of clemency.*

Edward's clemency was not very remarkable; he certainly did, at the earnest and tearful solicitation of his queen, abandon his ferocious purpose of executing the noble patriots who had surrendered themselves to him in order to save their fellow-townsmen, but he did not forego his vengeance on the ill-fated place. He drove out all the inhabitants of Calais, and repopulated it with his English subjects.

[40] *Doth vail the bonnet of his victory.*

In Bullockar's *English Expositor*, 1616, *to vail* is thus explained: "It means to put off the hat, to strike sail, to give signs of submission."

H. T.

Arden, of Feversham

The dramas written during the first thirty years of Elizabeth's reign are not easily arranged in categories. As Ashley H. Thorndike (45) points out, they deal with a variety of subjects, and they recall many different models. Any single play, in fact, is certain to reveal in some measure the conflicting influences of the two great traditions that were then struggling for mastery. The medieval religious drama, with its miracles and moralities, had been for centuries virtually the only existing dramatic tradition; but by 1559, in England as elsewhere in Europe, the new learning had brought to men's knowledge the tragedies and comedies of Greece and Rome.

Although the writing and performing of miracle plays had nearly ceased, their chief characteristics long survived: their epic structure, their mixture of the terrible and the ludicrous, their medley of persons from all walks in life, and their readiness to exhibit anything whatever on the stage. And, although moralities were already losing their pre-eminence, abstractions figuring as symbolic characters continued to be common until Shakespeare's time.

However, the classical models had begun to acquire imitators as well as admirers. For tragedy, the classical models adopted were not the Greek plays, but those of the Roman philosopher Seneca. The plays of Seneca are inferior rhetorical imitations of the Athenian masterpieces, but they had the unstinted admiration of the Renaissance. In England, as in every other nation of Western Europe, they were familiar to students, and, translated into the vernacular, they became the common property of all educated men. Although these plays were probably never acted in Rome, they were accepted by the Elizabethans as stage plays, and all their characteristics were applied to stage performance.

Their stories, which were drawn from the bloodiest and most violent of the Greek myths and which traced crimes to final horrible retribution, and their elaborate poetic diction delighted both scholars and public. However, the public theaters eventually created a popular demand that could not endure such solecisms, and fortunately they soon attracted independent-minded dramatists who preferred the license of the public taste to the narrow laws of the scholars.

Gorboduc, the first English tragedy, was a definite attempt to follow the examples of Italy and France and to initiate English tragedy in strict conformity to the Senecan model. It was written by Thomas Norton and Thomas Sackville, afterwards Lord Buckhurst, and was performed by the gentlemen of the Inner Temple as part of their elaborate Christmas entertainment for the Queen in 1561–62. The story of a fratricide and the resulting murders and wars was selected from English legend because of its likeness to Seneca's *Thebais.*

By the time Shakespeare began his theatrical career, nearly twenty years after the performance of *Gorboduc,* the companies of professional actors were securely established in London. They had built playhouses, won the favor of the court and the patronage of a large public, and begun to attract brilliant young men from the universities as playwrights.

Tragedy by this time was well established as a species of popular drama. To be sure, the species was not strictly defined, but it already comprised a number of plays that were written in ambitious verse and dealt with momentous and direful events, heroic and extraordinary persons, and atrocious crimes. Sensational and violent, they appealed to an audience that was familiar with cruelty and brutality in its daily life, and that welcomed verbal fireworks as well as gruesome murder.

Arden, of Feversham is in this tradition. Relating the history of a nearly contemporaneous homicide, it is the earliest domestic tragedy extant. It attempts to show the "dissimulation of a wicked woman, the insatiable desire of filthy lust (for her worthless paramour) and the shameful end of all murderers." The play is a dramatization of an actual crime, the facts of which it closely follows but at the same time animating them with great psychological insight. (The subject becomes especially pertinent when we remember that Shakespeare's mother was herself a member of the Arden family.)

There had probably been earlier dramatizations of notorious criminal cases; but *Arden* makes the most of the public's morbid curiosity, and its performances drew large audiences. But the playwright seems also to have designed it as protest against current dramatic fashions. The tragedies of the day were concerned mainly with kings and courts and state affairs, and Shakespeare himself wrote many such. It is conceivable that he would for once try his hand at writing of ordinary men and women and domestic affairs. Others were concerned with past events and remote scenes; he would write of English events of his own time. Others sought to render their stories impressive by means of all the graces of imagery and ornament; he would endeavor to tell the true story of an actual crime and let it point its own moral. Thus he opposed the romanticism of the day with the credo of the realist:

> Gentlemen, we hope you'll pardon this naked tragedy,
> Wherein no filéd points are foisted in
> To make it gracious to the ear or eye;
> For simple truth is gracious enough,
> And needs no other points of glozing stuff.
>
> [V. vi]

Arden, of Feversham is, in fine, a picture elaborated with scientific calculation of effect. Shakespeare relied on nature, trusting to the force inherent in his motive, which was to produce a work dramatizing a tragic episode in human life. All this he contrived to do without overpassing the strictest, the most self-denying realism. He succeeded in adding something of his own human emotion and inviting his audience to share the pathos that he felt. With this play, he broke fresh ground in the realistic domestic tragedy as well as in the drama of intrigue and revenge.

Arden was soon followed by a number of criminal plays, or what John Bakeless (*The Tragicall History of Christopher Marlowe*) calls "news plays," like *A Warning for Fair Women, A Yorkshire Tragedy,* Marlowe's *Massacre at Paris,* and Ben Jonson's *Page of Plymouth,* all of which dealt with exciting murders in the manner of the sensational press of today. These plays had for their audience the same sort of interest that any current sensation has for the modern reader of the tabloid newspapers. The main difference is that the modern reader insists on getting his thrills a little fresher.

Although the criminal play, influenced by *Arden,* was revived by George Lillo in the eighteenth century and perhaps motivated him in his *George Barnwell,* none of *Arden*'s successors has surpassed it in its vivid presentation of factual life and character. Its unquestioned triumph, as a strikingly effective murder play, lies in its portrayal of Alice Arden. No other evil woman in English drama before Lady Macbeth is comparable to her in villainy. *Arden* is the first as well as the best of several domestic dramas, and its peculiar excellence lies in the transformation of what F. E. Schelling (38) calls this "sordid material into a tragedy of such inherent worth that creditable critical opinion has again and again referred it to Shakespeare." It is no wonder that Swinburne (43) hails *Arden of Feversham* as one of the most admirable plays of that rich period:

> I cannot but finally take heart to say, even in the absence of all external or traditional testimony that it seems to me not pardonable merely nor permissible, but simply logical and reasonable, to set down this poem, a

young man's work on the face of it, as the possible work of no man's youthful hand but Shakespeare's.

However, it was not until 1770, long after the first appearance of *Arden, of Feversham* (1592), that the play was definitely coupled with the name of Shakespeare. This service we owe to a citizen of Feversham, Edward Jacob, who published a reprint of the first edition with a preface "in which some reasons are offered in favor of its being the earliest dramatic work of Shakespeare now remaining." The reasons that Jacob offers are encompassed in a list of phrases and words in *Arden* for which he cites Shakespeare's parallels, among which are: "such a taunting letter," "painted cloth," "mermaid's song," "basilisk," "lean-faced knave," "white-livered," "buy his merriment as dear," "a raven for a dove," "swear me on the interrogatories, "horned beast," "death makes amends for sin."

In considering the claim to Shakespearean authenticity of this work and others of this class, it is but fair to recognize, particularly on first perusal, the intoxicating effect of the poetry. According to Tucker Brooke (8), "there are in this work gorgeous poetic passages that grip the imagination and overwhelm the reason. There is nothing fitful or transitory about the true Shakespearean quality: his creations gain, instead of losing, by repeated and various examination."

PERSONS REPRESENTED.

———◆———

LORD CHEINY.

Appears, Act IV. sc. 2.

ARDEN, *a Gentleman of* Feversham.

Appears, Act I. sc. 1 ; sc. 2 ; sc. 3.   Act II. sc. 3.   Act III. sc. 1 ; sc. 3.   Act IV. sc. 2 ; sc. 3 ; sc. 4 ; sc. 5.   Act V. sc. 2.

FRANKLIN, *his Friend.*

Appears, Act I. sc. 1 ; sc. 2 ; sc. 3.   Act II. sc. 3.   Act III. sc. 1 ; sc. 3.   Act IV. sc. 2 ; sc. 3 ; sc. 4 ; sc. 5.   Act V. sc. 2 ; sc. 4 ; sc. 6.

MOSBIE, *the Paramour of* Arden's *Wife.*

Appears, Act I. sc. 2 ; sc. 3.   Act II. sc. 1.   Act IV. sc. 1 ; sc. 3 ; sc. 4 ; sc. 5.   Act V. sc. 1 ; sc. 2 ; sc. 4 ; sc. 6.

CLARKE, *a Painter, in Love with* Susan Mosbie.

Appears, Act I. sc. 2.   Act II. sc. 1.   Act IV. sc. 3.

GREENE, *a Townsman of* Feversham.

Appears, Act I. sc. 3.   Act II. sc. 2 ; sc. 3.   Act III. sc. 2 ; sc. 4.   Act IV. sc. 2 ; sc. 3 ; sc. 4.   Act V. sc. 1 ; sc. 2.

BRADSHAW, *a Goldsmith.*

Appears, Act II. sc. 2.   Act IV. sc. 1.   Act V. sc. 2 ; sc. 6.

ADAM FOWLE, *Landlord of the* Flower-de-luce.

Appears, Act I. sc. 1.   Act V. sc. 1.

DICK REDE, *a Townsman of* Feversham ; *ruined by* Arden.

A SAILOR, *his Companion.*

Appear, Act IV. sc. 5.

MICHAEL, *a Servant of* Arden's, *in Love with* Susan Mosbie.

Appears, Act I. sc. 1 ; sc. 3.   Act II. sc. 3.   Act III. sc. 1 ; sc. 3 ; sc. 4.   Act IV. sc. 2 ; sc. 3 ; sc. 5.   Act V. sc. 1 ; sc. 2 ; sc. 4 ; sc. 6.

BLACK WILL, *a Ruffian.*

Appears, Act II. sc. 2 ; sc. 3.   Act III. sc. 2 ; sc. 4.   Act IV. sc. 2 ; sc. 4 ; sc. 5.   Act V. se. 1 ; sc. 2 ; sc. 5.

SHAKEBAG, *his Companion.*

Appears, Act II. sc. 2 ; sc. 3.   Act III. sc. 2 ; sc. 4.   Act IV. sc. 2 ; sc. 4 ; sc. 5.   Act V. sc. 1 ; sc. 2 ; sc. 3.

MAYOR OF FEVERSHAM.

Appears, Act V. sc. 2 ; sc. 4 ; sc. 6.

A FERRYMAN.

Appears, Act IV. sc. 4.

A LONDON 'PRENTICE.

Appears, Act II. sc. 3.

ALICE, *Wife to* Arden.

Appears, Act I. sc. 1 ; sc. 2 ; sc. 3.   Act II. sc. 1.   Act IV. sc. 1 ; sc. 3 ; sc. 5.   Act V. sc. 1 ; sc. 2 ; sc. 4 ; sc. 6.

SUSAN, *Servant to* Alice, *and Sister to* Mosbie.

Appears, Act II. sc. 1.   Act V. sc. 2 ; sc. 4 ; sc. 6.

Watchmen, and Attendants on Lord Chieny.

SCENE.—*Chiefly at* FEVERSHAM *and* LONDON, *and the Road between them.*

Arden, of Feversham.

ACT I.

SCENE I.—*A Room in* Arden's *House.*

Enter ARDEN *and* FRANKLIN.

Frank. Arden, cheer up thy spirits, and droop
    no more :
My gracious lord, the duke of Somerset,
Hath freely given to thee and to thy heirs,
By letters patent from his Majesty,[1]
All the lands of the abbey of Feversham.
Here are the deeds, seal'd and subscrib'd with his
    name and the king's.
Read them ; and leave this melancholy mood.

   Arden. Franklin, thy love prolongs my weary
    life ;
And but for thee, how odious were this life ;
That shows me nothing, but torments my soul,
And those foul objects that offend mine eyes,
Which make me wish that for this vale of heaven,
The earth hung o'er my head and cover'd me.
Love-letters pass 'twixt Mosbie and my wife,
And they have privy meetings in the town :
Nay, on his finger did I spy the ring,
Which, at our marriage day, the priest put on ;
Can any grief be half so great as this ?

   Frank. Comfort thyself, sweet friend, it is not
    strange
That women will be false and wavering.

   Arden. Ay, but to doat on such a one as he,
Is monstrous, Franklin, and intolerable

   Frank. Why, what is he ?

   Arden. A botcher, and no better at the first,
Who, by base brokage, getting some small stock,
Crept into service of a nobleman ;
And by his servile flattery and fawning,
Is now become the steward of his house ;
And bravely jets it in his silken gown.

   Frank. No nobleman will countenance such a
    peasant.

   Arden. Yes, the lord Clifford ; he that loves
    not me :
But through his favour let him not grow proud ;

For were he by the lord Protector back'd,
He should not make me to be pointed at :
I am by birth a gentleman of blood ;[2]
And that injurious ribald that attempts
To violate my dear wife's chastity,
(For dear I hold her love, as dear as heaven,)
Shall, on the bed which he thinks to defile,
See his dissever'd joints and sinews torn ;
Whilst on the planchers[3] pants his weary body,
Smear'd in the channels of his lustful blood.

   Frank. Be patient, gentle friend, and learn of me
To ease thy grief, and save her chastity :
Entreat her fair ; sweet words are fittest engines
To raze the flint walls of a woman's breast.
In any case be not too jealous,
Nor make a question of her love to thee ;
But as securely, presently take horse,
And lie with me at London all this term :
For women, when they may, will not ;
But being kept back, straight grows outrageous.

   Arden. Though this abhors from reason, yet I'll
    try it,[4]
And call her forth, and presently take leave. How,
    Alice !

Enter ALICE.

   Alice. Husband, what mean you to get up so
    early ?
Summer nights are short, and yet you rise ere day ;
Had I been 'wake you had not rose so soon.

   Arden. Sweet love, thou knowest that we two,
    Ovid-like,
Have often chid the morn, when't 'gan to peep ;
And often wish'd that dark night's purblind steeds
Would pull her by the purple mantle back,
And cast her in the ocean to her love.
But this night, sweet Alice, thou hast kill'd my
    heart :
I heard thee call on Mosbie in thy sleep.

   Alice. 'Tis like I was asleep when I nam'd him,
For being awake he comes not in my thoughts.

Arden. Ay, but you started up, and suddenly,
Instead of him, caught me about the neck.

   Alice. Instead of him! why, who was there
      but you?
And where but one is, how can I mistake?

   Frank. Arden, forbear to urge her over far.

   Arden. Nay, love, there is no credit in a dream;
Let it suffice I know thou lov'st me well.

   Alice. Now I remember whereupon it came:
Had we no talk of Mosbie yesternight?

   Frank. Mistress Alice, I heard you name him
      once or twice.

   Alice. And thereof came it; therefore blame
      not me.

   Arden. I know it did, and therefore let it pass:
I must to London, sweet Alice, presently.

   Alice. But tell me; do you mean to stay there
      long?

   Arden. No longer there, till my affairs be done.

   Frank. He will not stay above a month at most.

   Alice. A month, ah me! sweet Arden, come
      again
Within a day or two, or else I die.

   Arden. I cannot long be from thee, gentle Alice.
Whilst Michael fetch our horses from the field,
Franklin and I will down unto the quay:
For I have certain goods there to unload.
Meanwhile, prepare our breakfast, gentle Alice;
For yet, ere noon, we'll take horse and away.
              [*Exeunt* ARDEN *and* FRANK.

   Alice. Ere noon he means to take horse and
      away:
Sweet news is this! Oh that some airy spirit
Would, in the shape and likeness of a horse,
Gallop with Arden across the Ocean,
And throw him from his back into the waves.
Sweet Mosbie is the man that hath my heart;
And he usurps it, having nought but this—
That I am tied to him by marriage.
Love is a god, and marriage is but words;
And therefore Mosbie's title is the best.
Tush; whether it be so or no, he shall be mine,
In spite of him, of Hymen, and of rites.

      Enter ADAM *of the Flower-de-luce.*

And here comes Adam of the Flower-de-luce;
I hope he brings me tidings of my love.
How now, Adam, what is the news with you?
Be not afraid; my husband is now from home.

   Adam. He whom ye wot of,—Mosbie, mistress
      Alice,
Is come to town; and sends you word by me,
In any case you may not visit him.

   Alice.   Not visit him?

   Adam. No, nor take knowledge of his being here.

   Alice. But tell me, is he angry or displeas'd.

   Adam. It should seem so, for he is wondrous sad.

   Alice. Were he as mad as raving Hercules,[5]
I'll see him, I; and were thy house of force,
These hands of mine should raze it to the ground;
Unless that thou wouldst bring me to my love.

   Adam. Nay, and you be so impatient, I'll be
      gone.

   Alice. Stay, Adam, thou wert wont to be my
      friend:
Ask Mosbie how I have incurr'd his wrath;
Bear him from me this pair of silver dice,[6]
With which we play'd for kisses many a time;
And when I lost, I won, and so did he:
Such winning, and such losing, Jove send me;
And bid him, if his love do not decline,
To come this morning but along my door,
And as a stranger, but salute me there:
This may he do without suspect or fear.

   Adam. I'll tell him what you say, and so fare-
      well.   [*Exit* ADAM.

   Alice. Do, and one day I'll make amends for all.
I know he loves me well, but dares not come,
Because my husband is so jealous:
And these my narrow prying neighbours blab,
Hinders our meetings when we would confer.
But if I live that block shall be remov'd;
And Mosbie, thou that comes to me by stealth,
Shall neither fear the biting speech of men,
Nor Arden's looks; as surely shall he die,
As I abhor him, and love only thee.

          Enter MICHAEL.

How now, Michael, whither are you going?

   Mich. To fetch my master's nag;
I hope you'll think on me.

   Alice. Ay, but Michael, see you keep your oath;
And be as secret as you are resolute.

   Mich. I'll see he shall not live above a week.

   Alice. On that condition, Michael, here's my
      hand:
None shall have Mosbie's sister but thyself.

   Mich. I understand the painter here hard by,
Hath made report that he and Sue is sure.

   Alice. There's no such matter, Michael, believe
      it not.

   Mich. But he hath sent a dagger sticking in a
      heart,
With a verse or two stolen from a painted cloth;
The which I hear the wench keeps in her chest:
Well, let her keep it, I shall find a fellow

That can both write and read, and make rhyme too;
And if I do,—well, I say no more:
I'll send from London such a taunting letter,
As shall eat the heart he sent with salt,
And fling the dagger at the painter's head.

   Alice. What needs all this? I say that Susan's
      thine.

   Mich. Why, then I say that I will kill my master,
Or any thing that you will have me do.

   Alice. But, Michael, see you do it cunningly.

   Mich. Why, say I should be took, I'll ne'er
      confess
That you know anything; and Susan being a maid,
May beg me from the gallows of the sheriff.

   Alice. Trust not to that, Michael.

   Mich. You cannot tell me; I have seen it, I;
But, mistress, tell her whether I live or die,
I'll make her more worth than twenty painters can.
For I will rid mine elder brother away;
And then the farm of Bocton is mine own.
Who would not venture upon house and land,
When he may have it for a right down blow?

   Alice. Yonder comes Mosbie; Michael get thee
      gone,
And let not him nor any know thy drift.

                 [*Exit* MICH.

SCENE II.—*Before* Arden's *House.*

Enter ALICE *from the House, meeting* MOSBIE.

   Alice. Mosbie, my love.

   Mos. Away, I say, and talk not to me now.

   Alice. A word or two, sweetheart, and then I
      will;
'Tis yet but early days, thou needst not fear.

   Mos. Where is your husband?

   Alice. 'Tis now high water, and he is at the
      quay.

   Mos. There let him be; henceforward know
      me not.

   Alice. Is this the end of all thy solemn oaths?
Is this the fruit thy reconcilement buds?
Have I for this given thee so many favours,
Incurr'd my husband's hate, and, out alas!
Made shipwreck of mine honour for thy sake?
And dost thou say, henceforward know me not?
Remember when I lock'd thee in my closet,
What were thy words and mine; did we not both
Decree, to murder Arden in the night?
The heavens can witness, and the world can tell,
Before I saw that falsehood look of thine,
'Fore I was 'tangled with thy 'ticing speech,
Arden to me was dearer than my soul,

And shall be still; base peasant, get thee gone,
And boast not of thy conquest over me,
Gotten by witchcraft, and mere sorcery.
For what hast thou to countenance my love,
Being descended of a noble house,
And match'd already with a gentleman,
Whose servant thou may'st be;—and so farewell.

   Mos. Ungentle and unkind Alice, now I see
That which I ever fear'd, and find too true:
A woman's love is as the lightning flame,
Which even in bursting forth consumes itself.
To try thy constancy have I been strange;
Would I had never tried, but liv'd in hope.

   Alice. What needs thou try me, whom thou
      ne'er found false.

   Mos. Yet pardon me, for love is jealous.

   Alice. So lists the sailor to the mermaid's song;
So looks the traveller to the basilisk:
I am content for to be reconcil'd,
And that I know will be mine overthrow.

   Mos. Thine overthrow? first let the world dis-
      solve.

   Alice. Nay, Mosbie, let me still enjoy thy love.
And happen what will, I am resolute,
My saving husband hordes up bags of gold,
To make our children rich, and now is he
Gone to unload the goods that shall be thine,
And he and Franklin will to London straight.

   Mos. To London, Alice, if thou'lt be rul'd by me,
We'll make him sure enough for coming there.

   Alice. Ah, would we could.

   Mos. I happen'd on a painter yesternight,
The only cunning man of Christendom:
For he can temper poison with his oil,
That whoso looks upon the work he draws,
Shall with the beams that issue from his sight,
Suck venom to his breast and slay himself.
Sweet Alice he shall draw thy counterfeit,
That Arden may, by gazing on it, perish.

   Alice. Ay, but Mosbie, that is dangerous:
For thou, or I, or any other else,
Coming into the chamber where it hangs, may die.

   Mos. Ay, but we'll have it covered with a cloth,
And hung up in the study for himself.

   Alice. It may not be, for when the picture's
      drawn,
Arden I know will come and show it me.

   Mos. Fear not, we will have that shall serve the
      turn:
This is the painter's house; I'll call him forth,

   Alice. But Mosbie, I'll have no such picture, I.

   Mos. I pray thee leave it to my discretion. How,
      Clarke.

Enter CLARKE.

O, you are an honest man of your word,
You served me well.

   Clarke. Why, Sir, I'll do it for you at any time,
Provided, as you have given your word,
I may have Susan Mosbie to my wife:
For as sharp-witted poets, whose sweet verse
Make heavenly gods break off their nectar draughts,
And lay their ears down to the lowly earth:
Use humble promise to their sacred muse,
So we that are the poet's favorites,
Must have a love.   Ay, love's the painter's muse,
That makes him frame a speaking countenance,
A weeping eye that witnesses heart's grief;
Then tell me, master Mosbie, shall I have her?

   Alice. 'Tis pity but he should, he'll use her well.

   Mos. Clarke, here's my hand, my sister shall be
     thine.

   Clarke. Then, brother, to requite this courtesy,
You shall command my life, my skill, and all.

   Alice. Ah, that thou could'st be secret.

   Mos. Fear him not, love, I have talk'd sufficient.

   Clarke. You know not me, that ask such ques-
     tions:
Let it suffice, I know you love him well,
And fain would have your husband made away:
Wherein, trust me, you show a noble mind,
That rather than you'll live with him you hate,
You'll venture life, and die with him you love.
The like will I do for my Susan's sake.

   Alice. Yet nothing could enforce me to the
     deed,
But Mosbie's love; might I without control,
Enjoy thee still, then Arden should not die:
But seeing I cannot, therefore let him die.

   Mos. Enough, sweet Alice; thy kind words make
     me melt,
Your trick of poisoned pictures we dislike,
Some other poison would do better far.

   Alice. Ay, such as might be put into his broth,
And yet in taste not to be found at all.

   Clarke. I know your mind, and here I have it for
     you,
Put but a dram of this into his drink,
Or any kind of broth that he shall eat:
And he shall die within an hour after.

   Alice. As I am a gentlewoman, Clarke, next day
Thou and Susan shall be married.

   Mos. And I'll make her dowry more than I'll
     talk of, Clarke.

   Clarke. Yonder 's your husband;— Mosbie, I'll
     be gone.

Enter ARDEN *and* FRANKLIN.

   Alice. In good time, see where my husband
     comes;
Master Mosbie ask him the question yourself.
                   [*Exit* CLARKE.

   Mos. Master Arden, being at London yester-
     night,
The Abbey lands whereof you are now possess'd,
Were offered me, on some occasion,
By Greene, one of Sir Antony Agers' men:
I pray you, sir, tell me, are not the lands yours?
Hath any other interest herein?

   Arden. Mosbie, that question we'll decide anon,
Alice, make ready my breakfast, I must hence.
                    [*Exit* ALICE.
As for the lands, Mosbie, they are mine,
By letters patent from his majesty:
But I must have a mandate for my wife,
They say you seek to rob me of her love;
Villain, what makes thou in her company,
She's no companion for so base a groom.

   Mos. Arden, I thought not on her; I came to
     thee,
But rather than I'll pocket up this wrong—

   Frank. What will you do, sir?

   Mos. Revenge it on the proudest of you both:
      [ARDEN *draws forth* Mos.'s *Sword.*

   Arden. So, sirrah, you may not wear a sword,
The statute makes against artificers,[7]
I warrant that I do;[8] now use your bodkin,
Your Spanish needle, and your pressing iron.
For this shall go with me;—and mark my words,—
You, goodman botcher, 'tis to you I speak,—
The next time that I take thee near my house,
Instead of legs I'll make thee crawl on stumps.

   Mos. Ah, master Arden, you have injur'd me,
I do appeal to God, and to the world.

   Frank. Why, canst thou deny thou wert a botcher
     once.

   Mos. Measure me what I am, not what I was.

   Arden. Why, what art thou now but a velvet
     drudge,
A cheating steward, and base-minded peasant?

   Mos. Arden, now thou hast belch'd and vomited
The rancorous venom of thy mis-swoln heart,
Hear me but speak: As I intend to live
With God, and his elected saints in heaven,
I never meant more to solicit her,
And that she knows, and all the world shall see.
I loved her once,—sweet Arden, pardon me,
I could not choose; her beauty fir'd my heart;
But time hath quench'd these over-raging coals,

And, Arden, though I now frequent thy house,
'Tis for my sister's sake her waiting maid,
And not for hers.   Mayest thou enjoy her long
Hell fire and wrathful vengeance light on me,
If I dishonour her or injure thee.

   Arden. Mosbie, with these thy protestations,
The deadly hatred of my heart's appeas'd,
And thou and I'll be friends if this prove true.
As for the base terms I gave thee lately,
Forget them, Mosbie: I had cause to speak;
When all the knights and gentlemen of Kent,
Make common table-talk of her and thee.

   Mos. Who lives that is not touch'd with slanderous tongues,

   Frank. Then Mosbie, to eschew the speech of
men,
Upon whose general bruit all honour hangs,
Forbear his house.

   Arden. Forbear it! Nay, rather frequent it
more,
The world shall see that I distrust her not.
To warn him on the sudden from my house,
Were to confirm the rumour that is grown.

   Mos. By my faith, sir, you say true,
And therefore will I sojourn here a while,
Until our enemies have talk'd their fill.
And then I hope they'll cease, and at last confess,
How causeless they have injur'd her and me.

   Arden. And I will lie at London all this term,
To let them see how light I weigh their words.
                [*Exeunt into the House.*

SCENE III.—*Room in* Arden's *House, as before.*

Enter ARDEN, FRANKLIN, MOSBIE, MICHAEL, *and*
ALICE.

   Alice. Husband sit down, your breakfast will be
cold.

   Arden. Come, Master Mosbie, will you sit with
us.

   Mos. I cannot eat, but I'll sit for company.

   Arden. Sirrah Michael, see my horse be ready.

   Alice. Husband why pause ye, why eat you not?

   Arden. I am not well, there's something in this
broth
That is not wholesome; didst thou make it, Alice?

   Alice. I did, and that's the cause it likes not you,
        [*She throws the Broth on the Ground.*
There's nothing that I do can please your taste,
You were best to say I would have poison'd you.
I cannot speak or cast aside my eye,
But he imagines, I have stept awry.
Here's he that you cast in my teeth so oft,

Now will I be convinced, or purge myself,
I charge thee speak to this mistrustful man,
Thou that wouldst see me hang;—thou, Mosbie,
thou,
What favour hast thou had more than a kiss,[10]
At coming or departing from the town?

   Mos. You wrong yourself and me, to cast these
doubts,
Your loving husband is not jealous.

   Arden. Why, gentle mistress Alice, can't I be ill,
But you'll accuse yourself.
Franklin, thou hast a box of methridate,
I'll take a little to prevent the worst.

   Frank. Do so, and let us presently take horse,
My life for yours ye shall do well enough.

   Alice. Give me a spoon, I'll eat of it myself,
Would it were full of poison to the brim;
Then should my cares and troubles have an end;
Was ever silly woman so tormented?

   Arden. Be patient, sweet love, I mistrust not
thee.

   Alice. God will revenge it, Arden, if thou dost,
For never woman lov'd her husband better, than I
thee.

   Arden. I know it, sweet Alice, cease to complain;
Lest that in tears I answer thee again.

   Frank. Come, leave this dallying, and let us away.

   Alice. Forbear to wound me with that bitter
word,
Arden shall go to London in my arms

   Arden. Loth am I to depart, yet I must go.

   Alice. Wilt thou to London, then, and leave me
here:
Ah, if thou love me, gentle Arden, stay,
Yet if thy business be of great import,
Go if thou wilt; I'll bear it as I may:
But write from London to me every week,
Nay, every day, and stay no longer there
Than thou must need, lest that I die for sorrow.

   Arden. I'll write unto thee every other tide,
And so farewell, sweet Alice, till we meet next.

   Alice. Farewell, husband, seeing you'll have
it so.
And master Franklin, seeing you take him hence,
In hope you'll hasten him home, I'll give you this.
                [*She kisses him.*

   Frank. And if he stay, the fault shall not be
mine;—
Mosbie, farewell; and see you keep your oath.

   Mos. I hope he is not jealous of me now.

   Arden. No, Mosbie, no; hereafter think of me,
As of your dearest friend, and so farewell.
       [*Exeunt* ARDEN, FRANK. *and* MICH.

Alice. I am glad he is gone, he was about to stay;
But did you mark me then how I broke off?

Mos. Ay, Alice, and it was cunningly performed:
But what a villain is this painter, Clarke!

Alice. Was it not a goodly poison that he gave?
Why he's as well now as he was before.
It should have been some fine confection,
That might have given the broth some dainty taste,
This powder was too gross and populous.

Mos. But had he eaten but three spoonfulls more,
Then had he died, and our love continued.

Alice. Why so it shall, Mosbie, albeit he live.

Mos. It is impossible, for I have sworn
Never hereafter to solicit thee,
Or, whilst he lives, once more importune thee.

Alice. Thou shalt not need, I will importune
    thee.
What! shall an oath make thee forsake my love?
As if I have not sworn as much myself,
And given my hand unto him in the church.
Tush, Mosbie, oaths are words, and words are wind,
And wind is mutable: Then I conclude,
'Tis childishness to stand upon an oath.

Mos. Well proved, mistress Alice; yet by your
    leave,
I will keep mine unbroken whilst he lives.

Alice. Aye, do, and spare not; his time is but
    short;
For if thou art as resolute as I,
We'll have him murdered as he walks the streets.
In London many alehouse ruffians keep,
Which, as I hear, will murder men for gold;
They shall be soundly fee'd to pay him home.

Mos. Alice, what's he that comes yonder, know-
    est thou him?

Alice. Mosbie, begone; I hope 'tis one that
    comes
To put in practice our intended drifts. [*Exit* Mos.

Enter GREENE.

Greene. Mistress Arden, you are well met;
I am sorry that your husband is from home,
When, as my purpos'd journey was to him:
Yet all my labour is not spent in vain;
For I suppose that you can full discourse,
And flat resolve me of the thing I seek.

Alice. What is it, master Greene? If that I may,
Or can, with safety, I will answer you.

Greene. I heard your husband hath the grant,
    of late,
Confirm'd by letters patent from the king,
Of all the lands of the abbey of Feversham,
Generally entitled; so that all former grants

Are cut off, whereof I myself had one;
But now my interest by that is void.
This is all, mistress Arden, is it true or no?

Alice. True, master Greene, the lands are his in
    state:
And whatsoever leases were before,
Are void for term of master Arden's life.
He hath the grant under the chancery seal.

Greene. Pardon me, mistress Arden, I must
    speak,
For I am touch'd. Your husband doth me wrong,
To wring from me the little land I have.
My living is my life, only that
Resteth remainder of my portion.
Desire of wealth is endless in his mind:
And he is greedy, gaping still for gain:
Nor cares he though young gentlemen do beg,
So he may scrape and hoard up in his pouch.
But seeing he hath taken my lands, I'll value life
As careless, as he is careful for to get:
And tell him this from me, I'll be reveng'd,
And so, as he shall wish the abbey lands
Had rested still within their former state.

Alice. Alas, poor gentleman, I pity you!
And woe is me that any man should want.
God knows, 'tis not my fault: But wonder not,
Though he be hard to others, when to me——
Ah, master Greene, God knows how I am used.

Greene. Why, mistress Arden, can the crabbéd
    churl
Use you unkindly? Respects he not your birth,
Your honourable friends, nor what you brought?
Why, all Kent knows your parentage, and what
    you are.

Alice. Ah, master Greene, be it spoken in secret
    here,
I never live good day with him alone:
When he's at home, then have I froward looks,
Hard words and blows, to mend the match withal:
And though I might content as good a man,
Yet doth he keep in every corner trulls
And, weary with his trugs at home,
Then rides he straight to London: there, forsooth,
He revels it among such filthy ones,
As counsel him to make away his wife.
Thus live I daily in continual fear,
In sorrow: so despairing of redress,
As every day I wish, with hearty prayer,
That he or I were taken forth the world.

Greene. Now trust me, mistress Alice, it griev-
    eth me,
So fair a creature should be so abused.
Why, who'd have thought the civil sir so sullen.

He looks so smoothly.   Fie upon him, churl;
And if he lives a day he lives too long.
But, frolic woman, I shall be the man
Shall set you free from all this discontent :
And if the churl deny my interest,
And will not yield my lease into my hand,
I 'll pay him home whatever hap to me.

    Alice. But speak you as you think ?

    Greene. Ay, God's my witness, I mean plain
    dealing;
For I had rather die than lose my land.

    Alice. Then, master Greene, be counselled by me;
Endanger not yourself for such a churl,
But hire some cutter for to cut him short :
And here's ten pounds to wager them withal;
When he is dead you shall have twenty more.

And the lands whereof my husband is possess'd,
Shall be entitled as they were before.

    Greene. Will you keep promise with me ?

    Alice. Or count me false and perjur'd whilst I
    live.

    Greene. Then here's my hand, I 'll have him so
    despatch'd :
I 'll up to London straight, I 'll thither post,
And never rest till I have compass'd it.
Till then, farewell.

    Alice. Good fortune follow all your forward
    thoughts.   [*Exit* GREENE.
And whosoever doth attempt the deed.
A happy hand I wish, and so farewell.
All this goes well.   Mosbie, I long for thee,
To let thee know all that I have contriv'd.

ACT II.

SCENE I.—*Before* Arden's *House.*

Enter MOSBIE *and* CLARKE, *meeting* ALICE.

    Mos. How now, Alice, what's the news ?

    Alice. Such as will content thee well, sweetheart.

    Mos. Well, let them pass awhile, and tell me,
    Alice,
How have you dealt and temper'd with my sister.
What, will she have my neighbour Clarke, or no ?

    Alice. What, master Mosbie! let him woo him-
    self !
Think you that maids look not for fair words ?
Go to her, Clarke, she's all alone within :
Michael, my man, is clean out of her books.

    Clarke. I thank you, mistress Arden, I will in ;
And if fair Susan and I can agree,
You shall command me to the uttermost,
As far as either goods or life may stretch.
                    [*Exit* CLARKE.

    Mos. Now, Alice, let's hear thy news.

    Alice. They be so good, that I must laugh for
    joy,
Before I can begin to tell my tale.

    Mos. Let's hear them, then, that I may laugh
    for company.

    Alice. This morning, master Greene, Dick Greene,
    I mean ;
From whom my husband had the abbey land,
Came hither, railing, for to know the truth,
Whether my husband had the lands by grant.
I told him all, whereat he storm'd amain,

And swore he would cry quittance with the churl ;
And if he did deny his interest,
Stab him, whatever did befal himself.
When, as I saw his choler thus to rise,
I whetted on the gentleman with words :
And to conclude, Mosbie, at last we grew
To composition for my husband's death.
I gave him ten pounds to hire knaves,
By some devise to make away the churl ;
When he is dead he should have twenty more,
And repossess his former lands again.
On this we agreed ; and he is ridden straight
To London, to bring his death about.

    Mos. But call you this good news ?

    Alice. Ay, sweetheart, be they not ?

    Mos. 'Twere cheerful news to hear the churl were
    dead :
But trust me, Alice, I take it passing ill
You would be so forgetful of our state,
To make recount of it to every groom.
What ! to acquaint each stranger with our drifts,
Chiefly in case of murder ; why, 'tis the way
To make it open unto Arden's self,
And bring thyself and me to ruin both :
Forewarn'd, forearm'd; who threats his enemy,
Lends him a sword to guard himself withal.

    Alice. I did it for the best.

    Mos. Well, seeing 'tis done, clearly let it pass.
You know this Greene ; is he not religious ?
A man, I guess, of great devotion.

    Alice. He is.

Mos. Then, sweet Alice, let it pass; I have a drift
Will quiet all, whatever is amiss.

Enter CLARKE *and* SUSAN.

Alice. How now, Clarke, have you found me false?
Did I not plead the matter hard for you?
Clarke. You did.
Mos.   And what; wil't be a match?
Clarke. A match! ay, faith, sir; ay, the day is mine.
The painter lays his colours to the life:
His pencil draws no shadows in his love.
Susan is mine.
Alice.   You make her blush.
Mos. What, sister, is it Clarke must be the man?
Susan. It resteth in your grant; some words are pass'd;
And happily we be grown unto a match,
If you be willing that it shall he so.
Mos. Ah, master Clarke, it resteth at my grant;
You see my sister's yet at my dispose;
But so you'll grant me one thing I shall ask,
I am content my sister shall be yours.
Clarke. What is it, master Mosbie?
Mos. I do remember once, in secret talk,
You told me how you could compound by art,
A crucifix impoisoned;
That whoso look'd upon it should wax blind,
And with the scent be stifled; that ere long
He should be poison'd that did view it well.
I would have you make me such a crucifix,
And then I'll grant my sister shall be yours.
Clarke. Though I am loth, because it toucheth life;
Yet rather or I'll leave sweet Susan's love,
I'll do it, and with all the haste I may
But for whom is it?
Alice. Leave that to us. Why, Clarke, is it possible
That you should paint and draw it out yourself,
The colours being baleful and impoisoned,
And no ways prejudice yourself withal?
Mos. Well questioned, Alice; Clarke, how answer you that?
Clarke. Very easily: I'll tell you straight,
How I do work of these impoison'd drugs.
I fasten on my spectacles so close,
As nothing can any way offend my sight;
Then, as I put a leaf within my nose,
So put I rhubarb, to avoid the smell,
And softly as another work I paint.

Mos. 'Tis very well; but against when shall I have it?
Clarke. Within these ten days.
Mos.   'Twill serve the turn.
Now Alice let's in, and see what cheer you keep.
I hope, now Master Arden is from home,
You'll give me leave to play your husband's part.
Alice. Mosbie, you know who's master of my heart,
As well may be the master of the house. [*Exeunt.*

SCENE II.—*Country between* Feversham *and* London.

Enter GREENE *and* BRADSHAW.

Brad. See you them that come yonder, Master Greene?
Greene. Ay, very well, do you know them?
Brad. The one I know not, but he seems a knave,
Chiefly for bearing the other company:
For such a slave, so vile a rogue as he,
Lives not again upon the earth.
Black Will is his name: I tell you, master Greene,
At Boulogne he and I were fellow-soldiers,
Where he played such pranks,
As all the camp fear'd him for his villany:
I warrant you he bears so bad a mind,
That for a crown he'll murder any man.
Greene. The fitter is he for my purpose, marry.
                                 [*Aside.*

Enter BLACK WILL *and* SHAKEBAG.

Will. How now, fellow Bradshaw,
Whither away so early?
Brad. O Will, times are changed, no fellows now,
Though we were once together in the field;
Yet thy friend, to do thee any good I can.
Will. Why, Bradshaw, was not thou and I
Fellow-soldiers at Boulogne:
Where I was a corporal, and thou but a base mercenary groom?
No fellows now, because you are a goldsmith,
And have a little plate in your shop.
You were glad to call me fellow Will,
And with a curtsey to the earth;
"One snatch, good corporal,"
When I stole the half ox from John the vit'ler,
And domineer'd with it amongst good fellows,
In one night.
Brad. Ay, Will, those days are past with me.
Will. Ay, but they be not past with me,
For I keep that same honourable mind still.

Good, neighbour Bradshaw, you are too proud to
    be my fellow;
But were it not that I see more company coming
    down
The hill, I would be fellows with you once more,
And share crowns with you too.
But let that pass, and tell me whither you go.

  Brad. To London, Will, about a piece of service,
Wherein happily thou mayst pleasure me.

  Will. What is it?

  Brad. Of late Lord Cheiny lost some plate,
Which one did bring, and sold it at my shop,
Saying he served sir Anthony Cooke.
A search was made, the plate was found with me,
And I am bound to answer at the 'size,
Now, lord Cheiny solemnly vows,
If law will serve him, he'll hang me for his plate.
Now I am going to London, upon hope,
To find the fellow; now, Will, I know
Thou art acquainted with such companions.

  Will. What manner of man was he?

  Brad. A lean-faced writhen knave,
Hawk-nosed, and very hollow-eyed,
With mighty furrows in his stormy brows;
Long hair down his shoulders curled,
His chin was bare, but on his upper lip,
A mutchado, which he wound about his ear.

  Will. What apparel had he?

  Brad. A watchet satin doublet all so torn,
The inner side did bear the greatest show;
A pair of threadbare velvet hose, seam rent,
A worsted stocking rent above the shoe,
A livery cloak, but all the lace was off,
'Twas bad, but yet it served to hide the plate.

  Will. Sirrah, Shakebag, canst thou remember
Since we trowled the bowl at Sittingburn,
Where I broke the tapster's head of the Lion
With a cudgel stick?

  Brad.   Aye, very well, Will.

  Will. Why, it was with the money that the plate
    was sold for;
Sirrah, Bradshaw, what wilt thou give him
That can tell thee who sold the plate?

  Brad. Who, I pray thee, good Will?

  Will. Why, 'twas one Jack Fitten,
He's now in Newgate for stealing a horse,
And shall be arraigned the next 'size.

  Brad. Why, then, let lord Cheiny seek Jack
    Fitten forth;
For I'll back and tell him who robbed him of his
    plate;
This cheers my heart; master Greene, I'll leave you,
For I must to the Isle of Sheppy with speed.

  Greene. Before you go, let me entreat you
To carry this letter to mistress Arden of Feversham,
And humbly recommend me to herself.

  Brad. That will I, master Greene, and so fare-
    well.
Here, Will, there's a crown for thy good news.
                         [*Exit.* BRAD.

  Will. Farewell, Bradshaw,
I'll drink no water for thy sake, whilst this lasts:
Now, gentlemen, shall we have your company to
    London?

  Greene. Nay, stay, sirs, a little more, I needs
    must use your help,
And in a matter of great consequence;
Wherein if you'll be secret and profound,
I'll give you twenty angels for your pains.

  Will. How! twenty angels? Give my fellow
George Shakebag and me twenty angels,
And if thou'lt have thine own father slain,
That thou mayst inherit his land; we'll kill him.

  Shake. Aye, thy mother, thy sister, thy brother,
    or all thy kin.

  Greene. Well, this it is; Arden of Feversham
Hath highly wrong'd me about the Abbey land,
That no revenge but death will serve the turn:
Will you two kill him? here are the angels down,
And I will lay the platform of his death.[11]

  Will. Plat me no platforms, give me the money,
And I'll stab him as he stands pissing against a wall,
But I'll kill him.

  Shake.   Where is he?

  Greene. He is now at London, in Aldersgate
    street.

  Shake. He's dead as if he had been condemn'd
By an act of parliament, if once Black Will and I
Swear his death.

  Greene. Here is ten pound, and when he is dead,
Ye shall have twenty more.

  Will. My fingers itch to be at the peasant.
Ah, that I might be set a work thus through the year,
And that murder would grow to an occupation;
That a man might without danger of law:
Zounds, I warrant I should be warden of the com-
    pany.
Come, let us be going, and we'll bate at Rochester,
Where I'll give thee a gallon of sack,
To hansel the match withal.   [*Exeunt.*

SCENE III.—London. *A Street near* St. Paul's.

Enter MICHAEL.

  Mich. I have gotten such a letter,
As will touch the painter: And thus it is.

Enter ARDEN *and* FRANKLIN, *and hear* MICHAEL *read this letter.*

My duty remembered, Mrs. Susan, hoping in God you be in good health, as I, Michael, was at the making hereof. This is to certify you, that as the turtle true, when she hath lost her mate, sitteth alone; so I, mourning for your absence, do walk up and down Paul's, till one day I fell asleep, and lost my master's Pantophelles.¹² Ah, mistress Susan, abolish that paltry painter, cut him off by the shins, with a frowning look of your crabbed countenance, and think upon Michael, who, drunk with the dregs of your favour, will cleave as fast to your love, as a plaster of pitch to a galled horse's back. Thus hoping you will let my passions penetrate, or rather impetrate mercy of your meek hands, I end

Your MICHAEL, or else not MICHAEL.

Arden. [*Coming forward*] Why, you paltry knave,
Stand you here loitering, knowing my affairs,
What haste my business craves to send to Kent?
Frank. Faith, friend Michael, this is very ill,
Knowing your master hath no more but you,
And do ye slack his business for your own?
Arden. Where is the letter, sirrah, let me see it.
[*He gives him the Letter.*
See, master Franklin, here is proper stuff,
Susan my maid, the painter, and my man.
A crew of harlots¹³ all in love forsooth,
Sirrah, let me hear no more of this,
Nor for thy life once write to her a word.

Enter GREENE, WILL, *and* SHAKEBAG.

Wilt thou be married to so base a trull?
'Tis Mosbie's sister: come I once at home,
I'll rouse her from remaining in my house.
Now, Master Franklin, let's go walk in Paul's,
Come, but a turn or two, and then away. [*Exeunt.*
Greene. The first is Arden, and that's his man,
The other is Franklin; Arden's dearest friend.
Will. Zounds! I'll kill them all three.
Greene. Nay, sirs, touch not his man in any case,
But stand close, and take you fittest standing,
And at his coming forth speed him:
To the Nag's Head, there is this coward's haunt;
But now I'll leave you till the deed be done.
[*Exit* GREENE.
Shake. If he be not paid his own, ne'er trust Shakebag.
Will. Sirrah, Shakebag, at his coming forth
I'll run him through, and then to the Blackfriars,
And there take water and away.
Shake. Why, that's the best; but see thou miss him not.
Will. How can I miss him, when I think on the forty
Angels I must have more.

Enter a PRENTICE.

Pren. 'Tis very late, I were best shut up my stall,
For here will be old filching,¹⁴ when the press comes forth
Of Paul's.
[*Lets down his Window, and it breaks* WILL's *Head.*¹⁵
Will. Zounds! draw, Shakebag, draw, I am almost kill'd.
Pren. We'll tame you, I warrant.
Will. Zounds! I am tame enough already.

Enter ARDEN, FRANKLIN, *and* MICHAEL.

Arden. What troublesome fray or mutiny is this?
Frank. 'Tis nothing but some babbling paltry fray,
Devis'd to pick men's pockets in the throng.
Arden. Is't nothing else? Come, Franklin, let us away. [*Exeunt.*
Will. What mends shall I have for my broken head?
Pren. Marry, this mends, that if you get you not away
All the sooner, you shall be well beaten, and sent to the compter.¹⁶ [*Exit* PREN.
Will. Well, I'll be gone, but look to your signs,
For I'll pull them down all.
Shakebag, my broken head grieves me not so much,
As by this means Arden hath escaped.

Enter GREENE.

Greene. I had a glimpse of him and his companion.
Why, sirs, Arden's as well as I.
I met him and Franklin going merrily to the ordinary again,
What, dare you not do it?
Will. Yes, sir, we dare do it, but were my consent to give,
We would not do it under ten pound more.
I value every drop of my blood at a French crown.
I have had ten pound to steal a dog,
And we have no more here to kill a man;
But that a bargain is a bargain, and so forth,
You should do it yourself.
Greene. I pray thee how came thy head broke?
Will. Why, thou seest it is broke, dost thou not?
Shake. Standing against a stall, watching Arden's coming,
A boy let down his shop window, and broke his head.

65

Whereupon arose a brawl, and in the tumult
Arden escap'd us, and passed by unthought on ;
But forbearance is no acquittance,
Another time we'll do it, I warrant thee.

    Greene. I pray thee Will, make clean thy bloody
        brow,
And let's bethink us on some other place,
Where Arden may be met with handsomely.
Remember how devoutly thou hast sworn
To kill the villain ; think upon thine oath.

    Will. Tush, I have broken five hundred oaths ;
But wouldst thou charm me to effect this deed,
Tell me of gold, my resolution's fee.
Say, thou seest Mosbie kneeling at my knees,
Offering me service for my high attempt :
And sweet Alice Arden, with a lap of crowns,
Come, with a lowly curtsey to the earth,
Saying, Take this : but for thy quarterage,
Such yearly tribute will I answer thee.
Why, this would steel soft-mettled cowardice,
With which Black Will was never tainted yet.
I tell thee, Greene, the forlorn traveller,
Whose lips are glued with summer's parching heat,
Ne'er long'd so much to see a running brook,
As I to finish Arden's tragedy.
Seest thou this gore that cleaveth to my face ?
From hence ne'er will I wash this bloody stain,
Till Arden's heart be panting in my hand.17

    Greene. Why that's well said, but what says
        Shakebag?

    Shake. I cannot paint my valour out with words,
But give me place and opportunity,
Such mercy as the starven lioness,
When she is dry-sucked of her eager young,
Shows to the prey that next encounters her,
On Arden so much pity would I take.

    Greene. So should it fare with men of firm re-
        solve.
And now, sirs, seeing this accident,
Of meeting him in Paul's, hath no success,
Let us bethink us on some other place,
Whose earth may swallow up this Arden's blood.
See, yonder comes his man, and wot you what,
The foolish knave's in love with Mosbie's sister,
And for her sake, whose love he cannot get,
Unless Mosbie solicit his suit,
The villain hath sworn the slaughter of his master.
We'll question him, for he may stead us much :

       Enter MICHAEL.

How now, Michael, whither are you going ?
    Mich. My master hath now supped,
And I am going to prepare his chamber.

    Greene. Where supped Master Arden ?
    Mich. At the Nag's Head, at the eighteen-penny
        ordinary.
How now, Master Shakebag !   What, Black Will !
God's dear lady, how chance your face is so bloody ?
    Will. Go too, sirrah, there is a chance in it,
This sauciness in you will make you be knock'd.
    Mich. Nay, and you be offended I'll be gone.
    Greene. Stay, Michael, you may not escape us so ;
Michael, I know you love your master well.
    Mich. Why so I do, but wherefore urge you
        that ?
    Greene. Because I think you love your mistress
        better.
    Mich. So think not I, but say, i'faith what if I
        should ?
    Shake. Come, to the purpose, Michael, we hear
You have a pretty love in Feversham.
    Mich. Why, have I two or three, what's that to
        thee ?
    Will. You deal too mildly with the peasant ;
        thus it is,
'Tis known to us that you love Mosbie's sister.
We know besides, that you have tak'n your oath,
To further Mosbie to your mistress' bed,
And kill your master, for his sister's sake.
Now, sir, a poorer coward than yourself,
Was never foster'd in the coast of Kent.
How comes it then, that such a knave as you
Dare swear a matter of such consequence ?
    Greene. Ah, Will!——
    Will. Tush, give me leave, there is no more but
        this,
Since thou hast sworn, we dare discover all ;
And hadst thou, or shouldst thou utter it,
We have devised a complot under hand,
Whatever shall betide to any of us,
To send thee roundly to the devil of hell.
And therefore thus : I am the very man,
Mark'd in my birth-hour by the destinies,
To give an end to Arden's life on earth ;
Thou but a member, but to whet the knife,
Whose edge must search the closet of his breast.
Thy office is but to appoint the place,
And train thy master to his tragedy.
Mine to perform it, when occasion serves.
Then be not nice, but here devise with us,
How, and what way, we may conclude his death.
    Shake. So shalt thou purchase Mosbie for thy
       friend,
And, by his friendship, gain his sister's love.
    Greene. So shall thy mistress be thy favourer,
And thou disburden'd of the oath thou made.

Mich. Well, gentlemen, I cannot but confess,
Since you have urged me so apparently,
That I have vowed my Master Arden's death;
And he, whose kindly love and liberal hand,
Doth challenge naught but good deserts of me,
I will deliver over to your hands.
This night come to his house at Aldersgate,
The doors I'll leave unlock'd against you come.
No sooner shall ye enter through the latch,
Over the threshold to the inner court,
But on your left hand shall you see the stairs,
That leads directly to my master's chamber.
There take him, and dispose him as you please.
Now it were good we parted company,
What I have promiséd I will perform.

    Will. Should you deceive us, 'twould go wrong
      with you.

    Mich. I will accomplish all I have reveal'd.

    Will. Come, let's go drink, choler makes me as
      dry as a dog.

           [*Exeunt* WILL, GREENE, *and* SHAKE.

    Mich. Thus feeds the lamb securely on the
      down,
Whilst through the thicket of an arbour brake,
The hunger-bitten wolf o'erpries his haunt,
And takes advantage for to eat him up.
Ah! harmless Arden, how hast thou misdone,
That thus thy gentle life is levell'd at?
The many good turns that thou hast done to me,
Now must I quittance with betraying thee.
I that should take the weapon in my hand,
And buckler thee from ill-intending foes,
Do lead thee, with a wicked fraudful smile,
As unsuspected, to the slaughter-house.
So have I sworn to Mosbie and my mistress;
So have I promised to the slaughtermen:
And should I not deal currently with them,
Their lawless rage would take revenge on me.
Tush, I will spurn at mercy for this once;
Let pity lodge where feeble women lie,
I am resolv'd, and Arden needs must die.

                   [*Exit* MICH.

ACT III.

SCENE I.—*A Room in* Franklin's *House, at*
Aldersgate.

Enter ARDEN *and* FRANKLIN.

    Arden. No, Franklin, no; if fear or stormy
      threats,
If love of me, or care of womanhood,
If fear of God, or common speech of men,
Who mangle credit with their wounding words,
And couch dishonour as dishonour buds,
Might join repentance in her wanton thoughts,
No question then but she would turn the leaf,
And sorrow for her dissolution:
But she is rooted in her wickedness;
Perverse and stubborn, not to be reclaim'd;
Good counsel is to her as rain to weeds,
And reprehension makes her vice to grow,
As hydra's head, that perish'd by decay.[18]
Her faults, methinks, are painted in my face,
For every searching eye to over-read;
And Mosbie's name a scandal unto mine,
Is deeply trenchéd in my blushing brow.
Ah! Franklin, Franklin, when I think on this,
My heart's grief rends my other powers,
Worse than the conflict at the hour of death.

    Frank. Gentle Arden, leave this sad lament,
She will amend, and so your griefs will cease,
Or else she'll die, and so your sorrows end.
If neither of these two do happily fall,
Yet let your comfort be, that others bear
Your woes twice doubled all with patience.

    Arden. My house is irksome, there I cannot rest.

    Frank. Then stay with me in London, go not
      home.

    Arden. Then that base Mosbie doth usurp my
      room,
And makes his triumph of my being thence.
At home, or not at home, where'er I be,
Here, here it lies; ah, Franklin, here it lies,
That will not out till wretched Arden dies.

Enter MICHAEL.

    Frank. Forget your griefs a while, here comes
      your man.

    Arden. What o'clock is't, sirrah?

    Mich.   Almost ten.

    Arden. See, see, how runs away the weary time.
Come, Master Franklin, shall we go to bed.

           [*Exeunt* ARDEN *and* MICH.

    Frank. I pray you go before, I'll follow you;
Ah, what a hell is fretful jealousy!
What pity-moving words! what deep-fetch'd sighs!

What grievous groans, and overlading woes,
Accompany this gentle gentleman!
Now will he shake his care-oppresséd head,
Then fix his sad eyes on the sullen earth,
Asham'd to gaze upon the open world.
Now will he cast his eyes up towards the heavens,
Looking that way for a redress of wrong:
Sometimes he seeketh to beguile his grief,
And tells a story with his careful tongue.
Then comes his wife's dishonour in his thoughts,
And in the middle cutteth off his tale;
Pouring fresh sorrow on his weary limbs.
So woe-begone, so inly charg'd with woe,
Was never any lived, and bare it so.

Re-enter MICHAEL.

Mich. My master would desire you come to bed.
Frank. Is he himself already in his bed?
Mich. He is, and fain would have the light away;
[*Exit* FRANK.
Conflicting thoughts encampéd in my breast,
Awake me with the echo of their strokes:
And I a judge to censure either side,
Can give to neither wishéd victory.
My master's kindness pleads to me for life,
With just demand, and I must grant it him,
My mistress she hath forced me with an oath,
For Susan's sake, the which I may not break;
For that is nearer than a master's love.
That grim-faced fellow, pityless black Will,
And Shakebag, stern in bloody stratagem,
(Two rougher ruffians never liv'd in Kent,)
Have sworn my death if I infringe my vow:
A dreadful thing to be consider'd of.
Methinks I see them with their bolster'd hair,
Staring and grinning in thy gentle face,
And in their ruthless hands their daggers drawn,
Insulting o'er thee with a peck of oaths;
Whilst thou, submissive, pleading for release,
Art mangled by their ireful instruments.
Methinks I hear them ask where Michael is;
And pityless black Will cries, "Stab the slave:
The peasant will detect the tragedy."
The wrinkles in his foul, death-threatening face,
Gape open wide, like graves to swallow men.
My death to him is but a merriment;
And he will murder me to make him sport.
He comes, he comes! ah, master Franklin, help!
Call up the neighbours, or we are but dead.

Re-enter FRANKLIN *and* ARDEN.

Frank. What dismal outcry calls me from my
     rest?

Arden. What hath occasion'd such a fearful cry?
Speak, Michael, hath any injur'd thee?
Mich. Nothing, sir; but as I fell asleep,
Upon the threshold leading to the stairs,
I had a fearful dream that troubled me;
And in my slumber thought I was beset
With murderous thieves, that came to rifle me.
My trembling joints witness my inward fear:
I crave your pardons for disturbing you.
Arden. So great a cry for nothing I ne'er heard:
What, are the doors fast lock'd, and all things safe?
Mich. I cannot tell; I think I lock'd the doors.
Arden. I like not this; but I'll go see myself:
Ne'er trust me, but the doors were all unlock'd.
This negligence not half contenteth me.
Get you to bed; and if you love my favour,
Let me have no more such pranks as these.
Come, master Franklin, let us go to bed.
Frank. Ay, by my faith, the air is very cold.
Michael, farewell; I pray thee dream no more.

SCENE II.—*Outside* Franklin's *House.*

Enter WILL, GREENE, *and* SHAKEBAG.

Shake. Black night hath hid the pleasure of the day;
And sheeting darkness overhangs the earth;
And with the black fold of her cloudy robe,
Obscures us from the eyesight of the world,
In which sweet silence such as we triumph.
The lazy minutes linger on their time,
As loth to give due audit to the hour:
Till in the watch our purpose be complete,
And Arden sent to everlasting night.
Greene, get you gone, and linger here about
And at some hour hence, come to us again,
Where we will give you instance of his death.
Greene. Speed to my wish, whose will soe'er
     says no;
And so I'll leave you for an hour or two.
[*Exit* GREENE.
Will. I tell thee, Shakebag, would this thing
     were done.
I am so heavy than I can scarce go:
This drowsiness in me bodes little good.
Shake. How now, Will, become a precisian?[19]
Nay, then, let's go sleep: when bugs and fears
Shall kill our courage with their fancy's work.
Will. Why, Shakebag, thou mistakes me much,
And wrong me too, in telling me of fear.
Were't not a serious thing we go about,
It should be slipp'd, till I had fought with thee:
To let thee know I am no coward, I!
I tell thee, Shakebag, thou abusest me.

Shake. Why, thy speech betray'd an inly kind
    of fear,
And savour'd of a weak, relenting spirit.
Go forward now in that we have begun;
And afterwards attempt me when thou darest.
    Will. And if I do not, heaven cut me off:
But let that pass, and show me to this house,
Where thou shalt see I'll do as much as Shakebag.
    Shake. This is the door; but soft, methinks 'tis
    shut!
The villain, Michael, hath deceived us.
    Will. Soft, let me see, Shakebag; 'tis shut in-
    deed.
Knock with thy sword: perhaps the slave will hear.
    Shake. It will not be; the white-liver'd peasant
    is gone to bed,
And laughs us both to scorn.
    Will. And he shall buy his merriment as dear,
As ever coistrel bought so little sport:
Ne'er let this sword assist me when I need,
But rust and canker after I have sworn;
If I, the next time that I meet the hind
Lop not away his leg, his arm, or both.
    Shake. And let me never draw a sword again,
Nor prosper in the twilight, cock-shut light,
When I would fleece the wealthy passenger,
But lie and languish in a loathsome den,
Hated, and spit at by the goers by,
And in that death may die unpitied,
If I, the next time that I meet the slave,
Cut not the nose from off the coward's face,
And trample on it for his villany.
    Will. Come, let's go seek out Greene; I know
    he'll swear.
    Shake. He were a villain and he would not swear;
'Twould make a peasant swear among his boys,
That ne'er durst say before but yea and no,
To be thus flouted of a coistrel.[20]
    Will. Shakebag, let's seek out Greene, and in
    the morning,
At the alehouse 'butting Arden's house,
Watch the out-coming of that prick-ear'd cur;
And then let me alone to handle him.   [*Exeunt.*

SCENE III.—*Room in* Franklin's *House, as
before.*

Enter ARDEN, FRANKLIN, *and* MICHAEL.

    Arden. Sirrah, get you back to Billingsgate,
And learn what time the tide will serve our turn;
Come to us in Paul's; first go make the bed,
And afterwards go hearken for the flood.
                           [*Exit* MICH.

Come, master Franklin, you shall go with me.
This night I dream'd, that being in a park,
A toil was pitch'd to overthrow the deer;
And I, upon a little rising hill,
Stood wistly watching for the herd's approach:
Even there, methought a gentle slumber took me,
And summon'd all my parts to sweet repose.
But, in the pleasure of this golden rest,
An ill-thew'd forester had remov'd the toil,
And rounded me with that beguiling home,
Which late, methought, was pitch'd to cast the
    deer;
With that he blew an evil-sounding horn,
And at the noise, another herdsman came,
With falchion drawn, and bent it at my breast,
Crying aloud, " Thou art the game we seek."
With this I wak'd, and trembled every joint,
Like one obscured in a little bush,
That sees a lion foraging about;
And when the dreadful forest king is gone,
He pries about with timorous suspect,
Throughout the thorny casements of the brake,
And will not think his person dangerless,
But quakes and shivers, though the cause be gone.
So trust me, Franklin, when I did awake,
I stood in doubt whether I waked or no:
Such great impression took this fond surprise.
God grant this vision deemed me any good.
    Frank. This phantasy doth rise from Michael's
    fear,
Who being awak'd with the noise he made,
His troubled senses yet could take no rest.
And this, I warrant you, procured your dream.
    Arden. It may be so; God frame it to the best;
But oftentimes my dreams presage too true.
    Frank. To such as note their nightly phantasies,
Some one in twenty may incur belief;
But use it not; 'tis but a mockery.
    Arden. Come, master Franklin, we'll now walk
    in Paul's,
And dine together at the ordinary,
And by my man's direction draw to the quay.
And with the tide go down to Feversham.
Say, master Franklin, shall it not be so?
    Frank. At your good pleasure, sir,
I'll bear you company.   [*Exeunt.*

SCENE IV.—Aldersgate.

Enter MICHAEL; *then enter* GREENE, WILL, *and*
    SHAKEBAG, *at another Door.*

    Will. Draw, Shakebag, for here's that villain
    Michael.

Greene. First, let's hear what he can say.

Will. Speak, milksop slave, and never after speak.

Mich. For God's sake, sirs, let me excuse myself,
For here I swear by heaven, and earth, and all,
I did perform the utmost of my task,
And left the doors unbolted and unlock'd.
But see the chance, Franklin and my master,
Were very late conferring in the porch,
And Franklin left his napkin where he sat,
With certain gold knit in it, as he said,
Being in bed, he did bethink himself,
And coming down, he found the doors unshut,
He lock'd the gates and brought away the keys,
For which offence my master rated me:
But now I am going to see what flood it is,
For with the tide my master will away,

Where you may front him well on Rainham Down,
A place well fitting such a stratagem.

Will. Your excuse hath somewhat mollified my
    choler:
Why, now Greene, 'tis better now than ere it was.

Greene. But Michael, is it true?

Mich. As true as I report it to be true.

Shake. Then Michael, this shall be your penance,
To feast us all at the Salutation,
Where we will plot our purpose thoroughly.

Greene. And Michael, you shall bear no news of
    this tide,
Because they two may be in Rainham Down before
    your master.

Mich. Why, I'll agree to any thing you'll have me,
So you will accept of my company.   [*Exeunt.*

ACT IV.

SCENE I.—Arden's *House at* Feversham.

Enter MOSBIE.

Mos. Disturbed thoughts drive me from company,
And dry my marrow with their watchfulness,
Continual trouble of my moody brain,
Feebles my body by excess of drink,
And nips me, as the bitter north-east wind
Doth check the tender blossoms in the spring.
Well fares the man howe'er his cates do taste,
That tables not with foul suspicion:
And he but pines amongst his delicates,
Whose troubled mind is stuft with discontent.
My golden time was, when I had no gold,
Though then I wanted, yet I slept secure;
My daily toil, begat me night's repose,
My night's repose made daylight fresh to me;
But since I climb'd the top-bough of the tree,
And sought to build my nest among the clouds,
Each gentle starry gale[21] doth shake my bed:
And makes me dread my downfall to the earth,
But whither doth contemplation carry me?
The way I seek to find, where pleasure dwells,
Is hedged behind me, that I cannot back,
But needs must on, although to danger's gate;
Then Arden perish thou by that decree.
For Greene doth err the land,[22] and weed thee up,
To make my harvest nothing but pure corn.
And for his pains I'll heave him up a while,
And after smother him to have his wax.
Such bees as Greene must never live to sting.

Then is there Michael, and the painter too,
Chief actors to Arden's overthrow:
Who, when they see me sit in Arden's seat,
They will insult upon me for my mead,
Or fright me by detecting of his end.
I'll none of that, for I can cast a bone,
To make these curs pluck out each other's throat,
And then am I sole ruler of mine own:
Yet mistress Arden lives, but she's myself,
And holy chuch-rites make us two but one,
But what for that, I may not trust you, Alice,
You have supplanted Arden for my sake,
And will extirpen me to plant another:
'Tis fearful sleeping in a serpent's bed;
And I will cleanly rid my hands of her.

Enter ALICE.

But here she comes, and I must flatter her.
How now, Alice? What, sad and passionate?
Make me partake of thy pensiveness:
Fire divided burns with lesser force.

Alice. But I will damn that fire within my
    breast,[23]
Till by the force thereof my part consume; ah,
    Mosbie!

Mos. Such deep pathairs,[24] like to a cannon's
    burst,
Discharg'd against a ruinated wall,
Break my relenting heart in thousand pieces.
Ungentle Alice, thy sorrow is my sore,
Thou know'st it well, and 'tis thy policy

To forge distressful looks, to wound a breast,
Where lies a heart, that dies when thou art sad;
It is not love, that loves to anger love.

   Alice. It is not love that loves to murder love.

   Mos. How mean you that?

   Alice. Thou knowest how dearly Arden loved me.

   Mos. And then——

   Alice. And then, conceal the rest, for 'tis too bad,
Lest that my words be carried with the wind,
And publish'd in the world to both our shames,
I pray thee, Mosbie, let our spring-time wither,
Our harvest else will yield but loathsome weeds.
Forget, I pray thee, what hast pass'd betwixt us,
For now I blush, and tremble at the thought.

   Mos. What, are you chang'd?

   Alice. Ay! to my former happy life again:
From title of an odious strumpet's name,
To honest Arden's wife, not Arden's honest wife.
Ah! Mosbie, 'tis thou hast rifled me of that,
And made me slanderous to all my kin:
Even in my forehead is thy name engraven,
A mean artificer, that low-born name.
I was bewitched, woe worth the hapless hour,
And all the causes that enchanted me.

   Mos. Nay, if thou ban, let me breathe curses forth,
And if you stand so nicely at your fame,
Let me repent the credit I have lost.
I have neglected matters of import,
That would have stated me above thy state
Forslow'd advantages,[25] and spurn'd at time.
Ay, fortune's right hand Mosbie hath forsook,
To take a wanton giglot[26] by the left.
I left the marriage of an honest maid,
Whose dowry would have weighed down all thy
    wealth,
Whose beauty and demeanour far exceeded thee.
This certain good I lost for changing bad,
And wrap'd my credit in thy company.
I was bewitch'd! that is no theme of thine,
And thou unhallowed hast enchanted me:
But I will break thy spells and exorcisms,
And put another sight upon these eyes,
That show'd my heart a raven for a dove.
Thou art not fair, I view'd thee not till now,
Thou art not kind, till now I knew thee not.
And now the rain hath beaten off thy gilt,
Thy worthless copper shows thee counterfeit.
It grieves me not to see how foul thou art,
But mads me that I ever thought thee fair.
Go, get thee gone, a copesmate for thy hinds,
I am too good to be thy favourite.

   Alice. Ay, now I see, and too soon find it true,
Which often hath been told me by my friends:
That Mosbie loves me not, but for my wealth,
Which, too incredulous, I ne'er believ'd.
Nay, hear me speak, Mosbie, a word or two,
I'll bite my tongue if it speak bitterly:
Look on me, Mosbie, or I'll kill myself,
Nothing shall hide me from thy stormy look:
If thou cry war, there is no peace for me,
I will do penance for offending thee,
And burn this prayer-book, where I here use,
The holy word that had converted me.
See, Mosbie, I will tear away the leaves,
And all the leaves, and in this golden cover
Shall thy sweet phrases and thy letters dwell,
And thereon will I chiefly meditate,
And hold no other sect but such devotion.
Wilt not thou look? is all thy love o'erwhelm'd?
Wilt thou not hear? what malice stops thine ears?
Why speak'st thou not? what silence ties thy
    tongue?
Thou hast been sighted, as the eagle is,
And heard as quickly as the fearful hare:
And spoke as smoothly as an orator,
When I have bid thee hear, or see, or speak.
And art thou sensible in none of these?
Weigh all my good turns, with this little fault,
And I deserve not Mosbie's muddy looks.
A sense of trouble is not thicken'd, still
Be clear again; I'll ne'er more trouble thee.

   Mos. O no, I am a base artificer;
My wings are feather'd for a lowly flight.
Mosbie, fie, no; not for a thousand pound,
Make love to you, why, 'tis unpardonable!
We beggars must not breathe where gentles are.

   Alice. Sweet Mosbie is as gentle as a king,
And I too blind to judge him otherwise;
Flowers do sometimes spring in fallow lands,
And weeds in gardens, roses grow on thorns.
So whatsoe'er my Mosbie's father was,
Himself is valued gentle by his worth.

   Mos. Ah, how you women can insinuate,
And clear a trespass with your sweet-set tongue!
I will forget this quarrel, gentle Alice,
Provided I'll be tempted so no more.

   Alice. Then with thy lips seal up this new made
    match.

   Mos. Soft, Alice, for here comes somebody.

Enter BRADSHAW.

   Alice. How now, Bradshaw, what's the news
    with you?

   Brad. I have little news, but here's a letter,
That master Greene importuned me to give you.

   Alice. Go in Bradshaw, call for a cup of beer,

'Tis almost supper time, thou shalt stay with us.
[*Exit.* BRAD.

[*Reads.*] We have missed of our purpose at London, but shall perform it by the way. We thank our neighbour Bradshaw. Yours, RICHARD GREENE.

How likes my love the tenor of this letter?
Mos. Well, were his date completed and expir'd.
Alice. Ah, would it were.
Then comes my happy hour;
Till then my bliss is mix'd with bitter gall.
Come, let us in, to shun suspicion.
Mos. Ay, to the gates of death to follow thee.
[*Exeunt.*

SCENE II.—*Country near* Rochester.

Enter GREENE, WILL, *and* SHAKEBAG.

Shake. Come, Will, see thy tools be in readiness,
Is not thy powder dank,
Or will thy flint strike fire?
Will. Then ask me if my nose be on my face,
Or whether my tongue be frozen in my mouth.
Zounds, here's a coil, you were best swear me on the
Interrogatories, how many pistols I have took in
hand,
Or whether I love the smell of gunpowder,
Or dare abide the noise the dag[27] will make,
Or will not wink at flashing of the fire.
I pray thee, Shakebag, let this answer thee,
That I have took more purses in this Down,
Than e'er thou handledst pistols in thy life.
Shake. Ay, haply thou hast pick'd more in a
throng,
But should I brag what booties I have took,
I think the overplus that's more than thine,
Would 'mount to a greater sum of money,
Than either thou, or all thy kin are worth.
Zounds, I hate them as I hate a toad,
That carry a muscado in their tongue,
And scarce a hurting weapon in their hand.
Will. O, Greene, intolerable.
It is not for mine honour to bear this.
Why, Shakebag, I did serve the king at Boulogne,
And thou canst brag of nothing that thou hast
done.
Shake. Why, so can Jack of Feversham,
That swooned for a fillip on the nose;
When he that gave it him hollowed in his ear,
And he supposed a cannon bullet hit him.
[*They fight.*
Greene. I pray you, sirs, list to Æsop's talk:
Whilst two stout dogs were striving for a bone,
There comes a cur, and stole it from them both.

So while you stand striving on these terms of manhood,
Arden escapes us, and deceives us all.
Shake. Why, he begun.
Will. And thou shalt find I'll end.
I do but slip it until better time;
But if I do forget ——
[*He kneels down, and holds up his Hands to Heaven.*
Greene. Well, take your fittest standings, and
once more
Lime well your twigs to catch this wary bird.
I'll leave you, and at your dag's discharge,
Make towards, like the longing water dog,
That coucheth till the fowling-piece be off,
Then seizeth on the prey with eager mood.
Ah, might I see him stretching forth his limbs,
As I have seen them beat their wings ere now.
Shake. Why, that thou shalt see, if he comes
this way.
Greene. Yes, that he doth, Shakebag, I warrant
thee:
But brawl not when I am gone in any case;
But, sirs, be sure to speed him when he comes,
And in that hope I'll leave you for an hour.
[*Exit* GREENE; WILL *and* SHAKE. *hide themselves.*

Enter ARDEN, FRANKLIN, *and* MICHAEL.

Mich. 'Twere best that I went back to Rochester:
The horse halts downright; it were not good
He travelled in such pain to Feversham;
Removing of a shoe may happily help it.
Arden. Well, get you back to Rochester; but,
sirrah, see ye
Overtake us ere we come to Rainham Down,
For it will be very late ere we get home.
Mich. Ay, God knows, and so doth Will and
Shakebag,
That thou shalt never go further than that Down;
And therefore have I prick'd the horse on purpose,
Because I would not view the massacre. [*Aside.*
[*Exit* MICH.
Arden. Come, master Franklin, onward with your
tale.
Frank. I assure you, sir, you task me much:
A heavy blood is gathered at my heart;
And on the sudden is my wind so short,
As hindereth the passage of my speech;
So fierce a qualm yet ne'er assailed me.
Arden. Come, master Franklin, let us go on
softly.
The annoyance of the dust, or else some meat

You eat at dinner, cannot brook with you:
I have been often so, and soon amended.

Frank. Do you remember where my tale did
    leave?

Arden. Ay, where the gentleman did check his
    wife.

Frank. She being reprehended for the fact,
Witness produced, that took her with the deed,
Her glove brought in, which there she left behind,
And many other assured arguments,
Her husband ask'd her whether it were not so.

Arden. Her answer then? I wonder how she
    look'd,
Having forsworn it with such vehement oaths,
And at the instant so approv'd upon her.

Frank. First did she cast her eyes down to the
    earth,
Watching the drops that fell amain from thence;
Then softly draws she forth her handkerchief,
And modestly she wipes her tear-stain'd face;
Then hemm'd she out, to clear her voice should
    seem,
And with a majesty address'd herself,
To encounter all their accusations;——
Pardon me, master Arden, I can no more;
This fighting at my heart makes short my wind.

Arden. Come, we are almost now at Rainham
    Down.
Your pretty tale beguiles the weary way:
I would you were in state to tell it out.

Shake. Stand close, Will; I hear them coming.

Enter LORD CHEINY, *with his* Men.

Will. Stand to it, Shakebag, and be resolute.

L. Ch. Is it so near night as it seems?
Or will this black-faced evening have a shower?
What, master Arden! you are well met:
I have long'd this fortnight's day to speak with
    you;
You are a stranger, man, in the isle of Sheppey.

Arden. Your honour's always bound to do you
    service.

L. Ch. Come you from London, and ne'er a man
    with you?

Arden. My man's coming after.
But here's my honest friend that came along with
    me.

L. Ch. My lord Protector's man, I take you
    to be.

Frank. Ay, my good lord, and highly bound to
    you.

L. Ch. You and your friend come home and sup
    with me.

Arden. I beseech your honour, pardon me;
I have made a promise to a gentleman,
My honest friend, to meet him at my house;
The occasion is great, or else would I wait on
    you.

L. Ch. Will you come to-morrow and dine with
    me,
And bring your honest friend along with you:
I have divers matters to talk with you about.

Arden. To-morrow we will wait upon your honour.

L. Ch. One of you stay my horse at the top of
    the hill.
What, Black Will, for whose purse wait you?
Thou wilt be hang'd in Kent, when all is done.

Will. Not hang'd, God save your honour:
I am your beadsman,[28] bound to pray for you.

L. Ch. I think thou ne'er saidst prayer in all thy
    life.
One of you give him a crown:
And, sirrah, leave this kind of life.
If thou art tainted for a penny matter,
And come in question, surely thou wilt truss.
Come, master Arden, let us be going;
Your way and mine lies four miles together.

    [*Exeunt all but* WILL. *and* SHAKE.

Will. The devil break all your necks at four
    miles end.
Zounds, I could kill myself for very anger.
His lordship chops me in, even when
My dag was level'd at his heart.
I would his crown were molten down his throat.

Shake. Arden, thou hast wondrous holy luck.
Did ever man escape as thou hast done?
Well, I'll discharge my pistol at the sky;
For by this bullet Arden might not die.

Re-enter GREENE.

Greene. What, is he down? Is he despatch'd?

Shake. Ay, in health, towards Feversham, to
    shame us all.

Greene. The devil he is; why, sirs, how 'scap'd
    he?

Shake. When we were ready to shoot,
Comes my lord Cheiny to prevent his death.

Greene. The Lord of heaven hath preserv'd
    him.

Will. Preserv'd a fig! the lord Cheiney hath
    preserv'd him,
And bids him to a feast, at his house at Shurland.
But by the way, once more I'll meet with him;
And if all the Cheineys in the world say no,
I'll have a bullet in his breast to-morrow;
Therefore come Greene, and let us to Feversham.

Greene. Ay, and excuse ourselves to mistress
    Arden.
O, how she 'll chafe when she hears of this !
    Shake. Why, I 'll warrant you she 'll think we
    dare not do it.
    Will. Why then, let us go, and tell her all the
    matter ;
And plot the news to cut him off to-morrow.
                       [*Exeunt.*

SCENE III.—Arden's *House at* Feversham.

Enter ARDEN *and his* Wife, FRANKLIN, *and*
        MICHAEL.

Arden. See how the hours, guardians of heaven's
    gate,
Have by their toil remov'd the darksome clouds,
That Sol may well discern the trampled pace,
Wherein he wont to guide his golden car ;
The season fits ; come, Franklin, let's away.
    Alice. I thought you did pretend some special
    hunt,
That made you thus cut short the time of rest.
    Arden. It was no chase that made me rise so
    early,
But, as I told thee yesternight, to go to the Isle of
    Sheppey,
There to dine with my lord Cheiney ;
For so his honour late commanded me.
    Alice. Ay, such kind husbands seldom want
    excuses.
Home is a wild cat to a wandering wit :
The time hath been, would God it were not pass'd,
That honours, title, nor a lord's command,
Could once have drawn you from these arms of mine :
But my deserts, or your deserves decay,
Or both ; yet if true love may seem desert,
I merit still to have thy company.
    Frank. Why, I pray you, sir, let her go along
    with us ;
I am sure his honour will welcome her
And us the more for bringing her along.
    Arden. Content, sirrah, saddle your mistress'
    nag.
    Alice. No ; beg'd favour merits little thanks :
If I should go, our house would run away,
Or else be stolen ; therefore I 'll stay behind.
    Arden. Nay, see how mistaking you are ;
I pray thee go.
    Alice.   No, no, not now.
    Arden. Then let me leave thee satisfied in this,
That time, nor place, nor persons alter me,
But that I hold thee dearer than my life.

    Alice. That will be seen soon, by your quick re-
    turn.
    Arden. And that shall be ere night, and if I
    live.
Farewell, sweet Alice, we mind to sup with thee.
                      [*Exit* ALICE.
    Frank. Come, Michael, are our horses ready ?
    Mich. Ay, your horses are ready, but I am not
    ready,
For I have lost my purse,
With six and thirty shillings in it,
With taking up of my mistress' nag.
    Frank. Why, I pray you, let us go before,
Whilst he stays behind to seek his purse.
    Arden. Go to, sirrah, see you follow us to the
    isle of Sheppey,
To my lord Cheiney's where we mean to dine.
            [*Exeunt* ARDEN *and* FRANK.
    Mich. So, fair weather after you ;
For before you lies Black Will and Shakebag,
In the broom close, too close for you ;
They'll be your ferrymen to a long home.

        Enter CLARKE.

But who is this ? the painter, my corival,
That would needs win mistress Susan.
    Clarke. How now, Michael, how doth my mis-
    tress,
And all at home ?
    Mich. Who, Susan Mosbie ? she is your mistress
    too.
    Clarke. Ay, how doth she, and all the rest ?
    Mich. All's well but Susan, she is sick.
    Clarke. Sick, of what disease ?
    Mich. Of a great fear.
    Clarke. A fear, of what ?
    Mich. A great fever.
    Clarke. A fever ! God forbid.
    Mich. Yes, faith, and of a lordain, too,[29]
As big as yourself.
    Clarke. O, Michael, the spleen prickles you ;
Go to, you carry an eye over mistress Susan.
    Mich. Ay, faith, to keep her from the painter.
    Clarke. Why more from the painter, than from
    a serving creature like yourself ?
    Mich. Because you painters make but a paint-
    ing-table of a pretty wench, and spoil her
    beauty with blotting.
    Clarke. What mean you by that ?
    Mich. Why, that you painters paint lambs in
    the linings of wenches' petticoats,
And we serving-men put horns to them, to make
    them become sheep,

Clarke. Such another word will cost you a cuff or a knock.

Mich. What, with a dagger made of a pencil?
Faith, 'tis too weak;
And therefore thou too weak to win Susan.

Clarke. Would Susan's love lay upon this stroke.
[*He breaks* MICHAEL's *Head.*

Enter MOSBIE, GREENE, *and* ALICE.

Alice. I'll lay my life, this is for Susan's love;
Staid you behind your master to this end?
Have you no other time to brable in
But now, when serious matters are in hand?
Say, Clarke, hast thou done the thing thou promis'd?

Clarke. Ay, here it is, the very touch is death.

Alice. Then this I hope, if all the rest do fail,
Will catch master Arden,
And make him wise in death, that liv'd a fool.
Why should he thrust his sickle in our corn;
Or what hath he to do with thee, my love?
Or govern me, that am to rule myself?
Forsooth, for credit sake, I must leave thee.
Nay, he must leave to live, that we may love:
May live, may love, for what is life but love?
And love shall last as long as life remains;
And life shall end, before my love depart.

Mos. Why, what is love without true constancy?
Like to a pillar built of many stones,
Yet neither with good mortar, well compact,
Nor cement to fasten it in the joints;
But that it shakes with every blast of wind,
And being touch'd, straight falls unto the earth,
And buries all his haughty pride in dust.
No, let our love be rocks of adamant,
Which time, nor place, nor tempest can asunder.

Greene. Mosbie, leave protestations now,
And let's bethink us what we have to do;
Black Will and Shakebag I have placed
In the broom, close watching Arden's coming,
Let's to them, and see what they have done.
[*Exeunt.*

SCENE IV.—*The Kentish Coast opposite the* Isle
of Sheppey.

Enter ARDEN *and* FRANKLIN.

Arden. Oh, ferryman, where art thou?

Enter Ferryman.

Fer. Here, here, go before to the boat,
And I will follow you.

Arden. We have great haste, I pray thee come
away.

Fer. Fie! what a mist is here.

Arden. This mist, my friend, is mystical,
Like to a good companion's smoky brain,
That was half-drowned with new ale over night.

Fer. 'Twere pity but his scull were opened,
To make more chimney room.

Frank. Friend, what's thy opinion of this mist?

Fer. I think 'tis like to a curst wife in a little
house,
That never leaves her husband till she have driven
Him out at doors, with a wet pair of eyes;
Then looks he as if his house were a-fire,
Or some of his friends dead.

Arden. Speak'st thou this of thine own experience?

Fer. Perhaps aye, perhaps no: for my wife is as
other women,
That is to say, governed by the moon.

Frank. By the moon! how, I pray thee?

Fer. Nay, thereby lies a bargain,
And you shall not have it fresh and fasting.

Arden. Yes, I pray thee, good ferryman.

Fer. Then for this once, let it be midsummer
moon,
But yet my wife has another moon.

Frank. Another moon?

Fer. Ay, and it hath influences, and eclipses.

Arden. Why then, by this reckoning, you sometimes
Play the man in the moon.

Fer. Ay, but you had not best to meddle with
that moon,
Lest I scratch you by the face, with my bramble
bush.

Arden. I am almost stifled with this fog; come,
let's away.

Frank. And, sirrah, as we go, let us have some
more of your bold yeomanry.

Fer. Nay, by my troth, sir, but flat knavery.
[*Exeunt.*

Enter WILL *and* SHAKEBAG *at opposite Sides.*

Shake. Oh Will, where art thou?

Will. Here, Shakebag, almost in hell's mouth,
Where I cannot see my way for smoke.

Shake. I pray thee speak still, that we may meet
by the sound, or I shall fall into some ditch or
other, unless my feet see better than my eyes.

Will. Did'st thou ever see better weather to run
away with another man's wife, or play with a wench
at potfinger?

Shake. No, this were a fine world for chandlers,
If this weather would last, for then a man
Should never dine nor sup without candle light.
But, sirrah, Will, what horses are those that pass'd?
    Will. Why, didst thou hear any?
    Shake. Ay, that I did.
    Will. My life for thine, it was Arden and his
        companion,
And then all our labour's lost.
    Shake. Nay, say not so, for if it be they, they
May happily lose their way as we have done,
And then we may chance meet with them.
    Will. Come, let us go on like a couple of blind
pilgrims.   [SHAKE. *falls into a Ditch.*
    Shake. Help, Will, help, I am almost drown'd!

Enter the Ferryman.

    Fer. Who's that, that calls for help?
    Will. 'Twas none here, 'twas thou thyself.
    Fer. I came to help him that call'd for help.
Why, how now? who is this that's in the ditch?
You are well enough serv'd, to go without a guide,
        such weather as this.
    Will. Sirrah, what company hath passed your ferry
this morning?
    Fer. None but a couple of gentlemen, that went
to dine at my lord Cheiney's.
    Will. Shakebag, did I not tell thee as much?
    Fer. Why, sir, will you have any letters carried
to them?
    Will. No, sir, get you gone.
    Fer. Did you ever see such a mist as this?
    Will. No, nor such a fool as will rather be
houghed than get his way.[30]
    Fer. Why, sir, this is no hough Monday, you are
        deceiv'd.
What's his name, I pray you sir?
    Shake. His name is Black Will.
    Fer. I hope to see him one day hang'd upon a hill.
                                    [*Exit* Fer.
    Shake. See how the sun hath cleared the foggy
        mist,
Now we have miss'd the mark of our intent.

Enter GREENE, MOSBY, *and* ALICE.

    Mos. Black Will and Shakebag, what make you
        here?
What, is the deed done? is Arden dead?
    Will. What could a blinded man perform in
        arms?
Saw you not how till now, the sky was dark,
That neither horse nor man could be discerned?
Yet did we hear their horses as they passed.

    Greene. Have they escap'd you then, and passed
        the ferry?
    Shake. Ay, for a while, but here we two will stay,
And at their coming back, meet with them once
        more.
Zounds, I was ne'er so toiled in all my life,
In following so slight a task as this.
    Mos. How cam'st thou so beraid?[31]
    Will. With making false footing in the dark.
He needs would follow them without a guide.
    Alice. Here's to pay for a fire and good cheer;
Get you to Feversham to the Flower de-luce,
And rest yourselves until some other time.
    Greene. Let me alone, it most concerns my state.
    Will. Ay, mistress Arden, this will serve the turn,
In case we fall into a second fog.
            [*Exeunt* GREENE, WILL, *and* SHAKE.
    Mos. These knaves will never do it, let us give it
        over.
    Alice. First tell me how you like my new device?
Soon when my husband is returning back,
You and I both marching arm in arm,
Like loving friends, we'll meet him on the way,
And boldly beard and brave him to his teeth:
When words grow hot, and blows begin to rise,
I'll call those cutters forth your tenement,
Who in a manner to take up the fray,
Shall wound my husband hornsbie to the death.[32]
    Mos. Ah, fine device, why this deserves a kiss.
                                    [*Exeunt.*

SCENE V.—*The Open Country.*

Enter DICK REDE *and a* Sailor.

    Sailor. Faith, Dick Rede, it is to little end,
His conscience is too liberal,[33] and he too niggardly
To part from any thing may do thee good.
    Rede. He is coming from Shurland as I understand.
Here I'll intercept him, for at his house
He never will vouchsafe to speak with me:
If prayers and fair entreaties will not serve,
Or make no battery in his flinty breast,
I'll curse the carl and see what that will do;
See where he comes, to further my intent.

Enter FRANKLIN, ARDEN, *and* MICHAEL.

Master Arden, I am now bound to the sea;
My coming to you was about the plot of ground
Which wrongfully you detain from me:
Although the rent of it be very small,
Yet will it help my wife and children:
Which here I leave in Feversham; God knows,
Needy and bare; for Christ's sake let them have it.

Arden. Franklin, hearest thou this fellow speak?
That which he craves I dearly bought of him,
Although the rent of it was ever mine.
Sirrah, you that ask these questions,
If with thy clamorous impeaching tongue
Thou rail on me, as I have heard thou dost,
I'll lay thee up so close a twelve months' day,
As thou shalt neither see the sun nor moon.
Look to it, for as surely as I live,
I'll banish pity if thou use me thus.
   Rede. What! wilt thou do me wrong, and threat
     me too?
Nay, then I'll tempt thee, Arden; do thy worst.
God, I beseech thee, show some miracle
On thee or thine, in plaguing thee for this.
That plot of ground, which thou detainest from me,—
I speak it in an agony of spirit,—
Be ruinous and fatal unto thee:
Either there be butcher'd by thy dearest friends,
Or else be brought for men to wonder at,
Or thou or thine miscarry in that place,
Or there run mad, and end thy cursed days.
   Frank. Fie, bitter knave, bridle thine envious
     tongue,
For curses are like arrows shot upright,
Which falling down light on the shooter's head.
   Rede. Light where they will, were I upon the sea,
As oft I have in many a bitter storm,
And saw a dreadful southern flaw at hand,
The pilot quaking at the doubtful storm,
And all the sailors praying on their knees,
Even in that fearful time would I fall down,
And ask of God, whate'er betide of me,
Vengeance on Arden, or some mis-event,
To show the world what wrong the carl hath done.
This charge I'll leave with my distressful wife:
My children shall be taught such prayers as these,
And thus I go, but leave my curse with thee.
           [*Exeunt* REDE *and* Sailor.
   Arden. It is the railingest knave in Christendom;
And oftentimes the villain will be mad:
It greatly matters not what he says;
But I assure you I ne'er did him wrong.
   Frank. I think so, master Arden.
   Arden. Now that our horses are gone home be-
     fore,
My wife may haply meet me on the way;
For God knows she's grown passing kind of late,
And greatly changed from the old humour
Of her wonted frowardness;
And seeks by fair means to redeem old faults.
   Frank. Happy the change that alters for the
     best;

But see in any case you make no speech
Of the cheer we had at my lord Cheiney's,
Although most bounteous and liberal;
For that will make her think herself more wrong'd,
In that we did not carry her along;
For sure she grieved that she was left behind.
   Arden. Come, Franklin, let us strain to mend
     our pace,
And take her unawares, playing the cook,

     Enter ALICE *and* MOSBIE.

For I believe she'll strive to mend our cheer.
   Frank. Why, there's no better creatures in the
     world
Than women are when they are in good humours.
   Arden. Who is that? Mosbie, what, so familiar?
Injurious strumpet, and thou ribald knave,
Untwine those arms.
   Alice. Ay, with a sugar'd kiss, let them untwine.
   Arden. Ah, Mosbie, perjur'd beast; bear this
     and all.
   Mos. And yet no horned beast; the horns are
     thine.
   Frank. O monstrous: Nay, then, 'tis time to draw.
   Alice. Help, help! they murder my husband

     Enter WILL *and* SHAKEBAG.

   Shake. Zounds, who injures master Mosbie?
   [WILL, SHAKE. *and* MOS. *attack* ARDEN *and*
     FRANK., *the* Ruffians *are driven back.*
Help, Will, I am hurt.
   Mos. I may thank you, mistress Arden, for this
     wound. [*Exeunt* MOS., WILL, *and* SHAKE.
   Alice. Ah, Arden, what folly blinded thee?
Ah, jealous harebrain'd man! what hast thou done?
When we to welcome thy intended sport,
Came lovingly to meet thee on thy way,
Thou drewest thy sword, enraged with jealousy,
And hurt thy friend,
Whose thoughts were free from harm;
All for a worthless kiss, and joining arms,
Both done but merrily, to try thy patience.
And me unhappy that devised the jest,
Which though begun in sport, yet ends in blood.
   Frank. Marry, God defend me from such a jest.
   Alice. Couldst thou not see us friendly smile on
     this,
When we join'd arms, and when I kiss'd his cheek.
Hast thou not lately found me over kind?
Didst thou not hear me cry they murder thee?
Call'd I not help to set my husband free?
No, ears and all were 'witch'd; ah me, accurs'd,
To link in liking with a frantic man!

Henceforth I 'll be thy slave, no more thy wife;
For with that name I never shall content thee.
If I be merry, thou straightways think me light.
If sad, thou sayest the sullens trouble me.
If well attired, thou thinks I will be gadding.
If homely, I seem sluttish in thine eye.
Thus am I still, and shall be while I live,
Poor wench abused by thy misgovernment.

 Arden. But is it for truth, that neither thou nor he,
Intendest malice in your misdemeanor.

  Alice. The heavens can witness of our harmless
   thoughts.

 Arden. Then pardon me, sweet Alice, and for-
  give this fault:
Forget but this, and never see the like.
Impose me penance, and I will perform it:
For in thy discontent I find a death,
A death tormenting more than death itself.

  Alice. Nay, hadst thou lov'd me as thou dost
   pretend,
Thou wouldst have mark'd the speeches of thy friend,
Who, going wounded from the place, he said
His skin was pierc'd only through my device;
And if sad sorrow taint thee for this fault,
Thou wouldst have followed him and seen him
  dress'd,
And cried him mercy whom thou hast misdone;
Ne'er shall my heart be eas'd till this be done.

 Arden. Content thee, sweet Alice, thou shalt
  have thy will,

Whate'er it be, for that I injur'd thee
And wrong'd my friend; shame scourgeth my offence:
Come thou, thyself, and go along with me,
And be a mediator 'twixt us two.

  Frank. Why, master Arden, know you what you do?
Will you follow him that hath dishonour'd you?

  Alice. Why, canst thou prove that I have been
   disloyal?

  Frank. Why Mosbie taunt your husband with
   the horn?

  Alice. Ay, after he had revil'd him,
By the injurious name of perjured beast:
He knew no wrong could spite a jealous man
More than the hateful naming of the horn.

  Frank. Suppose 'tis true, yet is it dangerous
To follow him whom he hath lately hurt.

  Alice. A fault confess'd is more than half amends.
But men of such ill spirit as yourself,
Work crosses and debates 'twixt man and wife.

 Arden. I pray thee, gentle Franklin, hold thy peace;
I know my wife counsels me for the best.
I 'll seek out Mosbie, where his wound is dress'd,
And salve this hapless quarrel if I may.
       [*Exeunt* ARDEN *and* ALICE.

  Frank. He whom the devil drives must go per-
   force.
Poor gentleman, how soon he is bewitch'd;
And yet because his wife's the instrument,
His friends must not be lavish in their speech.
            [*Exit* FRANK.

ACT V.

SCENE I.—*A Street in* Feversham.

Enter BLACK WILL, SHAKEBAG, *and* GREENE.

 Will. Sirrah Greene, when was I so long in
  killing a man?

 Greene. I think we shall never do it;
Let us give it over.

 Shake. Nay, zounds, we 'll kill him,
Though we be hang'd at his door for our labour.

 Will. Thou knowest, Greene, that I have liv'd in
London these twelve years,
Where I have made some go upon wooden legs,
For taking the wall on me.
Divers with silver noses, for saying,
There goes Black Will.
I have cracked as many blades,
As thou hast done nuts.

 Greene. O monstrous lie!

 Will. Faith in a manner I have.
The bawdy-houses have paid me tribute;
There durst not a whore set up, unless she have
  agreed
With me first, for opening her shop windows.
For a cross word of a tapster,
I have pierced one barrel after another, with my
  dagger,
And held him by the ears till all his beer hath run
  out.
In Thames-street a brewer's cart was like to have
  run
Over me; I made no more ado, but went to the clerk,
And cut all the natches of his tallies,
And beat them about his head.
I, and my company, have taken the constable from
  his watch,
And carried him about the fields on a coltstaff.

I have broken a sergeant's head with his own mace,
And bail'd whom I list with my sword and buckler.
All the tenpenny alehouse men would stand every
    morning,
With a quart pot in their hands,
Saying, will it please your worship drink:
He that had not done so had been sure to have had
    his
Sign pull'd down, and his lattice borne away the
    next night.
To conclude, what have I not done? yet cannot
    do this,
Doubtless he is preserved by miracle.

Enter ALICE *and* MICHAEL.

Greene. Hence, Will, here comes mistress Arden.
Alice. Ah, gentle Michael, art thou sure they're
    friends?
Mich. Why, I saw them when they both shook
    hands,
When Mosbie bled, he even wept for sorrow:
And rail'd on Franklin that was cause of all.
No sooner came the surgeon in at doors,
But my master took to his purse and gave him
    money.
And to conclude, sent me to bring you word,
That Mosbie, Franklin, Bradshaw, Adam Fowle,
With divers of his neighbours, and his friends,
Will come and sup with you at our house this night.
Alice. Ah, gentle Michael, run thou back again,
And when my husband walks into the fair,
Bid Mosbie steal from him and come to me.
And this night shall thou and Susan be made sure.
Mich. I'll go tell him.
Alice. And as thou goest, tell John Cooke of our
    guests,
And bid him lay it on, spare for no cost. [*Exit* MICH.
Will. Nay, and there be such cheer, we will bid
    ourselves,
Mistress Arden, Dick Greene and I do mean to
    sup with you.
Alice. And welcome shall you be. Ah, gentlemen,
How miss'd you of your purpose yesternight?
Greene. 'Twas long of Shakebag, that unlucky
    villain.
Shake. Thou dost me wrong, I did as much as
    any.
Will. Nay, then, mistress Alice, I'll tell you how
    it was.
When he should have lock'd with both his hilts,
He in a bravery flourish'd over his head;
With that comes Franklin at him lustily,
And hurts the slave, with that he slinks away.

Now his way had been to have come hand and feet,
One and two round at his costerd.[34]
He like a fool bears his sword point half a yard out
Of danger, I lie here for my life.
If the devil come, and he have no more strength
    than fence,
He shall never beat me from this ward.
I'll stand to it, a buckler in a skilful hand,
Is as good as a castle.
Nay, 'tis better than a sconce,[35] for I have tried it.
Mosbie perceiving this, began to faint.
With that comes Arden with his arming sword,
And thrust him through the shoulder in a trice.
Alice. Ay, but I wonder why you both stood still.
Will. Faith I was so amazed I could not strike.
Alice. Ah, sirs, had he yesternight been slain,
For every drop of his detested blood,
I would have crammed in angels in thy fist,
And kiss'd thee too, and hug'd thee in my arms.
Will. Patient yourself, we cannot help it now,
Greene, and we two, will dodge him through the fair,
And stab him in the crowd, and steal away.

Enter MOSBIE.

Alice. It is impossible; but here comes he,
That will, I hope, invent some surer means.
Sweet Mosbie, hide thy arm, it kills my heart.
Mos. Ay, mistress Arden, this is your favour.
Alice. Ah, say not so, for when I saw thee hurt,
I could have took the weapon thou let'st fall,
And run at Arden, for I have sworn,
That these mine eyes, offended with his sight,
Shall never close, till Arden's be shut up.
This night I rose and walk'd about the chamber,
And twice or thrice, I thought to have murdered
    him.
Mos. What, in the night! then had we been
    undone.
Alice. Why, how long shall he live?
Mos. Faith, Alice, no longer than this night.
Black Will and Shakebag, will you two
Perform the complot that I have laid.
Will. Ay, or else think me as a villain.
Greene. And rather than you shall want,
I'll help myself.
Mos. You, master Greene, shall single Franklin
    forth,
And hold him with a long tale of strange news,
That he may not come home till supper time.
I'll fetch master Arden home, and we like friends
Will play a game or two at tables here.
Alice. But what of all this? How shall he be
    slain?

Mos. Why, Black Will and Shakebag, lock'd
　　　within the counting-house,
Shall, at a certain watchword given, rush forth.
　Will. What shall the watchword be?
　Mos. Now I take you, that shall be the word,
But come not forth before in any case.
　Will. I warrant you, but who shall lock me in?
　Alice. That will I do, thou'st keep the key thyself.
　Mos. Come, master Greene, go you along with me.
See all things ready, Alice, against we come.
　Alice. Take no care for that, send you him home,
　　　　　　　　　　[Exeunt Mos. *and* GREENE.
And if he ere go forth again, blame me.
Come, Black Will, that in mine eyes art fair,
Next unto Mosbie do I honour thee.
Instead of fair words and large promises,
My hands shall play you golden harmony.
How like you this? say, will you do it, sirs?
　Will. Ay, and that bravely too, mark my device.
Place Mosbie, being a stranger, in a chair,
And let your husband sit upon a stool,
That I may come behind him cunningly,
And with a towel pull him to the ground;
Then stab him till his flesh be as a sieve
That done bear him behind the Abbey,
That those that find him murder'd, may suppose,
Some slave or other kill'd him for his gold.
　Alice. A fine device, you shall have twenty pound,
And when he is dead, you shall have forty more.
And lest you might be suspected staying here,
Michael shall saddle you two lusty geldings.
Ride whether you will, to Scotland or to Wales.
I'll see you shall not lack, where'er you be.
　Will. Such words would make one kill a thousand
　　　men.
Give me the key; which is the counting-house?
　Alice. Here would I stay, and still encourage you,
But that I know how resolute you are.
　Shake. Tush, you are too faint-hearted, we must
　　　do it.
　Alice. But Mosbie will be there, whose very looks
Will add unwonted courage to my thought,
And make me the first, that shall adventure on him.
　Will. Tush, get you gone, 'tis we must do the
　　　deed.
When this door opens next look for his death.
　Alice. Ah, would he now were here, that it might
　　　open.
I shall no more be closed in Arden's arms,
That like the snakes of black Tisiphone,
Sting me with their embracings.[36]　Mosbie's arms
Shall compass me, and were I made a star,
I would have none other spheres but those.

There is no nectar, but in Mosbie's lips;
Had chaste Diana kiss'd him, she, like me,
Would grow love-sick, and from her watery bower,
Fling down Endimion and snatch him up:[37]
Then blame not me, that slay a silly man,
Not half so lovely as Endimion.

SCENE II.—*A Room in* Arden's *House.*

Enter MICHAEL *and* ALICE.

　Mich. Mistress, my master is coming hard by.
　Alice. Who comes with him?
　Mich. Nobody but Mosbie.
　Alice. That's well, Michael, fetch in the tables,
And when thou hast done, stand before the count-
　　　ing-house door.
　Mich. Why so?
　Alice. Black Will is lock'd within to do the deed.
　Mich. What, shall he die to-night?
　Alice. Ay, Michael.
　Mich. But shall not Susan know it?
　Alice. Yes, for she'll be as secret as ourselves.
　Mich. That's brave, I'll go fetch the tables.
　Alice. But, Michael, hark to me a word or two.
When my husband is come in, lock the street-door:
He shall be murdered or e'er the guests come in.
　　　　　　　　　　　　　　[Exit. MICH.

Enter ARDEN *and* MOSBIE.

Husband, what mean you to bring Mosbie home?
Although I wish'd you to be reconciled,
'Twas more for fear of you, than love of him.
Black Will and Greene are his companions,
And they are cutters, and may cut you short;
Therefore I thought it good to make you friends.
But wherefore do you bring him hither now?
You have given me my supper with his sight.
　Mos. Master Arden, methinks your wife would
　　　have me gone.
　Arden. No, good master Mosbie, women will be
　　　prating.
Alice, bid him welcome; he and I are friends.
　Alice. You may enforce me to it, if you will
But I had rather die than bid him welcome.
His company hath purchas'd me ill friends;
And therefore will I ne'er frequent it more.
　Mos. Oh, how cunningly she can dissemble!
　　　　　　　　　　　　　　[Aside.
　Arden. Now he is here you will not serve me so.
　Alice. I pray you be not angry or displeas'd;
I'll bid him welcome, seeing you'll have it so;
You are welcome, master Mosbie; will you sit
　　　down?

Mos. I know I am welcome to your loving husband,
But for yourself, you speak not from your heart.
    Alice. And if I do not, sir, think I have cause.
    Mos. Pardon me, master Arden, I 'll away.
    Arden. No, good master Mosbie.
    Alice. We shall have guests enough, though you
go hence.
    Mos. I pray you, master Arden, let me go.
    Arden. I pray thee, Mosbie, let her prate her fill.
    Alice. The doors are open, sir, you may be gone.
    Mich. Nay, that 's a lie, for I have lock'd the
doors.   [*Aside.*
    Arden. Sirrah, fetch me a cup of wine ;
I 'll make them friends.
And, gentle mistress Alice, seeing you are so stout,
You shall begin ; frown not, I 'll have it so.
    Alice. I pray you meddle with that you have
to do.
    Arden. Why, Alice, how can I do too much for
him,
Whose life I have endangered without cause.
    Alice. 'Tis true ; and seeing 'twas partly through
my means,
I am content to drink to him for this once.
Here, master Mosbie, and I pray you henceforth,
Be you as strange to me as I to you :
Your company hath purchas'd me ill friends ;
And I for you, God knows, have undeserved
Been ill spoken of in every place :
Therefore, henceforth frequent my house no more.
    Mos. I 'll see your husband in despite of you :
Yet, Arden, I protest to thee by heaven,
Thou ne'er shall see me more, after this night.
I 'll go to Rome rather than be forsworn.
    Arden. Tush, I 'll have no such vows made in
my house.
    Alice. Yes, I pray you, husband, let him swear ;
And on that condition, Mosbie, pledge me here.
    Mos. Ay, as willingly as I mean to live.
    Arden. Come, Alice, is our supper ready yet ?
    Alice. It will by then you have played a game
at tables.
    Arden. Come, master Mosbie, what shall we
play for ?
    Mos. Three games for a French crown, sir,
And please you.
    Arden.   Content.   [*They play at Tables.*
    Will. Can he not take him yet ? what a spite is
that ?
    Alice. Not yet, Will ; take heed he see thee not.
    Will. I fear he will espy me as I am coming.
    Mich. To prevent that, creep betwixt my legs.

    Mos. One ace, or else I lose the game.
    Arden. Marry, sir, there's two for failing.
    Mos. Ah, master Arden, now I can take you.[38]
    [BLACK WILL. and SHAKE. *enter from the
Counting-house ;* WILL. *pulls* ARDEN *down
with a Towel.*
    Arden. Mosbie ! Michael ! Alice ! what will
you do ?
    Will. Nothing but take you up, sir, nothing else.
    Mos. There's for the pressing-iron you told me of.
                [*Stabs him.*
    Shake. And there's for the ten pound in my
sleeve.   [*Stabs him.*
    Alice. What, groanest thou ? nay, then, give me
the weapon :
Take this for hindering Mosbie's love and mine.
                [*She stabs him.*
    Mich. O, mistress !
    Will. Ah ! that villain will betray us all.
    Mos. Tush, fear him not, he will be secret.
    Mich. Why, dost thou think I will betray my-
self ?
    Shake. In Southwark dwells a bonny northern
lass ;
The widow Chambley ; I 'll to her house now,
And if she will not give me harbour,
I 'll make booty of the quean even to her smock.
    Will. Shift for yourselves ; we two will leave
you now.
    Alice. First lay the body in the counting-house.
    [*They lay the Body in the Counting-house.*
    Will. We have our gold, mistress Alice, adieu :
Mosbie, farewell ; and Michael, farewell too.
                [*Exeunt.*

Enter SUSAN.

    Susan. Mistress, the guests are at the doors.
Hearken, they knock ; what, shall I let them in ?
    Alice. Mosbie, go thou and bear them company :
                [*Exit* Mos.
And, Susan, fetch water and wash away the blood.
    Susan. The blood cleaveth to the ground, and
will not out.
    Alice. But with my nails I 'll scrape away the
blood :
The more I strive the more the blood appears.
    Susan. What's the reason, mistress, can you tell ?
    Alice. Because I blush not at my husband's death.

Re-enter MOSBIE.

    Mos. How now, what's the matter ? is all well ?
    Alice. Ay, well, if Arden were alive again :
In vain we strive ; for here his blood remains.

Mos. Why, strew rushes on it, can you not ?
This wench doth nothing : fall unto the work.

   Alice. 'Twas thou that made me murder him !

   Mos. What of that ?

   Alice. Nay, nothing, Mosbie, so it be not known.

   Mos. Keep thou it close, and 'tis impossible.

   Alice. Ah, but I cannot ; was he not slain by me ?
My husband's death torments me at the heart.

   Mos. It shall not long torment thee, gentle Alice
I am thy husband ; think no more of him.

Enter ADAM FOWLE *and* BRADSHAW.

   Brad. How now, mistress Arden ? what ail you
      weep ?

   Mos. Because her husband is abroad so late.
A couple of ruffians threaten'd him yesternight ;
And she, poor soul, is afraid he should be hurt.

   Adam. Is 't nothing else ? tush, he 'll be here
      anon.

Enter GREENE.

   Greene. Now, mistress Arden, lack you any
      guests ?

   Alice. Ah, master Greene, did you see my hus-
      band lately ?

   Greene. I saw him walking behind the abbey
      even now.

Enter FRANKLIN.

   Alice. I do not like this being out so late :
Master Franklin, where did you leave my husband ?

   Frank. Believe me I saw him not since morning.
Fear you not, he 'll come anon ; mean time
You may do well to bid his guests sit down.

   Alice. Ay, so they shall ; master Bradshaw, sit
      you there :
I pray you be content ; I 'll have my will.
Master Mosbie, sit you in my husband's seat.

   Mich. Susan, shall thou and I wait on them ?
Or, and thou sayest the word, let us sit down too.

   Susan. Peace ; we have other matters now in
      hand.
I fear me, Michael, all will be betray'd.

   Mich. Tush, so it be known that I shall marry
      thee in the
Morning, I care not though I be hang'd ere night.
But to prevent the worst, I 'll buy some ratsbane.

   Susan. Why, Michael, wilt thou poison thyself ?

   Mich. No, but my mistress, for I fear she 'll tell.

   Susan. Tush, Michael, fear not her ; she 's wise
      enough.

   Mos. Sirrah Michael, give us a cup of beer :
Mistress Arden, here 's to your husband.

   Alice. My husband ?

   Frank. What ails you, woman, to cry so suddenly r

   Alice. Ah, neighbours, a sudden qualm came
      o'er my heart :
My husband's being forth torments my mind.
I know something 's amiss ; he is not well,
Or else I should have heard of him ere now.

   Mos. She will undo us through her foolishness.

   Greene. Fear not, mistress Arden, he is well
      enough.

   Alice. Tell not me ; I know he is not well.
He was not wont for to stay thus late.
Good master Franklin, go and seek him forth,
And if you find him, send him home to me ;
And tell him what a fear he hath put me in.

   Frank. I like not this ; I pray God all be well.
I 'll seek him out, and find him if I can.

       [*Exeunt* FRANK, MOS., *and* GREENE.

   Alice. Michael, how shall I do to rid the rest
      away ?

   Mich. Leave that to my charge ; let me alone
'Tis very late, master Bradshaw,
And there are many false knaves abroad,
And you have many narrow lanes to pass.

   Brad. Faith, friend Michael, and thou sayest true.
Therefore, I pray thee, light 's forth, and lend 's a
      link. [*Exeunt* BRAD., ADAM, *and* MICH.

   Alice. Michael, bring them to the doors, but do
      not stay :
You know I do not love to be alone.
Go, Susan, and bid thy brother come ;
But wherefore should he come ? Here is nought
      but fear.
Stay, Susan, stay, and help to counsel me.

   Susan. Alas, I counsel ! fear frights away my wits.

      [*They open the Counting-house Door, and look
      upon* ARDEN.

   Alice. See, Susan, where thy quondam master lies ;
Sweet Arden, smear'd in blood and filthy gore.

   Susan. My brother, you, and I, shall rue this deed.

   Alice. Come, Susan, help to lift his body forth ;
And let our salt tears be his obsequies.

Re-enter MOSBIE *and* GREENE.

   Mos. How now, Alice, whither will you bear him ?

   Alice. Sweet Mosbie, art thou come ? Then weep
      that will.
I have my wish in that I joy thy sight.

   Greene. Well, it 'hoves us for to be circumspect.

   Mos. Ay, for Franklin thinks that we have mur-
      dered him.

   Alice. Ay, but he cannot prove it for his life :
We 'll spend this night in dalliance and in sport.

Re-enter MICHAEL.

Mich. O, mistress! the mayor and all the watch
Are coming towards our house with glaves and bills.
    Alice. Make the door fast; let them not come in
    Mos. Tell me, sweet Alice, how shall I escape
    Alice. Out at the back door, over the pile of wood,
And, for one night, lie at the Flower-de-luce.
    Mos. That is the next way to betray myself.
    Greene. Alas, mistress Arden, the watch will take
    me here,
And cause suspicion, where else would be none.
    Alice. Why, take that way that master Mosbie
    doth:
But first convey the body to the fields.
    Mos. Until to-morrow, sweet Alice, now farewell;
And see you confess nothing in any case.
    Greene. Be resolute, mistress Alice, betray us not,
But cleave to us as we will stick to you.
    [*Exeunt* Mos. *and* GREENE, *bearing away the*
      Body.
    Alice. Now let the judge and juries do their
    worst:
My house is clear; and now I fear them not.
    Susan. As we went it snow'd all the way,
Which makes me fear our footsteps will be spied.
    Alice. Peace, fool; the snow will cover them
    again.
    Susan. But it had done before we came back
    again.
    Alice. Hark! hark! they knock:
Go, Michael, let them in.

    Enter the Mayor *and the* Watch.

How now, master mayor, have you brought my
    husband home?
    Mayor. I saw him come into your house an hour
    ago.
    Alice. You are deceiv'd, it was a Londoner.
    Mayor. Mistress Arden, know you not one
That is called Black Will?
    Alice. I know none such; what mean these
    questions?
    Mayor. I have the counsel's warrant to appre-
    hend him.
    Alice. I am glad it is no worse.   [*Aside.*
Why, master mayor, think you I harbour any such?
    Mayor. We are inform'd that here he is;
And therefore pardon us, for we must search.
    Alice. Ay, search and spare you not, through
    every room;
Were my husband at home, you would not offer
    this.

    Enter FRANKLIN.

Master Franklin, what mean you come so sad?
    Frank. Arden, thy husband, and my friend, is
    slain.
    Alice. Ah! by whom? master Franklin, can
    you tell?
    Frank. I know not; but behind the abbey
There he lies murder'd in most piteous case.
    Mayor. But, master Franklin, are you sure 'tis he?
    Frank. I am too sure; would God I were de-
    ceiv'd.
    Alice. Find out the murderers, let them be known.
    Frank. Ay, so they shall, come you along with us.
    Alice. Wherefore?
    Frank. Know you this hand-towel and this knife?
    Susan. Ah, Michael, through this thy negligence,
Thou hast betrayed and undone us all.   [*Aside.*
    Mich. I was so afraid, I knew not what I did,
I thought I had thrown them both into the well.
                   [*Aside.*
    Alice. It is the pig's blood we had to supper.
But wherefore stay you? find out the murderers.
    Mayor. I fear me you'll prove one of them your-
    self.
    Alice. I one of them! what mean such questions?
    Frank. I fear me he was murder'd in this house,
And carried to the fields; for from that place,
Backwards and forwards, may you see,
The print of many feet within the snow.
And look about this chamber where we are,
And you shall find part of his guiltless blood,
For in his slip-shoe did I find some rushes,
Which argueth he was murdered in this room.
    Mayor. Look in the place where he was wont to
    sit.
See, see, his blood; it is too manifest.
    Alice. It is a cup of wine that Michael shed.
    Mich. Ay, truly.
    Frank. It is his blood, which, strumpet, thou
    hast shed.
But if I live, thou and thy 'complices
Which have conspiréd, and wrought his death,
Shall rue it.
    Alice. Ah, master Franklin, God and heaven can
    tell,
I lov'd him more than all the world beside.
But bring me to him, let me see his body.
    Frank. Bring that villain, and Mosbie's sister
    too,
And one of you go to the Flower-de-luce.
And seek for Mosbie, and apprehend him.
                   [*Exeunt.*

SCENE III.—*An obscure Street in* London.

Enter SHAKEBAG.

Shake. The widow Chambly in her husband's
days I kept,
And now he's dead, she has grown so stout,
She will not know her old companions:
I came thither, thinking to have had
Harbour, as I was wont,
And she was ready to thrust me out at doors,
But whether she would or no, I go me up,
And as she followed me I spurn'd her down the
stairs,
And broke her neck; and cut her tapster's throat.
And now I am going to fling them in the Thames
I have the gold, what care I though it be known?
I'll cross the water, and take sanctuary.   [*Exit.*

SCENE IV.—Arden's *House at* Feversham.

Enter the Mayor, MOSBIE, ALICE, FRANKLIN,
MICHAEL, *and* SUSAN.

Mayor. See, mistress Arden, where your husband
lies,
Confess this foul fault and be penitent,
   Alice. Arden, sweet husband, what shall I say?
The more I sound his name, the more he bleeds;[39]
This blood condemns me, and in gushing forth,
Speaks as it falls, and asks me why I did it.
Forgive me Arden, I repent me now;
And would my death save thine, thou shouldst not die.
Rise up, sweet Arden, and enjoy thy love,
And frown not on me, when we meet in heaven.
In heaven I'll love thee, though on earth I did not.
   Mayor. Say, Mosbie, what made thee murder him
   Frank. Study not for an answer, look not down,
His purse and girdle found at thy bed's head.
Witness sufficiently thou didst the deed.
It bootless is to swear thou didst it not.
   Mos. I hired Black Will and Shakebag, ruffians
both,
And they and I have done this murderous deed.
But wherefore stay we?
Command and bear me hence.
   Frank. Those ruffians shall not escape.
I will to London and get the counsel's warrant
To apprehend them.   [*Exeunt.*

SCENE V.—*The* Kentish *Coast.*

Enter BLACK WILL.

Will. Shakebag, I hear hath taken sanctuary,
But I am so pursued with hues and cries,
For petty robberies that I have done:
That I can come unto no sanctuary:
Therefore must I in some oyster boat,
At last be fain to go aboard some hoy,
And so to Flushing; there is no staying here.
At Sittingburn the watch was like to take me,
And had not I with my buckler cover'd my head,
And ran full blank at all adventures,
I am sure I had ne'er gone further than that place,
For the constable had twenty warrants to appre-
hend me.
Besides that, I robbed him and his man once at
Gad's-hill.
Farewell England, for I'll to Flushing now. [*Exit.*

SCENE VI.—*Justice Room at* Feversham.

Enter the Mayor, MOSBIE, ALICE, MICHAEL,
SUSAN, *and* BRADSHAW.

Mayor. Come, make haste, and bring away the
prisoners.
   Brad. Mistress Arden, you are now going to God,
And I am by the law condemn'd to die,
About a letter I brought from master Greene
I pray you, mistress Arden, speak the truth:
Was I ever privy to your intent or no?[40]
   Alice. What should I say?
You brought me such a letter,
But I dare swear thou knewest not the contents.
Leave now to trouble me with worldly things,
And let me meditate upon my Saviour, Christ,
Whose blood must save me for the blood I shed.
   Mos. How long shall I live in this hell of grief?
Convey me from the presence of that strumpet.
   Alice. Ah! but for thee I had never been a
strumpet.
What cannot oaths and protestations do,
When men have opportunity to woo?
I was too young to sound thy villanies;
But now I find it and repent too late.
   Susan. Ah, gentle brother, wherefore should I
die?
I knew not of it till the deed was done.
   Mos. For thee I mourn more than for myself:
Let it suffice I cannot save thee now.
   Mich. And if your brother, and my mistress,
Had not promised me you in marriage,
I had never given consent to this foul deed.
   Mayor. Leave to accuse each other now,
And listen to the sentence I shall give.
Bear Mosbie and his sister to London straight,
Where they in Smithfield must be executed.

Bear mistress Arden unto Canterbury;
Where, as her sentence is, she must be burnt.
Michael and Bradshaw in Feversham
Must suffer death.

Alice. Let my death make amends for all my sin.

Mos. Fie upon women, this shall be my song;
But bear me hence, for I have liv'd too long.

Susan. Seeing no hope on earth, in heaven is my
hope.

Mich. Faith I care not, seeing I die with Susan.

Brad. My blood be on his head who gave the
sentence.

Mayor. To speedy execution with them all.

                         [*Exeunt.*

Enter FRANKLIN.

Frank. Thus have you seen the truth of Arden's
death

As for the ruffians Shakebag and Black Will,
The one took sanctuary, and being sent for out,
Was murder'd in Southwark, as he pass'd
To Greenwich, where the lord Protector lay.
Black Will was burnt in Flushing, at a stake;
Greene was hang'd at Ospringe in Kent;
The painter fled; and how he died we know not.
But this above the rest is to be noted:
Arden lay murder'd in that plot of ground,
Which he by force and violence held from Rede;
And in the grass his body's print was seen
Two years and more after the deed was done.
Gentlemen, we hope you'll pardon this naked
         tragedy,
Wherein no filéd points are foisted in,
To make it gracious to the ear or eye;
For simple truth is gracious enough,
And needs no other points of glozing stuff.

NOTES TO ARDEN, OF FEVERSHAM.

—◆—

¹ *By letters patent from his majesty.*

The murder on which this tragedy was founded took place in the year 1551; therefore the sovereign here alluded to was Edward the Sixth, the singularly amiable son of that bloated savage, Henry the Eighth. The Duke of Somerset, just before mentioned, was, in consequence of the king being a minor, Lord Protector of the kingdom.

² *A gentleman of blood;* i.e. of a good family.

³ *Whilst on the planchers.*

The *planchers* were the boards of which the flooring of a room was composed. From *plancher*, French.

⁴ *Though this abhors from reason, yet I'll try it.*

That is, although the plan you propose is repugnant to, and condemned by, my reason, still I will try it with a faint hope that as all ordinary and likely methods of winning back my wife's affection have failed, an extraordinary and unlikely one may perhaps succeed.

⁵ *Were he as mad as raving Hercules.*

It is related that Hercules, having shot the centaur, Nessus, with a poisoned arrow, because he offered violence to his wife, Dejanira, the dying monster, eager for revenge, gave the lady his tunic, which was covered with blood, poisoned and infected by the arrow, and told her that the garment had the power of recalling a faithless husband from unlawful loves. An occasion for testing the virtue of the dress soon arrived: Hercules had seized a princess of the name of Iole, with whom he was passionately in love, and he took her to Mount Œta, where he intended to offer a sacrifice to Jupiter. Not having a proper garment in which to officiate, he sent to his wife for one. Dejanira sent him the dress which had belonged to the centaur; and Hercules, having put it on, was seized with a raving madness. As he also suffered the acutest torments from the poison having penetrated to his bones, he mounted a funeral pile, and ordering it to be set on fire, perished in the flames.

⁶ *Bear him from me these pair of silver dice.*

Whimsical as this incident may be, it was an actual occurrence; the poet has here literally followed the chronicler. Holinshed tells us: "It happened this Mosbie, upon some mistaking to fall out with her (Alice); but she being desirous to be in favour with him again, sent him a pair of *silver dice* by one Adam Foule, dwelling at the Flower-de-luce, in Feversham. After which he resorted to her again, and oftentimes lay in Arden's house; and although (as it was said) Arden perceived right well their mutual familiarity to be much greater than

their honesty, yet because he would not offend her, and so lose the benefit he hoped to gain at some of her friends' hands, in bearing with her lewdness, which he might have lost had he fallen out with her, he was contented to wink at her filthy disorder, and both permitted and also invited Mosbie very often to lodge in his house. And thus it continued a good space before any practice was begun by them against Master Arden. She at length, inflamed in love with Mosbie, and loathing her husband, wished, and after practised, the means how to hasten his end."

⁷ *The statute makes against artificers.*

To *make*, in ancient phraseology usually meant to do; *makes* is here used in the sense of decides against. The law forbade any under the rank of a gentleman to wear a sword.

⁸ *I warrant that I do;* i.e. the law justifies my act.

⁹ *She throws the broth on the ground.*

This, the first attempt of Alice upon her husband's life, is thus related by Holinshed; the reader will perceive how closely the poet has followed the track of the historian:—"Now, Master Arden purposing that day to ride to Canterbury, his wife brought him his breakfast; which was wont to be milk and butter. He, having received a spoonful or two of the milk, misliked the taste and colour thereof, and said to his wife, 'Mistress Alice, what milk have you given me here?' Wherewithal she tilted it over with her hand, saying, 'I ween nothing can please you.' Then he took horse and rode towards Canterbury, and by the way fell into extreme sickness, and so escaped for that time."

¹⁰ *What favour hast thou had more than a kiss?*

In those days a kiss was merely a salutation, and not, as now, an act of familiarity and affection.

¹¹ *The platform of his death;* i.e. the scheme or plan of it.

¹² *My master's pantophelles;* i.e. his slippers.

¹³ *A crew of harlots.*

Harlot was a reproachful term which in former times was sometimes applied to men as well as to women. It is so used by Chaucer, Shakspere, and Ben Jonson; it was probably a name addressed to lewd, unmanly triflers.

¹⁴ *Old filching;* i.e. excessive filching.

¹⁵ *It breaks Black Will's head.*

This incident gives a lively idea of some of the inconveniences of London in old times.

[16] *You shall be well beaten and sent to the compter.*

Some may perhaps be surprised at the insolence of the 'prentice, and the comparatively submissive manner of the ruffian, Black Will, who is represented as a man not likely to put up with the slightest injury without resenting it. But they must remember that the apprentices of London were, in the age referred to, a very formidable body, and that a cry for " clubs" would have brought hundreds of these young gentlemen, ever ready for and delighting in a fray, to the assistance of their comrade.

[17] *Till Arden's heart be panting in my hand.*

It has been objected that the language of Black Will and Shakebag in this scene is more poetical than natural, that it is not appropriately given to men so sunk in intellectual and moral darkness. This must to some extent be admitted ; too great a licence in this direction is ever the fault of young poets. Energy of mind and warmth of imagination, must be directed by experience, and chastened by maturity, before they become real poetic power.

[18] *As Hydra's head, that perish'd by decay.*

I think we should read, *nourished* by decay ; the fable being, that as soon as one head of the hydra was cut off, two sprang up in its place.

[19] *How now, Will, become a precisian?*

A *precisian* is one who pretends to a more than ordinary degree of sanctity. It was a name frequently bestowed upon the Puritans. In Dr. Faustus, 1604, we have :—

I will set my countenance like a *precisian*.

And in Ben Jonson's *Case is Altered :*—

It is *precisianism* to alter that,
With austere judgment, which is given by nature.

[20] *A coistrel ;* i.e. a coward, a runaway.

[21] *Each gentle starry gale.*

That is, *stirring* gale. Our word star is supposed to be derived from *stir-an,* a Saxon word, signifying to move.

[22] *For Greene doth erre the land.*

This may mean that Greene *heirs* or inherits the land, or that he *ears ;* i.e. ploughs it.

[23] *But I will dam that fire within my breast.*

That is, close it up within my own breast. Alice is meditating a separation from Mosbie, and therefore says she will close up her affection within her own heart.

[24] *Such deep pathairs.*

That is, moving sighs ; sighs which from their intensity have a pathetic power.

[25] *Forslow'd advantages.*

That is, neglected, delayed, or hindered them.

[26] *A wanton giglot.*

A *giglot,* or *giglet,* is a frivolous and lascivious woman.

[27] *The dag.*

An obsolete term anciently applied both to a pistol and a dagger.

[28] *I am your beadsman.*

That is, your dependent, who in return for charitable assistance, constantly renders up prayers for your welfare.

[29] *And of a lordain too.*

I have not met this word elsewhere, but I suppose it means a looby, an awkward lout. The meaning, then, is, Susan is sick of a fever arising from the fear of your presence.

[30] *As will rather be houghed than get his way.*

To *hough* a man, was to hamstring him, to disable him, by cutting the sinews of his hams. Black Will, desirous of getting rid of the ferryman, utters this brutal threat.

[31] *Beraide ;* i.e. mud-bespattered.

[32] *Shall wound my husband hornsbie to the death.*

I suppose she means, shall wound my *cuckold* husband.

[33] *His conscience is too liberal.*

That is, too licentious; too easy and indifferent to be aroused by your words.

[34] *His costard ;* i.e. his head.

[35] *A sconce ;* i.e. a helmet ; a protection for the sconce.

[36] *That like the snakes of black Tisiphone,*
Sting me with their embracings.

According to the Greek mythology, Tisiphone was one of the furies, and dealt out the vengeance of the gods when they were offended with mankind. She was a wholesale dispenser of plagues and famines, and was also entrusted with the amiable office of scourging the spirits of the wicked in Tartarus. She was represented with a whip in her hand, and a serpent hanging from among her hair ; these venomous reptiles were also encircled round her wrists in the manner of bracelets.

[37] *Fling down Endymion and snatch him up.*

The passion of Alice for Mosbie, in its wild extravagance, certainly borders upon sensual madness. She adorns this " black, swart man" with all the manly graces that a vivid imagination can conceive; she does not so much love him as she loves the being, which in her heated fancy he appears. Actuated by this feeling she compares him to Endymion, who was reported to be so exceedingly beautiful that the goddess Diana became enamoured of him as he slept naked on Mount Latmos, and descended from her starry habitation that she might enjoy his love. Some have said that this fable of Endymion's amours with Diana, or the moon, had its origin in his knowledge of astronomy, and that as he passed the night upon some mountain, gazing in an attitude of admiration upon the heavenly bodies, it was reported that he was courted by the radiant queen of night.

[38] *Ah ! master Arden, now I take you.*

The curious reader will be interested in the account given by Holinshed, of the circumstances of this savage murder:—"They conveyed Black Will into Master Arden's house, putting him into a closet at the end of his parlour. Before this they had sent out of the house all the servants, those excepted which were privy to the devised murder. Then went Mosbie to the door, and there stood in a nightgown of silk girded about him, and this was betwixt six and seven of the clock at night. Master Arden, having been at a neighbour's house of his, named Dumpkin, and having cleared certain reckonings betwixt them, came home, and, finding Mosbie standing at the door, asked him if it were supper-time ? I think not, (quoth Mosbie,) it is not yet ready. Then let us go and play a game at the tables in the mean season, said Master Arden. And so they went straight into the parlour: and as they came by through the hall, his wife was walking there, and Master Arden said, How now, Mistress Alice ? But she made small answer to him. In the meantime, one chained the wicket-door of the entry. When they came into the parlour, Mosbie sat down on the bench, having his face toward the place where Black Will stood. Then Michael, Master Arden's man, stood at his master's back, holding a candle in his hand, to shadow Black Will, that Arden might by no means perceive him coming forth. In their play Mosbie said thus (which seemed to be the watchword for Black Will's coming.) Now I may take you, sir, if I will. Take me ? quoth Master Arden ; which way ? With that Black Will stepped forth, and cast a towel about his neck, so as to stop his breath and strangle him.

Then Mosbie, having at his girdle a pressing iron of fourteen pounds weight, struck him on the head with the same, so that he fell down, and gave a great groan, insomuch that they thought he had been killed."

[39] *The more I sound his name, the more he bleeds.*

An allusion to an ancient and widely-spread superstition that the body of a murdered man bled again in the presence of his assassin. It was supposed that even inanimate objects were revolted at the crime of murder ; and, departing from the course of nature, in some mysterious manner pointed out the criminal. A modern poet, and one who was a poet of great pathetic and tragic power, though commonly regarded as a humorist only—I mean the late Thomas Hood—thus refers to the superstition alluded to in the text :—

> Oh, God ! it made me quake to see
> Such sense within the slain ;
> For when I touched the lifeless clay,
> The blood gushed out amain :
> For every clot, a burning spot
> Was scorching in my brain.

[40] *Was I ever privy to your intent or no ?*

Bradshaw, it appears both from the Chronicle and the drama, was innocent of the murder, although he was by no means a very estimable and unspotted character. However, he suffered the same punishment as the others, namely, that of death. There is a venerable saying, that men are judged of by their associates ; and in the case of this poor goldsmith, the evil reputation and actions of his companions brought him to a violent and ignominious end.

H. T.

The Merry Devil
of Edmonton

Romantic comedy, of which this play is an example, ran in no other channel so purely as in that which Shakespeare made for it; and with every allowance for difference and inferiority, no veritable contemporaneous analogues are to be found to his work—so, at least, claims F. E. Schelling (38). Indeed, save for Shakespeare's comedies, the examples are rare of plays in which the comic spirit enters otherwise than by way of relief or in support of some other motif, historical, tragic, or realistic. Without here attempting to enumerate all the comedies that fall within this favored decade, we may name at least a few.

Two anonymous surviving plays mentioned in Henslowe's performance lists are *A Knack to Know a Knave* and *A Knack to Know an Honest Man.* The former, which treats, in somewhat belated moral tone, King Edgar and Saint Dunstan, is enlivened with "Kempe's applauded merriments of the men of Gotham." The latter, a companion play in title but not in subject matter, is a typically naïve old-time comedy involving duels, banishments, and tests of love and friendship. *The Weakest Goes to the Wall* is derived from one of the stories of Barnabe Rich's *Farewell to the Military Profession,* which also supplied the story for *The Merry Wives of Windsor.* It begins with a dumb show and progresses through a variety of incidents to unexpected discovery and reconciliation.

A tendency to imitate and repeat certain characters, scenes, and situations is characteristic of the comedies, as of the tragedies, in the last decade of Elizabeth's reign. In *The Merry Wives of Windsor,* for example, broken English is used in the speech of the Welsh Sir Hugh and the French doctor

Caius; and this device becomes a feature also of the three captains Fluellen, Macmorris, and Jamy in *Henry V*. Haughton's *Englishmen for My Money,* in which three foreigners court three English girls, each in a jargon of his own, dates from the same period as these plays of Shakespeare. And still again, the "group of irregular humorists" of *The Merry Wives*—the Welsh parson, the French doctor, and the host of the Garter with the group around him, is closely followed in *The Merry Devil of Edmonton*. Finally, there is in this play, as in *The Merry Wives,* a merry landlord. These two plays likewise make much of scenes of wandering and cross-purposes at night—the one in Windsor Forest, the other in Enfield Chase—in which the action also represents persons mistaking one another on account of the dark, and hence becoming involved in all kinds of entanglements.

The Merry Devil of Edmonton is, aside from *The Merry Wives of Windsor,* by far the best of the many romantic comedies in all these aspects, as well as in its happy, wholesome love tale, a touch of the threatened supernatural, and the "humors" of low comedy to which Jonson had just given a new turn—perhaps explaining why this play was so popular on the English stage.

According to J. M. Manley and M. C. Bradbrook (4), the source of *The Merry Devil of Edmonton* is in the chapbook of *Friar Bacon and Friar Bungay,* a play that was sufficiently popular to evoke a second part, the fragmentary *John of Bordeaux*. It is a play of revelry among the country folk of Suffolk, with a good deal of local color from Bungay, Fressingfield, and Beccles. Prince Edward hands over his part to the Fool, while he goes wooing a country maid. The key word of the play is "frolic": it occurs again and again. The king and courtiers make merry in an atmosphere of curds and cream, deer hunting and practical jokes; though Robin Hood does not appear, his spirit rules. The rival magicians conjure largely by way of entertainment: the play is full of shows. When Friar Bacon's magic glass brings about the death of two Oxford scholars, he abjures magic, only to resume it in order that the Devil may carry off the Clown to hell. And the play concludes with a resounding prophecy of the birth of Queen Elizabeth.

In comedy, as Madeleine Doran (13) points out, one seldom finds so damaging a conflict of aims as in tragedy. That may be partly because norms of social behavior are easier to manage than philosophical assumptions about the universe. It may also be because we expect less, are more willing to accept implausible action for the sake of a lively story, more willing to accept any mixture in an *olla podrida* of fun. The moral function of comedy could be, and often was, quite as easily interpreted to be purgation of melancholy as instruction in manners and morals. And of course the purging of melancholy is synonymous with being agreeably diverted.

Finally, in addition to *The Merry Devil of Edmonton* and other works involving conjuring and magic, the King's Men presented a variety of Shakespeare's plays, ranging from *Othello* to *The Winter's Tale,* from *The Tempest* to *Much Ado About Nothing*. They also produced *Julius Caesar* and two plays called *Hotspur* and *Sir John Falstaff*, which must be the two parts of *Henry IV*. In addition to Shakespeare's plays, the King's Men presented Jonson's comedy *The Alchemist*, which they first produced in 1611 with Burbage and Heminges playing the leads. Most strongly represented, next to Shakespeare, was that successful new team of playwrights, Beaumont and Fletcher.

PERSONS REPRESENTED.

———◆———

SIR ARTHUR CLARE.
HENRY CLARE, *his Son.*
Appear, sc. 2; sc. 4; sc. 5; sc. 6; sc. 7; sc. 9.

SIR RICHARD MOUNCHENSEY.
Appears, sc. 2; sc. 4.

RAYMOND MOUNCHENSEY, *his Son.*
Appears, sc. 2; sc. 4; sc. 6; sc. 9.

SIR RALPH JERNINGHAM.
Appears, sc. 2; sc. 5; sc. 7; sc. 9.

FRANK JERNINGHAM, *his Son.*
Appears, sc. 2; sc. 4; sc. 5; sc. 6; sc. 7; sc. 9.

SIR JOHN, *the Priest of* Enfield.
Appears, sc. 3; sc. 7; sc. 8; sc. 9.

BANKS, *a Miller.*
Appears, sc. 3; sc. 7; sc. 8.

SMUG, *a Smith.*
Appears, sc. 3; sc. 7; sc. 9.

BILBO, *Servant to* Sir Arthur Clare.
Appears, sc. 2; sc. 4; sc. 5; sc. 9.

BLAGUE, *the Host of the* George Inn.
Appears, sc. 2; sc. 3; sc. 7; sc. 8; sc. 9.

BRIAN, *a Forest-keeper.*
RALPH, *his Man.*
Appear, sc. 7.

SEXTON.
Appears, sc. 8.

FRIAR HILDERSHAM.
BENEDIC, *a Novice.*
CHAMBERLAIN.
Appear, sc. 9.

PETER FABEL, *a Scholar and Magician, surnamed* " the Merry Devil."
Appears, sc. 1; sc. 2; sc. 4; sc. 6; sc. 9.

COREB, *an Evil Spirit.*
Appears, sc. 1.

LADY CLARE.
Appears, sc. 2; sc. 4; sc. 5; sc. 6.

MILLISENT, *her Daughter.*
Appears, sc. 2; sc. 4; sc. 5; sc. 6; sc. 7; sc. 9.

ABBESS OF CHESTON PRIORY.
Appears, sc. 5.

Nuns and Attendants.

SCENE.—EDMONTON, *and the Surrounding Country.*

The Merry Devil of Edmonton.

THE PROLOGUE.

YOUR silence and attention, worthy friends,
That your free spirits may with more pleasing
    sense
Relish the life of this our active scene:
To which intent, to calm this murmuring breath,
We ring this round with our invoking spells;
If that your list'ning ears be yet prepar'd
To entertain the subject of our play,
Lend us your patience.
'Tis Peter Fabel, a renowned scholar,[1]
Whose fame hath still been hitherto forgot
By all the writers of this latter age.
In Middlesex his birth and his abode,
Not full seven miles from this great famous city;
That, for his fame in slights and magic won,
Was call'd the merry fiend of Edmonton.
If any here make doubt of such a name,
In Edmonton yet fresh unto this day,
Fix'd in the wall of that old ancient church,
His monument remaineth to be seen:
His memory yet in the mouths of men,
That whilst he liv'd he could deceive the devil.
Imagine now, that whilst he is retir'd
From Cambridge back unto his native home,
Suppose the silent sable-visag'd night
Casts her black curtain over all the world;
And whilst he sleeps within his silent bed,
Toil'd with the studies of the passéd day,
The very time and hour wherein that spirit,
That many years attended his command,
And oftentimes 'twixt Cambridge and that town
Had in a minute borne him thro' the air,
By composition 'twixt the fiend and him,
Comes now to claim the scholar for his due.
                    [Draw the Curtains.
Behold him here laid on his restless couch!
His fatal chime prepared at his head,
His chamber guarded with these sable slights,
And by him stands that necromantic chair,
In which he makes his direful invocations,
And binds the fiends that shall obey his will.
Sit with a pleased eye, until you know
The comic end of our sad tragic show.

SCENE I.—Fabel's *Chamber, supplied with Books and Necromantic Instruments.*

The chime goes, in which time FABEL *is oft seen to stare about him and hold up his hands.*

  Fabel. What means the tolling of this fatal
    chime?
O what a trembling horror strikes my heart!
My stiffen'd hair stands upright on my head,
As do the bristles of a porcupine.

Enter COREB, *a Spirit.*

  Coreb. Fabel, awake! or I will bear thee hence
Headlong to hell.
  Fabel.   Ha, ha, why dost thou wake me?
Coreb, is it thou?
  Coreb.   'Tis I.
  Fabel. I know thee well, I hear the watchful dogs
With hollow howling tell of thy approach:
The lights burn dim, affrighted with thy presence;
And this distemper'd and tempestuous night
Tells me the air is troubled with some devil.
  Coreb. Come, art thou ready?
  Fabel.   Whither, or to what?
  Coreb. Why, scholar, this the hour my date ex-
    pires;
I must depart, and come to claim my due.
  Fabel. Hah! what is thy due?
  Coreb.   Fabel, thyself.
  Fabel. O let not darkness hear thee speak that
    word,
Lest that with force it hurry hence amain,
And leave the world to look upon my woe:
Yet overwhelm me with this globe of earth,
And let a little sparrow with her bill,
Take but so much as she can bear away,
That every day thus losing of my load,
I may again, in time, yet hope to rise.
  Coreb. Didst thou not write thy name with thine
    own blood?
And drew'st the formal deed 'tixt thee and me?
And is it not recorded now in hell?
  Fabel. Why com'st thou in this stern and horrid
    shape?
Not in familiar sort as thou wast wont?

Coreb. Because the date of thy command is out,
And I am master of thy skill and thee.

Fabel. Coreb, thou angry and impatient spirit,
I have earnest business for a private friend :
Reserve me, spirit, until some farther time.

    Coreb. I will not for the mines of all the earth.

    Fabel. Then let me rise, and ere I leave the
       world,
Dispatch some business that I have to do ;
And in mean time repose thee in that chair.

    Coreb. Fabel, I will.   [*Sits down.*

    Fabel. O that this soul, that cost so dear a price
As the dear precious blood of her Redeemer,
Inspir'd with knowledge, should by that alone,
Which makes a man so mean unto the powers,
Ev'n lead him down into the depth of hell ;
When men in their own pride strive to know more
Than man should know !
For this alone God cast the angels down.
The infinity of arts is like a sea,
Into which when man will take in hand to sail
Farther than reason (which should be his pilot)
Hath skill to guide him ; losing once his compass,
He falleth to such deep and dangerous whirlpools,
As he doth lose the very sight of heaven :
The more he strives to come to quiet harbour,
The farther still he finds himself from land.
Man striving still to find the depth of evil,
Seeking to be a God, becomes a devil.

    Coreb. Come, Fabel, hast thou done ?

    Fabel. Yes, yes, come hither.

    Coreb. Fabel, I cannot.

    Fabel. Cannot ! what ails your hollowness ?

    Coreb. Good Fabel, help me.

    Fabel. Alas ! where lies your grief ?—Some aqua
       vitæ !
The devil's very sick, I fear he'll die,
For he looks very ill.

    Coreb. Dar'st thou deride the minister of dark-
       ness ?
In Lucifer's great name, Coreb conjures thee
To set him free.

    Fabel. I will not for the mines of all the earth,
Unless thou give me liberty to see
Seven years more, before thou seize on me.

    Coreb. Fabel, I give it thee.

    Fabel.   Swear, damned fiend.

    Coreb. Unbind me, and by hell I will not touch
       thee
Till seven years, from this hour, be full expir'd.

    Fabel. Enough, come out.

    Coreb.   A vengeance take thy art !
Live, and convert all piety to evil ;

Never did man thus over-reach the devil.
No time on earth, like Phætontic flames,
Can have perpetual being.   I'll return
To my infernal mansion : but be sure,
Thy seven years done, no trick shall make me tarry ;
But, Coreb, thou to hell shalt Fabel carry.

    Fabel. Then thus between us two this variance
       ends ;
Thou to thy fellow-fiends, I to my friends.

                    [*Exeunt.*

SCENE II. — *A Room in the George Inn, at
       Waltham.*

Enter SIR ARTHUR CLARE, DORCAS *his Lady ;*
   MILLISENT *his Daughter*, Young HARRY CLARE ;
   *the men booted, the Gentlewomen in Cloaks and
   Safe-guards :*[2] BLAGUE, *the merry Host of the
   George, comes in with them.*

    Host. Welcome, good knight, to the George at
Waltham ; my freehold, my tenements, goods, and
chattels.   Madam, here's a room is the very Homer
and Iliads of a lodging, it hath none of the four
elements in it ; I built it out of the centre, and I
drink ne'er the less sack.—Welcome,—my little
waste of maidenheads : what ? I serve the good
duke of Norfolk.

    Clare. God a mercy, my good host Blague :
Thou hast a good seat here.

    Host. 'Tis correspondent, or so : there's not a
Tartarian,[3] nor a carrier, shall breathe upon your
geldings : they have villanous rank feet, the
rogues, and they shall not sweat in my linen.
Knights and lords too have been drunk in my
house, I thank the destinies.

    H. Clare. Pr'ythee, good sinful inn-keeper, will
that corruption, thine hostler,[4] to look well to my
gelding—Hay ! a pox of these rushes.[5]

    Host. You, St. Dennis, your gelding shall walk
without doors, and cool his feet for his master's
sake.   By the body of Saint George, I have an excellent intellect to go steal some venison :[6] now
when wast thou in the forest ?

    H. Clare. Away, you stale mess of white broth.
Come hither, sister, let me help you.

    Clare. Mine host, is not Sir Richard Mounchen-
sey come yet, according to our appointment when
we last dined here ?

    Host. The knight's not yet apparent — marry
here's a fore-runner that summons a parley, and
faith he'll be here top and top-gallant presently.

    Clare. 'Tis well ; good mine host, go down and
see breakfast be provided.

Host. Knight, thy breath hath the force of a woman, it takes me down; I am for the baser element of the kitchen: I retire like a valiant soldier, face point-blank to the foe-man; or like a courtier, that must not shew his prince his posteriors: vanish to know my canvasadoes, and my interrogatories, for I serve the good duke of Norfolk.

[*Exit.*

Clare. How doth my lady? are you not weary, madam?
Come hither, I must talk in private with you;
My daughter Millisent must not over-hear.

Mill. Ay! whispering! pray God it tend to my good!
Strange fear assails my heart, usurps my blood.

Clare. You know, our meeting with the knight Mounchensey
Is to assure our daughter to his heir.

Dorcas. 'Tis without question.

Clare. Two tedious winters have pass'd o'er, since first
These couple lov'd each other, and in passion
Glew'd first their naked hands with youthful moisture;
Just so long, on my knowledge.

Dorcas.   And what of this

Clare. This morning should my daughter lose her name,
And to Mounchensey's house convey our arms,
Quarter'd within his 'scutcheon: the affiance made
'Twixt him and her, this morning should be seal'd.

Dorcas. I know it should.

Clare. But there are crosses, wife; here's one in Waltham,
Another at the Abbey, and a third
At Cheston; and it is ominous to pass
Any of these without a pater-noster.
Crosses of love still thwart this marriage,
Whilst that we two like spirits walk in night,
About those stony and hard-hearted plots.

Mill. O God! what means my father? [*Aside.*

Clare. For look you wife, the riotous old knight
Hath over-run his annual revenue,
In keeping jolly Christmas all the year:
The nostrils of his chimneys are still stuff'd
With smoke, more chargeable than cane tobacco;
His hawks devour his fattest dogs, whilst simple,
His leanest curs eat his hounds' carrion.
Besides, I heard of late his younger brother,
A Turkey-merchant, hath sure suck'd the knight,
By means of some great losses on the sea;
That (you conceive me) before God, all's naught,

His seat is weak: thus each thing rightly scann'd,
You'll see a flight, wife, shortly of his land.

Mill. Treason to my heart's truest sovereign:
How soon is love smother'd in foggy gain! [*Aside.*

Dorcas. But how shall we prevent this dangerous match?

Clare. I have a plot, a trick, and this it is.
Under this colour I'll break off the match;
I'll tell the knight, that now my mind is chang'd
For marrying of my daughter; for I intend
To send her unto Cheston nunnery.

Mill. O me accursed! [*Aside.*

Clare. There to become a most religious nun.

Mill. I'll first be buried quick. [*Aside.*

Clare. To spend her beauty in most private prayers.

Mill. I'll sooner be a sinner in forsaking
Mother and father. [*Aside.*

Clare. How dost like my plot?

Dorcas. Exceeding well: but is it your intent
She shall continue there?

Clare. Continue there? ha, ha, that were a jest:
You know a virgin may continue there
A twelve-month and a day, only on trial.
There shall my daughter sojourn some three months,
And in meantime I'll compass a fair match
'Twixt youthful Jerningham, the lusty heir
Of Sir Ralph Jerningham, dwelling in the forest.
I think they'll both come hither with Mounchensey.

Dorcas. Your care argues the love you bear our child;
I will subscribe to any thing you'll have me.

[*Exeunt* CLARE *and* DORCAS.

Mill. You will subscribe to it?—good, good, 'tis well;
Love hath two chairs of state, heaven and hell.
My dear Mounchensey, thou my death shalt rue,
Ere to thy heart Millisent prove untrue. [*Exit.*

Enter BLAGUE.

Host. Hostlers, you knaves and commanders, take the horses of the knights and competitors: your honourable hulks have put into harbour, they'll take in fresh water here, and I have provided clean chamber-pots. *Via*—they come.[7]

Enter SIR RICHARD MOUNCHENSEY, SIR RALPH JERNINGHAM, Young FRANK JERNINGHAM, RAYMOND MOUNCHENSEY, PETER FABEL, *and* BILBO.

Host. The destinies be most neat chamberlains to these swaggering puritans, knights of the subsidy.

Sir Rich. God a mercy, good mine-host.

Sir Ralph. Thanks, good host Blague.

Host. Room for my case of pistols, that have Greek and Latin bullets in them: let me cling to your flanks, my nimble Giberalters, and blow wind in your calves to make them swell bigger. Ha; I'll caper in mine own fee-simple; away with punctilios and orthography, I serve the good duke of Norfolk.

Bilbo. Tityre, tu patulæ recubans sub tegmine fagi.[8] Truly, mine host, Bilbo, though he be somewhat out of fashion, will be your only blade still; I have a villanous sharp stomach to slice a breakfast.

Host. Thou shalt have it without any more discontinuance, releases, or attournment—what! we know our terms of hunting, and the sea card.

Bilbo. And do you serve the good duke of Norfolk still?

Host. Still, and still, and still, my soldier of Saint Quintin's. Come follow me, I have Charles's-wain below in a butt of sack, I will glister like your crab-fish.

Bilbo. You have fine scholar-like terms: your Cooper's Dictionary is your only book to study in a cellar,[9] a man shall find very strange words in it. Come, my host, let's serve the good duke of Norfolk.

Host. And still, and still, and still, my boy, I'll serve the good duke of Norfolk.

[*Exeunt* Host *and* BILBO.

Enter SIR ARTHUR CLARE, HARRY CLARE, *and* MILLISENT.

Sir Ralph. Good Sir Arthur Clare!

Clare. What gentleman is that? I know him not.

Sir Rich. 'Tis Mr. Fabel, sir, a Cambridge scholar, My son's dear friend.

Clare. Sir, I entreat you know me.

Fabel. Command me, sir, I am affected to you For your Mounchensey's sake.

Clare. Alas! for him, I not respect whether he sink or swim! A word in private, Sir Ralph Jerningham.

Ray. Methinks your father looketh strangely on me:
Say, love, why are you sad?

Mill. I am not, sweet;
Passion is strong, when woe with woe doth meet.

Clare. Shall's in to breakfast? After we'll conclude,
The cause of this our coming: in and feed,
And let that usher a more serious deed. [*Exit.*

Mill. Whilst you desire his grief, my heart shall bleed. [*Exit.*

H. Clare. Raymond Mounchensey, come, be frolic, friend;
This is the day thou hast expected long.

Ray. Pray God, dear Harry Clare, it prove so happy!

H. Clare. There's nought can alter it; be merry, lad.

Fabel. There's nought shall alter it; be lively, Raymond:
Stand any opposition 'gainst thy hope,
Art shall confront it with her largest scope. [*Exeunt.*

PETER FABEL, *solus.*

Fabel. Good old Mounchensey, is thy hap so ill,
That for thy bounty, and thy royal parts,
Thy kind alliance should be held in scorn;
And after all these promises by Clare,
Refuse to give his daughter to thy son,
Only because thy revenues cannot reach
To make her dowage of so rich a jointure
As can the heir of wealthy Jerningham?
And therefore is the false fox now in hand
To strike a match betwixt her and the other;
And the old gray-beards now are close together,
Plotting it in the garden. Is't even so?
Raymond Mounchensey, boy, have thou and I
Thus long at Cambridge read the liberal arts,
The metaphysics, magic, and those parts
Of the most secret deep philosophy?
Have I so many melancholy nights
Watch'd on the top of Peter-house highest tower,
And come we back unto our native home,
For want of skill to lose the wench thou lov'st?
We'll first hang Envil in such rings of mist
As never rose from any dampish fen;
I'll make the brinéd sea to rise at Ware,
And drown the marshes unto Stratford-bridge:
I'll drive the deer from Waltham in their walks,
And scatter them, like sheep, in every field.
We may perhaps be cross'd; but if we be,
He shall cross the devil that but crosses me.

Enter RAYMOND *and* Young JERNINGHAM.

But here comes Raymond, disconsolate and sad;
And here's the gallant that must have the wench.

Jer. I pry'thee, Raymond, leave these solemn dumps,
Revive thy spirits; thou that before hast been
More watchful than the day-proclaiming cock,
As sportive as a kid, as frank and merry
As mirth herself.

If aught in me may thy content procure,
It is thine own, thou may'st thyself assure.

Ray. Ha! Jerningham, if any but thyself
Had spoke that word, it would have come as cold
As the bleak northern winds upon the face
Of winter.
From thee, they have some power upon my blood;
Yet being from thee, had but that hollow sound
Come from the lips of any living man,
It might have won the credit of mine ear;
From thee it cannot.

Jer. If I understand thee, I am a villain:
What! dost thou speak in parables to thy friend?

Enter HARRY CLARE.

Come, boy, and make me this same groaning love,
Troubled with stitches and the cough o'th lungs,
That wept his eyes out when he was a child,
And ever since hath shot at hoodman-blind:
Make her leap, caper, jerk, and laugh, and sing,
And play me horse tricks.
Make Cupid wanton as his mother's dove;
But in this sort, boy, I would have thee love.

Fabel. Why, how now, madcap? what, my lusty
    Frank,
So near a wife, and will not tell your friend?
But you will to this gear in hugger-mugger:[10]
Art thou turn'd miser, rascal, in thy loves?

Jer. Who I? z'blood, what should all you see
in me, that I should look like a married man? ha!
am I bald? are my legs too little for my hose? if
I feel any thing in my forehead, I am a villain.
Do I wear a night-cap? do I bend in the hams?
What dost thou see in me, that I should be towards marriage? ha?

H. Clare. What, thou married? let me look upon
thee; rogue, who has given this out of thee? how
cam'st thou into this ill name? what company
hast thou been in, rascal?

Fabel. You are the man, sir, must have Millisent,
The match is making in the garden now;
Her jointure is agreed on, and the old men,
Your fathers, mean to launch their busy bags;[11]
But in the mean time to thrust Mounchensey off.
For colour of this new-intended match,
Fair Millisent to Cheston must be sent,
To take the approbation for a Nun,
Ne'er look upon me, lad, the match is done.

Jer. Raymond Mounchensey, now I touch thy
    grief
With the true feeling of a zealous friend.
And as for fair and beauteous Millisent,
With my vain breath I will not seek to slubber[12]

Her angel-like perfections: but thou know'st
That Essex hath the saint that I adore:
Where e'er didst meet me, that we two were jovial,
But like a wag thou hast not laugh'd at me,
And with regardless jesting mock'd my love?
How many a sad and weary summer's night,
My sighs have drunk the dew from off the earth,
And I have taught the nightingale to wake,
And from the meadows sprung the early lark
An hour before she should have list to sing:
I have loaded the poor minutes with my moans,
That I have made the heavy slow-pac'd hours
To hang like heavy clogs upon the day.
But, dear Mounchensey, had not my affection
Seiz'd on the beauty of another dame,
Before I'd wrong the chase, and leave the love
Of one so worthy, and so true a friend,
I will abjure both beauty and her sight,
And will in love become a counterfeit.

Moun. Dear Jerningham, thou hast begot my
    life,
And from the mouth of hell, where now I sate,
I feel my spirit rebound against the stars,
Thou hast conquer'd me, dear friend, in my free
    soul,
There time, nor death, can by their power controul.

Fabel. Frank Jerningham, thou art a gallant
    boy:
And were he not my pupil, I would say,
He were as fine a metal'd gentleman,
Of as free spirit, and of as fine a temper,
As is in England; and he is a man
That very richly may deserve thy love.
But, noble Clare, this while of our discourse,
What may Mounchensey's honour to thyself
Exact upon the measure of thy grace?

H. Clare. Raymond Mounchensey, I would have
    thee know,
He does not breathe this air, whose love I cherish,
And whose soul I love more than Mounchensey's:
Nor ever in my life did see the man
Whom, for his wit and many virtuous parts,
I think more worthy of my sister's love.
But since the matter grows unto this pass,
I must not seem to cross my father's will;
But when thou list to visit her by night,
My horse is saddled, and the stable door
Stands ready for thee: use them at thy pleasure.
In honest marriage wed her frankly, boy,
And if thou gett'st her, lad, God give thee joy.

Moun. Then, care away! let fate my fall pre-
    tend,
Back'd with the favours of so true a friend.

Fabel. Let us alone, to bustle for the set;
For age and craft with wit and art have met.
I'll make my spirits to dance such nightly jigs
Along the way 'twixt this and Tot'nam Cross,
The carriers' jades shall cast their heavy packs,
And the strong hedges scarce shall keep them in:
The milk-maids' cuts[13] shall turn the wenches off,
And lay their dossers[14] tumbling in the dust:
The frank and merry London 'prentices,
That come for cream and lusty country cheer,
Shall lose their way; and scrambling in the ditches
All night, shall whoop and hollow, cry and call,
Yet none to other find the way at all.
    Moun. Pursue the project scholar, what we can
        do
To help endeavour, join our lives thereto. [*Exeunt.*

SCENE III.—*The House of* Banks, *the Miller, at*
Waltham.

Enter BANKS, SIR JOHN, *and* SMUG.

    Banks. Take me with you, good Sir John[15]: a
plague on thee, Smug, and thou touchest liquor thou
art foundered straight—What! are your brains
always water-mills? must they ever run round?
    Smug. Banks, your ale is as a Philistine fox;—
nouns! there's fire i' th' tail on't;—you are a rogue
to charge us with mugs i' th' rearward;—a plague
of this wind, O, it tickles our catastrophe.
    Sir John. Neighbour Banks of Waltham, and
goodman Smug, the honest smith of Edmonton, as
I dwell betwixt you both, at Enfield, I know the
taste of both your ale-houses; they are good both,
smart both.——Hem, grass and hay,—we are all
mortal,—let's live 'till we die, and be merry, and
there's an end.
    Banks. Well said, sir John, you are of the same
humour still; and doth the water run the same way
still, boy?
    Smug. Vulcan was a rogue to him;—Sir John,
lock, lock, lock fast, sir John;—So, sir John, I'll
one of these years, when it shall please the god-
desses and the destinies, be drunk in your company;
that's all now, and God send us health.—Shall I
swear I love you?
    Sir John. No oaths, no oaths, good neighbour
        Smug,
We'll wet our lips together, and hug;
Carouse in private, and elevate the heart, and the
liver, and the lights, and the lights; mark you me,
within us for—hem—grass and hay,—we are all
mortal,—let's live till we die, and be merry, and
there's an end.

    Banks. But to our former motion about stealing
some venison; whither go we?
    Sir John. Into the forest, neighbour Banks; into
Brian's walk, the mad-keeper.
    Smug. Blood! I'll tickle your keeper.
    Banks. I'faith, thou art always drunk, when we
have need of thee.
    Smug. Need of me! heart, you shall have need
of me always, while there is iron in an anvil.
    Banks. Mr. Parson, may the Smith go (think
you) being in this taking?
    Smug. Go! I'll go, in spite of all the bells in
Waltham.
    Sir John. The question is, good neighbour Banks
—let me see, the moon shines to night,—there's not
a narrow bridge betwixt this and the forest,—his
brain may be settled ere night,—he may go, he may
go, neighbour Banks. Now we want none but the
company of mine host Blague, of the George at
Waltham: if he were here, our consort were full.
Look where comes my good host, the duke of Norfolk's man! and how? and how? A hem—grass
and hay—we are not yet mortal; let us live till we
die, and be merry, and there's an end.

Enter Host.

    Host. Ha! my Castilian dialogues; and art thou
in breath still, boy? Miller, doth the match hold?
Smith, I see by thy eyes thou hast been reading a
little Geneva print:[16] but wend we merrily to the
forest, to steal some of the king's deer? I'll meet
you, at the time appointed. Away, I have knights
and colonels at my house, and must tend the Hungarians.[17] If we be scared in the forest, we'll meet
in the church-porch at Enfield: is't correspondent?
    Banks. 'Tis well; but how if any of us should be
taken?
    Smug. He shall have ransom by my sword.
    Host. Tush, the knaves keepers are my bona so-
cias, and my pensioners—Nine o'clock—Be valiant,
my little Gogmagogs;—I'll fence with all the justices in Hertfordshire—I'll have a buck till I die;
I'll slay a doe while I live—Hold your bow strait
and steady; I serve the good duke of Norfolk.
    Smug. O rare! who, ho, ho, boy.
    Sir John. Peace, neighbour Smug! You see this
boor, a boor of the country, an illiterate boor, and
yet the citizen of good-fellows. Come, let's provide: a hem—grass and hay,—we are not yet all
mortal; we'll live till we die, and be merry, and
there's an end: come, Smug.
    Smug. Good night, Waltham—who, ho, ho, boy.
                    [*Exeunt.*

SCENE IV.— *A Room in the George Inn.*

Enter the Knights *and* Gentlemen *from Breakfast again.*

O. Moun. Nor I for thee, Clare, not of this:
What! hast thou fed me all this while with shalls?
And com'st to tell me now, thou lik'st it not?
Clare. I do not hold thy offer competent:
Nor do I like the assurance of thy land,
The title is so brangled with thy debts.[18]
O. Moun. Too good for thee: and, knight, thou
　　know'st it well,
I fawn'd not on thee for thy goods, not I,
'Twas thine own motion; that thy wife doth know.
L. Clare. Husband, it was so; he lies not in that.
Clare. Hold thy chat, quean.
O. Moun. To which I hearkened willingly, and
　　the rather,
Because I was persuaded it proceeded
From love thou bor'st to me and to my boy;
And gav'st him free access unto thy house,
Where he hath not behav'd him to thy child
But as befits a gentleman to do:
Nor is my poor distresséd state so low
That I'll shut up my doors, I warrant thee.
Clare. Let it suffice, Mounchensey, I mislike it;
Nor think thy son a match fit for my child.
O. Moun. I tell thee, Clare, his blood is good
　　and clear
As the best drop that panteth in thy veins:
But for this maid, thy fair and virtuous child,
She is no more disparag'd by thy baseness,
Than the most orient and the precious jewel,
Which still retains his lustre and his beauty,
Although a slave were owner of the same.
Clare. She is the last is left me to bestow;
And her I mean to dedicate to God.
O. Moun. You do, sir?
Clare.　　　　Sir, sir, I do; she is mine own.
O. Moun. And pity she is so:
Damnation dog thee and thy wretched pelf. [*Aside.*
Clare. Not thou, Mounchensey, shalt bestow my
　　child.
O. Moun. Neither shouldst thou bestow her
　　where thou meanest.
Clare. What wilt thou do?
O. Moun.　　　　No matter, let that be;
I will do that, perhaps, shall anger thee:
Thou hast wrong'd my love, and, by God's bless'd
　　angel,
Thou shalt well know it.
Clare.　　　　Tut, brave not me.

O. Moun. Brave thee, base churl! were't not for
　　manhood sake—
I say no more, but that there be some by
Whose blood is hotter than ours is,
Which, being stirr'd might makes us both repent
This foolish meeting.　But Harry Clare,
Although thy father hath abus'd my friendship,
Yet I love thee, I do, my noble boy,
I do, i'faith.
L. Clare. Ay, do, do, fill all the world with talk
of us, man; man, I never look'd for better at your
hands.
Fabel. I hop'd your great experience, and your
　　years,
Would have prov'd patience rather to your soul,
Than with this frantic and untamed passion
To whet their skeens;[19] and, but for that
I hope their friendships are too well confirm'd,
And their minds tempered with more kindly heat,
Than for their forward parent's frowardness,
That they should break forth into public brawls.
Howe'er the rough hand of the untoward world
Hath moulded your proceedings in this matter,
Yet I am sure the first intent was love:
Then since the first spring was so sweet and warm,
Let it die gently, ne'er kill it with a scorn.
Ray. O thou base world! how leprous is that
　　soul
That is once lim'd in that polluted mud!
O sir Arthur! you have startled his free active
　　spirit
With a too sharp spur for his mind to bear.
Have patience, sir; the remedy to woe,
Is, to leave that of force we must forego.
Mill. And I must take a twelvemonth's appro-
　　bation,
That in the meantime this sole and private life,
At the year's end may fashion me a wife.
But, sweet Mounchensey, ere this year be done,
Thou'st be a friar, if that I be a nun.
And, father, ere young Jerningham's I'll be,
I will turn mad, to spite both him and thee. [*Aside.*
Clare. Wife, come to horse; and, housewife,
　　make you ready:
For if I live, I swear by this good light,
I'll see you lodg'd in Cheston-house to-night.
　　　　　　　　　　　　　　　　　[*Exeunt.*
O. Moun. Raymond, away, thou see'st how mat-
　　ters fall.
Churl, hell consume thee, and thy pelf and all!
　　　　　　　　　　　　　　　　　[*Exit.*
Fabel. Now, Mr. Clare, you see how matters
　　fadge;[20]

Your Millisent must needs be made a nun.
Well, sir, we are the men must ply the match:
Hold you your peace, and be a looker-on:
And send her unto Cheston, where he will,
I'll send me fellows of a handful high
Into the cloisters where the nuns frequent,
Shall make them skip like does about the dale;
And make the lady prioress of the house
To play at leap-frog naked in their smocks,
Until the merry wenches at their mass
Cry teehee, weehee;
And tickling these mad lasses in their flanks,
Shall sprawl and squeak, and pinch their fellow
    nuns.
Be lively, boys, before the wench we lose,
I'll make the abbess wear the canon's hose. [*Exeunt.*

   Re-enter HARRY CLARE, FRANK JERNINGHAM,
     PETER FABEL, *and* MILLISENT.

H. Clare. Spite now hath done her worst; sister,
    be patient.
   Jer. Forewarn'd poor Raymond's company! O
    heaven!
When the composure of weak frailty meet
Upon this mart of dirt, O then weak love
Must in her own unhappiness be silent,
And wink on all deformities.
   Mill.   'Tis well:
Where's Raymond, brother? Where's my dear
    Mounchensey?
Would we might weep together, and then part,
Our sighing parley would much ease my heart.
   Fabel. Sweet beauty, fold your sorrows in the
    thought
Of future reconcilement: let your tears
Show you a woman, but be no farther spent
Than from the eyes: for sweet experience says,
That love is firm that's flatter'd with delays.
   Mill. Alas, sir, think you I shall e'er be his?
   Fabel. As sure as parting smiles on future bliss.
Yond comes my friend; see, he hath doated
So long upon your beauty, that your want
Will with a pale retirement waste his blood:
For in true love music doth sweetly dwell;
Sever'd, these less worlds bear within them hell.

     Enter MOUNCHENSEY.

   Moun. Harry and Frank, you are enjoined to
    wean
Your friendship from me, we must part; the breath
Of all advis'd corruption; pardon me,
Faith, I must say so; you may think I love you,
I breathe not rougher spite do sever us;

We'll meet by stealth, sweet friend, by stealth you
    twain;
Kisses are sweetest got by struggling pain.
   Jer. Our friendship dies not, Raymond.
   Moun. Pardon me:
I am busied; I have lost my faculties,
And buried them in Millisent's clear eyes.
   Mill. Alas! sweet love, what shall become of
    me?
I must to Cheston to the nunnery,
I shall ne'er see thee more.
   Moun.   How, sweet!
I'll be thy votary, we'll often meet:
This kiss divides us, and breathes soft adieu—
This be a double charm to keep both true.
   Fabel. Have done, your fathers may chance spy
    your parting.
Refuse not you by any means, good sweetness,
To go into the nunnery, for from hence
Must we beget your loves sweet happiness:
You shall not stay there long, your harder bed
Shall be more soft, when nun and maid are dead.

     Enter BILBO.

   Moun. Now, sirrah, what's the matter?
   Bilbo. Marry, you must to horse presently; that
villanous old gouty churl, sir Arthur Clare, longs
till he be at the nunnery.
   H. Clare. How, sir?
   Bilbo. O, I cry you mercy, he is your father, sir,
indeed; but I am sure, that there's less affinity
betwixt your two natures, than there is between
a broker and a cutpurse.
   Moun. Bring me my gelding, sirrah.
   Bilbo. Well, nothing grieves me, but for the
poor wench; she must now cry vale to lobster
pies, artichokes, and all such meats of mortality.
Poor gentlewoman! the sign must not be in Virgo
any longer with her, and that me grieves: farewell.
     Poor Millisent
      Must pray and repent;
        O fatal wonder!
      She'll now be no fatter,
       Love must not come at her,
        Yet she shall be kept under. [*Exit.*
   Jer. Farewell dear Raymond.
   H. Clare.   Friend, adieu.
   Mill.   Dear sweet,
No joy enjoys my heart till we next meet. [*Exeunt.*
   Fabel. Well, Raymond, now the tide of discon-
    tent
Beats in thy face; but ere't be long, the wind
Shall turn the flood. We must to Waltham-abbey,

And as fair Millisent in Cheston lives
A most unwilling nun, so thou shalt there
Become a beardless novice; to what end,
Let time and future accidents declare:
Taste thou my sleights, thy love I'll only share.

   Moun. Turn friar? Come, my good counsellor,
      let's go,
Yet that disguise will hardly shroud my woe.
                                [Exeunt.

SCENE V.—*A Room in* Cheston (i. e. Cheshunt)
                Priory.

Enter the PRIORESS OF CHESTON, *with a* Nun *or
two,* SIR ARTHUR CLARE, SIR RALPH JERNING-
HAM, HENRY *and* FRANK, *the* Lady *and* BILBO,
with MILLISENT.

   L. Clare. Madam,
The love unto this holy sisterhood,
And our confirm'd opinion of your zeal,
Hath truly won us to bestow our child
Rather on this than any neighbouring cell.

   Pri. Jesus' daughter, Mary's child,
Holy matron, woman mild,
For thee a mass shall still be said,
Every sister drop a bead;
And those again succeeding them,
For you shall sing a *Requiem.*

   Frank. The wench is gone, Harry, she is no more
a woman of this world—Mark her well, she looks
like a nun already: what think'st on her?

   H. Clare. By my faith, her face comes handsomely
to't.
But peace, let's hear the rest.

   Clare. Madam, for a twelvemonth's approba-
      tion,
We mean to make this trial of our child.
Your care, and our dear blessing in mean time,
We pray may prosper this intended work.

   Pri. May your happy soul be blithe,
That so truly pay your tithe:
He that many children gave,
'Tis fit that he one child should have.
Then, fair virgin, hear my spell,
For I must your duty tell.

   Mill. Good men and true, stand together,
And hear your charge.

   Pri. First, a mornings take your book,
The glass wherein yourself must look;
Your young thoughts, so proud and jolly,
Must be turn'd to motions holy;
For your busk attires, and toys,
Have your thoughts on heavenly joys;

And for all your follies past,
You must do penance, pray, and fast.

   Bilbo. Let her take heed of fasting; and if ever
she hurt herself with praying, I'll ne'er trust
beast.

   Mill. This goes hard, by'r lady.   *[Aside.*

   Pri. You shall ring the sacring bell,[21]
Keep your hours and tell your knell,
Rise at midnight to your matins,
Read your psalter, sing your latins;
And when your blood shall kindle pleasure,
Scourge yourself in plenteous measure.

   Mill. Worse and worse, by St. Mary. *[Aside.*

   Frank. Sirrah, Hal, how does she hold her countenance?—well, go thy ways, if ever thou prove a
nun, I'll build an abbey.

   H. Clare. She may be a nun; but if ever she
prove an anchoress, I'll dig her grave with my
nails.

   Frank. To her again, mother.

   H. Clare. Hold thine own, wench.

   Pri. You must read the morning mass,
You must creep unto the cross,[22]
Put cold ashes on your head,
Have a hair-cloth for your bed.

   Bilbo. She had rather have a man in her bed.

   Pri. Bind your beads, and tell your needs,
Your holy aves and your creeds:
Holy maid, this must be done,
If you mean to live a nun.

   Mill. The holy maid will be no nun. *[Aside.*

   Clare. Madam, we have some business of im-
      port,
And must be gone:
Will 't please you take my wife into your closet,
Who farther will acquaint you with my mind:
And so, good madam, for this time adieu.
              [Exeunt Women, *and* CLARE.

   Sir R. Well now, Frank Jerningham, how sayest
      thou?
To be brief.
What wilt thou say for all this, if we two,
Her father and myself, can bring about,
That we convert this nun to be a wife,
And thou the husband to this pretty nun?
How then, my lad? ha, Frank; it may be done.

   H. Clare. Ay, now it works.

   Frank. O God, sir! you amaze me at your
      speech,[23]
Think with yourself, sir, what a thing it were
To cause a recluse to remove her vow
A maimèd, contrite, and repentant soul,
Ever mortified with fasting and with prayer,

101

Whose thoughts, even as her eyes, are fix'd on
    heaven;
To draw a virgin thus devout with zeal,
Back to the world; O impious deed!
Nor by the canon law can it be done,
Without a dispensation from the church:
Besides, she is so prone unto this life,
As she 'll even shriek to hear a husband nam'd.
    Bilbo. Ay, a poor innocent she!—well, here 's
    no knavery;
He flouts the old fools to their teeth.   [*Aside.*
    Sir R. Boy, I am glad to hear
Thou mak'st such scruple of that conscience
And in a man so young as is yourself,
I promise you 'tis very seldom seen.
But Frank, this is a trick, a mere device,
A sleight plotted betwixt her father and myself,
To thrust Mounchensey's nose beside the cushion;
That being thus debarr'd of all access,
Time yet may work him from her thoughts,
And give thee ample scope to thy desires.
    Bilbo. A plague on you both for a couple of
    Jews.   [*Aside.*
    H. Clare. How now, Frank, what say you to that?
    Frank. Let me alone, I warrant thee.
                      [*To* H. Clare.
Sir, assured that this motion doth proceed
From your most kind and fatherly affection,
I do dispose my liking to your pleasure:
But for it is a matter of such moment
As holy marriage, I must crave thus much,
To have some conference with my ghostly father,
Friar Hildersham, here by, at Waltham abbey
To be absolv'd of things, that it is fit
None only but my confessór should know.
    Sir R. With all my heart, he is a reverend man:
And to-morrow morning we will meet all at the
    abbey,
Where, by the opinion of that reverend man,
We will proceed; I like it passing well.
Till then we part, boy; ay, think of it, farewell:
A parent's care no mortal tongue can tell. [*Exeunt.*

SCENE VI.—*Before the Gate of the* Priory.

Enter Sir Arthur Clare, *and* Raymond Moun-
    chensey, *like a* Friar.

    Clare. Holy young novice, I have told you now
My full intent, and do refer the rest
To your professed secrecy and care:
And see,
Our serious speech hath stolen upon the way,
That we are come unto the abbey gate.

Because I know Mounchensey is a fox,
That craftily doth overlook my doings,
I 'll not be seen, not I; tush, I have done,
I had a daughter, but she 's now a nun:
Farewell, dear son, farewell.   [*Exit.*
    Moun. Fare you well--Ay, you have done:
Your daughter, sir, shall not be long a nun.
O my rare tutor! never mortal brain
Plotted out such a plot of policy;
And my dear bosom is so great with laughter,
Begot by his simplicity and error,
My soul is fall'n in labour with her joy.
O my friends, Frank Jerningham, and Clare!
Did you but know but how this jest takes fire,
That good sir Arthur, thinking me a novice,
Hath even pour'd himself into my bosom,
O you would vent your spleens with tickling mirth.
But, Raymond, peace, and have an eye about,
For fear perhaps some of the nuns look out.
    Peace and charity within,
Never touch'd with deadly sin;
I cast holy water pure
On this wall, and on this door,
That from evil shall defend,
And keep you from the ugly fiend:
Evil sprite, by night nor day,
Shall approach, or come this way;
Elf nor fairy, by this grace,
Day nor night shall haunt this place.
    Holy maidens—   [*Knocks.*
    [*Answer within.*] Who 's that which knocks? ha,
    who 's there?
    Moun. Gentle nun, here is a friar.

Enter Nun.

    Nun. A friar without? now Christ us save:
Holy man, what would'st thou have?
    Moun. Holy maid, I hither come
From friar and father Hildersham,
By the favour and the grace
Of the Prioress of this place,
Amongst you all to visit one
That 's come for approbation;
Before she was as now you are,
The daughter of sir Arthur Clare;
But since she now became a nun,
Call'd Millisent of Edmonton.[24]
    Nun. Holy man, repose you there,
This news I 'll to our abbess bear,
To tell what a man is sent,
And your message, and intent.
    Moun. Benedicite.
    Nun.   Benedicite.   [*Exit.*

Moun. Do, my good plump wench; if all fall
  right,
I 'll make your sisterhood one less by night.
Now, happy fortune, speed this merry drift,
I like a wench comes roundly to her shrift.

Enter LADY CLARE *and* MILLISENT.

L. Clare. Have friars recourse then to the house
  of nuns ?
Mill. Madam, it is the order of this place,
When any virgin comes for approbation,
(Lest that for fear, or such sinister practice,
She should be forc'd to undergo this veil,
Which should proceed from conscience and devotion)
A visitor is sent from Waltham house,
To take the true confession of the maid.
   L. Clare. Is that the order ? I commend it well :
You to your shrift, I 'll back unto the cell.   [*Exit.*
   Moun. Life of my soul ! bright angel !
   Mill. What means the friar ?
   Moun. O Millisent, 'tis I.
   Mill. My heart misgives me ; I should know that
  voice.
You ? who are you ? the holy virgin bless me !
Tell me your name : you shall ere you confess me.
   Moun. Mounchensey, thy true friend.
   Mill. My Raymond ! my dear heart !
Sweet life, give leave to my distracted soul
To wake a little from this swoon of joy.
By what means cam'st thou to assume this shape ?
   Moun. By means of Peter Fabel, my kind tutor,
Who in the habit of friar Hildersham,
Frank Jerningham's old friend and confessor,
Plotted by Frank, by Fabel, and myself,
And so delivered to sir Arthur Clare,
Who brought me here unto the abbey gate,
To be his nun-made daughter's visitor.
   Mill. You are all sweet traitors to my poor old
  father.
O my dear life, I was a dreamed to-night,
That as I was praying in my psalter,
There came a spirit unto me as I kneel'd,
And by his strong persuasions tempted me
To leave this nunnery : and methought
He came in the most glorious angel shape,
That mortal eye did ever look upon.
Ha ! thou art sure that spirit, for there 's no form
Is in mine eye so glorious as thine own.
   Moun. O thou idolatress, that dost this worship
To him whose likeness is but praise of thee !
Thou bright unsetting star, which through this veil,
For very envy, mak'st the sun look pale.
   Mill. Well, visitor, lest that perhaps my mother

Should think the friar too strict in his decrees,
I this confess to my sweet ghostly father ;
If chaste pure love be sin, I must confess,
I have offended three years now with thee.
   Moun. But do you yet repent you of the same ?
   Mill. I'faith I cannot.
   Moun.   Nor will I absolve thee
Of that sweet sin, though it be venial :
Yet have the penance of a thousand kisses ;
And I enjoin you to this pilgrimage :—
That in the evening you bestow yourself
Here in the walk near to the willow ground,
Where I 'll be ready both with men and horse
To wait your coming, and convey you hence
Unto a lodge I have in Enfield Chase :
No more reply if that you yield consent :
I see more eyes upon our stay are bent.
   Mill. Sweet life, farewell, 'tis done, let that
  suffice ;
What my tongue fails, I send thee by mine eyes.
                         [*Exit.*

Enter FABEL, HARRY CLARE, *and* JERNINGHAM.

   Jer. Now, visitor, how does this new-made nun ?
   H. Clare. Come, come, how does she, noble
  capuchin ?
   Moun. She may be poor in spirit, but for the
  flesh
'Tis fat and plump, boys. Ah, rogues, there is
A company of girls would turn you all friars.
   Fabel. But how, Mounchensey, how, lad, for
  the wench ?
   Moun. Zounds, lads (i'faith I thank my holy
  habit,)
I have confess'd her, and the lady prioress
Hath given me ghostly counsel, with her blessing.
And how say ye, boys,
If I be chose the weekly visitor !
   H. Clare. Blood ! she 'll have ne'er a nun un-
bag'd to sing mass then.
   Jer. The abbot of Waltham will have as many
children to put to nurse, as he has calves in the
marsh.
   Moun. Well, to be brief, the nun will soon at
night turn Lippit ; if I can but devise to quit her
cleanly of the nunnery, she is mine own.
   Fabel. But sirrah, Raymond, what news of Peter
Fabel at the house ?
   Moun. Tush, he is the only man, a necromancer,
and a conjuror, that works for young Mounchensey
altogether ; and if it be not for friar Benedic, that
he can cross him by his learned skill, the wench is
gone, Fabel will fetch her out by very magic.

Fabel. Stands the wind there, boy? keep them in
          that key,
The wench is ours before to-morrow day.
Well, Harry and Frank, as ye are gentlemen,
Stick to us close this once; you know your fathers
Have men and horse lie ready still at Cheston,
To watch the coast be clear, to scout about,
And have an eye unto Mounchensey's walks
Therefore you two may hover thereabouts,
And no man will suspect you for the matter:
Be ready but to take her at our hands,
Leave us to scamble,[25] for her getting out.

Jer. Blood! if all Hertfordshire were at our
heels, we'll carry her away in spite of them.

H. Clare. But whither, Raymond?

Moun. To Brian's upper lodge in Enfield Chase;
He is mine honest friend, and a tall-keeper:[26]
I'll send my man unto him presently,
To acquaint him with your coming and intent.

Fabel. Be brief, and secret.

Moun.   Soon at night, remember
You bring your horses to the willow ground.

Jer. 'Tis done, no more.

H. Clare.   We will not fail the hour,
My life and fortune now lie in your power.

Fabel. About our business! Raymond, let's away,
Think of your hour, it draws well off the day.
                                    [*Exeunt.*

SCENE VII.—Enfield Chase.

Enter BLAGUE, BANKS, SMUG, *and* SIR JOHN.

Blague. Come, ye Hungarian pilchers,[27] we are
once more come under the Zona Torrida of the
forest; let's be resolute; let's fly to and again;
and the devil come, we'll put him to his interrogatories, and not budge a foot. What! foot, I'll
put fire into you, ye shall all three serve the good
duke of Norfolk.

Smug. Mine host, my bully, my precious consul,
my noble Holofernes, I have been drunk in thy
house twenty times and ten; all's one for that:
I was last night in the third heaven, my brain was
poor, it had yeast in't, but now I am a man of
action; is't not so, lad?

Banks. Why, now thou hast two of the liberal
sciences about thee, wit and reason, thou mayest
serve the duke of Europe.

Smug. I will serve the duke of Christendom, and
do him more credit in his cellar, than all the plate
in his buttery; is't not so, lad?

Sir John. Mine host, and Smug, stand there:
Banks, you and your horse keep together, but lie
close, show no tricks for fear of the keeper. If we
be scar'd, we'll meet in the church-porch at Enfield.

Smug. Content, sir John.

Banks. Smug, dost not thou remember the tree
thou fellest out of last night.

Smug. Tush, and't had been as high as an abbey,
I should ne'er have hurt myself; I have fall'n into
the river, coming home from Waltham, and 'scaped
drowning.

Sir John. Come, sever, fear no spirits, we'll have
a buck presently; we have watch'd later than this
for a doe, mine host.

Host. Thou speakest as true as velvet.

Sir John. Why then come—grass and hay, &c.
                                    [*Exeunt.*

Enter HARRY CLARE, JERNINGHAM, *and*
MILLISENT.

H. Clare. Frank Jerningham!

Jer. Speak, softly, rogue, how now?

H. Clare. 'Sfoot, we shall lose our way, it's so
dark: whereabouts are we?

Jer. Why man, at Porter's gate,
The way lies right: hark, the clock strikes at Enfield, what's the hour?

H. Clare. Ten, the bell says.

Jer. A lie's in's throat, it was but eight when
we set out of Cheston; sir John and his sexton are
at their ale to-night, the clock runs at random.

H. Clare. Nay, as sure as thou liv'st, the villanous vicar is abroad in the chase this dark night:
the stone priest steals more venison than half the
country.

Jer. Millisent, how dost thou?

Mill.   Sir, very well.
I would to God we were at Brian's lodge.

H. Clare. We shall anon—nouns, hark!
What means this noise?

Jer.   Stay, I hear horsemen.

H. Clare.   I hear footmen too.

Jer. Nay then I have it: we have been discovered,
And we are followed by our father's men.

Mill. Brother, and friend, alas! what shall
          we do?

H. Clare. Sister, speak softly, or we are descry'd,
They are hard upon us, whatsoe'er they be;
Shadow yourself behind this brake of fern,
We'll get into the wood, and let them pass.

Enter SIR JOHN, BLAGUE, SMUG, *and* BANKS; *one
after another.*

Sir John. Grass and hay, we are all mortal! the
keeper's abroad, and there's an end.

Banks. Sir John!

Sir John. Neighbour Banks, what news?

Banks. Zounds, sir John, the keepers are abroad; I was hard by 'em.

Sir John. Grass and hay, where's mine host Blague?

Blague. Here, metropolitan; the Philistines are upon us, be silent: let us serve the good duke of Norfolk.—But where is Smug?

Smug. Here: a pox on you all, dogs; I have killed the greatest buck in Brian's walk:—Shift for yourselves, all the keepers are up; let's meet in Enfield church porch:—Away, we are all taken else. [*Exeunt.*

Enter BRIAN, *with his man* RALPH *and his Hound.*

Brian. Ralph, hear'st thou any stirring?

Ralph. I heard one speak here hard by in the bottom. Peace, master, speak low—nouns, if I did not hear a bow go off and the buck bray, I never heard deer in my life.

Brian. When went your fellows into their walks?

Ralph. An hour ago.

Brian. Life! is there stealers abroad, and we cannot hear of them?
Where the devil are my men to-night?
Sirrah, go up and wind toward Buckley's lodge:
I'll cast about the bottom with my hound,
And I will meet thee under Cony-oak.

Ralph. I will, sir. [*Exit.*

Brian. How now! by the mass, my hound stays upon something; hark, hark, Bowman, hark, hark there.

Mill. Brother, Frank Jerningham, brother Clare!

Brian. Peace: that's a woman's voice—Stand; who's there? Stand, or I'll shoot.

Mill. O Lord! hold your hands, I mean no harm, sir.

Brian. Speak, who are you?

Mill. I am a maid, sir—who? master Brian?

Brian. The very same: sure I should know her voice—Mistress Millisent!

Mill. Ay; it is I, sir.

Brian. God for his passion! what make you here alone? I look'd for you at my lodge an hour ago. What means your company to leave you thus? Who brought you hither?

Mill. My brother, sir, and master Jerningham; who, hearing folks about us in the chase, feared it had been sir Arthur my father, who had pursued us, and thus dispers'd ourselves till they were past us.

Brian. But where be they?

Mill. They be not far off, here about the grove.

Enter HARRY CLARE *and* JERNINGHAM.

H. Clare. Be not afraid, man; I hear Brian's tongue, that's certain.

Jer. Call softly for your sister.

H. Clare. Millisent!

Mill. Ay, brother, here.

Brian. Master Clare!

H. Clare. I told you it was Brian.

Brian. Who is that, Master Jerningham? You are a couple of hot-shots: does a man commit his wench to you, to put her to grass at this time of night?

Jer. We heard a noise about us in the chase,
And fearing that our fathers had pursu'd us,
Severed ourselves.

H. Clare. 　　　Brian, how hapdst thou on her?

Brian. Seeking for stealers that are abroad to-night,
My hound stay'd on her, and so found her out.

H. Clare. They were these stealers that affrighted us;
I was hard upon them when they hors'd their deer,
And I perceive they took me for a keeper.

Brian. Which way took they?

Jer. Towards Enfield.

Brian. A plague upon't, that's the damn'd priest, and Blague of the George, he that serves the good duke of Norfolk.
[*A noise within.*] Follow, follow, follow.

H. Clare. Peace; that's my father's voice.

Brian. Nouns, you suspected them, and now they are here indeed.

Mill. Alas! what shall we do?

Brian. If you go to the lodge, you are surely taken:
Strike down the wood to Enfield presently,
And if Mounchensey come, I'll send him to you.
Let me alone to bustle with your fathers;
I warrant you that I will keep them play
Till you have quit the chase; away, away.
Who's there?

Enter the Knights.

Sir R. In the king's name pursue the ravisher.

Brian. Stand, or I'll shoot.

Clare. Who's there?

Brian. I am the keeper, that do charge you stand;
You have stolen my deer.

Clare. We stolen thy deer? we do pursue a thief.

Brian. You are arrant thieves, and ye have stolen my deer.

Clare. We are knights; sir Arthur Clare, and sir Ralph Jerningham.

Brian. The more your shame, that knights should be such thieves.

Clare. Who, or what art thou?

Brian. My name is Brian, keeper of this walk.

Clare. O Brian, a villain!
Thou hast receiv'd my daughter to thy lodge.

Brian. You have stolen the best deer in my walk to-night: my deer

Clare. My daughter—
Stop not my way.

Brian. What make you in my walk? you have stolen the best buck in my walk to-night.

Clare. My daughter—

Brian. My deer—

Sir R. Where is Mounchensey?

Brian. Where is my buck?

Clare. I will complain me of thee to the king.

Brian. I'll complain unto the king, you spoil his game: 'tis strange that men of your account and calling will offer it. I tell you true, sir Arthur and sir Ralph, that none but you have only spoil'd my game.

Clare. I charge you stop us not.

Brian. I charge you both get out of my ground. Is this a time for such as you, men of place, and of your gravity, to be abroad a thieving? 'tis a shame; and afore God if I had shot at you, I had served you well enough. 　　　　　　*[Exeunt.*

SCENE VIII.—*Before the Porch of* Enfield *Church.*

Enter BANKS, *the Miller, wet on his Legs.*

Banks. Foot, here's a dark night indeed: I think I have been in fifteen ditches between this and the forest—Soft, here's Enfield church: I am so wet with climbing over into an orchard, for to steal some filberts—Well, here I'll sit in the church-porch, and wait for the rest of my consorts.

Enter Sexton.

Sex. Here's a sky as black as Lucifer, God bless us. Here was goodman Theophilus buried, he was the best nut-cracker that ever dwelt in England—Well, 'tis nine o'clock, 'tis time to ring curfew. Lord bless us, what a white thing is that in the church-porch! O Lord, my legs are too weak for my body, my hair is too stiff for my night-cap, my heart fails; this is the ghost of Theophilus:

O Lord, it follows me, I cannot say my prayers and one would give me a thousand pound. Good spirit! I have bowled and drunk and followed the hounds with you a thousand times, though I have not the spirit now to deal with you—O Lord!

Enter Priest.

Sir John. Grass and hay! we are all mortal; who's there?

Sex. We are grass and hay indeed: I know you to be master parson, by your phrase.

Sir John. Sexton!

Sex. I, sir.

Sir John. For mortality's sake, what's the matter?

Sex. O Lord, I am a man of another element; master Theophilus's ghost is in the church porch. There was an hundred cats, all fire, dancing even now, and they are clomb up to the top of the steeple: I'll not into the belfry for a world.

Sir John. O goodman Solomon, I have been about a deed of darkness to-night: O Lord! I saw fifteen spirits in the forest like white bulls; if I lie, I am an errant thief: mortality haunts us—grass and hay! the devil's at our heels, and let's hence to the parsonage. 　　　　　　*[Exeunt.*

　　[The Miller *comes out very softly.*

Miller. What noise was that? 'tis the watch; sure that villanous unlucky rogue Smug is ta'en, upon my life, and then all our knavery comes out: I heard one cry, sure.

Enter Host BLAGUE.

Host. If I go steal any more venison, I am a paradox: foot, I can scarce bear the sin of my flesh in the day, 'tis so heavy: if I turn not honest, and serve the good duke of Norfolk as a true mareterraneum skinker[28] should do, let me never look higher than the element of a constable.

Miller. By the mass there are some watchmen; I hear them name master constable: I would my mill were an eunuch, and wanted her stones, so I were hence.

Host. Who's there?

Miller. 'Tis the constable, by this light: I'll steal hence, and if I can meet mine host Blague, I'll tell him how Smug is ta'en, and will him to look to himself. 　　　　　　*[Exit.*

Host. What the devil is that white thing? this same is a church-yard, and I have heard that ghosts and villanous goblins have been seen here.

Enter Sexton *and* Priest.

Sir John. Grass and hay! oh that I could conjure! we saw a spirit here in the church-yard; and in the fallow field there's the devil with a man's body upon his back in a white sheet.

Sex. It may be a woman's body, sir John.

Sir John. If she be a woman, the sheets damn her.

Lord bless us, what a night of mortality is this!

Host. Priest!

Sir John. Mine host!

Host. Did you not see a spirit all in white cross you at the stile?

Sex. O no, mine host! but there sat one in the porch: I have not breath enough left to bless me from the devil.

Host. Who's that?

Sir John. The sexton, almost frighted out of his wits: Did you see Banks, or Smug?

Host. No, they are gone to Waltham, sure. I would fain hence; come, let's to my house; I'll ne'er serve the duke of Norfolk in this fashion again whilst I breathe. If the devil be among us, it's time to hoist sail, and cry roomer. Keep together; sexton, thou art secret. What! let's be comfortable one to another.

Sir John. We are all mortal, mine host.

Host. True; and I'll serve God in the night hereafter, afore the duke of Norfolk.　　*[Exeunt.*

SCENE IX.—*A Room in a House opposite the George Inn.*

Enter SIR ARTHUR CLARE, *and* SIR RALPH JERNINGHAM, *trussing their Points, as newly up.*

Sir R. Good-morrow, gentle knight;
A happy day after your short night's rest.

Clare. Ha, ha, sir Ralph, stirring so soon indeed?
By'r lady, sir, rest would have done right well:
Our riding late last night has made me drowsy.
Go to, go to, those days are gone with us.

Sir R. Sir Arthur, sir Arthur, care go with those days,
Let 'em even go together, let 'em go;
'Tis time, i'faith, that we were in our graves,
When children leave obedience to their parents
When there's no fear of God, no care, no duty.
Well, well, nay it shall not do, it shall not:
No, Mounchensey, thou'lt hear on't, thou shalt,
Thou shalt, i'faith;
I'll hang thy son, if there be law in England.
A man's child ravish'd from a nunnery!
This is rare! well, there's one gone for friar Hildersham.

Clare. Nay, gentle knight, do not vex thus, it will but hurt your heat; you cannot grieve more than I do, but to what end; but hark you, sir Ralph, I was about to say something; it makes no matter: but hark you, in your ear; the friar's a knave: but God forgive me, a man cannot tell neither: 'sfoot, I am so out of patience, I know not what to say.

Sir R. There's one went for the friar an hour ago. Comes he not yet? 'Sfoot, if I do find knavery under's cowl, I'll tickle him, I'll ferk him —Here, here, he's here, he's here. Good-morrow, friar; good morrow, gentle friar.

Enter HILDERSHAM.

Clare. Good-morrow, father Hildersham, good-morrow.

Hild. Good-morrow, reverend knights, unto you both.

Clare. Father, how now? You hear how matters go;
I am undone, my child is cast away;
You did your best, at least I think the best:
But we are all cross'd; flatly, all is dash'd.

Hild. Alas! good knights, how might the matter be?
Let me understand your grief, for charity.

Clare. Who does not understand my grief?
Alas! alas!
And yet you do not: will the church permit
A nun, in approbation of her habit,
To be ravished?

Hild. A holy woman, Benedicite!
Now God forefend that any should presume
To touch the sister of a holy house.

Clare. Jesus deliver me!

Sir R. Why, Millisent, the daughter of this knight,
Is out of Cheston taken this last night.

Hild. Was that fair maiden late become a nun?

Sir R. Was she, quoth a? Knavery, knavery, knavery, knavery; I smell it, I smell it, i'faith; is the wind in that door? Is it even so? Dost thou ask me that now?

Hild. It is the first time that e'er I heard of it.

Clare. That's very strange.

Sir R. Why, tell me friar, tell me, thou art counted a holy man; do not play the hypocrite with me, (nor bear with me)[29] I cannot dissemble: did I aught but by thy own consent? by thy allowance? nay, farther, by thy warrant?

Hild. Why, reverend knight—

Sir R. Unreverend friar—

Hild. Nay, then give me leave, sir, to depart in
  quiet:
I had hop'd you had sent for me to some other end.

 Clare. Nay, stay, good friar, if anything hath hap'd
About this matter, in thy love to us,
That thy strict order cannot justify,
Admit it to be so, we will cover it;
Take no care, man:
Disclaim not yet my counsel and advice,
The wisest man that is may be o'er-reach'd.

 Hild. Sir Arthur, by my order, and my faith,
I know not what you mean.

 Sir R. By your order, and by your faith? this
is most strange of all: why tell me, friar, are not
you confessor to my son Frank?

 Hild. Yes, that I am.

 Sir R. And did not this good knight here, and
  myself,
Confess with you, being his ghostly father,
To deal with him about th' unbanded marriage
Betwixt him and that fair young Millisent?

 Hild. I never heard of any match intended.

 Clare. Did not we break our minds that very
  time,
That our device in making her a nun
Was but a colour, and a very plot
To put by young Mounchensey? Is't not true?

 Hild. The more I strive to know what you
  should mean,
The less I understand you.

 Sir R. Did not you tell us still, how Peter Fabel
At length would cross us, if we took not heed?

 Hild. I have heard of one that is a great magician,
But he's about the university.

 Sir R. Did you not send your novice, Benedic,
To persuade the girl to leave Mounchensey's love,
To cross that Peter Fabel in his art,
And to that purpose made him visitor?

 Hild. I never sent my novice from my house,
Nor have we made our visitation yet.

 Clare. Never sent him! nay, did he not go?
and did not I direct him to the house, and confer
with him by the way? and did not he tell me what
charge he had received from you, word by word, as
I requested at your hands?

 Hild. That you shall know; he came along
  with me,
And stays without:—Come hither, Benedic.

Enter BENEDIC.

Young Benedic, were you e'er sent by me
To Cheston nunnery for a visitor?

 Ben. Never, sir, truly.

 Sir R. Stranger than all the rest!

 Clare. Did not I direct you to the house,
Confer with you from Waltham abbey
Unto Cheston wall?

 Ben. I never saw you, sir, before this hour.

 Sir R. The devil thou did'st not!—Ho, Chamberlain!

Enter Chamberlain.

 Cham. Anon, anon.

 Sir R. Call mine host Blague hither.

 Cham. I will send one over, sir, to see if he be
up: I think he be scarce stirring yet.

 Sir R. Why, knave, didst thou not tell me an
hour ago mine host was up?

 Cham. Ay, sir, my master's up.

 Sir R. You knave, is he up, and is he not up?
Dost thou mock me?

 Cham. Ay, sir, my master is up; but I think
master Blague indeed be not stirring.

 Sir R. Why, who's thy master? Is not the
master of the house thy master?

 Cham. Yes, sir, but master Blague dwells over
the way.

 Clare. Is not this the George? Before Jove
there's some villany in this.

 Cham. Foot, our sign's remov'd; this is strange!

Enter BLAGUE, *trussing his Points.*

 Host. Chamberlain, speak up to the new lodgings.
Bid Nell look well to the bak'd meat.
How now, my old Jenerts bank, my horse,
My castle;[30] lie in Waltham all night, and
Not under the canopy of your host Blague's house?

 Clare. Mine host, mine host, we lay all night at
the George in Waltham; but whether the George
be your fee-simple or no, 'tis a question: look upon
your sign.

 Host. Body of St. George, this is mine over-
thwart neighbour hath done this to seduce my blind
customers. I'll tickle his catastrophe for this; if
I do not indict him at the next assizes for bur-
glary, let me die of the yellows,[31] for I see it is no
boot in these days to serve the good duke of Norfolk: the villanous world is turn'd manger; one
jade deceives another, and your hostler plays his
part commonly for the fourth share. Have we
comedies in hand, you whorson, villanous male
London-letcher?

 Clare. Mine host, we have had the moilingest
night of it,[32] that ever we had in our lives.

 Host. Is it certain?

Clare. We have been in the forest all night almost.

Host. Foot, how did I miss you? Heart! I was stealing of a buck there.

Clare. A plague on you; we were staid for you.

Host. Were you, my noble Romans? Why you shall share; the venison is a footing, *sine Cerere et Baccho friget Venus;* that is, there is a good breakfast provided for a marriage that is in my house this morning.

Clare. A marriage, mine host!

Host. A conjunction copulative; a gallant match between your daughter and Raymond Mounchensey, young *juventus.*

Clare. How?

Host. 'Tis firm; 'tis done.
We'll show you a precedent in the civil law for't.

Sir R. How! married?

Host. Leave tricks and admiration, there's a cleanly pair of sheets on the bed in the orchard-chamber, and they shall lie there—What? I'll do it, I serve the good duke of Norfolk.

Clare. Thou shalt repent this, Blague.

Sir R. If any law in England will make thee smart for this, expect it with all severity.

Host. I renounce your defiance; if you parley so roughly, I'll barricado my gates against you. Stand fair, bully; priest, come off from the rear-ward: what can you say now? 'Twas done in my house; I have shelter in the court for 't. Do you see yon bay window? I serve the good duke of Norfolk, and 'tis his lodging. Storm, I care not, serving the good duke of Norfolk: thou art an actor in this, and thou shalt carry fire in thy face eternally.

Enter SMUG, MOUNCHENSEY, HARRY CLARE, *and* MILLISENT.

Smug. Fire! nouns, there's no fire in England like your Trinidado sack. Is any man here humorous?[33] We stole the venison, and we'll justify it: say you now.

Host. In good sooth, Smug, there's more sack on the fire, Smug.

Smug. I do not take any exceptions against your sack; but if you'll lend me a pike staff, I'll cudgel them all hence, by this hand.

Host. I say thou shalt into the cellar.

Smug. 'Sfoot, mine host, shall's not grapple? Pray you, pray you; I could fight now for all the world like a cockatrice's egg. Shall's not serve the duke of Norfolk?   [*Exit.*

Host. In, skipper, in.

Clare. Sirrah! hath young Mounchensey married your sister?

H. Clare. 'Tis certain, sir; here's the priest that coupled them, the parties joined, and the honest witness that cry'd amen.

Moun. Sir Arthur Clare, my new-created father, I beseech you hear me.

Clare. Sir, sir, you are a foolish boy, you have done that you cannot answer; I dare be bold to seize her from you, for she's a professed nun

Mill. With pardon, sir, that name is quite undone;
This true-love knot cancels both maid and nun.
When first you told me I should act that part,
How cold and bloody it crept o'er my heart.
To Cheston with a smiling brow I went,
But yet, dear sir, it was to this intent,
That my sweet Raymond might find better means
To steal me thence. In brief, disguis'd he came,
Like novice to old father Hildersham;
His tutor, here, did act that cunning part,
And in our love hath join'd much wit to art.

Clare. Is it even so?

Mill. With pardon, therefore, we entreat your smiles?
Love thwarted, turns itself to thousand wiles.

Clare. Young master Jerningham, were you an actor
In your own love's abuse?

Jern.   My thoughts, good sir,
Did labour seriously unto this end,
To wrong myself, ere I'd abuse my friend.

Host. He speaks like a bachelor of music; all in numbers. Knights, if I had known you would have let this covey of partridges sit thus long upon their knees under my sign post, I would have spread my door with coverlids.

Clare. Well, sir, for this your sign was removed, was it?

Host. Faith, we followed the directions of the devil, master Peter Fabel; and Smug (Lord bless us) could never stand upright since.

Clare. You, sir, 'twas you was his minister that married them.

Sir John. Sir, to prove myself an honest man, being that I was last night in the forest stealing venison; now, sir, to have you stand my friend, if the matter should be called in question, I married your daughter to this worthy gentleman.

Clare. I may chance to requite you, and make your neck crack for't.

Sir John. If you do, I am as resolute as my neighbour vicar of Waltham-abbey—a hem—grass and hay, we are all mortal; let's live till we be hang'd, mine host, and be merry, and there's an end.

Enter FABEL.

Fabel. Now, knights, I enter; now my part begins.
To end this difference, know, at first I knew
What you intended, ere your love took flight
From old Mounchensey : you, sir Arthur Clare,
Were minded to have married this sweet beauty
To young Frank Jerningham : to cross this match
I us'd some pretty sleights, but I protest,
Such as but sat upon the skirts of art;
No conjurations, nor such weighty spells
As tie the soul to their performancy :
These, for his love who once was my dear pupil,
Have I effected.   Now, methinks 'tis strange
That you, being old in wisdom, should thus knit
Your forehead on this match; since reason fails,
No law can curb the lover's rash attempt;
Years, in resisting this, are sadly spent :
Smile then upon your daughter and kind son,
And let our toil to future ages prove,
The devil of Edmonton did good in love.

Clare. Well, 'tis in vain to cross the providence :
Dear son, I take thee up into my heart ;
Rise, daughter, this is a kind father's part.

Host. Why, sir George, send for Spindle's noise presently :[34]
Ha! ere't be night I'll serve the good duke of Norfolk.

Sir John. Grass and hay, mine host, let's live till we die, and be merry, and there's an end.

Clare. What, is breakfast ready, mine host?

Host. 'Tis, my little Hebrew.

Clare. Sirrah! ride straight to Cheston nunnery,
Fetch thence my lady ; the house, I know,
By this time misses their young votary.
Come, knights, let's in.

Bilbo. I will to horse presently, sir.—A plague on my lady, I shall miss a good breakfast.—Smug, how chance you cut so plaguely behind, Smug?

Smug. Stand away, I'll founder you else.

Bilbo. Farewell, Smug, thou art in another element.

Smug. I will be, by and by; I will be Saint George again.

Clare. Take heed the fellow do not hurt himself.

Sir R. Did we not last night find two Saint Georges here?

Fabel. Yes, knights, this martialist was one of them.

Clare. Then thus conclude your night of merriment.   [*Exeunt omnes.*

NOTES TO THE MERRY DEVIL OF EDMONTON.

[1] *'Tis Peter Fabel, a renowned scholar.*

In *Weever's Funeral Monuments*, 1631, we have the following brief account of the hero of this drama:—" Here (i.e. at Edmonton) lieth interred under a seemely tome without inscription, the body of Peter Fabell (as the report goes) upon whom this fable was fathered, that he by his wittie devises beguiled the devill; belike he was some ingenious conceited gentleman, who did use some sleighty trickes for his owne disports. He lived and died in the raigne of Henry the Seventh, saith the booke of his merry pranks." Again, in the *Speculum Britanniæ*, Middlesex; Norden says: "There is a fable of one Peter Fabell that lyeth in the same church also, who is saide to have beguiled the devill by pollicie for money."

Fuller also, in his *Worthies*, thus alludes to the visionary and traditionary hero of this drama:—" I shall probably offend the gravity of some to insert, and certainly curiosity of others to omit him. Some make him a friar, others a lay gentleman, all a conceited (i.e. a witty, ingenious) person, who, with his merry devices, deceived the devil, who by grace may be resisted, not deceived by wit. If a grave bishop in his sermon, speaking of Brute's coming into this land, said it was but a *bruit*, I hope I may say without offence, that this Fabel was but a *fable*, supposed to live in the reign of King Henry the Sixth."

[2] *The gentlewomen in cloaks and safe-guards.*

Safe-guards were a kind of outer petticoat formerly worn by ladies who rode on horseback; they had their name from their being used to preserve the other clothes from mud.

[3] *A Tartarian*, i.e. a cant name for a thief.

[4] *Will that corruption, thine ostler, &c.*

To *will* him is to desire him to do any service.

[5] *Hay! a pox of these rushes.*

I have before mentioned, that previously to the introduction of carpets into England, it was customary to strew the floors of rooms with rushes. Numerous allusions to this practice may be found in our ancient dramatists; thus Shakspere, in *Henry IV.*, Part I.:—

> She bids you
> Upon the wanton rushes lay you down.

Again, in Ben Jonson's *Cynthia's Revels*:—"All the ladies and gallants lye languishing upon the rushes, like so many pounded cattle i' the midst of harvest." And in Dekkar's *Bel-man of London*:—" the windowes were spread with hearbs, the chimney drest up with greene boughes, and the floore strewed with bulrushes, as if some lasse were that morning to be married."

[6] *I have an excellent intellect to go steal some venison.*

That is, I have a good mind to do so.

[7] *Via—they come.*

A cant phrase, common in our old plays, expressive of exultation or defiance. Mr. Tollet supposes it to be taken from the Italian *via*, and to be used on occasions to quicken or pluck up courage. It is sometimes used in the sense of *away*.

[8] *Tityre, tu patulæ recubans sub tegmine fagi.*

The first line of Virgil's *Eclogues*.

[9] *Your Cooper's Dictionary is your only book to study in a cellar.*

A very poor quibble, alluding to the wine-casks made by a cooper, and also to Thomas Cooper's *Thesaurus linguæ Latinæ*, printed in folio, 1584.

[10] *But will you to this gear in hugger-mugger.*

That is, in private, or with secrecy. Thus, in *Hamlet*, the King, speaking of the death of Polonius, says:—

> ———— We have done but greenly,
> In *hugger-mugger* to inter him.

Again, in *The Revenger's Tragedy*, 1609:—"He died like a politician, in *hugger-mugger*, made no man acquainted with it." The word is graceless enough, but, as Dr. Johnson remarks, "If phraseology is to be changed as words grow uncouth by disuse, or gross by vulgarity, the history of every language will be lost; we shall no longer have the words of any author; and, as these alterations will be often unskilfully made, we shall in time have very little of his meaning."

[11] *Mean to launch their busy bags.*

Thus the quartos; Mr. Dodsley reads *pursy*.

[12] *I will not seek to slubber
Her angel-like perfections.*

That is, to describe them in an imperfect or neglectful manner; to obscure. This rather inelegant word occurs in Shakspere's *Othello*.

[13] *The milk-maid's cuts.*

That is, horses. Anciently a horse was frequently called *cut*, but the word was also a vulgar term of abuse. Mr. Gilchrist remarks: "It appears probable to me that the opprobrious epithet, *cut*, arose from the practice of cutting the hair of convicted thieves, which was anciently the custom in England, as appears from the edicts of John de Northampton against adulterers, who thought, with Paulo Migante, that

> ' England ne'er would thrive,
> Till all the whores were burnt alive.' '

[14] *Dossers*, i.e. panniers.

[15] *Take me with you, good Sir John.*

That is, explain your meaning, let my apprehension follow your words. Thus, in the first part of *Henry the Fourth*, Falstaff, pretending not to understand the Prince, exclaims: " I would your grace would take me with you, whom means your grace?"

[16] *I see by thy eyes thou hast been reading a little Geneva print.*

A quibble, meaning that Smug's eyes were red from drinking gin, commonly called Geneva.

[17] *And must tend the Hungarians.*

By the *Hungarians*, the host, whose conversation is full of puns and quibbles, means his *hungry* guests.

[18] *The title is so brangled with thy debts.*

That is, choked up, lost, overgrown, and hidden by them.

[19] *To whet their skeins.*

Skein is the Irish word for a knife or dagger. So in *Soliman and Persida*, 1599 :—

> Against the light-foot Irish have I serv'd
> And in my skin bear tokens of the *skeins*.

[20] *You see how matters fadge.*

That is, *go, proceed :* though it is usually employed in the sense of *succeed.* Thus, in Haughton's *Englishmen for any Money :*—

> But, sirra Ned, what sayes Mathea to thee ?
> Wilt *fadge ?* Wilt *fadge ?* What, wilt it be a match ?

[21] *The sacring bell.*

The little bell which is rung to give notice of the approach of the Host when it is carried in procession. It is also mentioned in *Henry the Eighth.*

[22] *You must creep unto the cross.*

A practice, I believe, still in use in religious houses attached to the Romish church. The penitents creep on their hands and knees to the foot of a crucifix, in token of their remorse for sin, and their humiliation of spirit. The custom is thus alluded to in Warner's *Albion's England*, 1602 :—

We offer tapers, pay our tythes and vowes ; we pilgrims goe,
To every sainct, at every shrine we offerings doe bestow ;
We kiss the pix, we *creepe the cross*, our beades we over-runne,
The convent hath a legacie, who so is left undone.

[23] *You amaze me at your speech.*

I am responsible for the last word of this line ; the old copies read :—You amaze me at your ——. A word equivalent to that I have supplied, had evidently been dropped by the compositor.

[24] *Call'd Millisent of Edmonton.*

When a novice entered a religious house for the sake of becoming a monk or nun, they gave up the name by which they had been known in the outward world, and some new cognomen was bestowed upon them.

[25] *Leave us to scamble.*

Scamble is an obsolete word, having the same meaning as scramble.

[26] *And a tall keeper.*

The word *tall*, here and in many other places in our ancient writers, is not designed to give an idea of height or bulk, but signifies stout, bold, or courageous.

[27] *Come, ye Hungarian pilchers.*

Hungarian was a cant term used to express contempt. It does not appear to have had any strictly defined meaning. Mr. Tollet observes, that " the Hungarians, when infidels, overran Germany and France, and would have invaded England if they could have come to it. See Stowe, in the year 930 ; and Holinshed's *Invasions of Ireland*, p. 56. Hence their name might become a proverb of baseness."

[28] *As a true mareterraneum skinker.*

A *skinker* is a tapster, or drawer. Mr. Steevens says, it is derived from the Dutch word *schenken*, which signifies, to fill a cup or glass. The word *mareterraneum* I cannot explain, but suspect it is a coinage of the bombastic host's, and not intended to possess any definite meaning.

[29] *Nor bear with me.*

Perhaps we should read,—" *Now* bear with me."

[30] *How now, my old Jenert's bank, my horse, my castle.*

An anonymous critic observes :—" I once suspected this passage of corruption, but have found reason to change my opinion. The merry host seems willing to assemble ideas expressive of *trust* and *confidence*. The old quartos begin the word *jenert* with a capital letter ; and therefore, we may suppose *Jenert's bank* to have been the shop of some banker, in whose possession money could be deposited with security. The Irish still say—as sure as *Burton's Bank ;* and our own countrymen—as safe as the *Bank of England*. We might read, my *house*, instead of my *horse*, as the former agrees better with *castle*. The services of a *horse* are of all things the most uncertain."

[31] *Let me die of the yellows.*

A disease peculiar to horses. So in Shakspere's *Taming of a Shrew :*—

> His horse sped with spavins, and raied with the *yellows*.

[32] *We have had the moilingest night of it.*

That is, the most toilsome and dirty ; to *moil*, is to labour wearily through the mire.

[33] *Is any man here humourous ?*

That is, capricious, changeable. Thus, in the *Spanish Tragedy*, 1607 :—

> You know that women oft are *humourous*.

In *Cynthia's Revels*, by Ben Jonson, we have :—" A

nymph of a most wandering and giddy disposition, *humourous* as the air,*" &c. Again, in the comedy of *The Silent Woman* :—*" As proud as May, and as *humourous* as April.*" And in Dekkar's *Satiromastrix*, 1600 :—

——— All our understanding faculties,
Sit there in their high court of parliament,
Enacting laws to sway this *humourous* world,
This little isle of man.

By the Elizabethan writers the word *humour* was frequently used for peculiarities of manner. Whalley observes—" The word was new ; the use, or rather abuse of it was excessive. It was applied upon all occasions with as little judgment as wit. Every coxcomb had it always in his mouth ; and every particularity he affected was denominated by the name of *humour*. To redress this extravagance, Jonson is exact in describing the true meaning and proper application of the term." Jonson's description and definition will be both interesting and valuable to the readers of our ancient drama ; I therefore subjoin it. It is contained in the induction to his comedy of *Every Man Out of his Humour* :—

Why humour, as 'tis ens (i.e. *as it is an existence*) we thus
      define it,
To be a quality of air, or water,
And in itself holds these two properties,
Moisture and fluxure : as, for demonstration,
Pour water on this floor, 'twill wet and run :
Likewise the air, forced through a horn or trumpet,

Flows instantly away, and leaves behind
A kind of dew ; and hence we do conclude,
That whatsoe'er hath fluxture and humidity,
As wanting power to contain itself,
Is humour. So in every human body,
The choler, melancholy, phlegm, and blood,
By reason that they flow continually
In some one part, and are not continent,
Receive the name of humours. Now thus far
It may, by metaphor, apply itself
Unto the general disposition :
As when some one peculiar quality
Doth so possess a man, that it doth draw
All his affects, his spirits, and his powers,
In their confluctions, all to run one way,
This may be truly said to be a humour.
But that a rook, by wearing a pyed feather,
The cable hatband, or the three-piled ruff,
A yard of shoe-tye, or the Switzer's knot
On his French garters, should affect a humour :
O, it is more than most ridiculous.

[34] *Send for Spindle's noise presently.*

A band of music was formerly called a *noise* of music. Thus, in *Henry the Fourth* (Part II.) :—" See if thou canst find out Sneak's noise ; mistress Tearsheet would fain hear some music." And in Cartwright's comedy of *The Ordinary*, 1651 :—

Hang shop-books ; give us some wine ! *hey for a noise
Of fiddlers now.*

H. T.

A Yorkshire Tragedy

Of all the plays in the Shakespeare apocrypha, according to Baldwin Maxwell (27), it is for *A Yorkshire Tragedy* that there is the strongest external evidence of Shakespeare's authorship. Not only was it printed in 1608 with the declaration on the title page that it had been written by "W. Shakespeare" and "Acted by his majesty's Players at the Globe," but it was in the same year entered upon the Register of the Stationers' Company as a work by "Wylliam Shakespere."

Although the omission of *A Yorkshire Tragedy* from the First Folio, the obviously unscrupulous dealings of its publisher, Thomas Pavier, and the suspicions occasioned by the inexplicable entry of the author's name in the Register, may be regarded as grounds for doubting Shakespeare's authorship of the play, they cannot be said to indicate that Shakespeare might not, when the play was being prepared for the stage, have introduced here and there lines that he thought would render it more effective. That he might well have done (as he did often) for any play presented by his company; and a number of critics, though convinced that Shakespeare's part in the play was very small indeed, have persuaded themselves from the external evidence that he must have had at least some connection with it.

The struggle engendered by the conflict between the internal evidence of the play itself and what they considered to be the strong external evidence is reflected in the discussions of J. P. Collier, Hermann Ulrici, F. G. Fleay, A. W. von Schlegel, and others.

Collier expresses the belief that Shakespeare must have been "concerned" in the play, but the great weight he gives to the external evidence is suggested in his claim that "the internal evidence . . . of Shakespeare's authorship is nearly as strong as the external, and there are some speeches which could scarcely have proceeded from any other pen"; and, recognizing that such "has not been the general opinion of commentators," he suggests that perhaps Shakespeare yielded to the necessity of the case and contributed this one of "four plays" presented the same night.

Ulrici (*Über Shakespeares dramatische Kunst,* 1839), whose discussion though largely drawn for Collier's, is stated with greater boldness, expresses the conviction that "every unprejudiced reader of the *Yorkshire Tragedy* will . . . recognize the hand of Shakespeare, not only in the composition, in spite of its great simplicity, but also in the characters and the 'language'; some passages can have proceeded from no other pen than Shakespeare's." Yet apparently not wholly satisfied, Ulrici suggests that Shakespeare might have undertaken the play at the request of his brother actors, who wished to gratify the momentary excitement of the public with regard to this sensational crime.

The peculiarity of domestic tragedy to England at this period is an interesting testimony both to the relative freedom of the English stage from critical dominance and to the large middle-class element in its audience. Alfred Harbage's revealing study (20) shows that the public theatres must have drawn on a wide cross section of the population of London for their audience, excluding only the very poor. Domestic tragedy has therefore the characteristics of bourgeois literature in its heavy moral emphasis and in its **combination** of sensationalism and sentiment (as, for example, in *Arden, of Feversham* and *A Yorkshire Tragedy*).

The ethical pattern of temptation, sin, repentance, and punishment that domestic tragedy inherited from the morality play was one widely familiar to everybody through persistent Christian teaching. Harbage points out that it was given precise and elaborate form in the official book of homilies prescribed for weekly reading in every church, and it was echoed in sermons and moralizing pamphlets, even in the broadside ballads commemorating striking crimes that served in that day in place of sensational journalism. It is interesting to note that *A Yorkshire Tragedy* follows closely the conventional portrayal of the Prodigal Son (a theme that was a favorite in both Elizabethan and Jacobean comedy). In this play a husband seeks a wife's dowry "to give new life / Unto those pleasures which I most affect" (Scene ii), refuses a place at court with "Shall I that dedicated myself to pleasure, be now confin'd in service?" (Scene iii) and later realizes that he has been "zany to a swine,—to show tricks in the mire" (Scene iv).

Thus, as A. P. Rossiter (36) informs us, by following the medieval tradition we see the domestic tragedy as a particular branch of moral history, in which impressive middle-class murder stories were dramatized with the usual suggestion that "blood will have blood," as *The Mirror for Magistrates* had phrased it. An example is *A Yorkshire Tragedy,* which is concerned with a highly sensational contemporary crime.

The perpetrator of the sordid murders in this play is Walter Calverly, a gentleman of ancient and honorable family (married to the daughter of Sir Henry Cobham, a lineal descendant of that Sir John Oldcastle who was the original prototype of Falstaff). In a fit of madness Calverly wounded his wife and slew two of his three children. It is noteworthy, as Maxwell points out, that (except for the servants appearing in Scene i) none of the characters is identified by other than a type designation: Husband, Wife, Knight, Servant, and the like. Before the story was told in the 1607 edition of Stow's *Chronicles,* entries had been made upon the Stationers' Register in 1605 of, first, "A Book Called Two Unnatural Murders, the one practiced by master Calverly, a Yorkshire gent upon his wife . . . and on his children. . . ." and, a month later, "A Ballad of Lamentable Murder Done in Yorkshire by a gent upon 2 of his own children sore wounding his Wife and Nurse."

Few critics have failed to recognize the dramatic effectiveness of *A Yorkshire Tragedy.* To Maxwell, as to most critics, its bare realism, and its fierce dramatic power distinguish *A Yorkshire Tragedy* and set it among the few truly great domestic tragedies of its age. Swinburne (43) declares it full

> to overflowing of fierce animal power, and hot as with the furious breath of some caged wild beast. . . . It is and must always be unsurpassable for pure potency of horror; and the breathless heat of its action, its raging rate of speed, leaves actually no breathing-time for disgust; it consumes our very sense of repulsion with fire. 'Tis a very excellent piece of work.

We finish reading *A Yorkshire Tragedy,* wrote J. A. Symonds (44),

> with the same kind of impression as that left upon our sight by a flash of lightning revealing some grim object in a night of pitchy darkness. The mental retina has been all but seared and blinded; yet the scene discovered in that second shall not be forgotten.

The most recent editor of the play, Tucker Brooke (8), declares: "The barbaric force of the play and the splendour of some of the prose it contains cannot fail to impress the reader." And the same dramatic effectiveness is recognized by Allardyce Nicoll (*Shakespeare,* 1953), who writes of it as "a truly great play" wherein "the crude realism . . . is given something of a monumental tone by [Husband's] villainy, repentance, and final series of ghastly murders." There is an advance here on the characterization of *Arden, of Feversham* (another domestic tragedy), and there seems, in spite of the shortness of the piece, an attempt at securing some broader and loftier appeal.

In fact, the powerful effect of the play on most readers is due in large part, as Maxwell suggests, to the play's brevity and to the swiftness with which it reaches its climax. He feels, moreover, that there are some deeply thoughtful and well-expressed speeches that have contributed to the widely accepted view that Shakespeare either was the author of the play or had some share in its composition. The dramatist, whoever he was, obviously had a mature, even an inquiring mind. Not content merely to relate what had happened, he sought to answer the question of why Husband had behaved as he had. Husband himself is made to give the only possible psychological expla-

nation and to voice the prayer that the devil that had possessed him might be
bound by:

> . . . you blessed angels,
> In that pit bottomless! Let him not rise
> To make men act unnatural tragedies;
> To spread into a father, and in fury
> Make him his childrens executioner;
> Murder his wife, his servants, and who not?—
> For that man's dark, where heaven is quite forgot.
>
> [Scene x]

Madeleine Doran (13) claims that direct self-explanation is a dramatic
shortcut, useful when action is full and complicated and characters are many.
Momentous conflicts of passion and of purpose that change the course of the
speaker's life are set down in the barest terms and decided in a moment.
When, for example, Faustus determines to devote his life to black magic, and
thus takes the first step to damnation, he arrives at the decision after the most
perfunctory review and rejection of all the other fields of learning—logic,
medicine, law, divinity. In the same swift way Calverly, in *A Yorkshire Tragedy,* has a moment of repentance for his wasted youth and of tenderness for
one of his children before beginning his mad course of slaughtering his family.
The scene actually reveals brilliant psychological insight into the alternate
clarity and confusion of an unbalanced mind; but it is done almost in short-
hand, without preparation or without sequel, without any suggestion that such
a state was typical of many in Calverly's experience. It is a kind of synecdoche
of construction, a commonplace of Elizabethan dramatic technique, especially
in domestic tragedy.

Tragedy (epic or domestic), as defined by Ian Scott-Kilvert (40), deals
in absolutes. The typically tragic situation is the act of self-will pursued,
whether in ignorance or knowledge. It is the determination of a tragic hero,
such as Oedipus or Faustus or Macbeth (or, to a lesser degree, Calverly), to
refuse compromise and to hold to his course. It springs from the paradox that
men's desires and ambitions vastly exceed their limitations in which its
central theme is the meaning of suffering and the mystery of evil.

In fine, the true material of tragedy is the fate of "the man in the middle"
(in the Aristotelian phrase), the hero who is allowed no unsullied choice, but
is torn by conflicting impulses and is forced to act, to suffer, to bear the load
of guilt, and finally to attain self-knowledge. Thus tragedy makes its impact
not as doctrine but as discovery, however unwelcome or unpleasant, by virtue
of its truth to our experience and its uncompromising confrontation of the
worst that life can do to man. But in order to arrive at this knowledge, it is
necessary that the inner conflict between the forces of good and evil should
be left free to play itself out, not be predetermined in the interests of divine
or poetic justice.

PERSONS REPRESENTED.

————◆————

HUSBAND.
Appears, sc. 2 ; sc. 3 ; sc. 4 ; sc. 5 ; sc. 6 ; sc. 8 ; sc. 9 ; sc. 10.

MASTER OF A COLLEGE.
Appears, sc. 4 ; sc. 6 ; sc. 7 ; sc. 8 ; sc. 9 ; sc. 10.

A KNIGHT, *a Magistrate.*
Appears, sc. 9.

SEVERAL GENTLEMEN.
Appear, sc. 2 ; sc. 8 ; sc. 9 ; sc. 10.

OLIVER,
RALPH,   } *Servants.*
SAMUEL,

Appear, sc. 1.

OTHER SERVANTS.
Appear, sc. 2 ; sc. 3 ; sc. 4 ; sc. 5 ; sc. 7.

OFFICERS.
Appear, sc. 8 ; sc. 9 ; sc. 10.

A LITTLE BOY.
Appears, sc. 4 ; sc. 5.

WIFE.
Appears, sc. 2 ; sc. 3 ; sc. 5 ; sc. 7 ; sc. 10.

MAID-SERVANT.
Appears, sc. 5.

The Tragedy is complete in One Act.

SCENE.—CALVERLY, *in* YORKSHIRE.

A Yorkshire Tragedy.

———◆———

SCENE I.—*A Room in a Country House.*

Enter Oliver *and* Ralph.[1]

Oliv. Sirrah Ralph, my young mistress is in such a pitiful passionate humour for the long absence of her love——

Ralph. Why, can you blame her? Why, apples hanging longer on the tree than when they are ripe, makes so many fallings; viz. mad wenches, because they are not gathered in time, are fain to drop of themselves, and then 'tis common you know for every man to take them up.

Oliv. Mass thou say'st true, 'tis common indeed. But sirrah, is neither our young master return'd, nor our fellow Sam come from London?

Ralph. Neither of either, as the puritan bawd says.[2] 'Slid I hear Sam. Sam's come: here he is; tarry;—come i'faith: now my nose itches for news.

Oliv. And so does mine elbow.

Sam. [*Within.*] Where are you there? Boy, look you walk my horse with discretion. I have rid him simply: I warrant his skin sticks to his back with very heat. If he should catch cold and get the cough of the lungs, I were well served, were I not?

Enter Sam.

What Ralph and Oliver!

Both. Honest fellow Sam, welcome i'faith. What tricks hast thou brought from London?

Sam. You see I am hang'd after the truest fashion: three hats, and two glasses bobbing upon them; two rebato wires[3] upon my breast, a cap-case by my side, a brush at my back, an almanack in my pocket, and three ballads in my codpiece. Nay, I am the true picture of a common serving-man.

Oliv. I'll swear thou art; thou may'st set up when thou wilt: there's many a one begins with less I can tell thee, that proves a rich man ere he dies. But what's the news from London, Sam?

Ralph. Ay, that's well said; what's the news

from London, sirrah? My young mistress keeps such a puling for her love.

Sam. Why the more fool she; ay, the more ninny-hammer she.

Oliv. Why, Sam, why?

Sam. Why, he is married to another long ago.

Both. I'faith? You jest.

Sam. Why, did you not know that till now? Why, he's married, beats his wife, and has two or three children by her. For you must note, that any woman bears the more when she is beaten.[4]

Ralph. Ay, that's true, for she bears the blows.

Oliv. Sirrah Sam, I would not for two years' wages my young mistress knew so much: she'd run upon the left hand of her wit, and ne'er be her own woman again.

Sam. And I think she was blest in her cradle, that he never came in her bed. Why, he has consum'd all, pawn'd his lands, and made his university brother stand in wax for him: there's a fine phrase for a scrivener. Puh! he owes more than his skin is worth.

Oliv. Is't possible?

Sam. Nay, I'll tell you moreover, he calls his wife whore, as familiarly as one would call Moll and Doll; and his children bastards, as naturally as can be.—But what have we here? I thought 'twas something pull'd down my breeches; I quite forgot my two poking-sticks:[5] these came from London. Now any thing is good here that comes from London.

Oliv. Ay, far fetch'd, you know, Sam,[6]—But speak in your conscience, i'faith; have not we as good poking-sticks i' the country as need to be put in the fire?

Sam. The mind of a thing is all; the mind of a thing is all; and as thou said'st even now, far-fetch'd are the best things for ladies.

Oliv. Ay, and for waiting-gentlewomen too.

Sam. But Ralph, what, is our beer sour this thunder?

Ralph. No, no, it holds countenance yet.

Sam. Why then follow me; I'll teach you the

finest humour to be drunk in : I learn'd it at London last week.

Both. I' faith ?　Let 's hear it, let 's hear it.

Sam. The bravest humour! 'twould do a man good to be drunk in it : they call it knighting in London, when they drink upon their knees.

Both. 'Faith that 's excellent.

Sam. Come follow me; I 'll give you all the degrees of it in order.　　　　　　　　[*Exeunt.*

SCENE II.—*An Apartment in* Calverly Hall.

Enter Wife.[7]

Wife. What will become of us ?　All will away :
My husband never ceases in expense,
Both to consume his credit and his house;
And 'tis set down by heaven's just decree,
That riot's child must needs be beggary.
Are these the virtues that his youth did promise ?
Dice and voluptuous meetings, midnight revels,
Taking his bed with surfeits; ill beseeming
The ancient honour of his house and name ?
And this not all, but that which kills me most,
When he recounts his losses and false fortunes,
The weakness of his state so much dejected,
Not as a man repentant, but half mad.
His fortunes cannot answer his expense,
He sits, and sullenly locks up his arms;
Forgetting heaven, looks downward; which makes
　　him
Appear so dreadful that he frights my heart :
Walks heavily, as if his soul were earth;
Not penitent for those his sins are past,
But vexed his money cannot make them last
A fearful melancholy, ungodly sorrow.
O, yonder he comes; now in despite of ills
I 'll speak to him, and I will hear him speak,
And do my best to drive it from his heart.

Enter Husband.

Hus. Pox o'the last throw !　It made five hundred
　　angels
Vanish from my sight.　I am damn'd, I'm damn'd;
The angels have forsook me.[8]　Nay it is
Certainly true; for he that has no coin
Is damn'd in this world; he is gone, he 's gone.

Wife. Dear husband.

Hus. O! most punishment of all, I have a wife.

Wife. I do entreat you, as you love your soul,
Tell me the cause of this your discontent.

Hus. A vengeance strip thee naked! thou art
　　cause,
Effect, quality, property; thou, thou, thou. [*Exit.*

Wife. Bad turn'd to worse; both beggary of the
　　soul
And of the body ;—and so much unlike
Himself at first, as if some vexed spirit
Had got his form upon him.　He comes again.

Re-enter Husband.

He says I am the cause : I never yet
Spoke less than words of duty and of love.

Hus. If marriage be honourable, then cuckolds are honourable, for they cannot be made without marriage.　Fool! what meant I to marry to get beggars ?　Now must my eldest son be a knave or nothing; he cannot live upon the fool, for he will have no land to maintain him.　That mortgage sits like a snaffle upon mine inheritance, and makes me chew upon iron.　My second son must be a promoter,[9] and my third a thief, or an underputter; a slave pander.　Oh beggary, beggary, to what base uses dost thou put a man! I think the devil scorns to be a bawd; he bears himself more proudly, has more care of his credit.—Base, slavish, abject, filthy poverty !

Wife. Good sir, by all our vows I do beseech
　　you,
Show me the true cause of your discontent.

Hus. Money, money, money; and thou must supply me.

Wife. Alas, I am the least cause of your discontent,
Yet what is mine either in rings or jewels,
Use to your own desire; but I beseech you,
As you are a gentleman by many bloods,[10]
Though I myself be out of your respect,
Think on the state of these three lovely boys
You have been father to.

Hus. Puh! bastards, bastards, bastards;[11] begot in tricks, begot in tricks.

Wife. Heaven knows how those words wrong
　　me : but I may
Endure these griefs among a thousand more.
O call to mind your lands already mortgag'd,
Yourself wound into debts, your hopeful brother
At the university in bonds for you,
Like to be seiz'd upon; and——

Hus. Have done, thou harlot,
Whom though for fashion-sake I married,
I never could abide.　Think'st thou, thy words
Shall kill my pleasures ?　Fall off to thy friends;
Thou and thy bastards beg; I will not bate
A whit in humour.　Midnight, still I love you,
And revel in your company !　Curb'd in,
Shall it be said in all societies,

That I broke custom? that I flagg'd in money?
No, those thy jewels I will play as freely
As when my state was fullest.

Wife. Be it so.

Hus. Nay I protest (and take that for an earnest)
                         [*Spurns her.*
I will for ever hold thee in contempt,
And never touch the sheets that cover thee,
But be divorc'd in bed, till thou consent
Thy dowry shall be sold, to give new life
Unto those pleasures which I most affect.

Wife. Sir, do but turn a gentle eye on me,
And what the law shall give me leave to do,
You shall command.

Hus. Look it be done. Shall I want dust,
And like a slave wear nothing in my pockets
              [*Holds his hands in his pockets.*
But my bare hands, to fill them up with nails?
O much against my blood!¹² Let it be done;
I was never made to be a looker on,
A bawd to dice; I'll shake the drabs myself,
And make them yield: I say, look it be done.

Wife. I take my leave: it shall.   [*Exit.*

Hus. Speedily, speedily.
I hate the very hour I chose a wife:
A trouble, trouble! Three children, like three evils,
Hang on me. Fie, fie, fie! Strumpet and bastards!

Enter three Gentlemen.

Strumpet and bastards!

1st Gent. Still do these loathsome thoughts jar
     on your tongue?
Yourself to stain the honour of your wife,
Nobly descended? Those whom men call mad,
Endanger others; but he's more than mad
That wounds himself; whose own words do pro-
     claim
Scandals unjust, to soil his better name.
It is not fit; I pray, forsake it.

2nd Gent. Good sir, let modesty reprove you.

3rd Gent. Let honest kindness sway so much
     with you.

Hus. Good den; I thank you, sir; how do you?
     Adieu!
I am glad to see you. Farewell instructions, ad-
     monitions!   [*Exeunt* Gentlemen.

Enter a Servant.

How now, sirrah? What would you?

Ser. Only to certify you, sir, that my mistress
was met by the way, by them who were sent for
her up to London¹³ by her honourable uncle, your
worship's late guardian.

Hus. So, sir, then she is gone; and so may you be;
But let her look the thing be done she wots of,
Or hell will stand more pleasant than her house
At home.   [*Exit* Serv.

Enter a Gentleman.

Gent. Well or ill met, I care not.

Hus. No, nor I.

Gent. I am come with confidence to chide you.

Hus. Who? me?
Chide me? Do't finely then; let it not move me:
For if thou chid'st me angry, I shall strike.

Gent. Strike thine own follies, for 'tis they
     deserve
To be well beaten. We are now in private;
There's none but thou and I. Thou art fond and
     peevish;¹⁴
An unclean rioter; thy lands and credit
Lie now both sick of a consumption:
I am sorry for thee. That man spends with shame,
That with his riches doth consume his name;
And such art thou.

Hus. Peace.

Gent. No, thou shalt hear me further.
Thy father's and forefathers' worthy honours,
Which were our country monuments, our grace,
Follies in thee begin now to deface.
The spring-time of thy youth did fairly promise
Such a most fruitful summer to thy friends,
It scarce can enter into men's beliefs,
Such dearth should hang upon thee. We that see it,
Are sorry to believe it. In thy change,
This voice into all places will be hurl'd—
Thou and the devil have deceiv'd the world.

Hus. I'll not endure thee.

Gent. But of all the worst,
Thy virtuous wife, right honourably allied,
Thou hast proclaim'd a strumpet.

Hus. Nay then I know thee;
Thou art her champion, thou; her private friend;
The party you wot on.

Gent. O ignoble thought!
I am past my patient blood. Shall I stand idle,
And see my reputation touch'd to death?

Hus. It has gall'd you, this; has it?

Gent. No, monster; I will prove
My thoughts did only tend to virtuous love.

Hus. Love of her virtues? there it goes.

Gent. Base spirit,
To lay thy hate upon the fruitful honour
Of thine own bed!
        [*They fight, and the* Hus. *is hurt.*

Hus. Oh!

Gent. Wilt thou yield it yet?

Hus. Sir, sir, I have not done with you.

Gent. I hope, nor ne'er shall do.

[*They fight again.*

Hus. Have you got tricks? Are you in cunning with me?

Gent. No, plain and right:

He needs no cunning that for truth doth fight.

[Hus. *falls down.*

Hus. Hard fortune! am I levell'd with the ground?

Gent. Now, sir, you lie at mercy.

Hus. Ay, you slave.

Gent. Alas, that hate should bring us to our grave!

You see, my sword's not thirsty for your life:

I am sorrier for your wound than you yourself.

You're of a virtuous house; show virtuous deeds;

'Tis not your honour, 'tis your folly bleeds.

Much good has been expected in your life;

Cancel not all men's hopes: you have a wife,

Kind and obedient; heap not wrongful shame

On her and your posterity; let only sin be sore,

And by this fall, rise never to fall more.

And so I leave you. [*Exit.*

Hus. Has the dog left me then,

After his tooth has left me? O, my heart

Would fain leap after him. Revenge I say;

I'm mad to be reveng'd. My strumpet wife,

It is thy quarrel that rips thus my flesh,

And makes my breast spit blood;—but thou shalt bleed.

Vanquish'd? got down? unable even to speak?

Surely 'tis want of money makes men weak:

Ay, 'twas that o'erthrew me: I'd ne'er been down else. [*Exit.*

SCENE III.—*Another room in the same.*

Enter Wife,[15] *and a* Servant.

Ser. 'Faith, mistress, if it might not be presumption

In me to tell you so, for his excuse

You had small reason, knowing his abuse.

Wife. I grant I had; but alas,

Why should our faults at home be spread abroad?

'Tis grief enough within doors. At first sight

Mine uncle could run o'er his prodigal life

As perfectly as if his serious eye

Had number'd all his follies:

Knew of his mortgag'd lands, his friends in bonds,

Himself wither'd with debts; and in that minute

Had I added his usage and unkindness,

'Twould have confounded every thought of good:

Where now, fathering his riots on his youth,

Which time and tame experience will shake off,—

Guessing his kindness to me, (as I smooth'd him

With all the skill I had, though his deserts

Are in form uglier than an unshap'd bear,)

He's ready to prefer him to some office

And place at court; a good and sure relief

To all his stooping fortunes. 'Twill be a means, I hope,

To make new league between us, and redeem

His virtues with his lands.

Ser. I should think so, mistress. If he should not now be kind to you, and love you, and cherish you up, I should think the devil himself kept open house in him.

Wife. I doubt not but he will. Now pr'ythee leave me; I think I hear him coming.

Ser. I am gone. [*Exit.*

Wife. By this good means I shall preserve my lands,

And free my husband out of usurers' hands.

Now there's no need of sale; my uncle's kind;

I hope, if aught, this will content his mind.

Here comes my husband.

Enter Husband.

Hus. Now, are you come? Where's the money? Let's see the money. Is the rubbish sold? those wise-acres, your lands? Why when? The money? Where is it? Pour it down; down with it, down with it: I say pour 't on the ground; let's see it, let's see it.

Wife. Good sir, keep but in patience, and I hope my words shall like you well. I bring you better comfort than the sale of my dowry.

Hus. Ha! What's that?

Wife. Pray do not fright me, sir, but vouchsafe me hearing. My uncle, glad of your kindness to me and mild usage (for so I made it to him), hath in pity of your declining fortunes, provided a place for you at court, of worth and credit; which so much overjoy'd me—

Hus. Out on thee, filth! over and overjoy'd, when I'm in torment? [*Spurns her.*] Thou politic whore, subtiler than nine devils, was this thy journey to nunck? to set down the history of me, of my state and fortunes? Shall I that dedicated myself to pleasure, be now confin'd in service? to crouch and stand like an old man i' the hams, my hat off? I that could never abide to uncover my head i' the church? Base slut! this fruit bear thy complaints.

Wife. O, heaven knows
That my complaints were praises, and best words,
Of you and your estate. Only, my friends
Knew of your mortgag'd lands, and were possess'd
Of every accident before I came.
If you suspect it but a plot in me,
To keep my dowry, or for mine own good,
Or my poor children's, (though it suits a mother
To show a natural care in their reliefs,)
Yet I'll forget myself to calm your blood:
Consume it, as your pleasure counsels you.
And all I wish even clemency affords ;
Give me but pleasant looks, and modest words.

Hus. Money, whore, money, or I'll—
                              [*Draws a dagger.*

Enter a Servant *hastily.*

What the devil! How now! thy hasty news?

Ser. May it please you, sir—

Hus. What! may I not look upon upon my dagger? Speak, villain, or I will execute the point on thee: Quick, short.

Ser. Why, sir, a gentleman from the university stays below to speak with you.   [*Exit.*

Hus. From the university? so; university:— that long word runs through me.   [*Exit.*

Wife. Was ever wife so wretchedly beset?
Had not this news stepp'd in between, the point
Had offer'd violence unto my breast.
That which some women call great misery,
Would show but little here; would scarce be seen
Among my miseries. I may compare
For wretched fortunes, with all wives that are.
Nothing will please him, until all be nothing.
He calls it slavery to be preferr'd ;
A place of credit, a base servitude.
What shall become of me, and my poor children,
Two here, and one at nurse? my pretty beggars!
I see how Ruin with a palsied hand
Begins to shake this ancient seat to dust:
The heavy weight of sorrow draws my lids
Over my dankish eyes :[16] I can scarce see ;
Thus grief will last ;—it wakes and sleeps with me.
                              [*Exit.*

SCENE IV.—*Another Apartment in the same.*

Enter Husband *and the* Master of a College.

Hus. Please you draw near, sir ; you're exceeding welcome.

Mast. That's my doubt ; I fear I come not to be welcome.

Hus. Yes, howsoever.

Mast. 'Tis not my fashion, sir, to dwell in long circumstance, but to be plain and effectual ; therefore to the purpose. The cause of my setting forth was piteous and lamentable. That hopeful young gentleman your brother, whose virtues we all love dearly, through your default and unnatural negligence lies in bond executed for your debt,—a prisoner ; all his studies amazed,[17] his hope struck dead, and the pride of his youth muffled in these dark clouds of oppression.

Hus. Umph, umph, umph!

Mast. O you have kill'd the towardest hope of all our university : wherefore, without repentance and amends, expect ponderous and sudden judgments to fall grievously upon you. Your brother, a man who profited in his divine employments, and might have made ten thousand souls fit for heaven, is now by your careless courses cast into prison, which you must answer for ; and assure your spirit it will come home at length.

Hus. O God! oh!

Mast. Wise men think ill of you ; others speak ill of you ; no man loves you: nay, even those whom honesty condemns, condemn you: And take this from the virtuous affection I bear your brother ; never look for prosperous hour, good thoughts, quiet sleep, contented walks, nor any thing that makes man perfect, till you redeem him. What is your answer? How will you bestow him? Upon desperate misery, or better hopes ?—I suffer till I hear your answer.

Hus. Sir, you have much wrought with me ; I feel you in my soul: you are your art's master. I never had sense till now ; your syllables have cleft me. Both for your words and pains I thank you. I cannot but acknowledge grievous wrongs done to my brother ; mighty, mighty, mighty, mighty, wrongs. Within, there.

Enter a Servant.

Hus. Fill me a bowl of wine.   [*Exit Ser.*
Alas, poor brother, bruis'd with an execution for my sake !

Mast. A bruise indeed makes many a mortal sore, Till the grave cure them.

Re-enter Servant *with wine.*

Hus. Sir, I begin to you ; you've chid your welcome.

Mast. I could have wish'd it better for your sake. I pledge you, sir :—To the kind man in prison.

Hus. Let it be so. Now, sir, if you please to spend but a few minutes in a walk about my grounds below, my man here shall attend you. I doubt not but by that time to be furnish'd of a sufficient answer, and therein my brother fully satisfied.

Mast. Good sir, in that the angels would be pleas'd,
And the world's murmurs calm'd; and I should say,
I set forth then upon a lucky day.
                                [Exeunt Mast. *and* Ser.

Hus. O thou confused man! Thy pleasant sins have undone thee; thy damnation has beggar'd thee. That heaven should say we must not sin, and yet made women! give our senses way to find pleasure, which being found, confounds us! Why should we know those things so much misuse us? O, would virtue had been forbidden! We should then have prov'd all virtuous; for 'tis our blood to love what we are forbidden. Had not drunkenness been forbidden, what man would have been fool to a beast, and zany to a swine,—to show tricks in the mire? What is there in three dice, to make a man draw thrice three thousand acres into the compass of a little round table, and with the gentleman's palsy in the hand shake out his posterity thieves or beggars? 'Tis done; I have don 't i'faith: terrible, horrible misery!—How well was I left! Very well, very well. My lands show'd like a full moon about me; but now the moon's in the last quarter,—waning, waning; and I am mad to think that moon was mine; mine and my father's, and my fore-fathers'; generations, generations.— Down goes the house of us; down, down it sinks. Now is the name a beggar; begs in me. That name which hundreds of years has made this shire famous, in me and my posterity runs out. In my seed five are made miserable besides myself: my riot is now my brother's gaoler, my wife's sighing, my three boys' penury, and mine own confusion. Why sit my hairs upon my cursed head?
                                [Tears his hair.
Will not this poison scatter them?[18] O, my brother's
In execution among devils that
Stretch him and make him give; and I in want.
Not able for to live, nor to redeem him!
Divines and dying men may talk of hell,
But in my heart her several torments dwell;
Slavery and misery. Who, in this case,
Would not take up money upon his soul?
Pawn his salvation, live at interest?
I, that did ever in abundance dwell.
For me to want, exceeds the throes of hell.

Enter a little Boy *with a top and scourge.*

Son. What ail you, father? Are you not well? I cannot scourge my top as long as you stand so. You take up all the room with your wide legs. Puh! you cannot make me afraid with this; I fear no vizards, nor bugbears.[19]
    [He takes up the Child *by the skirts of his long*
        coat with one hand, and draws his dagger
        with the other.
Hus. Up, sir, for here thou hast no inheritance left.[20]
Son. O, what will you do, father? I am your white boy.
Hus. Thou shalt be my red boy; take that.
                                [Strikes him.
Son. O, you hurt me, father.
Hus. My eldest beggar,
Thou shalt not live to ask an usurer bread;
To cry at a great man's gate; or follow,
"Good your honour," by a coach; no, nor your brother:
'Tis charity to brain you.
Son. How shall I learn, now my head's broke?
Hus. Bleed, bleed,   *[Stabs him.*
Rather than beg. Be not thy name's disgrace:
Spurn thou thy fortunes first; if they be base,
Come view thy second brother's. Fates! My children's blood
Shall spin into your faces; you shall see,
How confidently we scorn beggary!
                                [Exit with his Son.

SCENE V.

A Maid *discovered with a* Child *in her arms; the* Mother *on a Couch by her asleep.*

Maid. Sleep, sweet babe; sorrow makes thy mother sleep:
It bodes small good when heaviness falls so deep.
Hush, pretty boy; thy hopes might have been better.
'Tis lost at dice, what ancient honour won:
Hard, when the father plays away the son!
Nothing but Misery serves in this house;
Ruin and Desolation.   Oh!

Enter Husband, *with his* Son *bleeding.*

Hus. Whore, give me that boy.
                [Strives with her for the Child.
Maid. O help, help! Out alas! murder, murder!
Hus. Are you gossiping, you prating, sturdy quean?

I 'll break your clamour with your neck.　Down
　　　　stairs ;
Tumble, tumble, headlong.　So :--
　　　　　　[He throws her down, and stabs the Child.
The surest way to charm a woman's tongue,
Is—break her neck : a politician did it.[21]
　Son. Mother, mother ; I am kill'd, mother.
　　　　　　　　　　　　　　[Wife awakes.
　Wife. Ha, who 's that cry'd ?　O me ! my children !
Both, both, bloody, bloody !
　　　　　　[Catches up the youngest Child.
　Hus. Strumpet, let go the boy ; let go the
　　　beggar.
　Wife. O my sweet husband !
　Hus. Filth, harlot.
　Wife. O, what will you do, dear husband ?
　Hus. Give me the bastard.
　Wife. Your own sweet boy—
　Hus. There are too many beggars.
　Wife. Good my husband—
　Hus. Dost thou prevent me still ?
　Wife. O God !
　Hus. Have at his heart.
　　　　　　[Stabs at the Child *in her arms.*
　Wife. O, my dear boy !
　Hus. Brat, thou shalt not live to shame thy
　　　house—
　Wife. Oh heaven !　*[She is hurt, and sinks down.*
　Hus. And perish !—Now be gone :
There 's whores enough, and want would make thee
　　　one.

　　　　　　Enter a Servant.

　Ser. O sir, what deeds are these ?
　Hus. Base slave, my vassal !
Com'st thou between my fury to question me ?
　Ser. Were you the devil, I would hold you, sir.
　Hus. Hold me ?　Presumption !　I 'll undo thee
　　　for it.
　Ser. 'Sblood, you have undone us all, sir.
　Hus. Tug at thy master ?
　Ser. Tug at a monster.
　Hus. Have I no power ?　Shall my slave fetter
　　　me ?
　Ser. Nay then the devil wrestles ; I am thrown.
　Hus. O villain ! now I 'll tug thee, now I 'll tear
　　　thee ;
Set quick spurs to my vassal ; bruise him, trample
　　　him.
So ; I think thou wilt not follow me in haste.
My horse stands ready saddled.　Away, away ;
Now to my brat at nurse, my sucking beggar :
Fates, I 'll not leave you one to trample on !　*[Exit.*

SCENE VI.—*Court before the House.*

Enter Husband ; *to him the* Master of the College.

　Mast. How is it with you, sir ?
Methinks you look of a distracted colour.
　Hus. Who, I, sir ?　'Tis but your fancy.
Please you walk in, sir, and I 'll soon resolve you :
I want one small part to make up the sum,
And then my brother shall rest satisfied.
　Mast. I shall be glad to see it : Sir, I 'll attend
　　　you.　　　　　　　　　　　*[Exeunt.*

SCENE VII.—*A Room in the House.*

The Wife, Servant, *and* Children *discovered.*

　Ser. Oh, I am scarce able to heave up myself,
He has so bruis'd me with his devilish weight,
And torn my flesh with his blood hasty spur :
A man before of easy constitution,
Till now Hell power supplied, to his soul's wrong :
O how damnation can make weak men strong !

Enter the Master of the College *and two* Servants.

　Ser. O the most piteous deed, sir, since you
　　　came !
　Mast. A deadly greeting !　Hath he summ'd up
　　　these
To satisfy his brother ?　Here 's another ;
And by the bleeding infants, the dead mother.
　Wife. Oh ! oh !
　Mast. Surgeons ! surgeons ! she recovers life :--
One of his men all faint and bloodied !
　1st Ser. Follow ; our murderous master has took
　　　horse
To kill his child at nurse.　O, follow quickly.
　Mast. I am the readiest ; it shall be my charge
To raise the town upon him.[22]
　1st Ser. Good sir, do follow him.
　　　　　　[Exeunt Master *and two* Servants.
　Wife. O my children !
　1st Ser. How is it with my most afflicted mis-
　　　tress ?
　Wife. Why do I now recover ?　Why half live,
To see my children bleed before mine eyes ?
A sight able to kill a mother's breast, without
An executioner.—What, art thou mangled too ?
　1st Ser. I, thinking to prevent what his quick
　　　mischiefs
Had so soon acted, came and rush'd upon him.
We struggled ; but a fouler strength than his
O'erthrew me with his arms ;[23] then did he bruise
　　　me,

And rent my flesh, and robb'd me of my hair;
Like a man mad in execution,
Made me unfit to rise and follow him.

   Wife. What is it has beguil'd him of all grace,
And stole away humanity from his breast?
To slay his children, purpose to kill his wife,
And spoil his servants—

           Enter a Servant.

   Ser. Please you to leave this most accursed place:
A surgeon waits within.

   Wife. Willing to leave it?
'Tis guilty of sweet blood, innocent blood:
Murder has took this chamber with full hands,
And will ne'er out as long as the house stands.
                      [Exeunt.

       SCENE VIII.--*A high Road.*

      Enter Husband.   *He falls.*

   Hus. O stumbling jade! The spavin overtake
thee!
The fifty diseases stop thee![24]
Oh, I am sorely bruis'd! Plague founder thee!
Thou run'st at ease and pleasure. Heart of chance!
To throw me now, within a flight o' the town,
In such plain even ground too! 'Sfoot, a man
May dice upon it, and throw away the meadows.
Filthy beast!
   [*Cry within.*] Follow, follow, follow.
   Hus. Ha! I hear sounds of men, like hue and
cry.
Up, up, and struggle to thy horse; make on;
Dispatch that little beggar, and all's done.
   [*Cry within.*] Here, here; this way, this way.
   Hus. At my back? Oh,
What fate have I! my limbs deny me go.
My will is 'bated; beggary claims a part.
O could I here reach to the infant's heart!

Enter the Master of the College, *Three* Gentlemen, *and* Attendants *with Halberds.*

   All. Here, here; yonder, yonder.
   Mast. Unnatural, flinty, more than barbarous!
The Scythians, even the marble-hearted Fates,
Could not have acted more remorseless deeds,
In their relentless natures, than these of thine.
Was this the answer I long waited on?
The satisfaction for thy prison'd brother?
   Hus. Why he can have no more of us than our
skins,
And some of them want but fleaing.
   1st Gent. Great sins have made him impudent.

   Mast. He has shed so much blood, that he can-
not blush.
   2nd Gent. Away with him; bear him to the
justice's.
A gentleman of worship dwells at hand:
There shall his deeds be blaz'd.
   Hus. Why all the better.
My glory 'tis to have my action known;
I grieve for nothing, but I miss'd of one.
   Mast. There's little of a father in that grief:
Bear him away.   *[Exeunt.*

   SCENE IX.—*A Room in the House of a*
              Magistrate.

   Enter a Knight, *and Three* Gentlemen.

   Knight. Endanger'd so his wife? murder'd his
children?
   1st Gent. So the cry goes.
   Knight. I am sorry I e'er knew him;
That ever he took life and natural being
From such an honour'd stock, and fair descent,
Till this black minute without stain or blemish.
   1st Gent. Here come the men.

Enter Master of the College, *&c., with the* Prisoner.

   Knight. The serpent of his house! I am sorry
For this time, that I am in place of justice.
   Mast. Please you, sir——
   Knight. Do not repeat it twice; I know too much:
Would it had ne'er been thought on! Sir, I bleed
for you.
   1st Gent. Your father's sorrows are alive in me.
What made you show such monstrous cruelty?
   Hus. In a word, sir, I have consum'd all, play'd
away long-acre; and I thought it the charitablest
deed I could do, to cozen beggary, and knock my
house o' the head.
   Knight. O, in a cooler blood you will repent it.
   Hus. I repent now that one is left unkill'd;
My brat at nurse. I would full fain have wean'd
him.
   Knight. Well, I do not think, but in to-mor-
row's judgment,
The terror will sit closer to your soul,
When the dread thought of death remembers you:
To further which, take this sad voice from me,
Never was act play'd more unnaturally.
   Hus. I thank you, sir.
   Knight. Go lead him to the gaol:
Where justice claims all, there must pity fail.
   Hus. Come, come; away with me.
                    [Exeunt Hus., *&c.*

Mast. Sir, you deserve the worship of your place:
Would all did so! In you the law is grace.
 Knight. It is my wish it should be so.—Ruinous man!
The desolation of his house, the blot
Upon his predecessors' honour'd name!
That man is nearest shame, that is past shame.
         [Exeunt.

SCENE X.—*Before* Calverly Hall.

Enter Husband *guarded,* Master of the College, Gentlemen, *and* Attendants.

 Hus. I am right against my house,—seat of my ancestors :[25]
I hear my wife 's alive, but much endanger'd.
Let me entreat to speak with her, before
The prison gripe me.

   His Wife *is brought in.*

 Gent. See, here she comes of herself.
 Wife. O my sweet husband, my dear distress'd husband,
Now in the hands of unrelenting laws,
My greatest sorrow, my extremest bleeding;
Now my soul bleeds.
 Hus. How now? Kind to me? Did I not wound thee?
Left thee for dead?
 Wife. Tut, far, far greater wounds did my breast feel;
Unkindness strikes a deeper wound than steel.
You have been still unkind to me.
 Hus. 'Faith, and so I think I have;
I did my murders roughly out of hand,
Desperate and sudden; but thou hast devis'd
A fine way now to kill me: thou hast given mine eyes
Seven wounds a-piece. Now glides the devil from me,
Departs at every joint; heaves up my nails.
O catch him torments, that were ne'er invented!
Bind him one thousand more, you blessed angels,
In that pit bottomless![26] Let him not rise
To make men act unnatural tragedies;
To spread into a father, and in fury
Make him his children's executioner;
Murder his wife, his servants, and who not?—
For that man's dark, where heaven is quite forgot.
 Wife. O my repentant husband!
 Hus. O my dear soul, whom I too much have wrong'd;
For death I die, and for this have I long'd.

 Wife. Thou should'st not, be assur'd, for these faults die
If the law could forgive as soon as I.
     [The two Children *laid out.*
 Hus. What sight is yonder?
 Wife. O, our two bleeding boys,
Laid forth upon the threshold.
 Hus. Here 's weight enough to make a heart-string crack.
O were it lawful that your pretty souls
Might look from heaven into your father's eyes,
Then should you see the penitent glasses melt,
And both your murders shoot upon my cheeks!
But you are playing in the angels' laps,
And will not look on me, who, void of grace,
Kill'd you in beggary.
O that I might my wishes now attain,
I should then wish you living were again,
Though I did beg with you, which thing I fear'd:
O, 'twas the enemy my eyes so blear'd![27]
O, would you could pray heaven me to forgive,
That will unto my end repentant live!
 Wife. It makes me even forget all other sorrows
And live apart with this.
 Off. Come, will you go?
 Hus. I 'll kiss the blood I spilt, and then I 'll go:
My soul is bloodied, well may my lips be so.
Farewell, dear wife; now thou and I must part;
I of thy wrongs repent me with my heart.
 Wife. O stay; thou shalt not go.
 Hus. That 's but in vain; you see it must be so.
Farewell ye bloody ashes of my boys!
My punishments are their eternal joys.[28]
Let every father look into my deeds,
And then their heirs may prosper, while mine bleeds. *[Exeunt* Hus. *and* Officers.
 Wife. More wretched am I now in this distress,
Than former sorrows made me.
 Mast. O kind wife,
Be comforted; one joy is yet unmurder'd;
You have a boy at nurse; your joy's in him.
 Wife. Dearer than all is my poor husband's life.
Heaven give my body strength, which is yet faint
With much expense of blood, and I will kneel,
Sue for his life, number up all my friends,
To plead for pardon for my dear husband's life.
 Mast. Was it in man to wound so kind a creature?
I 'll ever praise a woman for thy sake.
I must return with grief; my answer's set;[29]
I shall bring news weighs heavier than the debt.
Two brothers, one in bond lies overthrown,
This on a deadlier execution.[30] *[Exeunt omnes.*

NOTES TO A YORKSHIRE TRAGEDY.

---

[1] *Enter Oliver and Ralph.*

The dialogue between these servants appears to have no relation to the plot; it probably refers to some incident which the author at first contemplated and afterwards abandoned. The young mistress who so deplores the long absence of her love cannot be Mrs. Calverly, the wife of the principal character, for the third servant says that this lover is married to another woman, that he "beats his wife, and has two or three children by her." On which Oliver remarks—"I would not for two years' wages my young mistress knew so much." This language must refer to some young lady who has been abandoned by Mr. Calverly; but it is strange that he should have been married to another for some years, and she remain unacquainted with the circumstance, especially as this rival resides in her own neighbourhood. No allusion is made to this slighted fair one after the first scene, which, indeed, might be omitted without injury to the story. The author possibly intended to write a longer drama, but finding that he had not sufficient materials, or becoming tired of his subject, hurried it to a conclusion.

[2] *Neither of either, as the puritan bawd says.*

An expression intended to ridicule the affected preciseness of expression used by the puritans. This quiet good-humoured little sarcasm is in the manner of Shakspere, who, in many of his plays, has expressed his dislike of that formal sect; but it cannot be used as evidence that he was the author of this brief drama, as a hit at the growing puritanism of the age seems in his time to have been relished in the theatre. This probably induced Ben Jonson to write his long farce of *Bartholomew Fair*, in which the puritans are so mercilessly laughed at. When, in after times, the saints swayed the destinies of the country, they closed the theatres, and possibly a sense of retaliation for the ridicule they were there treated with, may have had as much influence in causing this severity towards the players as the stern principles of religion professed by the dominant party. The dull man who feels a sarcasm, and cannot retort it, is tempted to a rougher and more violent revenge.

[3] *Two rebato wires.*

Wires employed in producing the plaits of the ancient ruff; *rebato* was the name of a frilled head-dress.

[4] *For you must note, that any woman bears the more she is beaten.*

An allusion to the unmannerly old proverb—

A woman, a dog, and a walnut-tree,
The more you beat 'em they better they be.

[5] *I quite forgot my two poking-sticks.*

A *poking-stick* was an instrument of the nature of the modern Italian-iron; it was used to adjust the plaits of the great ruffs formerly worn.

[6] *Ay, far fetch'd, you know Sam.*

A proverbial saying. On the books of the Stationers' Company, 1566, is entered "A playe intituled *Farre fetched and deare bowght ys good for ladies.*"

[7] *Enter Wife.*

To none of the characters, except the three servants, has the author given any names; it should be remembered that the drama is founded on a murder which actually occurred, and, as Mr. Steevens states, the author might not think himself at liberty to use the real names belonging to his characters, and at the same time was of opinion that fictitious ones would appear unsatisfactory, as the true were universally known.

[8] *The angels have forsook me.*

A pun is here intended between an *angel* a messenger of heaven, and an *angel* a gold coin of ten shillings value. So in *The Merry Wives of Windsor*—"She hath a legion of angels."

[9] *A promoter*, i.e. an informer.

[10] *As you are a gentleman by many bloods.*

That is, related to many high families.

[11] *Puh! bastards, bastards, bastards.*

"Though Shakspere has thought it necessary (says Mr. Steevens) to deviate from his story as it is still related in Yorkshire, yet here he seems to have had the original cause of this unhappy gentleman's rashness in his mind. Mr. Calverly is represented to have been of a passionate disposition, and to have struck one of his children in the presence of his wife, who pertly told him, *to correct children of his own when he could produce any.* On this single provocation he is said to have immediately committed all the bloody facts that furnish matter for the tragedy before us. He died possessed of a large estate."

[12] *O much against my blood.*

That is, against my nature or inclination. So afterwards—

For 'tis our *blood* to love what we 're forbidden.

[13] *My mistress was met by the way, by those who were sent for her up to London.*

She was met by those who were sent to conduct her up to London.

[14] *Fond and peevish*, i.e. weak and silly

[15] *Enter Wife.*

The quarto adds—" in a riding suit," the lady having just returned from her visit to her uncle at London.

[16] *My dankish eyes*, i.e. eyes moistened with tears.

[17] *All his studies amazed*, i.e. confounded, stunned.

[18] *Will not this poison scatter them?*

Alluding to the effects of some kinds of poison, which, even when not powerful enough to kill, cause the sufferer to lose his hair. In Leicester's *Commonwealth* is an instance of this effect of a poison. The author, in speaking of a page who had tasted a potion prepared by Leicester for the earl of Essex, says, " yet was he like to have lost his life, but escaped in the end (being young) with *the losse onely of his haire.*"

[19] *I fear no vizards, nor bugbears.*

Here I should suppose that the father gazes fixedly on the child he was about to murder, who, ignorant of the design, mistakes the distortions of real passion and excitement for grimaces made with a playful intention of frightening him.

[20] *Up, sir, for here thou hast no inheritance left.*

" I believe," says Malone, " he means, that his child having nothing left on earth, he will send him to heaven."

[21] *The surest way to charm a woman's tongue,*
Is—break her neck; a politician did it.

The politician alluded to was Queen Elizabeth's favourite, the earl of Leicester, the death of whose first wife is thus described in the celebrated libel entitled his *Commonwealth* :—

" The death of Leicester's first lady and wife.—For first his lordship hath a speciall fortune, that when he desireth any woman's favour, then what person soever standeth in his way, hath the luck to dye quickly for the finishing of his desire. As for example, when his lordship was in full hope to marry her majesty, and his owne wife stood in his light, as he supposed; he did but send her aside to the house of his servant Forster, of Cumner, by Oxford, where shortly after she had the chance to *fall from a paire of stairs, and so to break her neck*, but yet without hurting of her hood that stood upon her head. But Sir Richard Varney, who by commandment remained with her that day alone, with one man onely, and had sent away perforce all her servants from her to a market two miles off, he (I say) with his man, can tell how she died, which man being taken afterwards for a fellony in the marches of Wales, and offering to publish the manner of the said murder, was made away privily in the prison: and Sir Richard himself dying about the same time in London, cried piteously and blasphemed God, and said to a gentleman of worship of mine acquaintance, not long before his death that all the devils in hell did teare him in

pieces. The wife also of Bald Butler, kinsman to my lord, gave out the whole fact a little before her death. But to return unto my purpose, this was my lord's good fortune to have his wife dye at that time, when it was like to turne most to his profit."

" Lest it should be objected," says Mr. Steevens, " to the probability of Shakspere's having written the *Yorkshire Tragedy*, that he would not, on account of his intimacy with the friend of Essex, have treated the memory of Leicester with so much freedom, let me mention, that the former was executed in 1600, and our author was therefore left at full liberty to adopt the common sentiments relative to this great but profligate statesman."

When, for political reasons, this book was republished, in 1641, a metrical monologue, called *Leicester's Ghost*, was printed with it. The assumed murder is there thus alluded to :—

> My first wife she fell downe a paire of staires
> And brake her necke, and so at Conmore dyed,
> Whilst her true servants led with small affaires,
> Unto a fayre at Abbingdon did ride ;
> This dismall happ did to my wife betyde ;
> Whether ye call yt chance or destinie,
> Too true yt is, she did untimely dye.

[22] *To raise the town upon him.*

The town of Calverly is said to be about a mile from the scene of these murders.

[23] ———— *A fouler strength than his*
O'erthrew me with his arms.

The servant supposes his master to be possessed by a devil, who lends him supernatural strength for the accomplisment of evil purposes.

[24] *The fifty diseases stop thee.*

An expression which alludes to the delicate nature of horses and the great number (not literally fifty) of diseases to which they are subject. There is, however, an old book by one Gervase Markham, entitled, *The Fifty Diseases of a Horse.*

[25] *I am right against my house,—seat of my ancestors.*

The following note by Mr. Steevens will prove of interest to most readers :—" I am told, such general horror was inspired by the fact on which this play is founded, that the mansion of Mr. Calverly was relinquished by all his relations, and being permitted to decay, has never since proved the residence of persons of fashion or estate, being at present no more than a farm-house. They say also, it would be difficult even now to persuade some of the common people in the neighbourhood, but that the unfortunate master of Calverly Hall underwent the fate of Regulus, and was rolled down the hill before his own seat, enclosed in a barrel stuck with nails. Such is one of the stories current among the yeomanry of the circumjacent villages, where it is likewise added, that the place of Mr. Calverly's interment was never exactly known, several coffins supposed to be filled with sand having been deposited in various parishes, that his remains might elude the pursuit of the populace, who threatened to expose them to public infamy on a gibbet. They were imagined, however, at last to have been clandestinely conveyed into the family vault in Calverly church, where the bodies of his children lie; and it was long believed that his ghost rode every night with dreadful cries through the adjoining woods, to the terror of those whose business compelled them to travel late at night, or early in the morning. I have related all this mixture of truth and fable, only to gain an opportunity of observing that no murders were ever more deeply execrated, or bid fairer for a lasting remembrance."

[26] *Bind him one thousand more, you blessed angels,*
In that pit bottomless.

The author alludes to the event related in the first three verses of the twentieth chapter of the *Revelations*, " And I saw an angel come down from heaven, having the key of the bottomless pit and a great chain in his hand. And he laid hold on the dragon, that old serpent, which is the Devil, and Satan, and bound him a thousand years," &c.

[27] *O, 'twas the enemy my eyes so blear'd.*

To *blear*, is to make dim the sight; he means, that the enemy, i.e. the Devil, the common enemy of mankind, had dimmed and deceived his mind, and thus led him to the terrible crimes he had committed. The Hebrew word, signifying Satan, also means the adversary.

[28] *Farewell ye bloody ashes of my boys !*
My punishments are their eternal joys.

The meaning may be, the crime for which I am to suffer has proved their introduction to everlasting happiness; or, that the spirits of the children will rejoice in the punishment of their murderer. In the third part of *Henry the Sixth*, we have a similar idea :—

And happy always was it for that son,
Whose father for his hoarding went to hell.

That is, the son, like the children of Mr. Calverly, was rendered happy by not being punished for the sins of the father who himself expiated them.

[29] *My answer's set.*

That is, fixed, settled. A metaphor from the fixing of colours.

[30] *Two brothers, one in bond lies overthrown,*
This on a deadlier execution.

A quibble between *execution*, the writ in law, and *execution*, or death, by public justice.

H. T.

Locrine

In Holinshed's *Chronicles,* the great repository of English history, Shakespeare found an account of a King Kymbeline or Cymbeline, who is said to have been educated at Rome and there knighted by the Emperor Augustus, under whom he served in several campaigns. He reigned thirty-five years, and was buried in London. The name of Cymbeline's daughter, Imogen, occurs in Holinshed's story of Brutus and his son Locrine. In *The Tragedy of Locrine,* which dates from 1595, Imogen is mentioned as the wife of Brutus.

The play *Locrine,* as well as *Thomas, Lord Cromwell* and *The Puritan,* is advertised on its title pages as having been written by "W. S." Although the three plays, like many others, were omitted by Heminges and Condell from the First Shakespearean Folio of 1623, they appeared in the Third Folio of 1664—their inclusion there being according to Baldwin Maxwell (27), the earliest recorded suggestion that by the latter half of the seventeenth century the "W. S." of their title pages had been accepted as evidence of Shakespeare's whole or partial authorship.

It is interesting to note that the Third Folio, published during the Restoration, was believed to be such an improvement over its predecessors that, as Marchette Chute (11) points out, the Bodleian Library disposed of its copy of the First Folio and bought the new edition of 1664 instead—one in which "seven new plays, never printed before in folio" were added. These included *A Yorkshire Tragedy, Pericles,* and *Sir John Oldcastle,* and four other plays attributed to Shakespeare or to "W. S."in early quartos: *The London Prodigal, Locrine, Thomas, Lord Cromwell,* and *The Puritan.* In assigning only seven more plays to Shakespeare, the publisher of the Third Folio was actually showing great restraint, since the first volume of King Charles's own collection of Shakespeare's plays included *Fair Em, Mucedorus,* and *The Merry Devil of Edmonton.*

The truth was that no one during the Restoration knew what Shakespeare had written and what he had not; and, as soon as the authority of Heminges and Condell was ignored, there was no limit to the number of early plays that could be attributed to him. The Fourth Folio, which was published in 1685, also included the seven plays added to the Third Folio, as did the handsome illustrated edition of Nicholas Rowe at the beginning of the eighteenth century.

Of the three plays mentioned above, the earliest bearing the initials "W. S." is *Locrine*. It was published by Thomas Creede in 1595. Although it was not Creede's habit to give credit to a dramatist, he followed here what was becoming common practice of the time. As there were no copyright laws assuring that a playwright would be credited with his own work or protected against having another's work ascribed to him, Creede in citing the author's initials was doing more than was necessary or perhaps expected. Possibly because a play was regarded as the property of the company that had bought it rather than of the author who had sold it, two-thirds of the plays printed from 1590 to 1595 (including those by dramatists other than Shakespeare), have no statement concerning authorship but cite initials only.

The list concludes, for example, the first printed plays by B. J(onson), J. M(arston), T. M(iddleton), G. P(eele), R. W.(ilmot), and, of course, W. S(hakespeare).

When *Cromwell* (1602) and *The Puritan* (1607) were published, there can be no doubt that Shakespeare's name upon a printed play would have definitely assisted its sale. Maxwell is certain that it would also have done so when Creede published *Locrine* in 1595, although the printers seem to have been tardy in recognizing the value of his name. For instance, before the publication of *Locrine,* there had been two, possibly three, editions of *Venus and Adonis* and one of *The Rape of Lucrece,* all bearing Shakespeare's **full** name; but the only play by Shakespeare to have been printed was *Titus Adronicus,* which had been published anonymously. Indeed, no printed play was to cite Shakespeare as author for at least another two or three years; and it seems odd that, if his initials were then thought sufficient to increase the sale of a printed play, within three years immediately following the appearance of *Locrine* the quartos of *Richard II* (1597), *Richard III* (1597), *Romeo and Juliet* (1597), and *1 Henry IV* (1598) were all printed without mention of Shakespeare's authorship. It is uncertain, moreover, whether "W. S." is claimed to have been the author or merely the reviser. But, regardless of differing opinion, it was only after the appearance and success of *Locrine* that Shakespeare was identified as its author (and from three years after this, all his other works, early and late, made their first appearance in print under his full name).

To Edward Arber (2) and other critics, however, there is no question that Shakespeare either wrote *Locrine* or had a hand in revising it for the stage.

Such also seems to have been the idea of F. G. Fleay (*A Chronicle History of the Life and Work of William Shakespeare,* 1886) when he wrote: "I have faith in the view that W. S., who saw this play through the press, was William Shakespeare, and that he did it from charity to his old coadjutor [Peele], 'long sick and in necessity.'" Moreover, according to F. S. Moorman, the words "newly set forth, overseen and corrected by W. S." on the title page indicate that *Locrine* was an old play revised in 1591. Baldwin Maxwell (27), however, challenges this conclusion, declaring that

> the simplest and most reasonable interpretation of the statement "newly set forth, overseen and corrected by W. S." is, certainly, that the text there printed is that of a play as it had been reworked and revised. The original need not have been an old play. There are, indeed, many and strong reasons for thinking that the text of the tragedy as it has come down to us represents a revision of an earlier play—a revision which includes the insertion of several scenes. . . .

In this view, he seems to be supported by Arthur Acheson in *Shakespeare, Chapman, and Sir Thomas More,* who suggests that *Locrine* was originally penned by Greene in 1585–86 and later corrected by Shakespeare, though

> the only correction made by Shakespeare . . . was in the fourth line from the end, where the words "eight and thirty years" which coincide with the date of publication in 1595, took the place of a number indicating either its date of composition or of its previous presentation.

Acheson argues that Creede's statement about the play's having been "newly set forth, overseen and corrected by W.S." was not only authorized by but actually dictated by Shakespeare. Acheson is referring to an allusion to the queen in the closing speech of the play, which suggests that the quarto did not appear before late 1595 or 1596:

> So let us pray for that renowned maid
> That eight and thirty years the sceptre sway'd,
> In quiet peace and sweet felicity. . . .
> [V. iv]

Considerable controversy has arisen in connection with the different sources of *Locrine*. Various critics and historians have, according to Maxwell, noted the drama's debt to the history of Geoffrey of Monmouth, which the dramatist (ostensibly Shakespeare), supplemented with the histories of Caxton and Holinshed. Other sources were *The Complaint of Elstred,* by Thomas

Lodge, *The Mirror for Magistrates,* Edmund Spenser's *Complaints, Ruins of Rome; Visions of the World's Vanity,* and *The Faerie Queene,* with which Carrie A. Harper, in 1913, found a close parallel.

Willard Farnham took the position of the dramatist's having made some use of the *Mirror,* basing his argument principally upon the close affinity of play and *Mirror* in a "tragic pattern and philosophy of life," which are not, in Maxwell's view, shared by the chronicles. There are in the very first scene of *Locrine,* lines that seem unquestionably to have been inspired by similar lines in the tragedy of Albanact in *The Mirror for Magistrates.*

Frank G. Hubbard, after noting *Locrine*'s indebtedness to a line in Greene's *Menaphon* ("the arm-strong darling of doubled night"), quotes three passages from *Locrine* and one from *Selimus* also borrowed apparently from Greene:

> The arm-strong offspring of the doubled night,
> Stout Hercules, Alcamena's mighty son,
> That tam'd the monsters of the three-fold world. . . .
> > [*Locrine* III. iv (ll. 1253–55)]

> Stout Hercules, the mirror of the world,
> Son to Alcamena and great Jupiter,
> After so many conquests won in field,
> After so many monsters quell'd by force,
> Yielded his valiant heart to Omphale. . . .
> > [Ibid., IV. i (ll. 1362–66)]

> Now sit I like the mighty god of war,
> When, armed with his coat of adamant. . . .
> > [Ibid., III. iv (ll. 1225–26)]

> Now sit I like the arm-strong son of Jove
> When after he had all his monsters quelled,
> He was received in heaven amongst the gods,
> And had fair Hebe for his lovely bride.
> > (*Selimus,* lines 1671–74)

Maxwell, though, admits to some uncertainty as to just what may have been the relationship of the two plays. Attention was first called to this relationship by A. P. Daniel (in a brief note to the Atheneum dated April 16, 1898), who observed that several passages in the two plays were practically identical. About three years later, Charles Crawford likewise called attention to similar passages in both plays noting that among them were several that had been lifted from Spenser's *Complaints.* Thinking that he recognized a difference in the use made of Spenser's lines in the two plays (he believed the author of *Locrin* had sought to vary Spenser's language while the author of *Selimus* was content not to), Crawford concluded that *Locrine* had borrowed from *Selimus*. However, in 1905 Emil Koeppel published the result of his study of the parallels cited by Crawford, in which he reached the opposite conclusion: that *Selimus* had borrowed from *Locrine*. Koeppel was strongly supported in *The Cambridge History of English Literature* by J. W. Cunliffe with an argument based largely on the then unpublished study by Hubbard, which when it was later published, seems to have established the view that the author of *Selimus* was the borrower.

According to the point of view of Madeleine Doran, (13) the *de casibus,* or Gothic, conception of tragedy took form after an infusion of Stoicism from Seneca's tragedies. The constant theme of the former is the spectacle of the fall of illustrious men as showing the uncertainty of worldly power and the danger of coveting it; the latter center on the crucial conflict between the Stoic absolutes of Passion and Reason, and the impact on the world of moral evil in an individual soul. And these two ways of regarding tragic catastrophe —the Stoic and the Christian—are both to be looked for in Elizabethan tragedy.

Actually, they do not form a simple contradiction. They can be, and sometimes were, reconciled theologically. Both views were components of the Christian tradition; different men and different ages, or sometimes even the same man at different times, reflected more strongly now one, now the other intuition about the world. In Elizabethan plays, we sometimes find the two views operating, as in *The Lamentable Tragedy of Locrine*, in what seems to us unassimilated juxtaposition. (Other examples exhibiting a similar Senecan influence are *Gorboduc,* 1561; Gascoigne's *Jocasta,* 1566; Thomas Hughes's *Misfortunes of Arthur,* 1588; and Robert Wilmot's *Gismond of Salerne,* acted in 1567–68, revised for publication in 1591–92 under the title *Tancred and Gismund*.) More often, according to Miss Doran, we find something more complex, with both Stoic and Christian views present but with an emphasis of mood in one direction or the other.

However, a way to intensify tragedy was found by a shift of emphasis in the Christian ethical scheme from its theological to its psychological aspect. Potentiality for tragedy lay in the disruptive force of runaway passion. It was the psychological side of the scheme, the conflict between reason and passion, that widened the possibilities for tragedy in the Elizabethan period. The highly developed psychological theories of the passions, in which there was at the same time such great interest, provided dramatists with a means of deepening motivation and of intensifying internal conflict. But the dramatists did not lose sight of the stage upon which the battle was fought. In Marlowe, Shakespeare, Jonson, and Chapman—all heirs to the *de casibus* tradition—the simple old theme deepened into an awareness of the complex tensions between man's individual desires and the divine order between the central irony of the disproportion of the price mah sets on worldly power and its actual worth, and hence an awareness of profound tragic irony (which *Locrine,* among others, illustrates).

In the tragedies of these dramatists, death and the devil are common symbols. Death is present in the midst of life, and the devil has taken over the world. The special irony in the tragedy of ambition is in the final helplessness of man, in spite of his godlike aspirations to power, before an inexorable universe. The special irony in the tragedy of sex (or love) is in man's betrayal by his passions into a world of evil. A supreme realization of this irony is *Othello,* in which a man rich in all that we most admire in character —emotional depth, integrity, idealism, frankness, and generosity—is led by his very eagerness into self-betrayal by cynicism, malice, and intelligence directed toward evil ends. This attitude is reflected in Davies' summary view of man as a proud and yet wretched thing, and also in the disenchanted humanism of Hamlet (*Mirum in Modum,* England, 1878).

In short, the emotional restlessness of the age is most apparent in its concentration upon death as a subject for the theatre. The thought of death was a gathering point for men's fears and ambitions, a theme on which every writer could be eloquent and moving, particularly with the example of Seneca before him. Even a mediocre playwright like Henry Chettle can be pathetic and sententious:

> . . . the King and Captain are in this alike,
> None has free hold of life, but they are still,
> When death, heaven's steward comes, tenants at will.
> I lay me down, and rest in You my trust,
> If I wake never more, till all flesh rise
> I sleep a happy sleep, sin in me dies . . .

while Romeo laments Juliet with the passionate outcry of the sonneteers:

> . . . O my Love! my wife!
> Death, that has suck'd the honey of thy breath,
> Hath had no power yet upon thy beauty.
> Thou art not conquer'd. Beauty's ensign yet
> Is crimson in thy lips and in thy cheeks,
> And death's pale flag is not advanced there.
> [V. iii. 91–96]

Thus the stoical defiance of death on the stage brought to a head the inner tensions of the Renaissance. The frailty of human pride and reason seems more poignant to the Elizabethans, more calamitous, than to Chaucer or to the writer of *Everyman,* but return to the Middle Ages was neither possible nor desired. And the crucial feature of Jacobean tragedy is not disillusionment with the Renaissance but affirmation, however strained or perplexed, of it in not attempting such a return; restlessness and its splendor come from the same origins. The classical conception of tragedy as a fall from greatness underlies all these plays, with Seneca's as their exemplar; and (as noted by Miss Doran), however differently the responsibility for failure is assessed, and however differently power and greatness are valued, the idea lends constant irony of its own to two such insurgents as, for instance, *Richard III* and an Edward, evil troublers of the poor world's peace, and to Bussy's tragedy no less than to Macbeth's, in which Shakespeare's construction is, as Salinger points out, still based, in important features, on the tradition of which the moralities were part; and to this they owe their opportunity of appealing with universal and yet immediate significance. At the center of his tragedies are the familiar metaphors of man as "a little kingdom," and the state as "a body politic," both reflecting in little the plan of nature.

In this same context Shakespeare summed it all up magnificently in these succinct lines:

> When in disgrace with fortune and man's eyes
> I all alone beweep my outcast state.

PERSONS REPRESENTED.

BRUTUS, *King of* Britain.
Appears, Act I. sc. 1.

LOCRINE, *Son to* Brutus.
Appears, Act I. sc. 1; sc. 3. Act III. sc. 1; sc. 4. Act IV. sc. 1; sc. 3. Act V. sc. 1; sc. 3; sc. 4.

CAMBER, *Son of* Brutus.
Appears, Act I. sc. 1; sc. 3. Act II. sc. 5. Act III. sc. 1; sc. 4. Act IV. sc. 1. Act V. sc. 1.

ALBANACT, *Son to* Brutus.
Appears, Act I. sc. 1; sc. 3. Act II. sc. 3; sc. 4; sc. 5.

CORINEUS, *Brother to* Brutus.
Appears, Act I. sc. 1; sc. 3. Act III. sc. 1; sc. 4; sc. 5. Act IV. sc. 1.

ASSARACUS, *Brother to* Brutus.
Appears, Act I. sc. 1; sc. 3. Act III. sc. 1; sc. 4. Act IV. sc. 1. Act V. sc. 1; sc. 3; sc. 4.

THRASIMACHUS, *Son of* Corineus.
Appears, Act I. sc. 1; sc. 3. Act II. sc. 2; sc. 3; sc. 5. Act III. sc. 1; sc. 4. Act IV. sc. 1. Act V. sc. 1; sc. 2; sc. 4.

DENON, *an old British Officer.*
Appears, Act I. sc. 1; sc. 3. Act II. sc. 3; sc. 5.

HUMBER, *King of the* Scythians.
Appears, Act II. sc. 1; sc. 4; sc. 5; sc. 6. Act III. sc. 2; sc. 6. Act IV. sc. 2; sc. 4.

HUBBA, *his Son.*
Appears, Act II. sc. 1; sc. 4; sc. 5; sc. 6. Act III. sc. 2; sc. 5.

SEGAR, *a Scythian Commander.*
Appears, Act II. sc. 1; sc. 4; sc. 6. Act III. sc. 2; sc. 5.

THRASSIER, *a Scythian Commander.*
Appears, Act II. sc. 4; sc. 6. Act III. sc. 2.

STRUMBO, *a Cobbler.*
Appears, Act I. sc. 2. Act II. sc. 2; sc. 3; sc. 4; sc. 5. Act III. sc. 3. Act IV. sc. 2.

TROMPART, *his Servant.*
Appears, Act I. sc. 2. Act II. sc. 2; sc. 3; sc. 5. Act III. sc. 3.

OLIVER, *a Clown.*
WILLIAM, *his Son.*
Appear, Act III. sc. 3.

GUENDOLEN, *Daughter of* Corineus, *and Wife of* Locrine.
Appears, Act I. sc. 1; sc. 3. Act III. sc. 1. Act V. sc. 2; sc. 4.

MADAN, *Daughter of* Locrine, *and* Guendolen.
Appears, Act V. sc. 1; sc. 4.

ESTRILD, *Wife to* Humber.
Appears, Act II. sc. 1; sc. 6. Act III. sc. 2. Act. IV. sc. 1. Act V. sc. 1; sc. 3; sc. 4.

SABREN, *Daughter of* Locrine *and* Estrild.
Appears, Act. V. sc. 1; sc. 3; sc. 4.

DOROTHY, Strumbo's *Wife.*
Appears, Act I. sc. 2. Act II. sc. 2.

MARGERY, *Daughter of* Oliver.
Appears, Act III. sc. 3.

GHOST OF ALBANACT.
Appears, Act III. sc. 2; sc. 6. Act IV. sc. 2.

GHOST OF CORINEUS.
Appears, Act V. sc. 4.

ATE, *the Goddess of Revenge, as* Chorus.
Appears before each Act, and at the conclusion.

Lords, a Captain, Soldiers, a Page, and other Attendants.

SCENE.—BRITAIN.

Locrine.

———◆———

ACT I.

DUMB SHOW.

Thunder and lightning.   Enter ATE *in black, with a burning torch in one hand, and a bloody sword in the other. Presently let there come forth a lion running after a bear; then come forth an archer, who must kill the lion in a dumb show, and then depart.* ATE *remains.*

   Até. In poenam sectatur et umbra.
A mighty lion, ruler of the woods,
Of wondrous strength and great proportion,
With hideous noise scaring the trembling trees,
With yelling clamours shaking all the earth,
Travers'd the groves, and chas'd the wand'ring
     beasts :
Long did he range amid the shady trees,
And drave the silly beasts before his face;
When suddenly from out a thorny bush
A dreadful archer, with his bow y-bent,
Wounded the lion with a dismal shaft ;
So he him struck, that it drew forth the blood,
And fill'd his furious heart with fretting ire.
But all in vain he threatneth teeth and paws,
And sparkleth fire from forth his flaming eyes,
For the sharp shaft gave him a mortal wound :
So valiant Brute, the terror of the world,
Whose only looks did scare his enemies,
The archer Death brought to his latest end.
O, what may long abide above this ground,
In state of bliss and healthful happiness !   [*Exit.*

SCENE I.

Enter BRUTUS, *carried in a chair;* LOCRINE, CAMBER, ALBANACT, CORINEUS, GUENDOLEN, ASSARACUS, DEBON, *and* THRASIMACUS.

   Bru. Most loyal lords, and faithful followers,
That have with me, unworthy general,
Passed the greedy gulf of Ocean,
Leaving the confines of fair Italy,
Behold, your Brutus draweth nigh his end,
And I must leave you, though against my will.
My sinews shrink, my numbed senses fail,
A chilling cold possesseth all my bones ;
Black ugly Death with visage pale and wan
Presents himself before my dazzled eyes,
And with his dart prepared is to strike.
These arms, my lords, these never-daunted arms,
That oft have quelled the courage of my foes,
And eke dismay'd my neighbours' arrogance,
Now yield to death, o'erlaid with crooked age,
Devoid of strength and of their proper force.
Even as the lusty cedar worn with years,
That far abroad her dainty odour throws,
'Mongst all the daughters of proud Lebanon,
This heart, my lords, this ne'er-appalled heart,
That was a terror to the bordering lands,
A doleful scourge unto my neighbour kings,
Now by the weapons of unpartial death
Is clove assunder, and bereft of life :
As when the sacred oak with thunderbolts,
Sent from the fiery circuit of the heavens,
Sliding along the air's celestial vaults,
Is rent and cloven to the very roots.
In vain therefore I struggle with this foe ;
Then welcome death, since God will have it so.

   Assar. Alas ! my lord, we sorrow at your case,
And grieve to see your person vexed thus.
But whatsoe'er the Fates determined have,
It lieth not in us to disannul ;
And he that would annihilate their minds,
Soaring with Icarus too near the sun,
May catch a fall with young Bellerophon.[1]
For when the fatal Sisters have decreed
To separate us from this earthly mould,
No mortal force can countermand their minds.
Then, worthy lord, since there's no way but one,
Cease your laments, and leave your grievous moan.

   Cor. Your highness knows how many victories,
How many trophies I erected have
Triumphantly in every place we came.
The Grecian monarch, warlike Pandrasus,

And all the crew of the Molossians;
Goffarius the arm-strong king of Gauls,
Have felt the force of our victorious arms,
And to their cost beheld our chivalry.
Where-e'er Aurora, handmaid of the sun,
Where-e'er the sun, bright guardian of the day,
Where-e'er the joyful day with cheerful light,
Where-e'er the light illuminates the world,
The Trojans' glory flies with golden wings,
Wings that do soar beyond fell Envy's flight.
The fame of Brutus and his followers
Pierceth the skies, and, with the skies, the throne
Of mighty Jove, commander of the world.
Then, worthy Brutus, leave these sad laments:
Comfort yourself with this your great renown,
And fear not Death, though he seem terrible.

Bru. Nay, Corineus, you mistake my mind,
In construing wrong the cause of my complaints,
I fear'd to yield myself to fatal death;
God knows it was the least of all my thought.
A greater care torments my very bones,
And makes me tremble at the thought of it;
And in you, lordings, doth the substance lie.

Thra. Most noble lord, if aught your loyal peers
Accomplish may, to ease your ling'ring grief,
I, in the name of all, protest to you,
That we will boldly enterprise the same,
Were it to enter to black Tartarus,
Where triple Cerberus, with his venomous throat,
Scareth the ghosts with high-resounding noise.
We'll either rent the bowels of the earth,
Searching the entrails of the brutish earth,
Or, with Ixion's over-daring son,
Be bound in chains of ever-during steel.

Bru. Then hearken to your sovereign's latest
words,
In which I will unto you all unfold
Our royal mind and resolute intent.
When golden Hebe, daughter to great Jove,
Cover'd my manly cheeks with youthful down,
The unhappy slaughter of my luckless sire
Drove me and old Assaracus, mine eame,[2]
As exiles from the bounds of Italy;
So that perforce we were constrain'd to fly
To Græcia's monarch, noble Pandrasus.
There I alone did undertake your cause,
There I restor'd your antique liberty,
Though Græcia frown'd, and all Molossia storm'd;
Though brave Antigonus, with martial band,
In pitched field encounter'd me and mine;
Though Pandrasus and his contributaries,
With all the route of their confederates,
Sought to deface our glorious memory,

And wipe the name of Trojans from the earth:
Him did I captivate with this mine arm,
And by compulsion forc'd him to agree
To certain articles we did propound.
From Græcia through the boisterous Hellespont
We came unto the fields of Lestrygon,
Whereas our brother Corineus was;
Since when we passed the Cilician gulf,
And so transfreting[3] the Illyrian sea,
Arrived on the coasts of Acquitain;
Where, with an army of his barbarous Gauls,
Goffarius and his brother Gathelus
Encountering with our host, sustain'd the foil;
And for your sakes my Turinus there I lost,
Turinus, that slew six hundred men at arms,
All in an hour, with his sharp battle-axe.
From thence upon the stronds of Albion
To Corus' haven happily we came,
And quell'd the giants, come of Albion's race,
With Gogmagog, son to Samotheus,[4]
The cursed captain of that damned crew;
And in that isle at length I placed you.
Now let me see, if my laborious toils,
If all my care, if all my grievous wounds,
If all my diligence, were well employ'd.

Cor. When first I follow'd thee and thine, brave
king,
I hazarded my life and dearest blood
To purchase favour at your princely hands;
And for the same, in dangerous attempts,
In sundry conflicts, and in divers broils,
I shew'd the courage of my manly mind.
For this I combated with Gathelus,
The brother to Goffarius of Gaul:
For this I fought with furious Gogmagog,
A savage captain of a savage crew;
And for these deeds brave Cornwall I receiv'd,
A grateful gift given by a gracious king;
And for this gift, his life and dearest blood
Will Corineus spend for Brutus' good.

Deb. And what my friend, brave prince, hath
vow'd to you,
The same will Debon do unto his end.

Bru. Then, loyal peers, since you are all agreed,
And resolute to follow Brutus' hests,
Favour my sons, favour these orphans, lords,
And shield them from the dangers of their foes.
Locrine, the column of my family,
And only pillar of my weaken'd age,
Locrine, draw near, draw near unto thy sire,
And take thy latest blessings at his hands:
And, for thou art the eldest of my sons,
Be thou a captain to thy brethren,

And imitate thy aged father's steps,
Which will conduct thee to true honour's gate :
For if thou follow sacred virtue's lore,[5]
Thou shalt be crowned with a laurel branch,
And wear a wreath of sempiternal fame,[6]
Sorted amongst the glorious happy ones.[7]

    Loc. If Locrine do not follow your advice,
And bear himself in all things like a prince
That seeks to amplify the great renown
Left unto him for an inheritage
By those that were his glorious ancestors,
Let me be flung into the ocean,
And swallow'd in the bowels of the earth :
Or let the ruddy lightning of great Jove
Descend upon this my devoted head.

    Bru. But for I see you all to be in doubt,
Who shall be matched with our royal son,
Locrine, receive this present at my hand ;
                [*Taking* GUEN. *by the hand.*
A gift more rich than are the wealthy mines
Found in the bowels of America.[8]
Thou shalt be spoused to fair Guendolen :
Love her, and take her, for she is thine own,
If so thy uncle and herself do please.

    Cor. And herein how your highness honours me
It cannot now be in my speech express'd ;
For careful parents glory not so much
At their own honour and promotion,
As for to see the issue of their blood
Seated in honour and prosperity.

    Guen. And far be it from any maiden's thoughts
To contradict her aged father's will.
Therefore, since he to whom I must obey,
Hath given me now unto your royal self,
I will not stand aloof from off the lure,
Like crafty dames that most of all deny
That which they most desire to possess.

    Bru. Then now, my son, thy part is on the stage,
           [*Turning to* Loc. *who kneels.*
For thou must bear the person of a king.
           [*Puts the Crown on his Head.*
Locrine stand up, and wear the regal crown,
And think upon the state of majesty,
That thou with honour well may'st wear the crown :
And if thou tend'rest these my latest words,
As thou requir'st my soul to be at rest,
As thou desir'st thine own security,
Cherish and love thy new-betrothed wife

    Loc. No longer let me well enjoy the crown,
Than I do honour peerless Guendolen.

    Bru. Camber.

    Cam. My lord.

    Bru. The glory of mine age,

And darling of thy mother Innogen,
Take thou the South for thy dominion.
From thee there shall proceed a royal race,
That shall maintain the honour of this land,
And sway the regal sceptre with their hands.
And Albanact, thy father's only joy,
Youngest in years, but not the young'st in mind,
A perfect pattern of all chivalry,
Take thou the North for thy dominion ;
A country full of hills and ragged rocks,
Replenished with fierce, untamed, beasts,
As correspondent to thy martial thoughts.
Live long, my sons, with endless happiness,
And bear firm concordance among yourselves.
Obey the counsels of these fathers grave,
That you may better bear out violence.—
But suddenly, through weakness of my age,
And the defect of youthful puissance,
My malady increaseth more and more,
And cruel Death hasteneth his quickened pace,
To dispossess me of my earthly shape.
Mine eyes wax dim, o'er-cast with clouds of age,
The pangs of death compass my crazed bones ;
Thus to you all my blessings I bequeath,
And, with my blessings, this my fleeting soul.
My soul in haste flies to the Elysian fields :
My glass is run, and all my miseries
Do end with life ; death closeth up mine eyes. [*Dies.*

    Loc. Accursed stars, damn'd and accursed stars,
To abbreviate my noble father's life !
Hard-hearted gods, and too envious fates,
Thus to cut off my father's fatal thread !
Brutus, that was a glory to us all,
Brutus, that was a terror to his foes,
Alas ! too soon by Demogorgon's knife
The martial Brutus is bereft of life :
No sad complaints may move just Æacus.

    Cor. No dreadful threats can fear judge Rhadamanth.[9]
Wert thou as strong as mighty Hercules,
That tam'd the hugy monsters of the world,
Play'dst thou as sweet on the sweet-sounding lute
As did the spouse of fair Eurydice,
That did enchant the waters with his noise,
And made stones, birds, and beasts, to lead a
    dance,
Constrain'd the hilly trees to follow him,
Thou could'st not move the judge of Erebus,
Nor move compassion in grim Pluto's heart ;
For fatal Mors expecteth all the world,[10]
And every man must tread the way of death.
Brave Tantalus, the valiant Pelops' sire,
Guest to the gods, suffer'd untimely death ;

And old Tithonus, husband to the morn,
And eke grim Minos, whom just Jupiter
Deign'd to admit unto his sacrifice.
The thund'ring trumpets of blood-thirsty Mars,
The fearful rage of fell Tisiphone,
The boisterous waves of humid ocean,
Are instruments and tools of dismal death.
Then, noble cousin, cease to mourn his chance,
Whose age and years were signs that he should
      die,
It resteth now that we inter his bones,
That was a terror to his enemies.
Take up the corse, and princes hold him dead,
Who while he lived upheld the Trojan state.
Sound drums and trumpets; march to Troynovant,
There to provide our chieftain's funeral.

                        [*Exeunt.*

SCENE II.

Enter STRUMBO *above, in a Gown, with Ink and
Paper in his hand.*

Strum. Either the four elements, the seven
planets, and all the particular stars of the pole
antastic, are adversative against me, or else I was
begotten and born in the wane of the moon, when
every thing, as Lactantios in his fourth book of
Constultations[11] doth say, goeth a—ward. Ay,
masters, ay, you may laugh, but I must weep; you
may joy, but I must sorrow; shedding salt tears
from the watry fountains of my most dainty-fair
eyes along my comely and smooth cheeks, in as
great plenty as the water runneth from the buck-
ing-tubs, or red wine out of the hogsheads. For
trust me, gentlemen and my very good friends, and
so forth, the little god, nay the desperate god,
Cuprit, with one of his vengible bird-bolts, hath
shot me into the heel: so not only, but also, (oh
fine phrase!) "I burn, I burn, and I burn-a; in
love, in love, and in love-a.[12] Ah! Strumbo, what
hast thou seen? not Dina with the ass, Tom?[13]
Yea, with these eyes thou hast seen her; and
therefore pull them out, for they will work thy
bale. Ah! Strumbo, what hast thou heard? not
the voice of the nightingale, but a voice sweeter
than hers; yea, with these ears hast thou heard it,
and therefore cut them off, for they have caus'd thy
sorrow. Nay, Strumbo, kill thyself, drown thyself,
hang thyself, starve thyself. O, but then I shall
leave my sweetheart. Oh my heart! Now, pate, for
thy master! I will 'dite an aliquant love-pistle to
her, and then she hearing the grand verbosity of
my scripture, will love me presently. [*Writes.*

My pen is nought; gentlemen, lend me a knife;[14]
I think the more haste the worst speed.

           [*Writes again, and then reads.*

So it is, mistress Dorothy, and the sole essence of my soul,
that the little sparkles of affection kindled in me towards your
sweet self, hath now increas'd to a great flame, and will, ere it
be long, consume my poor heart, except you with the pleasant
water of your secret fountain quench the furious heat of the
same. Alas, I am a gentleman of good fame and name, in
person majestical, in 'parel comely, in gait portly. Let not
therefore your gentle heart be so hard as to despise a proper
tall young man of a handsome life; and by despising him, not
only but also, to kill him. Thus expecting time and tide, I
bid you farewell.

          Your servant,

             SIGNIOR STRUMBO.[15]

  O wit! O pate! O memory! O hand! O ink!
O paper! Well, now I will send it away. Trompart, Trompart. What a villain is this? Why sirrah,
come when your master calls you. Trompart.

            Enter TROMPART.

  Trom. Anon, sir.
  Strum. Thou knowest, my pretty boy, what a
good master I have been to thee ever since I took
thee into my service.
  Trom. Ay, sir.
  Strum. And how I have cherished thee always,
as if thou hadst been the fruit of my loins, flesh of
my flesh, and bone of my bone.
  Trom. Ay, sir.
  Strum. Then show thyself herein a trusty servant;
and carry this letter to mistress Dorothy, and tell
her——   [*Whispers him. Exit* TROM.
  Strum. Nay, masters, you shall see a marriage by
and by. But here she comes. Now must I frame
my amorous passions.

    Enter DOROTHY *and* TROMPART.

  Dor. Signior Strumbo, well met. I receiv'd your
letters by your man here, who told me a pitiful
story of your anguish; and so understanding your
passions were so great, I came hither speedily.
  Strum. Oh, my sweet and pigsney, the fecundity
of my ingeny[16] is not so great that may declare unto
you the sorrowful sobs and broken sleeps that I
suffer'd for your sake; and therefore I desire you
to receive me into your familiarity:

        For your love doth lie
          As near and as nigh
           Unto my heart within,
        As mine eye to my nose,
        My leg unto my hose,
          And my flesh unto my skin.

Dor. Truly, Master Strumbo, you speak too learnedly for me to understand the drift of your mind; and therefore tell your tale in plain terms, and leave off your dark riddles.

Strum. Alas, mistress Dorothy, this is my luck, that when I most would, I cannot be understood; so that my great learning is an inconvenience unto me. But to speak in plain terms, I love you, mistress Dorothy, if you like to accept me into your familiarity.

Dor. If this be all, I am content.

Strum. Say'st thou so, sweet wench, let me lick thy toes. Farewell, mistress. If any of you be in love, [*Turning to the Audience*] provide ye a cap-case full of new-coin'd words, and then shall you soon have the "succado de labres,"[17] and something else.

[*Exeunt.*

SCENE III.

Enter LOCRINE, GUENDOLEN, CAMBER, ALBANACT, CORINEUS, ASSARACUS, DEBON, *and* THRASIMACHUS.

Loc. Uncle, and princes of brave Britanny,
Since that our noble father is entomb'd,
As best beseem'd so brave a prince as he,
If so you please, this day my love and I,
Within the temple of Concordia,
Will solemnize our royal marriage.

Thra. Right noble lord, your subjects every one
Must needs obey your highness at command;
Especially in such a case as this,
That much concerns your highness' great content.

Loc. Then frolic, lordings, to fair Concord's walls,
Where we will pass the day in knightly sports,
The night in dancing and in figur'd masks,
And offer to god Risus[18] all our sports. [*Exeunt.*

ACT II.

Enter ATE *as before. After a little lightning and thundering, let there come forth this show. Enter at one door* PERSEUS *and* ANDROMEDA, *hand in hand, and* CEPHEUS *also, with swords and targets. Then let there come out of another door* PHINEUS, *in black armour, with Æthiopians after him, driving in* PERSEUS; *and having taken away* ANDROMEDA, *let them depart.* ATE *remains.*

Até. Regit omnia numen.
When Perseus married fair Andromeda,
The only daughter of king Cepheus,
He thought he had establish'd well his crown,
And that his kingdom should for aye endure.
But lo! proud Phineus with a band of men,
Contriv'd of sun-burnt Æthiopians,
By force of arms the bride he took from him,
And turn'd their joy into a flood of tears.
So fares it with young Locrine and his love;
He thinks this marriage tendeth to his weal,
But this foul day, this foul accursed day,
Is the beginning of his miseries.
Behold where Humber and his Scythians
Approacheth nigh with all his warlike train.
I need not, I, the sequel shall declare,
What tragic chances fall out in this war.

[*Exit.*

SCENE I.

Enter HUMBER, HUBBA, ESTRILD, SEGAR, *and their Soldiers.*

Hum. At length the snail doth climb the highest tops,
Ascending up the stately castle walls;
At length the water with continual drops
Doth penetrate the hardest marble stone;
At length we are arriv'd in Albion.
Nor could the barbarous Dacian sovereign,
Nor yet the ruler of brave Belgia,
Stay us from cutting over to this isle,
Whereas I hear a troop of Phrygians
Under the conduct of Posthumius' son,
Have pitched up lordly pavilions,
And hope to prosper in this lovely isle.
But I will frustrate all their foolish hope,
And teach them that the Scythian emperor
Leads Fortune tied in a chain of gold,
Constraining her to yield unto his will,
And grace him with their regal diadem;
Which I will have, maugre their treble hosts,
And all the power their petty kings can make.

Hub. If she that rules fair Rhamnus' golden gate[19]
Grant us the honour of the victory,

As hitherto she always favour'd us,
Right noble father, we will rule the land
Enthronized in seats of topaz stones;
That Locrine and his brethren all may know,
None must be king but Humber and his son.

Hum. Courage, my son; Fortune shall favour us,
And yield to us the coronet of bay,
That decketh none but noble conquerors.
But what saith Estrild to these regions?
How liketh she the temperature thereof?
Are they not pleasant in her gracious eyes?

Est. The plains, my lord, garnish'd with Flora's
wealth,
And over-spread with party-colour'd flowers,
Do yield sweet contentation to my mind.
The airy hills enclos'd with shady groves,
The groves replenish'd with sweet chirping birds,
The birds resounding heavenly melody,
Are equal to the groves of Thessaly;
Where Phœbus with the learned ladies nine,
Delight themselves with music's harmony,
And from the moisture of the mountain tops
The silent springs dance down with murmuring
streams,
And water all the ground with crystal waves.
The gentle blasts of Eurus' modest wind,
Moving the pittering leaves[20] of Silvan's woods,
Do equal it with Tempe's paradise;
And thus consorted all to one effect,
Do make me think these are the happy isles,
Most fortunate, if Humber may them win.

Hub. Madam, where resolution leads the way,
And courage follows with embolden'd pace,
Fortune can never use her tyranny:
For valiantness is like unto a rock,
That standeth in the waves of ocean;
Which though the billows beat on every side,
And Boreas fell, with his tempestuous storms,
Bloweth upon it with a hideous clamour,
Yet it remaineth still unmoveable.

Hum. Kingly resolv'd, thou glory of thy sire.
But, worthy Segar, what uncouth novelties
Bring'st thou unto our royal majesty?

Seg. My lord, the youngest of all Brutus' sons,
Stout Albanact, with millions of men,
Approacheth nigh, and meaneth ere the morn
To try your force by dint of fatal sword.

Hum. Tut, let him come with millions of hosts,
He shall find entertainment good enough,
Yea, fit for those that are our enemies;
For we'll receive them at the lances' points,
And massacre their bodies with our blades:
Yea, though they were in number infinite,

More than the mighty Babylonian queen,
Semiramis, the ruler of the West,
Brought 'gainst the emperor of the Scythians,
Yet would we not start back one foot from them,
That they might know we are invincible.

Hub. Now, by great Jove, the supreme king of
heaven,
And the immortal gods that live therein,
When as the morning shews his cheerful face,
And Lucifer, mounted upon his steed,
Brings in the chariot of the golden sun,
I'll meet young Albanact in the open field,
And crack my lance upon his burgonet,
To try the valour of his boyish strength.
There will I shew such ruthful spectacles,
And cause so great effusion of blood,
That all his boys shall wonder at my strength:
As when the warlike queen of Amazons,
Penthesilea, armed with her lance,
Girt with a corslet of bright-shining steel,
Coop'd up the faint-heart Grecians in the camp.

Hum. Spoke like a warlike knight, my noble
son;
Nay, like a prince that seeks his father's joy.
Therefore to-morrow, ere fair Titan shine,
And bashful Eos, messenger of light,
Expels the liquid sleep from out men's eyes,
Thou shalt conduct the right wing of the host,
The left wing shall be under Segar's charge
The rearward shall be under me myself.
And lovely Estrild, fair and gracious,
If Fortune favour me in mine attempts,
Thou shalt be queen of lovely Albion.
Fortune shall favour me in mine attempts,
And make thee queen of lovely Albion.
Come, let us in, and muster up our train,
And furnish up our lusty soldiers;
That they may be a bulwark to our state,
And bring our wished joys to perfect end.

[*Exeunt.*

SCENE II.

Enter STRUMBO, DOROTHY, *and* TROMPART,
cobbling shoes, and singing.

Trom. We cobblers lead a merry life:
All. Dan, dan, dan, dan.
Strum. Void of all envy and of strife:
All. Dan diddle dan.
Dor. Our ease is great, our labour small:
All. Dan, dan, dan, dan.
Strum. And yet our gains be much withal:
All. Dan diddle dan.

Dor. With this art so fine and fair :

All. Dan, dan, dan, dan.

Trom. No occupation may compare :

All. Dan diddle dan.

Dor. For merry pastime and joyful glee :
Dan, dan, dan, dan.

Strum. Most happy men we cobblers be :
Dan diddle dan.

Trom. The can stands full of nappy ale :
Dan, dan, dan, dan.

Strum. In our shop still withouten fail :
Dan diddle dan.

Dor. This is our meat, this is our food :
Dan, dan, dan, dan.

Trom. This brings us to a merry mood :
Dan diddle dan.

Strum. This makes us work for company :
Dan, dan, dan, dan.

Dor. To pull the tankards cheerfully :
Dan diddle dan.

Trom. Drink to thy husband, Dorothy :
Dan, dan, dan, dan.

Dor. Why then my Strumbo there's to thee :
Dan diddle dan.

Strum. Drink thou the rest, Trompart, amain :
Dan, dan, dan, dan.

Dor. When that is gone, we'll fill't again :
Dan diddle dan.

Enter a Captain.

Capt. The poorest state is farthest from annoy :
How merrily he sitteth on his stool !
But when he sees that needs he must be press'd,
He'll turn his note, and sing another tune.
Ho, by your leave, master cobbler.

Strum. You are welcome, gentleman. What
will you any old shoes or buskins, or will you have
your shoes clouted ? I will do them as well as any
cobbler in Cathness whatsoever.

Capt. O master cobbler, you are far deceiv'd in
me ; for don't you see this ? [*Shewing him press-
money.*] I come not to buy any shoes, but to buy
yourself. Come, sir, you must be a soldier in the
king's cause.

Strum. Why, but hear you, sir. Has your king
any commission to take any man against his will ?
I promise you, I can scant believe it : or did he
give you commission ?

Capt. O, sir, you need not care for that ; I need
no commission. Hold here. I command you, in
the name of our king Albanact, to appear to-morrow in the town-house of Cathness.

Strum. King Nactaball ! I cry God mercy ;
what have we to do with him, or he with us ? But
you, sir, master Capontail, draw your pasteboard, or

else I promise you, I'll give you a canvasado with
a bastinado over your shoulders, and teach you to
come hither with your implements.

Capt. I pray thee, good fellow, be content ; I do
the king's command.

Strum. Put me out of your book then.

Capt. I may not.

Strum. No ! Well, come, sir, will your stomach
serve you ? By gogs blue-hood and halidom,[21] I
will have a bout with you.

[*Strum. snatches up a staff. They fight.*

Enter THRASIMACHUS.

Thra. How now !
What noise, what sudden clamour's this ?
How now !
My captain and the cobbler so hard at it !
Sirs, what is your quarrel ?

Capt. Nothing, sir, but that he will not take
press-money.

Thra. Here, good fellow, take it at my command,
Unless you mean to be stretch'd.

Strum. Truly, master gentleman, I lack no
money : if you please I will resign it to one of
these poor fellows.

Thra. No such matter.
Look you be at the common house to-morrow.

[*Exeunt* THRA. *and* CAPT.

Strum. O wife, I have spun a fair thread ! If I
had been quiet, I had not been press'd, and therefore well may I waiment.[22] But come, sirrah, shut
up, for we must to the wars. [*Exeunt.*

SCENE III.

Enter ALBANACT, DEBON, THRASIMACHUS,
and Lords.

Alba. Brave cavaliers, princes of Albany,
Whose trenchant blades, with our deceased sire
Passing the frontiers of brave Græcia,
Were bathed in our enemies' lukewarm blood,
Now is the time to manifest your wills,
Your haughty minds and resolutions.
Now opportunity is offered
To try your courage and your earnest zeal,
Which you always protest to Albanact ;
For at this time, yea at this present time,
Stout fugitives, come from the Scythians' bounds,
Have pester'd every place with mutinies.
But trust me, lordings, I will never cease
To persecute the rascal runagates,
Till all the rivers, stained with their blood,
Shall fully shew their fatal overthrow.

Deb. So shall your highness merit great renown,
And imitate your aged father's steps.

Alba. But tell me, cousin, cam'st thou through
the plains?
And saw'st thou there the faint-heart fugitives,
Mustering their weather-beaten soldiers?
What order keep they in their marshalling?

Thra. After we passed the groves of Caledon,
Where murmuring rivers slide with silent streams,
We did behold the straggling Scythians' camp,
Replete with men, stor'd with munition.
There might we see the valiant-minded knights,
Fetching careers along the spacious plains.
Humber and Hubba arm'd in azure blue,
Mounted upon their coursers white as snow,
Went to behold the pleasant flowering fields:
Hector and Troilus, Priamus' lovely sons,
Chasing the Grecians over Simois,
Were not to be compar'd to these two knights.

Alba. Well hast thou painted out in eloquence
The portraiture of Humber and his son.
As fortunate as was Polycrates,[23]
Yet should they not escape our conquering swords,
Or boast of aught but of our clemency.

Enter STRUMBO *and* TROMPART, *crying often,*

" Wild-fire and pitch, wild-fire and pitch."

Thra. What, sirs, what mean you by these
clamours made,
These outcries raised in our stately court?

Strum. Wild-fire and pitch, wild-fire and pitch.

Thra. Villains, I say, tell us the cause hereof.

Strum. Wild-fire and pitch, wild-fire and pitch.

Thra. Tell me, you villains, why you make this
noise,
Or with my lance I'll prick your bowels out.

Alba. Where are your houses? where's your
dwelling-place?

Strum. Place! Ha, ha, ha! laugh a month and
a day at him. Place! I cry God mercy: Why do
you think that such poor honest men as we be,
hold our habitacles in kings' palaces? Ha, ha, ha!
But because you seem to be an abominable chief-
tain, I will tell you our state:
From the top to the toe,
From the head to the shoe,
From the beginning to the ending,
From the building to the brenning.[24]
This honest fellow and I had our mansion-cottage
in the suburbs of this city, hard by the temple of
Mercury; and by the common soldiers of the
Shittens, the Scythians, (what do you call them?)

with all the suburbs, were burnt to the ground;
and the ashes are left there for the country wives
to wash bucks withal:
And that which grieves me most,
My loving wife,
(O cruel strife!)
The wicked flames did roast.
And therefore, captain Crust,
We will continually cry,
Except you seek a remedy,
Our houses to re-edify,
Which now are burnt to dust.
[*Both cry* " Wild-fire and pitch, wild-fire and
pitch."

Alba. Well, we must remedy these outrages,
And throw revenge upon their hateful heads.
And you, good fellows, for your houses burnt,
We will remunerate you store of gold,
And build your houses by our palace-gate.

Strum. Gate! O petty treason to my person, no
where else but by your backside? Gate! O how I
am vexed in my choler! Gate! I cry God mercy.
Do you hear, master king? If you mean to
gratify such poor men as we be, you must build
our houses by the tavern.

Alba. It shall be done, sir.

Strum. Near the tavern; ay, by our lady. Sir,
it was spoken like a good fellow. Do you hear,
sir? when our house is builded, if you do chance to
pass or re-pass that way, we will bestow a quart of
the best wine upon you.
[*Exeunt* STRUM. *and* TROM.

Alba. It grieves me, lordings, that my subjects'
goods
Should thus be spoiled by the Scythians,
Who, as you see, with lightfoot foragers,
Depopulate the places where they come:
But, cursed Humber, thou shalt rue the day,
That e'er thou cam'st unto Cathnesia. [*Exeunt.*

SCENE IV.

Enter HUMBER, HUBBA, SEGAR, THRASSIER, *and*
their Forces.

Hum. Hubba, go take a coronet of our horse,[25]
As many lanciers, and light-armed knights,
As may suffice for such an enterprise,
And place them in the grove of Caledon:
With these, when as the skirmish doth increase,
Retire thou from the shelters of the wood,
And set upon the weaken'd Trojans' backs;
For policy, joined with chivalry,
Can never be put back from victory. [*Exit* HUB.

Enter ALBANACT; STRUMBO *and* Clowns *with him.*

Alba. Thou base-born Hun, how durst thou be
    so bold,
As once to menace warlike Albanact,
The great commander of these regions ?
But thou shalt buy thy rashness with thy death,
And rue too late thy over-bold attempts ;
For with this sword, this instrument of death,
That hath been drenched in my foe-men's blood,
I'll separate thy body from thy head,
And set that coward blood of thine abroach.

    Strum. Nay, with this staff, great Strumbo's in-
    strument,
I'll crack thy cockscomb, paltry Scythian.

    Hum. Nor reck I of thy threats, thou princox
    boy,[26]
Nor do I fear thy foolish insolency :
And, but thou better use thy bragging blade,
Than thou dost rule thy overflowing tongue,
Superbious[27] Briton, thou shalt know too soon
The force of Humber and his Scythians.

    [*They fight.* HUM. *and his* Soldiers *fly.* ALBA.
    and his Forces *follow.*

    Strum. O horrible, terrible !   [*Exit.*

SCENE V.

Alarum.   *Enter* HUMBER *and his* Soldiers.

    Hum. How bravely this young Briton, Alba-
    nact,
Darteth abroad the thunderbolts of war,
Beating down millions with his furious mood,
And in his glory triumphs over all,
Moving the massy squadrons off the ground !
Heaps hills on hills, to scale the starry sky :
As when Briareus, arm'd with an hundred hands,
Flung forth an hundred mountains at great
    Jove :
As when the monstrous giant Monychus
Hurl'd mount Olympus at great Marsis targe,
And shot huge cedars at Minerva's shield.
How doth he overlook with haughty front
My fleeting hosts, and lifts his lofty face
Against us all that now do fear his force !
Like as we see the wrathful sea from far,
In a great mountain heap'd, with hideous noise
With thousand billows beat against the ships,
And toss them in the waves like tennis balls.

                [*An alarum sounded.*
Ah me ! I fear my Hubba is surpris'd.

Alarum again. *Enter* ALBANACT, CAMBER, THRA-
SIMACHUS, DEBON, *and their Forces.*

    Alba. Follow me, soldiers, follow Albanact ;
Pursue the Scythians flying through the field.
Let none of them escape with victory ;
That they may know the Britons' force is more
Than all the power of the trembling Huns.

    Thra. Forward, brave soldiers, forward ; keep
    the chase.
He that takes captive Humber or his son,
Shall be rewarded with a crown of gold.

An alarum sounded ; then they fight. HUMBER
   and his army retreat. The Britons *pursue.*
   HUBBA *enters at their rear, and kills* DEBON :
   STRUMBO *falls down ;* ALBANACT *runs out, and
   afterwards enters wounded.*

    Alba. Injurious Fortune, hast thou cross'd me
    thus ?
Thus in the morning of my victories,
Thus in the prime of my felicity,
To cut me off by such hard overthrow !
Hadst thou no time thy rancour to declare,
But in the spring of all my dignities ?
Hadst thou no place to spit thy venom out,
But on the person of young Albanact ?
I that erewhile did scare mine enemies,
And drove them almost to a shameful flight ;
I that erewhile full lion-like did fare
Amongst the dangers of the thick-throng'd pikes,
Must now depart, most lamentably slain
By Humber's treacheries and Fortune's spites.
Cursed be her charms, damned be her cursed
    charms,
That do delude the wayward hearts of men,
Of men that trust unto her fickle wheel,
Which never leaveth turning upside-down !
O gods, O heavens, allot me but the place
Where I may find her hateful mansion.
I'll pass the Alps to watery Meroe,
Where fiery Phœbus in his chariot,
The wheels whereof are decked with emeralds,
Casts such a heat, yea such a scorching heat,
And spoileth Flora of her chequer'd grass ;
I'll overturn the mountain Caucasus,
Where fell Chimæra in her triple shape,
Rolleth hot flames from out her monstrous paunch,
Scaring the beasts with issue of her gorge ;
I'll pass the frozen zone, where icy flakes
Stopping the passage of the fleeting ships,
Do lie, like mountains, in the congeal'd sea :
Where if I find that hateful house of hers,

I'll pull the fickle wheel from out her hands,
And tie herself in everlasting bands.
But all in vain I breathe these threatenings;
The day is lost, the Huns are conquerors,
Debon is slain, my men are done to death,
The currents swift swim violently with blood,
And last, (O that this last might so long last!)
Myself with wounds past all recovery,
Must leave my crown for Humber to possess.

Strum. Lord have mercy upon us, masters, I
think this is a holiday; every man lies sleeping in
the fields: but God knows full sore against their
wills.

Thra. Fly, noble Albanact, and save thyself,
The Scythians follow with great celerity,
And there's no way but flight or speedy death;
Fly, noble Albanact, and save thyself.

                  [Exit THRA. *Alarum.*

Alba. Nay, let them fly that fear to die the death,
That tremble at the name of fatal Mors.
Ne'er shall proud Humber boast or brag himself,
That he hath put young Albanact to flight:
And lest he should triumph at my decay,
This sword shall reave his master of his life,
That oft hath saved his master's doubtful life:
But oh, my brethren, if you care for me,
Revenge my death upon his trait'rous head.

     Et vos queis domus est nigrantis regia Ditis,
     Qui regitis rigido Stygios moderamine lucos,
     Nox cæci regina poli, furialis Erinnys,
     Diique deæque omnes, Albanum tollite regem,
     Tollite flumineis undis rigidaque palude.
     Nunc me fata vocant, hoc condam pectore ferrum.

                  [Stabs himself.

       Enter TROMPART.

O, what hath he done? his nose bleeds; but I
smell a fox: look where my master lies. Master,
master.

Strum. Let me alone, I tell thee, for I am dead.

Trom. Yet one word, good master.

Strum. I will not speak, for I am dead, I tell thee.

Trom. And is my master dead?   *[Singing.*
  O sticks and stones, brickbats and bones,
    And is my master dead?
  O you cockatrices, and you bablatrices,
    That in the woods dwell:
  You briars and brambles, you cook-shops and shambles,
    Come howl and yell.

  With howling and screeking, with wailing and weeping,
    Come you to lament,
O colliers of Croydon, and rustics of Roydon,
    And fishers of Kent.
For Strumbo the cobbler, the fine merry cobbler
    Of Cathness town,
At this same stoure,[28] at this very hour,
    Lies dead on the ground.

O master, thieves, thieves, thieves!

Strum. Where be they? cox me tunny, bobekin!
let me be rising: be gone; we shall be robb'd by
and by.   *[Exeunt* STRUM. *and* TROM.

            SCENE VI.

Enter HUMBER, HUBBA, SEGAR, THRASSIER
       ESTRILD, *and* Soldiers.

Hum. Thus from the dreadful shocks of furious
    Mars,
Thundering alarums, and Rhamnusia's drum,[29]
We are retir'd with joyful victory.
The slaughtered Trojans, squeltering in their blood,
Infect the air with their carcasses,
And are a prey for every ravenous bird.

Est. So perish they that are our enemies!
So perish they that love not Humber's weal!
And, mighty Jove, commander of the world,
Protect my love from all false treacheries!

Hum. Thanks, lovely Estrild, solace to my soul.
But, valiant Hubba, for thy chivalry
Declar'd against the men of Albany,
Lo! here a flow'ring garland wreath'd of bay,
As a reward for this thy forward mind.

            [Sets it on HUB.'s *head.*

Hub. This unexpected honour, noble sire,
Will prick my courage unto braver deeds,
And cause me to attempt such hard exploits,
That all the world shall sound of Hubba's name.

Hum. And now, brave soldiers, for this good
    success,
Carouse whole cups of Amazonian wine,
Sweeter than Nectar or Ambrosia;
And cast away the clods of cursed care,
With goblets crown'd with Semeleius' gifts.[30]
Now let us march to Abis' silver streams,
That clearly glide along the champain fields,
And moist the grassy meads with humid drops.
Sound drums and trumpets, sound up cheerfully,
Sith we return with joy and victory.   *[Exeunt.*

ACT III.

Enter ATE *as before. Then this dumb show. A Crocodile sitting on a river's bank, and a little Snake stinging it. Both of them fall into the water.*

Até. Scelera in authorem cadunt.

High on a bank, by Nilus' boisterous streams,
Fearfully sat the Egyptian crocodile,
Dreadfully grinding in her sharp long teeth
The broken bowels of a silly fish.
His back was arm'd against the dint of spear,
With shields of brass that shin'd like burnish'd gold:
And as he stretched forth his cruel paws,
A subtle adder creeping closely near,
Thrusting his forked sting into his claws,
Privily shed his poison through his bones,
Which made him swell, that there his bowels burst,
That did so much in his own greatness trust.
So Humber having conquer'd Albanact,
Doth yield his glory unto Locrine's sword.
Mark what ensues, and you may easily see
That all our life is but a tragedy.   [*Exit.*

SCENE I.

Enter LOCRINE, GUENDOLEN, CORINEUS, ASSARA-
cus, THRASIMACHUS, *and* CAMBER.

Loc. And is this true? Is Albanactus slain?
Hath cursed Humber with his straggling host,
With that his army made of mongrel curs,
Brought our redoubted brother to his end?
O that I had the Thracian Orpheus' harp
For to awake out of the infernal shade
Those ugly devils of black Erebus,
That might torment the damned traitor's soul!
O that I had Amphion's instrument,
To quicken with his vital notes and tunes
The flinty joints of every stony rock,
By which the Scythians might be punished!
For, by the lightning of almighty Jove,
The Hun shall die, had he ten thousand lives:
And would to God he had ten thousand lives,
That I might with the arm-strong Hercules
Crop off so vile an hydra's hissing heads!
But say, my cousin, (for I long to hear)
How Albanact came by untimely death.

Thra. After the trait'rous host of Scythians
Enter'd the field with martial equipage,
Young Albanact, impatient of delay,
Led forth his army 'gainst the straggling mates;

Whose multitude did daunt our soldiers' minds.
Yet nothing could dismay the forward prince;
But with a courage most heroical,
Like to a lion 'mongst a flock of lambs,
Made havoc of the faint-heart fugitives,
Hewing a passage through them with his sword.
Yea, we had almost given them the repulse,
When, suddenly from out the silent wood,
Hubba, with twenty thousand soldiers,
Cowardly came upon our weaken'd backs,
And murdered all with fatal massacre:
Amongst the which old Debon, martial knight,
With many wounds was brought unto the death;
And Albanact, oppress'd with multitude,
Whilst valiantly he fell'd his enemies,
Yielded his life and honour to the dust.
He being dead, the soldiers fled amain;
And I alone escaped them by flight,
To bring you tidings of these accidents.

Loc. Not aged Priam, king of stately Troy,
Grand emperor of barbarous Asia,
When he beheld his noble-minded son
Slain trait'rously by all the Mirmidons,
Lamented more than I for Albanact.

Guen. Not Hecuba the queen of Ilion,
When she beheld the town of Pergamus,
Her palace, burned with all-devouring flames,
Her fifty sons and daughters, fresh of hue,
Murdered by wicked Pyrrhus' bloody sword,
Shed such sad tears as I for Albanact.

Cam. The grief of Niobe, fair Athens' queen,[31]
For her seven sons magnanimous in field,
For her seven daughters, fairer than the fairest,
Is not to be compar'd with my laments.

Cori. In vain you sorrow for the slaughtered prince,
In vain you sorrow for this overthrow.
He loves not most that doth lament the most,
But he that seeks to venge the injury.
Think you to quell the enemies' warlike train
With childish sobs and womanish laments?
Unsheath your swords, unsheath your conquering
swords,
And seek revenge, the comfort for this sore.
In Cornwall, where I hold my regiment
Even just ten thousand valiant men at arms
Hath Corineus ready at command.
All these and more, if need shall more require,
Hath Corineus ready at command.

Cam. And in the fields of martial Cambria,

Close by the boisterous Iscan's silver streams,
Where light-foot fairies skip from bank to bank,
Full twenty thousand brave courageous knights
Well exercis'd in feats of chivalry,
In manly manner most invincible,
Young Camber hath, with gold and victual.
All these and more, if need shall more require,
I offer up to venge my brother's death.

   Loc. Thanks, loving uncle, and good brother too;
For this revenge, for this sweet word, revenge,
Must ease and cease my wrongful injuries:
And by the sword of bloody Mars I swear,
Ne'er shall sweet quiet enter this my front,
Till I be venged on his trait'rous head,
That slew my noble brother Albanact.
Sound drums and trumpets; muster up the camp;
For we will straight march to Albania.   [*Exeunt.*

SCENE II.

Enter HUMBER, ESTRILD, HUBBA, THRASSIER, *and*
Soldiers.

   Hum. Thus are we come victorious conquerors
Unto the flowing current's silver streams,
Which, in memorial of our victory,
Shall be agnominated by our name,[32]
And talked of by our posterity:
For sure I hope before the golden sun
Posteth his horses to fair Thetis' plains,[33]
To see the water turned into blood,
And change his bluish hue to rueful red,
By reason of the fatal massacre
Which shall be made upon the virent plains.[34]

Enter the Ghost *of* ALBANACT.[35]

   Ghost. See how the traitor doth presage his
     harm;
See how he glories at his own decay;
See how he triumphs at his proper loss;
O Fortune vile, unstable, fickle, frail!

   Hum. Methinks I see both armies in the field.
The broken lances climb the crystal skies;
Some headless lie, some breathless, on the ground,
And every place is strew'd with carcasses:
Behold the grass hath lost his pleasant green,
The sweetest sight that ever might be seen.

   Ghost. Ay, trait'rous Humber, thou shalt find it
     so,
Yea to thy cost thou shalt the same behold,
With anguish, sorrow, and with sad laments.
The grassy plains, that now do please thine eyes,
Shall ere the night be colour'd all with blood.
The shady groves which now inclose thy camp,

And yield sweet savour to thy damned corps,
Shall ere the night be figur'd all with blood.
The profound stream that passeth by thy tents,
And with his moisture serveth all thy camp,
Shall ere the night converted be to blood,
Yea with the blood of those thy straggling boys:
For now revenge shall ease my lingering grief,
And now revenge shall glut my longing soul. [*Exit.*

   Hub. Let come what will, I mean to bear it out;
And either live with glorious victory,
Or die with fame renown'd for chivalry.
He is not worthy of the honey-comb,
That shuns the hives because the bees have stings.
That likes me best that is not got with ease,
Which thousand dangers do accompany;
For nothing can dismay our regal mind,
Which aims at nothing but a golden crown,
The only upshot of mine enterprises.
Were they enchanted in grim Pluto's court,
And kept for treasure 'mongst his hellish crew,
I would either quell the triple Cerberus,
And all the army of his hateful hags,
Or roll the stone with wretched Sysiphus.

   Hum. Right martial be thy thoughts, my noble
     son,
And all thy words savour of chivalry.

Enter SEGAR.

But, warlike Segar, what strange accidents
Make you to leave the warding of the camp?[36]

   Segar. To arms, my lord, to honourable arms;
Take helm and targe in hand: The Britons come
With greater multitude than erst the Greeks
Brought to the ports of Phrygian Tenedos.

   Hum. But what saith Segar to these accidents?
What counsel gives he in extremities?

   Segar. Why this, my lord, experience teacheth
     us,
That resolution's a sole help at need.
And this, my lord, our honour teacheth us,
That we be bold in every enterprise.
Then, since there is no way but fight or die,
Be resolute, my lord, for victory.

   Hum. And resolute, Segar, I mean to be.
Perhaps some blissfull star will favour us,
And comfort bring to our perplexed state.
Come, let us in, and fortify our camp,
So to withstand their strong invasion.   [*Exeunt.*

SCENE III.

Enter STRUMBO, TROMPART, OLIVER, *and* WILLIAM.

   Strum. Nay, neighbour Oliver, if you be so hot,

come, prepare yourself, you shall find two as stout fellows of us, as any in all the north.

Oliv. No, by my dorth,[37] neighbour Strumbo; Ich zee dat you are a man of small zideration, dat will zeek to injure your old vreends, one of your vamiliar guests; and derefore zeeing your pinion is to deal withouten reazon, Ich and my zon William will take dat course dat shall be fardest vrom reason. How zay you? will you have my daughter or no?

Strum. A very hard question, neighbour, but I will solve it as I may. What reason have you to demand it of me?

Will. Marry sir, what reason had you, when my sister was in the barn, to tumble her upon the hay, and to fish her belly?

Strum. Mass, thou say'st true. Well, but would you have me marry her therefore? No, I scorn her, and you, and you: ay, I scorn you all.

Oliv. You will not have her then?

Strum. No, as I am a true gentleman.

Will. Then will we school you, ere you and we part hence. [*They fight.*

Enter MARGERY. *She snatches the staff out of her Brother's hand, as he is fighting.*

Strum. Ay, you come in pudding-time, or else I had dress'd them.

Mar. You, master saucebox, lobcock, cockscomb; you, slopsauce, lickfingers, will you not hear?

Strum. Who speak you to? me?

Mar. Ay, sir, to you, John Lack-honesty, Littlewit. Is it you that will have none of me?

Strum. No, by my troth, mistress Nicebice. How fine you can nick-name me! I think you were brought up in the University of Bridewell,[38] you have your rhetoric so ready at your tongue's end, as if you were never well warn'd when you were young.

Mar. Why then, goodman Cod's-head, if you will have none of me, farewell.

Strum. If you be so plain, mistress Driggle-draggle, fare you well.

Mar. Nay, master Strumbo, ere you go from hence, we must have more words. You will have none of me? [*They fight.*

Strum. Oh my head, my head! Leave, leave, leave; I will, I will, I will.

Mar. Upon that condition I let thee alone.

Oliv. How now, master Strumbo? Hath my daughter taught you a new lesson?

Strum. Ay, but hear you, goodman Oliver; it will not be for my ease to have my head broken every day: therefore remedy this, and we shall agree.

Oliv. Well, zon, well, (for you are my zon now) all shall be remedied. Daughter, be friends with him.

[*They shake hands. Exeunt* OLIV., WILL., *and* MAR.

Strum. You are a sweet nut; the devil crack you! Masters, I think it be my luck. My first wife was a loving quiet wench; but this, I think, would weary the devil. I would she might be burnt, as my other wife was; if not, I must run to the halter for help. O codpiece, thou hast done thy master! this it is to be meddling with warm plackets. [*Exeunt.*

SCENE IV.

Enter LOCRINE, CAMBER, CORINEUS, THRASI-MACHUS, *and* ASSARACUS.

Loc. Now am I guarded with an host of men,
Whose haughty courage is invincible.
Now am I hemm'd with troops of soldiers,
Such as might force Bellona to retire,
And make her tremble at their puissance.
Now sit I like the mighty god of war,
When, armed with his coat of adamant,
Mounted his chariot drawn with mighty bulls,
He drove the Argives over Xanthus' streams.
Now, cursed Humber, doth thy end draw nigh.
Down goes the glory of his victories,
And all his fame, and all his high renown,
Shall in a moment yield to Locrine's sword.
Thy bragging banners cross'd with argent streams,
The ornaments of thy pavilions,
Shall all be captivated with this hand;
And thou thyself at Albanactus' tomb
Shalt offered be, in satisfaction
Of all the wrongs thou didst him when he liv'd.
But canst thou tell me, brave Thrasimachus,
How far we distant are from Humber's camp?

Thra. My lord, within yon foul accursed grove,
That bears the tokens of our overthrow,
This Humber hath entrench'd his damned camp.
March on, my lord, because I long to see
The treacherous Scythians squelt'ring in their
    gore.

Loc. Sweet Fortune, favour Locrine with a smile,
That I may venge my noble brother's death!
And in the midst of stately Troynovant,
I'll build a temple to thy deity,
Of perfect marble, and of jacinth stones,

That it shall pass the high pyramides,
Which with their top surmount the firmament.

    Cam. The arm-strong offspring of the doubled
        night,[39]
Stout Hercules, Alcmena's mighty son,
That tam'd the monsters of the three-fold world,
And rid the oppressed from the tyrants' yokes,
Did never shew such valiantness in fight,
As I will now for noble Albanact.

    Cor. Full fourscore years hath Corineus liv'd,
Sometimes in war, sometimes in quiet peace,
And yet I feel myself to be as strong
As erst I was in summer of mine age;
Able to toss this great unwieldy club,
Which hath been painted with my foe-men's brains:
And with this club I'll break the strong array
Of Humber and his straggling soldiers,
Or lose my life amongst the thickest press,
And die with honour in my latest days:
Yet, ere I die, they all shall understand,
What force lies in stout Corineus' hand.

    Thra. And if Thrasimachus detract the fight,[40]
Either for weakness, or for cowardice,
Let him not boast that Brutus was his eame,[41]
Or that brave Corineus was his sire.

    Loc. Then courage, soldiers, first for your safety,
Next for your peace, last for your victory.
                                  [*Exeunt.*

SCENE V.

Alarum.   *Enter* HUBBA *and* SEGAR *at one side of
the stage, and* CORINEUS *at the other.*

    Cor. Art thou that Humber, prince of fugitives,
That by thy treason slew'st young Albanact?

    Hub. I am his son that slew young Albanact;
And if thou take not heed, proud Phrygian,
I'll send thy soul unto the Stygian lake,
There to complain of Humber's injuries.

    Cor. You triumph, sir, before the victory,
For Corineus is not so soon slain.
But, cursed Scythians, you shall rue the day,
That e'er you came into Albania.
So perish they that envy Britain's wealth,
So let them die with endless infamy:
And he that seeks his sovereign's overthrow,
Would this my club might aggravate his woe.
      [*Strikes them with his club. Exeunt fighting.*

SCENE VI.

Enter HUMBER.

    Hum. Where may I find some desert wilderness,

Where I may breathe out curses as I would,
And scare the earth with my condemning voice;
Where every echo's repercussion
May help me to bewail mine overthrow,
And aid me in my sorrowful laments?
Where may I find some hollow uncouth rock,
Where I may damn, condemn, and ban my fill,
The heavens, the hell, the earth, the air, the
    fire;
And utter curses to the concave sky,
Which may infect the airy regions,
And light upon the Briton Locrine's head?
You ugly spirits that in Cocytus mourn,
And gnash your teeth with dolorous laments;
You fearful dogs, that in black Lethe howl,
And scare the ghosts with your wide open throats;
You ugly ghosts, that flying from these dogs
Do plunge yourselves in Puryflegethon;[42]
Come all of you, and with your shrieking notes
Accompany the Britons' conquering host.
Come, fierce Erinnys, horrible with snakes;
Come, ugly furies, armed with your whips;
You threefold judges of black Tartarus;
And all the army of your hellish fiends,
With new-found torments rack proud Locrine's
    bones!
O gods and stars! damn'd be the gods and
    stars,
That did not drown me in fair Thetis' plains!
Curst be the sea, that with outrageous waves,
With surging billows, did not rive my ships
Against the rocks of high Ceraunia,
Or swallow me into her wat'ry gulf!
Would God we had arriv'd upon the shore
Where Polyphemus and the Cyclops dwell;
Or where the bloody Anthropophagi[43]
With greedy jaws devour the wandering wights!

Enter the Ghost *of* ALBANACT.

But why comes Albanactus' bloody ghost,
To bring a corsive[44] to our miseries?
Is't not enough to suffer shameful flight,
But we must be tormented now with ghosts,
With apparitions fearful to behold?
    Ghost. Revenge, revenge for blood.
    Hum. So, nought will satisfy your wandering
      ghost
But dire revenge; nothing but Humber's fall;
Because he conquer'd you in Albany.
Now, by my soul, Humber would be condemn'd
To Tantal's hunger, or Ixion's wheel,
Or to the vulture of Prometheus,
Rather than that this murder were undone.

When as I die, I'll drag thy cursed ghost
Through all the rivers of foul Erebus,
Through burning sulphur of the limbo-lake,

To allay the burning fury of that heat,
That rageth in mine everlasting soul.
Ghost. Vindicta! vindicta!   [*Exeunt.*

ACT IV.

Enter ATE *as before.   Then* OMPHALE, *having a
club in her hand, and a lion's skin on her back;*
HERCULES *following with a distaff.* OMPHALE
turns about, and taking off her pantofle,[45] *strikes*
HERCULES *on the head; then they depart.* ATE
remains.

Até. Quem non argolici mandata severa tyranni,
Non potuit Juno vincere, vicit amor.
Stout Hercules, the mirror of the world,
Son to Alcmena and great Jupiter,
After so many conquests won in field,
After so many monsters quell'd by force,
Yielded his valiant heart to Omphale,
A fearful woman, void of manly strength.
She took the club, and wore the lion's skin;
He took the wheel, and maidenly 'gan spin.
So martial Locrine, cheer'd with victory,
Falleth in love with Humber's concubine,
And so forgetteth peerless Guendolen:
His uncle Corineus storms at this,
And forceth Locrine for his grace to sue.
Lo here the sum; the process doth ensue. [*Exit.*

SCENE I.

Enter LOCRINE, CAMBER, CORINEUS, ASSARACUS,
THRASIMACHUS, *and* Soldiers.

Loc. Thus from the fury of Bellona's broils,
With sound of drum, and trumpets' melody,
The Britain king returns triumphantly.
The Scythians slain with great occision,[46]
Do equalise the grass in multitude;
And with their blood have stain'd the streaming
brooks,
Offering their bodies, and their dearest blood,
As sacrifice to Albanactus' ghost.
Now, cursed Humber, hast thou paid thy due,
For thy deceits and crafty treacheries,
For all thy guiles, and damned stratagems,
With loss of life and ever-during shame.
Where are thy horses trapp'd with burnish'd gold?
Thy trampling coursers rul'd with foaming bits?
Where are thy soldiers strong and numberless?
Thy valiant captains, and thy noble peers?

Even as the country clowns with sharpest scythes
Do mow the wither'd grass from off the earth,
Or as the ploughman with his piercing share
Renteth the bowels of the fertile fields,
And rippeth up the roots with razors keen,
So Locrine, with his mighty curtle-axe
Hath cropped off the heads of all thy Huns:
So Locrine's peers have daunted all thy peers,
And drove thine host unto confusion,
That thou may'st suffer penance for thy fault,
And die for murdering valiant Albanact.
Cori. And thus, yea thus, shall all the rest be
serv'd
That seek to enter Albion 'gainst our wills.
If the brave nation of the Troglodytes,
If all the coal-black Æthiopians,
If all the forces of the Amazons,
If all the hosts of the Barbarian lands,
Should dare to enter this our little world,
Soon should they rue their over-bold attempts;
That after us our progeny may say,
There lie the beasts that sought to usurp our land.
Loc. Ay, they are beasts that seek to usurp our
land,
And like to brutish beasts they shall be serv'd.
For, mighty Jove, the supreme king of heaven,
That guides the concourse of the meteors,
And rules the motion of the azure sky,
Fights always for the Britons' safety.
But stay; methinks I hear some shrieking noise
That draweth near to our pavilion.

Enter Soldiers, *leading in* ESTRILD.

Est. What prince soe'er, adorn'd with golden
crown,
Doth sway the regal sceptre in his hand,
And thinks no chance can ever throw him down,
Or that his state shall everlasting stand,
Let him behold poor Estrild in this plight,
The perfect platform of a troubled wight.[47]
Once was I guarded with Mavortial bands,[48]
Compass'd with princes of the noble blood;
Now am I fallen into my foe-men's hands,
And with my death must pacify their mood.
O life, the harbour of calamities!

153

O death, the haven of all miseries!
I could compare my sorrows to thy woe,
Thou wretched queen of wretched Pergamus,
But that thou viewd'st thy enemies' overthrow.
Nigh to the rock of high Caphareus
Thou saw'st their death, and then departed'st
    thence:
I must abide the victors' insolence.
The gods that pitied thy continual grief,
Transform'd thy corps, and with thy corps thy care:
Poor Estrild lives, despairing of relief,
For friends in trouble are but few and rare.
What, said I, few? ay, few, or none at all,
For cruel Death made havoc of them all.
Thrice happy they, whose fortune was so good
To end their lives, and with their lives their woes!
Thrice hapless I, whom Fortune so withstood,
That cruelly she gave me to my foes!
O soldiers, is there any misery
To be compar'd to fortune's treachery?

  Loc. Camber, this same should be the Scythian
    queen.
  Cam. So may we judge by her lamenting words.
  Loc. So fair a dame mine eyes did never see;
With floods of woes she seems o'erwhelm'd to be.
  Cam. O, hath she not a cause for to be sad?
  Loc. [*Aside.*] If she have cause to weep for
    Humber's death,
And shed salt tears for her overthrow,
Locrine may well bewail his proper grief,
Locrine may move his own peculiar woe.
He, being conquer'd, died a speedy death,
And felt not long his lamentable smart:
I, being conqueror, live a lingering life,
And feel the force of Cupid's sudden stroke.
I gave him cause to die a speedy death;
He left me cause to wish a speedy death.
O, that sweet face, painted with nature's dye,
Those roseal cheeks mix'd with a snowy white,
That decent neck surpassing ivory,
Those comely breasts which Venus well might spite,
Are like to snares which wily fowlers wrought,
Wherein my yielding heart is prisoner caught!
The golden tresses of her dainty hair,
Which shine like rubies glittering with the sun,
Have so entrapp'd poor Locrine's love-sick heart,
That from the same no way it can be won.
How true is that which oft I heard declar'd,
One dram of joy must have a pound of care.
  Est. Hard is their fall, who from a golden crown
Are cast into a sea of wretchedness.
  Loc. Hard is their thrall, who by Cupido's frown
Are wrapp'd in waves of endless carefulness. [*Aside.*

  Est. O kingdom, object to all miseries![49]
  Loc. O love, the extream'st of all extremi-
    ties!   [*Aside. Goes into his chair.*
  Sold. My lord, in ransacking the Scythian tents,
I found this lady, and to manifest
That earnest zeal I bear unto your grace,
I here present her to your majesty.
  2nd Sold. He lies, my lord; I found the lady first,
And here present her to your majesty.
  1st Sold. Presumptuous villain, wilt thou take
    my prize?
  2nd Sold. Nay, rather thou depriv'st me of my
    right.
  1st Sold. Resign thy title, caitiff, unto me,
Or with my sword I'll pierce thy coward's loins.
  2nd Sold. Soft words, good sir; 'tis not enough
    to speak:
A barking dog doth seldom strangers bite.
  Loc. Unreverent villains, strive you in our sight?
Take them hence, jailor, to the dungeon;
There let them lie, and try their quarrel out.
But thou, fair princess, be no whit dismay'd,
But rather joy that Locrine favours thee.
  Est. How can he favour me that slew my spouse?
  Loc. The chance of war, my love, took him from
    thee.
  Est. But Locrine was the causer of his death.
  Loc. He was an enemy to Locrine's state,
And slew my noble brother Albanact.
  Est. But he was link'd to me in marriage-bond,
And would you have me love his slaughterer?
  Loc. Better to live, than not to live at all.[50]
  Est. Better to die renown'd for chastity,
Than live with shame and endless infamy.
What would the common sort report of me,
If I forget my love, and cleave to thee?
  Loc. Kings need not fear the vulgar sentences.
  Est. But ladies must regard their honest name.
  Loc. Is it a shame to live in marriage-bonds?
  Est. No, but to be a strumpet to a king.
  Loc. If thou wilt yield to Locrine's burning love,
Thou shalt be queen of fair Albania.
  Est. But Guendolen will undermine my state.
  Loc. Upon mine honour thou shalt have no harm.
  Est. Then lo! brave Locrine! Estrild yields to
    thee;
And, by the gods, whom thou dost invocate,
By the dread ghost of thy deceased sire,
By thy right-hand, and by thy burning love,
Take pity on poor Estrild's wretched thrall.
  Cori. Hath Locrine then forgot his Guendolen,
That thus he courts the Scythian's paramour?
What, are the words of Brute so soon forgot?

Are my deserts so quickly out of mind?
Have I been faithful to thy sire now dead?
Have I protected thee from Humber's hand,
And do'st thou quit me with ingratitude?
Is this the guerdon for my grievous wounds?
Is this the honour for my labours past?
Now, by my sword, Locrine, I swear to thee,
This injury of thine shall be repaid.

Loc. Uncle, scorn you your royal sovereign,
As if we stood for cyphers in the court?
Upbraid you me with those your benefits?
Why, 'twas a subject's duty so to do.
What you have done for our deceased sire,
We know; and all know, you have your reward.

Cori. Avaunt, proud princox! brav'st thou me
    withal?
Assure thyself, though thou be emperor,
Thou ne'er shalt carry this unpunished.

Camb. Pardon, my brother, noble Corineus.
Pardon this once, and it shall be amended.

Assa. Cousin, remember Brutus' latest words,
How he desired you to cherish them:
Let not this fault so much incense your mind,
Which is not yet passed all remedy.

Cori. Then, Locrine, lo I reconcile myself;
But as thou lov'st thy life, so love thy wife.
But if thou violate those promises,
Blood and revenge shall light upon thy head.
Come, let us back to stately Troynovant,
Where all these matters shall be settled.

Loc. Millions of devils wait upon thy soul! [*Aside.*
Legions of spirits vex thy impious ghost!
Ten thousand torments rack thy cursed bones!
Let everything that hath the use of breath,
Be instruments and workers of thy death! [*Exeunt.*

SCENE II.

Enter HUMBER, *his Hair hanging over his Shoulders, his Arms all bloody, and a Dart in his Hand.*

Hum. What basilisk was hatched in this place,
Where everything consumed is to nought?
What fearful fury haunts these cursed groves,
Where not a root is left for Humber's meat?
Hath fell Alecto, with envenom'd blasts,
Breathed forth poison in these tender plains?
Hath triple Cerberus, with contagious foam,
Sow'd aconitum 'mongst these wither'd herbs?
Hath dreadful Fames,[51] with her charming rods,
Brought barrenness on every fruitful tree?
What, not a root, no fruit, no beast, no bird,
To nourish Humber in this wilderness!
What would you more, you fiends of Erebus?

My very entrails burn for want of drink;
My bowels cry, Humber give us some meat;
But wretched Humber can give you no meat,
These foul accursed groves afford no meat,
This fruitless soil, this ground, brings forth no meat,
The gods, hard-hearted gods, yield me no meat:
Then how can Humber give you any meat?

Enter STRUMBO, *wearing a Scotch Cap, with a Pitchfork in his Hand.*

Strum. How do you, masters, how do you? how
have you scap'd hanging this long time? I'faith I
have scaped many a scouring this year; but I thank
God I have past them all with a good corraggio,
and my wife and I are in great love and charity
now, I thank my manhood and my strength. For
I will tell you, masters: Upon a certain day at
night I came home, to say the very truth, with my
stomach full of wine, and ran up into the chamber,
where my wife soberly sat rocking my little baby,
leaning her back against the bed, singing lullaby.
Now when she saw me come with my nose foremost, thinking that I had been drunk (as I was
indeed), she snatch'd up a faggot-stick in her hand,
and came furiously marching towards me, with a
big face, as though she would have eaten me at a
bit; thundering out these words unto me: "Thou
drunken knave, where hast thou been so long? I
shall teach thee how to benight[52] me another
time:" and so she began to play knaves trumps.
Now, although I trembled, fearing she would set
her ten commandments in my face, I ran within
her, and taking her lustily by the middle, I carried
her valiantly to the bed, and flinging her upon it,
flung myself upon her, and there I delighted her
so with the sport I made, that ever after she would
call me "sweet husband;" and so banish'd brawling for ever. And to see the good will of the
wench! she bought with her portion a yard of land,
and by that I am now become one of the richest
men in our parish. Well, masters, what's a'clock?
It is now breakfast time; you shall see what meat
I have here for my breakfast.
    [*Sits down, and takes out his victuals.*
Hum. Was ever land so fruitless as this land?
Was ever grove so graceless as this grove?
Was ever soil so barren as this soil?
Oh no: the land where hungry Fames dwelt,
May no ways equalize this cursed land;
No, even the climate of the torrid zone
Brings forth more fruit than this accursed grove.
Ne'er came sweet Ceres, ne'er came Venus here;
Triptolemus, the god of husbandmen,

Ne'er sow'd his seed in this foul wilderness.
The hunger-bitten dogs of Acheron,
Chas'd from the nine-fold Pyriphlegethon,
Have set their foot-steps in this damned ground.
The iron-hearted Furies, arm'd with snakes,
Scatter'd huge Hydras over all the plains ;
Which have consum'd the grass, the herbs, the trees,
Which have drunk up the flowing water-springs.

      [STRUM. *hearing his voice starts up, and puts*
         his meat in his pocket, endeavouring to hide
         himself.

   Hum. Thou great commander of the starry sky,
That guid'st the life of every mortal wight,
From the enclosures of the fleeting clouds
Rain down some food, or else I faint and die :
Pour down some drink, or else I faint and die.
O Jupiter, hast thou sent Mercury
In clownish shape to minister some food ?
Some meat, some meat, some meat.

   Strum. O alas, sir, you are deceiv'd. I am not
Mercury ; I am Strumbo.

   Hum. Give me some meat, villain ; give me some
      meat,
Or 'gainst this rock I'll dash thy cursed brains,
And rent thy bowels with my bloody hands.
Give me some meat, villain ; give me some meat.

   Strum. By the faith of my body, good fellow, I
had rather give an whole ox, than that thou should'st
serve me in that sort. Dash out my brains ! O
horrible ! terrible ! I think I have a quarry of stones
in my pocket.   [*Aside.*

     [*He makes as though he would give him some, and*
       as he puts out his hand, the Ghost of AL-
       BANACT *enters, and strikes him on the hand.*
       STRUM. *runs out,* HUM. *following him.*

   Ghost. Lo, here the gift of fell ambition,
Of usurpation and of treachery !
Lo, here the harms that wait upon all those
That do intrude themselves in others' lands,
Which are not under their dominion !   [*Exit.*

SCENE III.

Enter LOCRINE.

   Loc. Seven years hath aged Corineus liv'd
To Locrine's grief, and fair Estrilda's woe,
And seven years more he hopeth yet to live.
O supreme Jove, annihilate this thought !
Should he enjoy the air's fruition,
Should he enjoy the benefit of life,
Should he contemplate the radiant sun,
That makes my life equal to dreadful death ?
Venus, convey this monster from the earth,

That disobeyeth thus thy sacred hests !
Cupid, convey this monster to dark hell,
That disannuls thy mother's sugar'd laws !
Mars, with thy target, all beset with flames,
With murdering blade bereave him of his life,
That hindreth Locrine in his sweetest joys !
And yet, for all his diligent aspect,
His wrathful eyes, piercing likes lynxes' eyes,
Well have I overmatch'd his subtilty.
Nigh Durolitum,[53] by the pleasant Ley,
Where brackish Thamis slides with silver streams,
Making a breach into the grassy downs,
A curious arch of costly marble fraught
Hath Locrine framed underneath the ground ;
The walls whereof, garnish'd with diamonds,
With opals, rubies, glistering emeralds,
And interlac'd with sun-bright carbuncles,
Lighten the room with artificial day :
And from the Lee with water-flowing pipes
The moisture is deriv'd into this arch,
Where I have plac'd fair Estrild secretly.
Thither eftsoons, accompanied with my page,
I visit covertly my heart's desire,
Without suspicion of the meanest eye,
For love aboundeth still with policy.
And thither still means Locrine to repair,
'Till Atropos cut off mine uncle's life.   [*Exit.*

SCENE IV.

Enter HUMBER.

   Hum. O vita, misero ionga, felici brevis !
Eheu malorum fames extremum malum !
Long have I lived in this desert cave,
With eating haws and miserable roots,
Devouring leaves and beastly excrements.
Caves were my beds, and stones my pillowberes,
Fear was my sleep, and horror was my dream ;
For still, methought, at every boisterous blast,
Now Locrine comes, now, Humber, thou must die ;
So that for fear and hunger Humber's mind
Can never rest, but always trembling stands.
O, what Danubius now may quench my thirst ;
What Euphrates, what light-foot Euripus
May now allay the fury of that heat,
Which raging in my entrails eats me up ?
You ghastly devils of the ninefold Styx,
You dammed ghosts of joyless Acheron,
You mournful souls, vex'd in Abyssus' vaults,
You coal-black devils of Avernus' pond,
Come, with your flesh-hooks rent my famish'd arms,
These arms that have sustain'd their master's life.
Come, with your razors rip my bowels up,

With your sharp fire-forks crack my starved bones:
Use me as you will, so Humber may not live.
Accursed gods, that rule the starry poles,
Accursed Jove, king of the cursed gods,
Cast down your lightning on poor Humber's head,
That I may leave this death-like life of mine!
What! hear you not? and shall not Humber die?
Nay I will die, though all the gods say nay.
And, gentle Aby, take my troubled corpse,[54]
Take it, and keep it from all mortal eyes,
That none may say, when I have lost my breath,
The very floods conspir'd 'gainst Humber's death.
                [*Flings himself into the river.*

Enter the Ghost *of* ALBANACT.

   Ghost. En cædem sequitur cædes, in cæde quiesco.
Humber is dead. Joy heavens, leap earth, dance trees!
Now may'st thou reach thy apples, Tantalus,
And with them feed thy hunger-bitten limbs.
Now Sisyphus, leave the tumbling of thy rock,
And rest thy restless bones upon the same.
Unbind Ixion, cruel Rhadamanth,
And lay proud Humber on the whirling wheel.
Back will I post to hell-mouth Tænarus,
And pass Cocytus, to the Elysian fields,
And tell my father Brutus of this news.   [*Exit.*

ACT V.

Enter ATE *as before. Then enter* JASON, *leading* CREON's Daughter; MEDEA *following with a Garland in her hand. She puts the Garland on the head of* CREON's Daughter; *sets it on fire; and then killing her and* JASON, *departs.*

   Até. Non tam trinacriis exæstuat Ætna cavernis,
Læsæ furtivo quam cor Mulieris amore.
Medea seeing Jason leave her love,
And choose the daughter of the Theban king,
Went to her devilish charms to work revenge;
And raising up the triple Hecate,
With all the rout of the condemned fiends,
Framed a garland by her magic skill,
With which she wrought Jason and Creon's ill.
So Guendolen, seeing herself misus'd,
And Humber's paramour possess her place,
Flies to the dukedom of Cornubia,
And with her brother, stout Thrasimachus,
Gathering a power of Cornish soldiers,
Gives battle to her husband and his host,
Nigh to the river of great Mercia.
The chances of this dismal massacre
That which ensueth shortly will unfold.   [*Exit.*

SCENE I.

Enter LOCRINE, CAMBER, ASSARACUS, *and* THRASIMACHUS.

   Assa. But tell me, cousin, dy'd my brother so?
Now who is left to helpless Albion,
That as a pillar might uphold our state,
That might strike terror to our daring foes?
Now who is left to hapless Brittany,
That might defend her from the barbarous hands

Of those that still desire her ruinous fall,
And seek to work her downfal and decay?
   Cam. Ay uncle, death's our common enemy,
And none but death can match our matchless power.
Witness the fall of Albioneus' crew,
Witness the fall of Humber and his Huns;
And this foul death hath now increas'd our woe,
By taking Corineus from this life,
And in his room leaving us worlds of care.
   Thra. But none may more bewail his mournful hearse,
Than I that am the issue of his loins.
Now foul befal that cursed Humber's throat,
That was the causer of his ling'ring wound!
   Loc. Tears cannot raise him from the dead again.
But where's my lady mistress, Guendolen?
   Thra. In Cornwall, Locrine, is my sister now,
Providing for my father's funeral.
   Loc. And let her there provide her mourning weeds,
And mourn for ever her own widow-hood.
Ne'er shall she come within our palace gate,
To countercheck brave Locrine in his love.
Go, boy, to Durolitum, down the Ley,
Unto the arch where lovely Estrild lies;
Bring her and Sabren straight unto the court:
She shall be queen in Guendolena's room.
Let others wail for Corineus' death;
I mean not so to macerate my mind,[55]
For him that barr'd me from my heart's desire.
   Thra. Hath Locrine then forsook his Guendolen?
Is Corineus' death so soon forgot?
If there be gods in heaven, as sure there be,
If there be fiends in hell, as needs there must,

They will revenge this thy notorious wrong,
And pour their plagues upon thy cursed head.

Loc. What, prat'st thou, peasant, to thy sove-
    reign?
Or art thou strucken in some ecstasy?
Dost thou not tremble at our royal looks?
Dost thou not quake, when mighty Locrine frowns?
Thou beardless boy, were't not that Locrine scorns
To vex his mind with such a heartless child,
With the sharp point of this my battle-axe
I'd send thy soul to Pyriphlegethon.

Thra. Though I be young and of a tender age,
Yet will I cope with Locrine when he dares.
My noble father with his conquering sword
Slew the two giants, kings of Aquitain.
Thrasimachus is not so degenerate,
That he should fear and tremble at the looks
Or taunting words of a Venerean squire.[56]

Loc. Menacest thou thy royal sovereign?
Uncivil, not beseeming such as you.
Injurious traitor, (for he is no less
That at defiance standeth with his king)
Leave these thy taunts, leave these thy bragging
    words,
Unless thou mean'st to leave thy wretched life.

Thra. If princes stain their glorious dignity
With ugly spots of monstrous infamy,
They leese their former estimation,
And throw themselves into a hell of hate.

Loc. Wilt thou abuse my gentle patience,
As though thou didst our high displeasure scorn?
Proud boy, that thou may'st know thy prince is
    mov'd,
Yea, greatly mov'd at this thy swelling pride,
We banish thee for ever from our court.

Thra. Then, losel Locrine,[57] look unto thyself;
Thrasimachus will venge this injury.   [*Exit.*

Loc. Farewell, proud boy, and learn to use thy
    tongue.

Assa. Alas, my lord, you should have call'd to
    mind
The latest words that Brutus spake to you;
How he desir'd you, by the obedience
That children ought to bear unto their sire,
To love and favour Lady Guendolen.
Consider this, that if the injury
Do move her mind, as certainly it will,
War and dissension follows speedily.
What though her powers be not so great as yours?
Have you not seen a mighty elephant
Slain by the biting of a silly mouse?
Even so the chance of war inconstant is.

Loc. Peace, uncle, peace, and cease to talk hereof;

For he that seeks, by whispering this or that,
To trouble Locrine in his sweetest life,
Let him persuade himself to die the death.

Enter ESTRILD, SABREN, *and a* Page.

Est. O say me, page, tell me, where is the king.
Wherefore doth he send for me to the court?
Is it to die? is it to end my life?
Say me, sweet boy; tell me and do not feign.

Page. No, trust me, madam: if you will credit
the little honesty that is yet left me, there is no
such danger as you fear. But prepare yourself;
yonder's the king.

Est. Then, Estrild, lift thy dazzled spirits up,
And bless that blessed time, that day, that hour,
That warlike Locrine first did favour thee.
Peace to the king of Brittany, my love!
                       [*Kneeling.*
Peace to all those that love and favour him!

Loc. Doth Estrild fall with such submission
Before her servant, king of Albion?
Arise, fair lady, leave this lowly cheer;
                     [*Taking her up.*
Lift up those looks that cherish Locrine's heart,
That I may freely view that roseal face,
Which so entangled hath my love-sick breast.
Now to the court, where we will court it out,
And pass the night and day in Venus' sports.
Frolic, brave peers; be joyful with your king.
                        [*Exeunt.*

SCENE II.

Enter GUENDOLEN, THRASIMACHUS, MADAN,
and Soldiers.

Guen. You gentle winds, that with your modest
    blasts
Pass through the circuit of the heavenly vault,
Enter the clouds, unto the throne of Jove,
And bear my prayers to his all-hearing ears,
For Locrine hath forsaken Guendolen,
And learn'd to love proud Humber's concubine.
You happy sprites, that in the concave sky
With pleasant joy enjoy your sweetest love,
Shed forth those tears with me, which then you
    shed
When first you woo'd your ladies to your wills:
Those tears are fittest for my woeful case,
Since Locrine shuns my nothing-pleasant face.
Blush heavens, blush sun, and hide thy shining
    beams;
Shadow thy radiant locks in gloomy clouds;
Deny thy cheerful light unto the world,

Where nothing reigns but falsehood and deceit.
What said I? falsehood? ay, that filthy crime,
For Locrine hath forsaken Guendolen.
Behold the heavens do wail for Guendolen;
The shining sun doth blush for Guendolen;
The liquid air doth weep for Guendolen;
The very ground doth groan for Guendolen.
Ay, they are milder than the Britain king,
For he rejecteth luckless Guendolen.

 Thra. Sister, complaints are bootless in this
  cause.
This open wrong must have an open plague,
This plague must be repaid with grievous war,
This war must finish with Locrinus' death;
His death must soon extinguish our complaints.

 Guen. O no; his death will more augment my
  woes:
He was my husband, brave Thrasimachus,
More dear to me than the apple of mine eye;
Nor can I find in heart to work his scathe.

 Thra. Madam, if not your proper injuries,
Nor my exile, can move you to revenge,
Think on our father Corineus' words;
His words to us stand always for a law.
Should Locrine live, that caus'd my father's death?
Should Locrine live, that now divorceth you?
The heavens, the earth, the air, the fire reclaims;[58]
And then why should all we deny the same?

 Guen. Then henceforth farewell womanish com-
  plaints!
All childish pity henceforth then farewell!
But cursed Locrine, look unto thyself;
For Nemesis, the mistress of revenge,
Sits arm'd at all points on our dismal blades:
And cursed Estrild, that inflam'd his heart,
Shall, if I live, die a reproachful death.

 Mad. Mother, though nature makes me to la-
  ment
My luckless father's froward lechery,
Yet, for he wrongs my lady mother thus,
I, if I could, myself would work his death.

 Thra. See, madam, see! the desire of revenge
Is in the children of a tender age.
Forward, brave soldiers, into Mercia,
Where we shall brave the coward to his face.
          [*Exeunt.*

SCENE III.

Enter LOCRINE, ESTRILD, SABREN, ASSARACUS,
  and Soldiers.

 Loc. Tell me, Assaracus, are the Cornish chuffs[59]
In such great number come to Mercia?

And have they pitched there their petty host,
So close unto our royal mansion?

 Assa. They are, my lord, and mean incontinent
To bid defiance to your majesty.

 Loc. It makes me laugh, to think that Guendolen
Should have the heart to come in arms against
  me.

 Est. Alas, my lord, the horse will run amain,
When as the spur doth gall him to the bone:
Jealousy, Locrine, hath a wicked sting.

 Loc. Sayst thou so, Estrild, beauty's paragon?
Well, we will try her choler to the proof,
And make her know, Locrine can brook no braves.
March on, Assaracus; thou must lead the way,
And bring us to their proud pavilion.
          [*Exeunt.*

SCENE IV.

Thunder and Lightning. Enter the Ghost *of*
  CORINEUS.

 Ghost. Behold, the circuit of the azure sky
Throws forth sad throbs, and grievous suspires,
Prejudicating Locrine's overthrow.
The fire casteth forth sharp darts of flames;
The great foundation of the triple world
Trembleth and quaketh with a mighty noise,
Presaging bloody massacres at hand.
The wandering birds that flutter in the dark,
(When hellish night in cloudy chariot seated,
Casteth her mists on shady Tellus' face,
With sable mantles covering all the earth)
Now flies abroad amid the cheerful day,
Foretelling some unwonted misery.
The snarling curs of darken'd Tartarus,
Sent from Avernus' ponds by Rhadamanth,
With howling ditties pester every wood.
The wat'ry ladies,[60] and the lightfoot fawns,
And all the rabble of the woody nymphs,
All trembling hide themselves in shady groves,
And shroud themselves in hideous hollow pits.
The boisterous Boreas thund'reth forth revenge:
The stony rocks cry out on sharp revenge:
The thorny bush pronounceth dire revenge.
          [*Alarum.*
Now, Corineus, stay and see revenge,
And feed thy soul with Locrine's overthrow.
Behold they come; the trumpets call them forth;
The roaring drums summon the soldiers.
Lo where their army glistereth on the plains.
Throw forth thy lightning, mighty Jupiter,
And pour thy plagues on cursed Locrine's head!
          [*Stands aside.*

Enter LOCRINE, ESTRILD, ASSARACUS, SABREN, *and their* Soldiers *at one side;* THRASIMACHUS, GUENDOLEN, MADAN, *and their* Followers, *at another.*

Loc. What, is the tiger started from his cave?
Is Guendolen come from Cornubia,
That thus she braveth Locrine to the teeth?
And hast thou found thine armour, pretty boy,
Accompanied with these thy straggling mates?
Believe me, but this enterprise was bold,
And well deserveth commendation.
 Guen. Ay, Locrine, traitorous Locrine, we are
   come,
With full pretence to seek thine overthrow.
What have I done, that thou shouldst scorn me thus?
What have I said, that thou shouldst me reject?
Have I been disobedient to thy words?
Have I bewray'd thy arcane secrecy?[61]
Have I dishonoured thy marriage bed
With filthy crimes, or with lascivious lusts?
Nay, it is thou that hast dishonour'd it;
Thy filthy mind, o'ercome with filthy lusts,
Yieldeth unto affection's filthy darts.
Unkind, thou wrong'st thy first and truest feere;[62]
Unkind, thou wrong'st thy best and dearest friend;
Unkind, thou scorn'st all skilful Brutus' laws,
Forgetting father, uncle, and thyself.
 Est. Believe me, Locrine, but the girl is wise,
And well would seem to make a vestal nun:
How finely frames she her oration!
 Thra. Locrine, we came not here to fight with
   words,
Words that can never win the victory;
But, for you are so merry in your frumps,[63]
Unsheath your swords, and try it out by force,
That we may see who hath the better hand.
 Loc. Think'st thou to dare me, bold Thrasimachus?
Think'st thou to fear me with thy taunting braves?
Or do we seem too weak to cope with thee?
Soon shall I show thee my fine cutting blade,
And with my sword, the messenger of death,
Seal thee an acquittance for thy bold attempts.
         [Exeunt.

Alarum.   *Enter* LOCRINE, ASSARACUS, *and* Soldiers *at one Door;* GUENDOLEN, THRASIMACHUS, *and his* Forces *at another. They fight.* LOCRINE *and his* Followers *are driven back. Then re-enter* LOCRINE *and* ESTRILD.

 Loc. O fair Estrilda, we have lost the field;
Thrasimachus hath won the victory,
And we are left to be a laughing-stock,

Scoff'd at by those that are our enemies.
Ten thousand soldiers, arm'd with sword and shield,
Prevail against an hundred thousand men.
Thrasimachus, incens'd with fuming ire,
Rageth amongst the faint-heart soldiers,
Like to grim Mars, when, cover'd with his targe,
He fought with Diomedes in the field,
Close by the banks of silver Simois.   *[Alarum.*
O lovely Estrild, now the chase begins:
Ne'er shall we see the stately Troynovant,
Mounted on coursers garnish'd all with pearls;
Ne'er shall we view the fair Concordia,
Unless as captives we be thither brought.
Shall Locrine then be taken prisoner
By such a youngling as Thrasimachus?
Shall Guendolena captivate my love?
Ne'er shall mine eyes behold that dismal hour,
Ne'er will I view that ruthful spectacle;
For with my sword, this sharp curtle-axe,
I'll cut in sunder my accursed heart.
But, O you judges of the nine-fold Styx,
Which with incessant torments rack the ghosts
Within the bottomless abyssus' pits;
You gods, commanders of the heav'nly spheres,
Whose will and laws irrevocable stand,
Forgive, forgive, this foul accursed sin!
Forget, O gods, this foul condemned fault!
And now, my sword, that in so many fights
        [Kisses his sword.
Hast sav'd the life of Brutus and his son,
End now his life that wisheth still for death,
Work now his death that wisheth still for death,
Work now his death that hateth still his life!
Farewell, fair Estrild, beauty's paragon,
Fram'd in the front of forlorn miseries!
Ne'er shall mine eyes behold thy sun-shine eyes,
But when we meet in the Elysian fields:
Thither I go before with hasten'd pace.
Farewell, vain world, and thy enticing snares!
Farewell, foul sin, and thy enticing pleasures!
And welcome, death, the end of mortal smart,
Welcome to Locrine's over-burthen'd heart!
      [Stabs himself, and dies.
 Est. Break, heart, with sobs and grievous suspires!
Stream forth you tears from forth my watry eyes;
Help me to mourn for warlike Locrine's death!
Pour down your tears, you watry regions,
For mighty Locrine is bereft of life!
O fickle Fortune! O unstable world!
What else are all things that this globe contains,
But a confused chaos of mishaps?
Wherein, as in a glass, we plainly see
That all our life is but a tragedy;

Since mighty kings are subject to mishap,
(Ay, mighty kings are subject to mishap;)
Since martial Locrine is bereft of life.
Shall Estrild live then after Locrine's death?
Shall love of life bar her from Locrine's sword?
O no; this sword that hath bereft his life,
Shall now deprive me of my fleeting soul.
Strengthen these hands, O mighty Jupiter,
That I may end my woeful misery!
Locrine, I come; Locrine, I follow thee.

            [*Kills herself.*

Alarum. Enter SABREN.

   Sab. What doleful sight, what ruthful spectacle
Hath Fortune offer'd to my hapless heart?
My father slain with such a fatal sword,
My mother murder'd by a mortal wound!
What Thracian dog, what barbarous Myrmidon,
Would not relent at such a ruthful case?
What fierce Achilles, what hard stony flint,
Would not bemoan this mournful tragedy?
Locrine, the map of magnanimity,
Lies slaughter'd in this foul accursed cave.
Estrild, the perfect pattern of renown,
Nature's sole wonder, in whose beauteous breasts
All heavenly grace and virtue was enshrin'd,
Both massacred, are dead within this cave;
And with them dies fair Pallas and sweet Love.
Here lies a sword, and Sabren hath a heart;
This blessed sword shall cut my cursed heart,
And bring my soul unto my parents' ghosts,
That they that live and view our tragedy,
May mourn our case with mournful plaudite.

            [*Attempts to kill herself.*

Ah me, my virgin hands are too too weak!
To penetrate the bulwark of my breast.
My fingers, us'd to tune the amorous lute,
Are not of force to hold this steely glaive :[64]
So I am left to wail my parents' death,
Not able for to work my proper death.
Ah, Locrine, honour'd for thy nobleness,
Ah, Estrild, famous for thy constancy,
Ill may they fare that wrought your mortal ends!

Enter GUENDOLEN, THRASIMACHUS, MADAN,
and Soldiers.

   Guen. Search soldiers, search; find Locrine and
      his love,
Find the proud strumpet, Humber's concubine,
That I may change those her so pleasing looks
To pale and ignominious aspect.
Find me the issue of their cursed love.
Find me young Sabren, Locrine's only joy,

That I may glut my mind with lukewarm blood,
Swiftly distilling from the bastard's breast.
My father's ghost still haunts me for revenge,
Crying, "revenge my over-hasten'd death."
My brother's exile and mine own divorce
Banish remorse clean from my brazen heart,
All mercy from mine adamantine breasts.

   Thra. Nor doth thy husband, lovely Guendolen,
That wonted was to guide our stayless steps,
Enjoy this light : see where he murder'd lies
By luckless lot and froward frowning fate;
And by him lies his lovely paramour,
Fair Estrild, gored with a dismal sword,
And, as it seems, both murder'd by themselves;
Clasping each other in their feebled arms,
With loving zeal, as if for company
Their uncontented corps were yet content
To pass foul Styx in Charon's ferry-boat.

   Guen. And hath proud Estrild then prevented me?
Hath she escaped Guendolena's wrath,
By violently cutting off her life?
Would God she had the monstrous Hydra's lives,
That every hour she might have died a death
Worse than the swing of old Ixion's wheel,
And every hour revive to die again!
As Tityus, bound to houseless Caucasus,
Doth feed the substance of his own mishap,
And every day for want of food doth die,
And every night doth live, again to die.
But stay; methinks, I hear some fainting voice,
Mournfully weeping for their luckless death.

   Sab. You mountain nymphs which in these
      deserts reign,
Cease off your hasty chase of savage beasts!
Prepare to see a heart oppress'd with care;
Address your ears to hear a mournful style!
No human strength, no work can work my weal,
Care in my heart so tyrant-like doth deal.
You Dryades, and light-foot Satyri,
You gracious fairies, which at even-tide
Your closets leave, with heavenly beauty stor'd,
And on your shoulders spread your golden locks;
You savage bears, in caves and darken'd dens,
Come wail with me the martial Locrine's death;
Come mourn with me for beauteous Estrild's
      death!
Ah! loving parents, little do you know
What sorrow Sabren suffers for your thrall.

   Guen. But may this be, and is it possible?
Lives Sabren yet to expiate my wrath?
Fortune, I thank thee for this courtesy;
And let me never see one prosperous hour,
If Sabren die not a reproachful death.

Sab. Hard-hearted Death, that, when the wretch-
ed call,
Art farthest off, and seldom hear'st at all ;
But in the midst of fortune's good success
Uncalled com'st, and sheer'st our life in twain ;
When will that hour, that blessed hour draw nigh,
When poor distressed Sabren may be gone ?
Sweet Atropos, cut off my fatal thread !
What art thou, Death ? shall not poor Sabren die ?

Guen. Yes, damsel, yes, Sabren shall surely die,
Though all the world should seek to save her life.
And not a common death shall Sabren die,
But, after strange and grievous punishments
Shortly inflicted on thy bastard's head,
Thou shalt be cast into the cursed streams,
And feed the fishes with thy tender flesh.

Sab. And think'st thou then, thou cruel homi-
cide,
That these thy deeds shall be unpunished ?
No traitor, no ; the gods will venge these wrongs,
The fiends of hell will mark these injuries.
Never shall these blood-sucking mastiff curs
Bring wretched Sabren to her latest home.
For I myself, in spite of thee and thine,
Mean to abridge my former destinies ;
And that which Locrine's sword could not per-
form,
This present stream shall present bring to pass.
                  [*She drowns herself.*

Guen. One mischief follows on another's neck.
Who would have thought so young a maid as she
With such a courage would have sought her death ?

And, for because this river was the place
Where little Sabren resolutely died,
Sabren for ever shall this same be call'd.[65]
And as for Locrine, our deceased spouse,
Because he was the son of mighty Brute,
To whom we owe our country, lives, and goods,
He shall be buried in a stately tomb,
Close by his aged father Brutus' bones,
With such great pomp and great solemnity
As well beseems so brave a prince as he.
Let Estrild lie without the shallow vaults,
Without the honour due unto the dead,
Because she was the author of this war.
Retire, brave followers, unto Troynovant,
Where we will celebrate these exequies,
And place young Locrine in his father's tomb.
                        [*Exeunt.*

Enter ATE.

Até. Lo ! here the end of lawless treachery,
Of usurpation and ambitious pride.
And they that for their private amours dare
Turmoil our land, and set their broils abroach,
Let them be warned by these premises.
And as a woman was the only cause
That civil discord was then stirred up,
So let us pray for that renowned maid
That eight and thirty years the sceptre sway'd,
In quiet peace and sweet felicity ;
And every wight that seeks her grace's smart,
Would that this sword were pierced in his heart !
                        [*Exit.*

NOTES TO LOCRINE.

---

[1] *Soaring with Icarus too near the sun,*
May catch a fall with young Bellerophon.

This play abounds with classical allusions; the fate of Icarus is too well known to render any explanation necessary; but a word may be said of the fall of Bellerophon. He was a son of Glaucus, king of Ephyre, and the owner of the famous winged horse Pegasus, by the aid of which he attempted to fly to heaven; but it is said that Jupiter, enraged at his presumption, sent a venomous insect, which stung the horse, and caused it to throw its rider, who, falling to the earth, wandered about in great dejection until the day of his death.

[2] *Mine eame,* i.e. my uncle.

[3] *Transfreting,* i.e. passing over.

[4] *And quell'd the giants, come of Albion's race,*
With Gogmagog, son to Samotheus.

Albion was a son of Neptune, by Amphitrite. He is said to have seized upon our British island, and peopled it with a race of giants, who were subdued by Brutus when he sought refuge here after the destruction of Troy. Albion, says one legend, took the island from the Celts, who had resided in it upwards of three hundred years. They were governed successively by five kings, the first of whom was named Samothes, and said to be the eldest son of Japhet, and the same who is called by Moses, Meshech. From King Samothes Britain received its first name, that of Samothea. Gogmagog was a giant who reigned over the island. Most of this fabulous history was invented by an Italian friar, who published it about the end of the fifteenth century.

[5] *Sacred virtue's lore,* i.e. her teaching.

[6] *Sempiternal fame.*

Fame eternal in futurity; having beginning, but no end.

[7] *Sorted amongst the glorious happy ones.*

That is, having thy lot among them.

[8] *A gift more rich than are the wealthy mines*
Found in the bowels of America.

Here is an anachronism of more than two thousand six hundred years. The period to which this drama refers is shortly after the destruction of Troy by the Greeks, which event is attributed to the year 1184 *before* Christ, while America was not discovered by Columbus until the year 1494 A.D.

[9] *No dreadful threats can fear judge Rhadamanth.*

That is, can appal him. Rhadamanthus was fabled to be a son of Jupiter by Europa. He reigned over one of the group of islands called the Cyclades, and was so inflexibly just, that after his death he was supposed to have been created one of the judges of hell. Æacus, mentioned in the preceding line, was a son of Jupiter by another lady; he was king of the island of Œnopia, and on account of his integrity he also was supposed to preside on the judgment-seat of the infernal regions.

[10] *For fatal Mors expecteth all the world.*

The classical allusions throughout this play occur so constantly that I have considered it necessary to explain only the least familiar of them. *Mors* was one of the infernal deities, born of Night without a father; she seems to have been synonymous with our modern personification of death; and was sometimes represented as a skeleton, armed with a scythe and a scymitar.

[11] *Lactantius, in his fourth book of Constultations.*

Strumbo means *Consultations;* he is an ignorant cobbler, affecting long words and learning: thus, by mistake, he uses *aliquant* for eloquent, *cuprit* for Cupid, &c.

[12] *I burn, I burn, and I burn-a, &c.*

This appears to have been the burden of some old song.

[13] *Not Diana with the ass Tom.*

Probably meaning Diana and Acteon.

[14] *Gentlemen, lend me a knife.*

Here and in other places Strumbo addressed the groundlings, for whose amusement he seems to have been introduced. These appeals to the audience were very frequent in our ancient drama. In *King Lear,* the fool addresses a coarse jest to the spectators.

[15] *Signor Strumbo.*

Strumbo, who is an ancient Briton, gives himself a Spanish title.

[16] *My ingeny,* i.e. Strumbo's mistake for ingenuity.

[17] *Succedo de labres.*

A corrupt expression for the sweetness of lips.

[18] *Risus,* i.e. the deity who presided over mirth and laughter.

[19] *If she that rules fair Rhamnus' golden gate.*

That is, Fortuna, the goddess of fortune, to whom a temple was erected in Rhamnus, a town in Attica.

[20] *The pittering leaves.*

Pittering is a word coined to express the noise made by the fluttering of leaves.

[21] *By gogs blue-hood and halidom.*

Gogs blue-hood is a corruption of God's blood; *halidom* means our blessed lady. We have here an allusion to the Virgin Mary, in a period long prior to that of Christianity.

[22] *Well may I waiment.*

That is, lament. It is an old Saxon word, and used by the father of British poetry, Chaucer.

[23] *As fortunate as was Polycrates.*

Polycrates was a tyrant of Samos, who experienced such a constant flow of good fortune, that Amosis, the king of Egypt, thinking that some sudden calamity would befal him to balance so much good, advised him to sacrifice some valuable object in order to mitigate his great happiness. Polycrates consented, and threw a valuable jewel into the sea; but it seemed as if the fates would not permit him to suffer any loss; for a few days afterwards a large fish was presented to him, and in its belly the lost gem was found. Some time after he visited the governor of Magnesia, who put him to death, merely from an envious desire to terminate his prosperity.

Malone suggests that a line, preceding the above, has been lost; something of this import—

But were they brave as Phthia's arm-strong chief.

[24] *Brenning,* i.e. burning.

[25] *Go take a coronet of our horse.*

That is, a cornet's party of them.

[26] *Princox boy,* i.e. conceited fellow.

[27] *Superbius,* i. e. august, stately, magnificent. From the Latin *superbus.*

[28] *Stoure,* i.e. battle, tumult, incursion.

[29] *Rhamnusia's drum.*

Rhamnusia was one of the titles of Nemesis, the goddess of vengeance; it was bestowed upon her on account of her famous temple at Rhamnus.

[30] *With Semeleius' gifts.*

With the gifts of Bacchus, who was the son of Jupiter and Semele.

[31] *Of Niobe, fair Athens' queen.*

Niobe was the wife of Amphion, King of *Thebes;* perhaps the author wrote fair *Amphion's* queen.

[32] *Shall be agnominated by our name.*

Called by our name. Here is an instance of the extreme pedantry of the writer. This word (formed from the *agnomen* of the Romans) is, I believe, used by no other English writer.

[33] *Fair Thetis' plains,* i.e. the level of the sea.

[34] *Virent plains,* i.e. green plains.

[35] *Enter the Ghost of Albanact.*

" Why this personage (says Malone) is summoned from the dead, it is not easy to say. Though an interlocutor in the scene, he neither addresses Humber, nor is seen by him."

[36] *The warding of the camp.*

That is, the defence of it. So in *Titus Andronicus,* the unhappy father, when sending his severed hand to the emperor as a ransom for the lives of his two sons, exclaims—

Good Aaron, give his majesty my hand,
Tell him it was a hand that *warded* him
From thousand dangers.

[37] *By my dorth,* i.e. a provincial corruption of by my *troth.*

[38] *I think you were brought up in the University of Bridewell.*

Bridewell house of correction in ancient Britain! The author might with more reason have spoken of London Bridge or Westminster Abbey.

[39] *The arm-strong offspring of the doubled night.*

That is, of the night protracted to twice its usual length, while Jupiter begot Hercules.

[40] *Detract the fight,* i.e. withdraw from it.

[41] *His eame*—See note 2.

[42] *Puryflegethon.*

One of the infernal rivers, usually called Phlegethon.

[43] *Or where the bloody Anthropophagi.*

A supposed race of monstrous cannibals spoken of by Sir Walter Raleigh in his *Description of Guiana.* See note 20 to *Othello.*

[44] *A corsive.*

That is, a corrosive. So in *The Spanish Tragedy :—*
His son distrest, a *corsive* to his heart.

[45] *Pantofle,* i.e. slipper.

[46] *Occision.*

An affected word (probably coined by the author), meaning slaughter.

[47] *The perfect platform of a troubled wight.*

That is, the perfect representation of adversity; *platform* is a plan or model.

[48] *Mavortial bands.*

Another Latinism; *Mavors* is a poetical name for Mars; hence *Mavortial.*

[49] *Object to all miseries,* i.e. exposed to them.

[50] *Better to live than not to live at all.*

I think we should read—better to *love.* Malone, however, observes, " perhaps the author meant only to say— That it is better to live on any terms, than to die. He has many similar truisms in this play, delivered with the same pomp of versification."

[51] *Dreadful Fames,* i.e. hunger personified.

[52] *To benight me,* i.e. to come home so late at night.

[53] *Nigh Durolitum.*

According to Camden, *Durolitum* is Leyton, in Essex, a town upon the river Ley.

[54] *And, gentle Aby, take my troubled corpse.*

In a preceding scene the river has been called *Abis.* *Aber*, says Drayton, in his *Polyolbion*, signifies, in British, the mouth of a river. From Humber's suicide, tradition tells us the river took its present name, *the Humber.* Spencer says in describing this incident :—

> Whose bad condition yet it doth retain,
> Oft tossed with his storms, which therein still remain.

[55] *Macerate my mind*, i.e. mortify it.

[56] *A Venerean squire*, i.e. a wanton follower of women.

[57] *Then, losel Locrine*, i.e. base, unworthy wretch.

[58] *The earth, the air, the fire reclaims.*

That is, cries out against.

[59] *The Cornish chuffs.*

A contemptuous term; a *chuff* or *chough* being a thievish bird, that collects its prey by the sea-shore.

[60] *The wat'ry ladies.*

Fairies who haunt pools and fountains. Theobald would read *Naiads.*

[61] *Thy arcane secrecy.*

A mere repetition; thy secret secrecy.

[62] *Feere*, i.e. mate.

[63] *Frumps*, i.e. gibes, sneers.

[64] *This steely glaive*, i.e. sword.

[65] *Sabren for ever shall this same be call'd.*

The name of the unfortunate maiden has, we are told by Milton, been corrupted by time from Sabren to Sabrina, and thence to *Severn.* That noble poet also, in his *Masque of Comus*, thus alludes to this legend :—

> There is a gentle nymph not far from hence,
> That with moist curb sways the smooth Severn stream,
> Sabrina is her name, a virgin pure ;
> Whilom she was the daughter of Locrine,
> That had the sceptre from his father Brute.
> She, guiltless damsel, flying the mad pursuit
> Of her enraged step-dame Guendolen,
> Commended her fair innocence to the flood,
> That staid her flight with his cross-flowing course,
> The water-nymphs, that in the bottom play'd,
> Held up their pearled wrists, and took her in,
> Bearing her straight to aged Nereus' hall ;
> Who piteous of her woes, rear'd her lank head,
> And gave her to his daughters to imbathe
> In nectar'd lavers, strew'd with asphodel, &c.

H. T.

Mucedorus

The only external evidence in any degree sanctioning the attribution of this play to Shakespeare is the statement on the title page of the 1610 edition that it was written by "William Sh.," and that it belonged to the repertoire of the Globe Theatre. We also know that its public appeal was enormous. It was acted by strolling companies all over England as late as the eighteenth century, and it passed through seventeen editions between 1598 and 1700, a record unequaled in the history of pre-Restoration drama. The only play at all comparable with *Mucedorus* in popularity with the early book publishers is a considerably better comedy of a similar kind, *The Merry Devil of Edmonton* (also attributed to Shakespeare). Six quarto editions of the latter are recorded between 1608 and 1655.

Its antecedents, in the view of Hallett Smith, (42) lie in Philip Sidney's *Arcadia,* representative of the romance genre which Shakespeare was both responding to and embracing and which would dictate the character of his later plays.

In *Studies in English Renaissance Drama* George F. Reynolds points out that the prominence of the play dates from its revival by the King's Men in 1610; and reasons for its popularity, in addition to the parallel popularity of Sidney's *Arcadia,* are the "merry conceits" of the clown, Mouse, and perhaps the novelty of having the part of the bear taken by a real bear. On the question of the source of the play, Reynolds says, "It may also be in point to notice the growing popularity of the *Arcadia,*" since it does give in unconsecutive passages amounting to about five hundreds words the basic situation of *Mucedorus*: Mucedorus (son of the king of Valentia), disguised as a shepherd, rescues the faithful princess Amadine from a "horrible foul bear" and later elopes with her.

It is Hallett Smith's opinion that *Mucedorus* was revived sometime between 1603 and 1610, at which time additions were made to it by another hand. Advertised as a comedy, the material of the play is, in his view, equally that of romance.

Marvin Herrick (23) finds a close kinship between *Mucedorus* and Thomas Dekker's earliest extant dramatic work, *Old Fortunatus,* which is a comical tragedy with distinct elements of the morality play and with a few echoes of the pastoral:

> It is the story of the possessor of the inexhaustible purse and the wishing cap, with his consequent adventures and those of his sons. It is recorded as already an old play in 1596. With its Lylyan figure of the serving man, Shadow, first of the series of Dekker's rollicking humorists, and its reminiscences of Faust and Tamburlaine it may, according to Schelling, date earlier. It has been assumed, in the absence of an English version, that Dekker read the story of Fortunatus in German or perhaps Dutch when in the low countries; but his fancy has converted the old folk tale into a thing of fresh and almost childlike poetic beauty with a framework of an allegorical contest between Vice and Virtue, the woof of its "trimming for court."

Some of the characters in *Old Fortunatus*—namely the Sultan of Egypt, the King of England and his daughter, the Prince of Cyprus, and various nobles —belong, in Herrick's view, to the tradition of tragedy. The royal and noble persons are balanced by the humble Fortunatus and his two sons, whose servant Shadow is reminiscent of Davus and Parmeno in Roman comedy. There are several abstract characters, Fortune, Virtue, Vice, and the Three Destinies are reminiscent of the morality play and the *Christian Terence.* Fortune's speeches are often Senecan. A chorus of satyrs appears in both the second and fourth acts. Another chorus, appearing between the acts to explain the loosely arranged action, belongs to comedy and history. In the action itself, there is considerable horseplay, much moralizing, and some pathos. Old Fortunatus and both his sons perish before the end of the play, the sons meeting violent and wretched deaths in the last act.

The fashion of comical history, according to M. C. Bradbrook (4), involves a king's or prince's revelling and giving his friendship to a particular craft or a particular town, a strong love interest and a popular hero, magic and buffoonery, and songs and shows. A simple definition of comedy is stated in the Induction to *Mucedorus,* where the figure of Envy opposes that of Comedy, promising in the play martial exploits, severed legs and arms, and the cries of many thousands slain. It sounds indeed as if Envy had originally been Tragedy. Comedy replies:

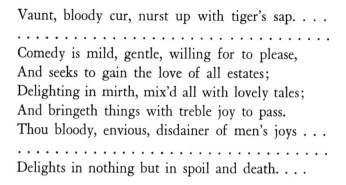

> Vaunt, bloody cur, nurst up with tiger's sap. . . .
>
> . . . .
>
> Comedy is mild, gentle, willing for to please,
> And seeks to gain the love of all estates;
> Delighting in mirth, mix'd all with lovely tales;
> And bringeth things with treble joy to pass.
> Thou bloody, envious, disdainer of men's joys . . .
>
> . . . .
>
> Delights in nothing but in spoil and death. . . .

It is probable that, from the middle of the fifteenth century, a popular romantic comedy-drama existed, closely related to ballads and festival games. This relationship indicates the kind of plays upon knights and monsters, fairy adventures and magic wonders, wishing wells, princesses and dragons, of which those two extremely successful works *Mucedorus* and *Pericles* were the descendants. These were among the most applauded plays of the time, and a debased version of *Mucedorus* was still being performed in Shropshire villages in the early nineteenth century. This is the kind of play that the mechanicals of *A Midsummer Night's Dream* are thinking of when Bottom wants to play either a tyrant or a lover and Flute hopes Thisbe is "a wandering knight."

In summary, this pretty little romance of *Mucedorus*, presented before King James by Shakespeare's company, relies for its drama and humor on the ancient formula of true love, disguise, wanderings in search of adventure, and such "conceits as clownage keeps in pay." And transplanted into the hall of a great house, popular comedy dissolved into pageant.

Shakespeare's success in the theatre was established in the final decade of Elizabeth's reign; and that success, aside from his great tragedies, was mainly dependent on his comedies. For comedy Shakespeare found no type already in vogue as he did for the history play, which explains why his earliest comic efforts were experimentally diverse. The elements of Shakespeare comedy are best revealed in *The Two Gentlemen of Verona* (and, to a lesser degree, *Mucedorus*): in atmosphere, romantic; in subject, devoted to love and adventure; in attitude, sympathetic to the personages involved; in quality, refined and poetic. If the two plays form "an aggregation of fascinating improbabilities," F. E. Schelling (38) reminds us that romance is improbability exploited by fancy; and its only demands are a continuous whetting of the curiosity in a rising scale and the maintenance of a lively interest, this last being the one tie of the veritably romantic to fact and that unascertainable thing that we call reality.

Shakespeare seems to have set little if any store on what we call inventive originality of subject, and he apparently believed that, with a known or borrowed story for subject, dramatic success is half won. But by and large, Shakespeare is always true to the passion evoked, and he is sincere and unerring in his representation of it. With personage, events, emotion, poetry welded into an artistic whole, we are beguiled into acceptance whether or not every detail answers to what we consider the law of probability and consistency, and whether or not it squares with our own experience.

Joseph Addison, in 1714, summed it up aptly when he wrote that:

anyone would rather read Shakespeare where there is not a single rule observed, than any production by a modern writer, where there is not one of them violated.

Finally, as for the conceivability of Shakespeare's having had a hand in the construction of *Mucedorus* or any of the other disputed plays, Tucker Brooke (8) suggests that when we consider the possibility of Shakespeare's cooperation in the capacity of reviser or elaborator, there is less cause for disbelief. Tucker Brooke points out that during his long and many-sided connection with the stage, the poet-actor would doubtless have had occasion to retouch and refine much of the work that came to his company. It is therefore at present a thoroughly permissible belief that some of the splendid passages in the best apocryphal plays are thus the hasty and fragmentary creation of the master's hand.

PERSONS REPRESENTED.

———◆———

ADRASTUS, *King of* Aragon.
Appears, sc. 4; sc. 7; sc. 13.

KING OF VALENTIA.
Appears, sc. 9; sc. 13.

MUCEDORUS, *Son of the* King of Valentia.
Appears, sc. 1; sc. 3; sc. 5; sc. 7; sc. 8; sc. 10; sc. 11; sc. 12; sc. 13.

ANSELMO, *a Noble in the confidence of* Prince Mucedorus.
Appears, sc. 1; sc. 9; sc. 13.

SEGASTO, *a wealthy Noble of* Aragon, *engaged to* Amadine.
Appears, sc. 3; sc. 5; sc. 7; sc. 8; sc. 11; sc. 12; sc. 13.

TREMELIO, *a Captain of* Aragon, *and Friend to* Segasto.
Appears, sc. 4; sc. 5.

COLLIN, *a Counsellor of the* King of Aragon.
Appears, sc. 4; sc. 13.

MOUSE, *the Clown.*
Appears, sc. 2; sc. 3; sc. 5; sc. 7; sc. 8; sc. 10; sc. 11; sc. 12; sc. 13.

BREMO, *a Wild Man.*
Appears, sc. 6; sc. 8; sc. 11; sc. 1...

RUMBELO, *a Soldier in the service of* Segasto.
Appears, sc. 11.

RODERIGO, } *Nobles attending on the* King of
BRACHIUS, } Valentia.
Appear, sc. 9; sc. 13.

AMADINE, *the Daughter of the* King of Aragon.
Appears, sc. 3; sc. 4; sc. 7; sc. 8; sc. 11; sc. 12; sc. 13.

ARIENA, Amadine's *Maid.*
Appears, sc. 7.

AN OLD WOMAN, *Keeper of an Alehouse.*
Appears, sc. 8.

COMEDY.
ENVY.
Appear, in the Induction and at the end of the piece.

Counsellors, a Prisoner, a Messenger, a Page, and Attendants.

SCENE.—*First at* VALENTIA, *afterwards at* ARAGON, *and a Forest near it.*

Mucedorus.

PROLOGUE.

Most sacred majesty,[1] whose great deserts,
Thy subject England, nay, the world admires;
Which heaven grant still increase, O may your praise
Multiplying with your hours, your fame still raise:
Embrace your council: Love, with Faith them guide,
That both as one bench, by the other's side.
So may your life pass on, and so run even,
That your firm zeal plant you a throne in heaven,

Where smiling angels shall your guardians be,
From blemish'd traitors stain'd with perjury:
And as the night's inferior to the day,
So be all earthly regions to your sway.
Be as the sun to day, the day to night;
For from your beams Europe shall borrow light.
Mirth drown your bosom, fair Delight your mind,
And may our pastime your contentment find.

INDUCTION.

Enter Comedy *joyfully, with a Garland of Bays on her Head.*

Com. Why so, thus do I hope to please:
Music revives, and mirth is tolerable:
Comedy, play thy part and please:
Make merry them that come to joy with thee:
Joy then good gentles, I hope to make you laugh:
Sound forth Bellona's silver tun'd strings,[2]
Time fits us well, the day and place is ours.

Enter Envy, *his Arms naked, besmeared with Blood.*

Envy. Nay, stay, minion, stay, there lies a block
What, all on mirth? I'll interrupt your tale,
And mix your music with a tragic end.
Com. What monstrous ugly hag is this,
That dares controul the pleasures of our will?
Vaunt, churlish cur, besmeared with gory blood,
That seem'st to check the blossom of delight,
And still the sound of sweet Bellona's breath:
Blush, monster, blush, and post away with shame,
That seek'st disturbance of a goddess' name.
Envy. Post hence thyself thou counterchecking trull,
I will possess this habit spite of thee,
And gain the glory of this wishéd part;
I'll thunder music shall appal the nymphs,

And make them shiver their clattering strings,
Flying for succour to their Danish caves.
  [*A sound of Drums within, and cries of* "Stab," "stab."
Hearken, thou shalt hear noise
Shall fill the air with shrilling sound:
And thunder music to the gods above:
Mars shall himself breathe down
A peerless crown upon brave Envy's head,
And raise his chival[3] with a lasting fame:
In this brave music Envy takes delight,
Where I may see them wallow in their blood,
To spurn at arms and legs quite shivered off,[4]
And hear the cries of many thousand slain:
How lik'st thou this my trull? 'tis sport alone for me.
Com. Vaunt, bloody cur, nurst up with tiger's sap,
That so dost quail a woman's mind:
Comedy is mild, gentle, willing for to please,
And seeks to gain the love of all estates;
Delighting in mirth, mix'd all with lovely tales;
And bringeth things with treble joy to pass.
Thou bloody, envious, disdainer of men's joys;
Whose name is wrought with bloody stratagems,
Delights in nothing but in spoil and death,
Where thou may'st trample in their luke-warm blood,

And grasp their hearts within thy curséd paws;
Yet vail thy mind, revenge thee not on me,
A silly woman begs it at thy hands.
Give me the leave to utter out my play:
Forbear this place, I humbly crave thee hence,
And mix not death amongst pleasing comedies,
That treat nought else but pleasure and delight:
If any spark of human rests in thee,
Forbear, begone, tender the suit of me.[5]

    Envy. Why so I will; forbearance shall be such,
As treble death shall cross thee with despite,
And make thee mourn where most thou joyest,
Turning thy mirth into a deadly dole,[6]
Whirling thy pleasures with a peal of death,
And drench thy methods in a sea of blood;
Thus will I do; thus shall I bear with thee,
And more to vex thee with a deeper spite,
I will with threats of blood begin the play,
Favouring thee with Envy and with Hate.

    Com. Then, ugly monster, do thy worst,
I will defend them in despite of thee;[7]
And though thou thinkest with tragic fumes
To prove my play unto my great disgrace,
I force it not,[8] I scorn what thou canst do:
I'll grace it so, thyself shall it confess,
From tragic stuff to be a pleasant comedy.

    Envy. Why then, Comedy, send the actors
        forth,
And I will cross the first step of their trade,
Making them fear the very dart of death.

    Com. And I'll defend them, maugre all thy
        spite:
So, ugly fiend, farewell till time shall serve,
That we may meet to parley for the best.

    Envy. Content, Comedy, I'll go spread my branch,
And scattered blossoms from my envious tree
Shall prove two monsters spoiling of their joys.

                   [*Exeunt.*

SCENE I.—*An Apartment at the Court of the*
    King of Valentia.

Enter MUCEDORUS, *and* ANSELMO, *his Friend.*

    Muc. Anselmo?
    Ansel.   My lord and friend,
Whose dear affections bosom with my heart,
And keep their domination in one orb;
Whence ne'er disloyalty shall root it forth,
But faith plant firmer in your choice respect.

    Muc. Much blame were mine if I should other
        deem,
Nor can coy fortune contrary allow;
But my Anselmo, loth I am to say, I must estrange
        that friendship.
Misconstrue not, 'tis from the realm, not thee:
Though lands part bodies, hearts keep company;
Thou know'st that I imparted often have,
Private relations with my royal sire,
Had, as concerning beauteous Amadine,
Rich Aragon's bright jewel; whose face (some say)
That blooming lilies never shone so gay;
Excelling, not excell'd; yet lest report
Does mangle verity, boasting of what is not,
Wing'd with desire, thither I'll straight repair,
And be my fortunes as my thoughts are fair.

    Ansel. Will you forsake Valentia? leave the
        court?
Absent you from the eye of sovereignty?
Do not, sweet prince, adventure on that task,
Since danger lurks each where, be won from it.

    Muc. Desist dissuasion,
My resolution brooks no battery,
Therefore if thou retain thy wonted form,
Assist what I intend.

    Ansel. Your miss[9] will breed a blemish in the court,
And throw a frosty dew upon that beard,
Whose front Valentia stoops to.

    Muc. If thou my welfare tender, then no more,
Let love's strong magic charm thy trivial phrase,
Wasted as vainly as to gripe the sun:
Augment not then more answer; lock thy lips,
Unless thy wisdom sure me with disguise,
According to my purpose.

    Ansel. That action craves no counsel,
Since what you rightly are, will more command,
Than best usurpéd shape.

    Muc. Thou still art opposite in disposition.
A more obscure servile habiliment
Beseems this enterprise.

    Ansel. Then like a Florentine or mountebank.

    Muc. 'Tis much too tedious, I dislike thy judg-
        ment,
My mind is grafted on a humbler stock.

    Ansel. Within my closet does there hang a
        cassock,
Though base the weed is, 'twas a shepherd's
Which I presented in lord Julius' mask.[10]

    Muc. That my Anselmo, and nought else but that,
Mask Mucedorus from the vulgar view:
That habit suits my mind, fetch me that weed.

                   [*Exit* ANSEL.

Better than kings have not disdain'd that state,
And much inferior to obtain their mate.

Re-enter ANSELMO *with a Shepherd's Coat.*

So, let our respect command thy secrecy,—
At once a brief farewell,
Delay to lovers is a second hell.   [*Exit* MUC.
   Ansel. Prosperity forerun thee: awkward chance,
Never be neighbour to thy wish's venture,
Content and fame advance thee.   Ever thrive,
And glory thy mortality survive.

SCENE II.—*The Outskirts of a Forest near* Aragon.

Enter MOUSE *with a Bottle of Hay.*[11]

   Mouse. O horrible, terrible! was ever poor gentleman so scar'd out of his seven senses? A bear?
Nay sure it cannot be a bear, but some devil in a
bear's doublet; for a bear could never have had
that agility to have frighted me. Well, I'll see
my father hang'd before I'll serve his horse any
more. Well, I'll carry home my bottle of hay,
and for once let my father's horse turn Puritan,
and observe fasting days, for he gets not a bit.
But soft, this way she followed me, therefore I'll
take the other path, and because I'll be sure to
have an eye to her, I will shake hands with some
foolish creditor, and make every step backward.

   [*As he goes backward the Bear comes in, and
      he tumbles over her, and runs away, leav-
      ing his bottle of hay behind him.*

SCENE III.—*Another part of the Forest.*

Enter SEGASTO *running, and* AMADINE *after him,
      being pursued by a Bear.*

   Seg. O fly madam, fly, or else we are but dead.
   Ama. Help, Segasto, help, help sweet Segasto, or
      else I die.
   Seg. Alas, madam, there is no way but flight;
Then haste and save yourself.   [*Exit running.*
   Ama. Why then I die. Oh! help me in distress.

Enter MUCEDORUS *like a Shepherd, with a Sword
      drawn, and a Bear's Head in his Hand.*

   Muc. Stay, lady, stay, and be no more dismay'd,
That cruel beast most merciless and fell,
Affrighted many with his hard pursues,
Prying from place to place to find his prey,
Prolonging thus his life by others' death:
His carcase now lies headless, void of breath.
   Ama. That foul deformèd monster, is he dead?
   Muc. Assure yourself thereof, behold his head,

Which if it please you, lady, to accept,
With willing heart I yield it to your majesty.
   Ama. Thanks, worthy shepherd, thanks a thou-
      sand times:
This gift, assure thyself, contents me more,
Than greatest bounty of a mighty prince,
Although he were the monarch of the world.
   Muc. Most gracious goddess, more than mortal
      wight,
Your heavenly hue of right imports no less;
Most glad am I, in that it was my chance
To undertake this enterprise in hand,
Which doth so greatly glad your princely mind.
   Ama. No goddess (shepherd), but a mortal wight,
A mortal wight distressèd as thou see'st;
My father here is king of Aragon,
I, Amadine, his only daughter am,
And after him sole heir unto the crown:
Now, whereas it is my father's will
To marry me unto Segasto,
One whose wealth, through father's former usury,
Is known to be no less than wonderful:
We both of custom oftentimes did use,
(Leaving the court) to walk within the fields
For recreation, especially the spring,
In that it yields great store of rare delights:
And passing farther than our wonted walks,
Scarce enterèd within these luckless woods,
But right before us down a steepfast hill,
A monstrous ugly bear did hie him fast
To meet us both: I faint to tell the rest,
Good shepherd; but suppose the ghastly looks,
The hideous fears, the hundred thousand woes
Which at this instant Amadine sustain'd.
   Muc. Yet, worthy princess, let thy sorrows cease
And let this sight your former joys revive.
   Ama. Believe me, shepherd, so it doth no less.
   Muc. Long may they last unto your heart's
      content;
But tell me, lady, what is become of him,
Segasto call'd,—what is become of him?
   Ama. I know not, I, that know the powers
      divine,
But God grant this, that sweet Segasto live.
   Muc. Yet hard-hearted he in such a case,
So cowardly to save himself by flight,
And leave so brave a princess to the spoil.
   Ama. Well, shepherd, for thy worthy valour
      tried,
Endangering thyself to set me free,
Unrecompensèd sure thou shalt not be:
In court thy courage shall be plainly known.
Bear thou the head of this most monstrous beast,

In open sight to every courtier's view:
So will the king, my father, thee reward.
Come, let's away, and guard me to the court.
 Muc. With all my heart.   [*Exeunt.*

Enter SEGASTO, *solus.*

 Seg. When heaps of harms do hover overhead,
'Tis time as then (some say) to look about,
And of ensuing harms to choose the least.
But hard, yea hapless is that wretch's chance,
Luckless his lot, and caitiff-like accurst,
At whose proceedings fortune ever frown
Myself I mean, most subject unto thrall:
For I, the more I seek to shun the worst,
The more by proof I find myself accurst.
Erewhiles assaulted with an ugly bear,
Fair Amadine in company all alone,
Forthwith by flight I thought to save myself,
Leaving my Amadine unto her shifts:
For death it was for to resist the bear,
And death no less of Amadine's harms to hear.
Accursèd I, in lingering life thus long:
In living thus, each minute of an hour
Doth pierce my heart with darts of thousand deaths:
If she by flight her fury doth escape,
What will she think?
Will she not say, yea flatly to my face,
Accusing me of mere disloyalty,—
A trusty friend is tried in time of need:
But I, when she in danger was of death,
And needed me, and cried, Segasto, help,
I turn'd my back and quickly ran away;
Unworthy I to bear this vital breath:
But what, what need these plaints?
If Amadine do live, then happy I,
She will in time forgive and so forget:
Amadine is merciful, not Juno-like,
In harmful hearts to harbour hatred long.

Enter MOUSE, *the Clown, running; crying* "Clubs!"

 Mouse. Clubs, prongs, pitchforks, bills! Oh help!
A bear, a bear, a bear!
 Seg. Still bears, and nothing but bears.
Tell me, sirrah, where she is.
 Mouse. O, sir, she is run down the woods;
I saw her white head, and her white belly.
 Seg. Thou talk'st of wonders to tell me of
  white bears;
But, sirrah, didst thou ever see any such?
 Mouse. No, faith, I never saw any such:
But I remember my father's words.
He bade me take heed I was not caught with the
  white bear.

 Seg. A lamentable tale, no doubt.
 Mouse. I'll tell you what, sir; as I was going
a-field to serve my father's great horse, and carried
a bottle of hay upon my head: now, do you see,
sir, I fast hood-wink'd that I should see nothing;
I, perceiving the bear coming, threw my hay into
the hedge, and ran away.
 Seg. What, from nothing?
 Mouse. I warrant you yes, I saw something; for
there was two loads of thorns besides my bottle of
hay, and that made three.
 Seg. But tell me, sirrah, the bear that thou didst
  see,
Did she not bear a bucket on her arm?
 Mouse. Ha, ha, ha, I never saw a bear go a-milk-
ing in all my life. But hark you, sir, I did not
look so high as her arm; I saw nothing but her
white head, and her white belly.
 Seg. But tell me, sirrah, where dost thou dwell?
 Mouse. Why, do you not know me?
 Seg. Why no; how should I know thee?
 Mouse. Why then you know nobody, and you
know not me: I tell you, sir, I am goodman Rats'
son, of the next parish over the hill.
 Seg. Goodman Rats' son, what's thy name?
 Mouse. Why, I am very near kin unto him.
 Seg. I think so; but what's thy name?
 Mouse. My name? I have a very pretty name.
I'll tell you what my name is; my name is Mouse.
 Seg. What, plain Mouse?
 Mouse. Ay, plain Mouse, without either welt or
gard.[12] But do you hear, sir, I am a very young
mouse, for my tail is scarce grown out yet; look
here else.
 Seg. But, I pray you, who gave you that name?
 Mouse. Faith, sir, I know not that, but if you
would fain know, ask my father's great horse, for
he hath been half-a-year longer with my father
than I have.
 Seg. This seems to be a merry fellow,
I care not if I take him home with me;
Mirth is a comfort to a troubled mind,
A merry man a merry master makes.
How say'st thou, sirrah, wilt thou dwell with me?
 Mouse. Nay, soft, sir, two words to a bargain.
Pray, what occupation are you?
 Seg. No occupation; I live upon my lands.
 Mouse. Your lands? away, you are no master
for me. Why, do you think that I am so mad to
go seek my living in the lands among the stones,
briers, and bushes, and tear my holiday apparel?
Not I, by your leave.
 Seg. Why, do I mean thou shalt?

Mouse. How then?

Seg. Why thou shalt be my man, and wait on me at court.

Mouse. What's that?

Seg. Where the king lies.

Mouse. What is that king, a man or a woman?

Seg. A man, as thou art.

Mouse. As I am? Hark you, sir, pray you what kin is he to goodman King, of our parish, the churchwarden?

Seg. No kin to him; he is king of the whole land.

Mouse. King of the whole land! I never saw him.

Seg. If thou wilt dwell with me, thou shalt see him every day.

Mouse. Shall I go home again to be torn in pieces with bears? No, not I; I will go home and put on a clean shirt, and then go drown myself.

Seg. Thou shalt not need; if thou wilt dwell with me thou shalt want nothing.

Mouse. Shall I not? then here's my hand, I'll dwell with you; and, hark you, sir, now you have entertained me, I'll tell you what I can do; I can keep my tongue from picking and stealing, and my hands from lying and slandering, I warrant you, as well as ever you had any man in your life.'

Seg. Now will I to court with sorrowful heart, rounded with doubts: If Amadine do live, then happy I; yea, happy I if Amadine do live. [*Exeunt.*

SCENE IV.—*Camp of the* King of Aragon.

Enter the KING, *with a young* Prisoner, AMADINE, TREMELIO, *with* COLLIN, *and* Counsellors.

King. Now, brave lords, our wars are brought to end,
Our foes the foil, and we in safety rest;
It us behoves to use such clemency in peace,
As valour in the wars;
'Tis as great honour to be bountiful at home,
As conquerors in the field.
Therefore, my lords, the more to my content,
Your liking and our country's safeguard,
We are dispos'd in marriage for to give
Our daughter unto lord Segasto here,
Who shall succeed the diadem after me,
And reign hereafter, as I to-fore have done,
Your sole and lawful king of Aragon.
What say you, lordlings? like you my advice?

Col. An't please your majesty, we do not only allow of your highness' pleasure, but also vow faithfully in what we may to further it.

King. Thanks, good my lords, if long Adrastus live,

He will at full requite your courtesies.
Tremelio, in recompense of your late valour done,
Take unto thee the Catalone, a prince,
Lately our prisoner, taken in the wars;
Be thou his keeper, his ransom shall be thine;
We'll think of it when leisure shall afford;
Meanwhile do use him well, his father is a king.

Tre. Thanks to your majesty; his usage shall be such,
As he thereat shall have no cause to grutch. [*Exit.*

King. Then march we on to court, and rest our wearied limbs.
But, Collin, I have a tale in secret fit for thee,
When thou shalt hear a watch-word from thy king,
Think then some weighty matter is at hand,
That highly shall concern our state;
Then, Collin, look thou be not far from me,
And for thy service thou to-fore hast done,
Thy truth and valour prov'd in every point,
I shall with bounties thee enlarge therefore.
So guard us to the court. [*Exeunt.*

SCENE V.—*Room at the Court of* Aragon.

Enter SEGASTO, *and* MOUSE, *with Weapons about him.*

Seg. Tell me, sirrah, how do you like your weapons?

Mouse. O very well, very well, they keep my sides warm.

Seg. They keep the dogs from your shins well, do they not?

Mouse. How keep the dogs from my shins? I would scorn but my shins should keep the dogs from them.

Seg. Well, sirrah, leaving idle talk, tell me, Dost thou know captain Tremelio's chamber?

Mouse. Ay, very well, it hath a door.

Seg. I think so, for so hath every chamber; But dost thou know the man?

Mouse. Ay, forsooth, he hath a nose on his face.

Seg. Why so hath every one.

Mouse. That's more than I know.

Seg. But dost thou remember the captain that was here with the king, that brought the young prince prisoner?

Mouse. O very well.

Seg. Go to him, and bid him come unto me; Tell him I have a matter in secret to impart to him.

Mouse. I will, master. What's his name?

Seg. Why, captain Tremelio.

Mouse. O, the meal-man; I know him very well,

He brings meal every Saturday; but hark you, master,
Must I bid him come to you, or must you come to him?

Seg. No, sirrah, he must come to me.

Mouse. Hark you, master, if he be not at home, What shall I do then?

Seg. Why then leave word with some of his folks.

Mouse. O, master, if there be nobody within, I will leave word with his dog.

Seg. Why, can his dog speak?

Mouse. I cannot tell, wherefore doth he keep his chamber else?

Seg. To keep out such knaves as thou art.

Mouse. Nay by lady, then go yourself.

Seg. You will go, sir, will you not?

Mouse. Yes, marry will I. O, 'tis come to my head: And if he be not within, I'll bring his chamber to you.

Seg. What, will you pluck down the king's house?

Mouse. No by lady, I'll know the price of it first. Master, it is such a hard name, I have forgotten it again; I pray you tell me his name?

Seg. I tell thee, captain Tremelio.

Mouse. O captain Treble-knave, captain Treble-knave.

Enter TREMELIO.

Tre. How now, sirrah, dost thou call me?

Mouse. You must come to my master, captain treble-knave.

Tre. My lord Segasto, did you send for me?

Seg. I did, Tremelio. Sirrah, about your business.

Mouse. Ay marry, what's that; can you tell?

Seg. No, not well.

Mouse. Marry then I can, straight to the kitchen-dresser to John the cook, and get me a good piece of beef and brewis,[13] and then to the buttery-hatch to Thomas the butler for a jake of beer: and there for an hour I'll so belabour myself, and therefore I pray you call me not till you think I have done, I pray you good master.

Seg. Well, sir, away.   [*Exit* MOUSE.
Tremelio; this it is, thou knowest the shepherd's fame is
Spread through all the kingdom of Aragon,
And such as have found triumph and favours
Never daunted at any time; but now a shepherd's,
Admired in court for worthiness,
And Segasto's honour laid aside:
My will therefore is this, thou dost find some means to work the shepherd's death; I know thy

strength sufficient to perform my desire, and thy love no otherwise than to revenge my injuries.

Tre. It is not the frowns of a shepherd that Tremelio scares:
Therefore account accomplish'd what I take in hand.

Seg. Thanks good Tremelio, and assure thyself, What I promise, that will I perform.

Tre. Thanks, good my lord: and in good time, See where he cometh; stand by a while,
And you shall see me put in practice your intended drift.
Have at thee swain, if that I hit thee right.

Enter MUCEDORUS.

Muc. Vild coward, so without cause to strike a man;
Turn, coward, turn; now strike and do thy worst.
                [MUC. *killeth him.*

Seg. Hold, shepherd, hold, spare him, kill him not:
Accurséd villain, tell me, what hast thou done?
Ah, Tremelio, trusty Tremelio, I sorrow for thy death,
And since that thou living didst prove faithful to Segasto,
So Segasto now living will honour the dead
Corpse of Tremelio with revenge.
Blood-thirsty villain, born and bred in merciless murder,
Tell me, how durst thou be so bold,
As once to lay thy hands upon the least of mine?
Assure thyself thou shalt be us'd according to the law.

Muc. Segasto cease, these threats are needless,
Accuse me not of murder, that have done nothing,
But in mine own defence.

Seg. Nay shepherd, reason not with me,
I'll manifest thy fact unto the king;
Whose doom will be thy death, as thou deserv'st.
What ho! Mouse come away.

Enter MOUSE.

Mouse. Why, how now, what's the matter?
I thought you would be calling before I had done.

Seg. Come, help away with my friend.

Mouse. Why is he drunk? can he not stand on his feet?

Seg. No, he is not drunk, he is slain.

Mouse. Flain? No, by lady he is not flain.

Seg. He's killed, I tell thee.

Mouse. What, do you use to kill your friends? I will serve you no longer.

Seg. I tell thee the shepherd killed him.

Mouse. O did he so? But master, I will have all his apparel if I carry him away.

Seg. Why so thou shalt.

Mouse. Come then, I will help: mass, master, I think his mother sung looby to him, he is so heavy.   [*Exeunt* SEG. *and* MOUSE *with the Body.*

Muc. Behold the fickle state of man, always mutable, never at one.

Sometime we feed our fancies with the sweet of our desires:

Sometimes again, we feel the heat of extreme miseries.

Now am I in favour about the court and country,

To-morrow those favours will turn to frowns.

To-day I live revengéd on my foe,

To-morrow I die, my foe revengéd on me.   [*Exit.*

SCENE VI.—*A Pathway in the Forest.*

Enter BREMO, *a wild Man.*

Bre. No passenger this morning? what, not one?

A chance that seldom doth befall,

What, not one? then lie thou there,

And rest thyself till I have further need:

Now Bremo, sith thy leisure so affords,

An endless thing, who knows not Bremo's strength,

Who like a king commands within these woods?

The bear, the boar, dare not abide his sight,

But haste away, to save themselves by flight.

The crystal waters in the bubbling brooks,

When I come by do swiftly slide away,

And clap themselves in closets under banks,

Afraid to look bold Bremo in the face.

The aged oaks at Bremo's breath do bow,

And all things else are still at my command.

Else what would I?

Rend them in pieces, and pluck them from the earth,

And each way else I would revenge myself.

Why who comes here, with whom dare I not fight?

Who fights with me, and doth not die the death?   Not one.

What favour shows this sturdy stick to those

That here within these woods are combatants with me?

Why, death, and nothing else but present death;

With restless rage I wander through these woods;

No creature here but feareth Bremo's force:

Man, woman, child, beast, and bird,

And everything that doth approach my sight,

Are forc'd to fall, if Bremo once do frown.

Come, cudgel, come, my partner in my spoils,

For here I see this day it will not be,

But when it falls that I encounter any,

One pat sufficeth for to work my will,

What, comes not one? then let's begone,

A time will serve when we shall better speed. [*Exit.*

SCENE VII.—Aragon. *A Room of State in the Court.*

Enter the KING, SEGASTO, MUCEDORUS, MOUSE, *and* Others.

King. Shepherd, thou hast heard thine accusers,

Murder is laid to thy charge:

What canst thou say? thou hast deservéd death.

Muc. Dread sovereign, I must needs confess,

I slew this captain in my own defence,

Not of any malice, but by chance:

But mine accuser hath a further meaning.

Seg. Words will not here prevail,

I seek for justice, and justice craves his death.

King. Shepherd, thine own confession hath condemned thee:

Sirrah, take him away, and do him to execution straight.

Mouse. So he shall, I warrant him:

But do you hear master king? he is kin to a monkey,

His neck is higher than his head.

Seg. Come, sirrah, away with him,

And hang him about the middle.

Mouse. Yes, forsooth, I warrant you; come you sirrah:

'A, so like a sheep-biter[14] 'a looks.

Enter AMADINE, *and a* Boy *with a Bear's Head.*

Ama. Dread sovereign, and well-belovéd sire,

On bended knee I crave the life of this condemned shepherd, which heretofore preserved the life of thy sometime distressed daughter.

King. Preserved the life of my sometime distressed daughter!

How can that be? I never knew the time,

Wherein was thou distrest: I never knew the day,

But that I have maintainéd thy estate,

As best beseem'd the daughter of a king,

I never saw the shepherd until now;

How comes it, then, that he preserv'd thy life?

Ama. Once walking with Segasto in the woods,

Further than our accustom'd manner was,

Right before us down a steepfall hill,

A monstrous ugly bear did hie him fast

To meet us both: now whether this be true,

I refer it to the credit of Segasto.

Seg. Most true, an't like your majesty.

King.   How then?

Ama. The bear being eager to obtain his prey,

Made forward to us with an open mouth,
As if he meant to swallow us both at once :
The sight whereof did make us both to dread ;
But specially your daughter Amadine,
Who for I saw no succour incident
But in Segasto's valour, I grew desperate,
And he most coward-like began to fly—
Left me distress'd to be devour'd of him ;
How say you, Segasto, is it not true ?

   King. His silence verifies it to be true : what
    then ?

   Ama. Then, I amaz'd, distresséd, all alone,
Did hie me fast, to 'scape that ugly bear,
But all in vain ; for why he reach'd after me,
And hardly I did oft escape his paws.
Till at the length this shepherd came,
And brought to me his head.
Come hither, boy ; lo, here it is, which I do present
    unto your majesty.

   King. The slaughter of this bear deserves great
    fame.

   Seg. The slaughter of a man deserves great
    blame.

   King. Indeed, occasion oftentimes so falls out.

   Seg. Tremelio in the wars (O king) preserved
    thee.

   Ama. The shepherd in the woods (O king) pre-
    served me.

   Seg. Tremelio fought when many men did yield.

   Ama. So would the shepherd had he been in field.

   Mouse. So would my master had he not run away.

   Seg. Tremelio's force sav'd thousands from the
    foe.

   Ama. The shepherd's force hath many thousands
    moe.

   Mouse. Aye, shipsticks,[15] nothing else.

   King. Segasto, cease to accuse the shepherd,
His worthiness deserves a recompense ;
All we are bound to do the shepherd good.
Shepherd, whereas it was my sentence thou shouldst
    die,
So shall my sentence stand, for thou shalt die.

   Seg. Thanks to your majesty.

   King. But soft, Segasto, not for this offence :
Long may'st thou live ; and when the sisters shall
    decree,
To cut in twain the twisted thread of life,
Then let him die ; for this I set him free,
And for thy valour I will honour thee.

   Ama. Thanks to your majesty.

   King. Come, daughter, let us now depart to
honour the worthy valour of the shepherd with our
rewards.   [*Exeunt* KING, AMAD., MUC., &c.

   Mouse. O master hear you, you have made a
    fresh hand now,
I thought you would, beshrew you : what will you
    do now ?
You have lost me a good occupation by this means :
Faith, master, now I cannot hang the shepherd,
I pray you let me take pains to hang you,
It is but half an hour's exercise.

   Seg. You are still in your knavery :
But sith I cannot have his life,
I will procure his banishment for ever.   Come on,
    sirrah.   [*Exeunt* SEG. *and* MOUSE.

Enter MUCEDORUS, *solus.*

   Muc. From Amadine, and from her father's court,
With gold and silver, and with rich rewards,
Flowing from the banks of gold and treasures :
More may I boast and say : but I ——[16]
Was never shepherd in such dignity.

Enter Messenger *and* MOUSE.

   Mess. All hail, worthy shepherd.

   Mouse. All rain, lousy shepherd.

   Muc. Welcome my friends, from whence come
    you ?

   Mess. The king and Amadine greet thee well ;
And after greeting done, bid thee depart the court.
Shepherd, begone.

   Mouse. Shepherd take law-legs, fly away shep-
    herd.

   Muc. Whose words are these ? come they from
    Amadine ?

   Mess. Ay, from Amadine.

   Mouse.   Ay, from Amadine.

   Muc. Oh luckless fortune, worse than Phæton's
    tale,
My former bliss is now become my bale.

   Mouse. What, wilt thou poison thyself ?

   Muc. My former heaven is now become my
    hell.

   Mouse. The worst ale-house that ever I came in
    in all my life.

   Muc. What shall I do ?

   Mouse.   Even go hang thyself.

   Muc. Can Amadine so churlishly command
To banish the shepherd from her father's court ?

   Mess. What should shepherds do in the court ?

   Mouse. What should shepherds do among us ?
Have we not lords enough on us in the court ?

   Muc. Why, shepherds are men, and kings are no
    more.

   Mess. Shepherds are men, and masters o'er their
    flocks.

Mouse. That's a lie; who pays them their wages
then?

Mess. Well, you are always interrupting me;
But you were best to look to him, lest you hang
for him when he is gone.   [*Exit.*

   Mouse. And you shall hang for company,   [*Sings.*
     For leaving me alone,
   Shepherd stand forth and hear my sentence,
    Shepherd begone, shepherd begone, begone, begone
   Begone shepherd, shepherd, shepherd.

                [*Exit* MOUSE.

Muc. And must I go? and must I needs depart?
Ye goodly groves, partakers of my songs,
In time before when fortune did not frown,
Pour forth your plaints, and wail awhile with me:
And thou, bright sun, the comfort of my cold,
Hide, hide thy face, and leave me comfortless:
Ye wholesome herbs and sweet smelling savours,
Yea, each thing else prolonging life of man,
Change, change your wonted course,
That I, wanting your aid, in woful sort may die.

   Enter AMADINE *and* ARIENA, *her Maid.*

Ama. Ariena, if anybody ask for me,
Make some excuse till I return.

Ari. What and Segasto call?

Ama. Do you the like to him; I mean not to
   stay long.   [*Exit* ARI.

Muc. This voice so sweet my pining spirit revives.

Ama. Shepherd well met, tell me how thou dost.

Muc. I linger life, yet wish for speedy death.

Ama. Shepherd, although thy banishment already
be decreed, and all against my will, yet Amadine—

Muc. Ah Amadine, to hear of banishment, is
   death:
Ay, double death to me: but since I must depart,
   one thing I crave.

Ama. Say on with all my heart.

Muc. That in absence either far or near,
You honour me as servant to your name.

Ama. Not so.

Muc.   And why?

Ama. I honour thee as sovereign of my heart.

Muc. A shepherd and a sovereign nothing like.[17]

Ama. Yes like enough, where there is no dislike.

Muc. Yet great dislike, or else no banishment.

Ama. Shepherd, it is only Segasto that procures
   thy banishment.

Muc. Unworthy wights are more in jealousy.

Ama. Would God they would free thee from
   banishment,
Or likewise banish me.

Muc. Amen, I say, to have your company.

Ama. Well, shepherd, sith thou sufferest for my
   sake,
With thee in exile also let me live;
On this condition, shepherd, thou canst love.

Muc. No longer love, no longer let me live.

Ama. Of late I loved one indeed, but now I love
   none but only thee.[18]

Muc. Thanks, worthy princess; burn likewise,
Yet smother up the blast,[19]
I dare not promise what I may perform.

Ama. Well, shepherd, hark what I shall say;
I will return unto my father's court,
There to provide me of such necessaries
As for my journey I shall think most fit;
This being done, I will return to thee;
Do thou therefore appoint the place
Where we may meet.

Muc. Down in the valley where I slew the bear,
And there doth grow a fair broad branched beech
That overshades a well; so who comes first,
Let them abide the happy meeting of us both.
How like you this?

Ama.   I like it well.

Muc. Now, if you please, you may appoint the
   time.

Ama. Full three hours hence, God willing, I will
   return.

Muc. The thanks that Paris gave the Grecian
   queen,
The like doth Mucedorus yield.

Ama. Then, Mucedorus, for three hours farewell.   [*Exit.*

Muc. Your departure, lady, breeds a privy pain.
                [*Exit.*

       Enter SEGASTO, *solus.*

Seg. 'Tis well, Segasto, that thou hast thy will;
Should such a shepherd, such a simple swain as he,
Eclipse thy credit, famous through the court?
No, ply, Segasto, ply; let it not in Aragon be said,
A shepherd hath Segasto's honour won.

   Enter MOUSE, *the Clown, calling his Master.*

Mouse. What ho, master, will you come away?

Seg. Will you come hither, I pray you; what is
the matter?

Mouse. Why, is it not past eleven of the clock?

Seg. How then, sir?

Mouse. I pray you come away to dinner.

Seg. I pray you come hither.

Mouse. Here's such ado with you; will you
never come?

Seg. I pray you, sir, what news of the message I sent you about?

Mouse. I tell you all the messes be on the table already. There wants not so much as a mess of mustard half-an-hour ago.

Seg. Come, sir, your mind is all upon your belly; You have forgotten what I bid you do.

Mouse. Faith, I know nothing, but you bade me go to breakfast.

Seg. Was that all?

Mouse. Faith I have forgotten it, the very scent of the meat hath made me forget it quite.

Seg. You have forgot the errand I bid you do.

Mouse. What errand? an arrant knave, or an arrant whore?

Seg. Why thou knave, did I not bid thee banish the shepherd?

Mouse. O, the shepherd's bastard.

Seg. I tell thee the shepherd's banishment.

Mouse. I tell you the shepherd's bastard shall be well kept, I'll look to it myself; but I pray you come away to dinner.

Seg. Then you will not tell me whether you have banished him or no?

Mouse. Why I cannot say banishment if you would give me a thousand pounds to say so.

Seg. Why your whoreson slave, have you forgotten that I sent you and another to drive away the shepherd?

Mouse. What an ass are you? here's a stir indeed: Here's message, arrant, banishment, and I cannot tell what.

Seg. I pray you, sir, shall I know whether you have drove him away?

Mouse. Faith I think I have; and you will not believe me, ask my staff.

Seg. Why, can thy staff tell?

Mouse. Why, he was with me too.

Seg. Then happy I that have obtain'd my will.

Mouse. And happier I if you would go to dinner.

Seg. Come, sirrah, follow me.

Mouse. I warrant you, I will not lose an inch of you now you are going to dinner: I promise you I thought seven years before I could get him away.

SCENE VIII.—*Beside the Well in the Forest.*

Enter AMADINE.

Ama. God grant my long delay procures no harm,
For this my tarrying frustrates my pretence:
My Mucedorus surely stays for me,
And thinks me over-long; at length I come,
My present promise to perform:
Ah, what a thing is firm, unfeignéd love!
What is it which true love does not attempt?
My father he may make, but I must match:
Segasto loves, but Amadine must like
Where likes her best: compulsion is a thrall:
No, no, the hearty choice is all in all.
The shepherd's virtue Amadine esteems.
But what, methinks the shepherd is not come;
I muse at that, the hour is at hand.
Well, here I'll rest till Mucedorus come.
[*She sits down.*

Enter BREMO, *looking about; hastily takes hold of her.*

Bre. A happy prey: now, Bremo, feed on flesh:
Dainties, Bremo, dainties, thy hungry paunch to fill;
Now glut thy greedy guts with lukewarm blood:
Come fight with me; I long to see thee dead.

Ama. How can she fight that weapons cannot wield?

Bre. What, canst not fight? then lie thee down and die.

Ama. What, must I die?

Bre. What needs these words? I thirst to suck thy blood.

Ama. Yet pity me, and let me live awhile.

Bre. No pity I, I'll feed upon thy flesh;
And tear thy body piece-meal, joint by joint.

Ama. Ah, now I want my shepherd's company.

Bre. I'll crush thy bones between two oaken trees.

Ama. Haste shepherd, haste, or else thou com'st too late.

Bre. I'll suck the sweetness from thy marrow bones.

Ama. Ah, spare, ah, spare, to shed my guiltless blood.

Bre. With this, my bat,[20] I will beat out thy brains;
Down, down, I say; prostrate thyself upon the ground,

Ama. Then Mucedorus farewell; my hoped joys farewell: [*She kneels.*
Yea, farewell life, and welcome present death;
To thee, O God, I yield my dying ghost.

Bre. Now Bremo play thy part.
How now? what sudden chance is this?
My limbs do tremble and my sinews shake,
My unweaken'd arms have lost their former force;
Ah, Bremo, Bremo, what a foil hadst thou,
That yet at no time was afraid,
To dare the greatest gods to fight with thee,

And now want strength for one down-driving blow.
[*He strikes.*

Ah how my courage fails when I should strike ;
Some new-come spirit abiding in my breast,
Saith, spare her, Bremo, spare her, do not kill :
Shall I spare her that never sparéd any ?
To it Bremo, to it, say again :——
I cannot wield my weapons in my hand ;
Methinks I should not strike so fair a one :
I think her beauty hath bewitch'd my force,
Or else with me altered nature's course.
Ay, woman, wilt thou live in woods with me ?

Ama. Fain would I live, yet loth to live in woods.

Bre. Thou shalt not choose, it shall be as I say,
And therefore follow me.   [*Exeunt* BRE. *and* AMA.

Enter MUCEDORUS.

Muc. It was my will an hour ago and more,
As was my promise for to make return ;
But other business hinder'd my pretence.
It is a world to see, when man appoints,
And purposely one certain thing decrees,
How many things may hinder his intent :
What one would wish, the same is farthest off ;
But yet the appointed time cannot be pass'd,
Nor hath her presence yet prevented me :
Well, here I'll stay and expect her coming.
          [*A cry within,* " Hold him, hold him !"
Some one or other is pursued no doubt,
Perhaps some search for me ; 'tis good to doubt
          the worst ;
Therefore I'll be gone.
          [*Exit.   A cry within,* " Hold him, hold him !"

Enter MOUSE, *the Clown, with a Pot.*

Mouse. Hold him, hold him, hold him ! here's
a stir indeed : here came hue after the crier ; and
I was set close at Mother Nips' house, and there
I called for three pots of ale, as 'tis the manner of
us courtiers.   Now, sirrah, I had taken the maidenhead of two of them, and as I was lifting up
the third to my mouth, there came, " Hold him,
hold him !"   Now I could not tell whom to catch
hold on, but I am sure I caught one, perchance a
may be in this pot.   Well, I'll see, mass, I cannot
see him yet : well, I'll look a little further ; mass,
he is a little slave if he be here ; why, here's nobody ; all this is well yet.   But if the old Trot
should come for her pot, ay, marry, there's the
matter : but I care not ; I'll face her out, and
call her old rusty, dusty, musty, fusty, crusty,
firebrand, and worse than all that, and so face her
out of her pot : but soft, here she comes.

Enter the Old Woman.

Old W. Come, you knave, where's my pot, you
knave ?

Mouse. Go look your pot ; come not to me for
your pot, 'twere good for you.

Old W. Thou liest, thou knave, thou hast my pot.

Mouse. You lie and you say it ; I your pot ?
I'll know what I'll say.

Old W. What wilt thou say ?

Mouse. But say I have it and thou dar'st.

Old W. Why, thou knave, thou hast not only my
pot but my drink unpaid for.

Mouse. You lie like an old ——, I will not say
whore.

Old W. Dost thou call me whore ? I'll cap thee
for my pot.

Mouse. Cap me and thou darest :
Search me whether I have it or no.
          [*She searcheth him and he drinketh over her
          Head, and casteth down the Pot ; she stum-
          bleth at it ; and then they fall together by
          the Ears ; she takes up her Pot and runs out.*

Enter SEGASTO.

Seg. How now, sirrah, what's the matter ?

Mouse. O flies, master, flies.

Seg. Flies, where are they ?

Mouse. O here, master, all about your face.

Seg. Why, thou liest ; I think thou art mad.

Mouse. Why, master, I have killed a dung-cart-
          full at the least.

Seg. Go to, sirrah, leave this idle talk, give care
          to me.

Mouse. How, give you one of my cares ?
Not an you were ten masters.

Seg. Why, sir, I pray you give ear to my words.

Mouse. I tell you I will not be made a curtall[21]
for no man's pleasure.

Seg. I tell thee attend what I say.
Go thy ways straight and rear the whole town.

Mouse. How, rear the whole town ? even go
yourself, it is more than I can do.   Why, do you
think I can rear a town that can scarce rear a pot
of ale to my head ?   I should rear a town, should
I not ?

Seg. Go to the constable, and make a privy
          search,
For the shepherd is run away with the king's
          daughter.

Mouse. How, is the shepherd run away with the
king's daughter, or is the king's daughter run away
with the shepherd ?

Seg. I cannot tell, but they are both gone together.

Mouse. What a fool is she to run away with the shepherd! Why, I think I am a little handsomer man than the shepherd myself: but tell me, master, must I make a privy search, or search in the privy?

Seg. Why, dost thou think they will be there?

Mouse. I cannot tell.

Seg. Well then, search everywhere.

Leave no place unsearch'd for them.   [*Exit.* SEG.

Mouse. Oh, now I am in office; now will I to that old firebrand's house, and will not leave one place unsearch'd: nay, I'll to the ale-stand, and drink so long as I can stand; and when I have done, I'll let out all the rest, to see if he be not hid in the barrel; and if I find him not there, I'll to the cup board; I'll not leave one corner of her house unsearched; i'faith ye old crust I'll be with ye now.   [*Exit.*

SCENE IX.—*Room of State in the Court of* Valentia.

Enter the KING OF VALENTIA, ANSELMO, RODERIGO, LORD BRACHIUS, *with* Others.

K. Val. Enough of music, it but adds to torment.
Delights to vexéd spirits are as dates
Set to a sick man, which rather cloy than comfort:
Let me entreat you to entreat no more.

Rod. Let your strings sleep, have done there.
                   [*Music ceaseth.*

K. Val. Mirth to a soul disturb'd, are embers turn'd,
Which sudden gleam with molestation,
But sooner lose their light for't;
'Tis gold bestow'd upon a rioter,
Which not relieves but murders him.
'Tis a drug given to the healthful,
Which infects, not cures.
How can a father that hath lost his son,
A prince both wise, virtuous, and valiant,
Take pleasure in the idle acts of time?
No, no, till Mucedorus I shall see again,
All joy is comfortless, all pleasure pain.

Ansel. Your son, my lord, is well.

K. Val. I prythee speak that thrice.

Ansel. The prince, your son, is safe.

K. Val. O, where, Anselmo; surfeit me with that.

Ansel. In Aragon, my liege, and at his parting,
Bound my secrecy,
By his affection's love not to disclose it;

But care of him and pity of your age
Makes my tongue blab what my breast vow'd concealment.

K. Val. Thou not deceiv'st me,
I ever thought thee what I find thee now,
An upright, loyal man.
But what desire or young-fed humour,
Nursed within his brain,
Drew him so privately to Aragon?

Ansel. A forcing adamant,
Love mix'd with fear and doubtful jealousy,
Whether report gilded a worthless trunk,
Or Amadine deserved her high extolment.

K. Val. See our provision be in readiness,
Collect us followers of the comeliest hue,
For our chief guardians; we will thither wend;
The crystal eye of heaven shall not thrice wink,
Nor the green flood six times his shoulders turn,
Till we salute the Aragonian king.
Music speak loudly now, the season's apt
For former dolours are in pleasure wrapt.

SCENE X.—*The Forest.*

Enter MUCEDORUS.

Muc. Now, Mucedorus, whither wilt thou go?
Home to thy father, to thy native soil,
Or try some long abode within these woods?
Well, I will hence depart, and hie me home;
What, hie me home said I? that may not be:
In Amadine rests my felicity.
Then, Mucedorus, do as thou didst decree,
Attire thee hermit-like within these groves;
Walk often to the beech, and view the well,
Make settles there, and seat thyself thereon:
And when thou feel'st thyself to be athirst,
Then drink a hearty draught to Amadine.
No doubt she thinks on thee,
And will one day come pledge thee at this well.
                   [*He disguises himself.*
Come, habit, thou art fit for me:
No shepherd now, an hermit must I be;[22]
Methinks this fits me very well;
Now must I learn to bear a walking staff,
And exercise some gravity withal.

Enter MOUSE *the Clown.*

Muc. Here's through the woods and through the woods,
To look out a shepherd, and a stray king's daughter:
But soft, who have we here? what art thou?

Muc. I am a hermit.

Mouse. An emmet, I never saw such a big emmet in all my life before.

Muc. I tell you, sir, I am an hermit,
One that leads a solitary life within these woods.

Mouse. O, I know thee now, thou art he that eats up all the hips and haws: we could not have one piece of fat bacon for thee all this year.

Muc. Thou dost mistake me:
But I pray thee tell me, whom dost thou seek in these woods?

Mouse. What do I seek? for a stray king's daughter,
Run away with a shepherd.

Muc. A stray king's daughter, run away with a shepherd!
Wherefore, canst thou tell?

Mouse. Yes, that I can, 'tis this; my master and Amadine walking one day abroad, nearer these woods than they were used (about what I cannot tell), but towards them comes running a great bear. Now my master played the man, and ran away, and Amadine crying after him: now, sir, comes me a shepherd, and he strikes off the bear's head; now, whether the bear were dead before or no I cannot tell, for bring twenty bears before me, and bind their hands and feet, and I'll kill them all: now, ever since Amadine hath been in love with the shepherd, and for good will she's even run away with the shepherd.

Muc. What manner of man was he? canst thou describe him unto me?

Mouse. Scribe him, aye, I warrant you that I can; a was a little, low, broad, tall, narrow, big, well-favoured fellow, a jerkin of white cloth, and buttons of the same.

Muc. Thou describest him well, but if I chance to see any such, pray you where shall I find you, or what's your name?

Mouse. My name is called master Mouse.

Muc. O, master Mouse; I pray you what office might you bear in the court?

Mouse. Marry, sir, I am rusher of the stable.

Muc. Oh, usher of the table.

Mouse. Nay, I say rusher, and I'll prove mine office good; for, look you, sir, when any come from under the sea or so, and a dog chance to blow his nose backward, then with a whip I give him the good time of the day, and strow rushes presently; therefore I am a rusher; a high office, I promise ye.

Muc. But where shall I find you in the court?

Mouse. Why, where it is best being, either in the kitchen eating, or in the buttery, drinking; but if you come, I will provide for thee a piece of beef and brewes knuckle deep in fat; pray you take pains, remember master Mouse. [*Exit.*

Muc. Aye, sir, I warrant I will not forget you.
Ah, Amadine! what should become of her?
Whither shouldst thou go so long unknown?
With watch and ward each passage is beset,
So that she cannot long escape unknown.
Doubtless, she hath lost herself within these woods,
And wandering to and fro she seeks the well,
Which yet she cannot find, therefore will I seek
her out. [*Exit.*

SCENE XI.—*Another part of the Forest.*

Enter BREMO *and* AMADINE.

Bre. Amadine, how like you Bremo and his woods?

Ama. As like the woods of Bremo's cruelty,
Though I were dumb and could not answer him,
The beasts themselves would with relenting tears
Bewail thy savage and inhuman deeds.

Bre. My love, why dost thou murmur to thyself?
Speak louder, for thy Bremo hears thee not.

Ama. My Bremo! no, the shepherd is my love.

Bre. Have I not savéd thee from sudden death,
Given thee leave to live that thou might'st love,
And dost thou whet me on to cruelty?
Come, kiss me (sweet) for all my favours past.

Ama. I may not, Bremo, therefore pardon me.

Bre. See how she flies away from me;
I will follow and give attend to her.
Deny my love? a worm of beauty,
I will chastise thee: come, come,
Prepare thy head upon the block.

Ama. O, spare me, Bremo, love should limit life,
Not to be made a murderer of himself.[23]
If thou wilt glut thy loving heart with blood,
Encounter with the lion or the bear;
And, like a wolf, prey not upon a lamb.

Bre. Why then dost thou repine at me?
If thou wilt love me thou shalt be my queen,
I'll crown thee with a chaplet made of ivory,
And make the rose and lily wait on thee:
I'll rend the burly branches from the oak,
To shadow thee from the fierce burning sun,[24]
The trees shall spread themselves where thou dost go,
And as they spread, I'll trace along with thee.[25]

Ama. You may, for who but you?

Bre. Thou shalt be fed with quails and partridges,
With blackbirds, larks, thrushes, and nightingales;

Thy drink shall be goat's milk and crystal water;
Distilling from the fountains and the clearest
    springs;
And all the dainties that the woods afford,
I'll freely give thee to obtain thy love.

    Ama. You may, for who but you?

    Bre. The day I'll spend to recreate my love,
With all the pleasures that I can devise;
And in the night I'll be thy bedfellow,
And lovingly embrace thee in mine arms.

    Ama. One may, so may not you?

    Bre. The satyrs and the wood-nymphs shall at-
    tend on thee,
And lull thee asleep with music's gentle sound,[26]
And in the morning when thou dost awake,
The lark shall sing, good morrow to my queen;
And whilst he sings I'll kiss mine Amadine.

    Ama. You may, for who but you.

    Bre. When thou art up, the wood-lanes shall be
    strewed
With violets, cowslips, and sweet marigolds,
For thee to trample and to tread upon;
And I will teach thee how to kill the deer,
To chase the hart, and how to rouse the roe,
If thou wilt live to love and honour me.

    Ama. You may, for who but you?

    Enter MUCEDORUS.

    Bre. Welcome, sir, an hour ago I look'd for
    such a guest;
Be merry, wench, we'll have a frolic feast,
Here's flesh enough for to suffice us both.
Say, sirrah, wilt thou fight, or dost thou mean to
    die?

    Muc. I want a weapon! how then can I fight?

    Bre. Thou want'st a weapon, why then thou
    yield'st to die?

    Muc. I say not so, I do not yield to die.

    Bre. Thou shalt not choose, I long to see thee
    dead.

    Ama. Yet spare him, Bremo, spare him.

    Bre. Away, I say, I will not spare him.

    Muc. Yet give me leave to speak.

    Bre. Thou shalt not speak.

    Ama. Yet give him leave to speak for my sake.

    Bre. Speak on, but be not over-long.

    Muc. In time of yore, when men like brutish
    beasts
Did lead their lives in loathsome cells and woods,
And wholly give themselves to witless will;
A rude unruly rout: then man to man became
A present prey, then might prevailed,
The weakest ever then went to the wall.[27]

Right was unknown, for wrong was all in all.
As men thus lived in their great outrage,
Behold, one Orpheus came (as poets tell),
And them from rudeness unto reason brought,
Who led by reason soon forsook the woods.
Instead of caves, they built them castles strong,
Cities and towns were founded by them then:
Glad were they, they had found such ease,
And in the end they grew to perfect amity,
Waying their former wickedness,[28]
They term'd the time wherein they lived then,
A golden age, a good and golden age.
Now Bremo (for so I heard thee call'd),
If men which lived 'tofore, as thou dost now,
Wild in woods, addicted all to spoil,
Return'd were by worthy Orpheus' means,
Let me (like Orpheus) cause thee to return
From murder, bloodshed, and such-like cruelties:
What, should we fight before we have a cause?
No, let's live, and love together faithfully:
I'll fight for thee.

    Bre. Fight for me, or die; or fight, or else thou
    diest.[29]

    Ama. Hold Bremo, hold.

    Bre. Away, I say, thou troublest me.

    Ama. You promiséd to make me queen.

    Bre. I did, I mean no less.

    Ama. You promiséd that I should have my will.

    Bre. I did, I mean no less.

    Ama. Then save the hermit's life, for he may
    save us both.

    Bre. At thy request I'll save him, but never any
    after him;
Say, hermit, what canst thou do?

    Muc. I'll wait on thee, sometime upon thy queen,
Such service shalt thou have as Bremo never had.

    [*Exeunt* BRE., AMA., *and* MUC.

    Enter SEGASTO, MOUSE, *and* RUMBELO.

    Seg. Come, sirs, what, shall I never have you find
out Amadine and the shepherd?

    Mouse. I have been through the woods, and
through the woods, and could see nothing but an
emmet.

    Rum. Why, I see a thousand emmets; thou
meanest a little one.

    Mouse. Nay, that emmet that I saw was bigger
than thou art.

    Rum. Bigger than I? what a fool have you to
your man. I pray you, master, turn him away.

    Seg. But dost thou hear, was he not a man?

    Mouse. I think he was, for he said he did lead a
salt-seller's life round about the woods.

Seg. Thou would'st say a solitary life about the woods.

Mouse. I think it was indeed.

Rum. I thought what a fool thou art.

Mouse. Thou art a wise man: why, he did nothing but sleep since he went.

Seg. But tell me, Mouse, how did he go?

Mouse. In a white gown, and a white hat on his head, and a staff in his hand.

Seg. I thought so; he was an hermit, that walked a solitary life in the woods. Well, get you to dinner, and after, never leave seeking till you bring some news of them, or I'll hang you both.
[*Exit* SEG.

Mouse. How now, Rumbelo, what shall we do now?

Rum. Faith I'll home to dinner, and afterwards to sleep.

Mouse. Why then thou wilt be hanged.

Rum. Faith I care not, for I know I shall never find them: well, I'll once more abroad, and if I cannot find them I'll never come home again.

Mouse. I tell thee what, Rumbelo, thou shalt go in at one end of the wood, and I at the other, and we will both meet together in the midst.

Rum. Content; let's away to dinner. [*Exeunt.*

SCENE XII.—*The Forest near the Cave of the Wild Man.*

Enter MUCEDORUS.

Muc. Unknown to any, here within these woods,
With bloody Bremo do I lead my life:
The monster he doth murder all he meets,
He spareth none, and none doth him escape:
Who would continue, who but only I,
In such a cruel cut-throat's company?
Yet Amadine is there, how can I choose?
Ah silly soul, how oftentimes she sits,
And sighs, and calls, " Come, shepherd, come:
Sweet Mucedorus, come set me free;"
When Mucedorus (peasant) stands her by.
But here she comes. What news, fair lady,
As you walk these woods?

Enter AMADINE.

Ama.   Ah, hermit, none but bad,
And such as thou knowest.

Muc. How do you like your Bremo and his woods?

Ama. Not my Bremo, nor his, Bremo's, woods.

Muc. And why not yours? methinks he loves you well.

Ama. I like not him; his love to me is nothing worth.

Muc. Lady, in this methinks you offer wrong,
To hate the man that ever loves you best.

Ama. Ah, hermit, I take no pleasure in his love,
Neither doth Bremo like me best.

Muc. Pardon my boldness, fair lady, sith we both
May safely talk now out of Bremo's sight,
Unfold to me, if you please, the full discourse;
How, when, and why you came into these woods,
And fell into this bloody butcher's hands.

Ama. Hermit, I will: Of late a worthy shepherd
I did love.

Muc. A shepherd (lady), sure a man unfit to
match with you.

Ama. Hermit, this is true: and when we had——

Muc. Stay there; the wild man comes.
Refer the rest until another time.

Enter BREMO.

Bre. What secret tale is this? what whispering
have we here?
Villain, I charge thee tell thy tale again.

Muc. If needs I must, lo, here it is again.
When as we both had lost the sight of thee,
It griev'd us both, but 'specially thy queen,
Who in thy absence ever fears the worst,
Lest some mischance befal your royal grace.
" Shall my sweet Bremo wander through the wood,
Toil to and fro, for to redress my want,
Hazard his life, and all to cherish me?
I like not this," quoth she:
And thereupon did crave to know of me,
If I could teach her handle weapons well.
My answer was, " I had small skill therein:
But gladsome (mighty king) to learn of thee:"
And this was all.

Bre.   Was't so? none can mislike of this:
I'll teach you both to fight; but first my queen
begin.
Here, take this weapon, see how thou canst use it.

Ama. This is too big; I cannot wield it in mine
arm.

Bre. Is't so? we'll have a knotty crab-tree
staff for thee;
But, sirrah, tell me, what sayest thou?

Muc. With all my heart, I willing am to learn.

Bre. Then take my staff, and see how thou canst
wield it.

Muc. First teach me how to hold it in mine
hand.

Bre. Thou holdest it well; look how he doth;
Thou mayest the sooner learn.

Muc. Next tell how, and when 'tis best to strike.

Bre. 'Tis best to strike when time doth serve;
'Tis best to lose no time.

Muc. Then now or never it is time to strike.

Bre. And when thou strikest be sure to hit the
head.

Muc. The head?

Bre. 　　　　The very head.

Muc. Then have at thine—

　　　　　　　　[*He strikes him down dead.*

So, lie there and die; a death (no doubt) according
to desert,

Or else a worse, as thou deservest worse.

Ama. It glads my heart this tyrant's death to
see.

Muc. Now, lady, it remains in you
To end the tale you lately had begun,
Being interrupted by this wicked wight:
You said you lov'd a shepherd.

Ama. Ay, so I do, and none but only him:
And will do still as long as life shall last.

Muc. But tell me, lady, sith I set you free,
What course of life do you intend to take?

Ama. I will disguiséd wander through the world,
Till I have found him out.

Muc. How if you find your shepherd in these
woods?

Ama. Ah! none so happy then as Amadine.
　　　　　　　　[*He discloseth himself.*

Muc. In tract of time a man may alter much;
Say, lady, do you know your shepherd well?

Ama. My Mucedorus, hath he set me free?

Muc. He hath set thee free.

Ama. And liv'd so long unknown to Amadine?

Muc. Ay, that's a question whereof you may not
be resolv'd:
You know that I am banish'd from the court;
I know, likewise, each passage is beset,
So that we cannot long escape unknown;
Therefore my will is this; that we return,
Right through the thickets to the wild man's
cave,
And there awhile live on his provision,
Until the search and narrow watch be past:
This is my counsel, and I like it best.

Ama. I think the same.

Muc. 　　　　Come, let's begone.

Enter MOUSE, *searching; he falls over the* Wild
Man, *and so carries him away.*[30]

Mouse. Nay, soft, sir, are you here: a bots on
you;
I was like to be hang'd for not finding of you:

We would borrow a certain stray king's daughter
of you,
A wench, a wench, sir, we would have.

Muc. A wench of me? I'll make thee eat my
sword.

Mouse. O Lord, nay, and you are so lusty, I'll
call a cooling card for you: O master, master, come
away quickly.

Enter SEGASTO.

Seg. What's the matter?

Mouse. Look, Amadine and the shepherd: O
brave!

Seg. What, minion, have I found you out?

Mouse. Nay, that a lie, I found her out myself.

Seg. Thou gadding housewife, what cause hadst
thou
To gad abroad?
When, as thou knowest, our wedding day so nigh?

Ama. Not so, Segasto, no such thing in hand:
Show your assurance, then I'll answer you.

Seg. Thy father's promise my assurance is.

Ama. But what he promis'd he hath not perform'd.

Seg. It rests in thee for to perform the same.

Ama. Not I.

Seg. 　　　　And why?

Ama. So is my will, and therefore even no.

Mouse. Master with a none, none so.

Seg. Ah, wicked villain, art thou here?

Muc. What need these words? I weigh them not.

Seg. We weigh them not; proud shepherd, I scorn
thy company.

Muc. I scorn not thee, nor yet the least of thine.

Mouse. That's a lie, a would have kill'd me with
his pugs-nando.

Seg. This stoutness, Amadine, contents me not.

Ama. Then seek another that you may better
please.

Muc. Well, Amadine, it only rests in thee,
Without delay to make thy choice of three:
There stands Segasto, a second here,
There stands the third: now make thy choice.

Mouse. A lord, at the least I am.

Ama. My choice is made, for I will none but thee.

Seg. A worthy mate (no doubt) for such a wife.

Muc. And Amadine, why will thou none but me?
I cannot keep thee as thy father did;
I have no lands for to maintain thy state:
Moreover, if thou mean to be my wife,
Commonly this must be thy use,
To bed at midnight, up at four,
Drudge all day, and trudge from place to place,

Whereby our daily victual for to win;
And last of all, which is the worst of all,
No princess then, but a plain shepherd's wife.

Mouse. Then God give you good morrow, goody
    shepherd.

Ama. It shall not need, if Amadine do live,
Thou shalt be crownéd king of Aragon,

Mouse. O master, laugh, when he is a king, I'll
    be a queen.

Muc. Then know that which ne'ertofore was
    known:
I am no shepherd, no Aragonian I,
But born of royal blood: my father's of Valentia king,
My mother queen: who for thy sacred sake
Took this hard task in hand.

Ama. Oh, how I joy my fortune is so good.

Seg. Well, now I see Segasto shall not speed,
But Mucedorus, I as much do joy
To see thee here within our court of Aragon,
As if a kingdom had befall'n me at this time;
I with my heart surrender her to thee.
                [He gives her to him.
And look what right to Amadine I have.

Mouse. What barn's door, and born where my
father was constable? a bots on thee, how dost
thou?

Muc. Thanks Segasto, but you levell'd at the
    crown.

Mouse. Master, bear this and bear all.

Seg.   Why so, sirrah?

Mouse. He says you take a goose by the crown.

Seg. Go to, sirrah, away, post you to the king,
Whose heart is fraught with careful doubts,
Glad him up, and tell him these good news,
And we will follow as fast as we may.

Mouse. I go master, I run master.   *[Exeunt.*

SCENE XIII.—Aragon.   *Room of State in the
    Court.*

Enter the KING *and* COLLIN.

King. Break heart, and end my pallid woes,
My Amadine, the comfort of my life;
How can I joy except she were in sight?
Her absence breeds great sorrow to my soul,
And with a thunder breaks my heart in twain.

Collin. Forbear those passions, gentle king,
And you shall see 'twill turn unto the best,
And bring your soul to quiet and to joy.

King. Such joy as death, except of her I hear,
And that with speed, I cannot sigh thus long;
But what a tumult do I hear within?
          [They cry within, "Joy and happiness."

Collin. I hear a noise of over-passing joy
Within the court: my lord be of good comfort,
And here comes one in haste.

Enter MOUSE *running.*

Mouse.   A king, a king!

Collin. Why, how now, sirrah, what's the matter?

Mouse. O 'tis news for a king, 'tis worth money.

King. Why, sirrah, thou shalt have silver and
    gold if it be good.

Mouse. O 'tis good, 'tis good Amadine.

King. O what of her? tell me, and I will make
    thee a knight.

Mouse. How, a spright! no by lady, I will not
    be a spright.
Master get you away; if I be a spright, I shall be
    so lean
I shall make you all afraid.

Collin. Then, sot, the king means to make thee
    a gentleman.

Mouse. Why, I shall want 'parel.

King. Thou shalt want for nothing.

Mouse. Then stand away, strike up thyself, here
    they come.

Enter SEGASTO, MUCEDORUS, *and* AMADINE.

Ama. My gracious father, pardon thy disloyal
    daughter.

King. What, do mine eyes behold my daughter
    Amadine?
Rise up daughter, and let these embracing arms
Show some token of thy father's joy,
Which ever since thy departure hath languished in
    sorrow.

Ama. Dear father, never were your sorrows
Greater than my griefs.
Never you so desolate as I comfortless:
Yet, nevertheless, knowing myself
To be the cause of both, on bended knees
I humbly crave your pardon.

King. I'll pardon thee, dear daughter, but for
    him—

Ama. Ay, father, what of him?

King. As sure as I am king, and wear the crown,
I'll be reveng'd on that accurséd wretch.

Muc. Yet worthy prince, work not thy will in
    wrath; show favour.

King. Ay, such favour as thou deservest.

Muc. I do deserve the daughter of a king.

King. Oh impudent! a shepherd and so inso-
    lent.

Muc. No shepherd I, but a worthy prince.

King. In fair conceit, not princely born.

Muc. Yes, princely born; my father is a king,
My mother a queen, and of Valentia both.

King. What, Mucedorus! welcome to our court.
What cause hadst thou to come to me disguis'd?

Muc. No cause to fear, I caus'd no offence;
But this, desiring thy daughter's virtues for to see,
Disguis'd myself from out my father's court,
Unknown to any in secret, I did rest,
And passéd many troubles near to death:
So hath your daughter my partaker been,
As you shall know hereafter more at large;
Desiring you, you will give her to me,
Even as my own, and sovereign of my life,
Then shall I think my travels all well spent.

King. With all my heart; but this,
Segasto claims my promise made 'tofore,
That he should have her as his only wife,
Before my council when he came from war.
Segasto, may I crave thee, let it pass,
And give Amadine as wife to Mucedorus?

Seg. With all my heart, were it a far greater
　　thing,
And what I may to furnish up their rites,
With pleasing sport and pastimes you shall see.

King. Thanks good Segasto, I will think of this.

Muc. Thanks, good my lord, and whilst I live
Account of me in what I can or may.

Ama. Good Segasto, these great courtesies
Shall not be forgot.

Mouse. Why, hark you, master, bones! what
have you done? what, given away the wench you
made me take such pains for? You are wise indeed. Mass! and I had known of that, I would
have had her myself; faith, master, now we may
go to breakfast with a woodcock pie.

Seg. Go to, sirrah, you were best to leave this
　　knavery.

King. Come on, my lords, let's now to court,
Where we may finish up the joyfullest day
That ever happ'd to a distresséd king:
Were but thy father, the Valentia lord,
Present in view of this combined knot——
　　　　　　　　　　　　　　[*A shout within.*

Enter Messenger.

What shout was that?

Mess.　　　　My lord, the great Valentia king,
Newly arriv'd, entreats your presence.

Muc.　　　　　　　　　My father?

King. Preparéd welcomes give him entertain-
　　ment;
A happier planet never reign'd than that
Which governs at this hour.　　　　　　[*Music.*

Enter the KING OF VALENTIA, ANSELMO, RODERIGO,
　BRACHIUS, *with* Others. *The* King *runs and
　embraces his* Son.

K. Val. Rise, honour of my age, food to my rest;
Condemn not, mighty king of Aragon,
My rude behaviour, so compell'd by nature,
That manners stood unacknowledgéd.

King. What we have to recite would tedious prove
By declaration, therefore in and feast;
To-morrow the performance shall explain
What words conceal; till then drums speak, bells
　　ring,
Give plausive welcomes to our brother king.
　[*Flourish of Drums and Trumpets.　Exeunt Omnes.*

Enter COMEDY and ENVY.

Com. How now, Envy! what, blushest thou al-
　　ready?
Peep forth, hide not thy head with shame,
But with courage praise a woman's deeds;
Thy threats were vain, thou couldst do me no hurt,
Although thou seem'st to cross me with despite,
I overwhelm'd and turn'd upside down thy blocks,
And made thyself to stumble at the same.

Envy. Though stumbled, yet not overthrown,
Thou canst not draw my head to mildness;
Yet must I needs confess thou hast done well,
And play'd thy part with mirth and pleasant glee:
Say all this; yet canst thou not conquer me,
Although this time thou hast a triumph got,[31]
Yet not the conquest neither,
A double revenge another time I'll have.

Com. Envy spit thy gall;
Plot, work, contrive, create new fallacies,
Teem from thy womb each minute a black traitor,
Whose blood and thoughts have twin conception;
Study to act deeds yet unchronicled,
Cast native monsters in the moulds of men;
Case vicious devils under sancted robes;
Unhasp the wicket where all perjuries roost,
And swarm this ball[32] with treasons, do thy worst,
Thou canst not, hell-hound, cross my stear[33] to-
　　night,
Nor blind that glory where I will delight.

Envy. I can, I will.

Com.　　　　　　　Nefarious hag begin,
And let us tug till one the mastery win.

Envy. Comedy, thou art a shallow goose,
I'll overthrow thee in thine own intent,
And make thy fall my comic merriment.

Com. Thy policy wants gravity, thou art too weak;
Speak friend, as how?

Envy.   Why thus,
From my foul study will I hoist a wretch,
A lean and hungry meagre cannibal,
Whose jaws swell to his eyes with chewing malice;
And him I'll make a poet.

Com. What's that to the purpose?

Envy. This scrambling raven with his needy
    beard,
Will I whet on to write a comedy;
Wherein shall be compos'd dark sentences,
Pleasing to factious brains;
And every otherwhere place me a jest,
Whose high abuse shall more torment than blows,
Then I myself (quicker than lightning,)
Will fly me to the puissant magistrate,
And waiting with a trencher at his back,
In midst of jollity rehearse those gauls
With some additions) so lately vented in your the-
    atre;
He on this cannot but make complaint
To your great danger, or at least restraint.

Com. Ha, ha, ha, I laugh to hear thy folly:
This is a trap for boys, not men, not such,
Especially deceitful in their doings,
Whose staid discretion rules their purposes:

I and my faction do eschew those vices:
But see, O see, the weary sun for rest,
Hath lain his golden compass to the west,
Where he perpetual bide, and ever shine,
As David's offspring in this happy clime.[34]
Stoop, Envy, stoop, bow to the earth with me,
Let's beg our pardon on our bended knee.

                              [*They kneel.*

Envy. My power hath lost her might, Envy's
    date's expired,
And I amazed am.   [*Falls down and quakes.*

Com. Glorious and wise Arch-Cæsar on this earth,
At whose appearance Envy's stricken dumb,
And all bad things cease operation:
Vouchsafe to pardon our unwilling error,
So late presented to your gracious view,
And we'll endeavour with excess of pain,
To please your senses in a choicer strain.
Thus we commit you to the arms of night,
Whose spangled carcase would for your delight,
Strive to excel the day: be blessed then,
Who other wishes, let him never speak.

Envy.   Amen.
To fame and honour we commend your rest,
Live still more happy, every hour more blest,

NOTES TO MUCEDORUS.

◆

¹ *Most sacred majesty.*

This prologue appears to have been an occasional one, spoken when the comedy was performed before the king. It was witnessed by James the First, and was also revived and played before Charles, after the Restoration. Ben Jonson's prologue to his comedy of *The Poetaster*, bears some resemblance to this, and may have been suggested by it. There Envy arises in the midst of the stage, and in the course of a long speech informs us :—

> For I am risse here with a covetous hope,
> To blast your pleasures and destroy your sports,
> With wrestings, comments, applications,
> Spy-like suggestions, privy whisperings,
> And thousand such promoting slights as these.

Envy then invokes all ill-disposed authors, all "poet-asses," to render him their assistance in condemning the play :—

> You know what dear and ample faculties
> I have endow'd you with : I 'll lend you more.
> Here, take my snakes among you, come and eat,
> And while the squeez'd juice flows in your black jaws,
> Help me to damn the author.   Spit it forth
> Upon his lines, and show your rusty teeth
> At every word, or accent : or else choose
> Out of my longest vipers, to stick down
> In your deep throats ; and let the heads come forth
> At your rank mouths ; that he may see you arm'd
> With triple malice, to hiss, sting, and tear
> His work and him ; to forge, and then declaim,
> Traduce, corrupt, apply, inform, suggest ;
> O, these are gifts wherein your souls are blest.

As the authors do not appear, Envy, as in the present comedy, is baffled, and then descends slowly to his legitimate habitation.

² *Sound forth Bellona's silver tunéd strings.*

The author has here, I think, fallen into error; what was Comedy to do with Bellona? The latter was the goddess of war, not of pastime. She was the sister of Mars ; or, according to other writers, his wife or daughter. Ancient poets described her as appearing in battle with dishevelled hair flowing wildly behind her, while in one hand she held a whip to scourge cowards, and in the other a flaming torch to animate the brave. At the gate of the temple erected to her at Rome was a small pillar called the column of war, against which the priests threw a spear whenever war was declared against an enemy. Among other superstitions which they practised, was the following barbarous and disgusting one : in moments of fanatical excitement they inflicted deep gashes on their bodies, particularly on the thigh, and receiving the blood which flowed from the wound, in their hands, offered it as an acceptable sacrifice to the goddess.   In paroxysms of wild excitement they frequently predicted war and slaughter, the defeat of enemies, and the desolation of nations.

³ *His chival ;* i.e. his reputation.

⁴ *To spurn at arms and legs quite shivered off.*

Should we not read, *slivered* off? Sliver is a common word in the north, where it means to cut a piece or slice. In *Macbeth* we have

> ——— Slips of yew,
> Sliver'd in the moon's eclipse.

⁵ *Tender the suit of me.*

That is, respect it, regard it with kindness.

⁶ *A deadly dole ;* i.e. a gloomy lamentation.

⁷ *I will defend them in despight of thee.*

Comedy has not mentioned whom she will defend, but I presume she alludes to the actors, who were threatened with an extinction of their calling by the Puritans, whom I suspect the author here intended to personify under the name of Envy.

⁸ *I force it not ;* i.e. do not obtrude it on unwilling listeners.

⁹ *Your miss ;* i.e. your absence.

¹⁰ *Which I presented in Lord Julius' mask.*

Those who love to reflect on the customs and pleasures of a past and brilliant age, will not quarrel with me for introducing the following extract from an interesting paper on *Masques*, in D'Israeli's *Curiosities of Literature :*—" It sometimes happens in the history of national amusements, that a name survives, while the thing itself is forgotten.   This has been remarkably the case with our COURT MASQUES, respecting which our most eminent writers long ventured on so many false opinions, with a perfect ignorance of the nature of those compositions, which combined all that was exquisite in the imitative arts of poetry, painting, music, song, dancing, and machinery, at a period when our public theatre was in its rude infancy.   * * * Warburton said on *Masques*, that ' Shakspere was an enemy to these *fooleries*, as appears by his writing none !'   This opinion was among the many which that singular critic threw out as they arose at the moment, for Warburton forgot that Shakspere characteristically introduces one in the *Tempest's* most fanciful scene.   Granger, who had not much time to study the manners of the age, whose personages he was so well acquainted with, in a note on Milton's masque, said that, ' These compositions were trifling and perplexed allegories; the persons of which are fantastical to the last degree. Ben Jonson, in his *Masque of Christmas*, has introduced *Minced Pie*, and *Babie Cake*, who act their parts in the drama. But the most wretched performances of this kind could please by the help of music, machinery, and dancing. Granger blunders, describing by two farcical characters a species of composition of which farce was not the characteristic; such personages as he notices would enter into the *Anti-Masque*, which was a humorous parody, of the more solemn masque, and sometimes relieved it. Malone, whose fancy was not vivid, condemns masques and the age of masques, in which he says, echoing Granger's epithet, ' the wretched taste of the times found amusement.' And lastly comes Mr. Todd, whom the splendid fragment of the *Arcades*, and the entire masque, which we have by heart, could not warm; while his neutralizing criticism fixes him at the freezing point of the thermometer.' ' This dramatic entertainment, performed not without prodigious expense in machinery and decoration, to *which humour* we certainly owe the entertainment of *Arcades*, and the inimitable mask of *Comus*.' *Comus*, however, is only a fine dramatic poem, retaining scarcely any features of the masque." Notwithstanding Mr. D'Israeli's eulogy of this obsolete entertainment, I incline greatly to the opinion of Dr. Warburton, nor can I think that Shakspere's introduction of a brief masque, or allegorical dance, in one of the scenes of *The Tempest*, any evidence that he approved of the masque as an entertainment in itself.

[11] *Enter Mouse with a bottle of hay.*

The term *bottle* was anciently applied to a quantity of hay or grass bundled up together.

[12] *Ay, plain mouse, without either welt or gard.*

That is, without any addition or ornament.

[13] *Of beef and brewis.*

Brewis is a piece of bread soaked in boiling fat pottage, made of salted meat. It seems anciently also to have meant some kind of broth. Thus, in Beaumont and Fletcher's *Dioclesian:*—

What an ocean of *brewis* shall I swim in.

[14] *A sheepbiter;* i.e., a petty thief.

[15] *Aye, shipsticks.*

I suppose he means *sheep-stakes*. The shepherd's vigilance had saved many sheep-stakes or hurdles from being stolen.

[16] *More may I boast and say; but I ——*

Mucedorus means, not only may I boast of favour and rewards from the king, but also of the affection of the princess Amadine; and he then breaks off abruptly, implying that it is not prudent to speak upon such a subject.

[17] *A shepherd and a sovereign nothing like.*

I see no sense in this line as it stands; should we not read:—A shepherd *is* a sovereign nothing like; i.e., no-way resembles him.

[18] *Of late I loved on indeed, but now I love none but only thee.*

This is very ambiguous; perhaps we should read:—
Of late I loved another, now I love only thee.

[19] ————*Burn likewise,*
Yet smother up the blast.

The prince should speak this aside; he is addressing his own heart, and saying to it,—burn thou with an equal affection to that which inspires Amadine, but for the present hide thy feelings; do not compel me to divulge my disguise.

[20] *My bat,* i. e. club.

[21] *I will not be made a curtall.*

A *curtall*, or *curtail*, is a dog of small value, who having had his tail cut off, misses his game. The tail is counted necessary to the agility of a greyhound. Mouse is quibbling on the previous observation of his master, namely, " give *ear* to my words;" to which he answers, " he will not give his ears;" that is, be curtailed, or deprived of them for any man's pleasure.

[22] *Come, habit, thou art fit for me:*
No shepherd now, an hermit must I be.

The dress of a hermit was suitable to his depressed state of mind, being expressive of loneliness and sadness.

[23] *O spare me, Bremo, love should limit life,*
Not to be made a murderer of himself.

I cannot understand this: Amadine is not begging the savage to limit or destroy her life, but to save it. She seems to say the reverse of what it is evident she means In these dramas a little conjectural emendation may very fairly be indulged in, especially if not introduced into the text; I would therefore suggest that the passage should read thus:

O spare me, Bremo, love should *not* limit life,
And thus be made a murderer of *itself*.

[24] *To shadow thee from the fierce burning sun.*

The old copy reads, *from burning sun.* I have interpolated the words, *the fierce,* as they, or something like them, appear to have been accidentally omitted, and the metre thus rendered defective.

[25] *I'll trace along with thee.*

That is, follow in thy very footsteps.

[26] *With music's gentle sound.*

Old copy reads—with music's sound.

[27] *The weakest ever then went to the wall.*

The old copy, which is evidently corrupt, reads:

The weakest went to walls.

The correction I have made is essential, but I think it proper to mention it.

²⁸ *Waying their former wretchedness.*

That is, doing away with, or abandoning it.

²⁹ *Fight for me, or die : or fight, or else thou diest.*

I suspect this line is corrupted ; it should read :—

Fight me or die : fight, or else thou diest.

³⁰ *Enter Mouse, searching ; he falls over the wild*
man, and so carries him away.

This was a primitive way of getting the supposed dead man off the stage. The players of those times having no scenes, could not shut the corpse out from the view of the audience. Malone, in his *Historical Account of the English Stage*, says :—" How little the imaginations of the audience were assisted by scenical deception, and how much necessity an author had to call on them ' to piece out imperfections with their thoughts, may be collected from Sir Philip Sidney, who, describing the state of the drama and the stage, in his time, (about the year 1583,) says, ' Now, you shall have three ladies walk to gather flowers, and then we must believe the stage to be a garden. By-and-by we hear news of shipwreck in the same place; then we are to blame if we accept it not for a rock. Upon the back of that comes out a hideous monster with fire and smoke ; and then the miserable beholders are bound to take it for a cave ; while, in the mean time, two armies fly in, represented with four swords and bucklers, and then what hard heart will not receive it for a pitched field.'

" The first notice that I have found of anything like moveable scenes being used in England, is in the narrative of the entertainment given to King James at Oxford, in August, 1605, when three plays were performed in the hall of Christ Church, of which we have the following account by a contemporary writer : ' The stage (he tells us) was built close to the upper end of the hall, as it seemed at the first sight : but indeed it was but a false wall, faire painted, and adorned with stately pillars, which pillars would turn about; by reason whereof, and with the help of other *painted clothes*, their stage did vary three times in the acting of one tragedy ;" that is, in other words, there were three scenes employed in the exhibition of the piece."

³¹ *Although this time thou hast a triumph got.*

The old copy reads, " This time thou hast got." I have interpolated the words *a triumph*, which were essential both to sense and metre.

³² *This ball*, i.e. this world.

³³ *Thou canst not, hell-hound, cross my stear.*

Perhaps we should read *steer*, i.e. my course, or progress onward.

³⁴ *As David's offspring in this happy clime.*

The old copy reads, *his* happy clime. This gives no meaning. The line is an allusion to King James, in whose presence the comedy was performed. James was, by his flatterers, called the Modern Solomon, and is therefore here alluded to as, in a metaphorical sense, the offspring of David; his descendant, because inheriting his wisdom and great qualities. The character of Solomon has been far too highly estimated by both ancient and modern writers, it has been drawn by the pen of devotion rather than by that of history, but let us make what deduction we please, it is still an insult to the memory of the wise, worldly, voluptuous, and gorgeous Hebrew monarch to compare him with that scoff of sovereignty, the vulgar, tyrannical, and pedantic James the First.

H. T.

London Prodigal

In his notes on *London Prodigal* Tucker Brooke (8) writes that it appears not to have been entered on the Stationers' Books. The first quarto (the only early one) was published in 1605 with the title: "The London Prodigal. As it was played by the Kings Majesty's servants. By William Shakespeare, London. Printed by T. C. for Nathanial Butter. . . ." It was next published in the Third and Fourth Shakespearean Folios, in supplements to Rowe's and Pope's editions of Shakespeare, and in separate reprints by R. Walker and J. Tonson.

All these editions ascribe the comedy unreservedly to Shakespeare, and their unanimous testimony gains weight from the fact that *London Prodigal* was performed by Shakespeare's company and that the quarto was printed for Butter, the publisher of *King Lear,* bearing Shakespeare's name as the author during his lifetime.

London Prodigal deals entirely with humors and manners. Like *The Puritan,* which it resembles in many points, it depends for its value and effect on the bare plot and the admirable delineation of the externalities of contemporary life. Shakespeare's catholicity and psychological insight are conspicuously absent, and every principle of his dramatic morality is outraged in the treatment of the prodigal's career. The only supposition on which the attribution can at all be justified is that put forward by F. G. Fleay—namely, that Shakespeare "plotted" the comedy roughly and then left his vague design to be executed by another.

Considered with regard to general spirit, *London Prodigal,* so full of intimate details of domestic life, shows as much affinity perhaps to the early works of Thomas Dekker or of John Marston as to the writings of any other well-known dramatist of the period.

The theme of prodigal youth had long been a favorite in Elizabethan and Jacobean comedy, where scenes of low life are, according to Madeleine Doran (13), frequently the liveliest in realistic representation. Thomas Middleton's comedies are an example of this genre. Henning describes them as full of the scuffle for money, where impecunious prodigals prey upon their rich relatives, and the relatives in turn are often eager to ruin the young men. Enough of the older moral attitudes survive to be recognized as unmistakable links with Prodigal Son morality or *Christian Terence*, or both. Miss Doran defines this type of play as "education drama," exemplified by the treatment of the Prodigal Son story in Italian *sacre rappresentazioni* or in English interludes, which set it, or some other story of riotous youth, in the abstract frame of the morality play. Some examples of the latter are Gascoigne's *Glass of Government*, Thomas Ingelond's *Disobedient Child*, and the anonymous *Nice Wanton* and *Misogonus*, which combines the three forms: Prodigal Son story, morality play, and Latin comedy.

In *London Prodigal*, Matthew Flowerdale, the prodigal son of a merchant father, is a libertine, gambler, swearer, brawler, drinker, and thief. Pretending to be a wealthy man, he wins the daughter of a knight as his wife, but is arrested for debt on his wedding day. Although she is abominably treated, the wife remains loyal and finally moves her dissolute husband to repentance and reform. *London Prodigal* is, in short, within the tradition of the morality play, with its focus on a serious moral problem that is brought to a happy ending in spiritual salvation.

PERSONS REPRESENTED.

FLOWERDALE, *Senior, a Merchant.*

Appears, Act I. sc. 1 ; sc. 2. Act II. sc. 1 ; sc. 4. Act III. sc. 2 ; sc. 3. Act IV. sc. 3. Act V. sc. 1.

MATTHEW FLOWERDALE, *his Son.*

Appears, Act I. sc. 1 ; sc. 2. Act II. sc. 1. Act III. sc. 2 ; sc. 3. Act IV. sc. 2. Act V. sc. 1.

FLOWERDALE, *Junior, Brother to the* Merchant.

Appears, Act I. sc. 1. Act III. sc. 2 ; sc. 3. Act V. sc. 1.

SIR LANCELOT SPURCOCK.

Appears, Act I. sc. 2. Act II. sc. 1 ; sc. 2 ; sc. 4. Act III. sc. 2 ; sc. 3. Act IV. sc. 1. Act V. sc. 1.

SIR ARTHUR GREENSHIELD, *a Military Officer, in love with* Luce.

Appears, Act II. sc. 1 ; sc. 3. Act III. sc. 3. Act IV. sc. 1 ; sc. 2. Act V. sc. 1.

OLIVER, *a* Devonshire *Clothier, also in love with* Luce.

Appears, Act II. sc. 1 ; sc. 4. Act III. sc. 3. Act IV. sc. 1 ; sc. 2. Act V. sc. 1.

WEATHERCOCK, *a Parasite to* Sir Lancelot Spurcock.

Appears, Act I. sc. 2. Act II. sc. 1 ; sc. 2 ; sc. 4. Act III. sc. 2 ; sc. 3. Act IV. sc. 1. Act V. sc. 1.

CIVET, *in love with* Frances.

Appears, Act I. sc. 2. Act III. sc. 1 ; sc. 3. Act IV. sc. 1 ; sc. 3. Act V. sc. 1.

AN ANCIENT CITIZEN.

Appears, Act V. sc. 1.

DAFFODIL, *Servant to* Sir Lancelot Spurcock.

Appears, Act I. sc. 2. Act II. sc. 2. Act III. sc. 3.

ARTICHOKE, *also a Servant to* Sir Lancelot Spurcock.

Appears, Act I. sc. 2. Act II. sc. 1 ; sc. 4. Act IV. sc. 2 ; sc. 3. Act V. sc. 1.

DICK,
RALPH, } *Two cheating Gamesters.*

Appear, Act V. sc. 1.

RUFFIAN, *a Pander.*

Appears, Act V. sc. 1.

DELIA, *Daughter to* Sir Lancelot Spurcock.

Appears, Act III. sc. 1. Act IV. sc. 1 ; sc. 2 ; sc. 3. Act V. sc. 1.

FRANCES, *Daughter to* Sir Lancelot Spurcock.

Appears, Act I. sc. 2. Act II. sc. 1. Act III. sc. 1 ; sc. 3. Act IV. sc. 1 ; sc. 3. Act V. sc. 1.

LUCE, *Daughter to* Sir Lancelot Spurcock.

Appears, Act I. sc. 2. Act II. sc. 1 ; sc. 2 ; sc. 3. Act III. sc. 3. Act IV. sc. 3. Act V. sc. 1.

CITIZEN'S WIFE.

Appears, Act V. sc. 1.

Sheriff and Officers ; Lieutenant and Soldiers ; Drawers, and other Attendants.

SCENE.—LONDON, *and the Country adjacent.*

London Prodigal.

ACT I.

SCENE I.—London. *A Room in* Flowerdale *Junior's House.*

Enter FLOWERDALE *Senior, and* FLOWERDALE *Junior.*

Flow. Sen. Brother, from Venice, being thus disguis'd,
I come, to prove the humours of my son.
How hath he borne himself since my departure,
I leaving you his patron and his guide?

Flow. Jun. I'faith, brother, so, as you will grieve to hear,
And I almost ashamed to report it.

Flow. Sen. Why how is't, brother? What, doth he spend beyond the allowance I left him?

Flow. Jun. How! beyond that? and far more. Why, your exhibition[1] is nothing. He hath spent that, and since hath borrow'd: protested with oaths, alleged kindred, to wring money from me,— " by the love I bore his father,—by the fortunes might fall upon himself,"—to furnish his wants: that done, I have had since, his bond, his friend and friend's bond. Although I know that he spends is yours, yet it grieves me to see the unbridled wildness that reigns over him.

Flow. Sen. Brother, what is the manner of his life? how is the name of his offences? If they do not relish altogether of damnation, his youth may privilege his wantonness. I myself ran an unbridled course till thirty, nay, almost till forty:—well, you see how I am. For vice once look'd into with the eyes of discretion, and well balanced with the weights of reason, the course past seems so abominable, that the landlord of himself, which is the heart of his body, will rather entomb himself in the earth, or seek a new tenant to remain in him; which once settled, how much better are they that in their youth have known all these vices, and left them, than those that knew little, and in their age run into them? Believe me, brother, they that die most virtuous, have in their

youth liv'd most vicious; and none knows the danger of the fire more than he that falls into it.—But say, how is the course of his life? let's hear his particulars.

Flow. Jun. Why I'll tell you, brother; he is a continual swearer, and a breaker of his oaths; which is bad.

Flow. Sen. I grant indeed to swear is bad, but not in keeping those oaths is better;[2] for who will set by a bad thing? Nay by my faith, I hold this rather a virtue than a vice. Well, I pray proceed.

Flow. Jun. He is a mighty brawler, and comes commonly by the worst.

Flow. Sen. By my faith this is none of the worst neither; for if he brawl and be beaten for it, it will in time make him shun it; for what brings man or child more to virtue than correction?—What reigns over him else?

Flow. Jun. He is a great drinker, and one that will forget himself.

Flow. Sen. O best of all! vice should be forgotten: let him drink on, so he drink not churches. Nay, an this be the worst, I hold it rather a happiness in him, than any iniquity. Hath he any more attendants?

Flow. Jun. Brother, he is one that will borrow of any man.

Flow. Sen. Why you see, so doth the sea; it borrows of all the small currents in the world to increase himself.

Flow. Jun. Ay, but the sea pays it again, and so will never your son.

Flow. Sen. No more would the sea neither, if it were as dry as my son.

Flow. Jun. Then, brother, I see you rather like these vices in your son, than any way condemn them.

Flow. Sen. Nay mistake me not, brother; for though I slur them over now, as things slight and nothing, his crimes being in the bud, it would gall my heart, they should ever reign in him.

196

M. Flow. [*Within.*] Ho! who's within ho?
[M. FLOW. *knocks within.*

Flow. Jun. That's your son; he is come to borrow more money.

Flow. Sen. For God's sake give it out I am dead; see how he'll take it. Say I have brought you news from his father. I have here drawn a formal will, as it were from myself, which I'll deliver him.

Flow. Jun. Go to, brother, no more: I will.

M. Flow. Uncle, where are you, uncle? [*Within.*

Flow. Jun. Let my cousin in there.

Flow. Sen. I am a sailor come from Venice, and my name is Christopher.

Enter M. FLOWERDALE.

M. Flow. By the lord, in truth, uncle——

Flow. Jun. In truth would have serv'd, cousin, without the lord.

M. Flow. By your leave, uncle, the Lord is the Lord of truth. A couple of rascals at the gate set upon me for my purse.

Flow. Jun. You never come, but you bring a brawl in your mouth.

M. Flow. By my truth, uncle, you must needs lend me ten pound.

Flow. Jun. Give my cousin some small beer here.

M. Flow. Nay look you, you turn it to a jest now. By this light, I should ride to Croydon Fair, to meet Sir Lancelot Spurcock; I should have his daughter Luce: and for scurvy ten pound, a man shall lose nine hundred threescore and odd pounds, and a daily friend beside! By this hand, uncle, 'tis true.

Flow. Jun. Why, any thing is true for aught I know.

M. Flow. To see now!—why you shall have my bond, uncle, or Tom White's, James Brock's, or Nick Hall's; as good rapier-and-dagger-men, as any be in England; let's be damn'd if we do not pay you: the worst of us all will not damn ourselves for ten pound. A pox of ten pound.

Flow. Jun. Cousin, this is not the first time I have believ'd you.

M. Flow. Why trust me now, you know not what may fall. If one thing were but true, I would not greatly care; I should not need ten pound;—but when a man cannot be believ'd, there's it.

Flow. Jun. Why what is it, cousin?

M. Flow. Marry, this uncle. Can you tell me if the *Catharine and Hugh* be come home or no?

Flow. Jun. Ay marry is't.

M. Flow. By God I thank you for that news. What is't in the Pool can you tell?

Flow. Jun. It is; what of that?

M. Flow. What? why then I have six pieces of velvet sent me; I'll give you a piece, uncle: for thus said the letter;—A piece of ash-colour, a three-pil'd black, a colour de roy, a crimson, a sad green,[3] and a purple: yes i'faith.

Flow. Jun. From whom should you receive this?

M. Flow. From whom? why from my father; with commendations to you, uncle; and thus he writes. I know, (saith he,) thou hast much troubled thy kind uncle, whom, God willing, at my return I will see amply satisfied; amply, I remember was the very word: so God help me.

Flow. Jun. Have you the letter here?

M. Flow. Yes, I have the letter here, here is the letter: no,—yes—no;—let me see; what breeches wore I o' Saturday? Let me see: o' Tuesday, my calamanco; o' Wednesday, my peach-colour satin; o' Thursday my velure; o' Friday my calamanco again; on Saturday,—let me see,—o' Saturday,—for in those breeches I wore o' Saturday is the letter—O, my riding breeches, uncle, those that you thought had been velvet; in those very breeches is the letter.

Flow. Jun. When should it be dated?

M. Flow. Marry, decimo tertio Septembris—no, no; decimo tertio Octobris; ay, Octobris, so it is.

Flow. Jun. Decimo tertio Octobris! and here receive I a letter that your father died in June. How say you, Kester?[4]

Flow. Sen. Yes truly, sir, your father is dead; these hands of mine help to wind him.

M. Flow. Dead?

Flow. Sen. Ay, sir, dead.

M. Flow. 'Sblood, how should my father come dead?

Flow. Sen. I' faith sir, according to the old proverb:
The child was born, and cried,
Became a man, after fell sick, and died.

Flow. Jun. Nay, cousin, do not take it so heavily.

M. Flow. Nay, I cannot weep you extempore: marry, some two or three days hence I shall weep without any stintance.[5]—But I hope he died in good memory.

Flow. Sen. Very well, sir, and set down every thing in good order; and the *Catharine and Hugh* you talk'd of, I came over in; and I saw all the bills of lading; and the velvet that you talk'd of, there is no such aboard.

M. Flow. By God, I assure you,[6] then there is knavery abroad.

Flow. Sen. I 'll be sworn of that: there 's knavery abroad, although there were never a piece of velvet in Venice.

M. Flow. I hope he died in good estate.

Flow. Sen. To the report of the world he did; and made his will, of which I am an unworthy bearer.

M. Flow. His will! have you his will?

Flow. Sen. Yes, sir, and in the presence of your uncle I was will'd to deliver it. [*Delivers the will.*

Flow. Jun. I hope, cousin, now God hath blessed you with wealth, you will not be unmindful of me.

M. Flow. I 'll do reason, uncle: yet i'faith I take the denial of this ten pound very hardly.

Flow. Jun. Nay, I deny'd you not.

M. Flow. By God you deny'd me directly.

Flow. Jun. I 'll be judg'd by this good fellow.

Flow. Sen. Not directly, sir.

M. Flow. Why, he said he would lend me none, and that had wont to be a direct denial, if the old phrase hold. Well, uncle, come, we'll fall to the legacies. [*reads.*] "In the name of God, Amen.— Item, I bequeath to my brother Flowerdale, three hundred pounds, to pay such trivial debts as I owe in London.

" Item, to my son Mat. Flowerdale, I bequeath two bale of false dice, videlicit, high men and low men, fulloms, stop-cater-traies, and other bones of function."[7] 'Sblood what doth he mean by this?

Flow. Jun. Proceed, cousin.

M. Flow. " These precepts I leave him : Let him borrow of his oath; for of his word no body will trust him. Let him by no means marry an honest woman; for the other will keep herself. Let him steal as much as he can, that a guilty conscience may bring him to his destinate repentance :"—I think he means hanging. An this were his last will and testament, the devil stood laughing at his bed's feet while he made it. 'Sblood, what doth he think to fob off his posterity with paradoxes?

Flow. Sen. This he made, sir, with his own hands.

M. Flow. Ay, well; nay come, good uncle, let me have this ten pound: imagine you have lost it, or were robb'd of it, or misreckon'd yourself so much; any way to make it come easily off, good uncle.

Flow. Jun. Not a penny.

Flow. Sen. I'faith lend it him, sir. I myself have an estate in the city worth twenty pound; all

that I 'll engage for him: he saith it concerns him in a marriage.

M. Flow. Ay marry doth it. This is a fellow of some sense, this: come, good uncle.

Flow. Jun. Will you give your word for it, Kester?

Flow. Sen. I will, sir, willingly.

Flow. Jun. Well, cousin, come to me an hour hence, you shall have it ready.

M. Flow. Shall I not fail?

Flow. Jun. You shall not, come or send.

M. Flow. Nay I 'll come myself.

Flow. Sen. By my troth, would I were your worship's man.

M. Flow. What? would'st thou serve?

Flow. Sen. Very willingly, sir.

M. Flow. Why I 'll tell thee what thou shalt do. Thou say'st thou hast twenty pound: go into Birchin-lane, put thyself into clothes: thou shalt ride with me to Croydon fair.

Flow. Sen. I thank you, sir, I will attend you.

M. Flow. Well, uncle, you will not fail me an hour hence.

Flow. Jun. I will not, cousin.

M. Flow. What 's thy name? Kester.

Flow. Sen. Ay, sir.

M. Flow. Well, provide thyself: uncle, farewell till anon. [*Exit* M. Flow.

Flow. Jun. Brother, how do you like your son?

Flow. Sen. I'faith brother, like a mad unbridled colt,

Or as a hawk, that never stoop'd to lure:

The one must be tamed with an iron bit,

The other must be watch'd, or still she's wild.

Such is my son; a while let him be so;

For counsel still is folly's deadly foe.

I 'll serve his youth, for youth must have his course;

For being restrain'd, it makes him ten times worse:

His pride, his riot, all that may be nam'd,

Time may recall, and all his madness tam'd.

[*Exeunt.*

SCENE II.—*The high street in* Croydon. *An Inn appearing, with an open Drinking-booth before it.*

Enter Sir Lancelot Spurcock, Weathercock, Daffodil, Artichoke, Luce, *and* Frances.

Sir Lanc. Sirrah, Artichoke, get you home before;

And as you prov'd yourself a calf in buying,

Drive home your fellow calves that you have bought.

Art. Yes, forsooth: Shall not my fellow Daffodil go along with me?

Sir Lanc. No, sir, no; I must have one to wait on me.

Art. Daffodil, farewell, good fellow Daffodil. You may see, mistress, I am set up by the halves; Instead of waiting on you, I am sent to drive home calves.   [*Exit.*

Sir Lanc. I 'faith, Franke, I must turn away this Daffodil;
He 's grown a very foolish saucy fellow.

Fran. Indeed la, father, he was so since I had him:
Before, he was wise enough for a foolish serving-man.

Weath. But what say you to me, sir Lancelot?

Sir Lanc. O, about my daughters?—well, I will go forward.
Here 's two of them, God save them; but the third,
O she 's a stranger in her course of life:
She hath refus'd you, master Weathercock.

Weath. Ay by the rood, sir Lancelot, that she hath; but had she try'd me, she should have found a man of me indeed.

Sir Lanc. Nay be not angry, sir, at her denial;
She hath refus'd seven of the worshipfull'st
And worthiest house-keepers this day in Kent:
Indeed she will not marry, I suppose.

Weath. The more fool she.

Sir Lanc. What, is it folly to love chastity?

Weath. No, no, mistake me not, sir Lancelot;
But 'tis an old proverb, and you know it well,
That women dying maids, lead apes in hell.

Sir Lanc. That is a foolish proverb and a false.

Weath. By the mass, I think it be, and there-fore let it go: but who shall marry with mistress Frances?

Fran. By my troth they are talking of marry-ing me, sister.

Luce. Peace, let them talk:
Fools may have leave to prattle as they walk.

Daff. Sentences still, sweet mistress![8]
You have a wit, an it were your alabaster.[9]

Luce. I 'faith and thy tongue trips trenchmore.[10]

Sir Lanc. No of my knighthood, not a suitor yet.
Alas, God help her, silly girl, a fool, a very fool;
But there 's the other black-brows, a shrewd girl,
She hath wit at will, and suitors two or three;
Sir Arthur Greenshield one, a gallant knight,
A valiant soldier, but his power but poor:
Then there 's young Oliver, the De'nshire lad,[11]
A wary fellow, marry full of wit,
And rich by the rood: But there 's a third, all air,

Light as a feather, changing as the wind;
Young Flowerdale.

Weath. O he, sir, he 's a desperate Dick indeed;
Bar him your house.

Sir Lanc. Fie, sir, not so: he 's of good pa-rentage.

Weath. By my fay[12] and so he is, and a proper man.

Sir Lanc. Ay, proper enough, had he good qualities.

Weath. Ay marry, there 's the point, sir Lan-celot: for there 's an old saying,

Be he rich, or be he poe,
Be he high, or be he low:
Be he born in barn or hall,
'Tis manners make the man and all.

Sir Lanc. You are in the right, master Weather-cock.

Enter Civet.

Civ. 'Soul, I think I am sure cross'd, or witch'd with an owl.[13] I have haunted them, inn after inn, booth after booth, yet cannot find them. Ha, yonder they are; that 's she. I hope to God 'tis she: nay, I know 'tis she now, for she treads her shoe a little awry.

Sir Lanc. Where is this inn? We are past it, Daffodil.

Daf. The good sign is here, sir, but the back gate is before.

Civ. Save you, sir. I pray may I borrow a piece of a word with you?

Daf. No pieces, sir.

Civ. Why then the whole. I pray, sir. what may yonder gentlewomen be?

Daf. They may be ladies, sir, if the destinies and mortality work.

Civ. What 's her name, sir?

Daf. Mistress Frances Spurcock, sir Lancelot Spurcock's daughter.

Civ. Is she a maid, sir?

Daf. You may ask Pluto and dame Proserpine that: I would be loath to be riddled, sir.[14]

Civ. Is she married, I mean, sir?

Daf. The fates know not yet what shoe-maker shall make her wedding shoes.

Civ. I pray where inn you, sir? I would be very glad to bestow the wine of that gentlewoman.[15]

Daf. At "the George," sir.

Civ. God save you, sir.

Daf. I pray your name, sir?

Civ. My name is master Civet, sir.

Daf. A sweet name! God be with you, good master Civet.   [*Exit* Civ.

Sir Lanc. Ha, have we spy'd you stout St. George? For all
Your dragon, you had best sell us good wine
That needs no ivy-bush. Well, we'll not sit by it,
As you do on your horse: This room shall serve:—
Drawer.

Enter Drawer.

Let me have sack for us old men:
For these girls and knaves small wines are the best.
A pint of sack,—no more.

Draw. A quart of sack in the Three Tuns. [*Exit.*

Sir Lanc. A pint, draw but a pint. Daffodil, call for wine to make yourselves drink.

Fran. And a cup of small beer, and a cake, good Daffodil.

[DAFF. *goes into the house, and returns with wine, &c.*

Enter M. FLOWERDALE, *and* FLOWERDALE, *Senior, as his servant.*

M. Flow. How now! fie, sit in the open room? Now, good sir Lancelot, and my kind friend, worshipful master Weathercock! What at your pint? A quart for shame.

Sir Lanc. Nay royster,[16] by your leave we will away.

M. Flow. Come, give us some music, we'll go dance. Be gone, sir Lancelot! what, and Fair day too?

Sir Lanc. 'Twere folly done, to dance within the Fair.

M. Flow. Nay if you say so, fairest of all Fairs, then I'll not dance. A pox upon my tailor, he hath spoil'd me a peach-coloured satin suit, cut upon cloth of silver; but if ever the rascal serve me such another trick, I'll give him leave, i'faith, to put me in the calendar of fools, and you, and you, sir Lancelot, and master Weathercock. My goldsmith too on t'other side — I bespoke thee, Luce, a carcanet of gold,[17] and thought thou should'st have had it for a fairing; and the rogue

puts me in rerages for orient pearl:[18] but thou shalt have it by Sunday night, wench.

Re-enter Drawer.

Draw. Sir, here is one hath sent you a pottle of Rhenish wine, brewed with rose-water.

M. Flow. To me?

Draw. No, sir; to the knight; and desires his more acquaintance.

Sir Lanc. To me? what's he that proves so kind?

Daf. I have a trick to know his name, sir. He hath a month's mind here to mistress Frances; his name is master Civet.

Sir Lanc. Call him in, Daffodil. [*Exit* DAF

M. Flow. O, I know him, sir; he is a fool, but reasonable rich: his father was one of these leasemongers, these corn-mongers,[19] these money-mongers; but he never had the wit to be a whoremonger.

Enter CIVET.

Sir Lanc. I promise you, sir, you are at too much charge.

Civ. The charge is small charge, sir; I thank God, my father left me wherewithal. If it please you, sir, I have a great mind to this gentlewoman here, in the way of marriage.

Sir Lanc. I thank you, sir. Please you to come to Lewsham,
To my poor house, you shall be kindly welcome.
I knew your father; he was a wary husband.[20]—
To pay here, drawer.

Draw. All is paid, sir; this gentleman hath paid all.

Sir Lanc. I'faith you do us wrong;
But we shall live to make amends ere long.
Master Flowerdale, is that your man?

M. Flow. Yes 'faith, a good old knave.

Sir Lanc. Nay then I think
You will turn wise, now you take such a servant:
Come, you'll ride with us to Lewsham; let's away;
'Tis scarce two hours to the end of day. [*Exeunt.*

ACT II.

SCENE I.—*A Road near* Sir Lancelot Spurcock's *house, in* Kent.

Enter SIR ARTHUR GREENSHIELD, OLIVER, Lieutenant, *and* Soldiers.

Sir Arth. Lieutenant, lead your soldiers to the ships,
There let them have their coats; at their arrival
They shall have pay. Farewell: look to your charge.

Sol. Ay, we are now sent away, and cannot so much as speak with our friends.

Oli. No man! what e'er you used a zuch a fashion, thick you cannot take your leave of your vreens.

Sir Arth. Fellow, no more: lieutenant lead them off.

Sol. Well, if I have not my pay and my clothes, I'll venture a running away, though I hang for't.

Sir Arth. Away, sirrah: charm your tongue.
[*Exeunt* Lieut. *and* Soldiers.

Oli. Bin you a presser, sir?

Sir Arth. I am a commander, sir, under the king?[21]

Oli. 'Sfoot man, and you be ne'er zutch a commander, shud 'a spoke with my vreens before I chid 'a gone: so shud.

Sir Arth. Content yourself man; my authority will stretch to press so good a man as you.

Oli. Press me? I devy; press scoundrels, and thy messels.[22] Press me! che scorns thee i'faith; for seest thee, here's a worshipful knight knows, cham not to be pressed by thee.

Enter SIR LANCELOT, WEATHERCOCK, M. FLOWERDALE, FLOWERDALE, *Senior,* LUCE, *and* FRANCES.

Sir Lanc. Sir Arthur, welcome to Lewsham; welcome by my troth. What's the matter man? why are you vext?

Oli. Why man, he would press me.

Sir Lanc. O fie, sir Arthur, press him? he is a man of reckoning.

Weath. Ay, that he is, sir Arthur; he hath the nobles, the golden ruddocks he.

Sir Arth. The fitter for the wars: and were he not
In favour with your worships, he should see
That I have power to press so good as he.

Oli. Chill stand to the trial, so chill.

M. Flow. Ay marry shall he. Press cloth and kersey, white-pot and drowsen broth![23] tut, tut, he cannot.

Oli. Well, sir, though you see vlouten cloth and karsey, che 'a zeen zutch a karsey-coat wear out the town sick a zilken jacket as thick a one you wear.

M. Flow. Well said vlittan vlattan.[24]

Oli. Ay, and well said cocknell, and Bow-bell too.[25] What do'st think cham aveard of thy zilken-coat? no vear vor thee.

Sir Lanc. Nay come, no more: be all lovers and friends.

Weath. Ay, 'tis best so, good master Oliver.

M. Flow. Is your name master Oliver, I pray you?

Oli. What tit and be tit, and grieve you.

M. Flow. No, but I'd gladly know if a man might not have a foolish plot out of master Oliver to work upon.

Oli. Work thy plots upon me! Stand aside: work thy foolish plots upon me, chil so use thee, thou wert never so used since thy dame bound thy head. Work upon me!

M. Flow. Let him come, let him come.

Oli. Zyrrha, Zyrrha, if it were not vor shame, che would 'a given thee zutch a whister-poop under the ear, che would have made thee a vanged another at my feet: Stand aside, let me loose; cham all of a vlaming fire-brand; stand aside.

M. Flow. Well, I forbear you for your friends' sake.

Oli. A vig for all my vreens: do'st thou tell me of my vreens?

Sir Lanc. No more, good master Oliver; no more, Sir Arthur. And, maiden, here in the sight
Of all your suitors, every man of worth,
I'll tell you whom I fainest would prefer
To the hard bargain of your marriage-bed.
Shall I be plain among you, gentlemen?

Sir Arth. Ay, sir, it is best.

Sir Lanc. Then, sir, first to you.
I do confess you a most gallant knight,
A worthy soldier, and an honest man:
But honesty maintains not a French-hood;[26]
Goes very seldom in a chain of gold;
Keeps a small train of servants; hath few friends.
And for this wild oats here, young Flowerdale,
I will not judge. God can work miracles;

But he were better make a hundred new,
Than thee a thrifty and an honest one.

Weath. Believe me he hath hit you there; he
hath touch'd you to the quick; that he hath.

M. Flow. Woodcock o' my side![27] Why, master
Weathercock, you know I am honest, howsoever
trifles—

Weath. Now by my troth I know no otherwise.
O, your old mother was a dame indeed;
Heaven hath her soul, and my wife's too, I trust:
And your good father, honest gentleman,
He is gone a journey, as I hear, far hence.

M. Flow. Ay, God be praised, he is far enough;
He is gone a pilgrimage to Paradise,
And left me to cut a caper against care.
Luce, look on me that am as light as air.

Luce. I'faith I like not shadows, bubbles, breath;
I hate a *Light o' love*, as I hate death.

Sir Lanc. Girl, hold thee there: look on this
De'nshire lad;
Fat, fair, and lovely, both in purse and person.

Oli. Well, sir, cham as the Lord hath made me.
You know me well ivin; cha have threescore pack
of karsey at Blackem-Hall,[28] and chief credit
beside; and my fortunes may be so good as
another's, zo it may.

Luce. 'Tis you I love, whatsoever others say.

Sir Arth. Thanks, fairest.

M. Flow. What, would'st thou have me quarrel
with him?

Flow. Sen. Do but say he shall hear from you.

Sir Lanc. Yet, gentlemen, howsoever I prefer
This De'nshire suitor, I'll enforce no love:
My daughter shall have liberty to choose
Whom she likes best. In your love-suit proceed:
Not all of you, but only one must speed.

Weath. You have said well; indeed right well.

Enter ARTICHOKE.

Art. Mistress; here's one would speak with
you. My fellow Daffodil hath him in the cellar
already; he knows him; he met him at Croydon fair.

Sir Lanc. O, I remember; a little man.

Art. Ay, a very little man.

Sir Lanc. And yet a proper man.

Art. A very proper, very little man.

Sir Lanc. His name is Monsieur Civet.

Art. The same, sir.

Sir Lanc. Come, gentlemen; if other suitors
come,
My foolish daughter will be fitted too:
But Delia my saint, no man dare move.

[*Exeunt all but* M. FLOW., OLI., *and* FLOW. *Sen.*

M. Flow. Hark you, sir, a word.

Oli. What han you say to me now?

M. Flow. You shall hear from me, and that very
shortly.

Oli. Is that all? vare thee well: che vere thee
not a vig.   [*Exit* OLI.

M. Flow. What if he should come more?[29] I
am fairly dress'd.

Flow. Sen. I do not mean that you shall meet
with him;
But presently we'll go and draw a Will,
Where we'll set down land that we never saw;
And we will have it of so large a sum,
Sir Lancelot shall entreat you take his daughter.
This being form'd, give it master Weathercock,
And make Sir Lancelot's daughter heir of all:
And make him swear never to show the will
To any one, until that you be dead.
This done, the foolish changing Weathercock
Will straight discourse unto Sir Lancelot
The form and tenor of your testament.
Ne'er stand to pause of it; be rul'd by me:
What will ensue, that shall you quickly see.

M. Flow. Come, let's about it: if that a Will,
sweet Kit,
Can get the wench, I shall renown thy wit.

[*Exeunt.*

SCENE II.—*A Room in* Sir Lancelot's *House.*

Enter DAFFODIL *and* LUCE.

Daf. Mistress! still froward? No kind looks
unto your Daffodil? Now by the gods—

Luce. Away you foolish knave; let my hand go.

Daf. There is your hand; but this shall go with
me:
My heart is thine; this is my true love's fee.

[*Takes off her bracelet.*

Luce. I'll have your coat stripp'd o'er your ears
for this,
You saucy rascal.

Enter SIR LANCELOT *and* WEATHERCOCK.

Sir Lanc. How now, maid! what is the news
with you?

Luce. Your man is something saucy.

[*Exit* LUCE.

Sir Lanc. Go to, sirrah; I'll talk with you anon.

Daf. Sir, I am a man to be talked withal; I am
no horse, I trow. I know my strength, then no
more than so.

Weath. Ay, by the makins, good sir Lancelot; I
saw him the other day hold up the bucklers,[30] like

an Hercules. I'faith God-a-mercy, lad, I like thee well.

Sir Lanc. Ay, ay, like him well. Go, sirrah, fetch me a cup of wine,
That ere I part with master Weathercock,
We may drink down our farewell in French wine.
                             [*Exit* DAF.

Weath. I thank you, sir; I thank you, friendly knight.
I'll come and visit you; by the mouse-foot I will :[31]
In the mean time, take heed of cutting Flowerdale :[32]
He is a desperate Dick, I warrant you.

Re-enter DAFFODIL.

Sir Lanc. He is, he is. Fill, Daffodil, fill me some wine. Ha! what wears he on his arm? My daughter Luce's bracelet? ay, 'tis the same. Ha' to you, master Weathercock.

Weath. I thank you, sir. Here, Daffodil; an honest fellow, and a tall, thou art. Well; I'll take my leave good knight; and I hope to have you and all your daughters at my poor house; in good sooth I must.

Sir Lanc. Thanks, master Weathercock; I shall be bold to trouble you, be sure.

Weath. And welcome. Heartily farewell.
                             [*Exit* WEATH.

Sir Lanc. Sirrah, I saw my daughter's wrong, and withal her bracelet on your arm. Off with it, and with it my livery too. Have I care to see my daughter match'd with men of worship? and are you grown so bold? Go, sirrah, from my house, or I'll whip you hence.

Daf. I'll not be whipp'd sir; there's your livery: This is a servingman's reward: what care I? I have means to trust to; I scorn service, I.
                             [*Exit* DAF.

Sir Lanc. Ay, a lusty knave; but I must let him go:
Our servants must be taught what they should know.   [*Exit.*

SCENE III.—*Another Room in the same.*

Enter SIR ARTHUR, *and* LUCE.

Luce. Sir, as I am a maid, I do affect
You above any suitor that I have;
Although that soldiers scarce know how to love.

Sir Arth. I am a soldier, and a gentleman
Knows what belongs to war, what to a lady.
What man offends me, that my sword shall right;
What woman loves me, I'm her faithful knight.

Luce. I neither doubt your valour, nor your love.
But there be some that bear a soldier's form,
That swear by him they never think upon;
Go swaggering up and down from house to house,
Crying, " God pays all." [33]

Sir Arth. I'faith, lady, I'll descry you such a man.
Of them there be many which you have spoke of
That bear the name and shape of soldiers,
Yet, God knows, very seldom saw the war:
That haunt your taverns and your ordinaries,
Your ale-houses sometimes, for all alike,
To uphold the brutish humour of their minds,
Being mark'd down for the bondmen of despair:
Their mirth begins in wine, but ends in blood;
Their drink is clear, but their conceits are mud.

Luce. Yet these are great gentlemen soldiers.

Sir Arth. No, they are wretched slaves,
Whose desperate lives doth bring them timeless graves.

Luce. Both for yourself, and for your form of life,
If I may choose, I'll be a soldier's wife. [*Exeunt.*

SCENE IV.—*Another Room in the same.*

Enter SIR LANCELOT and OLIVER.

Oli. And tyt trust to it, so then.

Sir Lanc. Assure yourself
You shall be married with all speed we may:
One day shall serve for Frances and for Luce.

Oli. Why che wou'd vain know the time, for providing wedding raiments.

Sir Lanc. Why no more but this. First get your assurance made touching my daughter's jointure; that dispatch'd, we will in two days make provision.

Oli. Why man, chil have the writings made by to-morrow.

Sir Lanc. To-morrow be it then: let's meet at the King's Head in Fish-street.

Oli. No, fie man, no: let's meet at the Rose at Temple-Bar; that will be nearer your counsellor and mine.

Sir Lanc. At the Rose be it then, the hour nine: He that comes last forfeits a pint of wine.

Oli. A pint is no payment; let it be a whole quart, or nothing.

Enter ARTICHOKE.

Art. Master, here is a man would speak with Master Oliver; he comes from young Master Flowerdale.

Oli. Why, chil speak with him, chil speak with him.

Sir Lanc. Nay, son Oliver, I will surely see
What young Flowerdale hath sent unto you.
I pray God it be no quarrel.

Oli. Why man, if he quarrel with me, chil give
him his hands full.

Enter FLOWERDALE, *Senior.*

Flow. Sen. God save you, good sir Lancelot.

Sir Lanc. Welcome honest friend.

Flow. Sen. To you and yours my master wisheth
　　health ;
But unto you, sir, this, and this he sends :
There is the length, sir, of his rapier ;
And in that paper shall you know his mind.

　　　　　　　　　　　[Delivers a letter.

Oli. Here ? chil meet him, my vriend, chil meet
him.

Sir Lanc. Meet him ! you shall not meet the
　　ruffian, fie.

Oli. An I do not meet him, chil give you leave
to call me cut. Where is't, sirrah ? where is't ?
where is't ?

Flow. Sen. The letter showeth both the time
　　and place ;
And if you be a man, then keep your word.

Sir Lanc. Sir, he shall not keep his word ; he
　　shall not meet.

Flow. Sen. Why let him choose ; he'll be the
　　better known
For a base rascal, and reputed so.

Oli. Zirrah, zirrah, an 'twere not an old fellow,
and sent after an errant, chid give thee something,
but chud be no money : but hold thee, for I see
thou art somewhat testern ;[34] hold thee ; there's
vorty shillings : bring thy master a-veeld, chil give
thee vorty more. Look thou bring him : chil maul
him, tell him ; chil mar his dancing tressels ; chil
use him, he was ne'er so us'd since his dame bound
his head ; chil mar him for capering any more, che
vore thee.[35]

Flow. Sen. You seem a man, sir, stout and reso-
　　lute ;
And I will so report, whate'er befall.

Sir Lanc. And fall out ill, assure thy master this,
I'll make him fly the land, or use him worse.

Flow. Sen. My master, sir, deserves not this of
　　you ;
And that you'll shortly find.

Sir Lanc. Thy master is an unthrift, you a knave,
And I'll attach you first,[36] next clap him up :
Or have him bound unto his good behaviour.

Oli. I wou'd you were a sprite, if you do him
any harm for this. An you do, chil nere see you,

nor any of yours, while chil have eyes open. What
do you think, chil be abaffelled up and down the
town for a messel, and a scoundrel ?[37] no che voro
you. Zirrha, chil come ; zay no more : chil come,
tell him.

Flow. Sen. Well, sir, my master deserves not
　　this of you,
And that you'll shortly find.

Oli. No matter ; he's an unthrift ; I defy him.

　　　　　　　　　　　[Exit FLOW. *Sen.*

Sir Lanc. Now gentle son, let me know the place.

Oli. No, che vore you.

Sir Lanc. Let me see the note.

Oli. Nay, chil watch you for zuch a trick. But
if che meet him, zo ; if not, zo : chil make him
know me, or chil know why I shall not ; chil vare
the worse.

Sir Lanc. What ! will you then neglect my
　　daughter's love ?
Venture your state and hers for a loose brawl ?

Oli. Why man, chil not kill him : marry chil
veeze him too and again ;[38] and zo God be with
you, vather. What, man ! we shall meet to-morrow. 　　　　　　　　　　　　*[Exit.*

Sir Lanc. Who would have thought he had been
　　so desperate ?
Come forth, my honest servant Artichoke.

Enter ARTICHOKE.

Arti. Now, what's the matter ? some brawl toward, I warrant you.

Sir Lanc. Go get me thy sword bright scour'd,
thy buckler mended. O for that knave ! that villain Daffodil would have done good service. But
to thee——

Arti. Ay, this is the tricks of all you gentlemen,
when you stand in need of a good fellow. "O for
that Daffodil ! O, where is he ?" But if you be
angry, an it be but for the wagging of a straw,
then—"Out o' doors with the knave ; turn the
coat over his ears." This is the humour of you all.

Sir Lanc. O for that knave, that lusty Daffodil !

Arti. Why there 'tis now : our year's wages and
our vails will scarce pay for broken swords and
bucklers that we use in our quarrels. But I'll
not fight if Daffodil be o' t'other side, that's flat.

Sir Lanc. 'Tis no such matter, man. Get wea-
　　pons ready,
And be at London ere the break of day :
Watch near the lodging of the De'nshire youth,
But be unseen ; and as he goeth out,
As he will go out, and that very early without
　　doubt——

Arti. What, would you have me draw upon him, as he goes in the street?

Sir Lanc. Not for a world, man.
Into the fields; for to the field he goes,
There to meet the desperate Flowerdale.
Take thou the part of Oliver my son,
For he shall be my son, and marry Luce:
Dost understand me, knave?

Arti. Ay, sir, I do understand you; but my young mistress might be better provided in matching with my fellow Daffodil.

Sir Lanc. No more; Daffodil is a knave. That Daffodil is a most notorious knave.   [*Exit* ARTI.

Enter WEATHERCOCK.

Master Weathercock, you come in happy time; the desperate Flowerdale hath writ a challenge; and who think you must answer it, but the Devonshire man, my son Oliver.

Weath. Marry I am sorry for it, good sir Lancelot. But if you will be rul'd by me, we'll stay their fury.

Sir Lanc. As how, I pray?

Weath. Marry I'll tell you; by promising young Flowerdale the red-lip'd Luce.

Sir Lanc. I'll rather follow her unto her grave.

Weath. Ay, sir Lancelot, I would have thought so too;
But you and I have been deceiv'd in him.
Come read this will, or deed, or what you call it,
I know not: Come, come; your spectacles I pray.
                  [*Gives him the Will.*

Sir Lanc. Nay, I thank God, I see very well.

Weath. Marry, God bless your eyes: mine have been dim almost this thirty years.

Sir Lanc. Ha! what is this? what is this?
                          [*Reads.*

Weath. Nay there's true love indeed:
He gave it to me but this very morn,
And bade me keep it unseen from any one.
Good youth! to see how men may be deceiv'd!

Sir Lanc. Passion of me,
What a wretch am I to hate this loving youth!

He hath made me, together with my Luce
He loves so dear, executors of all
His wealth.

   Weath. All, all, good man, he hath given you all.

   Sir. Lanc. Three ships now in the Straits, and
       homeward-bound;
Two lordships of two hundred pound a year,
The one in Wales, the other Gloucestershire:
Debts and accounts are thirty thousand pound;
Plate, money, jewels, sixteen thousand more;
Two housen furnish'd well in Coleman-street;
Beside whatsoe'er his uncle leaves to him,
Being of great domains and wealth at Peckham.

   Weath. How like you this, good knight? How like you this?

   Sir Lanc. I have done him wrong, but now I'll
       make amends;
The De'nshire man shall whistle for a wife.
He marry Luce! Luce shall be Flowerdale's.

   Weath. Why that is friendly said. Let's ride
       to London,
And straight prevent their match, by promising
Your daughter to that lovely lad.

   Sir Lanc. We'll ride to London:—or it shall
       not need;
We'll cross to Deptford-strand, and take a boat.
Where be these knaves? what Artichoke! what
       fop!

Enter ARTICHOKE.

   Art. Here be the very knaves, but not the merry knaves.

   Sir Lanc. Here take my cloak: I'll have a walk to Deptford.

   Art. Sir, we have been scouring of our swords and bucklers for your defence.

   Sir Lanc. Defence me no defence; let your swords rust, I'll have no fighting: ay, let blows alone. Bid Delia see all things be in readiness against the wedding: we'll have two at once, and that will save charges, master Weathercock.

   Art. Well we will do it, sir.   [*Exeunt.*

ACT III.

SCENE I.—*A Walk before* Sir Lancelot's *House.*

Enter CIVET, FRANCES, *and* DELIA.

Civ. By my truth this is good luck; I thank God for this. In good sooth I have even my heart's desire. Sister Delia—now I may boldly call you so, for your father hath frank and freely given me his daughter Franke.

Fran. Ay, by my troth, Tom, thou hast my good will too; for I thank God I long'd for a husband; and, would I might never stir, for one whose name was Tom.

Del. Why, sister, now you have your wish.

Civ. You say very true, sister Delia; and I pr'ythee call me nothing but Tom, and I'll call thee sweetheart, and Franke. Will it not do well, sister Delia?

Del. It will do very well with both of you.

Fran. But Tom, must I go as I do now, when I am married?

Civ. No, Franke; I'll have thee go like a citizen, in a guarded gown[39] and a French hood.

Fran. By my troth, that will be excellent indeed.

Del. Brother, maintain your wife to your estate.
Apparel you yourself like to your father,
And let her go like to your ancient mother:
He, sparing got his wealth, left it to you.
Brother, take heed of pride; it soon bids thrift
  adieu.

Civ. So as my father and my mother went! that's a jest indeed. Why she went in a fring'd gown, a single ruff, and a white cap; and my father in a mocado coat,[40] a pair of red satin sleeves, and a canvass back.

Del. And yet his wealth was all as much as yours.

Civ. My estate, my estate, I thank God, is forty pound a year in good leases and tenements; besides twenty mark a year at Cuckold's-haven; and that come to us all by inheritance.

Del. That may indeed; 'tis very fitly 'ply'd.
I know not how it comes, but so it falls out,
That those whose fathers have died wond'rous rich,
And took no pleasure but to gather wealth,
Thinking of little that they leave behind
For them they hope will be of their like mind—
But it falls out contrary: forty years' sparing
Is scarce three seven years spending; never caring
What will ensue, when all their coin is gone.
And, all too late, when thrift is thought upon,

Oft have I heard that pride and riot kiss'd,
And then Repentance cries—" for had I wist."

Civ. You say well, sister Delia, you say well; but I mean to live within my bounds: for look you, I have set down my rest thus far,[41] but to maintain my wife in her French hood and her coach, keep a couple of geldings and a brace of grey-hounds; and this is all I'll do.

Del. And you'll do this with forty pounds a-year?

Civ. Ay, and a better penny, sister.[42]

Fran. Sister, you forget that at Cuckold's-haven.

Civ. By my troth well remember'd, Franke; I'll give thee that to buy thee pins.

Del. Keep you the rest for points.[43] Alas the day!
Fools shall have wealth though all the world say nay.
Come, brother, will you in? Dinner stays for us.

Civ. Ay, good sister, with all my heart.

Fran. Ay, by my troth, Tom, for I have a good stomach.

Civ. And I the like, sweet Franke. No sister, do not think I'll go beyond my bounds.

Del. God grant you may not.   [*Exeunt.*

SCENE II.—London. *The Street before young Flowerdale's House.*

Enter M. FLOWERDALE *and* FLOWERDALE, *Senior.*

M. Flow. Sirrah, Kit, tarry thou there; I have spied sir Lancelot and old Weathercock coming this way: they are hard at hand; I will by no means be spoken withal.

Flow. Sen. I'll warrant you: go, get you in.
         [*Exit* M. FLOW.

Enter SIR LANCELOT *and* WEATHERCOCK.

Sir Lanc. Now, my honest friend, thou dost belong to master Flowerdale?

Flow. Sen. I do, sir.

Sir Lanc. Is he within, my good fellow?

Flow. Sen. No, sir, he is not within.

Sir Lanc. I pr'ythee, if he be within, let me speak with him.

Flow. Sen. Sir, to tell you true, my master is within, but indeed would not be spoke withal. There be some terms that stand upon his reputation; therefore he will not admit any conference till he hath shook them off.

Sir Lanc. I pr'ythee tell him his very good

friend, sir Lancelot Spurcock, entreats to speak with him.

Flow. Sen. By my troth, sir, if you come to take up the matter between my master and the Devonshire man, you do but beguile your hopes, and lose your labour;—

Sir Lanc. Honest friend, I have not any such thing to him. I come to speak with him about other matters.

Flow. Sen. For my master, sir, hath set down his resolution, either to redeem his honour, or leave his life behind him;—

Sir Lanc. My friend, I do not know any quarrel touching thy master or any other person. My business is of a different nature to him; and I pr'ythee so tell him.

Flow. Sen. For howsoever the Devonshire man is, my master's mind is bloody. That's a round O;[44] and therefore, sir, entreaty is but vain.

Sir Lanc. I have no such thing to him, I tell thee once again.

Flow. Sen. I will then so signify to him.

[*Exit* FLOW. *Sen.*

Sir Lanc. A sirrah! I see this matter is hotly carried; but I'll labour to dissuade him from it.

Enter M. FLOWERDALE *and* FLOWERDALE, *Senior.*

Good morrow, master Flowerdale.

M. Flow. Good morrow, good sir Lancelot; good morrow, master Weathercock. By my troth, gentlemen, I have been reading over Nick Machiavel; I find him good to be known, not to be followed. A pestilent human fellow! I have made certain annotations on him, such as they be. And how is 't, sir Lancelot? ha! how is 't? A mad world! men cannot live quiet in it.

Sir Lanc. Master Flowerdale, I do understand there is some jar between the Devonshire man and you.

Flow. Sen. They, sir? they are good friends as can be.

M. Flow. Who master Oliver and I? as good friends as can be.

Sir Lanc. It is a kind of safety in you to deny it, and a generous silence, which too few are endued withal: but, sir, such a thing I hear, and I could wish it otherwise.

M. Flow. No such thing, sir Lancelot, on my reputation; as I am an honest man.

Sir Lanc. Now I do believe you then, if you do engage your reputation there is none.

M. Flow. Nay I do not engage my reputation there is not. You shall not bind me to any con-

dition of hardness; but if there be any thing between us, then there is; if there be not, then there is not. Be or be not, all is one.

Sir Lanc. I do perceive by this, that there is something between you; and I am very sorry for it.

M. Flow. You may be deceiv'd, sir Lancelot. The Italian hath a pretty saying. *Questo*—I have forgot it too; 'tis out of my head: but in my translation, if it hold, thus. If thou hast a friend, keep him; if a foe, trip him.

Sir Lanc. Come, I do see by this there is somewhat between you; and before God I could wish it otherwise.

M. Flow. Well, what is between us, can hardly be alter'd. Sir Lancelot, I am to ride forth to-morrow. That way which I must ride, no man must deny me the sun: I would not by any particular man be denied common and general passage. If any one saith, Flowerdale, thou passest not this way; my answer is, I must either on, or return; but return is not my word; I must on: if I cannot then make my way, nature hath done the last for me; and there's the fine.[45]

Sir Lanc. Master Flowerdale, every man hath one tongue, and two ears. Nature in her building is a most curious work-master.

M. Flow. That is as much as to say, a man should hear more than he should speak.

Sir Lanc. You say true; and indeed I have heard more than at this time I will speak.

M. Flow. You say well.

Sir Lanc. Slanders are more common than truths, master Flowerdale; but proof is the rule for both.

M. Flow. You say true. What-do-you-call-him hath it there in his third canton.

Sir Lanc. I have heard you have been wild; I have believ'd it.

M. Flow. 'Twas fit, 'twas necessary.

Sir Lanc. But I have seen somewhat of late in you, that hath confirm'd in me an opinion of goodness toward you.

M. Flow. I'faith, sir, I'm sure I never did you harm:

Some good I have done, either to you or your's,
I am sure you know not; neither is it my will
You should.

Sir Lanc. Ay, your will, sir:

M. Flow. Ay, my will, sir. 'Sfoot do you know ought of my will? By God an you do, sir, I am abus'd.

Sir Lanc. Go, master Flowerdale; what I know, I know: and know you thus much out of my knowledge, that I truly love you. For my daughter, she's yours. And if you like a marriage better than a brawl, all quirks of reputation set aside, go with me presently; and where you should fight a bloody battle, you shall be married to a lovely lady.

M. Flow. Nay but, sir Lancelot—

Sir Lanc. If you will not embrace my offer, yet assure yourself thus much; I will have order to hinder your encounter.

M. Flow. Nay but hear me, sir Lancelot.

Sir Lanc. Nay, stand not you upon imputative honour. 'Tis merely unsound, unprofitable, and idle inference. Your business is to wed my daughter; therefore give me your present word to do it. I'll go and provide the maid; therefore give me your present resolution; either now or never.

M. Flow. Will you so put me to it?

Sir Lanc. Ay, afore God, either take me now, or take me never. Else what I thought should be our match, shall be our parting: so fare you well for ever.

M. Flow. Stay; fall out, what may fall, my love is above all: I will come.

Sir Lanc. I expect you; and so fare you well.

[*Exeunt* SIR LANC. *and* WEATH.

Flow. Sen. Now, sir, how shall we do for wedding apparel?

M. Flow. By the mass that's true. Now help Kit: the marriage ended, we'll make amends for all.

Flow. Sen. Well, well, no more; prepare you for your bride:
We will not want for clothes, whate'er betide.

M. Flow. And thou shalt see, when once I have my dower,
In mirth we'll spend full many a merry hour:
As for this wench, I not regard a pin,
It is her gold must bring my pleasures in. [*Exit.*

Flow. Sen. Is't possible he hath his second living?[46]
Forsaking God, himself to the devil giving?
But that I knew his mother firm and chaste,
My heart would say, my head she had disgrac'd;
Else would I swear, he never was my son:
But her fair mind so foul a deed did shun.

Enter FLOWERDALE, *Junior.*

Flow. Jun. How now, brother! how do you find your son?

Flow. Sen. O brother, heedless as a libertine;
Even grown a master in the school of vice:
One that doth nothing, but invent deceit;
For all the day he humours up and down,[47]
How he the next day might deceive his friend.

He thinks of nothing but the present time.
For one groat ready down, he'll pay a shilling;
But then the lender must needs stay for it.
When I was young, I had the scope of youth,
Both wild and wanton, careless and desperate;
But such mad strains as he's possess'd withal
I thought it wonder for to dream upon.

Flow. Jun. I told you so, but you would not believe it.

Flow. Sen. Well I have found it: but one thing comforts me.
Brother, to-morrow he is to be married
To beauteous Luce, sir Lancelot Spurcock's daughter.

Flow. Jun. Is't possible?

Flow. Sen. 'Tis true, and thus I mean to curb him.
This day, brother, I will you shall arrest him:
If any thing will tame him, it must be that;
For he is rank in mischief, chain'd to a life
That will increase his shame, and kill his wife.

Flow. Jun. What, arrest him on his wedding day? That
Were an unchristian, and unhuman part.
How many couple even for that very day
Have purchas'd seven years' sorrow afterward!
Forbear it then to-day; do it to-morrow;
And this day mingle not his joy with sorrow.

Flow. Sen. Brother, I'll have it done this very day,
And in the view of all, as he comes from church.
Do but observe the course that he will take;
Upon my life he will forswear the debt.
And, for we'll have the sum shall not be slight,
Say that he owes you near three thousand pound:
Good brother, let it be done immediately.

Flow. Jun. Well, seeing you will have it so,
Brother, I'll do't, and straight provide the shrieve.

Flow. Sen. So brother, by this means shall we perceive
What sir Lancelot in this pinch will do,
And how his wife doth stand affected to him,
(Her love will then be try'd to the uttermost)
And all the rest of them. Brother, what I will do,
Shall harm him much, and much avail him too.

[*Exeunt.*

SCENE III.—*A High Road near* London.

Enter OLIVER; *afterwards* SIR ARTHUR GREEN-
SHIELD.

Oli. Cham assured thick be the place that the scoundrel appointed to meet me. If 'a come, zo:

if 'a come not, zo. And che were avise he would
make a coystrel on us, ched veese him, and ched
vang him in hand; che would hoyst him, and give
it him to and again, zo chud. Who been 'a there?
sir Arthur? chil stay aside. [*Goes aside.*

Sir Arth. I have dog'd the De'nshire man into
the field,

For fear of any harm that should befal him.
I had an inkling of that yesternight,
That Flowerdale and he should meet this morning.
Though, of my soul, Oliver fears him not,
Yet for I'd see fair play on either side,
Made me to come, to see their valours try'd.—
Good morrow to master Oliver.

Oli. God and good morrow.

Sir Arth. What, master Oliver, are you angry?

Oli. What an it be, tyt and grieven you?

Sir Arth. Not me at all, sir; but I imagine by
Your being here thus arm'd, you stay for some
That you should fight withal.

Oli. Why an he do? che would not desire you
to take his part.

Sir Arth. No, by my troth, I think you need it
not;

For he you look for, I think, means not to come.

Oli. No! an che were assure of that, ched veeze
him in another place.

Enter DAFFODIL.

Daff. O, sir Arthur, master Oliver, ah me!
Your love, and your's, and mine, sweet mistress
Luce,
This morn is married to young Flowerdale.

Sir Arth. Married to Flowerdale! 't is impossible.

Oli. Married, man? che hope thou dost but jest,
to make a vlowten merriment[48] of it.

Daff. O 't is too true! here comes his uncle.

Enter FLOWERDALE, *Junior, with* Sheriff *and* Officers.

Flow. Jun. Good morrow, sir Arthur; good morrow, master Oliver.

Oli. God and good morn, master Flowerdale. I
pray you tellen us, is your scoundrel kinsman married?

Flow. Jun. Master Oliver, call him what you will,
but he is married to sir Lancelot's daughter here.

Sir Arth. Unto her?

Oli. Ay, ha' the old yellow zerved me thick a
trick? why man, he was a promise, chil chud 'a had
her: is 'a zutch a vox? chil look to his water, che
vore him.

Flow. Jun. The music plays; they are coming
from the church.
Sheriff, do your office: fellows, stand stoutly to it.

Enter SIR LANCELOT SPURCOCK, M. FLOWERDALE, WEATHERCOCK, CIVET, LUCE, FRANCES, FLOWER-DALE, *Senior, and* Attendants.

Oli. God give you joy, as the old zaid proverb
is, and some zorrow among. You met us well, did
you not?

Sir Lanc. Nay, be not angry, sir; the fault is in
me. I have done all the wrong; kept him from
coming to the field to you, as I might, sir; for I
am a justice, and sworn to keep the peace.

Weath. Ay marry is he, sir, a very justice, and
sworn to keep the peace: you must not disturb the
weddings.

Sir Lanc. Nay, never frown nor storm, sir; if
you do, I 'll have an order taken for you.

Oli. Well, well, chil be quiet.

Weath. Master Flowerdale, sir Lancelot; look
you who here is? master Flowerdale.

Sir Lanc. Master Flowerdale, welcome with all
my heart.

M. Flow. Uncle, this is she i' faith.—Master
Under-sheriff, arrest me? At whose suit?—Draw,
Kit.

Flow. Jun. At my suit, sir.

Sir Lanc. Why, what 's the matter, master
Flowerdale?

Flow. Jun. This is the matter, sir. This unthrift here hath cozen'd you, and hath had of me
in several sums three thousand pound.

M. Flow. Why, uncle, uncle.

Flow. Jun. Cousin, cousin, you have uncled me;
and if you be not staid, you 'll prove a cozener unto
all that know you.

Sir Lanc. Why, sir, suppose he be to you in debt
Ten thousand pound, his state to me appears
To be at least three thousand by the year.

Flow. Jun. O, sir, I was too late inform'd of that
plot;
How that he went about to cozen you,
And form'd a will, and sent it
To your good friend there, master Weathercock,
In which was nothing true, but brags and lies.

Sir Lanc. Ha! hath he not such lordships, lands,
and ships?

Flow. Jun. Not worth a groat, not worth a halfpenny he.

Sir Lanc. I pray tell us true; be plain, young
Flowerdale.

M. Flow. My uncle here 's mad, and dispos'd to

do me wrong; but here's my man, an honest fellow by the lord, and of good credit, knows all is true.

Flow. Sen. Not I, sir; I am too old to lie. I
   rather know
You forg'd a will, where every line you writ,
You studied where to quote your lands might lie.

Weath. And I pr'ythee where be they, honest
friend?

Flow. Sen. I' faith no where, sir, for he hath none
   at all.

Weath. Benedicite! We are o'er-reached, I believe.

Sir Lanc. I am cozen'd, and my hopefullest child
   undone.

M. Flow. You are not cozen'd, nor is she undone.
They slander me; by this light they slander me.
Look you, my uncle here's an usurer,
And would undo me; but I'll stand in law;
Do you but bail me, you shall do no more:
You brother Civet, and master Weathercook, do
   but bail me,
And let me have my marriage-money paid me,
And we'll ride down, and your own eyes shall see
How my poor tenants there will welcome me.
You shall but bail me, you shall do no more:—
And you, you greedy gnat, their bail will serve?

Flow. Jun. Ay, sir, I'll ask no better bail.

Sir Lanc. No, sir, you shall not take my bail,
   nor his,
Nor my son Civet's: I'll not be cheated, I.
Shrieve, take your prisoner; I'll not deal with
   him.
Let his uncle make false dice with his false bones;
I will not have to do with him: mock'd, gull'd, and
   wrong'd!
Come, girl, though it be late, it falls out well;
Thou shalt not live with him in beggar's hell.

Luce. He is my husband, and high heaven doth
   know
With what unwillingness I went to church;
But you enforc'd me, you compell'd me to it.
The holy church-man pronounc'd these words but
   now,
" I must not leave my husband in distress:"
Now I must comfort him, not go with you.

Sir Lanc. Comfort a cozener! on my curse forsake him.

Luce. This day you caus'd me on your curse to
   take him.
Do not, I pray, my grieved soul oppress:
God knows my heart doth bleed at his distress.

Sir Lanc. O master Weathercook,

I must confess I forc'd her to this match,
Led with opinion his false will was true.

Weath. Ah, he hath o'er-reach'd me too.

Sir Lanc. She might have liv'd
Like Delia, in a happy virgin's state.

Del. Father, be patient: sorrow comes too late.

Sir Lanc. And on her knees she begg'd and did
   entreat,
If she must needs taste a sad marriage life,
She crav'd to be sir Arthur Greenshield's wife.

Sir Arth. You have done her and me the greater
   wrong.

Sir Lanc. O, take her yet.

Sir Arth. Not I.

Sir Lanc. Or, master Oliver, accept my child,
And half my wealth is yours.

Oli. No, sir, chil break no laws.

Luce. Never fear, she will not trouble you.

Del. Yet, sister, in this passion
Do not run headlong to confusion:
You may affect him, though not follow him.

Fran. Do, sister; hang him, let him go.

Weath. Do 'faith, mistress Luce; leave him.

Luce. You are three gross fools; pray let me
   alone:
I swear, I'll live with him in all his moan.

Oli. But an he have his legs at liberty,
Cham aveard he will never live with you.

Sir Arth. Ay, but he is now in huckster's handling for running away.

Sir Lanc. Huswife, you hear how you and I are
   wrong'd,
And if you will redress it yet, you may:
But if you stand on terms to follow him,
Never come near my sight, nor look on me;
Call me not father, look not for a groat;
For all thy portion I will this day give
Unto thy sister Frances.

Fran. How say you to that, Tom? [*To* Civ.] I
shall have a good deal: besides, I'll be a good
wife; and a good wife is a good thing I can tell.

Civ. Peace, Franke. I would be sorry to see
thy sister cast away, as I am a gentleman.

Sir Lanc. What, are you yet resolv'd?

Luce. Yes, I am resolv'd.

Sir Lanc. Come then away; or now, or never
   come.

Luce. This way I turn; go you unto your feast;
And I to weep, that am with grief opprest.

Sir Lanc. For ever fly my sight: Come, gentlemen,
Let's in; I'll help you to far better wives than
her.

Delia, upon my blessing talk not to her.
Base baggage, in such haste to beggary!

Flow. Jun. Sheriff, take your prisoner to your
charge.

M. Flow. Uncle, by God you have us'd me very
hardly, by my troth, upon my wedding-day.

[*Exeunt* SIR LANC., CIV., WEATH., FRAN.,
DEL., *and their* Attendants.

Luce. O master Flowerdale, but hear me speak.

[*To* FLOW. *Jun.*

Stay but a little while, good master sheriff;
If not for him, for my sake pity him.
Good sir, stop not your ears at my complaint;
My voice grows weak, for women's words are faint.

M. Flow. Look you, uncle, she kneels to you.

Flow. Jun. Fair maid, for you, I love you with
my heart,
And grieve, sweet soul, thy fortune is so bad,
That thou should'st match with such a graceless
youth.
Go to thy father, think not upon him,
Whom hell hath mark'd to be the son of shame.

Luce. Impute his wildness, sir, unto his youth,
And think that now's the time he doth repent.
Alas, what good or gain can you receive,
To imprison him that nothing hath to pay?
And where nought is, the king doth lose his due:
O pity him as God shall pity you.

Flow. Jun. Lady, I know his humours all too
well;
And nothing in the world can do him good,
But misery itself to chain him with.

Luce. Say that your debt were paid, then is he
free?

Flow. Jun. Ay, virgin; that being answer'd, I
have done.
But to him that is all as impossible,
As I to scale the high pyramides.
Sheriff, take your prisoner: maiden, fare thee
well.

Luce. O go not yet, good master Flowerdale:
Take my word for the debt, my word, my bond.

M. Flow. Ay, by God, uncle, and my bond too.

Luce. Alas, I ne'er ought nothing but I paid it;
And I can work: alas, he can do nothing.
I have some friends perhaps will pity me:
His chiefest friends do seek his misery.
All that I can, or beg, get, or receive,
Shall be for you. O do not turn away:
Methinks, within, a face so reverend,
So well experienc'd in this tottering world,
Should have some feeling of a maiden's grief:
For my sake, his father's and your brother's sake,

Ay, for your soul's sake, that doth hope for joy,
Pity my state; do not two souls destroy.

Flow. Jun. Fair maid, stand up: not in **regard**
of him,
But in pity of thy hapless choice, I
Do release him.   Master sheriff, I thank you;
And officers, there is for you to drink.
Here, maid, take this money; there is a hundred
angels:
And, for I will be sure he shall not have it,
Here, Kester, take it you, and use it sparingly;
But let not her have any want at all.
Dry your eyes, niece; do not too much lament
For him whose life hath been in riot spent:
If well he useth thee, he gets him friends,
If ill, a shameful end on him depends.

[*Exit* FLOW. *Jun.*

M. Flow. A plague go with you for an old fornicator! Come, Kit, the money; come, honest Kit.

Flow. Sen. Nay, by my faith, sir, you shall pardon me.

M. Flow. And why, sir, pardon you?   Give me
the money, you old rascal, or I will make you.

Luce. Pray hold your hands; give it him honest
friend.

Flow. Sen. If you be so content, with all my
heart.   [*Gives the money.*

M. Flow. Content, sir? 'sblood she shall be content whether she will or no.   A rattle-baby come
to follow me!   Go, get you gone to the greasy
chuff your father: bring me your dowry, or never
look on me.

Flow. Sen. Sir, she hath forsook her father, and
all her friends for you.

M. Flow. Hang thee, her friends and father, all
together.

Flow Sen. Yet part with something to provide
her lodging.

M. Flow. Yes, I mean to part with her and you;
but if I part with one angel, hang me at a post.
I'll rather throw them at a cast of dice, as I have
done a thousand of their fellows.

Flow. Sen. Nay then I will be plain: degenerate
boy,
Thou hadst a father would have been asham'd——

M. Flow. My father was an ass, an old ass.

Flow. Sen. Thy father? thou proud licentious
villain:
What are you at your foils? I'll foil with you.

Luce. Good sir, forbear him.

Flow. Sen. Did not this whining woman hang on
me,
I'd teach thee what it was to abuse thy father.

Go hang, beg, starve, dice, game; that when all's
     gone,
Thou may'st after despair and hang thyself.

Luce. O, do not curse him.

Flow. Sen. I do not curse him; and to pray for
     him were vain:
It grieves me that he bears his father's name.

M. Flow. Well, you old rascal, I shall meet with
you.[49] Sirrah, get you gone; I will not strip the
livery over your ears, because you paid for it: but
do not use my name, sirrah, do you hear? Look
you do not use my name, you were best.

Flow. Sen. Pay me the twenty pound then that I
lent you, or give me security when I may have it.

M. Flow. I'll pay thee not a penny,
And for security I'll give thee none.
Minckins,[50] look you do not follow me; look you
     do not:
If you do, beggar, I shall slit your nose.

Luce. Alas, what shall I do?

M. Flow. Why turn whore: that's a good trade;
And so perhaps I'll see thee now and then.
                   [*Exit* M. Flow.

Luce. Alas the day that ever I was born.

Flow. Sen. Sweet mistress, do not weep; I'll
     stick to you.

Luce. Alas, my friend, I know not what to
     do.
My father and my friends, they have despis'd
     me;
And I a wretched maid, thus cast away,
Know neither where to go, nor what to say.

Flow. Sen. It grieves me at the soul, to see her
     tears
Thus stain the crimson roses of her cheeks.
Lady, take comfort; do not mourn in vain.
I have a little living in this town,
The which I think comes to a hundred pound;
All that and more shall be at your dispose.
I'll straight go help you to some strange dis-
     guise,
And place you in a service in this town,
Where you shall know all, yet yourself unknown.
Come, grieve no more, where no help can be had;
Weep not for him, that is more worse than bad.

Luce. I thank you, sir.   [*Exeunt.*

ACT IV.

SCENE I.—*A Room in Sir Lancelot Spurcock's
House in Kent.*

Enter Sir Lancelot, Sir Arthur, Oliver,
Weathercock, Civet, Frances, *and* Delia.

Oli. Well, cha 'a bin zarved many a sluttish
trick, but such a lerripoop as thick ych was ne'er
yzarved.

Sir Lanc. Son Civet, daughter Frances, bear
     with me:
You see how I'm press'd down with inward
     grief,
About that luckless girl, your sister Luce.
But 'tis fallen out
With me, as with many families beside:
They are most unhappy, that are most belov'd.

Civ. Father, 'tis so, 'tis even fallen out so.
But what remedy? set hand to your heart,
And let it pass. Here is your daughter Frances
And I; and we'll not say, we will bring forth
As witty children, but as pretty children
As ever she was, though she had the prick
And praise for a pretty wench:[51] But father,
Dun is the mouse;[52] you'll come?

Sir Lanc. Ay, son Civet, I'll come.

Civ. And you, master Oliver?

Oli. Ay, for che a vext out this veast, chil see if
a gan make a better veast there.

Civ. And you, sir Arthur?

Sir Arth. Ay, sir, although my heart be full,
I'll be a partner at your wedding feast.

Civ. And welcome all indeed, and welcome.
Come Franke, are you ready?

Fran. Jesu, how hasty these husbands are! I
pray father, pray to God to bless me.

Sir Lanc. God bless thee! and I do. God make
     thee wise!
Send you both joy! I wish it with wet eyes.

Fran. But, father, shall not my sister Delia go
along with us? She is excellent good at cookery,
and such things.

Sir Lanc. Yes marry shall she: Delia, make you
ready.

Del. I am ready, sir. I will first go to Greenwich; from thence to my cousin Chesterfield's, and
so to London.

Civ. It shall suffice, good sister Delia, it shall
suffice; but fail us not, good sister: give order to

cooks and others; for I would not have my sweet Franke to soil her fingers.

Fran. No, by my troth, not I. A gentlewoman, and a married gentlewoman too, to be companion to cooks and kitchen-boys! Not I, i'faith; I scorn that.

Civ. Why, I do not mean thou shalt, sweet-heart; thou seest I do not go about it. Well, farewell to you.—God's pity, master Weathercock! we shall have your company too?

Weath. With all my heart, for I love good cheer.

Civ. Well, God be with you all. Come, Franke.

Fran. God be with you, father; God be with you. Sir Arthur, master Oliver, and master Weathercock, sister, God be with you all: God be with you, father; God be with you every one.

         [*Exeunt* CIV. *and* FRAN.

Weath. Why, how now, sir Arthur? all a-mort? Master Oliver, how now, man? Cheerly, sir Lancelot; and merrily say, Who can hold that will away?

Sir Lanc. Ay, she is gone indeed, poor girl, un-done; But when they'll be self-will'd, children must smart.

Sir Arth. But, sir, That she is wrong'd, you are the chiefest cause; Therefore, 'tis reason you redress her wrong.

Weath. Indeed you must, sir Lancelot, you must.

Sir Lanc. Must? who can compel me, master Weathercock? I hope I may do what I list.

Weath. I grant you may; you may do what you list.

Oli. Nay, but an you be well avisen, it were not good, by this vrampolness[53] and vrowardness, to cast away as pretty a Dowsabel as an should chance to see in a summer's day. Chil tell you what chall do; chil go spy up and down the town, and see if I can hear any tale or tidings of her, and take her away from thick a messel; vor cham assured, he'll but bring her to the spoil; and so vare you well. We shall meet at your son Civet's.

Sir Lanc. I thank you, sir; I take it very kindly.

Sir Arth. To find her out, I'll spend my dearest blood; So well I lov'd her, to affect her good.

         [*Exeunt* CIV. *and* SIR ARTH.

Sir Lanc. O master Weathercock, what hap had I, To force my daughter from master Oliver, And this good knight, to one that hath no good-ness In his thought?

Weath. Ill luck; but what remedy?

Sir Lanc. Yes, I have almost devis'd a remedy: Young Flowerdale is sure a prisoner.

Weath. Sure; nothing more sure.

Sir Lanc. And yet perhaps his uncle hath re-leas'd him.

Weath. It may be very like; no doubt he hath.

Sir Lanc. Well if he be in prison, I'll have war-rants To 'tach my daughter[54] till the law be tried; For I will sue him upon cozenage.

Weath. Marry may you, and overthrow him too.

Sir Lanc. Nay that's not so; I may chance to be scoff'd And sentence past with him.

Weath. Believe me, so it may; therefore take heed.

Sir Lanc. Well howsoever, yet I will have war-rants; In prison, or at liberty, all's one You will help to serve them, master Weathercock?

         [*Exeunt.*

SCENE II.—*A Street in* London.

Enter M. FLOWERDALE.

M. Flow. A plague of the devil! the devil take the dice! the dice and the devil and his dam go together! Of all my hundred golden angels, I have not left me one denier. A pox of "come, a five!" What shall I do? I can borrow no more of my credit: there's not any of my acquaintance, man nor boy, but I have borrowed more or less of. I would I knew where to take a good purse, and go clear away; by this light I'll venture for it. God's-lid, my sister Delia: I'll rob her, by this hand.

Enter DELIA *and* ARTICHOKE.

Del. I pr'ythee, Artichoke, go not so fast; The weather's hot, and I am something weary.

Art. Nay I warrant you, mistress Delia, I'll not tire you with leading; we'll go an extreme moderate pace.

M. Flow. Stand; deliver your purse.

Art. O lord, thieves, thieves!   [*Exit* ART.

M. Flow. Come, come, your purse; lady, your purse.

Del. That voice I have heard often before this time. What, brother Flowerdale become a thief!

M. Flow. Ay, plague on 't, I thank your father: but sister, Come, your money, come. What!

The world must find me; I am born to live;
'Tis not a sin to steal, where none will give.

Del. O God, is all grace banish'd from thy heart?
Think of the shame that doth attend this fact.

M. Flow. Shame me no shames. Come, give
me your purse;
I'll bind you, sister, lest I fare the worse.

Del. No, bind me not: hold, there is all I have;
And would that money would redeem thy shame.

Enter OLIVER, SIR ARTHUR, *and* ARTICHOKE.

Art. Thieves, thieves, thieves!

Oli. Thieves! where man? why how now, mistress Delia. Ha' you yliked to been yrobb'd?

Del. No, master Oliver; 'tis master Flowerdale;
he did but jest with me.

Oli. How, Flowerdale, that scoundrel? Sirrah,
you meten us well; vang thee that.[55] [*Strikes him.*

M. Flow. Well, sir, I'll not meddle with you,
because I have a charge.

Del. Here brother Flowerdale, I'll lend you
this same money.

M. Flow. I thank you, sister.

Oli. I wad you were ysplit, an you let the messel have a penny; but since you cannot keep it,
chil keep it myself.

Sir Arth. 'Tis pity to relieve him in this sort,
Who makes a triumphant life his daily sport.

Del. Brother, you see how all men censure you.
Farewell; and I pray God amend your life.

Oli. Come, chil bring you along, and you, safe
enough from twenty such scoundrels as thick a
one is. Farewell and be hanged, zyrrah, as I think
so thou wilt be shortly. Come, sir Arthur.
                              [*Exeunt all but* M. FLOW.

M. Flow. A plague go with you for a kersey rascal.
This De'nshire man I think is made all of pork:
His hands made only for to heave up packs;
His heart as fat and big as is his face;
As differing far from all brave gallant minds,
As I to serve the hogs, and drink with hinds;
As I am very near now. Well what remedy?
When money, means, and friends, do grow so small,
Then farewell life, and there's an end of all. [*Exit.*

SCENE III.—*Another Street. Before* Civet's
house.

Enter FLOWERDALE, *Senior,* LUCE, *like a Dutch*
Frow, CIVET, *and* FRANCES.

Civ. By my troth, God-a-mercy for this, good
Christopher. I thank thee for my maid; I like
her very well. How dost thou like her, Frances?

Fran. In good sadness, Tom, very well, excellent
well; she speaks so prettily:—I pray what's your
name?

Luce. My name, forsooth, be called Tanikin.

Fran. By my troth a fine name. O Tanikin,
you are excellent for dressing one's head a new
fashion.

Luce. Me sall do every ting about de head.

Civ. What countrywoman is she, Kester?

Flow. Sen. A Dutch woman, sir.

Civ. Why then she is outlandish, is she not?

Flow. Sen. Ay, sir, she is.

Fran. O then thou canst tell how to help me to
cheeks and ears.[56]

Luce. Yes, mistress, very well.

Flow. Sen. Cheeks and ears! why, mistress
Frances, want you cheeks and ears? methinks you
have very fair ones.

Fran. Thou art a fool indeed. Tom, thou knowest what I mean.

Civ. Ay, ay, Kester; 'tis such as they wear
a' their heads. I pr'ythee, Kit, have her in, and
show her my house.

Flow. Sen. I will, sir. Come Tanikin.

Fran. O Tom, you have not bussed me to-day,
Tom.

Civ. No Frances, we must not kiss afore folks.
God save me, Franke. See yonder; my sister
Delia is come.

Enter DELIA *and* ARTICHOKE.

Welcome, good sister.

Fran. Welcome, good sister. How do you like
the tire of my head?

Del. Very well, sister.

Civ. I am glad you're come, sister Delia, to
give order for supper: they will be here soon.

Art. Ay, but if good luck had not serv'd, she
had not been here now. Filching Flowerdale had
like to have pepper'd us: but for master Oliver,
we had been robb'd.

Del. Peace, sirrah, no more.

Flow. Sen. Robb'd! by whom?

Art. Marry by none but by Flowerdale; he is
turn'd thief.

Civ. By my faith, but that is not well; but God
be prais'd for your escape. Will you draw near,
sister?

Flow. Sen. Sirrah, come hither. Would Flowerdale, he that was my master, have robbed you? I
pr'ythee tell me true.

Art. Yes i' faith, even that Flowerdale that was
thy master.

Flow. Sen. Hold thee; there is a French crown, and speak no more of this.   [*Aside.*

Art. Not I, not a word.—Now do I smell knavery: in every purse Flowerdale takes, he is half; and gives me this to keep counsel:—not a word, I.

Flow Sen. Why God-a-mercy.

Fran. Sister, look here; I have a new Dutch maid, and she speaks so fine, it would do your heart good.

Civ. How do you like her, sister?

Del. I like your maid well.

Civ. Well, dear sister, will you draw near, and give directions for supper? Guests will be here presently.

Del. Yes, brother; lead the way, I'll follow you.   [*Exeunt all but* DEL. *and* LUCE. Hark you, Dutch frow, a word.

Luce. Vat is your vill wit me?

Del. Sister Luce, 'tis not your broken language, Nor this same habit, can disguise your face From I that know you. Pray tell me, what means this.

Luce. Sister, I see you know me; yet be secret. This borrowed shape that I have ta'en upon me, Is but to keep myself a space unknown, Both from my father, and my nearest friends; Until I see how time will bring to pass The desperate course of master Flowerdale.

Del. O he is worse than bad; I pr'ythee leave him;
And let not once thy heart to think on him.

Luce. Do not persuade me once to such a thought.
Imagine yet that he is worse than naught;
Yet one hour's time may all that ill undo
That all his former life did run into.
Therefore, kind sister, do not disclose my estate;
If e'er his heart doth turn, 'tis ne'er too late.

Del. Well, seeing no counsel can remove your mind,
I'll not disclose you that are wilful blind.

Luce. Delia, I thank you. I now must please her eyes,
My sister Frances' neither fair nor wise.
                    [*Exeunt.*

ACT V.

SCENE I.—*Street before* Civet's *House.*

Enter M. FLOWERDALE.

M. Flow. On goes he that knows no end of his journey. I have pass'd the very utmost bounds of shifting; I have no course now but to hang myself. I have liv'd since yesterday two o'clock on a spice-cake I had at a burial;[57] and for drink, I got it at an ale-house among porters, such as will bear out a man if he have no money indeed; I mean—out of their companies, for they are men of good carriage. Who comes here? the two coney-catchers[58] that won all my money of me. I'll try if they'll lend me any.

Enter DICK *and* RALPH.

What master Richard, how do you? How dost thou, Ralph? By God, gentlemen, the world grows bare with me; will you do as much as lend me an angel between you both? You know, you won a hundred of me the other day.

Ralph. How! an angel? God damn us if we lost not every penny within an hour after thou wert gone.

M. Flow. I pr'ythee lend me so much as will pay for my supper: I'll pay you again, as I am a gentleman.

Ralph. I 'faith, we have not a farthing, not a mite. I wonder at it, master Flowerdale, You will so carelessly undo yourself. Why you will lose more money in an hour, Than any honest man spends in a year. For shame betake you to some honest trade, And live not thus so like a vagabond.
                    [*Exeunt* DICK *and* RALPH.

M. Flow. A vagabond indeed; more villains you: They give me counsel that first cozen'd me. Those devils first brought me to this I am, And being thus, the first that do me wrong. Well, yet I have one friend left me in store. Nor far from hence there dwells a cockatrice,[59] One that I first put in a satin gown; And not a tooth that dwells within her head, But stands me at the least in twenty pound: Her will I visit now my coin is gone; And as I take it here dwells the gentlewoman.
                    [*Knocks.*
What ho, is mistress Apricock within?

Enter Ruffian.

Ruf. What saucy rascal's that which knocks so
    bold?
O, is it you, old spend-thrift? Are you here?
One that is turned cozener 'bout the town?
My mistress saw you, and sends this word by me;
Either be packing quickly from the door,
Or you shall have such a greeting sent you straight
As you will little like on: you had best be gone.
                                      [*Exit.*

M. Flow. Why so, this is as it should be; being
    poor,
Thus art thou serv'd by a vile painted whore.
Well, since thy damned crew do so abuse thee,
I'll try of honest men, how they will use me.

Enter an ancient Citizen.

Sir, I beseech you to take compassion of a man;
one whose fortunes have been better than at this
instant they seem to be: but if I might crave of
you so much little portion as would bring me to
my friends, I would rest thankful until I had
requited so great a courtesy.

Cit. Fie, fie, young man! this course is very bad.
Too many such have we about this city;
Yet for I have not seen you in this sort,
Nor noted you to be a common beggar,
Hold; there's an angel to bear your charges down.
Go to your friends; do not on this depend:
Such bad beginnings oft have worser end. [*Exit* Cit.

M. Flow. Worser end! nay, if it fall out no
worse than in old angels, I care not. Nay, now
I have had such a fortunate beginning, I'll not let
a sixpenny purse escape me:—By the mass here
comes another.

Enter a Citizen's Wife, *and a* Servant *with a torch
before her.*

God bless you, fair mistress. Now would it please
you, gentlewoman, to look into the wants of a
poor gentleman, a younger brother, I doubt not
but God will treble restore it back again; one that
never before this time demanded penny, halfpenny, nor farthing.

Cit. Wife. Stay, Alexander. Now by my troth
a very proper man; and 'tis great pity. Hold, my
friend; there's all the money I have about me, a
couple of shillings; and God bless thee.

M. Flow. Now God thank you, sweet lady. · If
you have any friend, or garden-house[60] where you
may employ a poor gentleman as your friend, I am
yours to command in all secret service.

Cit. Wife. I thank you good friend; I pr'ythee
let me see that again I gave thee; there is one of
them a brass shilling: give me them, and here is
half-a-crown in gold. [*He gives the money to her.*]
Now out upon thee, rascal: secret service! what
dost thou make of me? It were a good deed to
have thee whipp'd: Now I have my money again,
I'll see thee hang'd before I give thee a penny.
Secret service!—On, good Alexander.
            [*Exeunt* Cit.'s Wife *and* Serv.

M. Flow. This is villanous luck; I perceive dis-
honesty will not thrive. Here comes more. God
forgive me, sir Arthur and master Oliver. Afore
God I'll speak to them.

Enter SIR ARTHUR, *and* OLIVER.

God save you, sir Arthur; God save you, master
Oliver.

Oli. Been you there, zirrah? come will you
ytaken yourself to your tools, coystrel?

M. Flow. Nay, master Oliver, I'll not fight with
    you.
Alas, sir, you know it was not my doings;
It was only a plot to get sir Lancelot's daugh-
    ter:
By God I never meant you harm.

Oli. And where is the gentlewoman thy wife,
mezel? where is she, zirrah, ha?

M. Flow. By my troth, master Oliver, sick, very
sick: and God is my judge, I know not what
means to make for her, good gentlewoman.

Oli. Tell me true—is she sick? tell me true, ich
'vise thee.

M. Flow. Yes 'faith, I tell you true, master
Oliver: if you would do me the small kindness but
to lend me forty shillings, so God help me, I will
pay you so soon as my ability shall make me able;
—as I am a gentleman.

Oli. Well, thou zaist thy wife is zick; hold,
there's vorty shillings; give it to thy wife. Look
thou give it her, or I shall zo veeze thee, thou
wert not zo veezed this zeven year; look to it.

Sir Arth. I'faith, master Oliver, 'tis in vain
To give to him that never thinks of her.

Oli. Well, would che could yvind it.

M. Flow. I tell you true, sir Arthur, as I am a
gentleman.

Oli. Well, farewell zirrah: come, sir Arthur.
            [*Exeunt* SIR ARTH. *and* OLI.

M. Flow. By the lord, this is excellent;
Five golden angels compass'd in an hour:
If this trade hold, I'll never seek a new.
Welcome, sweet gold, and beggary adieu.

Enter FLOWERDALE, *Junior, and* FLOWERDALE, *Senior.*

Flow. Jun. See, Kester, if you can find the house.

M. Flow. Who's here? My uncle, and my man Kester? By the mass 'tis they. How do you uncle? how dost thou, Kester? by my troth, uncle, you must needs lend me some money. The poor gentle-woman my wife, so God help me, is very sick: I was robb'd of the hundred angels you gave me; they are gone.

Flow. Jun. Ay, they are gone indeed. Come, Kester, away.

M. Flow. Nay, uncle; do you hear, good uncle?

Flow. Jun. Out, hypocrite, I will not hear thee speak: come, leave him, Kester.

M. Flow. Kester, honest Kester.

Flow. Sen. Sir, I have nought to say to you. Open the door to me, 'Kin: thou had'st best lock it fast, for there's a false knave without.

       [FLOW. *Sen. and* FLOW. *Jun. go in.*

M. Flow. You are an old lying rascal, so you are.

Enter, from Civet's *House,* LUCE.

Luce. Vat is de matter? Vat be you, yonker?

M. Flow. By this light a Dutch Frow; they say they are called kind. By this light, I'll try her.

Luce. Vat bin you, yonker? why do you not speak?

M. Flow. By my troth, sweet-heart, a poor gen-tleman that would desire of you, if it stand with your liking, the bounty of your purse.

Re-enter FLOWERDALE, *Senior.*

Luce. O hear God! so young an armin![61]

M. Flow. Armin, sweet-heart? I know not what you mean by that; but I am almost a beggar.

Luce. Are you not a married man? vere bin your vife? Here is all I have; take dis.

M. Flow. What gold, young frow? this is brave.

Flow. Sen. If he have any grace, he'll now re-pent.

Luce. Why speak you not? vere be your vife?

M. Flow. Dead, dead; she's dead, 'tis she hath undone me. Spent me all I had, and kept rascals under my nose to brave me.

Luce. Did you use her vell?

M. Flow. Use her! there's never a gentle-woman in England could be better used than I did her. I could but coach her; her diet stood me in forty pound a month: but she is dead; and in her grave my cares are buried.

Luce. Indeed dat vas not scone.[62]

Flow. Sen. He is turn'd more devil than he was before.

M. Flow. Thou dost belong to master Civet here, dost thou not?

Luce. Yes, me do.

M. Flow. Why there's it! there's not a hand-ful of plate but belongs to me. God's my judge, if I had such a wench as thou art, there's never a man in England would make more of her, than I would do—so she had any stock.

       [*Within,* O, why Tanikin.

Luce. Stay; one doth call; I shall come by and by again.   [*Exit.*

M. Flow. By this hand, this Dutch wench is in love with me. Were it not admirable to make her steal all Civet's plate, and run away?

Flow. Sen. It were beastly. O master Flower-dale,

Have you no fear of God, nor conscience?

What do you mean by this vile course you take?

M. Flow. What do I mean? why, to live; that I mean.

Flow. Sen. To live in this sort? Fie upon the course:

Your life doth show you are a very coward.

M. Flow. A coward! I pray in what?

Flow. Sen. Why you will borrow sixpence of a boy.

M. Flow. 'Snails, is there such cowardice in that? I dare borrow it of a man, ay, and of the tallest man in England,—if he will lend it me: let me borrow it how I can, and let them come by it how they dare. And it is well known, I might have rid out[63] a hundred times if I would, so I might.

Flow. Sen. It was not want of will, but cowardice.

There is none that lends to you, but know they gain:

And what is that but only stealth in you?

Delia might hang you now, did not her heart

Take pity of you for her sister's sake.

Go get you hence, lest ling'ring here your stay,

You fall into their hands you look not for.

M. Flow. I'll tarry here, 'till the Dutch frow comes, if all the devils in hell were here.

       [FLOW. *Sen. goes into* Civet's *House.*

Enter SIR LANCELOT, MASTER WEATHERCOCK, *and* ARTICHOKE.

Sir Lanc. Where is the door? are we not past it, Artichoke?

Art. By the mass here's one; I'll ask him. Do you hear, sir? What, are you so proud? **Do you**

hear? Which is the way to master Civet's house?
What, will you not speak? O me! this is filching
Flowerdale.

Sir Lanc. O wonderful! is this lewd villain here?
O you cheating rogue, you cut-purse, coney-catcher!
What ditch, you villain, is my daughter's grave?
A cozening rascal, that must make a will,
Take on him that strict habit, very that,
When he should turn to angel; a dying grace.
I 'll father-in-law you, sir, I 'll make a will;
Speak, villain, where 's my daughter?
Poison'd, I warrant you, or knock'd o' the head:
And to abuse good master Weathercock,
With his forged will, and master Weathercock,
To make my grounded resolution;[64]
Then to abuse the De'nshire gentleman:
Go; away with him to prison.

M. Flow. Wherefore to prison? sir, I will not go.

Enter CIVET *and his* Wife, OLIVER, SIR ARTHUR,
FLOWERDALE, *Senior,* FLOWERDALE, *Junior, and*
DELIA.

Sir Lanc. O here 's his uncle: welcome, gentlemen, welcome all. Such a cozener, gentlemen, a
murderer too, for any thing I know! My daughter
is missing; hath been look'd for; cannot be found.
A vild upon thee!

Flow. Jun. He is my kinsman, though his life
be vile:
Therefore, in God's name, do with him what you will.

Sir Lanc. Marry to prison.

M. Flow. Wherefore to prison? snick-up.[65] I
owe you nothing.

Sir Lanc. Bring forth my daughter then: Away
with him.

M. Flow. Go seek your daughter. What do you
lay to my charge?

Sir Lanc. Suspicion of murder. Go; away with
him.

M. Flow. Murder your dogs! I murder your
daughter? Come, uncle, I know you 'll bail me.

Flow. Jun. Not I, were there no more than I
the gaoler, thou the prisoner.

Sir Lanc. Go; away with him.

Enter LUCE.

Luce. O' my life hear: where will you ha' de
man? Vat ha' de yonker done?

Weath. Woman, he hath kill'd his wife.

Luce. His wife! dat is not good; dat is not
seen.

Sir Lanc. Hang not upon him, huswife; if you
do, I 'll lay you by him.

Luce. Have me no oder way dan you have him;[66]
He tell me dat he love me heartily.

Fran. Lead away my maid to prison! why, Tom,
will you suffer that?

Civ. No, by your leave, father, she is no vagrant:
she is my wife's chamber-maid, and as true as the
skin between any man's brows here.

Sir Lanc. Go to, you 're both fools.
Son Civet, of my life this is a plot;
Some straggling counterfeit prefer'd to you,
No doubt to rob you of your plate and jewels:—
I 'll have you led away to prison, trull.

Luce. I am no trull, neither outlandish frow:
Nor he nor I shall to the prison go.
Know you me now? nay never stand amaz'd.
                    [*Throws off her Dutch dress.*
Father, I know I have offended you;
And though that duty wills me bend my knees
To you in duty and obedience,
Yet this way do I turn, and to him yield
My love, my duty, and my humbleness.

Sir Lanc. Bastard in nature! kneel to such a
                    slave?

Luce. O master Flowerdale, if too much grief
Have not stopp'd up the organs of your voice,
Then speak to her that is thy faithful wife;
Or doth contempt of me thus tie thy tongue?
Turn not away; I am no Æthiop,
No wanton Cressid, nor a changing Helen;
But rather one made wretched by thy loss.
What! turn'st thou still from me? O then
I guess thee wofull'st among hapless men.

M. Flow. I am indeed, wife, wonder among wives!
Thy chastity and virtue hath infus'd
Another soul in me, red with defame,
For in my blushing cheeks is seen my shame.

Sir Lanc. Out hypocrite! I charge thee trust
                    him not.

Luce. Not trust him? By the hopes of after-
                    bliss,
I know no sorrow can be compar'd to his.

Sir Lanc. Well, since thou wert ordain'd to beg-
                    gary,
Follow thy fortune: I defy thee, I.

Oli. I wood che were so well ydoussed as was
ever white cloth in a tocking mill,[67] an che ha' not
made me weep.

Flow. Sen. If he hath any grace, he 'll now repent.

Sir Arth. It moves my heart.

Weath. By my troth I must weep, I cannot
                    choose.

Flow. Jun. None but a beast would such a maid
                    misuse.

M. Flow. Content thyself, I hope to win his
    favour,
And to redeem my reputation lost:
And, gentlemen, believe me, I beseech you;
I hope your eyes shall behold such a change
As shall deceive your expectation.

Oli. I would che were ysplit now, but che believe
him.

Sir Lanc. How! believe him!

Weath. By the mackins, I do.

Sir Lanc. What do you think that e'er he will
    have grace?

Weath. By my faith it will go hard.

Oli. Well, che vore ye, he is chang'd: And, master Flowerdale, in hope you been so, hold, there's
vorty pound toward your zetting up. What! be
not ashamed; vang it, man, vang it: be a good husband, loven to your wife; and you shall not want
for vorty more, I che vor thee.

Sir Arth. My means are little, but if you'll fol-
    low me,
I will instruct you in my ablest power:
But to your wife I give this diamond,
And prove true diamond-fair in all your life.

M. Flow. Thanks, good sir Arthur: master Oli-
    ver,
You being my enemy, and grown so kind,
Binds me in all endeavour to restore—

Oli. What! restore me no restorings, man; I
have vorty pound more for Luce here; vang it:
zouth chil devy London else. What, do you think
me a mezel or a scoundrel, to throw away my
money? Che have an hundred pound more to pace
of any good spotation. I hope your under[68] and
your uncle will vollow my zamples.

Flow. Jun. You have guess'd right of me; if he
leave off this course of life, he shall be mine heir.

Sir Lanc. But he shall never get a groat of me.
A cozener, a deceiver, one that kill'd
His painful father, honest gentleman,
That pass'd the fearful danger of the sea,
To get him living, and maintain him brave.

Weath. What hath he kill'd his father?

Sir Lanc. Ay, sir, with conceit of his vile courses.

Flow. Sen. Sir, you are misinform'd.

Sir Lanc. Why, thou old knave, thou told'st me
so thyself.

Flow. Sen. I wrong'd him then: and towards my
    master's stock
There's twenty nobles for to make amends.

M. Flow. No, Kester, I have troubled thee, and
    wrong'd thee more;
What thou in love giv'st, I in love restore.

Fran. Ha, ha, sister! there you play'd bo-peep
with Tom. What shall I give her toward household? sister Delia, shall I give her my fan?

Del. You were best ask your husband.

Fran. Shall I, Tom?

Civ. Ay, do, Franke; I'll buy thee a new one
with a longer handle.[69]

Fran. A russet one, Tom.

Civ. Ay, with russet feathers.

Fran. Here, sister; there's my fan toward
household, to keep you warm.

Luce. I thank you, sister.

Weath. Why this is well; and toward fair
    Luce's stock
Here's forty shillings: and forty good shillings
    more,
I'll give her, marry. Come sir Lancelot,
I must have you friends.

Sir Lanc. Not I: all this is counterfeit; he will
consume it were it a million.

Flow. Sen. Sir, what is your daughter's dower
    worth?

Sir Lanc. Had she been married to an honest
    man,
It had been better than a thousand pound.

Flow. Sen. Pay it to him, and I'll give you my
    bond
To make her jointure better worth than three.

Sir Lanc. Your bond, sir! why, what are
    you?

Flow. Sen. One whose word in London, tho' I
    say it,
Will pass there for as much as yours.

Sir Lanc. Wert not thou late that unthrift's
    serving-man?

Flow. Sen. Look on me better, now my scar is
    off:
Ne'er muse, man, at this metamorphosy.

Sir Lanc. Master Flowerdale!

M. Flow. My father! O, I shame to look on
    him.
Pardon, dear father, the follies that are past.

Flow. Sen. Son, son, I do; and joy at this thy
    change,
And applaud thy fortune in this virtuous maid,
Whom heaven hath sent to thee to save thy soul.

Luce. This addeth joy to joy; high heaven be
    prais'd.

Weath. Master Flowerdale, welcome from death,
good master Flowerdale. 'Twas said so here, 'twas
said so here, good faith.

Flow. Sen. I caus'd that rumour to be spread
    myself,

Because I 'd see the humours of my son,
Which to relate the circumstance is needless.
And sirrah, see
You run no more into that same disease:
For he that 's once cur'd of that malady,
Of riot, swearing, drunkenness, and pride,
And falls again into the like distress,
That fever's deadly, doth till death endure:
Such men die mad, as of a calenture.

M. Flow. Heaven helping me, I'll hate the course
 as hell.

Flow. Jun. Say it. and do it, cousin, all is well.

Sir Lanc. Well, being in hope you 'll prove an
 honest man,
I take you to my favour. Brother Flowerdale,
Welcome with all my heart: I see your care
Hath brought these acts to this conclusion,
And I am glad of it. Come, let 's in, and feast.

Oli. Nay, zoft you awhile. You promis'd to
make sir Arthur and me amends: here is your
wisest daughter; see which on us she 'll have.

Sir Lanc. A God's name, you have my good will;
 get hers.

Oli. How say you then, damsel?

Del. I, sir, am yours.

Oli. Why, then send for a vicar, and chil have it
dispatched in a trice; so chil.

Del. Pardon me, sir; I mean that I am yours
In love, in duty, and affection;
But not to love as wife: it shall ne'er be said,
Delia was buried married, but a maid.

Sir Arth. Do not condemn yourself for ever, virtuous fair; you were born to love.

Oli. Why you say true, sir Arthur; she was
ybore to it, so well as her mother:—but I pray
you show us some zamples or reasons why you will
not marry?

Del. Not that I do condemn a married life,
(For 'tis no doubt a sanctimonious thing,)
But for the care and crosses of a wife;
The trouble in this world that children bring.
My vow 's in heaven, on earth to live alone;
Husbands, howsoever good, I will have none.

Oli. Why then, che will live a bachelor too.
Che zet not a vig by a wife, if a wife zet not a vig
by me.—Come, shall 's go to dinner?

Flow Sen. To-morrow I crave your companies in
 Mark-lane:
To-night we 'll frolic in master Civet's house,
And to each health drink down a full carouse.

NOTES TO LONDON PRODIGAL.

[1] *Your exhibition,* i.e. your allowance.

[2] *I grant indeed to swear is bad, but not in keeping these oaths is better.*

There seems some corruption here; perhaps we should read—but *the* not keeping those oaths is better. That is, to take an improper oath is wrong, but not to keep it shows some signs of amendment.

[3] *A colour de roy, a crimson, a sad green.*

The *colour de roy* was so named in honour of the king; a *sad green* is a grave dark green.

[4] *Kester,* i.e. an abbreviation of Christopher.

[5] *Any stintance,* i.e. any stop or remission.

[6] *By God, I assure you.*

Malone remarks, that " the sacred name is oftener introduced in this play than any that I remember to have read. Being published before the stat. 3 Jac. I., c. 21, neither the author or printer had any scruple on the subject."

[7] *High men and low men, fulloms, stop-cater-traies, and other bones of function.*

High fulloms are those dice which are loaded in such a manner as make them usually turn up four, five, or six; *low fulloms,* or low men, are those which generally run, one, two, or three. *Stop-cater-traies* were probably dice prepared in such a manner as frequently to exhibit a four and a three.

[8] *Sentences still, sweet mistress.*

Sentences are wise sayings; maxims.

[9] *You have a wit, an it were your alabaster.*

An affected simile; your wit is as beautiful, clear, and transparent as alabaster.

[10] *Thy tongue trips trenchmore.*

A reproof of his forward talkativeness; *trenchmore* was a rapid dance.

[11] *The De'nshire lad.*

The Devonshire lad; throughout this play Devonshire is used as a dissyllable.

[12] *By my fay,* i.e. by my faith.

[13] *'Soul, I think I am sure cross'd, or witch'd with an owl.*

An owl was frequently supposed to be animated by an evil spirit. This superstition is a very ancient one. See note 35, to *The Comedy of Errors.*

[14] *I would be loath to be riddled, sir.*

That is, to be questioned or sifted; in some counties a sieve is called a riddle.

[15] *I would be very glad to bestow the wine of that gentlewoman.*

To pay for what she may choose to drink; to send her a present of wine. A mode of introduction common in the time of Shakspere.

[16] *Royster,* i.e. a braggadocio or swaggerer.

[17] *A carcanet of gold.*

A *carcanet* was a necklace.

[18] *The rogue puts me in rerages for orient pearl.*

I have never met with the word *rerages,* and cannot explain it. Mr. Steevens says :—" Perhaps *rerages* has here the same meaning as *refuse.* The *rear* of an army is the *hindmost* division of it. *Rerages* therefore may signify such pearls as have been left behind, after all the better sort had been selected from them."

[19] *One of these lease-mongers, these corn-mongers.*

An allusion to the numerous monopolies so much complained of about the time that this play was written.

[20] *A wary husband,* i.e. a prudent manager.

[21] *I am a commander, sir, under the king.*

From this passage it is highly probable that the present play was written after the accession of King James. If it had been written during the reign of Elizabeth, it would in all likelihood have been " under the queen."

[22] *Press scoundrels, and thy messels.*

Such poor mean rascals as you can pick up. *Messel* was probably a corruption of *measle,* a term of contempt for a low wretch.

[23] *Press cloth and kersey, white-pot and drowsen broth.*

A contemptuous allusion to the occupation and fare of the Devonshire people; *white-pot* is a favourite dish among them; *drowsen broth* is the grounds of beer boiled up with herbs,—a common beverage among servants and others.

[24] *Well said, vlittan vlatten.*

Words expressive of contempt, apparently coined to ridicule the clothier's sounding an *f* like a *v.*

[25] *Ay, and well said cocknell, and Bow-bell too.*

A *cocknell* is an obsolete term for what we now call

a *cockney*,—a Londoner, born within the sound of Bow-bell.

26 *But honesty maintains not a French hood.*

That is, mere honesty will not provide finery and luxury. A *French hood* seems to have been a costly and fashionable garment. In Ben Jonson's *Tale of a Tub*:—

> Can you make me a lady?
> *Pol.* I can gi' you
> A silken gown, and a rich petticoat,
> And a *French-hood.*

27 *Woodcock o' my side.*

The meaning is, What! does this fool peck at me, too? A *woodcock* was a proverbial expression for a fool or dunce.

28 *Threescore pack of karsey at Blackem Hall.*

He means at *Blackwell Hall,* in London, a great repository of woollen goods.

29 *What if he should come more?*

Perhaps we should read—What if he should come *now?*

30 *I saw him the other day hold up the bucklers.*

He who was victorious in mock-combat was said to gain the bucklers. They were awarded to him as a prize.

31 *By the mouse-foot, I will.*

A ludicrous and unmeaning oath. It also occurs in *Soliman and Perseda,* 1599:—" By cock and pie, and *mouse-foot.*

32 *Take heed of cutting Flowerdale.*

A *cutter* is a swaggerer, an unprincipled ruffian.

33 *Crying, God pays all.*

That is, they never paid for anything, but spunged upon all into whose company they could intrude themselves; a practice common to the disbanded soldiers of that age.

34 *Thou art somewhat testern.*

Probably, needy-looking, shabby. A *testern* is a sixpence; it is still common to say a man is not worth sixpence, when it is intended to imply that he is almost destitute.

35 *Che vore thee,* i.e. I assure thee.

36 *I'll attach you first.*

To *attach* is a legal term meaning to arrest, to apprehend.

37 *What do you think, chil be abasselled up and down the town for a messel, and a scoundrel?*

Chil is the west-country corruption of *I will; abasselled,* is treated with contempt; a *messel* has been explained in note 22.

38 *Marry chil veeze him too and again.*

He means he will *feese* him, a cant term, meaning, beat him into shreds. To *pheeze,* or *fease,* is to separate a twist into single threads.

39 *I'll have thee go like a citizen, in a guarded gown.*

A gown with rich guards or facings seems to have been a favourite dress with the wives of wealthy citizens.

40 *A moscado coat.*

This material is mentioned in several of our old plays. So in the *Devil's Charter,* 1607—" Varlet of velvet, old heart of durance, *moccado* villain," &c.

41 *I have set down my rest thus far.*

That is, I have made up my mind to this; come to this resolution.

42 *Ay, and a better penny sister.*

That is, yes, and have something to spare.

43 *Keep you the rest for points.*

That is, literally speaking, for the tags used to fasten up the breeches; but the prudent Delia means, keep the rest for necessaries and unavoidable expenses.

44 *That's a round O.*

That is, a direct lie; a circle in arithmetic being the representative of *nothing,* unless in conjunction with other figures. These words appear to be spoken aside.

45 *And there's the fine,* i.e. there's an end.

46 *Is't possible he hath his second living?*

Is it possible that another person as abandoned as he is to be found?

47 *For all the day he humours up and down.*

That is, meditates, devises schemes.

48 *A vlowten merriment,* i.e. a flowting, or jeering merriment.

49 *I shall meet with you.*

That is, I shall retaliate, I shall be even with you.

50 *Minckins,* i.e. a diminutive of *minx.*

51 ——— *Though she had the prick And praise for a pretty wench.*

That is, though she was generally picked out and commended as a pretty girl. The comparison is borrowed from the sports of archery; the *prick* was the mark shot at.

52 *Dun is the mouse.*

A proverbial expression, the exact signification of which is lost sight of; Mr. Malone conjectures that it meant, *Peace, be still.* It occurs in *Romeo and Juliet,* see note 12 to that play. I have no authority for the supposition, but I think it was synonymous with saying, pluck up your spirits, keep a good heart. It is called the constable's own word, perhaps for this reason, that the constable might frequently say to the person whom he arrested—" I must do my duty, but do not be cast down; it may not be so bad as you expect, but, *Dun's the mouse.*"

53 *By this vrampolness.*

He means *frampoldness,* or peevishness. Thus in the

Merry Wives of Windsor, Mrs. Quickly says—" The sweet woman leads an ill-life with him ; a very *frampold* life.

[54] *To 'tach my daughter*, i.e. attach or apprehend her.

[55] *Vang thee that.*

To *vang*, in the Devonshire jargon, is to take or receive.

[56] *Help me to cheek and ears.*

From the context it appears that this was the name of a particular kind of head-dress.

[57] *I have liv'd since yesterday, two o'clock, on a spice-cake I had at a burial.*

These cakes were the usual refreshment given at funerals. Rich ones were given to the mourners, and plainer ones distributed to the populace, among whom the prodigal appears to have been one.

[58] *The two coney-catchers.*

Coney-catchers were cheats, deceivers of simple people.

[59] *A cockatrice*, i.e. a harlot.

[60] *A garden house.*

A summer-house surrounded by trees and flowers; these places were much used in former times for stolen meetings in affairs of gallantry.

[61] *So young an armin.*

That is, a beggar. *Arm* in Dutch means poor and needy. *Arm-worden*, to grow poor ; *arm-maken*, to impoverish.

[62] *Dat vas not scone.*

Schön, that is good or pretty.

[63] *I might have rid out.*

That is, might have been a highwayman ; a midnight ride was a cant term for a plundering expedition.

[64] —————— *And master Weathercock,*
To make my grounded resolution.

There is some inaccuracy here which renders the passage unintelligible. Malone suggests that probably the author wrote—

—————— *And by this artifice*
To *shake* my grounded resolution.

The words *master Weathercock* might have been caught by the compositor from the preceding line, and those of *by this artifice*, or some similar expression, thus omitted.

[65] *Snick up*, i.e. hang yourself.

[66] *Have me no oder way dan you have him.*

That is, take me the same way that you take him ; I will go with him.

[67] *A tocking mill*, i.e. a ducking mill, a fulling mill.

[68] *I hope your under.*

Probably a corruption of *vader*, meaning Sir Lancelot.

[69] *I'll buy thee a new one with a longer handle.*

In the age of Elizabeth fans were frequently made with silver handles, and the upper part of them composed of feathers.

H. T.

The Puritan: or, the Widow of Watling Street

Omitted from the folios of 1623 and 1632, *The Puritan* was first claimed as a work by Shakespeare in a list of plays offered for sale by the bookseller Edward Archer in 1656; eight years later it was accepted into the canon of his work and published in the Third Folio.

The full title of the play is *The Puritan: or, the Widow of Watling Street*. According to the investigation by Baldwin Maxwell (27), the neighborhood of Watling Street was a section heavily inhabited by Puritans. Lady Plus, her children, her brother-in-law, and her servants are all said to be of the society or brotherhood of Puritans. The servants are named Nicholas St. Antlings, Frailty, and Simon St. Mary-Overies. The name of the first servant was clearly drawn from the church which stood in Watling Street—St. Antlings (or St. Antholins), a center of Puritanism, later described by Sir William Dugdale as "the grand nursery whence most of the seditious preachers were after sent abroad throughout England to poison the people with their antimonarchial principles."

The play's alliterative subtitle may derive from a broadside ballad, both parts of which were entered on the Stationers' Register in 1597. To this broadside, however, the play owes little else. Part I of the ballad narrates how a father, tired of his son's dissolute practices, had refused to release him from debtors' prison but is persuaded by his wife to name him co-executor with her of his will. Upon the father's death, the son seeks to secure the whole estate for himself by accusing his mother of being a harlot and his two sisters bastards. In Part II, the widow appeals to the Council, whose sober countenances so frighten the false witnesses the son has gathered that they confess their earlier perjury. The son, sent to prison, hangs himself.

Slight indeed is the ballad's similarity to the play. In both, a recently made widow has daughters and one son who has no affection for his father. The one likeness worthy of comment is perhaps that both sons claim knowledge of the law. The son in the ballad, recognizing that a widow is permitted one-third of her husband's moveables, at first declares

> I grant what law does crave;
> But not a penny more will I
> discharge of my legacy . . .

and Edmond, in a soliloquy closing the first scene of the play, asserts

> I know the law in that point; no attorney can gull me. . . . I'll rule the roast myself. . . . the law's in mine own hands now. Nay, now I know my strength, I'll be strong enough for my mother, I warrant you.

In Maxwell's view, the implication of Edmond's speech is certainly that he will proceed to try to secure for himself the greater part of his father's estate. But he does not do so, and as the play progresses he bears no further resemblance to the son in the ballad. However, that he should speak such lines in so emphatic a place as a soliloquy that closes the opening scene suggests that the dramatist may at first have intended to give Edmond a more prominent role in the play and one more nearly resembling that of the wicked son of the ballad.

One of the chief features of *The Puritan* is the bitterness in its attacks upon the Puritans. There are repeated references to their hypocrisy and to their fondness for long sermons. Lady Plus's first husband, affectionately described by her as one who had overthrown the rightful heir to get lands and who "would deceive all the world to get riches" [I. i] would, she says, "keep church so duly; rise early, before his servants, and even for religious haste, go ungartered, unbuttoned, nay (sir reverence) untrussed, to morning prayer. . . . dine quickly upon high days; and when I had great guests, would even shame me, and rise from the table, to get a good seat at an afternoon Sermon." [II. i]

In this same period, Shakespeare, in his undoubted plays, makes sport of his adversaries the Puritans with incisive humor. In *As You Like It*, we find an allusion to them, when Rosalind says, "O most gentle pulpiter! what tedious homily of love have you wearied your parishioners withal, and never cried, 'Have patience, good people'!" [III. ii. 163–66]. In his next play, *Twelfth Night,* the typical solemn and self-righteous Puritan is held up to ridicule in the Don Quixote–like personage of the moralizing and pompous Malvolio, who is launched upon a billowy sea of burlesque situations. When Sir Toby has made some inquiry about Malvolio, the following conversation takes place:

MARIA: Marry, sir, sometimes he is a kind of Puritan.

SIR ANDREW: O! If I thought that, I'd beat him like a dog!

SIR TOBY: What, for being a Puritan? Thy exquisite reason, dear knight?

SIR ANDREW: I have no exquisite reason for 't, but I have reason good enough.

MARIA: The devil a Puritan that he is, or anything constantly but a time-pleaser; an affection'd ass, that cons state without book and utters it by great swarths. . . . [II. iii. 151–62]

So far as we know, Shakespeare took no interest whatever in any ecclesiastical or religious movements. He came into contact with Puritanism only in its narrow and fanatical hatred of his art, and in its severely intolerant condemnation and punishment of moral, and especially of sexual, frailties. All he saw was its Pharisaical aspect and its virtue that was often enough only simulated.

It was his indignation at this hypocritical piety that led him to write *Measure for Measure*. He treated the subject as he did because the interests of the theatre demanded that the woof of comedy should be interwoven with the severe and somber warp of tragedy. But one feels throughout, even in the comic episodes, Shakespeare's burning wrath at the moral hypocrisy of the chief character, the judge of public morality, what Georg Brandes (7) calls "the hard and stern *Censor morum*," who in his moral fanaticism believes that he can root out vice by persecuting its tools, and imagines that he can purify and reform society by punishing every transgression, however natural and comparatively harmless, as a capital crime. *Measure for Measure* shows us how this puritanical dissembler, as soon as a purely sensual passion takes possession of him, does not hesitate to commit, under the pretense of piety, a crime against real morality, in which such a man's desire, if it meets with opposition, reveals in him quite another being—a villain, a hypocrite—who allows himself actions worse than those which, in the calm superiority of a spotless conscience, he has hitherto punished in others with the utmost severity. It was this type of man who, in Shakespeare's view, exemplified the Puritan mentality.

Historically according to Marchette (11), there were various sects of Puritans, including those who wished to purify the Church of England from the inside and those who wished another kind of state church entirely; but the distinguishing mark of any Puritan was his alarming sense of sin. In his diary, he would even reproach himself for his adulterous dreams, and his waking life was spent in constant struggle to overcome the temptations of the flesh by hard work and prayer. Dancing was a very unsafe occupation for the godly, since it turned their thoughts in the wrong direction, and even music tended to incline the thoughts of its hearers to licentiousness. But nothing was better calculated to kindle the fire of inordinate lust in the tender minds of the young than to let them go to stage plays, and the Puritan opposition to the theatre ultimately became implacable. They firmly believed that "horrible enormities and swelling sins" were shown on the stage, and that the theatre as a whole was a sink of "theft and whoredom, pride and prodigality, villainy and blasphemy." To a Puritan, soberly intent upon the saving of his soul, there could hardly be worse sin than to indulge carnal desire by going to see a play; and, in time, the Puritan movement gathered sufficient force to destroy the theatre of England entirely.

In *A Mad World, My Masters*, Thomas Middleton epitomizes the situation of the theatre and actors at this time, particularly in regard to Puritans, when, in answer to his servant's announcement:

> There are certain players come to town, sir, and desire to interlude before your worship

Sir Bounteous says:

> Players? By the mass, they are welcome; they'll grace my entertainment well. But for certain players, there you lie, boy; they were never more uncertain in their lives. Now up and now down, they know not when to play, where to play, nor what to play; not when to play for fearful fools, where to play for Puritan fools, nor what to play for critical fools. Go, call 'em in. . . .

The actual habits of the audience in a London theatre may be surmised from more or less graphic accounts given by contemporary satirists. Stephen Gosson, for example, in *The School of Abuse* (1579) writes:

> In our assemblies at plays in London, you shall see such heaving and shoving, such itching and shouldering to sit by women; such care for their garments, that they may not be trod on; such eyes to their laps, that no chips light in them; such pillows to their backs, that they take no hurt; such masking in their ears, I know not what; such playing at foot-saunt without cards; such tickling, such toying, such smiling, such winking, and such manning them home when their sports are ended, that it is a right comedy to mark their behavior, to watch their conceits, as the cat for the mouse, as good as a course at the game itself to dog them a little, or follow aloof by the print of their feet and so discover by slot where the deer takes soil.

Philip Stubbes's *Anatomy of Abuses* (1583), may be quoted to like purpose:

> But mark the flocking and running to Theatres and Curtains, daily and hourly, night and day, time and tide, to see Plays and Interludes, where such wanton gestures, such bawdy speeches, such laughing and leering, such kissing and bussing, such clipping and culling, such winking and

glancing of wanton eyes and the like is used as is wonderful to behold. Then these goodly pageants being ended, every mate sorts to his mate, every one brings another homeward of their way very friendly, and in their secret conclaves they play the sodomites or worse.

Fortunately, however, this Puritan attitude towards playgoing did not find much support in the people of London, though it had the full support of the London Council. The mayor and the aldermen were not at this time Puritans; but they were all businessmen who were sufficiently prosperous to be able to afford politics, and as businessmen they took a very unfavorable view of the acting profession. Actors did not sell a legitimate, visible commodity or sell it under the rules of any guild. Consequently they were parasites or, to use a favorite phrase of the period, "caterpillars of the commonwealth," strutting about in fine clothes, which they got by luring the pennies out of the pockets of simple-minded apprentices who should have been home or working. It would even have been better for the apprentices if they had spent their money in taverns; for although the London Council or the Puritans did not necessarily encourage drinking, the taverners were at least selling a legitimate commodity and operating under "legitimate rules." Actors and dramatists offered no legitimate commodity and, in the view of the Puritan, had no place in any well-ordered Christian society.

Ironically, however, these pulpit attacks against the stage and its adherents had a certain promotional value to a manager who was trying to fill a large theatre; for the preachers depicted the sinful delights of that "gorgeous playing place" with such fascinated horror that they must have provided an excellent advertisement for the theatre. As the sober journal of Sir Roger Wilbraham indicates, the Elizabethan businessman was well aware of the value of this kind of publicity. He relates the case of a printer who found himself loaded with unsold copies of a certain book. "He caused the preacher in his sermon to inveigh against the vanity thereof; since which it has been six times under press, so much was it in request."

George Steevens, fresh from editing the plays of Shakespeare, contributed to an edition of *The Puritan* a lengthy list of verbal parallels between it and undoubted plays of Shakespeare, particularly *Macbeth*. Both E. K. Chambers and Baldwin Maxwell identify a passage in *The Puritan* as a probable allusion to *Macbeth*, which would seem to date the comedy no earlier than late 1606. Elated by what he regards as truly miraculous acts by Pyeboard and the captain—the recovery of his lost chain and the apparent raising of the dead corporal—Sir Godfrey at the end of Act IV, Scene iii, invites all present to a banquet:

Ay, and a banquet ready by this time, master sheriff; to which I most cheerfully invite you, and your late prisoner there. See you this goodly chain, sir? Mum! no more words; 'twas lost and is found again. Come, my inestimable bullies, we'll talk of your noble acts in sparkling charnico; and instead of a jester, we'll have the ghost in the white sheet sit at the upper end of the table.

To Chambers and Maxwell it is certainly not beyond question that there is an intended allusion to the ghost of Banquo in Sir Godfrey's promise to "have the ghost in the white sheet sit at the upper end of the table." His remark springs naturally from the event. Others than Sir Godfrey refer to the corporal as a ghost, because all but Pyeboard, who had administered the sleeping potion, assume that he has been raised from the dead. As the whole situation is part of the plan prepared by Pyeboard and as no device is more common among Elizabethan dramatists than the clearing of the stage by an invitation to dinner, it seems certain that we have here a deliberate reference to the appearance of Banquo's ghost at Macbeth's feast. On the other hand, the startling effectiveness of the banquet scene in *Macbeth,* more clearly alluded to in Francis Beaumont and John Fletcher's *Knight of the Burning Pestle* (1607), might tempt one to see an allusion here if it could be proved that *The Puritan* was later than *Macbeth.*

A date no earlier than 1606 could be definitely established for *The Puritan* if, as Maxwell speculates, it could be shown that Shakespeare drew upon *The Merry Conceited Jests of George Peele*, which was entered upon the Stationers' Register in 1605, and presumably was printed shortly there-after (although the earliest extant edition of the *Jests* carries the date 1607). The scholar of *The Puritan*, George Pyeboard, was, of course, intended to be recognized as George Peele (Master of Arts from Oxford, dramatist, and "the very artifex of poetry," who had died about 1597). A "peel" is a "pie-board," and is defined by Webster's as a "spade-shaped instrument used chiefly by bakers (as for getting loaves and pies into and out of an oven)." It may be possible that the jests of George Pyeboard as presented in *The Puritan* provided the original suggestion for a jestbook and that the compiler, taking at least two jests from the play, hastily brought together a number of others, some perhaps based on stories told of Peele, others previously un-connected with him.

The main subject of *The Puritan*, in which a widow and her daughters all make protestations against matrimony but finally succumb, is the conjuring tricks of an Oxford scholar, like those of the Merry Devil of Edmonton. Similarly Thomas Dekker, Middleton, and Fletcher all use the theme of the widow hunt. For example, *Keep The Widow Waking*, a lost play, de-picted the contemporary public scandal in which a wealthy woman was trapped into matrimony by a schemer.

Finally A. W. von Schlegel (39), seeking to explain the change in Shakes-peare's style in *The Puritan,* suggests that the poet might have wished for once to write a play in the style of Ben Jonson, thus accounting for the difference between the present piece and his usual manner.

PERSONS REPRESENTED.

————◆————

SIR GODFREY PLUS, *Brother-in-Law to the* Widow Plus.

Appears, Act I. sc. 1. Act II. sc. 1. Act III. sc. 3; sc. 6. Act IV. sc. 2; sc. 3. Act V. sc. 4

EDMOND, *Son to the* Widow.

Appears, Act I. sc. 1. Act III. sc. 6. Act IV. sc. 2; sc. 3. Act V. sc. 1; sc. 4.

SIR OLIVER MUCKHILL, *a rich City Knight, and Suitor to the* Widow.

Appears, Act II. sc. 1. Act IV. sc. 2. Act V. sc. 3; sc. 4.

SIR JOHN PENNYDUB, *a Country Knight, and Suitor to* Mary.

Appears, Act II. sc. 1. Act IV. sc. 1. Act V. sc. 2; sc. 4.

SIR ANDREW TIPSTAFF, *a Courtier, and Suitor to* Frances.

Appears, Act II. sc. 1. Act IV. sc. 2. Act V. sc. 3; sc. 4.

GEORGE PYEBOARD, *a Scholar.*

Appears, Act I. sc. 2; sc. 4. Act II. sc. 1. Act III. sc. 1; sc. 2; sc. 4; sc. 5; sc. 6. Act IV. sc. 2; sc. 3. Act V. sc. 1; sc. 4.

CAPTAIN IDLE, *a Highwayman.*

Appears, Act I. sc. 2; sc. 4. Act III. sc. 6. Act. IV. sc. 2; sc. 3. Act V. sc. 1; sc. 4.

PUTTOCK,
RAVENSHAW, } Sheriff's *Serjeants.*

DOGSON, *a Catchpole.*

Appear, Act III. sc. 4; sc. 5.

CORPORAL OATH, *a vain-glorious fellow.*

Appears, Act I. sc. 3; sc. 4. Act III. sc. 1. Act IV. sc. 3.

NICHOLAS ST. ANTLINGS, *a Servant to* Lady Plus *and* Sir Godfrey.

Appears, Act I. sc. 3; sc. 4. Act II. sc. 2. Act III. sc. 3. Act IV. sc. 2; sc. 3. Act V. sc. 4.

SIMON ST. MARY-OVERIES, *Servant to* Lady Plus *and* Sir Godfrey.

Appears, Act I. sc. 3. Act II. sc. 1. Act III. sc. 1.

FRAILTY, *Servant to* Lady Plus *and* Sir Godfrey.

Appears, Act I. sc. 3. Act II. sc. 1. Act III. sc. 1; sc. 3. Act IV. sc. 2; sc. 3. Act V. sc. 1; sc. 4.

PETER SKIRMISH, *an old Soldier.*

Appears, Act I. sc. 2; sc. 4. Act III. sc. 1. Act IV. sc. 3. Act V. sc. 3; sc. 4.

A NOBLEMAN.

Appears, Act V. sc. 4.

A GENTLEMAN.

Appears, Act III. sc. 5.

THE SHERIFF OF LONDON.

Appears, Act IV. sc. 3.

LADY PLUS, *a Citizen's Widow.*

Appears, Act I. sc. 1. Act II. sc. 1. Act III. sc. 3. Act IV. sc. 2; sc. 3. Act V. sc. 4.

FRANCES, *her eldest Daughter.*

Appears, Act I. sc. 1. Act II. sc. 1. Act III. sc. 3. Act IV. sc. 2; sc. 3. Act V. sc. 4.

MARY, *the* Widow's *youngest Daughter.*

Appears, Act I. sc. 1. Act II. sc. 1. Act III. sc. 3. Act IV. sc. 1. Act V. sc. 2; sc. 4.

Sheriff's Officers, Keeper of the Marshalsea Prison, Musicians, and Attendants.

SCENE.—LONDON.

The Puritan: or, the Widow of Watling Street.

ACT I.

SCENE I.—*A Garden behind the* Widow's *House.*

Enter the Widow Plus, Frances, Mary, Sir Godfrey, *and* Edmond, *all in mourning; the latter in a Cyprus Hat* [1]: *the* Widow *wringing her hands, and bursting out into passion, as newly come from the burial of her* Husband.

Wid. O, that ever I was born, that ever I was born!

Sir God. Nay, good sister, dear sister, sweet sister, be of good comfort; show yourself a woman now or never.

Wid. O, I have lost the dearest man, I have buried the sweetest husband, that ever lay by woman.

Sir God. Nay, give him his due, he was indeed an honest, virtuous, discreet, wise man. He was my brother, as right as right.

Wid. O, I shall never forget him, never forget him; he was a man so well given to a woman. Oh!

Sir God. Nay, but kind sister, I could weep as much as any woman; but alas, our tears cannot call him again. Methinks you are well read, sister, and know that death is as common as *homo,* a common name to all men. A man shall be taken when he's making water. Nay, did not the learned parson, master Pigman, tell us even now,—that all flesh is frail—We are born to die—Man has but a time—with such-like deep and profound persuasions? as he is a rare fellow, you know, and an excellent reader. And for example, (as there are examples abundance,) did not sir Humphrey Bubble die t'other day? There's a lusty widow! why she cry'd not above half an hour. For shame, for shame!—Then follow'd him old master Fulsome, the usurer: there's a wise widow; why she cry'd ne'er a whit at all.

Wid. O rank not me with those wicked women; I had a husband out-shin'd 'em all.

Sir God. Ay that he did, i'faith; he out-shin'd 'em all.

Wid. Dost thou stand there, and see us all weep, and not once shed a tear for thy father's death? oh thou ungracious son and heir thou!

Edm. Troth, mother, I should not weep I'm sure. I am past a child, I hope, to make all my old schoolfellows laugh at me; I should be mock'd, so I should. Pray let one of my sisters weep for me; I'll laugh as much for her another time.

Wid. O thou past-grace, thou! Out of my sight, thou graceless imp! thou grievest me more than the death of thy father. O thou stubborn only son! Hadst thou such an honest man to thy father —that would deceive all the world to get riches for thee, and canst thou not afford a little salt water? He that so wisely did quite overthrow the right heir of those lands, which now you respect not: up every morning betwixt four and five; so duly at Westminster-hall every term-time, with all his cards and writings,[2] for thee, thou wicked Absalon: O dear husband!

Edm. Weep, quoth-a? I protest I am glad he's church'd; for now he's gone, I shall spend in quiet.

Fran. Dear mother, pray cease; half your tears suffice;
'Tis time for you to take truce with your eyes:
Let me weep now.

Wid. O such a dear knight, such a sweet husband have I lost, have I lost! If blessed be the corse, the rain rains upon,[3] he had it pouring down.

Sir God. Sister, be of good cheer. We are all mortal ourselves; I come upon you freshly, I ne'er speak without comfort. Hear me what I shall say:—My brother has left you wealthy; you're rich.

Wid. Oh!

Sir God. I say you're rich: you are also fair.

Wid. Oh.

Sir God. Go to, you're fair; you cannot smother it; beauty will come to light. Nor are your years

231

so far enter'd with you, but that you will be sought after, and may very well answer another husband. The world is full of fine gallants; choice enough, sister; for what should we do with all our knights, I pray, but to marry rich widows, wealthy citizens' widows, lusty fair-brow'd ladies? Go to, be of good comfort, I say; leave snobbing and weeping.[4]—Yet my brother was a kind-hearted man. I would not have the elf see me now.[5]—Come, pluck up a woman's heart. Here stand your daughters, who be well estated, and at maturity will also be enquir'd after with good husbands; so all these tears shall be soon dry'd up, and a better world than ever. What, woman! you must not weep still; he's dead, he's buried:—yet I cannot choose but weep for him.

Wid. Marry again! no, let me be buried quick
     then!
And that same part o' the choir whereon I tread
To such intent, O may it be my grave!
And that the priest may turn his wedding prayers,
Even with a breath, to funeral dust and ashes!
O, out of a million of millions, I should ne'er find such a husband; he was unmatchable, unmatchable. Nothing was too hot, nor too dear for me. I could not speak of that one thing that I had not. Beside, I had keys of all, kept all, receiv'd all, had money in my purse, spent what I would, went abroad when I would, came home when I would, and did all what I would. O, my sweet husband! I shall never have the like.

Sir God. Sister, ne'er say so. He was an honest brother of mine, and so; and you may light upon one as honest again, or one as honest again may light upon you: that's the properer phrase indeed.

Wid. Never: O, if you love me, urge it not.
O may I be the by-word of the world,   [*Kneels.*
The common talk at table in the mouth
Of every groom and waiter, if e'er more
I entertain the carnal suit of man.

Mary. I must kneel down for fashion too.

Fran. And I, whom never man as yet hath
     seal'd,
Even in this depth of general sorrow, vow
Never to marry, to sustain such loss
As a dear husband seems to be, once dead.

Mary. I lov'd my father well too; but to say,
Nay, vow, I would not marry for his death,
Sure I should speak false Latin, should I not?
I'd as soon vow never to come in bed.
Tut! woman must live by the quick, and not by
     the dead.

Wid. Dear copy of my husband, O let me kiss
     thee!   [*Kisses her husband's picture.*

How like him is this model! This brief picture
Quickens my tears: my sorrows are renew'd
At this fresh sight.

Sir God. Sister—

Wid. Away!
All honesty with him is turn'd to clay.
O my sweet husband! Oh.

Fran. My dear father! [*Exeunt* WID. *and* FRAN.

Mary. Here's a puling indeed! I think my mother weeps for all the women that ever buried husbands; for if from time to time all the widowers' tears[6] in England had been bottled up, I do not think all would have fill'd a three-halfpenny bottle. Alas, a small matter bucks a handkerchief![7] and sometimes the 'spital stands too nigh Saint Thomas a' Waterings.[8] Well, I can mourn in good sober sort as well as another; but where I spend one tear for a dead father, I could give twenty kisses for a quick husband.   [*Exit.*

Sir God. Well, go thy ways, old sir Godfrey, and thou may'st be proud on't; thou hast a kind loving sister-in-law. How constant! how passionate! how full of April the poor soul's eyes are! Well, I would my brother knew on't; he should then know what a kind wife he had left behind him. 'Truth, an 'twere not for shame that the neighbours at the next garden should hear me, between joy and grief I should e'en cry outright.   [*Exit.*

Edm. So; a fair riddance; My father's laid in dust; his coffin and he is like a whole meat-pie, and the worms will cut him up shortly. Farewell, old dad, farewell! I'll be curb'd in no more. I perceive a son and heir may be quickly made a fool, and he will be one; but I'll take another order.[9] Now she would have me weep for him forsooth; and why? because he cozen'd the right heir being a fool, and bestow'd those lands on me his eldest son; and therefore I must weep for him; ha, ha! Why, all the world knows, as long as 'twas his pleasure to get me, 'twas his duty to get for me: I know the law in that point; no attorney can gull me. Well, my uncle is an old ass, and an admirable coxcomb. I'll rule the roast myself; I'll be kept under no more; I know what I may do well enough by my father's copy: the law's in mine own hands now. Nay, now I know my strength, I'll be strong enough for my mother, I warrant you.   [*Exit.*

SCENE II.—*A Street.*

Enter PYEBOARD, *and* SKIRMISH.

Pye. What's to be done now, old lad of war?

Thou that were wont to be as hot as a turnspit, as nimble as a fencer, and as lousy as a school-master, now thou art put to silence like a sectary. War sits now like a justice of peace, and does nothing. Where be your muskets, calivers and hot-shots? in Long-lane, at pawn, at pawn? Now keys are your only guns; key-guns, key-guns,—and bawds the gunners; who are your sentinels in peace, and stand ready charg'd to give warning with hems, hums, and pocky coughs: only your chambers are licens'd to play upon you,[10] and drabs enow to give fire to 'em.

Skir. Well, I cannot tell, but I am sure it goes wrong with me; for since the ceasure of the wars I have spent above a hundred crowns out of purse. I have been a soldier any time this forty years; and now I perceive an old soldier and an old courtier have both one destiny, and in the end turn both into hob-nails.

Pye. Pretty mystery for a beggar; for indeed a hob-nail is the true emblem of a beggar's shoe-sole.

Skir. I will not say but that war is a blood-sucker, and so; but in my conscience, (as there is no soldier but has a piece of one, though it be full of holes, like a shot ancient;[11] no matter,—'twill serve to swear by,) in my conscience, I think some kind of peace has more hidden oppressions, and violent heady sins, (though looking of a gentle nature,) than a profess'd war.

Pye. 'Troth, and for mine own part, I am a poor gentleman, and a scholar; I have been matriculated in the university, wore out six gowns there, seen some fools, and some scholars, some of the city, and some of the country, kept order, went bare-headed over the quadrangle, eat my commons with a good stomach, and battled with discretion;[12] at last, having done many sleights and tricks to maintain my wit in use, (as my brain would never endure me to be idle,) I was expell'd the university, only for stealing a cheese out of Jesus college.

Skir. Is 't possible?

Pye. O! there was one Welshman (God forgive him!) pursued it hard, and never left, till I turn'd my staff toward London; where when I came, all my friends were pit-hol'd, gone to graves; as indeed there was but a few left before. Then was I turn'd to my wits, to shift in the world, to tower, among sons and heirs,[13] and fools, and gulls, and ladies' eldest sons; to work upon nothing, to feed out of flint: and ever since has my belly been much beholden to my brain. But now to return to you, old Skirmish:—I say as you say, and for my part wish a turbulency in the world; for I have nothing to lose but my wits, and I think they are as mad as they will be: and to strengthen your argument the more, I say an honest war is better than a bawdy peace. As touching my profession; the multiplicity of scholars, hatch'd and nourish'd in the idle calms of peace, makes them, like fishes, one devour another; and the community of learning has so play'd upon affections, that thereby almost religion is come about to phantasy, and discredited by being too much spoken of, in so many and mean mouths. I myself being a scholar and a graduate, have no other comfort by my learning, but the affection of my words, to know how, scholar-like, to name what I want; and can call myself a beggar both in Greek and Latin. And therefore not to cog with peace, I'll not be afraid to say, 'tis a great breeder, but a barren nourisher; a great getter of children, which must either be thieves or rich men, knaves or beggars.

Skir. Well, would I had been born a knave then, when I was born a beggar! for if the truth was known, I think I was begot when my father had never a penny in his purse.

Pye. Puh! faint not, old Skirmish; let this warrant thee—*facilis descensus Averni*—'tis an easy journey to a knave; thou may'st be a knave when thou wilt: and Peace is a good madam to all other professions, and an errant drab to us. Let us handle her accordingly, and by our wits thrive in despite of her: For since the law lives by quarrels, the courtier by smooth good-morrows, and every profession makes itself greater by imperfections, why not we then by shifts, wiles, and forgeries? And seeing our brains are our only patrimonies, let's spend with judgment; not like a desperate son and heir, but like a sober and discreet Templar: one that will never march beyond the bounds of his allowance. And for our thriving means, thus:—I myself will put on the deceit of a fortune-teller.

Skir. A fortune-teller? Very proper.

Pye. And you a figure-caster, or a conjurer.

Skir. A conjurer?

Pye. Let me alone; I'll instruct you, and teach you to deceive all eyes, but the devil's.

Skir. O ay, for I would not deceive him, an I could choose, of all others.

Pye. Fear not, I warrant you. And so by those means we shall help one another to patients; as the condition of the age affords creatures enough for cunning to work upon.

Skir. O wondrous! new fools and fresh asses.

Pye. O, fit, fit; excellent.

Skir. What, in the name of conjuring?

Pye. My memory greets me happily with an admirable subject to graze upon. The lady widow, whom of late I saw weeping in her garden for the death of her husband, sure she has but a waterish soul, and half of 't by this time is dropp'd out of her eyes: device well manag'd may do good upon her: it stands firm; my first practice shall be there.

Skir. You have my voice, George.

Pye. She has a grey gull to her brother, a fool to her only son, and an ape to her youngest daughter. I overheard them severally, and from their words I'll derive my device; and thou, old Peter Skirmish, shalt be my second in all sleights.

Skir. Ne'er doubt me, George Pyeboard;—only you must teach me to conjure.

Pye. Puh! I'll perfect thee, Peter: How now! what's he?

[IDLE *pinioned, and attended by a Guard of Sheriff's Officers, passes over the Stage.*

Skir. O George! this sight kills me. 'Tis my sworn brother, captain Idle.

Pye. Captain Idle!

Skir. Apprehended for some felonious act or other. He has started out,—has made a night on't,—lack'd silver. I cannot but commend his resolution; he would not pawn his buff-jerkin, I would either some of us were employed, or might pitch our tents at usurers' doors, to kill the slaves as they peep out at the wicket.

Pye. Indeed, those are our ancient enemies; they keep our money in their hands, and make us to be hang'd for robbing of them. But come, let's follow after to the prison, and know the nature of his offence; and what we can stead him in, he shall be sure of it: and I'll uphold it still, that a charitable knave is better than a soothing Puritan. [*Exeunt.*

SCENE III.—*A Street.*

Enter NICHOLAS ST. ANTLINGS, SIMON ST. MARY-OVERIES, *and* FRAILTY, *in black scurvy mourning Coats, with Books at their Girdles, as coming from Church.* *To them* CORPORAL OATH.

Nich. What, corporal Oath! I am sorry we have met with you, next our hearts: you are the man that we are forbidden to keep company withal. We must not swear I can tell you, and you have the name for swearing.

Sim. Ay, corporal Oath, I would you would do so much as forsake us, sir: we cannot abide you; we must not be seen in your company.

Frail. There is none of us, I can tell you, but shall be soundly whipp'd for swearing.

Oath. Why how now, "we three?"[14] Puritanical scrape-shoes, flesh o'Good-Fridays, a hand. [*Shakes them by the hand.*

All. Oh!

Oath. Why Nicholas St. Antlings, Simon St. Mary-Overies, has the devil possess'd you, that you swear no better? you half-christen'd catamites, you un-godmother'd varlets.[15] Does the first lesson teach you to be proud, and the second to be coxcombs, proud coxcombs, not once to do duty to a man of mark?

Frail. A man of mark, quoth-a! I do not think he can show a beggar's noble.[16]

Oath. A corporal, a commander, one of spirit, that is able to blow you up all three with your books at your girdles.

Sim. We are not taught to believe that, sir; for we know the breath of man is weak. [*OATH breathes on* FRAIL.

Frail. Foh! you lie, Nicholas; for here's one strong enough. Blow us up, quoth-a! he may well blow me above twelve-score off on him: I warrant, if the wind stood right, a man might smell him from the top of Newgate to the leads of Ludgate.

Oath. Sirrah, thou hollow book of wax-candle—

Nich. Ay, you may say what you will, so you swear not.

Oath. I swear by the—

Nich. Hold, hold, good corporal Oath; for if you swear once, we shall all fall down in a swoon presently.

Oath. I must and will swear, you quivering coxcombs: my captain is imprison'd; and by Vulcan's leather codpiece-point—

Nich. O Simon, what an oath was there!

Frail. If he should chance to break it, the poor man's breeches would fall down about his heels; for Venus allows him but one point to his hose.

Oath. With these my bully feet I will thump ope the prison doors, and brain the keeper with the begging-box, but I'll set my honest sweet captain Idle at liberty.

Nich. How, captain Idle? my old aunt's son, my dear kinsman, in cappadochio?[17]

Oath. Ay, thou church-peeling, thou holy paring, religious outside, thou. If thou hadst any grace in thee, thou wouldst visit him, relieve him, swear to get him out.

Nich. Assure you, corporal, indeed-la, 'tis the first time I heard on't.

Oath. Why do 't now then, marmozet.[18] Bring forth thy yearly wages; let not a commander perish.

Sim. But if he be one of the wicked, he shall perish.

Nich. Well, corporal, I 'll e'en along with you, to visit my kinsman; if I can do him any good, I will: but I have nothing for him. Simon St. Mary-Overies and Frailty, pray make a lie for me to the knight my master, old sir Godfrey.

Oath. A lie! may you lie then?

Frail. O ay, we may lie, but we must not swear.

Sim. True, we may lie with our neighbour's wife; but we must not swear we did so.

Oath. O, an excellent tag of religion!

Nich. O, Simon, I have thought upon a sound excuse; it will go current: say that I am gone to a fast.

Sim. To a fast? very good.

Nich. Ay, to a fast, say, with master Full-belly the minister.

Sim. Master Full-belly? an honest man: he feeds the flock well, for he 's an excellent feeder.

[*Exeunt* OATH *and* NICH.

Frail. O ay; I have seen him eat a whole pig, and afterward fall to the pettitoes.

[*Exeunt* SIM. *and* FRAIL.

SCENE IV.—*A Room in the Marshalsea Prison.*

Enter IDLE; *to him afterwards* PYEBOARD *and* SKIRMISH.

Pye. [*Within.*] Pray turn the key.

Skir. [*Within.*] Turn the key, I pray.

Idle. Who should those be? I almost know their voices. [PYE. *and* SKIR. *enter.*] O my friends! you are welcome to a smelling room here. You newly took leave of the air; has it not a strange savour?

Pye. As all prisons have, smells of sundry wretches, who, though departed, leave their scents behind them. By gold, captain, I am sincerely sorry for thee.

Idle. By my troth, George, I thank thee; but pish—what must be, must be.

Skir. Captain, what do you lie in for? is 't great? what's your offence?

Idle. Faith, my offence is ordinary, common; a high-way: and I fear me my penalty will be ordinary and common too;—a halter.

Pye. Nay, prophesy not so ill; it shall go hard but I'll shift for thy life.

Idle. Whether I live or die, thou'rt an honest George. I'll tell you. Silver flow'd not with me, as it had done; for now the tide runs to bawds and flatterers. I had a start out, and by chance set upon a fat steward, thinking his purse had been as pursy as his body; and the slave had about him but the poor purchase of ten groats. Notwithstanding being descried, pursued, and taken, I know the law is so grim, in respect of many desperate, unsettled soldiers, that I fear me I shall dance after their pipe for't.[19]

Skir. I am twice sorry for you, captain; first, that your purchase was so small, and now that your danger is so great.

Idle. Pish; the worst is but death. Have you a pipe of tobacco about you?

Skir. I think I have thereabouts about me.

Idle. Here's a clean gentleman too, to receive.[20]

[IDLE *smokes a pipe.*

Pye. Well, I must cast about some happy sleight, Work brain, that ever didst thy master right.

[OATH *and* NICH. *knock within.*

Oath. [*Within.*] Keeper, let the key be turn'd.

Nich. [*Within.*] Ay, I pray, master keeper, give us a cast of your office.

Enter OATH *and* NICHOLAS.

Idle. How now? More visitants? What, corporal Oath?

Pye. ⎫
Skir. ⎬ Corporal.

Oath. In prison, honest captain? this must not be.

Nich. How do you, captain kinsman?

Idle. Good coxcomb, what makes that pure, starch'd fool here?

Nich. You see, kinsman, I am somewhat bold to call in, and see how you do. I heard you were safe enough; and I was very glad on't, that it was no worse.

Idle. This is a double torture now. This fool, by the book, doth vex me more than my imprisonment. What meant you, corporal, to hook him hither?

Oath. Who, he? he shall relieve thee, and supply thee; I'll make him do't.

Idle. Fie, what vain breath you spend? He supply! I'll sooner expect mercy from an usurer when my bond's forfeited, sooner kindness from a lawyer when my money's spent, nay, sooner charity from the devil, than good from a Puritan. I'll look for relief from him when Lucifer is restor'd to his blood,[21] and in heaven again.

Nich. I warrant my kinsman's talking of me, for my left ear burns most tyrannically.

Pye. Captain Idle, what's he there? he looks like a monkey upward, and a crane downward.

Idle. Psha! a foolish cousin of mine, I must thank God for him.

Pye. Why, the better subject to work a scape upon; thou shalt e'en change clothes with him, and leave him here, and so—

Idle. Pish! I publish'd him e'en now to my corporal: he will be damn'd ere he do me so much good. Why, I know a more proper, a more handsome device than that, if the slave would be sociable. Now, goodman Fleerface?

Nich. O, my cousin begins to speak to me now; I shall be acquainted with him again, I hope.

Skir. Look, what ridiculous raptures take hold of his wrinkles.

Pye. Then what say you to this device? a happy one, captain?

Idle. Speak low, George; prison-rats have wider ears than those in malt-lofts.

Nich. Cousin, if it lay in my power, as they say, to do——

Idle. 'Twould do me an exceeding pleasure indeed, that: but ne'er talk further on't; the fool will be hang'd e'er he do't.   [*To the* Corporal.

Oath. Pox, I'll thump him to't.

Pye. Why, do but try the fopster, and break it to him bluntly.

Idle. And so my disgrace will dwell in his jaws, and the slave slaver out our purpose to his master; for would I were but as sure on't, as I am sure he will deny to do't.

Nich. I would be heartily glad, cousin, if any of my friendships, as they say, might—stand, ha—

Pye. Why, you see he offers his friendship foolishly to you already.

Idle. Ay, that's the hell on't; I would he would offer it wisely.

Nich. Verily and indeed la, cousin—

Idle. I have took note of thy fleers a good while. If thou art minded to do me good, (as thou gap'st upon me comfortably, and giv'st me charitable faces,—which indeed is but a fashion in you all that are Puritans), will soon at night steal me thy master's chain?

Nich. Oh, I shall swoon.

Pye. Corporal, he starts already.

Idle. I know it to be worth three hundred crowns: and with the half of that I can buy my life at a broker's, at second-hand, which now lies in pawn to the law. If this thou refuse to do, being easy and

nothing dangerous, in that thou art held in good opinion of thy master, why 'tis a palpable argument thou hold'st my life at no price; and these thy broken and unjointed offers are but only created in thy lip: now born, and now buried; foolish breath only. What, wilt do 't? shall I look for happiness in thy answer?

Nich. Steal my master's chain, quoth-a? No, it shall ne'er be said, that Nicholas St. Antlings committed birdlime.

Idle. Nay, I told you as much, did I not? Though he be a Puritan, yet he will be a true man.

Nich. Why cousin, you know 'tis written, "Thou shalt not steal."

Idle. Why, and fool, "Thou shalt love thy neighbour," and help him in extremities.

Nich. Mass I think it be indeed: in what chapter's that, cousin?

Idle. Why in the first of Charity, the second verse.

Nich. The first of Charity, quoth-a? That's a good jest; there's no such chapter in my book.

Idle. No, I knew 'twas torn out of thy book, and that makes it so little in thy heart.

Pye. [*Takes* Nich. *aside.*] Come, let me tell you, you're too unkind a kinsman i'faith; the captain loving you so dearly, ay, like the pomewater of his eye, and you to be so uncomfortable: fie, fie.

Nich. Pray do not wish me to be hang'd. Any thing else that I can do, had it been to rob, I would have done 't; but I must not steal: that's the word, the literal "Thou shalt not steal;" and would you wish me to steal then?

Pye. No faith, that were too much, to speak truth: why, wilt thou nym it from him?[23]

Nich. That I will.

Pye. Why enough, bully; he will be content with that, or he shall have none: let me alone with him now.—Captain, I have dealt with your kinsman in a corner; a good, kind-natur'd fellow, methinks: go to; you shall not have all your own asking, you shall bate somewhat on 't: he is not contented absolutely, as you would say, to steal the chain from him, but to do you a pleasure, he will nym it from him.

Nich. Ay, that I will, cousin.

Idle. Well, seeing he will do no more, as far as I see, I must be contented with that

Oath. Here's no notable gullery!

Pye. Nay, I'll come nearer to you, gentleman. Because we'll have only but a help and a mirth on't, the knight shall not lose his chain neither, but it shall be only laid out of the way some one or two days.

Nich. Ay, that would be good indeed, kinsman.

Pye. For I have a farther reach, to profit us better by the missing of 't only, than if we had it outright; as my discourse shall make it known to you. When thou hast the chain, do but convey it out at a back-door into the garden, and there hang it close in the rosemary bank, but for a small season; and by that harmless device I know how to wind captain Idle out of prison: the knight thy master shall get his pardon, and release him, and he satisfy thy master with his own chain, and wondrous thanks on both hands.

Nich. That were rare indeed la. Pray let me know how.

Pye. Nay, 'tis very necessary thou should'st know, because thou must be employ'd as an actor.

Nich. An actor? O no; that's a player: and our parson rails against players mightily, I can tell you, because they brought him drunk upon the stage once;—as he will be horribly drunk.

Oath. Mass I cannot blame him then, poor church-spout.

Pye. Why, as an intermeddler then.

Nich. Ay, that, that.

Pye. Give me audience then. When the old knight, thy master, has raged his fill for the loss of the chain, tell him thou hast a kinsman in prison, of such exquisite art that the devil himself is French lackey to him, and runs bare-headed by his horse-belly, when he has one; whom he will cause, with most Irish dexterity,[23] to fetch his chain, though 'twere hid under a mine of sea-coal, and ne'er make spade or pick-axe his instruments: tell him but this, with farther instructions thou shalt receive from me, and thou showest thyself a kinsman indeed.

Oath. A dainty bully.

Skir. An honest book-keeper.

Idle. And my three-times thrice-honey cousin.

Nich. Nay, grace of God, I'll rob him on 't suddenly; and hang it in the rosemary bank; but I bear that mind, cousin, I would not steal any thing, methinks, for mine own father.

Skir. He bears a good mind in that, captain.

Pye. Why, well said; he begins to be an honest fellow, 'faith.

Oath. In troth he does.

Nich. You see, cousin, I am willing to do you any kindness; always saving myself harmless.

Idle. Why I thank thee. Fare thee well; I shall requite it.   [*Exit* NICH.

Oath. 'Twill be good for thee, captain, that thou hast such an egregious ass to thy cousin.

Idle. Ay, is he not a fine fool, corporal? But, George, thou talk'st of art and conjuring? How shall that be?

Pye. Pooh! be 't not in your care: Leave that to me and my directions. Well, captain, doubt not thy delivery now, Even with the vantage, man, to gain by prison, As my thoughts prompt me. Hold on brain and plot! I aim at many cunning far events, All which I doubt not but to hit at length. I'll to the widow with a quaint assault: Captain, be merry.

Idle. Who I? Kerry merry buff-jerkin.

Pye. Oh, I am happy in more sleights; and one will knit strong in another. Corporal Oath

Oath. Ho! bully!

Pye. And thou, old Peter Skirmish, I have a necessary task for you both.

Skir. Lay it upon us, George Pyeboard.

Oath. Whate'er it be, we'll manage it.

Pye. I would have you two maintain a quarrel before the lady widow's door, and draw your swords i' the edge of the evening: clash a little, clash, clash.

Oath. Fooh! Let us alone to make our blades ring noon, Though it be after supper.

Pye. I know you can: and out of that false fire, I doubt not but to raise strange belief. And, captain, to countenance my device the better, and grace my words to the widow, I have a good plain satin suit, that I had of a young reveller t' other night; for words pass not regarded now-a-days, unless they come from a good suit of clothes; which the Fates and my wits have bestowed upon me. Well, captain Idle, if I did not highly love thee, I would ne'er be seen within twelve score of a prison; for I protest, at this instant I walk in great danger of small debts. I owe money to several hostesses, and you know such jills will quickly be upon a man's jack.

Idle. True, George.

Pye. Fare thee well, captain. Come corporal and ancient. Thou shalt hear more news next time we greet thee.

Oath. More news?—Ay, by yon Bear at Bridge-foot in heaven, shalt thou.[24]

[*Exeunt* PYE., SKIR., *and* OATH.

Idle. Enough: my friends, farewell! This prison shows as ghosts did part in hell. [*Exit.*

ACT II.

SCENE I.—*A Room in the* Widow's *House.*

Enter MARY.

Mary. Not marry! forswear marriage! Why all women know 'tis as honourable a thing as to lie with a man; and I, to spite my sister's vow the more, have entertained a suitor already, a fine gallant knight of the last feather.[25] He says he will coach me too, and well appoint me; allow me money to dice withal; and many such pleasing protestations he sticks upon my lips. Indeed his short-winded father i' the country is wondrous wealthy, a most abominable farmer; and therefore he may do it in time. 'Troth I'll venture upon him. Women are not without ways enough to help themselves: if he prove wise, and good as his word, why I shall love him, and use him kindly; and if he prove an ass, why in a quarter of an hour's warning I can transform him into an ox:—there comes in my relief again.

Enter FRAILTY.

Frail. O, mistress Mary, mistress Mary!

Mary. How now? what's the news?

Frail. The knight your suitor, sir John Pennydub.

Mary. Sir John Pennydub? where? where?

Frail. He's walking in the gallery.

Mary. Has my mother seen him yet?

Frail. O no; she's spitting in the kitchen.[26]

Mary. Direct him hither softly, good Frailty: I'll meet him half way.

Frail. That's just like running a tilt; but I hope he'll break nothing this time.

[*Exit.*

Enter SIR JOHN PENNYDUB.

Mary. 'Tis happiness my mother saw him not. O welcome, good sir John.

Sir John. I thank you 'faith—Nay you must stand me till I kiss you: 'tis the fashion every where i' faith, and I came from court even now.

Mary. Nay, the Fates forefend that I should anger the fashion!

Sir John. Then, not forgetting the sweet of new ceremonies,[27] I first fall back; then recovering myself, make my honour to your lip thus; and then accost it.

[*Kisses her.*

Mary. Trust me, very pretty and moving; you're

worthy of it, sir.—O my mother, my mother! now she's here, we'll steal into the gallery.

[*Exeunt* SIR JOHN *and* MARY.

Enter WIDOW *and* SIR GODFREY.

Sir God. Nay, sister, let reason rule you; do not play the fool; stand not in your own light. You have wealthy offers, large tenderings; do not withstand your good fortune. Who comes a wooing to you, I pray? No small fool; a rich knight o' the city, sir Oliver Muckhill; no small fool, I can tell you. And furthermore, as I heard late by your maid-servants, (as your maid-servants will say to me any thing, I thank them,) both your daughters are not without suitors, ay, and worthy ones too: one a brisk courtier, sir Andrew Tipstaff, suitor afar off to your eldest daughter: and the third a huge wealthy farmer's son, a fine young country knight; they call him sir John Pennydub: a good name marry;—he may have it coin'd when he lacks money. What blessings are these, sister?

Wid. Tempt me not, Satan.

Sir God. Satan! do I look like Satan? I hope the devil's not so old as I, I trow.

Wid. You wound my senses, brother, when you name
A suitor to me. O, I cannot abide it;
I take in poison when I hear one nam'd.

Enter SIMON.

How now, Simon? where's my son Edmond?

Sim. Verily, madam, he is at vain exercise, dripping in the Tennis-Court.

Wid. At Tennis-Court? O, now his father's gone, I shall have no rule with him. Oh wicked Edmond! I might well compare this with the prophecy in the Chronicle, though far inferior: As Harry of Monmouth won all, and Harry of Windsor lost all; so Edmond of Bristow, that was the father, got all, and Edmond of London, that's his son, now will spend all.

Sir God. Peace, sister, we'll have him reform'd; there's hope of him yet, though it be but a little.

Enter FRAILTY.

Frail. Forsooth, madam, there are two or three archers at door would very gladly speak with your ladyship.

Wid. Archers?

Sir God. Your husband's fletcher I warrant.[28]

Wid. O,

Let them come near, they bring home things of his;

Troth I should have forgot them. How now villain!

Which be those archers?

Enter SIR ANDREW TIPSTAFF, SIR OLIVER MUCK-HILL, *and* SIR JOHN PENNYDUB.

Frail. Why, do you not see them before you? Are not these archers?—what do you call 'em—shooters? Shooters and archers are all one, I hope.[29]

Wid. Out, ignorant slave!

Sir Oliv. Nay, pray be patient, lady: We come in way of honourable love—

Sir And. } We do.
Sir John. }

Sir Oliv. To you.

Sir And. } And to your daughters.
Sir John. }

Wid. O, why will you offer me this, gentlemen, (indeed I will not look upon you) when the tears are scarce out of mine eyes, not yet washed off from my cheeks; and my dear husband's body scarce so cold as the coffin? What reason have you to offer it? I am not like some of your widows that will bury one in the evening, and be sure to have another ere morning. Pray away; pray take your answers, good knights. An you be sweet knights, I have vow'd never to marry; and so have my daughters too.

Sir John. Ay, two of you have, but the third's a good wench.

Sir Oliv. Lady, a shrewd answer, marry. The best is, 'tis but the first; and he's a blunt wooer, that will leave for one sharp answer.

Sir And. Where be your daughters, lady? I hope they'll give us better encouragement.

Wid. Indeed they'll answer you so; take it on my word, they'll give you the very same answer verbatim, truly la.

Sir John. Mum: Mary's a good wench still; I know what she'll do.

Sir Oliv. Well, lady, for this time we'll take our leaves; hoping for better comfort.

Wid. O never, never, an I live these thousand years. An you be good knights, do not hope; 'twill be all vain, vain. Look you put off all your suits, an you come to me again.

[*Exeunt* SIR JOHN *and* SIR AND.

Frail. Put off all their suits, quoth-a? ay, that's

the best wooing of a widow indeed, when a man's non-suited; that is, when he's a-bed with her.

Sir Oliv. Sir Godfrey, here's twenty angels more. Work hard for me; there's life in it yet.

Sir God. Fear not sir Oliver Muckhill; I'll stick close for you: leave all with me.

[*Exit* SIR OLIV.

Enter PYEBOARD.

Pye. By your leave, lady widow.

Wid. What another suitor now?

Pye. A suitor! No, I protest, lady, if you'd give me yourself, I'd not be troubled with you.

Wid. Say you so, sir? then you're the better welcome, sir.

Pye. Nay, heaven bless me from a widow, unless I were sure to bury her speedily!

Wid. Good bluntness. Well, your business, sir?

Pye. Very needful; if you were in private once.

Wid. Needful? Brother, pray leave us; and you, sir. [*Exit* SIR GOD.

Frail. I should laugh now, if this blunt fellow should put them all beside the stirrup, and vault into the saddle himself. I have seen as mad a trick. [*Exit* FRAIL.

Wid. Now, sir; here's none but we.

Enter MARY *and* FRANCES.

Daughters, forbear.

Pye. O no, pray let them stay; for what I have to speak importeth equally to them as to you.

Wid. Then you may stay.

Pye. I pray bestow on me a serious ear, For what I speak is full of weight and fear.

Wid. Fear?

Pye. Ay, if it pass unregarded, and unaffected; else peace and joy: I pray attention. Widow, I have been a mere stranger from these parts that you live in, nor did I ever know the husband of you, and father of them; but I truly know by certain spiritual intelligence, that he is in purgatory.

Wid. Purgatory! tuh; that word deserves to be spit upon. I wonder that a man of sober tongue, as you seem to be, should have the folly to believe there's such a place.

Pye. Well, lady, in cold blood I speak it; I assure you that there is a purgatory, in which place I know your husband to reside, and wherein he is like to remain, till the dissolution of the world, till the last general bonfire; when all the earth shall melt into nothing, and the seas scald their finny labourers: so long is his abidance, unless you alter the property of your purpose, together with each of your daughters theirs; that is, the purpose of single life in yourself and your eldest daughter, and the speedy determination of marriage in your youngest.

Mary. How knows he that? what, has some devil told him?

Wid. Strange he should know our thoughts.— Why, but daughter, have you purpos'd speedy marriage?

Pye. You see she tells you, ay, for she says nothing. Nay, give me credit as you please; I am a stranger to you, and yet you see I know your determinations, which must come to me metaphysically,[30] and by a supernatural intelligence.

Wid. This puts amazement on me.

Fran. Know our secrets?

Mary. I had thought to steal a marriage. Would his tongue had dropp'd out when he blabb'd it!

Wid. But, sir, my husband was too honest a dealing man to be now in any purgatories—

Pye. O do not load your conscience with untruths;
'Tis but mere folly now to gild him o'er,
That has past but for copper. Praises here
Cannot unbind him there. Confess but truth;
I know he got his wealth with a hard gripe:
O, hardly, hardly.

Wid. This is most strange of all: how knows he that?

Pye. He would eat fools and ignorant heirs clean up;
And had his drink from many a poor man's brow,
Even as their labour brew'd it. He would scrape
Riches to him most unjustly: the very dirt
Between his nails was ill got, and not his own.
O, I groan to speak on't; the thought makes me
Shudder, shudder!

Wid. It quakes me too, now I think on't. [*Aside.*
Sir, I am much griev'd, that you a stranger should so deeply wrong my dead husband!

Pye. O!

Wid. A man that would keep church so duly; rise early, before his servants, and even for religious haste, go ungartered, unbuttoned, nay (sir reverence)[31] untrussed, to morning prayer?

Pye. O, uff.

Wid. Dine quickly upon high days; and when I had great guests, would even shame me, and rise from the table, to get a good seat at an afternoon sermon.

Pye. There's the devil, there's the devil! True: he thought it sanctity enough, if he had kill'd a

man, so it had been done in a pew; or undone his neighbour, so it had been near enough to the preacher. O, a sermon's a fine short cloak of an hour long, and will hide the upper part of a dissembler.—Church! ay, he seem'd all church, and his conscience was as hard as the pulpit.

Wid. I can no more endure this.

Pye. Nor I, widow, endure to flatter.

Wid. Is this all your business with me?

Pye. No, lady, 'tis but the induction to it.
You may believe my strains; I strike all true;
And if your conscience would leap up to your tongue, yourself would affirm it. And that you shall perceive I know of things to come, as well as I do of what is present, a brother of your husband's shall shortly have a loss.

Wid. A loss? marry heaven forefend! Sir Godfrey, my brother!

Pye. Nay, keep in your wonders, till I have told you the fortunes of you all; which are more fearful, if not happily prevented. For your part and your daughters', if there be not once this day some blood shed before your door, whereof the human creature dies, two of you (the elder) shall run mad;—

Wid and Fran. Oh!

Mary. That's not I yet.

Pye. And, with most impudent prostitution, show your naked bodies to the view of all beholders.

Wid. Our naked bodies? fie for shame.

Pye. Attend me—and your younger daughter be strucken dumb.

Mary. Dumb? out, alas! 'tis the worst pain of all for a woman. I'd rather be mad, or run naked, or any thing. Dumb!

Pye. Give ear: Ere the evening fall upon hill, bog, and meadow, this my speech shall have past probation, and then shall I be believ'd accordingly.

Wid. If this be true, we are all sham'd, all undone.

Mary. Dumb! I'll speak as much as ever I can possibly before evening.

Pye. But if it so come to pass (as for your fair sakes I wish it may) that this presage of your strange fortunes be prevented by that accident of death and blood-shedding, (which I before told you of,) take heed, upon your lives, that two of you which have vow'd never to marry, seek out husbands with all present speed; and you, the third, that have such a desire to out-strip chastity, look you meddle not with a husband.

Mary. A double torment.[32]

Pye. The breach of this keeps your father in purgatory; and the punishments that shall follow you in this world, would with horror kill the ear should hear them related.

Wid. Marry! Why I vow'd never to marry.

Fran. And so did I.

Mary. And I vow'd never to be such an ass, but to marry. What a cross-fortune's this?

Pye. Ladies, though I be a fortune teller, I cannot better fortunes; you have them from me as they are reveal'd to me: I would they were to your tempers, and fellows with your bloods; that's all the bitterness I would you.

Wid. O! 'tis a just vengeance for my husband's hard purchases.

Pye. I wish you to bethink yourselves, and leave them.

Wid. I'll to sir Godfrey, my brother, and acquaint him with these fearful presages.

Fran. For, mother, they portend losses to him.

Wid. O ay, they do, they do.
If any happy issue crown thy words,
I will reward thy cunning.

Pye. 'Tis enough, lady; I wish no higher.
[*Exeunt* WID. *and* FRAN.

Mary. Dumb? and not marry? worse:
Neither to speak, nor kiss; a double curse. [*Exit*

Pye. So, all this comes well about yet. I play the fortune-teller as well as if I had had a witch to my grannam: for by good happiness, being in my hostess's garden, which neighbours the orchard of the widow, I laid the hole of mine ear to a hole in the wall, and heard them make these vows, and speak those words, upon which I wrought these advantages; and to encourage my forgery the more, I may now perceive in them a natural simplicity which will easily swallow an abuse, if any covering be over it: and to confirm my former presage to the widow, I have advis'd old Peter Skirmish, the soldier, to hurt corporal Oath upon the leg; and in that hurry I'll rush amongst them, and instead of giving the corporal some cordial to comfort him, I'll pour into his mouth a potion of a sleepy nature, to make him seem as dead; for the which the old soldier being apprehended, and ready to be borne to execution, I'll step in, and take upon me the cure of the dead man, upon pain of dying the condemned's death. The corporal will wake at his minute, when the sleepy force hath wrought itself; and so shall I get myself into a most admir'd opinion, and, under the pretext of that cunning, beguile as I see occasion. And if that foolish Nicholas St. Antlings keep true time with the chain, my plot will be sound, the captain deliver'd, and my wits applauded amongst scholars and soldiers for ever. [*Exit.*

SCENE II.—*A Garden.*

Enter NICHOLAS.

Nich. O, I have found an excellent advantage to take away the chain. My master put it off e'en now, to 'say on a new doublet;[33] and I sneak'd it away by little and little, most puritanically. We shall have good sport anon, when he has miss'd it, about my cousin the conjuror. The world shall see I'm an honest man of my word; for now I'm going to hang it between heaven and earth, among the rosemary branches. [*Exit.*

ACT III.

SCENE I.—*The Street before the* Widow's *House.*

Enter SIMON *and* FRAILTY.

Frail. Sirrah, Simon St. Mary-Overies, my mistress sends away all her suitors, and puts fleas in their ears.

Sim. Frailty, she does like an honest, chaste, and virtuous woman; for widows ought not to wallow in the puddle of iniquity.

Frail. Yet, Simon, many widows will do't, whatso comes on't.

Sim. True, Frailty; their filthy flesh desires a conjunction copulative. What strangers are within, Frailty?

Frail. There's none, Simon, but master Pilfer the tailor; he's above with sir Godfrey, 'praising of a doublet: and I must trudge anon to fetch master Suds the barber.

Sim. Master Suds:—a good man; he washes the sins of the beard clean.

Enter SKIRMISH.

Skir. How now, creatures? what's o'clock?

Frail. Why, do you take us to be Jacks o'the clock house?[34]

Skir. I say again to you, what is't o'clock?

Sim. Truly la, we go by the clock of our conscience. All worldly clocks we know go false, and are set by drunken sextons.

Skir. Then what is't o'clock in your conscience? —O I must break off; here comes the corporal.

Enter OATH.

Hum, hum: what is't o'clock?

Oath. O'clock? why past seventeen.

Frail. Past seventeen! Nay, he has met with his match now; corporal Oath will fit him.

Skir. Thou dost not balk or baffle me, dost thou? I am a soldier. Past seventeen!

Oath. Ay, thou art not angry with the figures, art thou? I will prove it unto thee: twelve and one is thirteen, I hope; two fourteen, three fifteen, four sixteen, and five seventeen; then past seventeen: I will take the dial's part in a just cause.

Skir. I say 'tis but past five then.

Oath. I'll swear 'tis past seventeen then. Dost thou not know numbers? Can'st thou not cast?

Skir. Cast? dost thou speak of my casting i'the street?[35]   [*They draw and fight.*

Oath. Ay, and in the market-place.

Sim. Clubs, clubs, clubs.   [*Simon runs away.*

Frail. Ay, I knew by their shuffling, clubs would be trump. Mass here's the knave, an he can do any good upon them: Clubs, clubs, clubs. [*Exit.*

Enter PYEBOARD.

Oath. O villain, thou hast open'd a vein in my leg.

Pye. How now? for shame, for shame, put up, put up.

Oath. By yon blue welkin,[36] 'twas out of my part, George, to be hurt on the leg.

Enter Officers.

Pye. O, peace now: I have a cordial here to comfort thee.

Offi. Down with 'em, down with 'em; lay hands upon the villain.

Skir. Lay hands on me?

Pye. I'll not be seen among them now.

                                        [*Exit* PYE.

Oath. I'm hurt, and had more need have surgeons lay hands upon me, than rough officers.

Offi. Go, carry him to be dress'd then: this mutinous soldier shall along with me to prison.

[*Exeunt some of the* Sheriff's *Officers with* OATH.

Skir. To prison? Where's George?

Offi. Away with him.

                [*Exeunt* Officers *with* SKIR.

SCENE II.—*The Same.*

Re-enter PYEBOARD.

Pye. So,

All lights as I would wish. The amaz'd widow
Will plant me strongly now in her belief,
And wonder at the virtue of my words:
For the event turns those presages from them
Of being mad and dumb, and begets joy
Mingled with admiration. These empty creatures,
Soldier and corporal, were but ordain'd
As instruments for me to work upon.
Now to my patient; here's his potion.   [*Exit.*

SCENE III.—*An Apartment in the* Widow's *House.*

Enter WIDOW, FRANCES, *and* MARY.

Wid. O wondrous happiness, beyond our thoughts!
O lucky fair event! I think our fortunes
Were blest even in our cradles. We are quitted
Of all those shameful violent presages
By this rash bleeding chance. Go, Frailty, run, and know
Whether he be yet living, or yet dead,
That here before my door receiv'd his hurt.

Frail. Madam, he was carried to the superior;[37] but if he had no money when he came there, I warrant he 's dead by this time.   [*Exit* FRAIL.

Fran. Sure that man is a rare fortune-teller; never look'd upon our hands, nor upon any mark about us: a wondrous fellow surely!

Mary. I am glad I have the use of my tongue yet, though of nothing else. I shall find the way to marry, too, I hope, shortly.

Wid. O where 's my brother sir Godfrey? I would he were here, that I might relate to him how prophetically the cunning gentleman spoke in all things.

Enter SIR GODFREY.

Sir God. O my chain, my chain! I have lost my chain. Where be these villains, varlets?

Wid. O, he has lost his chain.

Sir God. My chain, my chain!

Wid. Brother, be patient; hear me speak. You know I told you that a cunning-man told me that you should have a loss, and he has prophesy'd so true—

Sir God. Out! he's a villain to prophesy of the loss of my chain. 'Twas worth above three hundred crowns. Besides 'twas my father's, my father's father's, my grandfather's huge grandfather's: I had as lief have lost my neck, as the chain that hung about it. O my chain, my chain!

Wid. O, brother, who can be guarded against a misfortune? 'Tis happy 'twas no more.

Sir God. No more! O goodly godly sister, would you had me lost more? my best gown too, with the cloth of gold lace? my holiday gaskins, and my jerkin set with pearl? No more!

Wid. O brother, you can read—

Sir God. But I cannot read where my chain is. What strangers have been here? You let in strangers, thieves, and catch-poles. How comes it gone? There was none above with me but my tailor; and my tailor will not steal, I hope.

Mary. No; he's afraid of a chain.

Enter FRAILTY.

Wid. How now, sirrah? the news?

Frail. O, mistress, he may well be call'd a corporal now, for his corpse is as dead as a cold capon's.

Wid. More happiness.

Sir God. Sirrah, what's this to my chain? Where's my chain, knave?

Frail. Your chain, sir?

Sir God. My chain is lost, villain.

Frail. I would he were hang'd in chains that has it then for me. Alas, sir, I saw none of your chain, since you were hung with it yourself.

Sir God. Out varlet! it had full three thousand links;
I have oft told it over at my prayers;
Over and over: full three thousand links.

Frail. Had it so, sir! Sure it cannot be lost then; I'll put you in that comfort.

Sir God. Why? why?

Frail. Why, if your chain had so many links, it cannot choose but come to light.[38]

Enter NICHOLAS.

Sir God. Delusion! Now, long Nicholas, where is my chain?

Nich. Why about your neck, is't not, sir?

Sir God. About my neck, varlet? My chain is lost; 'tis stolen away; I'm robb'd.

Wid. Nay, brother, show yourself a man.

Nich. Ay, if it be lost or stole, if he would be patient, mistress, I could bring him to a cunning kinsman of mine that would fetch it again with a sesarara.[39]

Sir God. Canst thou? I will be patient: say, where dwells he?

Nich. Marry he dwells now, sir, where he would not dwell an he could choose; in the Marshalsea, sir. But he's an excellent fellow if he were out; has travell'd all the world over he, and been in the seven-and-twenty provinces:[40] why, he would make it be fetch'd, sir, if it were rid a thousand mile out of town.

Sir God. An admirable fellow! What lies he for?

Nich. Why, he did but rob a steward of ten groats t' other night, as any man would ha' done, and there he lies for 't.

Sir God. I'll make his peace. A trifle! I'll get his pardon,
Besides a bountiful reward. I'll about it.
But fee the clerks, the Justice will do much.
I will about it straight. Good sister pardon me;
All will be well, I hope, and turn to good:
The name of conjurer has laid my blood. [*Exeunt.*

SCENE IV.—*A Street.*

Enter PUTTOCK, RAVENSHAW,[41] and DOGSON.

Put. His hostess where he lies will trust him no longer. She hath feed me to arrest him; and if you will accompany me, because I know not of what nature the scholar is, whether desperate or swift, you shall share with me, serjeant Ravenshaw. I have the good angel to arrest him.[42]

Rav. 'Troth I'll take part with thee, then, serjeant; not for the sake of the money so much, as for the hate I bear to a scholar. Why, serjeant, 'tis natural in us you know to hate scholars,—natural; besides, they will publish our imperfections, knaveries, and conveyances, upon scaffolds and stages.

Put. Ay, and spitefully too. 'Troth I have wonder'd how the slaves could see into our breasts so much, when our doublets are button'd with pewter.

Rav. Ay, and so close without yielding. O, they're parlous fellows; they will search more with their wits, than a constable with his officers.

Put. Whist, whist, whist. Yeoman Dogson, yeoman Dogson.

Dog. Ha! what says serjeant?

Put. Is he in the 'pothecary's shop still?

Dog. Ay, ay.

Put. Have an eye, have an eye.

Rav. The best is, serjeant, if he be a true scholar, he wears no weapon, I think.

Put. No, no, he wears no weapon.

Rav. 'Mass, I am glad of that: it has put me

in better heart. Nay, if I clutch him once, let me alone to drag him, if he be stiff-necked. I have been one of the six myself, that has dragg'd as tall men of their hands, when their weapons have been gone, as ever bastinado'd a serjeant. I have done I can tell you.

Dog. Serjeant Puttock, serjeant Puttock.

Put. Ho.

Dog. He's coming out single.

Put. Peace, peace, be not too greedy; let him play a little, let him play a little; we'll jerk him up of a sudden: I ha' fish'd in my time.

Rav. Ay, and caught many a fool, serjeant.

Enter PYEBOARD.

Pye. I parted now from Nicholas: the chain's couch'd,
And the old knight has spent his rage upon't.
The widow holds me in great admiration
For cunning art: 'mongst joys, I'm even lost,
For my device can no way now be cross'd:
And now I must to prison to the captain,
And there—

Put. I arrest you, sir.

Pye. Oh—I spoke truer than I was aware; I must to prison indeed.

Put. They say you're a scholar.—Nay sir—yeoman Dogson, have care to his arms.—You'll rail against serjeants, and stage 'em? You'll tickle their vices?

Pye. Nay, use me like a gentleman; I'm little less.

Put. You a gentleman! that's a good jest i'faith. Can a scholar be a gentleman, when a gentleman will not be a scholar? Look upon your wealthy citizens' sons, whether they be scholars or no, that are gentlemen by their fathers' trades. A scholar a gentleman!

Pye. Nay, let fortune drive all her stings into me, she cannot hurt that in me. A gentleman is *accidens inseparabile* to my blood.

Rav. A rablement! nay, you shall have a bloody rablement upon you, I warrant you.

Put. Go, yeoman Dogson, before, and enter the action i'the Counter. [*Exit* Dog.

Pye. Pray do not handle me cruelly; I'll go whither you please to have me.

Put. Oh, he's tame; let him loose, serjeant.

Pye. Pray, at whose suit is this?

Put. Why, at your hostess's suit where you lie, mistress Conyburrow, for bed and board; the sum four pound five shillings and five pence.

Pye. I know the sum too true; yet I presum'd

Upon a farther day. Well, 'tis my stars,
And I must bear it now, though never harder.
I swear now my device is cross'd indeed:
Captain must lie by't: this is deceit's seed.

Put. Come, come away.

Pye. Pray give me so much time as to knit my garter, and I'll away with you.

Put. Well, we must be paid for this waiting upon you; this is no pains to attend thus.

     [PYE. *pretends to tie his garter.*

Pye. I am now wretched and miserable; I shall ne'er recover of this disease. Hot iron gnaw their fists! They have struck a fever into my shoulder, which I shall ne'er shake out again, I fear me, 'till with a true *habeas corpus* the sexton remove me. O, if I take prison once, I shall be press'd to death with actions; but not so happy as speedily: perhaps I may be forty years a pressing, till I be a thin old man; that looking through the grates, men may look through me. All my means are confounded. What shall I do? Have my wits served me so long, and now give me the slip (like a train'd servant) when I have most need of them? No device to keep my poor carcass from these puttocks?— Yes, happiness: have I a paper about me now? Yes, two: I'll try it, it may hit; "Extremity is the touchstone unto wit." Ay, ay.

Put. 'Sfoot, how many yards are in thy garters, that thou art so long a tying of them? Come away, sir.

Pye. 'Troth serjeant, I protest, you could never have took me at a worse time; for now at this instant I have no lawful picture about me.[43]

Put. 'Slid, how shall we come by our fees then?

Rav. We must have fees, sirrah.

Pye. I could have wish'd, i'faith, that you had took me half an hour hence for your own sake; for I protest, if you had not cross'd me, I was going in great joy to receive five pound of a gentleman, for the device of a mask here, drawn in this paper. But now, come, I must be contented; 'tis but so much lost, and answerable to the rest of my fortunes.

Put. Why, how far hence dwells that gentleman?

Rav. Ay, well said, serjeant; 'tis good to cast about for money.

Put. Speak; if it be not far—

Pye. We are but a little past it; the next street behind us.

Put. 'Slid, we have waited upon you grievously already. If you'll say you'll be liberal when you have it, give us double fees, and spend upon us, why we'll show you that kindness, and go along with you to the gentleman.

Rav. Ay, well said; still, serjeant, urge that.

Pye. 'Troth if it will suffice, it shall be all among you; for my part I'll not pocket a penny: my hostess shall have her four pounds five shillings, and bate me the five pence; and the other fifteen shillings I'll spend upon you.

Rav. Why, now thou art a good scholar.

Put. An excellent scholar i'faith; has proceeded very well a-late. Come, we'll along with you.

[*Exeunt* PUT., RAV., *and* PYE., *who knocks at the Door of a Gentleman's House at the inside of the Stage.*

SCENE V.—*A Gallery in a* Gentleman's *House.*

Enter a Servant.

Ser. Who knocks? Who's at door? We had need of a porter.   [*Opens the Door.*

Pye. [*Within.*] A few friends here. Pray is the gentleman your master within?

Ser. Yes; is your business to him?

                 [*Ser. opens the Door.*

Enter PYEBOARD, PUTTOCK, RAVENSHAW, *and* DOGSON.

Pye. Ay, he knows it, when he sees me: I pray you, have you forgot me?

Ser. Ay by my troth, sir; pray come near; I'll in and tell him of you. Please you to walk here in the gallery till he comes.   [*Exit* Ser.

Pye. We will attend his worship. Worship, I think; for so much the posts at his door should signify, and the fair coming-in, and the wicket; else I neither knew him nor his worship: but 'tis happiness he is within doors, whatsoe'er he be. If he be not too much a formal citizen, he may do me good. [*Aside.*]—Serjeant and yeoman, how do you like this house? Is't not most wholesomely plotted?[44]

Rav. 'Troth, prisoner, an exceeding fine house.

Pye. Yet I wonder how he should forget me,—for he never knew me. [*Aside.*] No matter; what is forgot in you, will be remember'd in your master.[45] A pretty comfortable room this, methinks: you have no such rooms in prison now?

Put. O, dog-holes to't.

Pye. Dog-holes, indeed. I can tell you, I have great hope to have my chamber here shortly, nay, and diet too; for he's the most free-heartedst gentleman, where he takes: you would little think

it. And what a fine gallery were here for me to walk and study and make verses?

Put. O, it stands very pleasantly for a scholar.

Enter Gentleman.

Pye. Look what maps, and pictures, and devices, and things, neatly, delicately—Mass here he comes; he should be a gentleman; I like his beard well.—All happiness to your worship.

Gent. You're kindly welcome, sir.

Put. A simple salutation.

Rav. Mass, it seems the gentleman makes great account of him.

Pye. I have the thing here for you, sir—[*Takes the* Gentleman *apart.*] I beseech you, conceal me, sir; I'm undone else. [*Aside.*] I have the mask here for you, sir; look you, sir. I beseech your worship, first pardon my rudeness, for my extremes make me bolder than I would be. I am a poor gentleman, and a scholar, and now most unfortunately fallen into the fangs of unmerciful officers; arrested for debt, which though small, I am not able to compass, by reason I am destitute of lands, money, and friends; so that if I fall into the hungry swallow of the prison, I am like utterly to perish, and with fees and extortions be pinch'd clean to the bone. Now, if ever pity had interest in the blood of a gentleman, I beseech you vouchsafe but to favour that means of my escape, which I have already thought upon.

Gent. Go forward.

Put. I warrant he likes it rarely.

Pye. In the plunge of my extremities, being giddy, and doubtful what to do, at last it was put into my labouring thoughts, to make a happy use of this paper; and to blear their unletter'd eyes, I told them there was a device for a mask drawn in 't, and that (but for their interception) I was going to a gentleman to receive my reward for 't. They, greedy at this word, and hoping to make purchase of me,[46] offer'd their attendance to go along with me. My hap was to make bold with your door, sir, which my thoughts show'd me the most fairest and comfortablest entrance; and I hope I have happened right upon understanding and pity. May it please your good worship then, but to uphold my device, which is to let one of your men put me out at a back-door, and I shall be bound to your worship for ever.

Gent. By my troth, an excellent device.

Put. An excellent device, he says: he likes it wonderfully.

Gent. O' my faith, I never heard a better.

Rav. Hark, he swears he never heard a better, serjeant.

Put. O, there's no talk on 't: he 's an excellent scholar, and especially for a mask.[47]

Gent. Give me your paper, your device: I was never better pleas'd in all my life: good wit, brave wit, finely wrought! Come in, sir, and receive your money, sir.   [*Exit.*

Pye. I 'll follow your good worship.—You heard how he lik'd it now?

Put. Pooh, we know he could not choose but like it. Go thy ways; thou art a witty fine fellow i'faith: thou shalt discourse it to us at the tavern anon; wilt thou?

Pye. Ay, ay, that I will. Look, serjeant, here are maps, and pretty toys: be doing in the mean time; I shall quickly have told out the money, you know.

Put. Go, go, little villain; fetch thy chink; I begin to love thee: I 'll be drunk to-night in thy company.

Pye. This gentleman I well may call a part
Of my salvation in these earthly evils,
For he has sav'd me from three hungry devils.
                              [*Exit* PYE.

Put. Sirrah serjeant, these maps are pretty painted things, but I could ne'er fancy them yet: methinks they 're too busy, and full of circles and conjurations. They say all the world 's in one of them; but I could ne'er find the Counter in the Poultry.

Rav. I think so: how could you find it? for you know it stands behind the houses.

Dog. Mass, that 's true; then we must look o' the back-side for 't. 'Sfoot here 's nothing; all 's bare.

Rav. I warrant thee, that stands for the Counter; for you know there 's a company of bare fellows there.

Put. 'Faith, like enough, serjeant; I never mark'd so much before. Sirrah serjeant, and yeoman, I should love these maps out o'cry now,[48] if we could see men peep out of door in 'em. O, we might have 'em in a morning to our breakfast so finely, and ne'er knock our heels to the ground a whole day for 'em.

Rav. Ay marry, sir, I' d buy one then myself. But this talk is by the way.—Where shall us sup to-night? Five pound receiv'd—let 's talk of that. I have a trick worth all. You two shall bear him to the tavern, whilst I go close with his hostess, and work out of her. I know she would be glad of the sum, to finger money, because she knows 'tis but a desperate debt, and full of hazard. What will you say, if I bring it to pass that the hostess shall be contented with one-half for all, and we to share t'other fifty shillings, bullies?

Put. Why, I would call thee king of serjeants, and thou should'st be chronicled in the Counter-book for ever.

Rav. Well, put it to me; we 'll make a night on 't, i'faith.

Dog. 'Sfoot, I think he receives more money, he stays so long.

Put. He tarries long indeed. May be I can tell you, upon the good liking on 't, the gentleman may prove more bountiful.

Rav. That would be rare; we 'll search him.

Put. Nay, be sure of it, we 'll search him, and make him light enough.

Enter Gentleman.

Rav. O, here comes the gentleman. By your leave, sir.

Gent. God you good den, sirs. Would you speak with me?

Put. No, not with your worship, sir; only we are bold to stay for a friend of ours that went in with your worship.

Gent. Who? not the scholar?

Put. Yes, e'en he, an it please your worship.

Gent. Did he make you stay for him? He did you wrong then: why, I can assure you he 's gone above an hour ago.

Rav. How, sir?

Gent. I paid him his money, and my man told me he went out at back door.

Put. Back-door?

Gent. Why, what 's the matter?

Put. He was our prisoner, sir; we did arrest him.

Gent. What? he was not?—You the sheriff's officers! You were to blame then. Why did not you make known to me as much? I could have kept him for you. I protest, he receiv'd all of me in Britain gold of the last coining.

Rav. Vengeance dog him with 't!

Put. 'Sfoot, has he gull'd us so?

Dog. Where shall we sup now, serjeants?

Put. Sup, Simon, now![49] eat porridge for a month.—Well, we cannot impute it to any lack of good will in your worship. You did but as another would have done. 'Twas our hard fortunes to miss the purchase;—but if e'er we clutch him again, the Counter shall charm him.

Rav. The Hole shall rot him.[50]

Dog. Amen.   [*Exeunt* Serjeants.

Gent. So;

Vex out your lungs without doors. I am proud
It was my hap to help him. It fell fit;
He went not empty neither for his wit.
Alas, poor wretch, I could not blame his brain,
To labour his delivery, to be free
From their unpitying fangs. I'm glad it stood
Within my power to do a scholar good.   [*Exit.*

SCENE VI.—*A Room in the* Marshalsea Prison.

Enter IDLE; *to him* PYEBOARD.

Idle. How now! Who's that? What are you?

Pye. The same that I should be, captain.

Idle. George Pyeboard? Honest George? Why
cam'st thou in half-fac'd, muffled so?

Pye. O captain, I thought we should ne'er have
laugh'd again, never spent frolic hour again.

Idle. Why? why?

Pye. I coming to prepare thee, and with news
As happy as thy quick delivery,
Was trac'd out by the scent; arrested, captain.

Idle. Arrested, George?

Pye. Arrested. Guess, guess, how many dogs
do you think I had upon me?

Idle. Dogs? I say, I know not.

Pye. Almost as many as George Stone, the
bear;[51] three at once, three at once.

Idle. How didst thou shake them off then?

Pye. The time is busy, and calls upon our
        wits.

Let it suffice.

Here I stand safe, and scap'd by miracle:
Some other hour shall tell thee, when we'll steep
Our eyes in laughter. Captain, my device
Leans to thy happiness; for ere the day
Be spent to the girdle,[52] thou shalt be free.
The corporal's in's first sleep; the chain is miss'd;
Thy kinsman has express'd thee;[53] and the old
        knight
With-palsy hams, now labours thy release.
What rests, is all in thee:—to conjure, captain.

Idle. Conjure? 'Sfoot, George, you know, the
devil a conjuring I can conjure.

Pye. The devil a conjuring? Nay, by my say,
I'd not have thee do so much, captain, as the
devil a conjuring. Look here; I have brought
thee a circle ready character'd and all.

Idle. 'Sfoot, George, art in thy right wits?
Dost know what thou say'st? Why dost talk to
a captain of conjuring? Didst thou ever hear of a
Captain Conjure in thy life? Dost call't a circle?

'Tis too wide a thing, methinks; had it been a
lesser circle, then I knew what to have done.

Pye. Why every fool knows that, captain. Nay
then I'll not cog with you, captain: if you'll stay
and hang the next sessions, you may.

Idle. No, by my faith, George. Come, come;
let's to conjuring.

Pye. But if you look to be released, (as my wits
have took pain to work it, and all means wrought
to further it,) besides, to put crowns in your purse,
to make you a man of better hopes: and whereas
before you were a captain or poor soldier, to make
you now a commander of rich fools, which is truly
the only best purchase peace can allow you, safer
than highways, heath, or cony-groves, and yet a far
better booty; for your greatest thieves are never
hang'd, never hang'd: for why? they're wise, and
cheat within doors: and we geld fools of more
money in one night, than your false-tail'd gelding[54]
will purchase in twelve months' running: which
confirms the old beldam's saying, "He's wisest,
that keeps himself warmest;" that is, he that robs
by a good fire.

Idle. Well open'd i'faith, George; thou hast
pull'd that saying out of the husk.

Pye. Captain Idle, 'tis no time now to delude or
delay. The old knight will be here suddenly; I'll
perfect you, direct you, tell you the trick on't: 'tis
nothing.

Idle. 'Sfoot, George, I know not what to say to't.
Conjure? I shall be hang'd ere I conjure.

Pye. Nay, tell not me of that, captain; you'll
ne'er conjure after you're hang'd, I warrant you.
Look you, sir; a parlous matter, sure! First to
spread your circle upon the ground, with a little
conjuring ceremony, (as I'll have an hackney-man's
wand silver'd o'er o' purpose for you;) then arriv-
ing in the circle, with a huge word, and a great
trample—as for instance—have you never seen a
stalking, stamping player, that will raise a tempest
with his tongue, and thunder with his heels?

Idle. O yes, yes, yes: often, often.

Pye. Why be like such a one. For any thing
will blear the old knight's eyes; for you must note,
that he'll ne'er dare to venture into the room;
only perhaps peep fearfully through the key-hole,
to see how the play goes forward.

Idle. Well, I may go about it when I will; but
mark the end on't; I shall but shame myself i'faith,
George. Speak big words, and stamp and stare,
and he look in at key-hole! why the very thought
of that would make me laugh outright, and spoil
all. Nay, I'll tell thee, George; when I appre-

hend a thing once, I am of such a laxative laughter, that if the devil himself stood by, I should laugh in his face.

Pye. Pooh! that's but the babe of a man,[55] and may easily be hush'd;—as to think upon some disaster, some sad misfortune;—as the death of thy father i' the country.

Idle. 'Sfoot, that would be the more to drive me into such an ecstasy, that I should ne'er lin laughing [56]

Pye. Why then think upon going to hanging.

Idle. Mass that's well remembered: Now I'll do well, I warrant thee; ne'er fear me now. But how shall I do, George, for boisterous words and horrible names?

Pye. Pooh! any fustian invocations, captain, will serve as well as the best, so you rant them out well: or you may go to a 'pothecary's shop, and take all the words from the boxes.

Idle. Troth, and you say true, George; there's strange words enough to raise a hundred quacksalvers, though they be ne'er so poor when they begin. But here lies the fear on't: how, if in this false conjuration a true devil should pop up indeed?

Pye. A true devil, captain? why there was ne'er such a one. Nay, i'faith he that has this place, is as false a knave as our last churchwarden.

Idle. Then he's false enough o' conscience, i'faith, George.

Prisoners cry within.] Good gentlemen over the way, send your relief: Good gentlemen over the way,—good, sir Godfrey!

Pye. He's come, he's come.

Enter SIR GODFREY, EDMOND, *and* NICHOLAS.

Nich. Master, that's my kinsman yonder in the buff-jerkin. Kinsman, that's my master yonder i' the taffaty hat. Pray salute him entirely.

　　[SIR GOD. *and* IDLE *salute, and* PYE. *salutes* EDM.

Sir God. Now my friend.

　　　　　　　[SIR GOD. *and* IDLE *talk aside.*

Pye. May I partake your name, sir?

Edm. My name is master Edmond.

Pye. Master Edmond? Are you not a Welshman, sir?

Edm. A Welshman? why?

Pye. Because master is your Christian name, and Edmond your surname.

Edm. O no: I have more names at home: master Edmond Plus is my full name at length.

Pye. O, cry you mercy, sir.

Idle. [*Aside to* SIR GODFREY.] I understand that you are my kinsman's good master; and in regard of that, the best of my skill is at your service. But had you fortun'd a mere stranger, and made no means to me by acquaintance, I should have utterly denied to have been the man: both by reason of the act of parliament against conjurers and witches,[57] as also, because I would not have my art vulgar, trite, and common.

Sir God. I much commend your care there, good captain conjuror: and that I will be sure to have it private enough, you shall do't in my sister's house; mine own house I may call it, for both our charges therein are proportion'd.

Idle. Very good, sir. What may I call your loss, sir?

Sir God. O you may call it a great loss, a grievous loss, sir; as goodly a chain of gold, though I say it, that wore it—How say'st thou, Nicholas?

Nich. O 'twas as delicious a chain of gold, kinsman, you know—

Sir God. You know? Did you know't captain?

Idle. Trust a fool with secrets!—Sir, he may say, I know. His meaning is, because my art is such, that by it I may gather a knowledge of all things.

Sir God. Ay, very true.

Idle. A pox of all fools! The excuse stuck upon my tongue like ship-pitch upon a mariner's gown, not to come off in haste. [*Aside.*] By'r lady, knight, to lose such a fair chain of gold, were a foul loss. Well, I can put you in this good comfort on't: if it be between heaven and earth, knight, I'll have it for you.

Sir God. A wonderful conjurer! O ay, 'tis between heaven and earth, I warrant you; it cannot go out of the realm: I know 'tis somewhere above the earth:—

Idle. Ay, nigher the earth than thou wot'st on.

　　　　　　　　　　　　　　　[*Aside.*

Sir God. For, first, my chain was rich, and no rich thing shall enter into heaven, you know.

Nich. And as for the devil, master, he has no need on't; for you know he has a great chain of his own.

Sir God. Thou say'st true, Nicholas, but he has put off that now; that lies by him.

Idle. 'Faith, knight, in few words, I presume so much upon the power of my art, that I could warrant your chain again.

Sir God. O dainty captain!

Idle. Marry, it will cost me much sweat; I were better go to sixteen hot-houses.[58]

Sir God. Ay, good man, I warrant thee.

Idle. Beside great vexation of kidney and liver.

Nich. O, 'twill tickle you hereabouts, cousin; because you have not been used to 't.

Sir God. No? have you not been us'd to 't, captain?

Idle. Plague of all fools still! [*Aside.*] Indeed, knight, I have not us'd it a good while, and therefore 'twill strain me so much the more, you know.

Sir God. O, it will, it will.

Idle. What plunges he puts me to? Were not this knight a fool, I had been twice spoil'd now. That captain's worse than accurs'd that has an ass to his kinsman. 'Sfoot, I fear he will drivel it out, before I come to 't.—Now, sir, to come to the point indeed: you see I stick here in the jaw of the Marshalsea, and cannot do 't.

Sir God. Tut, tut, I know thy meaning: thou would'st say thou 'rt a prisoner: I tell thee thou 'rt none.

Idle. How, none? why is not this the Marshalsea?

Sir God. Wilt thou hear me speak? I heard of thy rare conjuring:

My chain was lost; I sweat for thy release,
As thou shalt do the like at home for me:—
Keeper.

Enter Keeper.

Keep. Sir.

Sir God. Speak, is not this man free?

Keep. Yes, at his pleasure, sir, the fees discharg'd.

Sir God. Go, go; I'll discharge them, I.

Keep. I thank your worship.   [*Exit* Keep.

Idle. Now, trust me, you're a dear knight. Kindness unexpected! O, there's nothing to a free gentleman. I will conjure for you, sir, till froth come through my buff-jerkin.

Sir God. Nay, then thou shalt not pass with so little a bounty; for at the first sight of my chain again, forty fine angels shall appear unto thee.

Idle. 'Twill be a glorious show, i'faith knight; a very fine show. But are all these of your own house? Are you sure of that, sir?

Sir God. Ay, ay;—no, no. What's he yonder talking with my wild nephew? Pray heaven he give him good counsel.

Idle. Who, he? He's a rare friend of mine, an admirable fellow, knight; the finest fortune-teller.

Sir God. O! 'tis he indeed, that came to my lady sister, and foretold the loss of my chain: I am not angry with him now, for I see 'twas my fortune to lose it. By your leave, master fortune-teller, I had a glimpse of you at home, at my sister's the widow's; there you prophesy'd of the loss of a chain: simply, though I stand here, I was he that lost it.

Pye. Was it you, sir?

Edm. O' my troth, nuncle, he's the rarest fellow; has told me my fortune so right! I find it so right to my nature.

Sir God. What is't! God send it a good one.

Edm. O, 'tis a passing good one, nuncle; for he says I shall prove such an excellent gamester in my time, that I shall spend all faster than my father got it.

Sir God. There's a fortune, indeed.

Edm. Nay, it hits my humour so pat.

Sir God. Ay, that will be the end on't. Will the curse of the beggar prevail so much, that the son shall consume that foolishly which the father got craftily? Ay, ay, ay; 'twill, 'twill, 'twill.

Pye. Stay, stay, stay.

    [*Opens an Almanack, and takes* IDLE *aside.*

Idle. Turn over, George.

Pye. June—July—Here, July; that's this month; Sunday thirteen, yesterday fourteen, to-day fifteen.

Idle. Look quickly for the fifteenth day. If within the compass of these two days there would be some boisterous storm or other, it would be the best; I'd defer him off 'till then. Some tempest, an it be thy will.

Pye. Here's the fifteenth day, [*reads*] "Hot and fair."

Idle. Puh! would it had been "hot and foul."

Pye. The sixteenth day; that's to-morrow: [*reads*] "The morning for the most part fair and pleasant—

Idle. No luck.

Pye. "But about high-noon, lightning and thunder."

Idle. Lightning and thunder? admirable! best of all! I'll conjure to-morrow just at high-noon, George.

Pye. Happen but true to-morrow, almanack, and I'll give thee leave to lie all the year after.

Idle. Sir, I must crave your patience, to bestow this day upon me, that I may furnish myself strongly. I sent a spirit into Lancashire t'other day to fetch back a knave drover, and I look for his return this evening. To-morrow morning my friend here and I will come and breakfast with you

Sir God. O, you shall be most welcome.

Idle. And about noon, without fail, I purpose to conjure.

Sir God. Mid-noon will be a fine time for you.

Edm. Conjuring? Do you mean to conjure at our house to-morrow, sir?

Idle. Marry do I, sir; 'tis my intent, young gentleman.

Edm. By my troth, I'll love you while I live for't. O rare! Nicholas, we shall have conjuring to-morrow.

Nich. Puh! ay, I could ha' told you of that.

Idle. La, he could have told him of that! fool, coxcomb, could you?   [*Aside.*

Edm. Do you hear me, sir? I desire more acquaintance on you. You shall earn some money of me, now I know you can conjure:—but can you fetch any that is lost?

Idle. O, any thing that's lost.

Edm. Why look you, sir, I tell it you as a friend and a conjuror. I should marry a 'pothecary's daughter, and 'twas told me, she lost her maidenhead at Stony-Stratford: now if you'll do but so much as conjure for't, and make all whole again—

Idle. That I will, sir.

Edm. By my troth I thank you, la.

Idle. A little merry with your sister's son, sir.

Sir God. O, a simple young man, very simple. Come captain, and you, sir; we'll e'en part with a gallon of wine till to-morrow breakfast.

Pye. }
Idle. } Troth, agreed, sir.

Nich. Kinsman—scholar.

Pye. Why now thou art a good knave; worth a hundred Brownists.[59]

Nich. Am I indeed, la? I thank you heartily, la.
                    [*Exeunt.*

ACT IV.

SCENE I.—*An Apartment in the* Widow's *House.*

Enter MARY *and* SIR JOHN PENNYDUB.

Sir John. But I hope you will not serve a knight so, gentlewoman, will you? to cashier him, and cast him off at your pleasure! What do you think I was dubb'd for nothing? No, by my faith, lady's daughter.

Mary. Pray sir John Pennydub, let it be deferr'd awhile. I have as big a heart to marry as you can have; but as the fortune-teller told me—

Sir John. Pox o' the fortune-teller! Would Derrick had been his fortune seven years ago,[60] to cross my love thus! Did he know what case I was in? Why this is able to make a man drown himself in his father's fish-pond.

Mary. And then he told me moreover, sir John, that the breach of it kept my father in purgatory.

Sir John. In purgatory? why let him purge out his heart there; what have we to do with that? There's physicians enough there to cast his water: is that any matter to us? How can he hinder our love? Why let him be hang'd, now he's dead.— Well, have I rid post day and night, to bring you merry news of my father's death, and now—

Mary. Thy father's death? Is the old farmer dead?

Sir John. As dead as his barn-door, Moll.

Mary. And you'll keep your word with me now, sir John; that I shall have my coach and my coachman?

Sir John. Ay 'faith.

Mary. And two white horses with black feathers to draw it?

Sir John. Two.

Mary. A guarded lackey to run before it, and py'd liveries to come trashing after't.

Sir John. Thou shalt, Moll.

Mary. And to let me have money in my purse, to go whither I will.

Sir John. All this.

Mary. Then come; whatsoe'er comes on't, we'll be made sure together before the maids i'the kitchen.   [*Exeunt.*

SCENE II.—*A Room in the* Widow's *House, with a Door at the side, leading to another Apartment.*

Enter WIDOW, FRANCES, *and* FRAILTY.

Wid. How now? Where's my brother sir Godfrey? Went he forth this morning?

Frail. O no madam; he's above at breakfast, with (sir reverence) a conjuror.

Wid. A conjurer! What manner of fellow is he?

Frail. O, a wondrous rare fellow, mistress; very strongly made upward, for he goes in a buff-jerkin. He says he will fetch sir Godfrey's chain again, if it hang between heaven and earth.

Wid. What! he will not? Then he's an excellent fellow, I warrant. How happy were that woman to be blest with such a husband! A cunning man! How does he look, Frailty? Very swartly, I warrant; with black beard, scorch'd cheeks, and smoky eyebrows.

Frail. Fo! He's neither smoke-dried, nor scorch'd, nor black, nor nothing. I tell you, madam, he looks as fair to see to as one of us. I do not think but if you saw him once, you'd take him to be a Christian.

Fran. So fair, and yet so cunning! that's to be wonder'd at, mother.

Enter SIR OLIVER MUCKHILL, *and* SIR ANDREW TIPSTAFF.

Sir Oliv. Bless you, sweet lady.

Sir And. And you, fair mistress.

                         [*Exit* FRAIL.

Wid. Coades,[61] what do you mean, gentlemen? Fie, did I not give you your answers?

Sir Oliv. Sweet lady.

Wid. Well, I will not stick with you for a kiss: daughter, kiss the gentleman for once.

Fran. Yes, forsooth.

Sir And. I'm proud of such a favour.

Wid. Truly la, sir Oliver, you're much to blame, to come again when you know my mind so well delivered as a widow could deliver a thing.

Sir Oliv. But I expect a further comfort, lady.

Wid. Why la you now! did I not desire you to put off your suit quite and clean when you came to me again? How say you? Did I not?

Sir Oliv. But the sincere love which my heart bears you—

Wid. Go to, I'll cut you off:—And sir Oliver to put you in comfort afar off, my fortune is read me; I must marry again,

Sir Oliv. O blest fortune!

Wid. But not as long as I can choose:—nay, I'll hold out well.

Sir Oliv. Yet are my hopes now fairer.

Enter FRAILTY.

Frail. O madam, madam.

Wid. How now? what's the haste?

                  [FRAIL. *whispers her.*

Sir And. 'Faith, mistress Frances, I'll maintain you gallantly. I'll bring you to court; wean you among the fair society of ladies, poor kinswomen of mine, in cloth of silver: beside, you shall have your monkey, your parrot, and your musk-cat.

Fran. It will do very well.

Wid. What, does he mean to conjure here then? How shall I do to be rid of these knights?—Please you, gentlemen, to walk a while in the garden, to gather a pink, or a gilly-flower?

Both. With all our hearts, lady, and 'count us favour'd.

        [*Exeunt* SIR AND., SIR OLIV., *and* FRAIL. The WID. *and* FRAN. *go into the adjoining Room.*

Sir God. [*within.*] Step in, Nicholas; look, is the coast clear.

Nich. [*within.*] O, as clear as a cat's eye, sir.

Sir God. [*within.*] Then enter Captain Conjurer.

Enter SIR GODFREY, IDLE, PYEBOARD, EDMOND, *and* NICHOLAS.

Now, how like you your room, sir?

Idle. O, wonderful convenient.

Edm. I can tell you, captain, simply though it lies here, 'tis the fairest room in my mother's house: as dainty a room to conjure in, methinks— Why you may bid, I cannot tell how many devils welcome in't; my father has had twenty in't at once.

Pye. What! devils?

Edm. Devils! no; deputies,—and the wealthiest men he could get.

Sir God. Nay, put by your chats now; fall to your business roundly: the fescue of the dial is upon the christ-cross of noon.[62] But O, hear me, captain; a qualm comes o'er my stomach.

Idle. Why, what's the matter, sir?

Sir God. O, how if the devil should prove a a knave, and tear the hangings!

Idle. Foh! I warrant you, sir Godfrey.

Edm. Ay, nuncle, or spit fire upon the ceiling?

Sir God. Very true too, for 'tis but thin plaister'd, and 'twill quickly take hold o' the laths; and if he chance to spit downward too, he will burn all the boards.

Idle. My life for yours, sir Godfrey.

Sir God. My sister is very curious and dainty of this room, I can tell you; and therefore if he must needs spit, I pray desire him to spit in the chimney.

Pye. Why, assure you, sir Godfrey, he shall not be brought up with so little manners, to spit and spawl o' the floor.

Sir God. Why I thank you, good captain; pray have a care. [IDLE *and* PYE. *retire to the upper end of the Room.*] Ay, fall to your circle; we'll not trouble you I warrant you. Come, we'll into the next room; and because we'll be sure to keep him out there, we'll bar up the door with some of the godly's zealous works.

Edm. That will be a fine device, nuncle; and because the ground shall be as holy as the door,

I 'll tear two or three rosaries in pieces, and strew the pieces about the chamber. [*Lightning and Thunder.*] Oh! the devil already.

[SIR GOD. *and* EDM. *run into the adjoining Room.*

Pye. 'Sfoot, captain, speak somewhat for shame: it lightens and thunders before thou wilt begin. Why when—

Idle. Pray peace, George; thou 'lt make me laugh anon, and spoil all. [*Lightning and Thunder.*

Pye. O, now it begins again; now, now, now, captain.

Idle. "Rhumbos ragdayon pur pur colucundrion hois plois."

Sir God. [*At the Door.*] O admirable conjurer! he has fetch'd thunder already.

Pye. Hark, hark!—again captain.

Idle. "Benjamino gaspois kay gosgothoteron umbrois."

Sir God. [*At the Door.*] O, I would the devil would come away quickly; he has no conscience to put a man to such pain.

Pye. Again.

Idle. "Flowste kakopumpos dragone leloomenos hodge podge."

Pye. Well said, captain.

Sir God. [*At the Door.*] So long a coming? O, would I had ne'er begun it now! for I fear me these roaring tempests will destroy all the fruits of the earth, and tread upon my corn—[*Thunder*] oh—in the country.

Idle. "Gogdedog hobgoblin hunks hounslow hockleyte coomb-park."

Wid. [*At the Door.*] O brother, brother, what a tempest 's in the garden! Sure there 's some conjuration abroad.

Sir God. [*At the Door.*] 'Tis at home, sister.

Pye. By and by I 'll step in, captain.

Idle. "Nunc nunc rip-gaskins ips drip—dropite—"

Sir God. [*At the Door.*] He drips and drops, poor man: alas, alas!

Pye. Now, I come.

Idle. "O—sulphure sootface."

Pye. Arch-conjurer, what wouldest thou with me?

Sir God. [*At the Door.*] O, the devil, sister, in the dining-chamber! Sing, sister; I warrant you that will keep him out:—quickly, quickly, quickly.

Pye. So, so, so; I 'll release thee. Enough, captain, enough; allow us some time to laugh a little: They 're shuddering and shaking by this time, as if an earthquake were in their kidneys.

Idle. Sirrah George, how was 't, how was 't? Did I do 't well enough?

Pye. Woult believe me, captain? better than any conjurer; for here was no harm in this, and yet their horrible expectation satisfied well. You were much beholden to thunder and lightning at this time; it grac'd you well, I can tell you.

Idle. I must needs say so, George. Sirrah, if we could have convey'd hither cleanly a cracker or a fire-wheel, it had been admirable.

Pye. Blurt, blurt! there 's nothing remains to put thee to pain now, captain.

Idle. Pain? I protest, George, my heels are sorer than a Whitsun morris-dancer's.

Pye. All 's past now; only to reveal that the chain 's in the garden, where thou know'st it has lain these two days.

Idle. But I fear that fox Nicholas has reveal'd it already.

Pye. Fear not, captain; you must put it to the venture now. Nay 'tis time; call upon them, take pity on them; for I believe some of them are in a pitiful case by this time.

Idle. Sir Godfrey, Nicholas, kinsman. 'Sfoot, they 're fast at it still, George.—Sir Godfrey.

Sir God. [*At the Door.*] O, is that the devil's voice? How comes he to know my name?

Idle. Fear not, sir Godfrey; all 's quieted.

Enter SIR GODFREY, *the* WIDOW, FRANCES, *and* NICHOLAS.

Sir God. What, is he laid?

Idle. Laid: and has newly dropp'd your chain in the garden.

Sir God. In the garden? in our garden?

Idle. Your garden.

Sir God. O sweet conjurer! whereabouts there?

Idle. Look well about a bank of rosemary.

Sir God. Sister, the rosemary bank. Come, come; there 's my chain, he says.

Wid. Oh, happiness! run, run.

[*Exeunt* WID., SIR GOD., FRAN. *and* NICH.

Edm. [*At the Door.*] Captain Conjurer?

Idle. Who? master Edmond?

Edm. Ay, master Edmond. May I come in safely without danger, think you?

Idle. Pooh, long ago; it is all as 'twas at first. Fear nothing; pray come near: how now, man?

Enter EDMOND.

Edm. O! this room 's mightily hot i'faith. 'Slid, my shirt sticks to my belly already. What a steam the rogue has left behind him! Foh! this room must be air'd, gentlemen; it smells horribly of brimstone: let's open the windows.

Pye. 'Faith, master Edmond, 'tis but your conceit.

Edm. I would you could make me believe that, i'faith. Why do you think I cannot smell his savour from another? Yet I take it kindly from you, because you would not put me in a fear, i'faith. On my troth I shall love you for this the longest day of my life.

Idle. Pooh, 'tis nothing, sir; love me when you see more.

Edm. Mass, now I remember, I'll look whether he has sing'd the hangings or no.

Pye. Captain, to entertain a little sport till they come, make him believe, you'll charm him invisible. He's apt to admire any thing, you see. Let me alone to give force to it.

Idle. Go; retire to yonder end then.

Edm. I protest you are a rare fellow; are you not?

Idle. O master Edmond, you know but the least part of me yet. Why now at this instant I could but flourish my wand thrice o'er your head, and charm you invisible.

Edm. What! you could not? make me walk invisible, man! I should laugh at that i'faith. Troth, I'll requite your kindness, an you'll do't, good Captain Conjuror.

Idle. Nay, I should hardly deny you such a small kindness, master Edmond Plus. Why, look you, sir, 'tis no more but this, and thus, and again, and now you're invisible.

Edm. Am I i'faith? Who would think it?

Idle. You see the fortune-teller yonder at farther end o' the chamber. Go toward him; do what you will with him, he shall ne'er find you.

Edm. Say you so? I'll try that i'faith.

           [*Justles him.*

Pye. How now, captain? Who's that justled me?

Idle. Justled you? I saw nobody.

Edm. Ha, ha, ha! Say 'twas a spirit.

Idle. Shall I?—May be some spirit that haunts the circle.

       [EDM. *pulls* PYE. *by the nose.*

Pye. O my nose, again! Pray conjure then, captain.

Edm. Troth, this is excellent; I may do any knavery now, and never be seen. And now I remember, sir Godfrey, my uncle, abus'd me t'other day, and told tales of me to my mother. Troth now I'm invisible, I'll hit him a sound wherret on

the ear, when he comes out o' the garden. I may be reveng'd on him now finely.

Enter SIR GODFREY, *the* WIDOW, *and* FRANCES.

Sir God. I have my chain again; my chain's found again. O sweet captain! O admirable conjurer! [EDM. *strikes him.*] Oh! what mean you by that, nephew?

Edm. Nephew? I hope you do not know me, uncle?

Wid. Why did you strike your uncle, sir?

Edm. Why, captain, am I not invisible?

Idle. A good jest, George.—Not now you are not, sir. Why did not you see me, when I did uncharm you?

Edm. Not I, by my troth, captain.—Then pray you pardon me, uncle; I thought I'd been invisible when I struck you.

Sir God. So, you would do't? Go, you're a foolish boy;

And were I not o'ercome with greater joy,

I'd make you taste correction.

Edm. Correction! pish. No, neither you nor my mother shall think to whip me as you have done.

Sir God. Captain, my joy is such, I know not how to thank you: let me embrace you. O my sweet chain! gladness e'en makes me giddy. Rare man! 'twas just i'the rosemary-bank, as if one should have laid it there. O cunning, cunning!

Wid. Well, seeing my fortune tells me I must marry, let me marry a man of wit, a man of parts. Here's a worthy captain, and 'tis a fine title truly la to be a captain's wife. A captain's wife! it goes very finely: beside, all the world knows that a worthy captain is a fit companion to any lord; then why not a sweet bed-fellow for any lady? I'll have it so.

Enter FRAILTY.

Frail. O mistress — gentlemen — there's the bravest sight coming along this way.

Wid. What brave sight?

Frail. O, one going to burying, and another going to hanging.

Wid. A rueful sight.

Pye. 'Sfoot, captain, I'll pawn my life the corporal's coffin'd, and old Skirmish the soldier going to execution; and 'tis now full about the time of his waking. Hold out a little longer, sleepy potion, and we shall have excellent admiration; for I'll take upon me the cure of him.

           [*Exeunt.*

SCENE III.—*The Street before the* WIDOW'S *House.*

Enter, from the House, SIR GODFREY, *the* WIDOW, FRANCES, IDLE, PYEBOARD, EDMOND, FRAILTY, *and* NICHOLAS. *A Coffin with* Corporal OATH *in it, brought in. Then enter* SKIRMISH *bound, and led in by* Officers; *the* Sheriff, &c., *attending.*

Frail. O here they come, here they come!

Pye. Now must I close secretly with the soldier; prevent his impatience, or else all's discovered.

Wid. O lamentable seeing! These were those brothers, that fought and bled before our door.

Sir God. What! they were not, sister?

Skir. George, look to't; I'll peach at Tyburn else.

Pye. Mum.—Gentles all, vouchsafe me audience, And you especially, good master sheriff: Yon man is bound to execution, Because he wounded this that now lies coffin'd.

Sher. True, true; he shall have the law,—and I know the law.

Pye. But under favour, master sheriff, if this man had been cur'd and safe again, he should have been releas'd then?

Sher. Why make you question of that, sir?

Pye. Then I release him freely; and will take upon me the death that he should die, if within a little season I do not cure him to his proper health again.

Sher. How, sir! recover a dead man? That were most strange of all.

Fran. Sweet sir, I love you dearly, and could wish my best part yours. O do not undertake such an impossible venture!

Pye. Love you me? Then for your sweet sake I'll do't. Let me entreat the corpse to be set down.

Sher. Bearers, set down the coffin. This were wonderful, and worthy Stowe's *Chronicle.*

Pye. I pray bestow the freedom of the air upon our wholesome art. Mass his cheeks begin to receive natural warmth. Nay, good corporal, wake betime, or I shall have a longer sleep than you. 'Sfoot, if he should prove dead indeed now, he were fully reveng'd upon me for making a property of him: yet I had rather run upon the ropes,[63] than have a rope like a tetter run upon me. O, he stirs! he stirs again! look, gentlemen! he recovers! he starts, he rises!

Sher. O, O, defend us! Out, alas!

Pye. Nay, pray be still; you'll make him more giddy else. He knows nobody yet.

Oath. 'Zounds, where am I? Cover'd with snow! I marvel.

Pye. Nay, I knew he would swear the first thing he did as soon as ever he came to his life again.

Oath. 'Sfoot, hostess, some hot porridge. O, O!—lay on a dozen of faggots in the Moon parlour, there.

Pye. Lady, you must needs take a little pity of him i'faith, and send him in to your kitchen fire.

Wid. O, with all my heart, sir: Nicholas and Frailty, help to bear him in.

Nich. Bear him in, quoth-a! Pray call out the maids; I shall ne'er have the heart to do't, indeed la.

Frail. Nor I neither; I cannot abide to handle a ghost, of all men.

Oath. 'Sblood, let me see—where was I drunk last night? heh?

Wid. O, shall I bid you once again take him away?

Frail. Why we are as fearful as you, I warrant you. Oh.

Wid. Away, villains! bid the maids make him a caudle presently, to settle his brain,—or a posset of sack; quickly, quickly.

[*Exeunt* FRAIL. *and* NICH., *pushing in the* CORP.

Sher. Sir, whatsoe'er you are, I do more than admire you.

Wid. O ay, if you knew all, master sheriff, as you shall do, you would say then, that here were two of the rarest men within the walls of Christendom.

Sher. Two of them? O wonderful! Officers, I discharge you; set him free; all's in tune.

Sir God. Ay, and a banquet ready by this time, master sheriff; to which I most cheerfully invite you, and your late prisoner there. See you this goodly chain, sir? Mum! no more words; 'twas lost and is found again. Come, my inestimable bullies, we'll talk of your noble acts in sparkling charnico;[64] and instead of a jester, we'll have the ghost in the white sheet sit at the upper end of the table.[65]

Sher. Excellent, merry man, i'faith!

[*Exeunt all but* FRAN.

Fran. Well, seeing I am enjoin'd to love, and marry,
My foolish vow thus I cashier to air,
Which first begot it. Now, Love, play thy part;
The scholar reads his lecture in my heart. [*Exit.*

ACT V.

SCENE.I.—*The Street before the* Widow's *House.*

Enter EDMOND *and* FRAILTY.

Edm. This is the marriage-morning for my mother and my sister.

Frail. O me, master Edmond! we shall have rare doings.

Edm. Nay go, Frailty, run to the sexton; you know my mother will be married at Saint Antling's. Hie thee; 'tis past five; bid them open the church-door: my sister is almost ready.

Frail. What already, master Edmond?

Edm. Nay, go; hie thee. First run to the sexton, and run to the clerk; and then run to master Pigman the parson; and then run to the milliner, and then run home again.

Frail. Here's run, run, run.

Edm. But hark, Frailty.

Frail. What, more yet?

Edm. Have the maids remember'd to strew the way to the church?

Frail. Foh! an hour ago; I help'd them myself.

Edm. Away, away, away, away then.

Frail. Away, away, away, away then.

[*Exit* FRAIL.

Edm. I shall have a simple father-in-law, a brave captain, able to beat all our street; captain Idle. Now my lady mother will be fitted for a delicate name: my lady Idle, my lady Idle! the finest name that can be for a woman: and then the scholar, master Pyeboard, for my sister Frances, that will be mistress Frances Pyeboard; mistress Frances Pyeboard! they'll keep a good table, I warrant you. Now all the knights' noses are put out of joint; they may go to a bone-setter's now.

Enter IDLE *and* PYEBOARD, *with* Attendants.

Hark, hark! O, who come here with two torches before them! My sweet captain, and my fine scholar. O, how bravely they are shot up in one night! They look like fine Britons now methinks. Here's a gallant change i'faith! 'Slid, they have hir'd men and all, by the clock.[66]

Idle. Master Edmond; kind, honest, dainty master Edmond.

Edm. Foh, sweet captain father-in-law! A rare perfume i'faith!

Pye. What, are the brides stirring? May we steal upon them, think'st thou, master Edmond?

Edm. Foh, they're e'en upon readiness, I can assure you; for they were at their torch e'en now: by the same token I tumbled down the stairs.

Pye. Alas, poor master Edmond.

Enter Musicians.

Idle. O, the musicians! I pr'ythee, master Edmond, call them, and liquor them a little.

Edm. That I will, sweet captain father-in-law; and make each of them as drunk as a common fiddler. [*Exeunt.*

SCENE II.—*The Same.*

Enter MARY *in a Balcony. To her below,* SIR JOHN PENNYDUB.

Sir John. Whew! mistress Moll, mistress Moll.

Mary. Who's there?

Sir John. 'Tis I.

Mary. Who? sir John Pennydub? O you're an early cock i'faith. Who would have thought you to be so rare a stirrer?

Sir John. Pr'ythee, Moll, let me come up.

Mary. No by my faith, sir John; I'll keep you down; for you knights are very dangerous, if once you get above.

Sir John. I'll not stay i'faith.

Mary. I'faith you shall stay; for, sir John, you must note the nature of the climates: your northern wench in her own country may well hold out till she be fifteen; but if she touch the south once, and come up to London, here the chimes go presently after twelve.

Sir John. O thou'rt a mad wench, Moll: but I pr'ythee make haste, for the priest is gone before.

Mary. Do you follow him; I'll not be long after. [*Exeunt.*

SCENE III.—*A Room in* Sir Oliver Muckhill's *House.*

Enter SIR OLIVER MUCKHILL, SIR ANDREW TIPSTAFF, *and* SKIRMISH.

Sir Oliv. O monstrous, unheard-of forgery!

Sir And. Knight, I never heard of such villany in our own country, in my life.

Sir Oliv. Why, 'tis impossible. Dare you maintain your words?

Skir. Dare we? even to their weazon pipes. We know all their plots; they cannot squander with us. They have knavishly abus'd us, made only properties of us, to advance theirselves upon our shoulders; but they shall rue their abuses. This morning they are to be married.

Sir Oliv. 'Tis too true. Yet if the widow be not too much besotted on sleights and forgeries, the revelation of their villanies will make them loathsome. And to that end, be it in private to you, I sent late last night to an honourable personage, to whom I am much indebted in kindness, as he is to me; and therefore presume upon the payment of his tongue, and that he will lay out good words for me; and to speak truth, for such needful occasions I only preserve him in bond: and sometimes he may do me more good here in the city by a free word of his mouth, than if he had paid one half in hand, and took doomsday for t' other.

Sir And. In troth, sir, without soothing be it spoken, you have publish'd much judgment in these few words.

Sir Oliv. For you know, what such a man utters will be thought effectual, and to weighty purpose; and therefore into his mouth we'll put the approved theme of their forgeries.

Skir. And I'll maintain it, knight, if she'll be true.

Enter a Servant.

Sir Oliv. How now, fellow?

Ser. May it please you, sir, my lord is newly lighted from his coach.

Sir Oliv. Is my lord come already? His honour's early.
You see he loves me well. Up before seven!
Trust me, I have found him night-capp'd at eleven.
There's good hope yet: come, I ll relate all to him.
[*Exeunt.*

SCENE IV.—*A Street; a Church appearing.*

Enter IDLE, PYEBOARD, SIR GODFREY, *and* EDMOND; *the* WIDOW *in a Bridal Dress*; SIR JOHN PENNYDUB, MARY *and* FRANCES; NICHOLAS, FRAILTY, *and other* Attendants. *To them a* Nobleman, SIR OLIVER MUCKHILL, *and* SIR ANDREW TIPSTAFF.

Nob. By your leave, lady.

Wid. My lord, your honour is most chastely welcome.

Nob. Madam, though I came now from court, I come not to flatter you. Upon whom can I justly cast this blot, but upon your own forehead, that know not ink from milk? such is the blind besotting in the state of an unheaded woman that's a widow. For it is the property of all you that are widows (a handful excepted) to hate those that honestly and carefully love you, to the maintenance of credit, state, and posterity; and strongly to dote on those that only love you to undo you. Who regard you least, are best regarded; who hate you most are best beloved. And if there be but one man amongst ten thousand millions of men, that is accurst, disastrous, and evilly planeted; whom Fortune beats most, whom God hates most, and all societies esteem least, that man is sure to be a husband. Such is the peevish moon that rules your bloods. An impudent fellow best woos you, a flattering lip best wins you; or in a mirth, who talks roughliest, is most sweetest: nor can you distinguish truth from forgeries, mists from simplicity: witness those two deceitful monsters, that you have entertain'd for bridegrooms.

Wid. Deceitful!

Pye. All will out.

Idle. 'Sfoot, who has blabb'd, George? that foolish Nicholas.

Nob. For what they have besotted your easy blood withal, were nought but forgeries: the fortune-telling for husbands, the conjuring for the chain sir Godfrey heard the falsehood of, all, nothing but mere knavery, deceit, and cozenage.

Wid. O wonderful! indeed I wonder'd that my husband, with all his craft, could not keep himself out of purgatory.

Sir God. And I more wonder'd, that my chain should be gone, and my tailor had none of it.

Mary. And I wonder'd most of all, that I should be tied from marriage, having such a mind to it. Come, sir John Pennydub, fair weather on our side: The moon has chang'd since yesternight.

Pye. The sting of every evil is within me.

Nob. And that you may perceive I feign not with you, behold their fellow-actor in those forgeries; who full of spleen and envy at their so sudden advancements, reveal'd all their plot in anger.

Pye. Base soldier, to reveal us!

Wid. Is 't possible we should be blinded so, and our eyes open?

Nob. Widow, will you now believe that false which too soon you believ'd true?

Wid. O, to my shame I do.

Sir God. But, under favour, my lord, my chain was truly lost, and strangely found again.

Nob. Resolve him of that, soldier.

Skir. In few words, knight, then thou wert the arch-gull of all.

Sir God. How, sir?

Skir. Nay I'll prove it: for the chain was but hid in the rosemary-bank all this while; and thou got'st him out of prison to conjure for it, who did it admirably, fustianly; for indeed what needed any other, when he knew where it was?

Sir God. O villany of villanies! But how came my chain there?

Skir. Where's "Truly la, Indeed la," he that will not swear, but lie; he that will not steal, but rob; pure Nicholas Saint-Antlings?

Sir God. O villain! one of our society,
Deem'd always holy, pure, religious.
A puritan a thief! When was't ever heard?
Sooner we'll kill a man, than steal, thou know'st.
Out slave! I'll rend my lion from thy back,[67]
With mine own hands.

Nich. Dear master! O!

Nob. Nay knight, dwell in patience. And now, widow, being so near the church, 'twere great pity, nay uncharity, to send you home again without a husband. Draw nearer, you of true worship, state, and credit; that should not stand so far off from a widow, and suffer forged shapes to come between you. Not that in these I blemish the true title of a captain, or blot the fair margent of a scholar; for I honour worthy and deserving parts in the one, and cherish fruitful virtues in the other. Come lady, and you virgin, bestow your eyes and your purest affections upon men of estimation both in court and city, that have long wooed you, and both with their hearts and wealth sincerely love you.

Sir God. Good sister, do. Sweet little Franke, these are men of reputation: you shall be welcome at court; a great credit for a citizen.—Sweet sister.

Nob. Come, her silence does consent to't.

Wid. I know not with what face—

Nob. Poh, poh, with your own face; they desire no other.

Wid. Pardon me, worthy sirs: I and my daughter have wrong'd your loves.

Sir Oliv. 'Tis easily pardon'd, lady, if you vouchsafe it now.

Wid. With all my soul.

Fran. And I, with all my heart.

Mary. And I, sir John, with soul, heart, lights and all.

Sir John. They are all mine, Moll.

Nob. Now lady:
What honest spirit, but will applaud your choice,
And gladly furnish you with hand and voice?
A happy change, which makes even heaven rejoice.
Come, enter into your joys; you shall not want
For fathers, now; I doubt it not, believe me,
But that you shall have hands enough to give ye.

                         [*Exeunt omnes.*

NOTES TO THE PURITAN.

---

[1] *A Cyprus hat.*

A hat with a black crape band around it. So in the *Winter's Tale :—*

> *Cyprus* black as any crow.

[2] *With all his cards and writings.*

The word *cards* does not convey any meaning; Malone says, "I suspect the author wrote *charts*, i.e. papers."

[3] *If blessed be the corse the rain rains upon.*

This is a proverbial saying, based upon a superstition still commonly believed by the vulgar.

[4] *Leave snobbing and weeping.*

Dr. Percy remarks, that the word *snobbing* is still used in Shropshire for sobbing.

[5] *I would not have the elf see me now.*

Steevens rather simply asks, "Whom does he mean by the *elf?*—some invisible attendant, like Robin Good-fellow, or any of the characters present?" Elf is here used as a term of endearment, and Sir Godfrey applies it to the widow. He turns away to weep and speaks the above aside; he is anxious that she should not see him commit the weakness which he is persuading her to avoid.

[6] *If from time to time all the widower's tears.*

Steevens thinks we should read *widow's* tears, and Malone observes, that, "I think I have observed in old English books the word *widower* applied to both sexes." This may be, but I think the author here alludes to a widower in the sense we now use the word. Miss Mary's meaning is, all the tears that men have ever shed for the loss of their wives, would not fill a three-halfpenny bottle; why then should women distress themselves so greatly for the loss of a husband.

[7] *A small matter bucks a handkerchief.*

Wets, or washes it; a great wash of the household linen was anciently called a *bucking.*

[8] *Sometimes the 'spital stands too nigh Saint Thomas a' Waterings.*

A quibble appears to have been intended between *spittle*, the moisture of the mouth; and *spital*, a corruption of the word hospital. Malone observes: "I suppose the meaning is, that those widows who assume the greatest appearance of sorrow, and shed most tears, are sometimes guilty of such indiscretions as render them proper subjects for the public hospital. There seems to be a poor quibble on the word *waterings.*"

[9] *But I'll take another order*, i.e. I'll pursue another course.

[10] *Only your chambers are now licensed to play upon you.*

A quibble between chambers, small pieces of ordinance; and chambers, the abodes of profligate women.

[11] *Though it be full of holes, like a shot ancient.*

That is, a banner riddled with shot. An *ancient* formerly meant either a standard or a standard-bearer.

[12] *Eat my commons with a good stomach, and battled with discretion.*

Battling is the term used at Oxford to express what is called *sizing* at Cambridge; i.e. obtaining provisions from the college buttery upon credit. A matter that students of very slender means, or of spotted character, have, doubtless, often *battled* for earnestly enough. In the times of Elizabeth and James, the Universities appear to have been greatly burdened with needy and profligate scholars.

[13] *To tower among sons and heirs.*

That is, to rise by their means, to hover over and descend upon them, as a hawk does upon its prey.

[14] *Why how now, we three?*

An allusion to a device, commonly used as a sign in the time of Shakspere, in which were two men dressed as fools, with the words above quoted beneath them. The spectator or inquirer concerning its meaning was supposed to make the third.

[15] *You un-godmother'd varlets.*

The puritans objected to the practice of having either godfathers or godmothers in baptism.

[16] *A man of mark, quoth-a! I do not think he can show a beggar's noble.*

A quibble between *mark*, the ancient coin value 13s. 4d., and *mark*, a token of eminence. A *noble* was a coin of the value of 6s. 8d., but a *beggar's noble* was, I believe, a cant term for a farthing.

[17] *My dear kinsman in cappodochio.*

Cappodochio is a cant term for captivity. *Cappadoces* is often employed in Latin poetry for slaves, Cappadocia being a country famous for them.

[18] *Do't now then, marmozet.*

A *marmozet* is a small monkey; the corporal applies the term to Nicholas in contemptuous allusion to his lean and abortive appearance, more resembling a monkey than a man.

[19] *I shall dance after their pipe for it.*

That is, go the same way, incur the same punishment as they did, namely, be hanged. *To dance Jack Ketch's jig* is a vulgar phrase not yet altogether obsolete.

[20] *Here's a clean gentleman too, to receive.*

That is, here's a clean pipe to receive the tobacco.

[21] *When Lucifer is restored to his blood.*

That is, to his celestial connexions; when he is restored to the place he once held among obedient and happy spirits.

[22] *Wilt thou nym it from him?*

A cant word signifying to steal; hence the name of *Nym*, one of Falstaff's companions.

[23] *With most Irish dexterity.*

That is, with extreme swiftness; it is an allusion to the Irish running footmen kept as messengers by many of the nobles, in the time of Elizabeth and James.

[24] *Ay, by yon Bear at Bridge-foot in heaven, shalt thou.*

There is evidently some corruption here, for the sentence carries no meaning. Perhaps for *in heaven*, we should read, *in the even;* the sense would then be:— "Ay, by the sign of the Bear (a well known tavern at the foot of London Bridge) thou shalt hear from me in the evening." The corporal, who swears by all kinds of odd things, may very naturally be supposed to swear by the sign of a tavern he frequents.

[25] *A fine gallant knight of the last feather.*

That is, of the very newest fashion. The comparison seems to be derived from a practice of the fops of that period, who carried feathers in their hands as fans, as well as wore them in their hats.

[26] *She's spitting in the kitchen.*

The author does not mean that the wealthy widow was engaged in any culinary operation in the kitchen, for she immediately afterwards enters with Sir Godfrey. She was spitting out harsh words, scolding her servants. An angry cat is said to spit.

[27] *Then, not forgetting the sweet of my new ceremonies.*

This is not very intelligible. Malone suggests that the author might have written *suit*, the course, or train. On this Steevens remarks: "I am not sure that *suite* was used in its present sense when this comedy was produced. I would rather read, "— not forgetting the sweet, *in* new ceremonies:" i.e. not omitting the sweetest circumstance in salutation, though, in compliance with modern forms, it must be preceded by art of address and regularity of approach."

[28] *Your husband's fletcher, I warrant.*

A *fletcher* was a maker of arrows; from *Fleche,* French.

[29] *Shooters and archers are all one, I hope.*

Malone remarks, that, "from this and other passages in our old comedies, it appears that the words *suitors* and *shooters* were, in the age of Queen Elizabeth, not distinguished in pronunciation."

[30] *Which must come to me metaphysically.*

Metaphysically is not here used in its ordinary acceptation as relating to the science of the affections of being in general, or, the laws of mind; but is employed in the sense of *immaterially, spiritually, invisibly.* The word is constantly used in the same sense by Shakspere; thus, in *Macbeth:*—

> That fate and *metaphysical* aid do seem
> To have me crown'd withal.

[31] *Nay, sir reverence.*

"This singular phrase (says Malone) which occurs frequently in ancient English books, appears to have been equivalent to, and was perhaps originally a corruption of, another expression that was formerly in use— *save reverence.* This latter seems to be a Gallicism;— *sauve votre grandeur, votre dignité.*"

[32] *A double torment;* i.e. the being deprived both of speech and a husband.

[33] *To 'say on a new doublet;* i.e. to *essay*, or try it on.

[34] *Why, do you take us to be Jacks o' the clock house?*

Figures formerly placed in the great clocks of churches, which by mechanism struck the hours.

[35] *Cast? dost thou speak of my casting i'the street.*

This sentence involves a coarse quibble on the word *cast*, which meant to vomit as well as to reckon. Oath used it in the latter sense, but Skirmish pleases to understand it in the former.

[36] *By yon blue welkin;* i.e. by the sky.

[37] *Madam, he was carried to the superior.*

Probably the *superior* was the pastor or spiritual director of these sectaries; though as the word was one in use among the adherents of the Romish church, and therefore not very likely to be used by the puritans, it may have been an error of the compositor, who perhaps transformed the word *surgeon* to *superior.*

[38] *If your chain had so many links, it cannot choose but come to light.*

A quibble between the links of a chain, and links, or torches.

[39] *Fetch it again with a sesarara.*

Steevens says this is a corruption of the writ of *certiorari;* it is, I believe, a cant word equivalent to a vulgar phrase still in use, namely, *fetch it in no time.*

[40] *And had been in the seven and twenty provinces.*

An ignorant allusion to the seventeen provinces in the Low Countries, which were then the objects of general attention, on account of their long war with Spain.

[41] *Enter Puttock, Ravenshaw, &c.*

A *puttock* is a buzzard, a mean degenerate species of hawk; and a *ravenshaw* is a thicket where ravens assemble and build. The names of these worthy officers were intended to indicate their natures.

[42] *I have the good angel to arrest him.*

He means the coin so called; probably an obscure pun was intended, he was paid to arrest him, and he had the spirit (good angel) to do so.

[43] *At this moment I have no lawful picture about me.*

That is, he had no money about him; coins were vulgarly called king's or queen's pictures, on account of the likeness of the sovereign impressed upon them.

[44] *Is't not most wholesomely plotted?*

That is, is not the ground-plot of this house laid in a most wholesome situation?

[45] *No matter; what is forgot in you, will be remember'd in your master.*

That is, though you have forgotten me your master will not do so. The servant having gone to apprize his master of the presence of a visitor, Pyeboard throws out this observation in order to account to the bailiffs for the former's not knowing him.

[46] *And hoping to make purchase of me.*

Hoping to plunder him; in former times *purchase* was a cant name for theft.

[47] *He's an excellent scholar, and especially for a mask.*

Steevens has attached the following ingenious note to this passage:—"The hint for this scene was taken from *The Merrie Conceited Jests of George Peele, Gentleman, sometimes a Student in Oxford, &c.*, bl. 1, 1607, p. 7:—'At that time (says the author) he had the oversight of the *pageants.*' He escaped from one of his creditors by the same stratagem that is here practised by George Pyeboard, whose character might have been designed for that of George Peele. A circumstance that adds no inconsiderable weight to my conjecture is, that a *pyeboard* (i.e. a board on which bakers carry their pies to the oven) is still called a *peel.* The word is derived from *paelle*, Fr. 'instrument de patissier.' See Cotgrave, under both *peel, paelle*, &c. It is highly probable that the comedy of the *Puritan* was written while the idea of Peele, who died about 1597, was recent in the memory of ancient audiences."

[48] *I should love these maps out of cry now.*

That is, beyond everything, beyond expression, or as Shakspere says, "out of all whooping."

[49] *Sup, Simon, now.*

"This (says Steevens) alludes to the character of Simon of Southampton, alias Sup-broth, whom we read of in *Thomas of Reading, or the five worthy Yeomen of the West. Now the sixth time corrected and enlarged, by T. D.* (i.e. Thomas Decker) 1632."

[50] *The hole shall rot him.*

The *hole* was one of the most offensive apartments in the Counter prison. See *The Walks of Hogsdon*, with the Humours of Wood-street Compter, a comedy, 1657:—

> Next from the stocks, *the hole*, and little ease,
> Sad places which kind nature do displease,
> And from the rattling of the keeper's keys.
> *Libera nos, Domine.*

[51] *Almost as many as George Stone, the bear.*

George Stone was a noted bear exhibited at Paris Garden; so called from the name of his owner. *Sacarson*, the bear mentioned in *The Merry Wives of Windsor*, probably bore the name of his keeper.

[52] ———— *For ere the day*
Be spent to the girdle.

That is, before mid-day. So in *Hamlet*—
> In the dead *waist* and middle of the night.

[53] *Thy kinsman hath expressed thee.*

That is, spoken for thee, expressed thy meaning.

[54] *Your false-tail'd gelding.*

That is, a highwayman's horse, with a false tail to take on and off, to aid in preventing recognition.

[55] *Puh! that's the babe of a man.*

That is, an invention of man; a mere phantasm of the mind; the scholar wishes to overcome the doubts or fears of the highwayman, by denying the existence of such a being as the devil.

[56] *That I should ne'er lin laughing.*

A provincial expression, signifying, I should never *leave off* laughing.

[57] *By reason of the act of parliament against conjurors and witches.*

The act here alluded to passed in the first year of the reign of James (1604). From this passage it may be inferred that the present play did not make its appearance until after that period. There is a particular clause in the statute against all persons "taking upon them by witchcraft &c., to tell or declare in what place any treasure of gold or silver should or might be found or had in the earth or other secret places."

[58] *I were better go to sixteen hot-houses.*

A cant name for brothels.

[59] *Worth a hundred Brownists.*

A sect of eccentric christians named *Brownists*, from their leader, Robert Brown, who first advanced the doctrines held by them, about the year 1583. For an account of this sect see Fuller's *Church History*, b. ix. p. 268.

[60] *Would Derrick had been his fortune seven years ago.*

Derrick was the common hangman at the time this play was produced. He is alluded to in *The Bell-man of London*, 1616:—"he rides circuit with the devil, and *Derrick* must be his host, and Tyborne the inne at which he will light." Again, "if *Derrick's* cables do but hold." And in the ancient ballad entitled, *Upon the Earle of Essex, his death* :—

> Derick, thou know'st at Cales I sav'd
> Thy life, lost for a rape there done,
> Where thou thyself can'st testifye
> Thine own hand three-and-twenty hung.

Rare times those, for the hangman who (at least among the lower ranks of the people) was a far more active man than the schoolmaster. In these days, when the teacher and the printing-press are ever at work, crime has decreased almost in the same proportion as executions have.

[61] *Coades.*

I cannot explain this expression; perhaps it is a corruption of the press. Steevens says : "She may mean to call these confederate lovers *co-aids* ; but I rather think the word is a corruption of some oath."

[62] *The fescue of the dial is upon the christ-cross of noon.*

A *fescue* is a small wire, by which those who teach children to read, point out the letters. Dr. Percy observes, " The meridional line in the old dial plate was distinguished by a cross, which being also prefixed to the alphabet in the ancient primer, occasioned it to be denominated by the vulgar the *Christ-cross-row* here alluded to : and carrying on the same allusion, the gnomon of the dial is here called the *fescue* or long pin used in pointing out the letters of the alphabet to children."

[63] *I had rather run upon the ropes, &c.*

He means, he would rather play dangerous tricks, like a rope-dancer, than run the risk of being hanged.

[64] *In sparkling charnico.*

Charnico was a common sort of sweet wine, supposed to have some medicinal properties.

[65] *Instead of a jester we'll have the ghost in the white sheet sit at the upper end of the table.*

Dr. Farmer believed this to be a sneer, or an allusion to the introduction of the ghost of *Banquo*, in *Macbeth ;* in that supposition he was also supported by Malone.

[66] *'Slid, they have hired men and all by the clock.*

Perhaps he intends to say that they have hired their dresses and attendants by the hour, or he may mean to swear by the clock.

[67] *Out, slave ! I'll rend my lion from thy back.*

Wealthy people frequently had their crest wrought on the back of their servant's dress, but a puritan would scarcely have worn so ostentatious a distinction; it is probable that the word *lion* is a misprint for *livery.*

H. T.

The Life and Death of Thomas, Lord Cromwell

The amount and variety of Elizabethan literature bearing the nationalist and patriotic stamp are extraordinary. That literature ranges from the legendary Brute, eponymous founder of Britain, through Arthurian and Saxon history to Elizabeth herself and happenings within the memory of living men. It takes every event, every story or rumor, into account circumstantially or imaginatively: the doing of princes, their wars and intrigues, or their petty private crimes and escapades. It is moral and tragic in the verse narratives of *The Mirror for Magistrates*; controversial in John Foxe's *Book of Martyrs*; biographical in *Thomas, Lord Cromwell*, George Cavendish's *Life and Death of Thomas Wolsey*, and in the annals of the prose chronicles of Edward Halle, Raphael Holinshed, and John Stow.

In addition there were numerous collections in English—free translations of history and tragedy, usually with considerable moralizing additions—of Italian tales or their French versions. The most important were William Painter's *Palace of Pleasure* (1566–67, 1575), from a variety of authors including Giovanni Boccaccio, Matteo Bandello (both direct and through Pierre Boaistuau and François de Belleforest), Cinthio (Giovanni Battista Giraldi), and Marguerite of Navarre; Geoffrey Fenton's *Certain Tragical Discourses*, from Beleforest; George Turberville's *Tragical Tales* in verse, chiefly from Boccaccio; and George Whetstone's *Rock of Regard* and *Heptameron of Civil Discourses*. There were, besides, lesser collections and single tales. Spanish authors likewise translated and imitated the Italian tales and produced collections of their own, the finest being the *Novelas Ejemplares* of Miguel de Cervantes; this added to the Italian and French novelle a rich source, on the whole more suitable for romance than for tragedy, to be drawn on by later Jacobean and Caroline dramatists.

Thus the ground was not unprepared when the immediate predecessors of Shakespeare turned to national history and to romance to find subject matter for drama; and it is always to be remembered that the Elizabethan chronicle play was only one form, albeit the most striking, of an extensive and varied literature expressing the national spirit. In his dedication to *Perkin Warbeck*, John Ford says that he was attracted to the subject by "a perfection in the story." The Prologue, after touching upon the neglect that had recently fallen upon "studies of this nature," proceeds as follows:

> . . . We can say
> He shows a History couched in a Play!
> A history of noble mention, known,
> Famous, and true; most noble, 'cause our own;
> Not forged from Italy, from France, from Spain,
> But chronicled at home.

We may define a chronicle history, or chronicle play, as a piece out of the saga of England, dramatized and set on the stage. It is sometimes made to center about the personality of a king or other hero, and becomes essentially his story; but the scene is commonly filled with a multiplicity of personages, and proceeds from event to event much as a panorama moves from picture to picture. That a spirit of patriotism inspired the writing of many of these plays is not to be denied; but their leading impetus was that of character and love of story, and everything was staged, the prowess and glory of kings and heroes and their incompetence and mishap as well.

When we turn to the popular drama, we find that *The Famous Victories of Henry V* is the earliest extant specimen of an actual chronicle play. This curious report on the wild life of that king when a prince, with the humors of the tavern, its suggestion of the character of Sir John Oldcastle, and its rude delineation of the difficult relations between Prince Henry and his father was acted by the Queen's Men when they were most popular. It is interesting as a primitive example of its type, and likewise because in its scenes of comedy we have a transcript of contemporary everyday life.

Among pre-Shakespearean chronicle histories, there are several other interesting plays: George Peele's *Edward I,* the two dramas known as *The Troublesome Reign of King John* (the basis of Shakespeare's *Life and Death of King John*), the two parts of *The Contention of the Two Famous Houses of York and Lancaster* (later rewritten in Shakespeare's 2 and 3 *Henry VI's*), and *The True Tragedy of Richard III* (not wholly unrelated to Shakespeare's *Richard III*). To these may be added Shakespeare's *1 Henry VI,* although we now have it only in the later form he gave it when he made it a part of his trilogy on that unhappy monarch. The whole group was in print before 1595;

and, in accordance with the practice of this earlier time, in none of the early quartos is there any mention of the author.

The vogue for chronicle history was from 1599 to the end of Elizabeth's reign. During these years, the chronicle play led all other plays in popularity, extending its methods to plays of other kinds, especially the biographical chronicle. From the first, however, there was a frequent biographical emphasis in chronicle plays, and their subject matter was soon extended to heroes less than royal, some of them all but contemporary: Cardinal Wolsey and Lord Cromwell, powerful implements of the tyranny of Henry VIII and victims of it as well, and Sir Thomas Wyatt, who precipitately attempted an anticipation of Elizabeth's accession to the throne. (Besides Shakespeare's *Henry VIII* and Samuel Rowley's *When You See Me You Know Me,* Cardinal Wolsey figures in three lost plays by Henry Chettle and others mentioned in the papers of Philip Henslowe. Sir Thomas Wyatt appears in a play by Dekker and Webster in collaboration, which forms a sequel to the story of the reign of Edward VI.)

It also appears from various sources that many more plays on minor characters in English history were known to the Elizabethan public. J. A. Symonds (44) notes *Buckingham* (1593); Middleton's tragedy of *Randal, Earl of Chester* (1602); a *Duchess of Suffolk*; a *Duke Humphrey*; an *Earl of Gloucester*; a *Hotspur*; the fragment of Ben Jonson's *Mortimer*; *Gowry,* which was represented in the reign of James I; a play on Thomas Stukeley, a restless adventurer of Devon stock, like Hawkins and Raleigh, who planned to carve out for himself a kingdom in Florida but became the inevitable enemy of his queen and died fighting the Moors; and, finally, the appearance of Sir Thomas Gresham, financier of the queen and the founder of the Royal Exchange, as a character in Thomas Heywood's *If You Not Know Me, You Know Nobody* (1607).

But among these biographical chronicles, there is none so interesting as the fine play *Sir Thomas More,* recently the subject of renewed attention by reason of the effort to identify as Shakespeare's one of the six (or, according to F. J. Furnivall, perhaps seven) handwritings in which the manuscript is preserved. The insurrection scene of this play has been attributed to Shakespeare by a number of scholars, partly because of the handwriting but also because of the similarity of the political ideas expressed in this scene to Shakespeare's known opinions enunciated in his chronicle plays.

The concentration of biography on a single tragic motive opened possibilities of the highest dramatic importance; and this concentration we find for the first time in Marlowe's *Edward II,* on the stage in the earliest nineties. This tragedy, regarded as a biographical drama, must have created a sensation on first performance. The overpowering pathos of the concluding scenes reaches a poignancy that few of Marlowe's successors, with the sole exception of Shakespeare, ever approached, suggesting new possibilities of character portrayal and dramatic evocation for this form.

In 1602, after being entered upon the Stationers' Register, there was published a quarto with a title page reading: "The True Chronicle History of the whole life and death of Thomas Lord Cromwell. As it has been sundry times publicly acted by the Right Honorable the Lord Chamberlain his servants. Written by W. S."

Quoting at length Swinburne's criticism of this play, Baldwin Maxwell (27) nevertheless admits he is undeterred by Swinburne's harsh judgment of it because he is convinced "that all students of Shakespeare may have an interest in any play, however bad they may think it, which for a century or so was accepted as by William Shakespeare"—and because he suspects Swinburne has in this instance allowed his judgment to do a courtesy to his wrath and to his love of vigorous expression.

One may reject Swinburne's disapproval as unwarrantably severe without joining the camp of such nineteenth-century German critics as A. W. von Schlegel, who, with great confidence, declared *Thomas Lord Cromwell* to be not only unquestionably Shakespeare's but deserving to be classed among his best and maturest works. The play of Cromwell is, in fact, a loosely constructed but by no means untypical mixture of historical fact, fiction, hearsay, and propaganda, with (at least to Maxwell) little or no character portrayal but with a glorification of homely virtues and one or two most amusing bits of comedy.

After a second edition of the play was published in 1613—again as "written by W. S."—*Cromwell* was included in the Third and Fourth Shakespearean Folios of 1664 and 1685, reprinted by Shakespeare's first editor, Nicholas Rowe, in 1709, and issued separately in 1734 by R. Walker as "A Tragedy. By Shakespear."

PERSONS REPRESENTED.

DUKE OF NORFOLK.

Appears, Act IV. sc. 1; sc. 2; sc. 5. Act V. sc. 3; sc. 5.

DUKE OF SUFFOLK.

Appears, Act IV. sc. 1; sc. 2; sc. 4; sc. 5. Act V. sc. 3; sc. 5.

EARL OF BEDFORD.

Appears, Act III. sc. 2. Act IV. sc. 1; sc. 4; sc. 5. Act V. sc. 1; sc. 3; sc. 5.

CARDINAL WOLSEY.

Appears, Act III. sc. 3.

GARDINER, *Bishop of* Winchester.

Appears, Act III. sc. 3. Act IV. sc. 1; sc. 2; sc. 5. Act V. sc. 3; sc. 5.

SIR THOMAS MORE.
SIR CHRISTOPHER HALES.

Appear, Act III. sc. 3. Act IV. sc. 1.

SIR RALPH SADLER.
SIR RICHARD RATCLIFF.

Appear, Act V. sc. 5.

OLD CROMWELL, *a Blacksmith of* Putney.

Appears, Act I. sc. 2. Act IV. sc. 2; sc. 4.

THOMAS CROMWELL, *his Son.*

Appears, Act I. sc. 2. Act II. sc. 1; sc. 2. Act III. sc. 1; sc. 2; sc. 3. Act IV. sc. 1; sc. 2; sc. 4. Act V. sc. 1; sc. 2; sc. 3; sc. 5.

BANISTER, *an* English *Merchant.*

Appears, Act I. sc. 3. Act II. sc. 3. Act IV. sc. 2.

BOWSER, *an* English *Merchant.*

Appears, Act I. sc. 2. Act II. sc. 3.

NEWTON, } *Merchants.*
CROSBY, }

Appear, Act IV. sc. 3.

BAGOT, *a Money-broker.*

Appears, Act I. sc. 3. Act II. sc. 2; sc. 3.

FRESCOBALD, *a* Florentine *Merchant.*

Appears, Act I. sc. 3. Act III. sc. 1. Act IV. sc. 2; sc. 4.

The GOVERNOR *of the* English *Factory at* Antwerp

Appears, Act II. sc. 3.

GOVERNOR *and other* STATES *of* Bononia.

Appear, Act III. sc. 2.

MASTER OF AN HOTEL *in* Bononia.

Appears, Act III. sc. 2.

SEELY, *a Poor Man of* Houndslow.

Appears, Act IV. sc. 2; sc. 4.

LIEUTENANT OF THE TOWER.

Appears, Act V. sc. 3; sc. 5.

YOUNG CROMWELL, *a little Boy, the Son of* Thomas.

Appears, Act V. sc. 5.

HODGE, *a Smith, afterwards Servant to* Thomas Cromwell.

Appears, Act I. sc. 1; sc. 2. Act II. sc. 2. Act III. sc. 1; sc. 2. Act IV. sc. 2.

WILL, } *Smiths, in the employ of*
TOM, } Old Cromwell.

Appear, Act I. sc. 1; sc. 2.

TWO CITIZENS.

Appear, Act V. sc. 4.

TWO FALSE WITNESSES.

Appear, Act IV. sc. 5.

MRS. BANISTER.

Appears, Act I. sc. 3. Act II. sc. 1; sc. 3. Act IV. sc. 2.

JOAN, *Wife to* Seely.

Appears, Act IV. sc. 2.

A Serjeant-at-Arms, a Herald, an Executioner, a Post, Messengers, Officers, Ushers, and Attendants.

SCENE.—*Partly in* LONDON, *and the adjoining district; partly in* ANTWERP *and* BONONIA.

THE LIFE AND DEATH OF
Thomas, Lord Cromwell.

ACT I.

SCENE I.—Putney. *The entrance of a Smith's Shop.*

Enter HODGE, WILL, *and* TOM.

Hodge. Come, masters, I think it be past five o'clock ; is it not time we were at work? my old master he'll be stirring anon.

Will. I cannot tell whether my old master will be stirring or no ; but I am sure I can hardly take my afternoon's nap, for my young master Thomas. He keeps such a coil in his study, with the sun, and the moon, and the seven stars, that I do verily think he'll read out his wits.

Hodge. He skill of the stars? There's goodman Car of Fulham, (he that carried us to the strong ale,[1] where goody Trundel had her maid got with child) O, he knows the stars ; he 'll tickle you Charles's wain in nine degrees : that same man will tell goody Trundel when her ale shall miscarry, only by the stars.

Tom. Ay! that's a great virtue indeed ; I think Thomas be nobody in comparison to him.

Will. Well, masters, come ; shall we to our hammers?

Hodge. Ay, content : first let 's take our morning's draught, and then to work roundly.

Tom. Ay, agreed. Go in, Hodge. [*Exeunt.*

SCENE II.—*The Same.*

Enter Young CROMWELL.

Crom. Good morrow, morn ; I do salute thy brightness.
The night seems tedious to my troubled soul,
Whose black obscurity binds in my mind
A thousand sundry cogitations :
And now Aurora with a lively dye
Adds comfort to my spirit, that mounts on high ;
Too high indeed, my state being so mean.
My study, like a mineral of gold,
Makes my heart proud, wherein my hope's enroll'd :

My books are all the wealth I do possess,
And unto them I have engag'd my heart.
O, learning, how divine thou seem'st to me,
Within whose arms is all felicity!
     [*The smiths beat with their hammers within.*
Peace with your hammers! leave your knocking there!
You do disturb my study and my rest :
Leave off, I say : you mad me with the noise.

Enter HODGE, WILL, *and* TOM.

Hodge. Why, how now, master Thomas? how now? will you not let us work for you?

Crom. You fret my heart with making of this noise.

Hodge. How, fret your heart? ay, but Thomas, you'll fret your father's purse, if you let us from working.[2]

Tom. Ay, this 'tis for him to make him a gentleman. Shall we leave work for your musing? that 's well i'faith :—But here comes my old master now.

Enter Old CROMWELL.

Old Crom. You idle knaves, what are you loit'ring now?
No hammers walking, and my work to do!
What not a heat among your work to day?

Hodge. Marry, sir, your son Thomas will not let us work at all.

Old Crom. Why knave, I say, have I thus cark'd and car'd,[3]
And all to keep thee like a gentleman ;
And dost thou let my servants at their work,
That sweat for thee, knave, labour thus for thee?

Crom. Father, their hammers do offend my study.

Old Crom. Out of my doors, knave, if thou lik'st it not.
I cry you mercy ; are your ears so fine?
I tell thee, knave, these get when I do sleep ;
I will not have my anvil stand for thee.

Crom. There's money, father; I will pay your
　　men.　　　　　　[*Throws money among them.*
Old Crom. Have I thus brought thee up unto
　　my cost,
In hope that one day thou'd'st relieve my age;
And art thou now so lavish of thy coin,
To scatter it among these idle knaves?
　Crom. Father, be patient, and content yourself:
The time will come I shall hold gold as trash.
And here I speak with a presaging soul,
To build a palace where this cottage stands,
As fine as is king Henry's house at Sheen.
　Old Crom. You build a house? you knave, you'll
　　be a beggar.
Now afore God all is but cast away,
That is bestow'd upon this thriftless lad.
Well, had I bound him to some honest trade,
This had not been; but 'twas his mother's doing,
To send him to the university.
How? build a house where now this cottage stands,
As fair as that at Sheen?—They shall not hear me.
　　　　　　　　　　　　　　　[*Aside.*
A good boy Tom, I con thee thank Tom;
Well said Tom; gramercy Tom.—
In to your work, knaves; hence, you saucy boy.
　　　　　　[*Exeunt all but* Young CROM.
　Crom. Why should my birth keep down my
　　mounting spirit?
Are not all creatures subject unto time,
To time, who doth abuse the cheated world,
And fills it full of hodge-podge bastardy?
There's legions now of beggars on the earth,
That their original did spring from kings;
And many monarchs now, whose fathers were
The riff-raff of their age: for time and fortune
Wears out a noble train to beggary;
And from the dunghill minions do advance
To state and mark in this admiring world.
This is but course, which in the name of fate
Is seen as often as it whirls about.
The river Thames, that by our door doth pass,
His first beginning is but small and shallow;
Yet, keeping on his course, grows to a sea.
And likewise Wolsey, the wonder of our age,
His birth as mean as mine, a butcher's son;
Now who within this land a greater man?
Then, Cromwell, cheer thee up, and tell thy soul,
That thou may'st live to flourish and control.

Enter Old CROMWELL.

Old Crom. Tom Cromwell; what, Tom, I say.
Crom. Do you call, sir?
Old Crom. Here is master Bowser come to know

if you have dispatch'd his petition for the lords of
the council or no.
　Crom. Father, I have; please you to call him in.
　Old Crom. That's well said, Tom; a good lad, Tom.

Enter BOWSER.

　Bow. Now, master Cromwell, have you dispatch'd
this petition?
　Crom. I have, sir; here it is: please you peruse it.
　Bow. It shall not need; we'll read it as we go
By water.
And, master Cromwell, I have made a motion
May do you good, an if you like of it.
Our secretary at Antwerp, sir, is
Dead; and the merchants there have sent to me,
For to provide a man fit for the place:
Now I do know none fitter than yourself,
If with your liking it stand, master Cromwell.
　Crom. With all my heart, sir; and I much am
　　bound
In love and duty, for your kindness shown.
　Old Crom. Body of me, Tom, make haste, lest
some body get between thee and home, Tom. I
thank you, good master Bowser, I thank you for
my boy; I thank you always, I thank you most
heartily, sir: ho, a cup of beer here for master
Bowser.
　Bow. It shall not need, sir.—Master Cromwell,
will you go?
　Crom. I will attend you, sir.
　Old Crom. Farewell, Tom: God bless thee, Tom!
God speed thee, good Tom!　　　　　[*Exeunt.*

SCENE III.—London.　*A Street before* Fresco-
　　　　　　bald's *House.*

Enter BAGOT.

　Bag. I hope this day is fatal unto some,
And by their loss must Bagot seek to gain.
This is the lodging of master Frescobald,
A liberal merchant, and a Florentine;
To whom Banister owes a thousand pound,
A merchant-bankrupt, whose father was my master.
What do I care for pity or regard?
He once was wealthy, but he now is fallen:
And I this morning have got him arrested
At suit of this same master Frescobald;
And by this means shall I be sure of coin,
For doing this same good to him unknown:
And in good time, see where the merchant comes.

Enter FRESCOBALD.

Good morrow to kind master Frescobald.

Fres. Good morrow to yourself, good master
    Bagot:
And what's the news, you are so early stirring?
It is for gain, I make no doubt of that.
    Bag. 'Tis for the love, sir, that I bear to you,
When did you see your debtor Banister?
    Fres. I promise you, I have not seen the man
This two months day: his poverty is such,
As I do think he shames to see his friends.
    Bag. Why then assure yourself to see him
    straight,
For at your suit I have arrested him,
And here they will be with him presently.
    Fres. Arrest him at my suit? you were to blame.
I know the man's misfortunes to be such,
As he's not able for to pay the debt;
And were it known to some, he were undone.
    Bag. This is your pitiful heart to think it so;
But you are much deceiv'd in Banister.
Why, such as he will break for fashion-sake,
And unto those they owe a thousand pound,
Pay scarce a hundred. O, sir, beware of him.
The man is lewdly given to dice and drabs·
Spends all he hath in harlots' companies:
It is no mercy for to pity him.
I speak the truth of him, for nothing else,
But for the kindness that I bear to you.
    Fres. If it be so, he hath deceiv'd me much;
And to deal strictly with such a one as he,
Better severe than too much lenity.
But here is master Banister himself,
And with him, as I take it, the officers.

Enter Mr. *and* Mrs. Banister, *and Two* Officers.

    Ban. O, master Frescobald, you have undone me.
My state was well-nigh overthrown before;
Now altogether down-cast by your means.
    Mrs. Ban. O, master Frescobald, pity my hus-
    band's case.
He is a man hath liv'd as well as any,
Till envious fortune and the ravenous sea
Did rob, disrobe, and spoil us of our own.
    Fres. Mistress Banister, I envy not your husband,
Nor willingly would I have us'd him thus,
But that I hear he is so lewdly given;
Haunts wicked company, and hath enough
To pay his debts, yet will not be known thereof.
    Ban. This is that damned broker, that same
    Bagot,
Whom I have often from my trencher fed.
Ungrateful villain for to use me thus!
    Bag. What I have said to him is nought but
    truth.

    Mrs. Ban. What thou hast said springs from an
    envious heart:
A cannibal, that doth eat men alive!
But here upon my knee believe me, sir,
(And what I speak, so help me God, is true,)
We scarce have meat to feed our little babes.
Most of our plate is in that broker's hand:
Which, had we money to defray our debts,
O think, we would not 'bide that penury.
Be merciful, kind master Frescobald;
My husband, children, and myself will eat
But one meal a day; the other will we keep,
And sell, as part to pay the debt we owe you.
If ever tears did pierce a tender mind,
Be pitiful; let me some favour find.
    Fres. Go to, I see thou art an envious man,
Good mistress Banister, kneel not to me;
I pray rise up; you shall have your desire.
Hold officers; be gone; there's for your pains.
You know you owe to me a thousand pound:
Here, take my hand; if e'er God make you able,
And place you in your former state again,
Pay me; but yet if still your fortune frown,
Upon my faith I'll never ask a crown.
I never yet did wrong to men in thrall,
For God doth know what to myself may fall.
    Ban. This unexpected favour, undeserv'd,
Doth make my heart bleed inwardly with joy.
Ne'er may aught prosper with me is my own,
If I forget this kindness you have shown.
    Mrs. Ban. My children in their prayers, both
    night and day,
For your good fortune and success shall pray.
    Fres. I thank you both; I pray go dine with me.
Within these three days, if God give me leave,
I will to Florence, to my native home.
Hold, Bagot, there's a portague to drink,[4]
Although you ill deserv'd it by your merit.
Give not such cruel scope unto your heart;
Be sure the ill you do will be requited:
Remember what I say, Bagot: farewell.
Come, master Banister, you shall with me;
My fare's but simple, but welcome heartily.
                  [*Exeunt all but* Bag.
    Bag. A plague go with you! would you had eat
    your last!
Is this the thanks I have for all my pains?
Confusion light upon you all for me!
Where he had wont to give a score of crowns,
Doth he now foist me with a portague?
Well, I will be reveng'd upon this Banister.
I'll to his creditors; buy all the debts he owes,
As seeming that I do it for good will;

I am sure to have them at an easy rate:
And when 'tis done, in Christendom he stays not,
But I'll make his heart to ache with sorrow.

And if that Banister become my debtor,
By heaven and earth I'll make his plague the
    greater.   [*Exit.*

ACT II.

Enter CHORUS.

Cho. Now, gentlemen, imagine that young
    Cromwell's
In Antwerp, leiger for the English merchants;[5]
And Banister, to shun this Bagot's hate,
Hearing that he hath got some of his debts,
Is fled to Antwerp, with his wife and children;
Which Bagot hearing, is gone after them,
And thither sends his bills of debt before,
To be reveng'd on wretched Banister.
What doth fall out, with patience sit and see,
A just requital of false treachery.   [*Exit.*

SCENE I.—Antwerp.

CROMWELL *discovered in his Study, sitting at a
Table, on which are placed Money-bags and Books
of account.*

Crom. Thus far my reckoning doth go straight
    and even.
But, Cromwell, this same plodding fits not thee;
Thy mind is altogether set on travel,
And not to live thus cloister'd like a nun.
It is not this same trash that I regard:
Experience is the jewel of my heart.

Enter a POST.

Post. I pray, sir, are you ready to dispatch me?
Crom. Yes; here's those sums of money you
    must carry.
You go as far as Frankfort, do you not?
Post. I do, sir.
Crom. Well, pr'ythee make then all the haste
    thou canst;
For there be certain English gentlemen
Are bound for Venice, and may happily want,
An if that you should linger by the way:
But in the hope that you will make good speed,
There's two angels, to buy you spurs and wands.[6]
Post. I thank you, sir; this will add wings
    indeed.   [*Exit* Post.
Crom. Gold is of power to make an eagle's speed.

Enter MRS. BANISTER.

What gentlewoman is this that grieves so much?
It seems she doth address herself to me.
   Mrs. Ban. God save you, sir. Pray is your
name master Cromwell?
   Crom. My name is Thomas Cromwell, gentle-
    woman.
   Mrs. Ban. Know you one Bagot, sir, that's come
    to Antwerp?
   Crom. No, trust me, I ne'er saw the man; but
    here
Are bills of debt I have receiv'd against
One Banister, a merchant fall'n to decay.
   Mrs. Ban. Into decay indeed, 'long of that
    wretch.
I am the wife to woeful Banister,
And by that bloody villain am pursu'd,
From London, here to Antwerp. My husband
He is in the governor's hands; and God
Of heaven knows how he will deal with him.
Now, sir, your heart is fram'd of milder temper;
Be merciful to a distressed soul,
And God no doubt will treble bless your gain.
   Crom. Good mistress Banister, what I can, I will,
In any thing that lies within my power.
   Mrs. Ban. O speak to Bagot, that same wicked
    wretch:
An angel's voice may move a damned devil.
   Crom. Why is he come to Antwerp, as you hear?
   Mrs. Ban. I heard he landed some two hours
    since.
   Crom. Well, mistress Banister, assure yourself
I'll speak to Bagot in your own behalf,
And win him to all the pity that I can.
Mean time, to comfort you in your distress,
Receive these angels to relieve your need;
And be assur'd, that what I can effect,
To do you good, no way I will neglect.
   Mrs. Ban. That mighty God that knows each
    mortal's heart,
Keep you from trouble, sorrow, grief, and smart.
                   [*Exit* MRS. BAN.

Crom. Thanks, courteous woman, for thy hearty
　　prayer.
It grieves my soul to see her misery:
But we that live under the work of fate,
May hope the best, yet know not to what state
Our stars and destinies have us assign'd;
Fickle is Fortune, and her face is blind.　　[*Exit.*

SCENE II.—*A Street in* Antwerp.

Enter BAGOT.

Bag. So, all goes well; it is as I would have it.
Banister, he is with the governor,
And shortly shall have gyves upon his heels.
It glads my heart to think upon the slave;
I hope to have his body rot in prison,
And after hear his wife to hang herself,
And all his children die for want of food.
The jewels I have with me brought to Antwerp,
Are reckon'd to be worth five thousand pound;
Which scarcely stood me in three hundred pound.
I bought them at an easy kind of rate;
I care not much which way they came by them,
That sold them me; it comes not near my heart:
And lest they should be stolen, (as sure they are,)
I thought it meet to sell them here in Antwerp;
And so have left them in the governor's hand,
Who offers me within two hundred pound
Of all my price: but now no more of that.—
I must go see an if my bills be safe,
The which I sent before to master Cromwell;
That if the wind should keep me on the sea,
He might arrest him here before I came:
And in good time, see where he is.

Enter CROMWELL.

God save you sir.
　　Crom. And you.—Pray pardon me, I know you
　　not.
　　Bag. It may be so, sir; but my name is Bagot;
The man that sent to you the bills of debt.
　　Crom. O, you're the man that pursues Banister.
Here are the bills of debt you sent to me;
As for the man, you know best where he is.
It is reported you have a flinty heart,
A mind that will not stoop to any pity,
An eye that knows not how to shed a tear,
A hand that's always open for reward.
But, master Bagot, would you be rul'd by me,
You should turn all these to the contrary:
Your heart should still have feeling of remorse,[7]
Your mind, according to your state, be liberal
To those that stand in need and in distress;

Your hand to help them that do stand in want,
Rather than with your poise to hold them down:
For every ill turn show yourself more kind;
Thus should I do; pardon, I speak my mind.
　　Bag. Ay, sir, you speak to hear what I would
　　say;
But you must live, I know, as well as I.
I know this place to be extortion;[8]
And 'tis not for a man to keep safe here,
But he must lie, cog with his dearest friend,
And as for pity, scorn it; hate all conscience:—
But yet I do commend your wit in this,
To make a show of what I hope you are not;
But I commend you, and it is well done:
This is the only way to bring your gain.
　　Crom. My gain? I had rather chain me to an
　　oar,
And, like a slave, there toil out all my life,
Before I'd live so base a slave as thou.
I, like an hypocrite, to make a show
Of seeming virtue, and a devil within!
No, Bagot; if thy conscience were as clear,
Poor Banister ne'er had been troubled here.
　　Bag. Nay, good master Cromwell, be not angry,
　　sir,
I know full well that you are no such man;
But if your conscience were as white as snow,
It will be thought that you are otherwise.
　　Crom. Will it be thought that I am otherwise?
Let them that think so, know they are deceiv'd.
Shall Cromwell live to have his faith misconstru'd?
Antwerp, for all the wealth within thy town,
I will not stay here full two hours longer.—
As good luck serves, my accounts are all made even;
Therefore I'll straight unto the treasurer.
Bagot, I know you'll to the governor:
Commend me to him; say I am bound to travel,
To see the fruitful parts of Italy;
And as you ever bore a christian mind,
Let Banister some favour of you find.
　　Bag. For your sake, sir, I'll help him all I can—
To starve his heart out ere he gets a groat; [*Aside.*
So, master Cromwell, do I take my leave,
For I must straight unto the governor.
　　Crom. Farewell, sir; pray you remember what I
　　said.　　　　　　　　　　　　　　　[*Exit* BAG.
No, Cromwell, no; thy heart was ne'er so base,
To live by falsehood, or by brokery.
But it falls out well; I little it repent;
Hereafter time in travel shall be spent.

Enter HODGE.

Hodge. Your son Thomas, quoth you! I have

been Thomass'd.[9] I had thought it had been no such matter to ha' gone by water; for at Putney, I'll go you to Parish-Garden for two-pence; sit as still as may be, without any wagging or jolting in my guts, in a little boat too: here, we were scarce four miles in the great green water, but I, thinking to go to my afternoon's nuncheon, as 'twas my manner at home, felt a kind of rising in my guts. At last, one of the sailors spying of me—be of good cheer, says he; set down thy victuals, and up with it; thou hast nothing but an eel in thy belly. Well, to't went I, to my victuals went the sailors; and thinking me to be a man of better experience than any in the ship, ask'd me what wood the ship was made of: they all swore I told them as right as if I had been acquainted with the carpenter that made it. At last we grew near land, and I grew villanous hungry, and went to my bag. The devil a bit there was, the sailors had tickled me; yet I cannot blame them: it was a part of kindness; for I in kindness told them what wood the ship was made of, and they in kindness eat up my victuals; as indeed one good turn asketh another. Well, would I could find my master Thomas in this Dutch town! he might put some English beer into my belly.

Crom. What, Hodge, my father's man! by my hand welcome.

How doth my father? what's the news at home?

Hodge. Master Thomas, O God! Master Thomas, your hand, glove and all: This is to give you to understanding, that your father is in health, and Alice Downing here hath sent you a nutmeg, and Bess Make-water a race of ginger; my fellows Will and Tom hath between them sent you a dozen of points; and goodman Toll, of the goat, a pair of mittens: myself came in person; and this is all the news.

Crom. Gramercy good Hodge, and thou art welcome to me,

But in as ill a time thou comest as may be;

For I am travelling into Italy.

What say'st thou, Hodge? wilt thou bear me company?

Hodge. Will I bear thee company, Tom? what tell'st me of Italy? Were it to the farthest part of Flanders, I would go with thee, Tom: I am thine in all weal and woe; thy own to command. What, Tom! I have pass'd the rigorous waves of Neptune's blasts. I tell you, Thomas, I have been in danger of the floods; and when I have seen Boreas begin to play the ruffian with us, then would I down a' my knees, and call upon Vulcan.

Crom. And why upon him?

Hodge. Because, as this same fellow Neptune is god of the seas, so Vulcan is lord over the smiths; and therefore I, being a smith, thought his godhead would have some care yet of me.

Crom. A good conceit: but tell me, hast thou din'd yet?

Hodge. Thomas, to speak the truth, not a bit yet, I.

Crom. Come, go with me, thou shalt have cheer, good store;

And farewell, Antwerp, if I come no more.

Hodge. I follow thee, sweet Tom, I follow thee.

[*Exeunt.*

SCENE III.—*Another Street in the same.*

Enter the Governor of the English Factory, BAGOT, MR. *and* MRS. BANISTER, *and Two* Officers.

Gov. Is Cromwell gone then say you, master Bagot?

On what dislike, I pray you? what was the cause?

Bag. To tell you true, a wild brain of his own;

Such youth as he can't see when they are well.

He is all bent to travel, (that's his reason,)

And doth not love to eat his bread at home.

Gov. Well, good fortune with him, if the man be gone.

We hardly shall find such a one as he,

To fit our turns, his dealings were so honest.

But now, sir, for your jewels that I have—

What do you say? what, will you take my price?

Bag. O, sir, you offer too much under foot.[10]

Gov. 'Tis but two hundred pounds between us, man;

What's that in payment of five thousand pound?

Bag. Two hundred pound! by'r lady, sir, 'tis great;

Before I got so much, it made me sweat.

Gov. Well, master Bagot, I'll proffer you fairly.

You see this merchant, master Banister,

Is going now to prison at your suit;

His substance all is gone: what would you have?

Yet, in regard I knew the man of wealth,

(Never dishonest dealing, but such mishaps

Have fallen on him, may light on me or you)

There is two hundred pound between us two;

We will divide the same: I'll give you one,

On that condition you will set him free.

His state is nothing; that you see yourself;

And where nought is, the king must lose his right.

Bag. Sir, sir, I know you speak out of your love;

'Tis foolish love, sir, sure, to pity him.

Therefore content yourself; this is my mind;
To do him good I will not bate a penny.

    Ban. This is my comfort, though thou dost no good,
A mighty ebb follows a mighty flood.

    Mrs. Ban. O thou base wretch, whom we have fostered,
Even as a serpent, for to poison us!
If God did ever right a woman's wrong,
To that same God I bend and bow my heart,
To let his heavy wrath fall on thy head,
By whom my hopes and joys are butchered.

    Bag. Alas, fond woman! I pr'ythee pray thy worst;
The fox fares better still when he is curst.

Enter BOWSER.

    Gov. Master Bowser! you're welcome, sir, from England.
What's the best news? and how do all our friends?

    Bow. They are all well, and do commend them to you.
There's letters from your brother and your son:
So, fare you well, sir; I must take my leave:
My haste and business doth require so.

    Gov. Before you dine, sir? What, go you out of town?

    Bow. I'faith unless I hear some news in town,
I must away; there is no remedy.

    Gov. Master Bowser, what is your business? may I know it?

    Bow. You may so, sir, and so shall all the city.
The king of late hath had his treasury robb'd,
And of the choicest jewels that he had:
The value of them was seven thousand pounds.
The fellow that did steal these jewels is hang'd;
And did confess that for three hundred pound
He sold them to one Bagot dwelling in London.
Now Bagot's fled, and, as we hear, to Antwerp;
And hither am I come to seek him out;
And they that first can tell me of his news,
Shall have a hundred pound for their reward.

    Ban. How just is God to right the innocent!

    Gov. Master Bowser, you come in happy time:
Here is the villain Bagot that you seek,
And all those jewels have I in my hands:
Here, officers, look to him, hold him fast.

    Bag. The devil ought me a shame, and now hath paid it.

    Bow. Is this that Bagot? Fellows, bear him hence;
We will not now stand here for his reply.
Lade him with irons; we will have him try'd
In England, where his villanies are known.

    Bag. Mischief, confusion, light upon you all!
O hang me, drown me, let me kill myself;
Let go my arms, let me run quick to hell.

    Bow. Away; bear him away; stop the slave's mouth.   [*Exeunt* Officers *and* BAG.

    Mrs. Ban. Thy works are infinite, great God of heaven.

    Gov. I heard this Bagot was a wealthy fellow.

    Bow. He was indeed; for when his goods were seiz'd,
Of jewels, coin, and plate, within his house
Was found the value of five thousand pound;
His furniture fully worth half so much;
Which being all distrained for the king,
He frankly gave it to the Antwerp merchants;
And they again, out of their bounteous mind,
Have to a brother of their company,
A man decay'd by fortune of the seas,
Given Bagot's wealth, to set him up again,
And keep it for him; his name is Banister.

    Gov. Master Bowser, with this most happy news
You have reviv'd two from the gates of death:
This is that Banister, and this his wife.

    Bow. Sir, I am glad my fortune is so good
To bring such tidings as may comfort you.

    Ban. You have given life unto a man deem'd dead;
For by these news my life is newly bred.

    Mrs. Ban. Thanks to my God, next to my sovereign king;
And last to you, that these good news do bring.

    Gov. The hundred pound I must receive, as due
For finding Bagot, I freely give to you.

    Bow. And, master Banister, if so you please,
I'll bear you company, when you cross the seas.

    Ban. If it please you, sir;—my company is but mean:
Stands with your liking, I will wait on you.

    Gov. I am glad that all things do accord so well.
Come, master Bowser, let us in to dinner;
And, mistress Banister, be merry, woman.
Come, after sorrow now let's cheer your spirit;
Knaves have their due, and you but what you merit.   [*Exeunt.*

ACT III.

SCENE I.—*The principal Bridge at* Florence.

Enter Cromwell *and* Hodge *in their Shirts, and without Hats.*

Hodge. Call you this seeing of fashions? marry would I had staid at Putney still. O, master Thomas, we are spoil'd, we are gone.

Crom. Content thee, man; this is but fortune.

Hodge. Fortune! a plague of this fortune, it makes me go wet-shod; the rogues would not leave me a shoe to my feet.

    For my hose,
They scorn'd them with their heels:
But for my doublet and hat,
O lord, they embrac'd me,
And unlac'd me,
And took away my clothes.
And so disgrac'd me.

Crom. Well, Hodge, what remedy? What shift shall we make now?

Hodge. Nay I know not. For begging I am naught; for stealing worse. By my troth, I must even fall to my old trade, to the hammer and the horse-heels again:—But now the worst is, I am not acquainted with the humour of the horses in this country; whether they are not coltish, given much to kicking, or no: for when I have one leg in my hand, if he should up and lay t'other on my chaps, I were gone; there lay I, there lay Hodge.

Crom. Hodge, I believe thou must work for us both.

Hodge. O, master Thomas, have not I told you of this? Have not I many a time and often said, Tom, or master Thomas, learn to make a horse-shoe, it will be your own another day; this was not regarded.—Hark you, Thomas! what do you call the fellows that robb'd us?

Crom. The banditti.

Hodge. The banditti do you call them? I know not what they are call'd here, but I am sure we call them plain thieves in England. O, Tom, that we were now at Putney, at the ale there!

Crom. Content thee, man: here set up these two bills,
And let us keep our standing on the bridge.
The fashion of this country is such,
If any stranger be oppress'd with want,
To write the manner of his misery;

And such as are dispos'd to succour him,

       [Hodge *sets up the Bills.*

Will do it. What, Hodge, hast thou set them up?

Hodge. Ay, they are up; God send some to read them,[11] and not only to read them, but also to look on us: and not altogether look on us, but to relieve us. O, cold, cold, cold!

    [Crom. *stands at one end of the Bridge, and* Hodge *at the other.*

Enter Frescobald.

Fres. [*Reads the bills.*] What's here?
Two Englishmen, and robb'd by the banditti!
One of them seems to be a gentleman.
'Tis pity that his fortune was so hard,
To fall into the desperate hands of thieves:
I'll question him of what estate he is.
God save you, sir. Are you an Englishman?

Crom. I am, sir, a distressed Englishman.

Fres. And what are you, my friend?

Hodge. Who, I sir? by my troth I do not know myself, what I am now; but, sir, I was a smith, sir, a poor farrier of Putney. That's my master, sir, yonder; I was robb'd for his sake, sir.

Fres. I see you have been met by the banditti,
And therefore need not ask you how you came thus.
But Frescobald, why dost thou question them
Of their estate, and not relieve their need?
Sir, the coin I have about me is not much:
There's sixteen ducats for to clothe yourselves,
There's sixteen more to buy your diet with,
And there's sixteen to pay for your horse-hire.
'Tis all the wealth, you see, my purse possesses;
But if you please for to inquire me out,
You shall not want for aught that I can do.
My name is Frescobald, a Florence merchant,
A man that always lov'd your nation.

Crom. This unexpected favour at your hands,
Which God doth know, if e'er I shall requite—
Necessity makes me to take your bounty,
And for your gold can yield you nought but thanks.
Your charity hath help'd me from despair;
Your name shall still be in my hearty prayer.

Fres. It is not worth such thanks: come to my house;
Your want shall better be reliev'd than thus.

Crom. I pray, excuse me; this shall well suffice,
To bear my charges to Bononia,
Whereas a noble earl is much distress'd.

An Englishman, Russel the earl of Bedford,
Is by the French king sold unto his death.
It may fall out, that I may do him good;
To save his life, I 'll hazard my heart-blood.
Therefore, kind sir, thanks for your liberal gift;
I must be gone to aid him: there's no shift.

Fres. I 'll be no hinderer to so good an act.
Heaven prosper you in that you go about!
If fortune bring you this way back again,
Pray let me see you: so I take my leave;
All good a man can wish, I do bequeath.

[*Exit* FRES.

Crom. All good that God doth send, light on
your head!
There's few such men within our climate bred.
How say you Hodge? is not this good fortune?

Hodge. How say you? I 'll tell you what, master
Thomas; if all men be of this gentleman's mind,
let's keep our standings upon this bridge; we shall
get more here, with begging in one day, than I
shall with making horse-shoes in a whole year.

Crom. No, Hodge, we must be gone unto Bononia,
There to relieve the noble earl of Bedford:
Where, if I fail not in my policy,
I shall deceive their subtle treachery.

Hodge. Nay, I 'll follow you. God bless us from
the thieving banditti again.　　　　　　[*Exeunt.*

SCENE II.—Bononia.[12]　*A Room in an Hotel.*

Enter BEDFORD *and* Host.

Bed. Am I betray'd? was Bedford born to die
By such base slaves, in such a place as this?
Have I escap'd so many times in France,
So many battles have I overpass'd,
And made the French stir, when they heard my
name;
And am I now betray'd unto my death?
Some of their heart's-blood first shall pay for it.

Host. They do desire, my lord, to speak with you.

Bed. The traitors do desire to have my blood;
But by my birth, my honour, and my name,
By all my hopes, my life shall cost them dear.
Open the door; I 'll venture out upon them,
And if I must die, then I 'll die with honour.

Host. Alas, my lord, that is a desperate course;
They have begirt you round about the house.
Their meaning is, to take you prisoner,
And so to send your body unto France.

Bed. First shall the ocean be as dry as sand,
Before alive they send me unto France.
I 'll have my body first bored like a sieve,
And die as Hector, 'gainst the Myrmidons,

Ere France shall boast, Bedford's their prisoner.
Treacherous France! that 'gainst the law of arms,
Hath here betray'd thine enemy to death.
But be assur'd, my blood shall be reveng'd
Upon the best lives that remain in France.

Enter a Servant.

Stand back, or else thou run'st upon thy death.

Ser. Pardon, my lord: I come to tell your
honour,
That they have hir'd a Neapolitan,
Who by his oratory hath promis'd them,
Without the shedding of one drop of blood,
Into their hands safe to deliver you;
And therefore craves none but himself may enter,
And a poor swain that attends upon him.

Bed. A Neapolitan? bid him come in.

[*Exit* Ser.

Were he as cunning in his eloquence,
As Cicero, the famous man of Rome,
His words would be as chaff against the wind.
Sweet-tongu'd Ulysses, that made Ajax mad,
Were he and his tongue in this speaker's head,
Alive he wins me not; then 'tis no conquest, dead.

Enter CROMWELL *in a Neapolitan Habit, and*
HODGE.

Crom. Sir, are you the master of the house?

Host. I am, sir.

Crom. By this same token you must leave this
place,
And leave none but the earl and I together,
And this my peasant here to tend on us.

Host. With all my heart; God grant you do
some good.

[*Exit* Host, CROM. *shuts the door.*

Bed. Now, sir, what is your will with me?

Crom. Intends your honour not to yield yourself?

Bed. No, good-man goose, not while my sword
doth last.
Is this your eloquence for to persuade me?

Crom. My lord, my eloquence is for to save you
I am not, as you judge, a Neapolitan,
But Cromwell, your servant, and an Englishman.

Bed. How! Cromwell? not my farrier's son?

Crom. The same, sir; and am come to succour you.

Hodge. Yes 'faith, sir; and I am Hodge, your
poor smith: many a time and oft have I shod your
dapple-grey.

Bed. And what avails it me that thou art here?

Crom. It may avail, if you 'll be rul'd by me.
My lord, you know, the men of Mantua
And these Bononians are at deadly strife;

And they, my lord, both love and honour you.
Could you but get out of the Mantua port,[13]
Then were you safe, despite of all their force.

Bed. Tut, man, thou talk'st of things impossible;
Dost thou not see, that we are round beset?
How then is't possible we should escape?

Crom. By force we cannot, but by policy.
Put on the apparel here that Hodge doth wear,
And give him yours: The states, they know you
    not,[14]
(For, as I think, they never saw your face);
And at a watch-word must I call them in,
And will desire that we two safe may pass
To Mantua, where I'll say my business lies.
How doth your honour like of this device?

Bed. O, wond'rous good.—But wilt thou ven-
    ture, Hodge?

Hodge. Will I?

> O noble lord,
>   I do accord,
> In any thing I can:
>   And do agree,
>   To set thee free,
> Do Fortune what she can.

Bed. Come, then, let us change our apparel
    straight.

Crom. Go, Hodge; make haste, lest they should
    chance to call.

Hodge. I warrant you I'll fit him with a suit.
                    [*Exeunt* BED. *and* HODGE.

Crom. Heavens grant this policy doth take suc-
    cess,
And that the earl may safely 'scape away!
And yet it grieves me for this simple wretch,
For fear lest they should offer him violence:
But of two evils 'tis best to shun the greatest;
And better is it that he live in thrall,
Than such a noble earl as he should fall.
Their stubborn hearts, it may be, will relent,
Since he is gone, to whom their hate is bent.

> *Re-enter* BEDFORD *and* HODGE.

My lord, have you dispatch'd?

Bed. How dost thou like us, Cromwell? is it
    well?

Crom. O, my good lord, excellent. Hodge, how
dost feel thyself?

Hodge. How do I feel myself? why, as a nobleman should do. O how I feel honour come creeping on! My nobility is wonderful melancholy: Is
it not most gentleman-like to be melancholy?

Bed. Yes, Hodge; now go sit down in the study,
and take state upon thee.

Hodge. I warrant you, my lord; let me alone to
take state upon me: But hark, my lord, do you feel
nothing bite about you?

Bed. No, trust me, Hodge.

Hodge. Ay, they know they want their old pasture. 'Tis a strange thing of this vermin, they dare
not meddle with nobility.

Crom. Go take thy place, Hodge; I will call
    them in.
Now all is done:—Enter an if you please.

> *Enter the* Governor, *and other* States *and* Citizens
>   *of* Bononia, *and* Officers *with Halberts.*

Gov. What, have you won him? will he yield
    himself?

Crom. I have an't please you; and the quiet earl
Doth yield himself to be dispos'd by you.

Gov. Give him the money that we promis'd him;
So let him go, whither it please himself.

Crom. My business, sir, lies unto Mantua:
Please you to give me a safe conduct thither.

Gov. Go, and conduct him to the Mantua port,
And see him safe deliver'd presently.
                    [*Exeunt* CROM., BED., *and an* Officer.
Go draw the curtains, let us see the earl:—
                    [*An* Attendant *opens the Curtains.*
O, he is writing; stand apart a while,

Hodge. [*Reads.*] Fellow William, I am not as I have
been; I went from you a smith, I write to you as a lord. I
am at this present writing, among the Polonian sausages.[15] I
do commend my lordship to Ralph and to Roger, to Bridget
and to Dorothy, and so to all the youth of Putney.

Gov. Sure these are the names of English noble-
    men,
Some of his special friends, to whom he writes:—
                    [HODGE *sounds a note.*
But stay, he doth address himself to sing.
                    [HODGE *sings a Song.*
My lord, I am glad you are so frolic and so blithe:
Believe me, noble lord, if you knew all,
You'd change your merry vein to sudden sorrow.

Hodge. I change my merry vein? no, thou Bo-
    nonian, no;
I am a lord, and therefore let me go.
I do defy thee and thy sausages;
Therefore stand off, and come not near my
    honour.

Gov. My lord, this jesting cannot serve your
    turn.

Hodge. Dost think, thou black Bononian beast,
That I do flout, do gibe, or jest?
No, no, thou beer pot, know that I,
A noble earl, a lord par-dy— [*A Trumpet sounds.*

Gov. What means this trumpet's sound?

Enter a Messenger.

Cit. One is come from the states of Mantua.

Gov. What, would you with us? speak thou man
     of Mantua.

Mes. Men of Bononia, this my message is;
To let you know, the noble earl of Bedford
Is safe within the town of Mantua,
And wills you send the peasant that you have,
Who hath deceiv'd your expectation:
Or else the states of Mantua have vow'd,
They will recall the truce that they have made;
And not a man shall stir from forth your town,
That shall return, unless you send him back.

Gov. O this misfortune, how it mads my heart!
The Neapolitan hath beguil'd us all.
Hence with this fool. What shall we do with him,
The earl being gone? A plague upon it all!

Hodge. No, I 'll assure you, I am no earl, but a
     smith, sir, one Hodge, a smith at Putney, sir; one
     that hath gulled you, that hath bored you, sir.

Gov. Away with him; take hence the fool you
     came for.

Hodge. Ay, sir, and I 'll leave the greater fool
     with you.

Mes. Farewell, Bononians. Come, friend, along
     with me.

Hodge. My friend, afore; my lordship will fol-
     low thee.   [*Exeunt* Hodge *and* Mess.

Gov. Well, Mantua, since by thee the earl is
     lost,
Within few days I hope to see thee crost.
         [*Exeunt* Gov., States, Attendants, &c.

Enter CHORUS.

Cho. Thus far you see how Cromwell's fortune
     pass'd.
The earl of Bedford being safe in Mantua,
Desires Cromwell's company into France,
To make requital for his courtesy;
But Cromwell doth deny the earl his suit,
And tells him that those parts he meant to see,
He had not yet set footing on the land;
And so directly takes his way to Spain;
The earl to France; and so they both do part.
Now let your thoughts, as swift as is the wind,
Skip some few years that Cromwell spent in travel;
And now imagine him to be in England,
Servant unto the Master of the rolls;
Where in short time he there began to flourish:
An hour shall show you what few years did cherish.
                   [*Exit.*

SCENE III.—London. *A Room in* Sir Christopher
             Hales' *House.*

Music plays; then a Banquet is brought in. Enter
     SIR CHRISTOPHER HALES, CROMWELL, *and two*
     Servants.

Hales. Come, sirs, be careful of your master's
     credit;
And as our bounty now exceeds the figure
Of common entertainment, so do you,
With looks as free as is your master's soul,
Give formal welcome to the thronged tables,
That shall receive the cardinal's followers,
And the attendants of the great lord chancellor.
But all my care, Cromwell, depends on thee;
(Thou art a man differing from vulgar form,
And by how much thy spirit's rank'd 'bove these,
In rules of art, by so much it shines brighter
By travel, whose observance pleads his merit,
In a most learn'd, yet unaffecting spirit.
Good Cromwell, cast an eye of fair regard
'Bout all my house; and what this ruder flesh,[16]
Through ignorance, or wine, do miscreate,
Salve thou with courtesy. If welcome want,
Full bowls and ample banquets will seem scant.

Crom. Sir, as to whatsoever lies in me,
Assure you, I will show my utmost duty.

Hales. About it then; the lords will straight be
     here.   [*Exit* CROM.
Cromwell, thou hast those parts would rather suit
The service of the state than of my house:
I look upon thee with a loving eye,
That one day will prefer thy destiny.

Enter a Servant.

Ser. Sir, the lords be at hand.

Hales. They are welcome: bid Cromwell straight
     attend us,
And look you all things be in perfect readiness.
                       [*Exit* Ser.

The music plays. Enter CARDINAL WOLSEY, SIR
     THOMAS MORE, GARDINER, CROMWELL, *and*
     other Attendants.

Wol. O, sir Christopher,
You are too liberal: What! a banquet too?

Hales. My lords, if words could show the ample
     welcome
That my free heart affords you, I could then
Become a prater; but I now must deal
Like a feast-politician with your lordships:
Defer your welcome till the banquet end,

That it may then salve our defect of fare:
Yet welcome now, and all that tend on you.

Wol. Our thanks to the kind Master of the rolls.
Come and sit down; sit down sir Thomas More.
'Tis strange, how that we and the Spaniard differ;
Their dinner is our banquet after dinner,
And they are men of active disposition.
This I gather, that, by their sparing meat,
Their bodies are more fitter for the wars;
And if that famine chance to pinch their maws,
Being us'd to fast, it breeds in them less pain.

Hales. Fill me some wine; I'll answer cardinal
    Wolsey.
My lord, we English are of more freer souls,
Than hunger-starv'd and ill-complexion'd Spaniards.
They that are rich in Spain, spare belly-food,
To deck their backs with an Italian hood,
And silks of Seville: and the poorest snake,[17]
That feeds on lemons, pilchards, and ne'er heated
His palate with sweet flesh, will bear a case
More fat and gallant than his starved face.
Pride, the inquisition, and this belly-evil,
Are, in my judgment, Spain's three-headed devil.

More. Indeed it is a plague unto their nation,
Who stagger after in blind imitation.

Hales. My lords, with welcome, I present your
    lordships
A solemn health.

More. I love healths well; but when as healths
    do bring
Pain to the head, and body's surfeiting,
Then cease I healths:
Nay spill not friend; for though the drops be small,
Yet have they force to force men to the wall.

Wol. Sir Christopher, is that your man?

Hales. An't like
Your grace, he is a scholar, and a linguist;
One that hath travelled through many parts
Of Christendom, my lord.

Wol. My friend, come nearer: have you been a
    traveller?

Crom. My lord,
I have added to my knowledge, the Low Countries,
With France, Spain, Germany, and Italy;

And though small gain of profit I did find,
Yet it did please my eye, content my mind.

Wol. What do you think then of the several
    states
And princes' courts as you have travelled?

Crom. My lord, no court with England may
    compare,
Neither for state, nor civil government.
Lust dwells in France, in Italy, and Spain,
From the poor peasant, to the prince's train.
In Germany and Holland, riot serves;
And he that most can drink, most he deserves.
England I praise not for I here was born,
But that she laughs the others unto scorn.

Wol. My lord, there dwells within that spirit
    more
Than can be discern'd by the outward eye:—
Sir Christopher, will you part with your man?

Hales. I have sought to proffer him unto your
    lordship;
And now I see he hath preferr'd himself.

Wol. What is thy name?

Crom. Cromwell, my lord.

Wol. Then, Cromwell, here we make thee soli-
    citor
Of our causes, and nearest, next ourself:
Gardiner, give you kind welcome to the man.
              [GAR. *embraces him.*

More. My lord cardinal, you are a royal winner,
Have got a man, besides your bounteous dinner.
Well, my good knight, pray, that we come no
    more;
If we come often, thou may'st shut thy door.

Wol. Sir Christopher, hadst thou given me half
    thy lands,
Thou could'st not have pleas'd me so much as with
This man of thine.   My infant thoughts do spell,
Shortly his fortune shall be lifted higher;
True industry doth kindle honour's fire:
And so, kind master of the rolls, farewell.

Hales. Cromwell, farewell.

Crom. Cromwell takes his leave of you,
That ne'er will leave to love and honour you.
        [*Exeunt.   The Music plays as they go out.*

ACT IV.

Enter Chorus.

Cho. Now Cromwell's highest fortunes do begin.
Wolsey, that lov'd him as he did his life,
Committed all his treasure to his hands,
Wolsey is dead; and Gardiner, his man,
Is now created bishop of Winchester.
Pardon if we omit all Wolsey's life,
Because our play depends on Cromwell's death.
Now sit, and see his highest state of all,
His height of rising, and his sudden fall:
Pardon the errors are already past,
And live in hope the best doth come at last.
My hope upon your favour doth depend,
And looks to have your liking ere the end. [*Exit.*

SCENE I.—*The Same. A public Walk.*

Enter Gardiner Bishop of Winchester, *the* Dukes
of Norfolk *and of* Suffolk, Sir Thomas
More, Sir Christopher Hales, *and* Cromwell.

Nor. Master Cromwell, since cardinal Wolsey's
death,
His majesty is given to understand
There's certain bills and writings in your hand,
That much concern the state of England.
My lord of Winchester, is it not so?
Gar. My lord of Norfolk, we two were whilom
fellows:
And master Cromwell, though our master's love
Did bind us, while his love was to the king,
It is no boot now to deny those things,
Which may be prejudicial to the state:
And though that God hath raised my fortune higher
Than any way I look'd for, or deserv'd,
Yet may my life no longer with me dwell,
Than I prove true unto my sovereign!
What say you, master Cromwell? have you those
Writings, ay, or no?
Crom. Here are the writings;
And on my knees I give them up unto
The worthy dukes of Suffolk, and of Norfolk
He was my master, and each virtuous part
That liv'd in him, I tender'd with my heart;
But what his head complotted 'gainst the state,
My country's love commands me that to hate.
His sudden death I grieve for, not his fall,
Because he sought to work my country's thrall.

Suf. Cromwell, the king shall hear of this thy
duty;
Who, I assure myself, will well reward thee.
My lord, let's go unto his majesty,
And show those writings which he longs to see.
[*Exeunt* Nor. *and* Suf.

Enter Bedford *hastily.*

Bed. How now, who is this? Cromwell? By my
soul,
Welcome to England: thou once did'st save my life;
Didst not, Cromwell?
Crom. If I did so, 'tis greater glory for me
That you remember it, than for myself
Vainly to report it.
Bed. Well, Cromwell, now's the time,
I shall commend thee to my sovereign.
Cheer up thyself, for I will raise thy state;
A Russel yet was never found ingrate. [*Exit.*
Hales. O how uncertain is the wheel of state!
Who lately greater than the cardinal,
For fear and love? and now who lower lies?
Gay honours are but Fortune's flatteries;
And whom this day pride and ambition swells,
To-morrow envy and ambition quells.
More. Who sees the cob-web tangle the poor fly,
May boldly say, the wretch's death is nigh.
Gard. I knew his state and proud ambition
Were too too violent to last o'er long.
Hales. Who soars too near the sun with golden
wings,
Melts them; to ruin his own fortune brings.

Enter the Duke of Suffolk.

Suf. Cromwell, kneel down. In king Henry's
name arise
Sir Thomas Cromwell; thus begins thy fame.

Enter the Duke of Norfolk.

Nor. Cromwell, the gracious majesty of England,
For the good liking he conceives of thee,
Makes thee the master of the jewel-house,
Chief secretary to himself, and withal
Creates thee one of his highness' privy council.

Enter the Earl of Bedford.

Bed. Where is sir Thomas Cromwell? is he
knighted?
Suf. He is, my lord.

Bed. Then, to add honour to
His name, the king creates him the lord keeper
Of his privy seal,[18] and master of the rolls,
Which you, sir Christopher, do now enjoy:
The king determines higher place for you.

Crom. My lords,
These honours are too high for my desert.

   More. O content thee, man; who would not
     choose it?
Yet thou art wise in seeming to refuse it.

   Gard. Here's honours, titles and promotions:
I fear this climbing will have sudden fall.

   Nor. Then come, my lords; let's all together
     bring
This new-made counsellor to England's king.
                    [*Exeunt all but* GARD.

   Gard. But Gardiner means his glory shall be
     dimm'd.
Shall Cromwell live a greater man than I?
My envy with his honour now is bred:
I hope to shorten Cromwell by the head.   [*Exit.*

SCENE II.—London. *A Street before* Crom-
     well's *House.*

Enter FRESCOBALD.

   Fres. O Frescobald, what shall become of thee?
Where shalt thou go, or which way shalt thou turn?
Fortune, that turns her too unconstant wheel,
Hath turn'd thy wealth and riches in the sea.
All parts abroad wherever I have been
Grow weary of me, and deny me succour.
My debtors, they that should relieve my want,
Forswear my money,[19] say they owe me none;
They know my state too mean to bear out law:
And here in London, where I oft have been,
And have done good to many a wretched man,
I am now most wretched here, despis'd myself.
In vain it is more of their hearts to try;
Be patient therefore, lay thee down and die.
                    [*Lies down.*

Enter SEELY *and* JOAN.

   Seely. Come Joan, come; let's see what he'll
do for us now. I wis[20] we have done for him, when
many a time and often he might have gone a-
hungry to bed.

   Joan. Alas man, now he is made a lord, he'll
never look upon us; he'll fulfil the old proverb,
"Set beggars a horseback and they'll ride"—A
well-a-day for my cow! such as he hath made us
come behind hand; we had never pawn'd our cow
else to pay our rent.

   Seely. Well Joan, he'll come this way; and by
God's dickers I'll tell him roundly of it, an if he
were ten lords: 'a shall know that I had not my
cheese and my bacon for nothing.

   Joan. Do you remember, husband, how he would
mouch up my cheese-cakes? He hath forgot this
now; but now we'll remember him.[21]

   Seely. Ay, we shall have now three flaps with a
fox-tail: but i'faith I'll jibber a joint,[22] but I'll tell
him his own.—Stay, who comes here? O, stand up,
here he comes; stand up.

Enter HODGE *with a* Tip-staff; CROMWELL, *with
   the Mace carried before him; the* DUKES OF
   NORFOLK *and* SUFFOLK, *and* Attendants.

   Hodge. Come; away with these beggars here.
Rise up, sirrah; come out, good people; run afore
there ho.   [FRES. *rises, and stands at a distance.*

   Seely. Ay, we are kick'd away, now we come for
our own; the time hath been, he would ha' look'd
more friendly upon us: And you, Hodge, we know
you well enough, though you are so fine.

   Crom. Come hither, sirrah:—Stay, what men
     are these?
My honest host of Hounslow, and his wife?
I owe thee money, father, do I not?

   Seely. Ay, by the body of me, dost thou. Would
thou would'st pay me: good four pound it is; I
hav't o' the post at home.[23]

   Crom. I know 'tis true. Sirrah, give him ten
     angels:—
And look your wife and you do stay to dinner;[24]
And while you live, I freely give to you
Four pound a year, for the four pound I ought
     you.

   Seely. Art not chang'd? Art old Tom still?
Now God bless thee, good lord Tom. Home Joan,
home; I'll dine with my lord Tom to day, and
thou shalt come next week. Fetch my cow; home
Joan, home.

   Joan. Now God bless thee, my good lord Tom:
I'll fetch my cow presently.   [*Exit* JOAN.

Enter GARDINER.

   Crom. Sirrah, go to yon stranger; tell him, I
Desire him stay to dinner: I must speak
With him.   [*To* HODGE.

   Gard. My lord of Norfolk, see you this
Same bubble? that same puff? but mark the end,
My lord; mark the end.

   Nor. I promise you, I like not something he
     hath done:
But let that pass; the king doth love him well.

Crom. Good morrow to my lord of Winchester:
    I know
You bear me hard about the abbey lands.
    Gard. Have I not reason, when religion's
    wrong'd?
You had no colour for what you have done.
    Crom. Yes, the abolishing of antichrist,
And of his popish order from our realm.
I am no enemy to religion;
But what is done, it is for England's good.
What did they serve for, but to feed a sort
Of lazy abbots and of full-fed friars?
They neither plough nor sow, and yet they reap
The fat of all the land, and suck the poor.
Look, what was theirs is in king Henry's hands;
His wealth before lay in the abbey lands.
    Gard. Indeed these things you have alleg'd,
    my lord;
When, God doth know, the infant yet unborn
Will curse the time the abbeys were pull'd down.
I pray now where is hospitality?
Where now may poor distressed people go,
For to relieve their need, or rest their bones,
When weary travel doth oppress their limbs?
And where religious men should take them in,
Shall now be kept back with a mastiff dog;
And thousand thousand——
    Nor. O my lord, no more:
Things past redress 'tis bootless to complain.
    Crom. What, shall we to the convocation-house?
    Nor. We'll follow you, my lord; pray lead the
    way.

    Enter Old CROMWELL, *in the dress of a Farmer.*

    Old Crom. How! one Cromwell made lord keeper,
since I left Putney, and dwelt in Yorkshire? I
never heard better news: I'll see that Cromwell,
or it shall go hard.
    Crom. My aged father! State then set aside,
Father, upon my knee I crave your blessing.
One of my servants, go, and have him in;
At better leisure will we talk with him.
    Old Crom. Now if I die, how happy were the day!
To see this comfort, rains forth showers of joy.
              [*Exeunt* Old CROM. *and* Servant.
    Nor. This duty in him shows a kind of grace.
              [*Aside.*
    Crom. Go on before, for time draws on apace.
              [*Exeunt all but* FRES.
    Fres. I wonder what this lord would have with
    me,
His man so strictly gave me charge to stay:
I never did offend him to my knowledge.

Well, good or bad, I mean to bide it all;
Worse than I am, now never can befal.

    Enter BANISTER *and his* Wife.

    Ban. Come, wife,
I take it to be almost dinner time;
For master Newton, and master Crosby sent
To me last night, they would come dine with me,
And take their bond in. I pray thee, hie thee home,
And see that all things be in readiness.
    Mrs. Ban. They shall be welcome, husband; I'll
    go before:
But is not that man master Frescobald?
           [*She runs and embraces him.*
    Ban. O heavens! it is kind master Frescobald:
Say, sir, what hap hath brought you to this pass?
    Fres. The same that brought you to your misery.
    Ban. Why would you not acquaint me with your
    state?
Is Banister your poor friend then forgot,
Whose goods, whose love, whose life and all is
    yours?
    Fres. I thought your usage would be as the rest,
That had more kindness at my hands than you,
Yet look'd askance when as they saw me poor.
    Mrs. Ban. If Banister would bear so base a heart,
I ne'er would look my husband in the face,
But hate him as I would a cockatrice.
    Ban. And well thou might'st, should Banister
    deal so.
Since that I saw you, sir, my state is mended;
And for the thousand pounds I owe to you,
I have it ready for you, sir, at home;
And though I grieve your fortune is so bad,
Yet that my hap's to help you, makes me glad;
And now, sir, will it please you walk with me?
    Fres. Not yet I cannot, for the lord chancellor
Hath here commanded me to wait on him:
For what I know not; pray God it be for good.
    Ban. Never make doubt of that; I'll warrant you,
He is as kind a noble gentleman,
As ever did possess the place he hath.
    Mrs. Ban. Sir, my brother is his steward: if you
    please,
We'll go along and bear you company;
I know we shall not want for welcome there.
    Fres. With all my heart; but what's become of
    Bagot?
    Ban. He is hang'd for buying jewels of the king's.
    Fres. A just reward for one so impious.
The time draws on: sir, will you go along?
    Ban. I'll follow you, kind master Frescobald.
              [*Exeunt.*

SCENE III.—*The Same. Another Street.*

Enter NEWTON *and* CROSBY.

New. Now, master Crosby, I see you have a care
To keep your word, in payment of your money.

Cros. By my faith I have reason on a bond.
Three thousand pound is far too much to forfeit;
And yet I doubt not master Banister.

New. By my faith, sir, your sum is more than
    mine;
And yet I am not much behind you too,
Considering that to-day I paid at court.

Cros. Mass, and well remember'd: What is the
    reason
Lord Cromwell's men wear such long skirts upon
Their coats? they reach down to their very hams.

New. I will resolve you, sir; and thus it is:
The bishop of Winchester, that loves not Cromwell,
(As great men are envied as well as less)
A while ago there was a jar between them;
And it was brought to my lord Crowwell's ear
That bishop Gardiner would sit on his skirts:
Upon which word he made his men long blue coats,
And in the court wore one of them himself;
And meeting with the bishop, quoth he, my lord,
Here's skirts enough now for your grace to sit on;
Which vex'd the bishop to the very heart.
This is the reason why they wear long coats.[25]

Cros. 'Tis always seen, and mark it for a rule,
That one great man will envy still another;
But 'tis a thing that nothing concerns me :—
What, shall we now to master Banister's?

New. Ay, come, we'll pay him royally for our
    dinner. [*Exeunt.*

SCENE IV.—*The Same. A Room in* Cromwell's
House.

Enter the Usher *and the* Sewer.[26] *Several* Servants
cross the Stage with Dishes in their Hands.

Ush. Uncover there, gentlemen.

Enter CROMWELL, BEDFORD, SUFFOLK, Old CROM-
WELL, FRESCOBALD, SEELY, *and* Attendants.

Crom. My noble lords of Suffolk and of Bedford,
Your honours are welcome to poor Cromwell's
    house.
Where is my father? nay, be cover'd, father;
Although that duty to these noblemen
Doth challenge it, yet I'll make bold with them.
Your head doth bear the calendar of care.
What! Cromwell cover'd, and his father bare?

It must not be.—Now, sir, to you: is not
Your name Frescobald, and a Florentine?

Fres. My name was Frescobald, till cruel fate
Did rob me of my name, and of my state.

Crom. What fortune brought you to this country
    now?

Fres. All other parts have left me succourless,
Save only this. Because of debts I have,
I hope to gain for to relieve my want.

Crom. Did you not once upon your Florence
    bridge
Help a distress'd man, robb'd by the banditti?
His name was Cromwell.

Fres. I ne'er made my brain
A calendar of any good I did:
I always lov'd this nation with my heart.

Crom. I am that Cromwell that you there re-
    liev'd.
Sixteen ducats you gave me for to clothe me,
Sixteen to bear my charges by the way,
And sixteen more I had for my horse-hire.
There be those several sums justly return'd:
Yet it injustice were, that serving at
My need, to repay thee without interest:
Therefore receive of me four several bags;
In each of them there is four hundred marks:
And bring to me the names of all your debtors;
And if they will not see you paid, I will.
O God forbid that I should see him fall,
That help'd me in my greatest need of all.
Here stands my father that first gave me life;
Alas, what duty is too much for him?
This man in time of need did save my life;
I therefore cannot do too much for him.
By this old man I oftentimes was fed,
Else might I have gone supperless to bed.
Such kindness have I had of these three men,
That Cromwell no way can repay again.
Now in to dinner, for we stay too long;
And to good stomachs is no greater wrong.
    [*Exeunt.*

SCENE V.—*The Same. A Room in the* Bishop
of Winchester's *House.*

Enter GARDINER *and a* Servant.

Gard. Sirrah, where be those men I caus'd to
    stay?

Ser. They do attend your pleasure, sir, within.

Gard. Bid them come hither, and stay you with-
    out: [*Exit* Ser.
For by those men the fox of this same land,
That makes a goose of better than himself,

Must worried be unto his latest home;
Or Gardiner will fail in his intent.
As for the dukes of Suffolk and of Norfolk,
Whom I have sent for to come speak with me;
Howsoever outwardly they shadow it,
Yet in their hearts I know they love him not.
As for the earl of Bedford, he's but one,
And dares not gainsay what we do set down.

Enter the two Witnesses.

Now, my good friends, you know I sav'd your lives,
When by the law you had deserved death;
And then you promis'd me, upon your oaths,
To venture both your lives to do me good.

    Both Wit. We swore no more than that we will
      perform.

    Gard. I take your words; and that which you
      must do,
Is service for your God, and for your king;
To root a rebel from this flourishing land,
One that's an enemy unto the church:
And therefore must you take your solemn oaths,
That you heard Cromwell, the lord chancellor,
Did wish a dagger at king Henry's heart.[27]
Fear not to swear it, for I heard him speak it;
Therefore we'll shield you from ensuing harms.

    2nd Wit. If you will warrant us the deed is good,
We'll undertake it.

    Gard. Kneel down, and I will here absolve you
      both:
This crucifix I lay upon your heads,
And sprinkle holy water on your brows.
The deed is meritorious that you do,
And by it shall you purchase grace from heaven.

    1st Wit. Now sir we'll undertake it, by our
      souls.

    2nd Wit. For Cromwell never lov'd none of our
      sort.

    Gard. I know he doth not; and for both of you,
I will prefer you to some place of worth.
Now get you in, until I call for you,
For presently the dukes mean to be here.

                  [*Exeunt* Wit.
Cromwell, sit fast; thy time's not long to reign.
The abbeys that were pull'd down by thy means
Is now a mean for me to pull thee down.
Thy pride also thy own head lights upon,
For thou art he hath chang'd religion:—
But now no more, for here the dukes are come.

Enter SUFFOLK, NORFOLK, *and* BEDFORD.

    Suf. Good even to my lord bishop.
    Nor. How fares my lord? what, are you all alone?

    Gard. No, not alone, my lords; my mind is
      troubled.
I know your honours muse wherefore I sent,
And in such haste. What, came you from the
      king?

    Nor. We did, and left none but lord Cromwell
      with him.

    Gard. O what a dangerous time is this we
      live in?
There's Thomas Wolsey, he's already gone,
And Thomas More, he follow'd after him:
Another Thomas yet there doth remain,
That is far worse than either of those twain;
And if with speed, my lords, we not pursue it,
I fear the king and all the land will rue it.

    Bed. Another Thomas? pray God, it be not
      Cromwell.

    Gard. My lord of Bedford, it is that traitor
      Cromwell.

    Bed. Is Cromwell false? my heart will never
      think it.

    Suf. My lord of Winchester, what likelihood
Or proof have you of this his treachery?

    Gard. My lord, too much: call in the men
      within.

Enter the Witnesses.

These men, my lord, upon their oaths affirm
That they did hear lord Cromwell in his garden
Wishing a dagger sticking at the heart
Of our king Henry: what is this but treason?

    Bed. If it be so, my heart doth bleed with
      sorrow.

    Suf. How say you, friends? What, did you hear
      these words?

    1st Wit. We did, an't like your grace.

    Nor. In what place was lord Cromwell when he
      spake them?

    2nd Wit. In his garden; where we did attend
      a suit,
Which we had waited for two years and more.

    Suf. How long is't since you heard him speak
      these words?

    2nd Wit. Some half year since.

    Bed. How chance that you conceal'd it all this
      time?

    1st Wit. His greatness made us fear; that was
      the cause.

    Gard. Ay, ay, his greatness, that's the cause
      indeed.
And to make his treason here more manifest,
He calls his servants to him round about,
Tells them of Wolsey's life, and of his fall;

Says that himself hath many enemies,
And gives to some of them a park, or manor,
To others leases, lands to other some:
What need he do thus in his prime of life,
And if he were not fearful of his death?

Suf. My lord, these likelihoods are very great.

Bed. Pardon me, lords, for I must needs depart;
Their proofs are great, but greater is my heart.[28]

             [*Exit* BED.

Nor. My friends, take heed of that which you
     have said;
Your souls must answer what your tongues report:
Therefore take heed; be wary what you do.

2nd Wit. My lord, we speak no more but truth.

Nor. Let him
Depart, my lord of Winchester: and let
These men be close kept till the day of trial.

Gard. They shall, my lord: ho, take in these
     two men.   [*Exeunt* Witnesses, &c.
My lords, if Cromwell have a public trial,
That which we do, is void, by his denial:
You know the king will credit none but him.

Nor. 'Tis true; he rules the king even as he
     pleases.

Suf. How shall we do for to attach him then?

Gard. Marry, thus, my lords; by an act he made
     himself,
With an intent to entrap some of our lives;
And this it is: "If any counsellor
Be convicted of high treason, he shall
Be executed without public trial:"
This act, my lords, he caus'd the king to make.[29]

Suf. He did indeed, and I remember it;
And now 'tis like to fall upon himself.

Nor. Let us not slack it; 'tis for England's
     good:
We must be wary, else he'll go beyond us.[30]

Gard. Well hath your grace said, my good lord
     of Norfolk:
Therefore let us go presently to Lambeth;
Thither comes Cromwell from the court to-night.
Let us arrest him; send him to the Tower;
And in the morning cut off the traitor's head.

Nor. Come then, about it; let us guard the
     town:
This is the day that Cromwell must go down.

Gard. Along my lords. Well, Cromwell is half
     dead;
He shak'd my heart, but I will shake his head.

             [*Exeunt.*

ACT V.

SCENE I.—*A Street in* London.

Enter BEDFORD.

Bed. My soul is like a water troubled;
And Gardiner is the man that makes it so.
O Cromwell, I do fear thy end is near;
Yet I'll prevent their malice if I can:
And in good time, see where the man doth come,
Who little knows how near's his day of doom.

Enter CROMWELL, *with his Train.* BEDFORD *makes
as though he would speak to him.* CROMWELL
goes on.

Crom. You're well encounter'd, my good lord of
     Bedford.
I see your honour is address'd to talk.
Pray pardon me; I am sent for to the king,
And do not know the business yet myself:
So fare you well, for I must needs be gone.

             [*Exit* CROM., &c.

Bed. You must; well, what remedy?

I fear too soon you must be gone indeed.
The king hath business; but little dost thou know,
Who's busy for thy life: thou think'st not so.

Re-enter CROMWELL, *attended.*

Crom. The second time well met my lord of
     Bedford:
I am very sorry that my haste is such.
Lord marquis Dorset being sick to death,
I must receive of him the privy seal.
At Lambeth soon, my lord, we'll talk our fill.

             [*Exit.*

Bed. How smooth and easy is the way to death!

Enter a Messenger.

Mes. My lord, the dukes of Norfolk and of
     Suffolk,
Accompanied with the bishop of Winchester,
Entreat you to come presently to Lambeth,
On earnest matters that concern the state.

Bed. To Lambeth! so: go fetch me pen and ink;

I and lord Cromwell there shall talk enough :
Ay, and our last, I fear, an if he come.   [*Writes.*
Here, take this letter,[31] and bear it to lord Cromwell ;
Bid him read it ; say it concerns him near :
Away, be gone, make all the haste you can.
To Lambeth do I go a woeful man.   [*Exeunt.*

SCENE II.—*A Street near the* Thames.

Enter CROMWELL, *attended.*

Crom. Is the barge ready ? I will straight to
  Lambeth :
And, if this one day's business once were past,
I 'd take my ease to-morrow, after trouble.

Enter Messenger.

How now my friend, wouldest thou speak with me ?
  Mes. Sir, here 's a letter from my lord of Bedford.
    [*Gives him a letter.* CROM. *puts it in
    his pocket.*
Crom. O good my friend, commend me to thy lord ;
Hold, take those angels ; drink them for thy pains.
  Mes. He doth desire your grace to read it,
Because he says it doth concern you near.
  Crom. Bid him assure himself of that. Farewell.
To-morrow, tell him, he shall hear from me.
Set on before there, and away to Lambeth. [*Exeunt.*

SCENE III.—Lambeth.

Enter GARDINER, SUFFOLK, NORFOLK, BEDFORD,
  Lieutenant of the Tower, *a* Serjeant-at-Arms, *a*
  Herald, *and* Halberts.

  Gard. Halberts, stand close unto the water-side ;
Serjeant-at-arms, be you bold in your office ;
Herald, deliver your proclamation.

  Her. This is to give notice to all the king's subjects, the
late lord Cromwell, lord chancellor of England, vicar-general
over the realm, him to hold and esteem as a traitor against the
crown and dignity of England. So God save the king.

  Gard. Amen.
  Bed. Amen, and root thee from the land !
For whilst thou livest, the truth cannot stand.
  Nor. Make a lane there, the traitor is at hand.
Keep back Cromwell's men ; drown them, if they
  come on.
Serjeant, your office.

Enter CROMWELL, *attended. The* Halbert-men
  make a lane.

  Crom. What means my lord of Norfolk, by these
  words ?
Sirs, come along.

  Gard. Kill them, if they come on.
  Ser. Lord Thomas Cromwell, in king Henry's
  name,
I do arrest your honour of high treason.
  Crom. Serjeant, me of treason ?
    [CROMWELL's Attendants *offer to draw.*
  Suf. Kill them, if they draw a sword.
  Crom. Hold ; I charge you, as you love me, draw
  not a sword.
Who dares accuse Cromwell of treason now ?
  Gard. This is no place to reckon up your crime ;
Your dove-like looks were view'd with serpents'
  eyes.
  Crom. With serpents' eyes indeed, by thine they
  were.
But, Gardiner, do thy worst : I fear thee not.
My faith compar'd with thine, as much shall pass
As doth the diamond excel the glass.
Attach'd of treason, no accusers by !
Indeed what tongue dares speak so foul a lie ?
  Nor. My lord, my lord, matters are too well
  known ;
And it is time the king had note thereof.
  Crom. The king ! let me go to him face to face ;
No better trial I desire than that.
Let him but say, that Cromwell's faith was feign'd,
Then let my honour and my name be stain'd.
If e'er my heart against the king was set,
O let my soul in judgment answer it !
Then if my faith's confirmed with his reason,
'Gainst whom hath Cromwell then committed trea-
  son ?
  Suf. My lord, my lord, your matter shall be tried ;
Mean time with patience content yourself.
  Crom. Perforce I must with patience be con-
  tent :—
O dear friend Bedford, dost thou stand so near ?
Cromwell rejoiceth one friend sheds a tear.
And whither is't ? Which way must Cromwell now ?
  Gard. My lord, you must unto the Tower.
  Lieutenant,
Take him unto your charge.
  Crom. Well, where you please : but yet before
  I part,
Let me confer a little with my men.
  Gard. Ay, as you go by water, so you shall.
  Crom. I have some business present to impart.
  Nor. You may not stay : lieutenant, take your
  charge.
  Crom. Well, well, my lord, you second Gar-
  diner's text.
Norfolk, farewell ! thy turn will be the next.
    [*Exeunt* CROM. *and* Lieu.

Gard. His guilty conscience makes him rave, my
lord.

Nor. Ay, let him talk; his time is short enough.

Gard. My lord of Bedford, come; you weep for
him
That would not shed even half a tear for you.

Bed. It grieves me for to see his sudden fall.

Gard. Such success wish I unto traitors all.

[*Exeunt.*

SCENE IV.—London. *A Street.*

Enter two Citizens.

1st Cit. Why, can this news be true? is 't pos-
sible?
The great lord Cromwell arrested upon treason?
I hardly will believe it can be so.

2nd Cit. It is too true, sir. Would it were other-
wise,
Condition I spent half the wealth I have!
I was at Lambeth, saw him there arrested,
And afterward committed to the Tower.

1st Cit. What, was 't for treason that he was
committed?

2nd Cit. Kind, noble gentleman! I may rue the
time:
All that I have, I did enjoy by him:
And if he die, then all my state is gone.

1st Cit. It may be hoped that he shall not die,
Because the king did favour him so much.

2nd Cit. O sir, you are deceiv'd in thinking so:
The grace and favour he had with the king,
Hath caus'd him have so many enemies.
He that in court secure will keep himself,
Must not be great, for then he is envied at.
The shrub is safe, when as the cedar shakes;
For where the king doth love above compare,
Of others they as much more envied are.

1st Cit. 'Tis pity that this nobleman should fall,
He did so many charitable deeds.

2nd Cit. 'Tis true; and yet you see in each estate
There 's none so good, but some one doth him hate;
And they before would smile him in the face,
Will be the foremost to do him disgrace.
What, will you go along unto the court?

1st Cit. I care not if I do, and hear the news,
How men will judge what shall become of him.

2nd Cit. Some will speak hardly, some will speak
in pity.
Go you to the court; I 'll go into the city;
There I am sure to hear more news than you.

1st Cit. Why then soon will we meet again:
adieu!   [*Exeunt.*

SCENE V.—*A Room in the Tower.*

Enter CROMWELL.

Crom. Now, Cromwell, hast thou time to medi-
tate,
And think upon thy state, and of the time.
Thy honours came unsought, ay, and unlook'd for;
Thy fall as sudden, and unlook'd for too.
What glory was in England that had I not?
Who in this land commanded more than Cromwell?
Except the king, who greater than myself?
But now I see what after ages shall;
The greater men, more sudden is their fall.
But now I do remember, the earl of Bedford
Was very desirous for to speak to me;
And afterward sent unto me a letter,
The which I think I still have in my pocket,
Now may I read it, for I now have leisure;
And this I take it is.   [*Reads.*

> My lord, come not this night to Lambeth,
> For if you do, your state is overthrown;
> And much I doubt your life, an if you come:
> Then if you love yourself, stay where you are.

O God, O God! had I but read this letter,
Then had I been free from the lion's paw:
Deferring this to read until to-morrow,
I spurn'd at joy, and did embrace my sorrow.

Enter Lieutenant of the Tower, Officers, &c.

Now, master lieutenant, when's this day of death?

Lieu. Alas, my lord, would I might never see it!
Here are the dukes of Suffolk and of Norfolk,
Winchester, Bedford, and sir Richard Radcliff,
With others; but why they come I know not.

Crom. No matter wherefore. Cromwell is pre-
par'd,
For Gardiner has my life and state ensnar'd.
Bid them come in, or you shall do them wrong,
For here stands he who some think lives too long.
Learning kills learning, and, instead of ink
To dip his pen, Cromwell's heart-blood doth drink.

Enter the DUKES OF SUFFOLK *and* NORFOLK; *the*
EARL OF BEDFORD, GARDINER BISHOP OF WIN-
CHESTER, SIR RICHARD RADCLIFF, *and* SIR
RALPH SADLER.

Nor. Good morrow, Cromwell. What, alone so
sad?

Crom. One good among you, none of you are bad.
For my part, it best fits me be alone;
Sadness with me, not I with any one.
What, is the king acquainted with my cause?

Nor. He is; and he hath answer'd us, my lord.

Crom. How shall I come to speak with him myself?

Gard. The king is so advertis'd of your guilt,
He'll by no means admit you to his presence.

Crom. No way admit me! am I so soon forgot?
Did he but yesterday embrace my neck,
And said that Cromwell was even half himself?
And are his princely ears so much bewitch'd
With scandalous ignomy,[32] and slanderous speeches,
That now he doth deny to look on me?
Well, my lord of Winchester, no doubt but you
Are much in favour with his majesty:
Will you bear a letter from me to his grace?

Gard. Pardon me; I will bear no traitor's letters.

Crom. Ha!—Will you do this kindness then?
Tell him
By word of mouth what I shall say to you?

Gard. That will I.

Crom. But, on your honour will you?

Gard. Ay, on my honour.

Crom. Bear witness, lords. Tell him, when he hath known you,
And try'd your faith but half so much as mine,
He'll find you to be the falsest-hearted man
In England: pray, tell him this.

Bed. Be patient, good my lord, in these extremes.

Crom. My kind and honourable lord of Bedford,
I know your honour always lov'd me well:
But, pardon me, this still shall be my theme;
Gardiner's the cause makes Cromwell so extreme.
Sir Ralph Sadler, I pray a word with you;
You were my man, and all that you possess
Came by my means: sir, to requite all this,
Say will you take this letter here of me,
And give it with your own hands to the king?

Sad. I kiss your hand, and never will I rest
Ere to the king this be delivered.   [*Exit* SAD.

Crom. Why then yet Cromwell hath one friend in store.

Gard. But all the haste he makes shall be but vain.
Here is a discharge for your prisoner,
To see him executed presently: [*To the* Lieu.
My lord, you hear the tenure of your life.

Crom. I do embrace it; welcome my last date,
And of this glistering world I take last leave:
And, noble lords, I take my leave of you.
As willingly I go to meet with death,
As Gardiner did pronounce it with his breath.
From treason is my heart as white as snow;

My death procured only by my foe.
I pray commend me to my sovereign king,
And tell him in what sort his Cromwell dy'd,
To lose his head before his cause was try'd;[33]
But let his grace, when he shall hear my name,
Say only this; Gardiner procur'd the same.

Enter Young CROMWELL.

Lieu. Here is your son, sir, come to take his leave.

Crom. To take his leave? Come hither, Harry Cromwell.
Mark, boy, the last words that I speak to thee:[34]
Flatter not Fortune, neither fawn upon her;
Gape not for state, yet lose no spark of honour;
Ambition, like the plague, see thou eschew it;
I die for treason, boy, and never knew it.
Yet let thy faith as spotless be as mine,
And Cromwell's virtues in thy face shall shine:
Come, go along, and see me leave my breath,
And I'll leave thee upon the floor of death.

Son. O father, I shall die to see that wound,
Your blood being spilt will make my heart to swound.

Crom. How, boy! not dare to look upon the axe?
How shall I do then to have my head struck off?
Come on, my child, and see the end of all;
And after say, that Gardiner was my fall.

Gard. My lord you speak it of an envious heart;
I have done no more than law and equity.

Bed. O, my good lord of Winchester, forbear:
It would have better seem'd you to have been absent,
Than with your words disturb a dying man.

Crom. Who me, my lord? no: he disturbs not me.
My mind he stirs not, though his mighty shock
Hath brought more peers' heads down unto the block.
Farewell, my boy! all Cromwell can bequeath,—
My hearty blessing:—so I take my leave.

Exec. I am your death's-man; pray my lord forgive me.

Crom. Even with my soul. Why man, thou art my doctor,
And bring'st me precious physic for my soul.
My lord of Bedford, I desire of you
Before my death a corporal embrace.
Farewell, great lord; my love I do commend,
My heart to you; my soul to heaven I send.
This is my joy, that ere my body fleet,
Your honour'd arms are my true winding-sheet.
Farewell, dear Bedford; my peace is made in heaven.

Thus falls great Cromwell, a poor ell in length,
To rise to unmeasur'd height, wing'd with new
    strength,
The land of worms, which dying men discover :[35]
My soul is shrin'd with heaven's celestial cover.
                    [*Exeunt* Crom., Officers, &c.
  Bed. Well, farewell Cromwell! sure the truest
    friend
That ever Bedford shall possess again.
Well, lords, I fear that when this man is dead,
You'll wish in vain that Cromwell had a head.

     Enter an Officer *with* Cromwell's *Head.*

  Offi. Here is the head of the deceased Cromwell.
  Bed. Pray thee go hence, and bear his head
    away
Unto his body ; inter them both in clay.
                   [*Exit* Officer.

     Enter Sir Ralph Sadler.

  Sad. How now my lords? What, is lord Crom-
    well dead?
  Bed. Lord Cromwell's body now doth want a
    head.
  Sad. O God, a little speed had sav'd his life.
Here is a kind reprieve come from the king,
To bring him straight unto his majesty.[36]
  Suf. Ay, ay, sir Ralph, reprieves come now too
    late.
  Gard. My conscience now tells me this deed
    was ill.
Would Christ that Cromwell were alive again!
  Nor. Come let us to the king, who, well I
    know,
Will grieve for Cromwell, that his death was so.
                   [*Exeunt omnes.*

NOTES TO LORD CROMWELL.

[1] *He that carried us to the strong ale.*

That is, to the ale-house where strong ale was sold. In old times, an *ale* frequently signified a festival, so called from the liquor drank upon that occasion. Thus we hear of church-ales, whitsun-ales, &c.

[2] *If you let us from working,* i.e. prevent or hinder us.

[3] *Have I thus cark'd and car'd.*

To *cark* is an obsolete expression for to be anxious.

[4] *There's a portague to drink.*

" A *portague* (says Malone) was a gold coin of Portugal, worth about four pounds ten shillings sterling. *Portugaise,* Fr. This seems to have been too considerable a present to deserve the observation that Bagot makes on receiving it :—

Where he had wont to give a score of crowns,
Doth he now foist me with a portague ?

I suspect we ought to read *cardecue,* i.e. un quart d'ecu, *the fourth part of a crown.* The word is used by Fletcher in the *Elder Brother :*—

And in a suit not worth a *cardecue.*

[5] *In Antwerp, leiger for the English merchants.*

That is, a resident agent for the transaction of their business.

[6] *To buy you spurs and wands.*

Wands are switches to increase the speed of his horse.

[7] *Remorse,* a word anciently used for tenderness or pity.

[8] *I know this place to be extortion.*

There is probably some omission here—perhaps the author wrote *extortious,* or—

I know this place to be extortion's *nest.*

[9] *Your son Thomas, quoth you ! I have been Thomas'd.*

A cant quibble, meaning, I have been made a fool of. Hodge enters in the midst of a speculation on the unreasonableness of old Cromwell in sending him a long voyage to look for his son Thomas.

[10] *You offer too much under foot.*

You offer too low a price, under the real value.

[11] *God send some to read.*

Steevens pleasantly remarks, " Hodge seems to have formed his wish on the cant lines which were formerly written on the blank leaves at the beginning of school-books, &c.

" Philemon Holland, his book,
God give him grace therein to look ;
And not to look, but understand," &c.

[12] *Bononia.*

Bononia is the Latin name of Bolognia, a town in Italy.

[13] *Could you but get out of the Mantua port.*

The line is not very clearly expressed ; Bedford was in Bononia, and wanted to get to Mantua. The meaning is—could he but get out at the port leading to Mantua.

[14] *The states they know you not.*

A *state* is an obsolete term for a dignitary or statesman, a ruler or senator.

[15] *Among the Polonian sausages.*

Hodge contemptuously calls the inhabitants of Bononia, *sausages,* because they were famous for the production of that description of viand, which is still vulgarly called a *Polony.*

[16] *What this ruder flesh ?*

In saying this, we must suppose Sir Christopher points to the inferior servants, whom on account of their coarse natures and want of polish, he calls, in comparison with Cromwell, ruder flesh, or inferior natures.

[17] *And the poorest snake.*

That is, the meanest creature, a man who crawls insignificantly through the world, as a snake does through the grass, always level with the dust.

[18] ——— *The king creates him the lord keeper
Of his privy seal.*

The rise of Cromwell to the highest honours of the state was certainly sudden, but not quite so rapid as this author has represented. In 1531 he was made a privy counsellor, and master of the jewel-house, and the next year clerk of the hanaper, and chancellor of the exchequer. In 1534, principal secretary of state, and master of the rolls. The following year he was appointed vicar-general over all the spiritualities in England, under the king ; on the 2nd of July, 1536, lord keeper of the privy-seal ; and soon afterwards he was advanced to the dignity of a baron. In 1537 he was created knight of the garter, and in 1540, earl of Essex and lord high chamberlain of England.

[19] *My debtors, they that should relieve my want,
Forswear my money.*

That is, deny on oath that they are indebted to me.

[20] *I wis,* i.e. I know.

[21] *But now we'll remember him.*

A vulgarism for remind him.

[22] *Ay, we shall have now three flaps with a fox-tail; but i' faith I'll gibber a joint.*

To have three flaps with a fox-tail, means to be rebuffed with rudeness and cunning; the precise meaning of the latter part of the sentence is not so readily explained. Perhaps it means,—I'll suffer my joints to be torn asunder, if I do not tell him, &c.; or, I'll be contented to be spitted if, &c. Dr. Percy suggests that perhaps we ought to read—I'll gibbet a joint, &c., i.e. suffer one of my limbs to be gibbeted.

[23] *I hav't o' the post at home.*

That is, he had the particulars of the account chalked upon the post at his house. A primitive way of keeping accounts not yet altogether abandoned.

[24] *And look your wife and you do stay to dinner.*

Stowe, in his *Survey of London*, says that " he had himself often seen at Lord Cromwell's gate more than two hundred persons served twice every day with bread, meat, and drink sufficient."

[25] *This is the reason why they wear long coats.*

That Cromwell's household did wear coats with singularly long skirts, is thus attested by Stowe, in his *Survey of London*, he himself having been a witness of what he describes:—" The skirts of his yeomen in livery were large enough for their friends to sit upon them." We, however, nowhere learn that they wore these coats in consequence of any such dispute as the text describes between Cromwell and Bishop Gardiner. A similar story is told of the duke of Buckingham and Cardinal Wolsey, of which it has been suggested the author of this play had a confused recollection. It is as follows:—The duke, one day, in conformity with the duties of his office, was holding a basin for the king to wash, and as soon as his majesty had finished, the cardinal dipped his hands into the same water. The duke resented this as an indignity; he disdained to wait upon any one less exalted than the king, and he exhibited his annoyance by spilling some of the water in Wolsey's shoes. The cardinal was scarlet with anger at this ludicrous rebuff, and said to the duke in a threatening tone, *that he would sit on his skirts.* The next day Buckingham came to court very richly dressed, but without skirts to his doublet; at which Henry, being surprised, asked him what he meant by that strange fashion? to which he replied, that his purpose was to prevent Cardinal Wolsey from sitting upon his skirts.

[26] *Enter the Usher and the Sewer.*

The *Sewer* was the officer in the households of our ancient nobility who placed the dishes on the table. He and the carver stood on each side of their lord when he was seated at dinner.

[27] *Did wish a dagger at King Henry's heart.*

The author of this drama has not paid a very great regard to historical fact. Gardiner was the enemy of Cromwell, and contributed as much as he could to his downfall; but he was not guilty of the atrocity here attributed to him. The immediate cause of Cromwell's ruin was Henry's aversion to Anne of Cleeves, and his desire to marry Catherine Howard, niece to the duke of Norfolk, Cromwell's chief enemy. By him he was accused of high treason, and attainted, unheard in parliament, in the absence of Cranmer, the only person who had spirit and honesty enough to remonstrate with the king on the injustice of this proceeding. He was accused of having received bribes, and of encroaching upon the royal authority, by issuing commissions, giving pardons to criminals, and granting licences for the exportation of prohibited goods. He was also accused of betraying the cause of the Christian church by protecting preachers of heresy, and promoting the circulation of heretical books; and that to crown these monstrous acts, he had, in a private conversation about the new opinions, *drawn out his dagger*, and declared that he would maintain the cause of the Reformation even against the king himself.

[28] *Their proofs are great, but greater is my heart.*

That is, the proofs of Cromwell's guilt are indeed great, but my affection for him, and my hope that his innocence will yet be proved, are still greater.

[29] *This act my lord he caused the king to make.*

Malone says—" This is asserted by Saunders, in his book *de Scism. Angl.*, but no such act of parliament was made in Henry's reign." He is mistaken. When, in obedience to the savage wishes of the king, Cromwell was seeking to procure the condemnation of the aged Countess of Salisbury and her family, and found that he could not collect sufficient materials for a criminal information against them, he assembled the judges, and asked them whether parliament might not condemn persons accused of treason without any previous trial or confession? The spirit of Englishmen, the sense of justice, and even the commonest feelings of humanity, were dormant or extinguished in all who served the English Nero; and, to their eternal disgrace, these servile judges, after some little fencing and equivocation, told Cromwell that though it was a nice question, and one that no inferior tribunal could entertain, there was no doubt that the court of parliament was supreme, and that any attainder by it would be good in law. This atrocious bill was therefore brought before the parliament, the members of which, as they were reduced to such a state of abject bondage as for their decisions to be merely an expression of the king's will, of course readily passed it. This instrument of tyranny did its work; Sir Adrian Fortescue and Sir Thomas Dingley were immediately sent to the block without trial, and the aged countess, the nearest relative to the savage king, after two years' imprisonment, was brought forth and literally hewed to death upon the scaffold. But the eternal spirit of retribution never sleeps for long; and even before the death of the innocent and grey-haired countess, Cromwell, the ready instrument of tyranny, had perished by the operation of that law which he had devised for her destruction.

[30] *Else he'll go beyond us,* i.e. overreach us.

[31] *Here, take this letter.*

Malone remarks—" The author attended but little to his scenery. It is evident from the manner of Cromwell's passing and repassing in this scene, that Bedford must be here supposed to be in a street or other public place, not very well calculated for writing. But a letter is wanted, and one is accordingly written."

[32] *Ignomy,* i.e. a contraction of *ignominy* commonly used in our ancient dramas.

[33] *To lose his head before his cause was tried.*

Cromwell's appeal for a trial before his peers was denied; his enemies preferred to proceed by bill of attainder, which was accordingly hurried through the House of Lords, and received the royal assent four days before his execution.

[34] *Mark, boy, the last words that I speak to thee.*

Cromwell's son was not a boy at the time of his father's execution; not only had he arrived at manhood, but had been called up by summons to the house of peers four years before that event, by the title of Baron Cromwell, of Wimbleton, in the county of Surrey.

[35] *The land of worms, which dying men discover.*

Some omission or corruption is evident here. Perhaps we may read—land of *bliss.* The worms are not discovered by the dead, the living only are cognizant of them.

[36] *To bring him straight unto his majesty.*

No reprieve was sent for Cromwell, although the unhappy man endeavoured to soften the king by the most humble supplications. He wrote a pathetic letter to his ungrateful sovereign, which is said to have brought tears into the eyes of that merciless man, but it produced no other effect. It concluded thus—" I, a most woeful prisoner, am ready to submit to death when it shall please God and your majesty; and yet the frail flesh incites me to call to your grace for mercy and pardon of mine offences. Written at the Tower with the heavy heart and trembling hand of your highness's most miserable prisoner, and poor slave, Thomas Cromwell."

H. T.

The Birth of Merlin;
or, the Child hath found
his Father

The Birth of Merlin, which—like *King Arthur,* the elder *King Leir, Vortigern,* and others—belongs to the genre of mythical history plays, was printed in 1662 by Francis Kirkman, with an ascription to William Shakespeare and William Rowley. Little indeed is known about Rowley's life; but if he collaborated with Shakespeare, it must have been in the full maturity of that poet's powers, and we must suppose, as J. A. Symonds (44) notes, either that Rowley retouched an early piece in which Shakespeare was known to have had some hand, or that Shakespeare received this piece of Rowley's for his theatre with approval. There are definite Shakespearean qualities in *The Birth of Merlin,* but these can be accounted for by referring it to the post-Shakespearean epoch, when his manner had helped to create a style.

The intricacy of the plot and the intellectual vivacity are not altogether unlike the early work of Shakespeare. The cast of some soliloquies, with interjected philosophical reflections, the phrasing, and the occasional pregnancy of thought mark it out as, at the least, post-Shakespearean. It belongs, indeed, to the category of plays suggestive of Shakespeare's style and thus by legend attributed in part to his authorship.

Founded on the Arthurian cycle, *The Birth of Merlin* combines the tale of Uther Pendragon's wanderings and loves with the story of Merlin's diabolical parentage. In the guise of a court gallant, the devil begets a child on a simple peasant girl. When he is born, this son, who miraculously enters the world in full maturity and with more than a man's wisdom, consigns his father to a prison in a rock and addresses himself to Britain's affairs of state. These supernatural and romantic elements are, however, subordinate to a farcical medley in this pseudo-historical play, which smacks more of legend and folklore than history. Like the play on Robert, Earl of Huntingdon (otherwise known as Robin Hood) by Henry Chettle and Anthony Munday, *The Birth of Merlin* preserves an historical English atmosphere ruled by romance, whether veiled or frank, in which mythical historical interest is mixed with necromancy.

From a general consideration of the style of this popular play, we may proceed to quote some specimens typical of Shakespeare's style:

> O, my good sister, I beseech you hear me:
> This world is but a masque, catching weak eyes,
> With what is not ourselves but our disguise:
> A vizard that falls off, the dance being done,
> And leaves death's glass for all to look upon:
> Our best happiness here, lasts but a night,
> Whose burning tapers make false ware seem right;
> Who knows not this, and will not now provide
> Some better shift before his shame be spied,
> And knowing this vain world at last will leave him,
> Shake off these robes that help but to deceive him.
>
> [III. iii]

Prince Uther, in his love lunes, exclaims:

> . . . Oh you immortal powers, why has poor man so many entrances for sorrow to creep in at, when our sense is much too weak to hold his happiness? Oh, say I was born deaf; and let your silence confirm in me the knowing my defect; at least be charitable to conceal my sin, for hearing is no less in me, dear brother. [II. iii]

A hermit refuses to drink healths to a wedding feast:

> . . . temperate minds covet that health to drink which nature gives in every spring to man: he that doth hold

> His body but a tenement at will,
> Bestows no cost but to repair what's ill. . . .
>
> [Ibid.]

And the following soliloquy has a profound vein of thought almost reminiscent of the brooding despair of Hamlet:

> Noble and virtuous; could I dream of marriage, I should affect thee,

Edwin. Oh, my soul, here's something tells me that these best of creatures, these models of the world, weak man and woman, should have their souls, their making, life and being, to some more excellent use. If what the sense calls pleasure were our ends, we might justly blame great nature's wisdom, who reared a building of so much art and beauty to entertain a guest so far uncertain, so imperfect. If only speech distinguish us from beasts, who know no inequality of birth or place, but still to fly from goodness—oh, how base were life at such a rate! No, no! that power that gave to man his being, speech, and wisdom, gave it for thankfulness.

> To him alone that
> Made me thus, may I whence truly know,
> I'll pay to him, not man, the love I owe.
>
> [I. i]

Significant in this play is the opposition between good and evil, which was, as Madeleine Doran (13) informs us, a theme of both romance and the morality play. Conflict was typically between a noble hero and a malignant adversary—giant, dragon, enchanter, magician, Satan, the devil—symbolic in a rather general, conventional way of right and wrong, good and evil, beauty and ugliness.

Douglas L. Peterson (32) carries this premise a step further: he says if we are to evaluate the romances on their own terms, we must recognize that Shakespeare in turning from tragedy to tragicomedy made an equally decisive shift in thematic interests. He turned from the destructive power of evil to the restorative power of good. In so doing, he was not retreating into a comfortable world of pseudoproblems, happy coincidences, and convenient miracles. He was, rather, seeking more effective ways of dealing with the metaphysical and epistemological problems in which the tragedies had begun to involve him. The result was a radically new mode of tragicomedy, which, by appropriating the improbable fictions of romance, allowed him to celebrate the restorative power of the good and to affirm, in the face of growing Jacobean skepticism and despite all appearances to the contrary, a morally coherent universe.

The license of romance allows Shakespeare the freedom to go beyond phenomenal representation. He is able to shift his focus from the physical to the metaphysical (and the mythical), to deal decisively with the question of appearance and reality by representing directly the forces that govern phenomenal nature or that may transcend it.

PERSONS REPRESENTED.

———◆———

AURELIUS, *King of* Britain.
Appears, Act I. sc. 2. Act II. sc. 2. Act III. sc. 5.

VORTIGER, *King of* Wales.
Appears, Act IV. sc. 1; sc. 3.

UTER PENDRAGON, *the Prince, Brother to* Aurelius.
Appears, Act II. sc. 1; sc. 3. Act III. sc. 5. Act IV. sc. 2; sc. 3; sc. 4. Act V. sc. 2.

DONOBERT, *a British Noble.*
Appears, Act I. sc. 1; sc. 2. Act II. sc. 2. Act III. sc. 1; sc. 2; sc. 5. Act V. sc. 2.

EARL OF GLOSTER.
Appears, Act I. sc. 1; sc. 2. Act II. sc. 2. Act III. sc. 2. Act V. sc. 2.

EDOL, *Earl of* Chester, *and General to* King Aurelius.
Appears, Act II. sc. 2. Act III. sc. 5. Act IV. sc. 2; sc. 3; sc. 4. Act V. sc. 2.

CADOR, *Earl of* Cornwall, *and Suitor to* Constantia.

EDWIN, *Son to the* Earl of Gloster, *and Suitor to* Modestia.
Appear, Act I. sc. 1; sc. 2. Act II. sc. 2. Act III. sc. 1; sc. 2; sc. 5. Act IV. sc. 2; sc. 3; sc. 4. Act V. sc. 2.

TOCLIO, *a Gentleman attending on* King Aurelius.
Appears, Act I. sc. 1; sc. 2. Act II. sc. 1; sc. 2; sc. 3. Act III. sc. 1; sc. 2; sc. 5. Act IV. sc. 2; sc. 4. Act V. sc. 2.

OSWOLD, *a Gentleman attending on* King Aurelius.
Appears, Act I. sc. 2. Act II. sc. 1; sc. 2; sc. 3. Act III. sc. 2; sc. 5. Act V. sc. 2.

MERLIN, *the Prophet.*
Appears, Act III. sc. 4. Act IV. sc. 1; sc. 4. Act V. sc. 1; sc. 2.

ANSELME, *a Hermit.*
Appears, Act I. sc. 2. Act II. sc. 3. Act III. sc. 2. Act V. sc. 2.

SIR NICODEMUS NOTHING, *a Courtier.*
Appears, Act III. sc. 1.

CLOWN, *Brother to* Joan, *the Mother of* Merlin.
Appears, Act II. sc. 1. Act III. sc. 1; sc. 4. Act IV. sc. 1; sc. 4. Act V. sc. 2.

THE DEVIL, *Father of* Merlin.
Appears, Act III. sc. 1; sc. 3; sc. 4. Act V. sc. 1.

OSTORIUS, *King of the* Saxons, *and General of their Army.*

OCTA, *a Saxon Noble.*
Appear, Act II. sc. 2; sc. 3. Act III. sc. 5.

PROXIMUS, *a Saxon Magician.*
Appears, Act II. sc. 2; sc. 3. Act III. sc. 5. Act IV. sc. 1.

TWO GENTLEMEN, *Attendants on* King Vortiger.
Appear, Act IV. sc. 1.

ARMEL,
PLESGETH, } *Spirits raised by* Proximus.
Appear, Act II. sc. 3.

A LITTLE ANTIC SPIRIT.
Appears, Act IV. sc. 1.

ARTESIA, *Sister to* Ostorius.
Appears, Act I. sc. 1. Act II. sc. 2; sc 3. Act III. sc. 5 Act V. sc. 2.

CONSTANTIA, *Daughter to* Donobert.
Appears, Act I. sc. 1. Act II. sc. 2. Act III. sc. 2.

MODESTIA, *Daughter to* Donobert.
Appears, Act I. sc. 1; sc. 2. Act II. sc. 2. Act III. sc. 2.

JOAN GO-TO-'T, *Mother of* Merlin.
Appears, Act II. sc. 1. Act III. sc. 1; sc. 4. Act IV. sc. 1. Act V. sc. 1.

A GENTLEWOMAN, *Attending on* Queen Artesia.
Appears, Act II. sc. 3.

LUCINA, *the Goddess who presides over the Birth of Children.*
Appears, Act III. sc. 3.

Two Bishops, British *and Saxon Nobles, Gentlemen and Soldiers, Attendants, the three Fates, Spirits, &c.*

SCENE.—*In and near the* BRITISH COURT, *afterwards in* WALES.

The Birth of Merlin; or, the Child hath found his Father.

ACT I.

SCENE I.—*A Room in the Castle of* Lord Donobert.

Enter DONOBERT, GLOSTER, CADOR, EDWIN, CONSTANTIA, *and* MODESTIA.

Cador. You teach me language, sir, as one that knows the debt of love I owe unto their virtues, wherein, like a true courtier, I have fed myself with hope of fair success, and now attend your wished consent to my long suit.

Dono. Believe me, youthful lord, time could not give an opportunity more fitting your desires, always provided my daughter's love be suited with my grant.

Cador. 'Tis the condition, sir, her promise seal'd.

Dono. Is 't so, Constantia?

Con. I was content to give him words for oaths, he swore so oft he loved me.

Dono. That thou believest him?

Con. He is a man I hope.

Dono. That's in the trial, girl.

Con. However, I am a woman, sir.

Dono. The law's on thy side, then, sha't have a husband,—ay, and a worthy one.   Take her, brave Cornwall, and make our happiness great as our wishes.

Cador. Sir, I thank you.

Glos. Double the fortunes of the day, my lord, and crown my wishes too. I have a son here, who, in my absence, would protest no less unto your other daughter.

Dono. Ha, Gloster! is it so? what says lord Edwin? will she protest as much to thee?

Edwin. Else must she want some of her sister's faith, sir.

Mod. Of her credulity much rather, sir. My lord, you are a soldier, and methinks the height of that profession should diminish all heat of love's desires, being so late employed in blood and ruin.

Edwin. The more my conscience ties me to repair the world's losses in a new succession.

Mod. Necessity, it seems, ties your affections then, and that at rate I would unwillingly be thrust upon you; a wife is a dish soon cloys, sir.

Edwin. Weak and diseaséd appetites it may.

Mod. Most of your making have dull stomachs, sir.

Dono. If that be all girl, thou shalt quicken him: be kind to him Modestia; noble Edwin, let it suffice, what's mine in her, speaks yours;
For her consent, let your fair suit go on,
She is a woman, sir, and will be won.

Enter TOCLIO.

Edwin. You give me comfort, sir.

Dono. Now Toclio?

Toclio. The king, my honoured lords, requires your presence, and calls a council for return of answer unto the parling enemy,[1] whose ambassadors are on the way to court.

Dono. So suddenly! Chester it seems has plied them hard at war, they sue so fast for peace, which, by my advice, they ne'er shall have, unless they leave the realm.   Come, noble Gloster, let's attend the king; it lies, sir, in your son to do me pleasure, and save the charges of a wedding-dinner.
If you'll make haste to end your love affairs,
One cost may give discharge to both my cares.
[*Exeunt* DONO. *and* GLOS.

Edwin. I 'll do my best.

Cador. Now, Toclio, what stirring news at court?

Toclio. Oh, my lord, the court's all filled with rumour, the city with news, and the country with wonder; and all the bells i' th' kingdom must proclaim it; we have a new holiday a coming.

Con. A holiday! for whom? for thee?

Toclio. Me, madame! s'foot, I 'd be loath that any man should make a holy-day for me yet.[2] In brief 'tis thus: there's here arrived at court, sent by the earl of Chester to the king, a man of rare esteem for holiness, a reverend hermit, that by miracle not only saved our army, but without aid of man o'erthrew the pagan host, and with such wonder, sir, as might confirm a kingdom to his faith.

Edwin. This is strange news indeed! where is he?

Toclio. In conference with the king, that much respects him.

Mod. Trust me, I long to see him.

Toclio. Faith you will find no great pleasure in him for aught that I can see, lady; they say he is half a prophet too; would he could tell me any news of the lost prince; there's twenty talents offered to him that finds him.

Cador. Such news was breeding in the morning.

Toclio. And now it has birth and life, sir; if fortune bless me I'll once more search those woods where then we lost him; I know not yet what fate may follow me.   [*Exit.*

Cador. Fortune go with you, sir: come, fair mistress, your sister and lord Edwin are in game, and all their wits at stake to win the set.

Con. My sister has the hand yet, we had best leave them.
She will be out anon as well as I,
He wants but cunning to put in a die.
           [*Exeunt* CADOR *and* CON.

Edwin. You are a cunning gamester, madam.

Mod. It is a desperate game, indeed, this marriage, where there's no winning without loss to either.

Edwin. Why, what but your perfection, noble lady, can bar the worthiness of this my suit? If so you please I count my happiness from difficult obtaining, you shall see my duty and observance.

Mod. There shall be place to neither, noble sir. I do beseech you let this mild reply give answer to your suit, for here I vow, if ever I change my virgin name, by you it gains or loses.[3]

Edwin. My wishes have their own.

Mod. Let them confine you then, as to my promise you give faith and credence?

Edwin. In your command my willing absence speaks it.   [*Exit* EDWIN.

Mod. Noble and virtuous; could I dream of marriage, I should affect thee Edwin. Oh, my soul, here's something tells me that these best of creatures, these models of the world, weak man and woman, should have their souls, their making, life and being, to some more excellent use. If what the sense calls pleasure were our ends, we might justly blame great nature's wisdom, who reared a building of so much art and beauty to entertain a guest so far uncertain, so imperfect. If only speech distinguish us from beasts, who know no inequality of birth or place, but still to

fly from goodness—oh, how base were life at such a rate! No, no! that power that gave to man his being, speech, and wisdom, gave it for thankfulness. To him alone that
Made me thus, may I whence truly know,
I'll pay to him, not man, the love I owe.   [*Exit.*

SCENE II.—*The* British *Court.*

Flourish of Cornets. Enter AURELIUS, *King of* Britain; DONOBERT, GLOSTER, CADOR, EDWIN, TOCLIO, OSWOLD, *and* Attendants.

Aurel. No tidings of our brother yet? 'Tis strange, so near the court, and in our own land too, and yet no news of him! Oh, this loss tempers the sweetness of our happy conquests, with much untimely sorrow.

Dono. Royal sir, his safety being unquestioned, should to time leave the redress of sorrow; were he dead, or taken by the foe, our fatal loss had wanted no quick herald to disclose it.

Aurel. That hope alone sustains me, nor will we be so ungrateful unto heaven to question what we fear with what we enjoy. Is answer of our message yet returned from that religious man, the holy hermit, sent by the earl of Chester to confirm us in that miraculous act? For 'twas no less, our army being in rout, nay, quite o'erthrown, as Chester writes; even then this holy man, armed with his cross and staff, went smiling on, and boldly fronts the foe; at sight of whom the Saxons stood amazed; for to their seeming, above the hermit's head appeared such brightness, such clear and glorious beams, as if our men marched all in fire, wherewith the pagans fled, and by our troops were all to death pursued.

Glos. 'Tis full of wonder, sir.

Aurel. Oh, Gloster, he's a jewel worth a kingdom. Where's Oswold with his answer?

Os. 'Tis here, my royal lord.

Aurel. In writing! will he not sit with us?

Os. His orisons performed, he bade me say he would attend with all submission.

Aurel. Proceed to council then, and let some give order, the ambassadors being come, to take our answer they have admittance. Oswold, Toclio, be it your charge. [*Exeunt* Os. *and* TOCLIO.] And now, my lords, observe the holy counsel of this reverend hermit.   [*Reads.*

As you respect your safety, limit not that only power that hath protected you; trust not an open enemy too far;
> He's yet a loser; and knows you have won;
> Mischiefs not ended, are then but begun.
           ANSELME, the Hermit.

Dono. Powerful and pithy, which my advice confirms; no man leaves physic when his sickness slacks, but doubles the receipts; the word of peace seems fair to bloodshot eyes; but being applied with such a medicine as blinds all the sight, argues desire of cure, but not knowledge of art.[4]

Aurel. You argue from defects: if both the name and the condition of the peace be one, it is to be preferred; and in the offer made by the Saxon, I see nought repugnant.

Glos. The time of truce required for, thirty days, carries suspicion in it, since half that space will serve to strength their weakened regiments.

Cador. Who, in less time, will undertake to free our country from them?

Edwin. Leave that unto our fortune.

Dono. Is not our bold and hopeful general still master of the field—their legions fallen—the rest entrenched for fear, half starved, and wounded—and shall we now give o'er our fair advantage? 'Fore heaven, my lord, the danger is far more in trusting to their words than to their weapons.

Enter OSWOLD.

Os. The ambassadors are come, sir.

Aurel. Conduct them in: we are resolved, my lords, since policy failed in the beginning, it shall have no hand in the conclusion. That heavenly power that hath so well begun their fatal overthrow I know can end it; from which fair hope myself will give them answer.

Flourish of Cornets. Enter ARTESIA, *with the Saxon Lords.*

Dono. What's here?—a woman orator?

Aurel. Peace, Donobert. Speak, what are you, lady?

Artes. The sister of the Saxon general, warlike Ostorius, the East Angles king; my name Artesia; who, in terms of love, brings peace and health to great Aurelius, wishing the army may return as fair a present as she makes tender of.

Aurel. The fairest presence e'er mine eyes were blest with! Command a chair, there, for this Saxon beauty! Sit, lady, we'll confer: your warlike brother sues for a peace, you say?

Artes. With endless love unto your state and person.

Aurel. He's sent a moving orator, believe me: what think'st thou, Donobert?

Dono. Believe me, sir, were I but young again, this gilded pill might take my stomach quickly.

Aurel. True, thou art old: how soon we do

forget our own defects. Fair damsel,—oh, my tongue turns traitor, and will betray my heart,—sister to our enemy:—'sdeath, her beauty mazes me; I cannot speak if I but look on her. What's that we did conclude?

Dono. This royal lord ——

Aurel. Pish, thou canst not utter it. Fairest of creatures, tell the king, your brother, that we in love—ha! and honour to our country, command his armies to depart our realm; but if you please, fair soul——Lord Donobert, deliver you our pleasure.

Dono. I shall, sir: lady, return, and certify your brother ——

Aurel. Thou art too blunt, and rude: return so soon! fie! let her stay; and send some messenger to certify our pleasure.

Dono. What means your grace?

Aurel. To give her time of rest to her long journey: we would not willingly be thought uncivil.

Artes. Great king of Britain, let it not seem strange to embrace the princely offers of a friend, Whose virtues, with thine own, in fairest merit; Both states in peace and love may now inherit.

Aurel. She speaks of love again; sure 'tis my fear, she knows I do not hate her.

Artes. Be then, thyself, most great Aurelius; and let not envy, nor a deeper sin, in these thy counsellors, deprive thy goodness of that fair honour, we, in seeking peace, give first to thee, who never used to sue but force our wishes; yet, if this seem light, oh let my sex, though worthless your respect, take the report of thy humanity, Whose mild and virtuous life loud fame displays, As being o'ercome by one so worthy praise.

Aurel. She has an angel's tongue! speak still.

Dono. This flattery is gross, sir; hear no more on't. Lady, these childish compliments are needless: you have your answer; and believe it, madam, his grace, though young, doth wear within his breast too grave a counsellor to be seduced by smoothing flattery, or oily words.

Artes. I come not, sir, to woo him.

Dono. 'Twere folly if you should; you must not wed him: shame take thy tongue.[5]

Aurel. Shame take thy tongue; being old and weak thyself, thou doat'st; and, looking on thy own defects, speak'st what thoud'st wish in me: do I command the deeds of others, mine own act not free?

Be pleas'd to smile or frown, we respect neither; My will and rule shall stand and fall together.

Most fair Artesia, see, the king descends to give thee welcome with these warlike Saxons, and now on equal terms both sues and grants. Instead of truce, let a perpetual league seal our united bloods in holy marriage: send the East Angles king this happy news—that thou with me hast made a league for ever, and added to his state a friend and brother: speak, dearest love; dare you confirm this title?

Artes. I were no woman to deny so high and noble a proposal to my fame and country.[6]

Aurel. Live, then, a queen in Britain.

Glos. He means to marry her.

Dono. Death! he shall marry the devil first! marry a pagan—an idolater![7]

Cador. He has won her quickly.

Edwin. She was wooed afore she came, sure; or came of purpose to conclude the match.

Aurel. Who dares oppose our will? My lord of Gloster, be you ambassador unto our brother, the brother of our queen, Artesia; tell him, for such our entertainment looks him,[8] our marriage adding to the happiness
Of our intended joys, man's good or ill,
In this like waves agree—come double still.

Enter the Hermit.

Who's this? the hermit? Welcome my happiness, our country's hope: most reverend, holy man, I wanted but thy blessing to make perfect the infinite sum of my felicity.

Her. Alack, sweet prince; that happiness is yonder:
Felicity and thou art far asunder.
This world can never give it.

Aurel. Thou art deceived: see here what I have found—beauty, alliance, peace, and strength of friends; all in this all-exceeding excellence: the league's confirmed.

Her. With whom, dear lord?

Aurel. With the great brother of this beauteous woman, the royal Saxon king.

Her. Oh! then I see, and fear thou art too near thy misery. What magic could so link thee to this mischief? By all the good that thou hast reaped by me, stand further from destruction.

Aurel. Speak as a man, and I shall hope to obey thee.[9]

Her. Idolaters, get hence! fond king, let go! Thou hug'st thy ruin, and thy country's woe.

Dono. Well spoke, old father, to him; bait him soundly. Now, by heaven's blest lady, I can scarce keep patience.

1st S. Lord. What devil is this?

2nd S. Lord. That cursed Christian, by whose hellish charms our army was o'erthrown.

Her. Why do you dally, sir? Oh! tempt not heaven; warm not a serpent in your naked bosom; discharge them from your court.

Aurel. Thou speak'st like madness. Command the frozen shepherd to the shade when he sits warm i' the sun—the fever-sick to add more heat unto his burning pain—these may obey: 'tis less extremity than thou enjoin'st to me: cast but thine eyes upon this beauty; do it; I'll forgive thee, though jealousy in others finds no pardon; then say thou dost not love like me: I shall then swear thou'rt immortal, and no earthly man: Oh, blame then my mortality, not me.

Her. It is thy weakness brings thy misery, unhappy prince.

Aurel. Be milder in thy doom.

Her. 'Tis you that must endure heaven's doom, which fallen, remember 's just.

Artes. Thou shalt not live to see it: how fares my lord? If my poor presence breeds dislike, great prince, I am no such neglected soul, will seek to tie you to your word.

Aurel. My word, dear love! may my religion, crown, state, and kingdom fail when I fail thee. Command earl Chester to break up the camp, without disturbance to our Saxon friends; send every hour swift posts to hasten on the king, her brother, to conclude this league, this endless happy peace of love and marriage; till when, provide for revels; and give charge that nought be wanting which will make our triumphs
Sportful and free to all: if such fair blood
Engender ill, men must not look for good.

　　　　[Flourish. Exeunt all but the Hermit.

Enter MODESTIA, *reading in a Book.*

Mod. How much the oft report of this blest hermit hath won on my desires: I must behold him: and sure this should be he. Oh, the world's folly! proud earth and dust, how low a price bears goodness! all that should make man absolute shines in him. Much reverent sir, may I, without offence, give interruption to your holy thoughts?

Her. What would you, lady?

Mod. That which till now ne'er found a language in me: I am in love.

Her. In love! with what?

Mod. With virtue.

Her. There's no blame in that.

Mod. Nay, sir, with you! with your religious life. Your virtue, goodness, if there be a name to express affection greater,—that, that would I learn and utter. Reverend sir, if there be anything to bar my suit, be charitable and expose it: your prayers are the same orisons which I will number. Holy sir, keep not instruction back from willingness: possess me of that knowledge leads you on to this humility; for well I know were greatness good, you would not live so low.

Her. Are you a virgin?

Mod. Yes, sir!

Her. Your name?

Mod. Modestia.

Her. Your name and virtues meet, a modest virgin: live ever in the sanctimonious way to heaven and happiness. There's goodness in you— I must instruct you further. Come, look up: behold yon firmament! there sits a power whose footstool is this earth: oh learn this lesson— And practise it: he that will climb so high, Must let no joy beneath to move his eye.[10]

Mod. I apprehend you, sir: on heaven I fix my love:

Earth gives us grief; our joys are all above.

For this was man in innocence naked born,

To show us wealth hinders our sweet return.

                 [*Exeunt.*

ACT II.

SCENE I.—*A Forest.*

Enter Clown *and his* Sister, *great with Child.*

Clown. Away, follow me no further, I am none of thy brother; what, with child! great with child! and know not who's the father on't! I am ashamed to call thee sister.

Joan. Believe me, brother, he was a gentleman.

Clown. Nay, I believe that; he gives arms and legs too, and has made you the herald to blaze 'em; but Joan, Joan, sister Joan, can you tell me his name that did it? how shall we call my cousin, your bastard, when we have it?

Joan. Alas! I know not the gentleman's name, brother; I met him in these woods the last great hunting; he was so kind, and proffered me so much, as I had not the heart to ask him more.

Clown. Not his name, why this shows your country breeding now; had you been brought up i' th' city, you'd have got a father first, and the child afterwards: hast thou no marks to know him by?

Joan. He had most rich attire, a fair hat and feather, a gilt sword, and most excellent hangers.

Clown. Pox on his hangers! would he had been gelt for his labour.

Joan. Had you but heard him swear, you would have thought——

Clown. Ay, as you did, swearing and lying goes together still; did his oaths get you with child? we shall have a roaring boy then i'faith. Well, sister, I must leave you.

Joan. Dear brother stay, help me to find him out; I'll ask no further.

Clown. 'Sfoot, who should I find? who should I ask for?

Joan. Alas! I know not: he uses in these woods, and these are witness of his oaths and promise.

Clown. We are like to have a hot suit on't, when our best witness 's but a knight o' th' post.

Joan. Do but inquire this forest; I'll go with you, some happy fate may guide us till we meet him.

Clown. Meet him! and what name shall we have for him when we meet him? 'Sfoot, thou neither know'st him, nor canst tell what to call him; was ever man tied with such a business, to have a sister got with child, and know not who did it? well, you shall see him, I'll do my best for you, I'll make proclamation, if these woods and trees, as you say, will bear any witness, let them answer. Oh, yes. If there be any man that wants a name, will come in for conscience sake, and acknowledge himself to be a whoremaster, he shall have that laid to his charge in an hour, he shall not be rid on in an age; if he have lands he shall have an heir, if he have patience he shall have a wife, if he have neither lands nor patience, he shall have a whore. So ho, boy! so ho, so, so!

Prince Uter. [*Within.*] So ho, boy! so ho, illo ho, illo ho!

Clown. Hark, hark, sister; there's one holloas to us; what a wicked world's this; a man cannot so soon name a whore but a knave comes presently, and see where he is; stand close awhile, sister.

Enter PRINCE UTER.

Prince. How like a voice that echo spoke, but

ah, my thoughts are lost for ever in amazement; could I but meet a man to tell her beauties, these trees would bend their tops to kiss the air, that from my lips should give her praises up.

Clown. He talks of a woman, sister.

Joan. This may be he, brother.

Clown. View him well; you see he has a fair sword, but his hangers are fallen.

Prince. Here did I see her first, here view her beauty; oh, had I known her name, I had been happy.

Clown. Sister, this is he sure; he knows not thy name neither; a couple of wise fools i'faith, to get children and not know one another.

Prince. You weeping leaves, upon whose tender cheeks doth stand a flood of tears at my complaint, and heard my vows and oaths.

Clown. Law, law, he has been a great swearer too; 'tis he, sister.

Prince. For having overtook her, as I have seen a forward blood-hound, strip the swifter of the cry ready to seize his wished hopes, upon the sudden view struck with astonishment at his arrived prey, instead of seizure stands at fearful bay;
Or like to Marius' soldiers, who o'ertook
The eye-sight killing Gorgon, at one look
Made everlasting stand; so fear'd my power
Whose cloud aspir'd the sun, dissolv'd a shower:
Pygmalion, then I tasted thy sad fate,[11] whose ivory picture, and my fair were one, our dotage past imagination; I saw and felt desire.

Clown. Pox o' your fingering! did he feel, sister?

Prince. But enjoyed not; oh, fate, thou hadst thy days and nights to feed,
Or calm affection, one poor sight was all,
Converts my pleasure to perpetual thrall,
Embracing thine, thou losest breath and desire,
So I relating mine, will here expire;
For here I vow to you, ye mournful plants,
Who were the first made happy by her fame,
Never to part hence, till I know her name.

Clown. Give me thy hand, sister, the child has found his father; this is he sure, as I am a man; had I been a woman, these kind words would have won me; I should have had a great belly too, that's certain; well, I'll speak to him; most honest and fleshly-minded gentleman, give me your hand, sir.

Prince. Ha! what art thou, that thus rudely and boldly darest take notice of a wretch so much allied to misery as I am?

Clown. Nay, sir, for our alliance, I shall be found to be a poor brother-in-law of your worship's; the gentlewoman you spoke on is my sister; you see

what a clew she spreads; her name is Joan Go-too't, I am her elder, but she has been at it before me: 'tis a woman's fault; pox o' this bashfulness, come forward Jug, prythee speak to him.

Prince. Have you e'er seen me lady?

Clown. Seen ye, ha, ha! it seems she has felt you too; here's a young Go-to-'t a-coming, sir; she is my sister; we all love to go to 't as well as your worship; she's a maid yet,[12] but you may make her a wife when you please, sir.

Prince. I am amazed with wonder: Tell me, woman, what sin have you committed worthy this?[13]

Joan. Do you not know me, sir?

Prince. Know thee! as I do thunder, hell, and mischief; witch, stallion, hag!

Clown. I see he will marry her, he speaks so like a husband.

Prince. Death! I will cut out their tongues for this blasphemy. Strumpet, villain, where have you ever seen me?

Clown. Speak for yourself with a pox to ye.

Prince. Slaves! I'll make you curse yourselves for this temptation.

Joan. Oh, sir, if ever you did speak to me it was in smoother phrase, in fairer language.

Prince. Lightning consume me if I ever saw thee! my rage o'erflows my blood, all patience flies me.   [*Beats her.*[14]

Clown. Hold, I beseech you, sir; I have nothing to say to you.

Joan. Help, help! murder, murder!

Enter TOCLIO *and* OSWOLD.

Toclio. Make haste, sir; this way the sound came; it was a wood.

Os. See where she is, and the prince! the price of all our wishes.

Clown. The prince, say ye? he's made a poor subject of me, I am sure.

Toclio. Sweet prince, noble Uter, speak! how fare you, sir?

Os. Dear sir, recal yourself; your fearful absence hath won too much already on the grief of our sad king, from whom our labouring search hath had this fair success in meeting you.

Toclio. His silence and his looks argue distraction.

Clown. Nay, he's mad sure; he will not acknowledge my sister, nor the child neither.

Os. Let us entreat your grace along with us; your sight will bring new life to the king your brother.

Toclio. Will you go, sir ?

Prince. Yes, any whither, guide me, all's hell I see,

Man may change air, but not his misery.

                       [*Exeunt* PRINCE *and* TOCLIO.

Joan. Lend me one word with you, sir.

Clown. Well said, sister; he has a feather, and fair hangers too, this may be he.

Os. What would you, fair one ?

Joan. Sure I have seen you in these woods ere this ?

Os. Trust me never, I never saw this place till at this time my friend conducted me.

Joan. The more's my sorrow then.

Os. Would I could comfort you : I am a bachelor, but it seems you have a husband; you have been foully o'ershot else.

Clown. A woman's fault; we are all subject to go to't, sir.

Enter TOCLIO.

Toclio. Oswold, away; the prince will not stir a foot without you.

Os. I am coming; farewell, woman.

Toclio. Prithee make haste.

Joan. Good sir, but one word with you ere you leave us.

Toclio. With me fair soul ?

Clown. She'll have a fling at him, too; the child must have a father.

Joan. Have you ne'er seen me, sir ?

Toclio. Seen thee! 'Sfoot! I have seen many fair faces in my time; prithee look up, and do not weep so ; sure, pretty wanton, I have seen this face before.

Joan. It is enough, though you ne'er see me more.   [*Sinks down.*

Toclio. 'Sfoot she's fallen ; this place is enchanted sure ; look to the woman, fellow.   [*Exit.*

Clown. Oh, she's dead! she's dead! as you are a man stay and help, sir. Joan, Joan, sister Joan ! why Joan Go-to-'t, I say; will you cast away yourself, and your child, and me too ? What do you mean, sister ?

Joan. Oh, give me pardon, sir; 'twas too much joy oppressed my loving thoughts; I knew you were too noble to deny me ; ha! where is he ?

Clown. Who, the gentleman ? he's gone, sister.

Joan. Oh! I am undone, then ; run, and tell him I did but faint for joy ; dear brother, haste ; why dost thou stay ? oh, never cease till he give answer to thee.

Clown. He! which he ? what do you call him tro ?

Joan. Unnatural brother, show me the path he took. Why dost thou dally ? speak, oh, which way went he ?

Clown. This way, that way, through the bushes there.

Joan. Were it through fire, the journey's easy ; winged with sweet desire.   [*Exit.*

Clown. Hey day, there's some hope of this yet ; I'll follow her for kindred's sake ; if she miss of her purpose now, she'll challenge all she finds I see, for if ever we meet with a two-legged creature in the whole kingdom, the child shall have a father, that's certain.   [*Exit.*

SCENE II.—*An Ante-chamber at the* British *Court.*

Loud Music. Enter Two with the Sword and Mace ; CADOR, EDWIN, *Two* Bishops, AURELIUS, OSTORIUS, *leading* ARTESIA *crowned ;* CONSTANTIA, MODESTIA, OCTA, PROXIMUS *a Magician,* DONOBERT, GLOSTER, OSWOLD, TOCLIO, *all pass over the stage ; Manet,* DONOBERT, GLOSTER, EDWIN, *and* CADOR.

Dono. Come, Gloster, I do not like this hasty marriage.

Glos. She was quickly wooed and won; not six days since arrived an enemy to sue for peace, and now crowned queen of Britain! this is strange.

Dono. Her brother, too, made as quick speed in coming, leaving his Saxons and his starved troops, to take the advantage whilst 'twas offered; 'fore heaven, I fear the king's too credulous; our army is discharged too.

Glos. Yes, and our general commanded home. Son Edwin, have you seen him since ?

Edwin. He's come to court; but will not view the presence, nor speak unto the king, he's so discontent at this so strange alliance with the Saxon, as nothing can persuade his patience.

Cador. You know his humour will endure no check; no, if the king oppose it. All crosses feed both his spleen and his impatience; those affections are in him like powder, apt to inflame with every little spark, and blow up all his reason.

Glos. Edol of Chester is a noble soldier.

Dono. So is he by the rood,[15] ever most faithful to the king and kingdom, howe'er his passions guide him.

Enter EDOL with Captains.

Cador. See where he comes, my lord.

Omnes. Welcome to court, brave earl.

Edol. Do not deceive me by your flatteries. Is

not the Saxon here? the league confirmed? the marriage ratified? the court divided with pagan infidels? the least part Christians, at least in their commands? Oh, the gods![16] it is a thought that takes away my sleep, and dulls my senses so, I scarcely know you. Prepare my horses, I 'll away to Chester.

Cap. What shall we do with our companies, my lord?

Edol. Keep them at home to increase cuckolds, and get some cases for your captainships, smooth up your brows, the wars have spoiled your faces, and few will now regard you.

Dono. Preserve your patience, sir.

Edol. Preserve your honours, lords, your country's safety, your lives and lands from strangers. What black devil could so bewitch the king, so to discharge a royal army in the height of conquest—nay, even already made victorious—to give such credit to an enemy, a starved foe, a straggling fugitive, beaten beneath our feet, so low dejected, so servile, and so base, as hope of life had won them all to leave the land for ever?

Dono. It was the king's will.

Edol. It was your want of wisdom, that should have laid before his tender youth the dangers of a state, where foreign powers bandy for sovereignty with lawful kings, who being settled once, to assure themselves, will never fail to seek the blood and life of all competitors.

Dono. Your words sound well, my lord, and point at safety, both for the realm and us; but why did you, within whose power it lay, as general, with full commission to dispose the war, lend ear to parley with your weakened foe?

Edol. Oh, the good gods!

Cador. And on that parley came this embassy.

Edol. You will hear me.

Edwin. Your letters did declare it to the king, both of the peace, and all conditions brought by this Saxon lady, whose fond love has thus bewitched him.

Edol. I will curse you all as black as hell, unless you hear me; your gross mistake would make wisdom herself run madding through the streets, and quarrel with her shadow; death! why killed ye not that woman?

Dono.
Glos. } Oh, my lord!

Edol. The great devil take me quick, had I been by, and all the women of the world were barren, she should have died e'er he had married her on these conditions.

Cador. It is not reason that directs you thus.

Edol. Then I have none, for all I have directs me, never was man so palpably abused, so basely marted, bought and sold to scorn, my honour, fame, and hopeful victories, the loss of time, expenses, blood, and fortunes, all vanished into nothing.

Edwin. This rage is vain, my lord; what the king does, nor they, nor you can help.

Edol. My sword must fail me then.

Cador. 'Gainst whom will you expose it?

Edol. What's that to you? 'gainst all the devils in hell, to guard my country.

Edwin. These are airy words.

Edol. Sir, you tread too hard upon my patience.

Edwin. I speak the duty of a subject's faith, and say again, had you been here in presence,
What the king did, you had not dar'd to cross it.

Edol. I will trample on his life and soul that says it.

Cador. My lord!

Edwin. Come, come.

Edol. Now, before heaven!

Cador. Dear sir.

Edol. Not dare? thou liest beneath thy lungs.

Glos. No more, son Edwin.

Edwin. I have done, sir, I take my leave.

Edol. But thou shall not, you shall take no leave of me, sir.

Dono. For wisdom's sake, my lord.

Edol. Sir, I 'll leave him, and you, and all of you, the court and king, and let my sword and friends shuffle for Edol's safety. Stay you here, and hug the Saxons till they cut your throats, or bring the land to servile slavery.
Such yokes of baseness, Chester must not suffer,
Go, and repent betimes these foul misdeeds,
For in this league, all our whole kingdom bleeds,
Which I 'll prevent, or perish.

[*Exeunt* EDOL *and* Cap.

Glos. See how his rage transports him!

Cador. These passions set apart, a braver soldier breathes not i' th' world this day.

Dono. I wish his own worth do not court his ruin.
The king must rule, and we must learn to obey,
True virtue still directs the noble way.

SCENE III.—*Hall of State in the Palace.*

Loud Music. Enter AURELIUS, ARTESIA, OSTORIUS, OCTA, PROXIMUS, TOCLIO, OSWOLD, *and* Hermit.

Aurel. Why is the court so dull? methinks

each room and angle of our palace should appear stuck full of objects fit for mirth and triumphs, to show our high content. Oswold, fill wine; must we begin the revels. Be it so, then, reach me the cup; I'll now begin a health to our loved queen, the bright Artesia, and the royal Saxon king, our war-like brother; go and command all the whole court to pledge it; fill to the hermit there; most reverend Anselme, we'll do thee the honour first to pledge my queen.

Her. I drink no healths great king, and if I did, I would be loath to part with health, to those that have no power to give it back again.

Aurel. Mistake not; it is the argument of love and duty to our queen and us.

Artes. But he owes none, it seems.

Her. I do to virtue, madam: temperate minds covet that health to drink which nature gives in every spring to man: he that doth hold
His body but a tenement at will,
Bestows no cost but to repair what's ill;
Yet if your healths, or heat of wine, fair princess,
Could this old frame, or these craz'd limbs restore,
Or keep out death, or sickness, then fill more;
I'll make fresh way for appetite; if no,
On such a prodigal who would wealth bestow.

Osto. He speaks not like a guest to grace a wedding.

Enter TOCLIO.

Artes. No, sir; but like an envious impostor.

Octa. A Christian slave; a cynic.

Osto. What virtue could decline your kingly spirit to such respect of him whose magic spells met with your vanquished troops, and turned your arms to that necessity of fight; which but for the despair of any hope to stand but by his charms, had been defeated in a bloody conquest?

Octa. 'Twas magic, hell-bred magic, did it, sir; and that's a course, my lord, which we esteem in all our Saxon wars unto the last and lowest ebb of servile treachery.

Aurel. Sure you are deceived: it was the hand of heaven, that in his virtue gave us victory. Is there a power in man that can strike fear through a general camp, or create spirits, in recreant bosoms, above present sense?

Osto. To blind the sense there may, with apparition of well-armed troops, which in themselves are air, formed into human shapes; and such that day were by that sorcerer raised to cross our fortunes.

Aurel. There is a law tells us, that words want

force to make deeds void; examples must be shown by instances alike, ere I believe it.

Osto. 'Tis easily performed, believe me, sir. Propose your own desires, and give but way to what our magic here shall straight perform; and then let his or our deserts be censured.

Aurel. We could not wish a greater happiness than what this satisfaction brings with it: let him proceed, fair brother.

Osto. He shall, sir. Come, learned Proximus, this task be thine; let thy great charms confound the opinion this Christian, by his spells, hath falsely won.

Prox. Great king, propound your wishes, then: what persons—of what state—what numbers—or how armed: please your thoughts; they shall appear before you.

Aurel. Strange art! what think'st thou, reverent hermit?

Her. Let him go on, sir.

Aurel. Wilt thou behold his cunning?

Her. Right gladly, sir; it will be my joy to tell, That I was here to laugh at him and hell.

Aurel. I like thy confidence.

Artes. His saucy impudence; proceed to the trial.

Prox. Speak your desires, my lord; and be it placed in any angle beneath the moon, the centre of the earth, the sea, the air, the region of the fire, nay hell itself, and I'll present it.

Aurel. We'll have no sight so fearful, only this: if all thy art can reach it, show me here the two great champions of the Trojan war, Achilles and brave Hector, our great ancestor,[17] both in their warlike habits, armour, shields, and weapons then in use for fight.

Prox. 'Tis done, my lord: command a halt and silence, as each man will respect his life or danger. *Armel! Plesgeth!*

Enter Spirit.

Spirit. Quid vis?

Prox. Attend me.

Aurel. The apparition comes: on our displeasure let all keep place and silence.

Drums within beat Marches. Enter PROXIMUS, *bringing in* Hector, *attired and armed after the* Trojan *manner; with Target, Sword, and Battle-axe, a Trumpet before him, and a* Spirit *in flame Colours with a Torch; at the other Door* Achilles, *with his Spear and Falchion, a Trumpet and a* Spirit *in Black before him: Trumpets sound alarm, and they manage their Weapons to begin the fight. After some Charges the* Hermit *steps in between them, at which, seeming amazed, the* Spirits *tremble. Thunder within.*

Prox. What means this stay, bright Armel, Plesgeth? why fear you and fall back? Renew the alarms, and enforce the combat, or hell and darkness circles you for ever.

Armel. We dare not.

Prox. Ha!

Ples. Our charms are all dissolved; Armel, away; 'Tis worse than hell to us while here we stay.

[*Exeunt the* Spirits.

Her. What! at a nonplus, sir? command them back for shame.

Prox. What power o'erawes my spells? Return, you hell-hounds; Armel, Plesgeth, double damnation seize you: by all the infernal powers, the prince of devils is in this Hermit's habit; what else could force my spirits quake or tremble thus?

Her. Weak argument to hide your want of skill.

Does the devil fear the devil, or war with hell? They have not been acquainted long, it seems. Know, misbelieving pagan, even that Power That overthrew your forces, still lets you see, He only can control both hell and thee.

Prox. Disgrace and mischief! I 'll enforce new charms, new spells, and spirits raised from the low abyss of hell's unbottomed depths.

Aurel. We have enough, sir; give o'er your charms; we 'll find some other time to praise your art. I dare not but acknowledge that heavenly Power my heart stands witness to. Be not dismayed, my lords, at this disaster; nor thou, my fairest queen; we 'll change the scene to some more pleasing sports. Lead to your chamber: Howe'er in this thy pleasures find a cross, Our joy's too fixéd here to suffer loss.

Toclio. Which I shall add to, sir, with news I bring. The prince, your brother, lives.

Aurel. Ha!

Toclio. And comes to grace this high and heaven-knit marriage.

Aurel. Why dost thou flatter me, to make me think such happiness attends me?

Enter PRINCE UTER *and* OSWOLD.

Toclio. His presence speaks my truth, sir.

Dono. 'Fore me? 'tis he! look, Gloster.

Glos. A blessing beyond hope, sir.

Aurel. Ha! 'tis he; welcome, my second comfort. Artesia, dearest love, it is my brother—my princely brother—all my kingdom's hope: oh give him welcome, as thou lov'st my health.

Artes. You have so free a welcome, sir, from me, as this your presence has such power, I swear o'er me a stranger, that I must forget my country, name, and friends, and count this place my joy and birthright.

Prince. 'Tis she! 'tis she, I swear! oh ye good gods, 'tis she! That face, within those woods where first I saw her, captived my senses, and thus many months barred me from all society of men. How came she to this place, brother Aurelius? Speak that angel's name—her heaven-blest name: oh speak it quickly, sir.

Artes. It is Artesia, the royal Saxon princess.

Prince. A woman, and no deity: no feigned shape to mock the reason of admiring sense, on whom a hope as low as mine may live, love, and enjoy; dear brother, may it not?

Aurel. She is all the good or virtue thou canst name; my wife, my queen.

Prince. Ha! your wife?

Artes. Which you shall find, sir; if that time and fortune may make my love but worthy of your trial.

Prince. Oh!

Aurel. What troubles you, dear brother? Why with so strange and fixed an eye dost thou behold my joys?

Artes. You are not well, sir.

Prince. Yes, yes; oh you immortal powers, why has poor man so many entrances for sorrow to creep in at, when our sense is much too weak to hold his happiness? Oh, say I was born deaf; and let your silence confirm in me the knowing my defect; at least be charitable to conceal my sin, for hearing is no less in me, dear brother.

Aurel. No more; I see thou art a rival in the joys of my high bliss: come, my Artesia, The day's most prais'd when 'tis eclipsed by night, Great good must have as great ill opposite.

Prince. Stay, hear but a word;—yet now I think on't, This is your wedding-night, and were it mine, I should be angry with least loss of time.

Artes. Envy speaks no such words; has no such looks.

Prince. Sweet rest unto you both.

Aurel. Lights to our nuptial chamber.

Artes. Could you speak so, I would not fear how much my grief did grow.

Aurel. Lights to our chamber; on, on, set on.

[*Exeunt all except the* PRINCE.

Prince. " Could you speak so, I would not fear how much my griefs did grow." Those were her very words. Sure I am waking; she wrung me by the hand, and spake them to me with a most passionate affection; perhaps she loves, and now repents her choice in marriage with my brother. Oh fond man, how darest thou trust thy traitor's thoughts thus to betray thyself? 'Twas but a waking dream wherein thou madest thy wishes speak; not her, in which thy foolish hopes strive to prolong
A wretched being, so sickly children play
With health-lov'd toys, which for a time delay,
But do not cure the fit: be then a man;
Meet that destruction which thou canst not fly
From: not to live, make it thy best to die;
And call her now, whom thou didst hope to wed,
Thy brother's wife; thou art too near a kin,
And such an act above all name's a sin
Not to be blotted out, heaven pardon me;
She's banish'd from my bosom now for ever,
To lowest ebbs, men justly hope a flood,
When vice grows barren, all desires are good.

Enter a Waiting Gentlewoman, *with a Jewel.*

Gent. The noble Prince, I take it, sir?

Prince. You speak me what I should be, lady.

Gent. Know by that name, sir, queen Artesia greets you.

Prince. Alas, good virtue, how is she mistaken!

Gent. Commending her affection in this jewel, sir.

Prince. She binds my service to her: ha! a jewel; 'tis a fair one, trust me; and methinks it much resembles something I have seen with her.

Gent. It is an artificial crab, sir.

Prince. A creature that goes backward.

Gent. True, from the way it looks.

Prince. There is no moral in it alludes to herself?

Gent. 'Tis your construction gives you that, sir; she's a woman.

Prince. And like this may use her legs and eyes two several ways.

Gent. Just like the sea-crab, which on the mussel preys, whilst he bills at a stone.

Prince. Pretty in troth; prithee tell me, art thou honest?

Gent. I hope I seem no other, sir.

Prince. And those that seem so are sometimes bad enough.

Gent. If they will accuse themselves for want of witness, let them; I am not so foolish.

Prince. I see thou art wise; come, speak me truly; what is the greatest sin?

Gent. That which man never acted, what has been done
Is as the least, common to all as one.

Prince. Dost think thy lady is of thy opinion?

Gent. She's a bad scholar else; I have brought her up, and she dares owe me still.[18]

Prince. Ay, 'tis a fault in greatness: they dare owe many ere they pay one; but darest thou expose thy scholar to my examining?

Gent. Yes, in good troth, sir, and pray put her to 't too; 'tis a hard lesson if she answer it not.

Prince. Thou know'st the hardest.

Gent. As far as a woman may, sir.

Prince. I commend thy plainness; when wilt thou bring me to thy lady?

Gent. Next opportunity I attend you, sir.

Prince. Thanks, take this, and commend me to her.

Gent. Think of your sea-crab, sir, I pray. [*Exit.*

Prince. Oh, by any means, lady. What shall all this tend to? if it be love or lust that thus incites her, the sin is horrid and incestuous; if to betray my life, what hopes she by it? Yes, it may be a practice 'twixt themselves to expel the Britons and ensure the state through our destruction; all this may be valid with a deeper reach in villany than all my thoughts can guess at; however—
I will confer with her, and if I find
Lust hath given life to envy in her mind,
I may prevent the danger; so men wise
By the same step by which they fell, may rise.
Vices are virtues, if so thought and seen,[19]
And trees with foulest roots, branch soonest green.
[*Exit.*

ACT III.

SCENE 1.—*Before the Palace of* King Aurelius.

Enter Clown *and his* Sister.

Clown. Come, sister, thou art all fool, all mad-woman.

Joan. Prithee have patience, we are now at Court.

Clown. At court! ha, ha, that proves thy madness; was there ever any woman in thy taking travelled to court for a husband? 'slid, 'tis enough for them to get children, and the city to keep 'em, and the country to find nurses: everything must be done in his due place, sister.

Joan. Be but content awhile, for sure I know this journey will be happy. Oh, dear brother, this night my sweet friend came to comfort me; I saw him and embraced him in mine arms.

Clown. Why did you not hold him, and call me to help you?

Joan. Alas! I thought I had been with him still, but when I waked——

Clown. Ah, pox of all loggerheads! then you were but in a dream all this while, and we may still go look for him. Well, since we are come to court, cast your cat's-eyes about you, and either find him out you dreamed on, or some other, for I'll trouble myself no further.

Enter DONO, CADOR, EWIN, *and* TOCLIO.

See, see, here comes more courtiers; look about you; come, pray view 'em all well; the old man has none of the marks about him, the others have both swords and feathers; what thinkest thou of that tall young gentleman?

Joan. He much resembles him; but sure my friend, brother, was not so high of stature.

Clown. Oh, beast, wast thou got with child with a short thing too?

Dono. Come, come, I'll hear no more on't: go, lord Edwin, tell her this day her sister shall be married to Cador, earl of Cornwall; so shall she to thee, brave Edwin, if she'll have my blessing.

Edwin. She is addicted to a single life; she will not hear of marriage.

Dono. Tush, fear it not; go you from me to her; use your best skill, my lord; and if you fail, I have a trick shall do it: haste, haste about it.

Edwin. Sir, I am gone; my hope is in your help more than my own.

Dono. And, worthy Toclio, to your care I must commend this business, for lights and music, and what else is needful.

Toclio. I shall, my lord.

Clown. We would entreat a word, sir; come forward, sister. [*Exit* DONO, TOCLIO, *and* CADOR.

Edwin. What lackest thou, fellow?

Clown. I lack a father for a child, sir.

Edwin. How! a god-father?

Clown. No, sir, we mean the own father; it may be you, sir, for anything we know: I think the child is like you.

Edwin. Like me! prithee where is it?

Clown. Nay, 'tis not born yet, sir; 'tis forthcoming you see; the child must have a father: what do you think of my sister?

Edwin. Why I think if she ne'er had husband she's a whore, and thou a fool; farewell. [*Exit.*

Clown. I thank you, sir. Well, pull up thy heart, sister; if there be any law in the court this fellow shall father it, 'cause he uses me so scurvily. There's a great wedding towards they say; we'll among them for a husband for thee.

Enter SIR NICHODEMUS *with a Letter.*

If we miss there, I'll have another bout with him that abused me. See! look, there comes another hat and feather; this should be a close lecher; he's reading of a love-letter.

Sir Nich. Earl Cador's marriage, and a masque to grace it; so, so. This night shall make me famous for presentments. How now, what are you?

Clown. A couple of Great Britons, you may see by our bellies, sir.

Sir Nich. And what of this, sir?

Clown. Why thus the matter stands, sir. There's one of your courtiers' hunting nags has made a gap through another man's enclosure. Now, sir, here's the question; who should be at charge of a fur-bush to stop it?

Sir Nich. Ha, ha, this is out of my element; the law must end it.

Clown. Your worship says well; for surely I think some lawyer had a hand in the business, we have such a troublesome issue.

Sir Nich. But what's thy business with me now?

Clown. Nay, sir, the business is done already, you may see by my sister's belly.

Sir Nich. Oh, now I find thee, this gentlewoman it seems has been humbled.

Clown. As low as the ground would give her leave, sir, and your worship knows this; though there be many fathers without children, yet to have a child without a father were most unnatural.

Sir Nich. That's true i'faith, I never heard of a child yet that e'er begot his father.

Clown. Why, true, you say wisely, sir.

Sir Nich. And therefore I conclude, that he that got the child is, without all question, the father of it.

Clown. Ay, now you come to the matter, sir; and our suit is to your worship for the discovery of this father.

Sir Nich. Why, lives he in the court here?

Joan. Yes, sir, and I desire but marriage.

Sir Nich. And does the knave refuse it? Come, come, be merry, wench, he shall marry thee, and keep the child too, if my knighthood can do any-thing; I am bound by mine orders to help dis-tressed ladies, and can there be a greater injury to a woman with child, than to lack a father for 't? I am ashamed of your simpleness. Come, come, give me a courtier's fee for my pains, and I'll be thy advocate myself, and justice shall be found, nay, I'll sue the law for it; but give me my fee first.

Clown. If all the money I have i' the world will do it, you shall have it, sir.

Sir Nich. An angel does it.

Clown. Nay, there's two, for your better sight, sir.

Sir Nich. Why, well said; give me thy hand, wench, I'll teach thee a trick for all this shall get a father for thy child presently, and this it is, mark now; you meet a man as you meet me now, thou claimest marriage of me, and layest the child to my charge; I deny it; pish, that's nothing, hold thy claim fast, thy words carry it, and no law can with-stand it.

Clown. Is't possible?

Sir Nich. Past all opposition, her own word carries it; let her challenge any man, the child shall call him father;[20] there's a trick for your money now.

Clown. Troth, sir, we thank you, we'll make use of your trick, and go no further to seek a father, for we challenge you, sir. Sister, lay it to him, he shall marry thee, I shall have a worshipful old man to my brother.

Sir Nich. Ha, ha! I like thy pleasantness.

Joan. Nay, indeed, sir, I do challenge you.

Clown. You think we jest, sir?

Sir Nich. Ay, by my troth do I, I like thy wit,

i'faith, thou shalt live at court with me; didst never hear of Nichodemus Nothing? I am the man.

Clown. Nothing! 'slid we are out again, thou wert never got with child with nothing, sure.

Joan. I know not what to say.

Sir Nich. Never grieve, wench; show me the man, and process shall fly out.

Clown. 'Tis enough for us to find the children, we look that you should find the father; and there-fore, either do us justice, or we'll stand to our first challenge.

Sir Nich. Would you have justice without an adversary? unless you can show me the man, I can do no good in it.

Clown. Why, then, I hope you'll do us no harm, sir, you'll restore my money.

Sir Nich. What! my fee? marry, law forbid it; find out the party, and you shall have justice, your fault closed up, and all shall be amended, the child his father, and the law ended. [*Exit.*

Clown. Well, he has deserved his fee indeed, for he has brought our suit to a quick end, I promise you, and yet the child has never a father; nor have we more money to seek after him, a shame of all lecherous placcats; now you look like a cat had newly kittened, what will you do tro? Follow me no further, lest I beat your brains out.

Joan. Impose upon me any punishment, rather than leave me now.

Clown. Well, I think I am bewitched with thee. I cannot find in my heart to forsake her; there was never sister would have abused a poor brother as thou hast done; I have even pined away with fretting, there's nothing but flesh and bones about me; well, and I had my money again, it were some comfort—hark, sister, [*thunder*] does it not thunder?

Joan. Oh, yes, most fearfully, what shall we do brother?

Clown. Marry, e'en get some shelter e'er the storm catch us; away, let's away, I prithee.

Enter the Devil *in Man's Habit, richly attired, his Feet and his Head horrid.*

Joan. Ha! 'tis he, stay brother, dear brother stay.

Clown. What's the matter now?

Joan. My love, my friend is come; yonder he goes.

Clown. Where, where, show me where? I'll stop him, if the devil be not in him.

Joan. Look there, look yonder; oh, dear friend, pity my distress, for heaven and goodness do but speak to me.

Devil. She calls me, and yet drives me headlong
    from her,
Poor mortal, thou and I are much uneven,
Thou must not speak of goodness, nor of heaven,
If I confer with thee; but be of comfort;
Whilst men do breathe, and Britain's name be
    known,
The fatal fruit thou bear'st within thy womb,
Shall here be famous till the day of doom.

Clown. 'Slid, who's that talks so? I can see nobody.

Joan. Then thou art blind, or mad; see where
he goes, and beckons me to come; oh, lead me
forth, I'll follow thee in spite of fear or death. [*Exit.*

Clown. Oh brave, she'll run to the devil for a husband; she's stark mad sure, and talks to a shadow,
for I could see no substance. Well, I'll after her,
the child was got by chance, and the father must
be found at all adventure.   [*Exit.*

SCENE II.—*The Porch of a Church.*

Enter HERMIT, MODESTIA, *and* EDWIN.

Mod. Oh, reverend sir, by you my heart hath
reached at the large hopes of holy piety, and for
this I craved your company,
Here in your sight religiously to vow,
My chaste thoughts up to heaven, and make you now
The witness of my faith.

Her. Angels assist thy hopes!

Edwin. What means my love? thou art my
promised wife.

Mod. To part with willingly what friends and life
Can make no good assurance of.

Edwin. Oh find remorse,
Fair soul, to love and merit, and yet recant thy
    vow.

Mod. Never; this world and I are parted now
    for ever.

Her. To find the way to bliss, oh happy woman,
Thou'st learn'd the hardest lesson well I see;
Now show thy fortitude and constancy,
Let these thy friends thy sad departure weep,
Thou shalt but lose the wealth thou couldst not keep,
My contemplation calls me, I must leave ye.

Edwin. O reverend sir, persuade her not to leave
me.

Her. My lord, I do not, nor to cease to love you,
I only pray her faith may fixéd stand,
Marriage was blest, I know, with heaven's own
    hand.[21]   [*Exit.*

Edwin. You hear him, lady, 'tis not a virgin
state, but sanctity of life, must make you happy.

Mod. Good sir, you say you love me; gentle
Edwin, even by that love, I do beseech you leave me

Edwin. Think of your father's tears, your weeping friends, whom cruel grief makes pale and bloodless all for you.

Mod. Would I were dead to all.

Edwin. Why do you weep?

Mod. Oh, who would live to see
How men with care and cost seek misery.

Edwin. Why do you seek it then? What joy,
what pleasure can give you comfort in a single
life?

Mod. The contemplation of a happy death, which
is to me so pleasing that I think no torture could
divert me. What's this world wherein you'd have
me walk, but a sad passage to a dread judgment-
seat, from whence even now we are but bailed upon
our good abearing, till those great sessions come,
when death the crier
Will surely summon us, and all to appear,
To plead us guilty or our bail to clear. [*Soft music.*
What music's this?

Enter two Bishops, DONOBERT, GLOSTER, CADOR,
    CONSTANTIA, OSWOLD, *and* TOCLIO.

Edwin. Oh now resolve and think upon my love;
this sounds the marriage of your beauteous sister,
virtuous Constantia, with the noble Cador: look,
and behold this pleasure.

Mod. Cover me with night,
It is a vanity not worth the sight.

Dono. See, see, she's yonder; pass on son Cador.
Daughter Constantia, I beseech you all, unless
she first move speech, salute her not. Edwin, what
good success?

Edwin. Nothing as yet, unless this object take her.

Dono. See, see, her eye is fixed upon her sister;
Seem careless all, and take no notice of her:
On there afore; come, my Constantia.

Mod. Not speak to me, nor deign to cast an eye,
To look on my despiséd poverty?
I must be more charitable; pray stay, lady;
Are you not she whom I did once call sister?

Con. I did acknowledge such a name to one
Whilst she was worthy of it, in whose folly,
Since you neglect your fame and friends together,
In you I drown'd a sister's name for ever.

Mod. Your looks did speak no less.

Glos. It now begins to work; this sight has
moved her.

Dono. I knew this trick would take, or nothing.

Mod. Though you disdain in me a sister's name,
yet charity methinks should be so strong to in

struct ere you reject. I am a wretch, even follies
instance, who perhaps have erred, not having
known the goodness bears so high and fair a show
in you, which being expressed,
I may recant this low despisèd life,
And please those friends whom I moved to grief.

Cador. She is coming i'faith; be merry, Edwin.

Con. Since you desire instruction you shall
have it; what is it should make you thus desire
to live vowed to a single life?

Mod. Because I know I cannot fly from death;
O, my good sister, I beseech you hear me:
This world is but a masque, catching weak eyes,
With what is not ourselves but our disguise:
A vizard that falls off, the dance being done,
And leaves death's glass for all to look upon:
Our best happiness here, lasts but a night,
Whose burning tapers make false ware seem
    right;
Who knows not this, and will not now provide
Some better shift before his shame be spied,
And knowing this vain world at last will leave him,
Shake off these robes that help but to deceive him.

Con. Her words are powerful; I am amaz'd to
hear her!

Dono. Her soul's enchanted with infected spells.
Leave her, best girl, for now in thee
I'll seek the fruits of age, posterity.
Out of my sight; sure I was half asleep, or drunk,
    when I begot thee.

Con. Good sir, forbear. What say you to that,
    sister?
The joy of children, a blest mother's name!
Oh, who without much grief can lose such fame?

Mod. Who can enjoy it without sorrow rather?
And that most certain where the joys unsure,
Seeing the fruit that we beget endure
So many miseries, that oft we pray
The heavens to shut up their afflicted day;
At best we do but bring forth heirs to die,
And fill the coffins of our enemy.

Con. Oh, my soul!

Dono. Hear her no more, Constantia: she's
sure bewitched with error; leave her, girl.

Con. Then must I leave all goodness, sir:
away, stand off, I say.

Dono. How's this?

Con. I have no father, friend, no husband now;
all are but borrowed robes in which we masque to
waste and spend the time, when all our life is but
one good between two ague-days, which from the
first, ere we have time to praise, a second fever
takes us. Oh, my best sister! my soul's eternal

friend! forgive the rashness of my distempered
tongue; for how could she who knew not herself,
know thy felicity, from which worlds cannot now
remove me?

Dono. Art thou mad too, fond woman? What's
thy meaning?

Con. To seek eternal happiness in heaven, which
all this world affords not.

Cador. Think of thy vow: thou art my promised
wife.

Con. Pray trouble me no further.

Omnes. Strange alteration!

Cador. Why do you stand at gaze you sacred
priests? You holy man be equal to the gods, and
consummate my marriage with this woman.

Bishop. Herself gives bar, my lord, to your desires and our performance; 'tis against the law and
orders of the church to force a marriage.

Cador. How am I wronged! was this your trick,
my lord?

Dono. I am abused past sufferance; grief and
amazement strive which sense of mine shall lose
her being first; yet let me call thee daughter.

Cador. Me, wife!

Con. Your words are air, you speak of want to
    wealth,
And wish her sickness newly raised to health.

Dono. Bewitched girls, tempt not an old man's
fury, that hath no strength to uphold his feeble
age but what your sights give life to; oh, beware,
and do not make me curse you.

Mod. Dear father, here at your feet we kneel;
grant us but this, that in your sight and hearing
the good hermit may plead our cause; which, if it
shall not give such satisfaction as your age desires,
we will submit to you.

Con. You gave us life, save not our bodies but
our souls from death.

Dono. This gives some comfort yet; rise with
my blessings. Have patience, noble Cador; worthy
Edwin, send for the hermit that we may confer, for
sure religion ties you not to leave
Your careful father thus; if so it be,
Take you content, and give all grief to me.

SCENE III.—*A Cave in the Forest.*

Thunder and Lightning. Enter Devil.

Devil. Mix light and darkness, earth and heaven
dissolve, be of one piece again, and turn to chaos.
Break all your works you powers, and spoil the
world; or, if you will maintain earth still, give way
and life to this abortive birth now coming, whose

fame shall add unto your oracles. Lucina, Hecate, dreadful queen of night, bright Proserpine, be pleased from Ceres' love, from Stygian darkness summon up the fates,

And in a moment bring them quickly hither, Lest death do vent her birth and her together.

[*Thunder.*

Assist you spirits of infernal deeps, squint-ey'd Erietho, midnight Incubus!

Enter Lucina, *and the three* Fates.[22]

Rise, rise to aid this birth prodigious. Thanks, Hecate, hail sister to the gods, there lies your way, haste with the Fates, and help! Give quick despatch unto her labouring throes, to bring this mixture of infernal seed to human being. [*Exit* Fates. And to beguile her pains till back you come, Antics shall dance and music fill the room.

[*A dance of* Spirits.

Devil. Thanks, queen of shades.

Lucina. Farewell, great servant to the infernal king,

In honour of this child the Fates shall bring All their assisting powers of knowledge, arts, Learning, wisdom, all the hidden parts Of all-admiring prophecy, to foresee The event of times to come, his art shall stand A wall of brass to guard the Britain land; Even from this minute all his art appears Manlike in judgment, person, state, and years; Upon his breast the Fates have fix'd his name; And since his birth-place was this forest here, They now have named him Merlin Silvester.

Devil. And Merlin's name in Britain shall live, Whilst men inhabit here, or Fates can give Power to amazing wonder; Envy shall weep, And Mischief sit and shake her ebon wings, Whilst all the world of Merlin's magic sings.

[*Exeunt.*

SCENE IV.—*The Forest.*

Enter Clown.

Clown. Well, I wonder how my poor sister does after all this thundering! I think she's dead, for I can hear no tidings of her. These woods yield small comfort to her: I could meet nothing but a swineherd's wife, keeping hogs by the forest side; but neither she nor none of her sows would stir a foot to help us. Indeed, I think she durst not trust herself under the trees with me, for I must needs confess I offered some kindness to her: well, I would fain know what's become of my sister; if

she have brought me a young cousin, his face may be a picture to find his father by. So-ho, sister Joan! Joan Go-to-'t, where art thou?

Joan. [*Within.*] Here, here, brother; stay but a while; I come to thee.

Clown. O, brave! she's alive still. I know her voice; she speaks, and speaks cheerfully, methinks: how now? what moon-calf has she got with her?

Enter Joan *and* Merlin, *with a Book.*

Joan. Come, my dear Merlin, why dost thou fix thine eye so deeply on that book?

Mer. To sound the depths of art, of learning, wisdom, knowledge.

Joan. Oh, my dear, dear son, those studies fit thee when thou art a man.

Mer. Why, mother, I can be but half a man at best,

And that is your mortality, the rest In me is spirit; 'tis not meat, nor time, That gives this growth and bigness; no, my years Shall be more strange than yet my birth appears. Look, mother, there's my uncle.

Joan. How dost thou know him, son? thou never saw'st him?

Mer. Yet I know him; and know the pains he has taken for ye to find out my father. Give me your hand, good uncle.

Clown. Ha, ha, I'd laugh at that, i'faith! do you know me, sir?

Mer. Yes, by the same token that even now you kissed the swineherd's wife i' the woods, and would have done more if she would have let you, uncle.

Clown. A witch! a witch! a witch! Sister, rid him out of your company; he is either a witch or a conjuror; he could never have known this else.

Joan. Pray love him, brother; he is my son.

Clown. Ha, ha! this is worse than all the rest, i'faith! by his beard he is more like your husband: let me see, is your great belly gone?

Joan. Yes, and this the happy fruit.

Clown. What, this artichoke? A child born with a beard on his face?

Mer. Yes, and strong legs to go, and teeth to eat.

Clown. You can nurse up yourself, then. There's some charges saved for soap and candle: 'slid, I have heard of some that have been born with teeth, but never none with such a talking tongue before.

Joan. Come, come, you must use him kindly, brother; did you but know his worth you would make much of him.

Clown. Make much of a monkey! This is worse than Tom Thumb; a child to speak, eat, and go the first hour of his birth; nay, such a baby as had need of a barber before he was born, too; why, sister, this is monstrous, and shames all our kindred.

Joan. That thus 'gainst nature and our common births, he comes thus furnished to salute the world, is power of Fates, and gift of his great father.

Clown. Why, of what profession is your father, sir?

Mer. He keeps a hot-house in the Low Countries; will you see him, sir?

Clown. See him! why, sister, has the child found his father?

Mer. Yes, and I'll fetch him, uncle.   [*Exit.*

Clown. Do not uncle me till I know your kindred: 'fore my conscience some baboon begot thee: surely thou art horribly deceived, sister, this urchin cannot be of thy breeding: I shall be ashamed to call him cousin, though his father be a gentleman.

Re-enter MERLIN *and* Devil.

Mer. Now, my kind uncle, see,
The child has found his father—this is he.

Clown. The devil it is! ha, ha! is this your sweetheart, sister? Have we run through the country, haunted the city, and examined the court, to find out a gallant with a hat and feather, and a silken sword, and golden hangers, and do you now bring me to a ragamuffin with a face like a frying-pan?

Joan. Fie, brother, you mistake; behold him better.

Clown. How's this? Do you juggle with me; or are mine eyes matches? Hat and feather, sword, and hangers and all! this is a gallant, indeed, sister; this has all the marks of him we look for.

Devil. And you have found him now, sir; give me your hand; I now must call you brother.

Clown. Not till you have married my sister; for all this while she's but your whore, sir.

Devil. Thou art too plain; I'll satisfy that wrong to her, and thee, and all, with liberal hand. Come, why art thou fearful?

Clown. Nay, I am not afraid, and you were the devil, sir.

Devil. Thou need'st not; keep with thy sister still, and I'll supply your wants; you shall lack nothing that gold and wealth can purchase.

Clown. Thank you, brother; we have gone many a weary step to find you; you may be a husband for a lady, for you are far-fetched and dear bought, I assure you. Pray how should I call your son, my cousin, here?

Devil. His name is Merlin.

Clown. Merlin! Your hand, cousin Merlin: for your father's sake I accept you to my kindred: but if you grow in all things as your beard does, you will be talked on. By your mother's side, cousin, you come of the Go-to-'ts, Suffolk bred; but our standing house is at Hockley-i'the-Hole, and Layton-Buzzard. For your father, no doubt you may from him claim titles of worship, but I cannot describe it: I think his ancestors came first from Hell-bree, in Wales, cousin.

Devil. No matter whence we do derive our
     name;
All Brittany shall ring of Merlin's fame,
And wonder at his acts. Go hence to Wales;
There live awhile; there Vortiger, the king,
Builds castles and strongholds which cannot stand
Unless supported by young Merlin's hand.
There shall thy fame begin, wars are a breeding.
The Saxons practise treason, yet unseen,
Which shortly shall break out. Fair love, farewell:
Dear son, and brother, here must I leave you all;
Yet still I will be near at Merlin's call.   [*Exit.*

Mer. Will you go, uncle?

Clown. Yes, I'll follow you, cousin. Well, I do most horribly begin to suspect my kindred: this brother-in-law of mine is the devil, sure; and though he hide his horns with his hat and feather, I spied his cloven foot for all his cunning. [*Exeunt.*

SCENE V.—*The* British *Court.*

Enter OSTORIUS, OCTA, *and* PROXIMUS.

Osto. Come, come, time calls our close complots to action. Go, Proximus, with winged speed fly hence: hie thee to Wales; salute great Vortiger with these our letters: bid the king to arms: tell him we have new friends, more forces landed in Norfolk and Northumberland: bid him make haste to meet us: if he keep his word we'll part the realm between us.

Octa. Bend all thine art to quit that late disgrace the Christian hermit gave thee; make thy revenge both sure and home.

Prox. That thought, sir, spurs me on till I have wrought their swift destruction.   [*Exit.*

Osto. Go then, and prosper. Octa, be vigilant: speak, are the forts possessed? the guards made sure? Revolve, I pray, on how large consequence the bare event and sequel of our hopes jointly consists, that have embarked our lives upon the hazard of the least miscarriage.

Octa. All's sure; the queen your sister hath

contrived the cunning plot so sure, as at an instant the brothers shall be both surprised and taken.

Osto. And both shall die, yet one awhile must live, till we by him have gathered strength and power to meet bold Edol, their stern general, that now, contrary to the king's command, hath re-united all his cashiered troops, and this way beats his drums to threaten us.

Octa. Then our plot's discovered.

Osto. Come, thou'rt a fool: his army and his life is given unto us; where is the queen, my sister?

Octa. In conference with the prince.

Osto. Bring the guards nearer, all is fair and good,
Their conference I hope shall end in blood.

[*Exeunt.*

Enter PRINCE *and* ARTESIA.

Art. Come, come, you do but flatter; what you term love is but a dream of blood, wakes with enjoying, and with open eyes forgot, contemned, and lost.

Prince. I must be wary; her words are danger-ous.
True, we'll speak of love no more, then.

Art. Nay, if you will you may,
'Tis but in jest, and yet so children play
With fiery flames, and covet what is bright,
But feeling his effects, abhor the light;
Pleasure is like a building, the more high,
The narrower still it grows; cedars do die
Soonest at top.

Prince. How does your instance suit?

Art. From art and nature to make sure the root,
And lay a fast foundation, ere I try
The uncertain changes of a wavering sky.
Make your example thus—You have a kiss—was it not pleasing?

Prince. Above all name to express it.

Art. Yet now the pleasure's gone, and you have lost your joy's possession.

Prince. Yet when you please this flood may ebb again.

Art. But where it never ebbs, there runs the main.

Prince. Who can attain such hopes?

Art. I'll show the way to it; give me a taste once more of what you may enjoy. [*He kisses her.*

Prince. Impudent whore! [*Aside.*
I were more false than atheism can be,
Should I not call this high felicity.

Art. If I should trust your faith, alas! I fear you soon would change belief.

Prince. I would covet martyrdom to make it confirmed.

Art. Give me your hand on that; you'll keep your word?

Prince. I will.

Art. Enough; help, husband! king Aurelius, help! rescue betrayed Artesia!

Prince. Nay, then 'tis I that am betrayed, I see, Yet with thy blood I'll end thy treachery.

Art. How now! what troubles you? Is this you, sir, that but even now would suffer martyr-dom to win your hopes, and is there now such terror in names of men to fright you? nay, then, I see what mettle you are made on.

Prince. Ha! was it but trial? then I ask your pardon. What a dull slave was I to be so fearful? (*Aside.*) I'll trust her now no more, yet try the utmost. (*Aloud.*) I am resolved no brother, no man breathing, were he my blood's begetter, should withhold me from your love; I'd leap into his bosom, and from his breast pull forth that hap-piness.

Art. Ay, now you speak a lover like a prince. Treason! treason!

Prince. Again!

Art. Help, Saxon princes! treason!

Enter OSTORIUS, OCTA, &c.

Ostor. Rescue the queen! strike down the villain.

Enter EDOL, AURELIUS, DONOBERT, CADOR, EDWIN, TOCLIO; OSWOLD *at the opposite side.*

Edol. Call in the guards: the prince in danger! Fall back, dear sir, my breast shall buckler you.

Aurel. Beat down their weapons.

Edol. Slave, wert thou made of brass, my sword shall bite thee.

Aurel. Withdraw on pain of death: where is the traitor?

Art. Oh, save your life, my lord! let it suffice my beauty forced mine own captivity.

Aurel. Who did attempt to wrong thee?

Prince. Hear me, sir!

Aurel. Oh, my sad soul! was't thou?

Art. Oh, do not stay to speak; one minute's stay prevents a second speech for ever.

Aurel. Make our guards strong. My dear Ar-tesia, let us know thy wrongs, and our own dangers.

Art. The prince your brother, with these Briton lords, have all agreed to take me hence by force, and marry me to him.

Prince. The devil shall wed thee first: thy base-ness and thy lust confound and rot thee.

Art. He courted me even now, and in mine ear shamed not to plead his most dishonest love, and their attempts to seize your sacred person, either to shut you up within some prison, or, which is worse, I fear to murder you.

Omnes Britons. 'Tis false as hell.

Edol. And as foul as she is.

Art. You know me, sir?

Edol. Yes, deadly sin, we know you, and shall discover all your villany.

Aurel. Chester, forbear.

Osto. Their treasons, sir, are plain. Why are their soldiers lodged so near the court?

Octa. Nay, why came he in arms so suddenly?

Edol. You fleering antics, do not wake my fury.

Octa. Fury!

Edol. Ratsbane, do not urge me.

Art. Good sir, keep farther from them.

Prince. Oh my sick heart, she is a witch by nature, devil by art.

Aurel. Bite thine own slanderous tongue, 'tis thou art false; I have observed your passions long ere this.

Osto. Stand on your guard, my lord; we are your friends, and all our force is yours.

Edol. To spoil and rob the kingdom.

Aurel. Sir, be silent.

Edol. Silent! how long? till Doomsday? shall I stand by and hear mine honour blasted with foul treason, the state half-lost, and your life endangered, yet be silent?

Art. Yes, my blunt lord, unless you speak your treasons. Sir, let your guards, as traitors, seize them all, and then let tortures and devulsive racks force a confession from them.

Edol. Wild-fire and brimstone eat thee! Hear me, sir.

Aurel. Sir, I'll not hear you.

Edol. But you shall: not hear me! were the world's monarch, Cæsar, living, he should hear me. I tell you, sir, these serpents have betrayed your life and kingdom: does not every day bring tidings of more swarms of lousy knaves, the offal fugitives of barren Germany, that land upon our coasts, and have by our neglect settled in Norfolk and Northumberland.

Osto. They come as aids and safeguards to the king.

Octa. Has he not need, when Vortiger's in arms, and you raise powers, 'tis thought to join with him?

Edol. Peace, you pernicious rat.

Dono. Prithee forbear.

Edol. Away! suffer a gilded rascal, a low-bred despicable creeper, an insulting toad, to spit his poisoned venom in my face!

Octa. Sir, sir.

Edol. Do not reply, you cur, for, by the gods, though the king's presence guard thee, I shall break all patience, and like a lion roused to spoil, shall run foul-mouthed upon thee, and devour thee quick. Speak, sir, will you forsake these scorpions, or stay till they have stung you to the heart?

Aurel. You are traitors all; this is our wife, our queen; brother Ostorius, troop your Saxons up, we'll hence to Winchester, raise more powers, to man with strength the castle Camilot:[23] go hence false men, join you with Vortiger, the murderer of our brother Constantine: we'll hunt both him and you with dreadful vengeance,
Since Britain fails, we'll trust to foreign friends,
And guard our person from your traitorous ends.

　[*Exeunt* AUREL., OSTO., ART., TOCLIO, *and* OS.

Edwin. He's sure bewitched.

Glos. What counsel now for safety?

Dono. Only this, sir, with all the speed we can, preserve the person of the king and kingdom.

Cador. Which to effect, 'tis best march hence to Wales, and set on Vortiger before he joins his forces with the Saxons.

Edwin. On, then, with speed for Wales and Vortiger; that tempest once o'erblown, we come, Ostorius, to meet thy traitorous Saxons, thee and them, that with advantage thus have won the king to back your factions, and to work our ruin,
This by the gods, and my good sword, I'll set
In bloody lines upon thy burgonet.　　[*Exeunt.*

ACT IV.

SCENE I.—*Before a Ruined Castle in* Wales.

Enter CLOWN, MERLIN, *and a* Little Antic Spirit.

Mer. How now, uncle, why do you search your pockets so? do you miss anything?

Clown. Ha! cousin Merlin, I hope your beard does not overgrow your honesty; I pray remember you are made up of sister's thread; I am your mother's brother, whoever was your father.

Mer. Why, wherein can you task my duty, uncle?

Clown. Yourself, or your page it must be; I have kept no other company, since your mother bound your head to my protectorship; I do feel a fault of one side; either it was that sparrow-hawk, or a cast of Merlin's,[24] for I find a covey of cardecus[25] sprung out of my pocket.

Mer. Why, do you want any money, uncle? Sirrah, had you any from him?

Clown. Deny it not, for my pockets are witness against you.

Spirit. Yes, I had, to teach you better wit to look to it.

Clown. Pray use your fingers better, and my wit may serve as it is, sir.

Mer. Well, restore it.

Spirit. There it is.

Clown. Ay, there's some honesty in this; 'twas a token from your invisible father, cousin, which I would not have to go invisibly from me again.

Mer. Well, you are sure you have it now, uncle?

Clown. Yes, and mean to keep it now from your page's filching fingers too.

Spirit. If you have it so sure, pray show it me again.

Clown. Yes, my little juggler, I dare show it; ha! cleanly conveyance again; ye have no invisible fingers have ye? 'Tis gone certainly.

Spirit. Why, sir, I touched you not.

Mer. Why, look you, uncle, I have it now; how ill do you look to it! here, keep it safer.

Clown. Ha, ha! this is fine i'faith, I must keep some other company if you have these sleights of hand.

Mer. Come, come, uncle, 'tis all my art, which shall not offend you, sir, only I give you a taste of it to show you sport.

Clown. Oh, but 'tis ill jesting with a man's pocket though; but I am glad to see you cunning cousin, for now I will warrant thee a living till thou diest; you have heard the news in Wales here?

Mer. Uncle, let me prevent your care and counsel, 'twill give you better knowledge of my cunning; you would prefer me now in hope of gain to Vortiger, king of the Welsh Britons, to whom are all the artists summoned now, that seek the secrets of futurity, the bards, the druids,[26] wizards, conjurers, not an Aurasper with his whistling spells, no Capuomanster with his musty fumes,
No witch or juggler but is thither sent,
To calculate the strange and fear'd event
Of this prodigious castle now in building, where all the labours of the painful day are ruined still i' th' night, and to this place you would have me go.

Clown. Well, if thy mother were not my sister, I would say she was a witch that begot this; but this is thy father, not thy mother wit; thou hast taken away my tale into thy mouth, and spake my thoughts before me; therefore away, shuffle thyself amongst the conjurers, and be a made man before thou comest to age.

Mer. Nay, but stay, uncle, you overslip my dangers: the prophecies and all the cunning wizards have certified the king, that his castle can never stand, till the foundation's laid with mortar, tempered with the fatal blood of such a child whose father was no mortal.

Clown. What's this to thee? if the devil were thy father, was not thy mother born at Carmarden? Diggon for that then, and then it must be a child's blood, and who will take thee for a child with such a beard of thy face? Is there not diggon for that, too, cousin?

Mer. I must not go; lend me your ear awhile I'll give you reasons to the contrary.

Enter Two Gentlemen.

1st Gent. Sure this is an endless piece of work the king has sent us about!

2nd Gent. Kings may do it, man, the like has been done to find out the unicorn.

1st Gent. Which will be sooner found, I think, than this fiend-begotten child we seek for.

2nd Gent. Pox of those conjurers that would speak of such a one, and yet all their cunning could not tell us where to find him.

1st Gent. In Wales they said assuredly he lives; come, let's inquire further.

Mer. Uncle, your persuasions must not prevail with me; I know mine enemies better than you do.

Clown. I say thou art a bastard, then, if thou disobey thine uncle. Was not Joan Go-to-'t, thy mother, my sister? If the devil were thy father, what kin art thou to any man alive but bailies and brokers? and they are but brothers-in-law to thee neither.

1st Gent. How's this? I think we shall speed here.

2nd Gent. Ay, and unlooked for too; go near and listen to them.

Clown. Hast thou a beard to hide it? wilt thou show thyself a child? wilt thou have more hair than wit? wilt thou deny thy mother, because nobody knows thy father? or shall thine uncle be an ass?

1st Gent. Bless ye friend, pray what call you this small gentleman's name?

Clown. Small, sir! a small man may be a great gentleman, his father may be of an ancient house for aught we know, sir.

2nd Gent. Why, do you not know his father?

Clown. No, nor you neither, I think, unless the devil be in ye.

1st Gent. What is his name, sir?

Clown. His name is my cousin, his education is my sister's son, but his manners are his own.

Mer. Why ask ye, gentlemen? my name is Merlin.

Clown. Yes, and a goshawk was his father for aught we know, for I am sure his mother was a windsucker.

2nd Gent. He has a mother then?

Clown. As sure as I have a sister, sir.

1st Gent. But his father you leave doubtful?

Clown. Well, sir, as wise men as you doubt whether he had a father or no.

1st Gent. Sure this is he we seek for.

2nd Gent. I think no less; and, sir we let you know the king hath sent for you.

Clown. The more child he; and he had been ruled by me he should have gone before he was sent for.

1st Gent. May we not see his mother?

Clown. Yes, and feel her, too—if you anger her. A devilish thing, I can tell you, she has been. I'll go fetch her to ye. [*Exit.*

2nd Gent. Sir, it were fit you did resolve for speed: you must unto the king.

Mer. My service, sir, shall need no strict command; it shall obey most peaceably; but needless 'tis to fetch what is brought home. My journey may be stayed: the king is coming hither with the same quest you bore before him! Hark! this drum will tell ye. [*Drums within beat a slow march.*

1st Gent. This is some cunning, indeed, sir.

Flourish. Enter VORTIGER *reading a Letter;* PROXIMUS, *with Drum, and Soldiers, &c.*

Vorti. Still in our eye your message, Proximus, we keep to spur our speed.[27] Ostorius and Octa we shall salute with succour against Prince Uter and Aurelius, whom now we hear encamps at Winchester. There's nothing interrupts our way so much as doth the erection of this famous castle; that, spite of all our art and daily labour, the night still ruins.

Prox. As erst I did affirm, still I maintain, the fiend-begotten child must be found out, whose blood gives strength to the foundation; it cannot stand else.

Enter CLOWN, JOAN, *and* MERLIN.

Vorti. Ha! is't so? Then, Proximus, by this intelligence he should be found. Speak! is this he you tell of?

Clown. Yes, sir; and I his uncle, and she his mother.

Vorti. And who is his father?

Clown. Why, she, his mother, can best tell you that; and yet I think the child be wise enough, for he has found his father.

Vorti. Woman, is this thy son?

Joan. It is, my lord.

Vorti. What was his father, or where lives he?

Mer. Mother, speak freely and unastonished; That which you dar'd to act dread not to name.

Joan. In which I shall betray my sin and shame. But, since it must be so, then know, great king, all that myself yet knows of him is this: In pride of blood and beauty I did live; my glass the altar was, my face the idol. Such was my peevish love unto myself that I did hate all other; such disdain was in my scornful eye, that I supposed no mortal creature worthy to enjoy me; thus, with the peacock, I beheld my train, but never saw the blackness of my feet. Oft have I chid the the winds for breathing on me, and curs'd the sun, fearing to blast my beauty. In midst of this most leprous disease, a seeming fair young man appeared unto me, in all things suiting my aspiring pride, and with him brought along a conquering power, to which my frailty yielded, from whose embraces this issue came. What more he is I know not.

Vorti. Some Incubus, or spirit of the night, begot him, then; for sure no mortal did it.

Mer. No matter who, my lord: leave further quest, since 'tis as hurtful as unnecessary more to inquire. Go to the cause, my lord, why you have sought me thus.

Vorti. I doubt not but thou knowest; yet, to be plain, I sought thee for thy blood.

Mer. By whose direction?

Prox. By mine! My art infallible instructed me, upon thy blood must the foundation rise of the king's building; it cannot stand else.

Mer. Hast thou such leisure to inquire my fate, and let thine own hang careless over thee? Know'st thou what pendulous mischief roofs thy head—how fatal, and how sudden?

Prox. Pish, bearded abortive! Thou foretell my danger! My lord, he trifles to delay his own.

Mer. No, I yield myself; and here, before the king, make good thine augury, as I shall mine. If thy fate fall not, thou hast spoke all truth, and let my blood satisfy the king's desires. If thou thyself wilt write thine epitaph, despatch it quickly; there's not a minute's space 'twixt thee and death.

Prox. Ha, ha, ha! [*A stone falls and kills* PROX.

Mer. Aye, so thou mayst die laughing.

Vorti. Ha! this is above admiration. Look! is he dead?

Clown. Yes, sir; here's brains to make mortar on, if you'll use them. Cousin Merlin, there's no more of this stone fruit ready to fall, is there? I pray give your uncle a little fair warning.

Mer. Remove that shape of death. And now, my lord, for clear satisfaction of your doubts, Merlin will show the fatal cause that keeps your castle down and hinders your proceedings. Stand there, and, by an apparition, see the labour and end of all your destiny. Mother and uncle, you must be absent.

Clown. Is your father coming, cousin?

Mer. Nay, you must begone.

Joan. Come, you'll offend him, brother.

Clown. I would fain see my brother-in-law: if you were married, I might lawfully call him so.

[MER. *strikes his Wand. Thunder and Lightning; two Dragons appear, a white and a red; they fight awhile and pause.*

Mer. Be not amazed, my lord, for on the victory Of loss or gain, as these two champions ends, Your fate, your life and kingdom, all depends; Therefore, observe it well.

Vorti. I shall: heaven be auspicious to us.

[*Thunder. The two Dragons fight again, and the white Dragon drives off the red.*

Vorti. The conquest is on the white dragon's part: now, Merlin, faithfully expound the meaning.

Mer. Your grace must, then, not be offended with me.

Vorti. It is the weakest part I have found in thee to doubt of me so slightly. Shall I blame my prophet that foretells me of my dangers? Thy cunning I approve most excellent.

Mer. Then know, my lord, there is a dampish cave, the nightly habitation of these dragons, vaulted beneath where you would build your castle, whose enmity and nightly combats there maintain a constant ruin of our labour. To make it more plain—the dragons, then, yourself betoken, and the Saxon king; the vanquished red, is, sir, your dreadful emblem.

Vorti. Oh, my fate!

Mer. Nay, you must hear with patience, royal sir. You slew the lawful king, Constantius: 'twas a red deed; your crown his blood did cement. The English Saxon, first brought in by you for aid against Constantius' brethren, is the white horror, who, now knit together, have driven and shut you up in these wild mountains; and though they now seek to unite with friendship, it is to wound your bosom, not embrace it; and, with an utter extirpation, drive the Britons out and plant the English. Seek for your safety, sir, and spend no time to build the airy castles; for Prince Uter, armed with vengeance for his brother's blood, is hard upon you. If you mistrust me, and to my words crave witness, sir, then know here comes a messenger to tell you so.　　　　　　　　　　[*Exit* MER.

Enter Messenger.

Mes. My lord, Prince Uter!

Vorti. And who else, sir?

Mes. Edol, the great general.

Vorti. The great devil! They are coming to meet us?

Mes. With a full power, my lord.

Vorti. With a full vengeance they mean to meet us; so we are ready to their confront as full march double footing. We'll lose no ground, nor shall their numbers fright us.

If it be fate, it cannot be withstood;

We got our crown so, be it lost in blood. [*Exeunt.*

SCENE II.—*Open Country in* Wales.

Enter PRINCE UTER, EDOL, CADOR, EDWIN, *and* TOCLIO, *with Drum and* Soldiers.

Prince. Stay and advise. Hold, drum!

Edol. Beat, slave! why do you pause?—why make a stand? Where are our enemies? or do you mean we fight amongst ourselves?

Prince. Nay, noble Edol, let us here take counsel. It cannot hurt; it is the surest garrison to safety

Edol. Fie, on such slow delays! so fearful men, that are to pass over a flowing river, stand on the bank to parley of the danger till the tide rise, and they be swallowed. Is not the king in field?

Cador. Proud Vortiger, the traitor, is in field.

Edwin. The murderer and usurper.

Edol. Let him be the devil, so I may fight with him. For heaven's love, sir, march on. Oh, my patience! will you delay until the Saxons come to aid his party!   [*A Tucket sounded.*[28]

Prince. There's no such fear; prythee be calm awhile. Hark! it seems by this, he comes or sends to us.

Edol. If it be for parley I will drown the summons, if all our drums and hoarseness choke me not.

Enter a Captain.

Prince. Nay, prithee hear; from whence art thou?

Cap. From the king Vortiger.

Edol. Traitor, there's none such: alarum drum, strike slave, or by mine honour I will break thy head, and beat thy drum's heads both about thine ears.

Prince. Hold, noble Edol; let's hear what articles he can enforce.

Edol. What articles, or what conditions can you expect to value half your wrong, unless he kill himself by thousand tortures, and send his carcase to appease your vengeance for the foul murder of Constantius, and that's not a tenth part neither.

Prince. 'Tis true, my brother's blood is crying to me now:

I do applaud your counsel; hence, begone!
                       [*Exit* Cap.

We 'll hear no parley now but by our swords.

Edol. And those shall speak home in death-killing words.

Alarum to the fight! sound, sound the alarum!
                           [*Exeunt.*

SCENE III.—*A Field of Battle.*

Alarum.   *Enter* EDOL, *driving* VORTIGER's *Force before him; then enter* PRINCE UTER, *pursuing* VORTIGER.

Vort. Dost follow me?

Prince. Yes, to the death I will.

Vort. Stay, be advised; I would not be the only fall of princes: I slew thy brother.

Prince. Thou didst, black traitor; and in that vengeance I pursue thee.

Vorti. Take mercy for thyself, and flee my sword: save thine own life as satisfaction, which here I give thee for thy brother's death.

Prince. Give what's thine own—a traitor's heart and head; that's all thou art right lord of: the kingdom which thou usurp'st, thou most unhappy tyrant, is leaving thee; the Saxons which thou brought'st to back thy usurpations are grown great, and where they seat themselves, do hourly seek to blot the records of old Brute and Britons from memory of men, calling themselves Hingestmen,[29] and Hingest-land, that no more the Briton name be known; all this by thee, thou base destroyer of thy native country.

Enter EDOL.

Edol. What, are you talking? [*He attacks* VORTI.

Prince. Hold, Edol!

Edol. Hold out, my sword, and listen not to king or prince's word. There's work enough abroad; this task is mine.
             [*Exit* EDOL *and* VORTI. *fighting.*

Prince. Prosper thy valour as thy virtues shine.
                               [*Exit.*

Enter CADOR *and* EDWIN.

Cador. Bright Victory herself fights on our part; and, buckled in a golden beaver, rides triumphantly before us.

Edwin. Justice is with her, whoever takes the true and rightful cause; let us not lag behind them.

Enter PRINCE.

Cador. Here comes the prince: how goes our fortunes, sir?

Prince. Hopeful and fair, brave Cador; proud Vortiger, beat down by Edol's sword, was rescued by the following multitudes; and now for safety's fled unto a castle here standing on the hill; but I have sent a cry of hounds as violent as hunger, to break his strong walls, or if they fail,
We 'll send in wildfire to dislodge him thence,
Or burn them with all-flaming violence.   [*Exeunt.*

SCENE IV.—*Another part of the Field. A blazing Star appears.*

Flourish of Trumpets.   *Enter* PRINCE UTER, EDOL, CADOR, EDWIN, *and* TOCLIO, *with Drum and Soldiers.*

Prince. Look, Edol! still this fiery exhalation shoots his frightful horrors on the amazed world: see in the beam that's 'bout his flaming ring, a dragon's head appears, from out whose mouth two flaming snakes of fire stretch east and west.

Edol. And see, from forth the body of the star,

seven smaller blazing streams, directly point on this affrighted kingdom.

Cador. 'Tis a dreadful meteor.

Edwin. And doth portend strange fears.

Prince. This is no crown of peace; this angry fire hath something more to burn than Vortiger: if it alone were pointed at his fall, it would pull in its blazing pyramids and be appeased, for Vortiger is dead.[30]

Edol. These never come without their large effects.

Prince. The will of heaven be done; our sorrow's this; we want a mystic Python[31] to expound this fiery oracle.

Cador. Oh no, my lord; you have the best that ever Britain bred; and durst I prophesy of your prophet, sir, none like him shall succeed him.

Prince. You mean Merlin.

Cador. True, sir; wondrous Merlin: he met us in the way, and did foretel the fortunes of this day successful to us.

Edwin. He's sure about the camp; send for him, sir.

Cador. He told the bloody Vortiger his fate, and truly too; and if I could give faith to any wizard's skill, it should be Merlin.

Enter MERLIN *and* Clown.

Cador. And see, my lord; as if to satisfy your highness' pleasure, Merlin is come.

Prince. See, the comet's in his eye; disturb him not.

Edol. With what a piercing judgment he beholds it!

Mer. Whither will heaven and fate translate this kingdom!
What revolutions, rise and fall of nations,
Is figur'd yonder in that star, that sings
The change of Britain's fate and death of kings?
Ha! he's dead already; how swiftly mischief creeps![32]
Thy fatal end, sweet prince, even Merlin weeps.

Prince. He does foresee some evil; his action shows it; for ere he does expound, he weeps the story.

Edol. There's another weeps too. Sirrah, dost thou understand what thou lamentest for?

Clown. No, sir; I am his uncle, and weep because my cousin weeps; flesh and blood cannot forbear.

Prince. Gentle Merlin, speak thy prophetic knowledge in explanation of this fiery horror, from which we gather from thy mournful tears much sorrow and disaster in it.

Mer. 'Tis true, fair prince; but you must hear the rest with patience.

Prince. I vow I will, though it portend my ruin.

Mer. There's no such fear; this brought the fiery fall of Vortiger, and yet not him alone; this day is fallen a king more good—the glory of our land—the mild and gentle, sweet Aurelius.

Prince. Our brother!

Edwin. Forefend it, heaven.

Mer. He at his palace royal, sir, at Winchester, this day is dead and poisoned.

Cador. By whom? or by what means, Merlin?

Mer. By the traitorous Saxons.

Edol. I ever feared as much. That devil, Ostorius, and the damned witch, Artesia, sure have done it.

Prince. Poisoned! oh look further, gentle Merlin; behold the star again, and do but find revenge for me, though it cost thousand lives, and mine the foremost.

Mer. Comfort yourself; the heavens have given it fully: all the portentous ills to you are told; now hear a happy story, sir, from me to you and to your fair posterity.

Clown. Methinks I see something like a peeled onion; it makes me weep again.

Mer. Be silent, uncle; you'll be forced else.

Clown. Can you not find in the star, cousin, whether I can hold my tongue or no?

Edol. Yes; I must cut it out.

Clown. Phew! you speak without book, sir; my cousin Merlin knows.

Mer. True, I must tie it up: now speak your pleasure, uncle.

Clown. Hum—hum—hum—hum.

Mer. So, so! now observe my lord, and there behold above yon flame-haired beam that upward shoots, appears a dragon's head, out of whose mouth two streaming lights point their flame-feathered darts contrary ways, yet both shall have their aims. Again behold from the ignisirent body seven splendent and illustrious rays are spread, all speaking heralds to this Britain isle, and thus they are expounded. The dragon's head is the hieroglyphic that figures out your princely self, that here must reign a king, those bi-formed[33] fires that from the dragon's mouth shoot east and west, emblem two royal babes which shall proceed from you, a son and daughter; her pointed constellation northwest bending,
Crowns her a queen in Ireland, of whom first springs
That kingdom's title to the Britain kings.

Clown. Hum, hum, hum.

Mer. But of your son, thus fate and Merlin tells: all aftertimes shall fill their chronicles with fame of his renown,[34] whose warlike sword shall pass through fertile France and Germany, nor shall his conquering foot be forced to stand, till Rome's imperial wreath hath crowned his fame with monarch of the west, from whose seven hills, with conquest, and contributory kings,
He back returns to enlarge the Britain bounds,
His heraldry adorned with thirteen crowns.

Clown. Hum, hum, hum.

Mer. He to the world shall add another worthy, and as a loadstone for his prowess, draw a train of martial lovers to his court. It shall be then the best of knighthood's honour at Winchester to fill his castle hall, and at his royal table sit and feast—
In warlike orders, all their arms round hurl'd,
As if they meant to circumscribe the world.

[*He touches the* Clown's *Mouth with his Wand.*

Clown. Hum, hum, hum; oh that I could speak a little!

Mer. I know your mind, uncle, again be silent.
[*Strikes again.*

Prince. Thou speak'st of wonders, Merlin; prithee go on, declare at full this constellation.

Mer. Those seven beams pointing downwards, sir, betoken the troubles of this land, which then shall meet with other fate. War and dissension strive to make division till seven kings agree to draw this kingdom to a heptarchy.[35]

Prince. Thine art hath made such proof that we believe thy words authentical; be ever near us, my prophet, and the guide of all my actions.

Mer. My service shall be faithful to your person, and all my studies for my country's safety.

Clown. Hum, hum, hum.

Mer. Come, you are released, sir.

Clown. Cousin, pray help me to my tongue again: you do not mean I shall be dumb still, I hope?

Mer. Why, hast thou not thy tongue?

Clown. Ha! yes, I feel it now; I was so long dumb I could not well tell whether I spoke or no.

Prince. Is it thy advice we presently pursue the bloody Saxons, that have slain my brother?

Mer. With your best speed, my lord; prosperity will keep your company.

Cador. Take then your title with you, royal prince, 'twill add unto our strength; long live king Uter.

Edol. Put the addition to it that heaven hath given you. The dragon is your emblem, bear it bravely, and so live long and ever happy, styled Uter-Pendragon, lawful king of Britain.

Prince. Thanks, Edol, we embrace the name and title; and in our shield and standard shall the figure of a red dragon still be borne before us to fright the bloody Saxons. Oh, my Aurelius, sweet rest thy soul; let thy disturbed spirit
Expect revenge, think what it would, it hath,
The dragon's coming in his fiery wrath. [*Exeunt.*

ACT V.

SCENE I.—*A barren Waste, a huge Rock appearing.*

Thunder, then Music. Enter JOAN, *fearfully, the* Devil *following her.*

Joan. Hence, thou black horror, is thy lustful fire kindled again? not thy loud-throated thunder, nor thy adulterous infernal music shall e'er bewitch me more; oh, too, too much, is past already.

Devil. Why dost thou fly me? I come a lover to thee, to embrace, and gently twine thy body in mine arms.

Joan. Out, hell-hound.

Devil. What hound soe'er I be,
Fawning and sporting as I would with thee,
Why should not I be strok'd and play'd withal?
Wilt thou not thank the lion might devour thee,
If he shall let thee pass?

Joan. Yes, thou art he; free me, and I'll thank thee.

Devil. Why, whither wouldst? I am at home with thee, thou art mine own, have we not charge of family together? where is your son?

Joan. Oh, darkness cover me.

Devil. There is a pride which thou hast won by me, the mother of a fame shall never die. Kings shall have need of written chronicles to keep their name alive, but Merlin none; ages to ages shall, like Sabalists—
Report the wonders of his name and glory,
While there are tongues and times to tell his story.

Joan. Oh, rot my memory before my flesh; let him be called some hell or earth-bred monster, that ne'er had hapless woman for his mother. Sweet death deliver me—hence from my sight—why shouldst thou now appear? I had no pride nor lustful thought about me to conjure and call thee to my ruin, when as at first thy cursed person became visible.

Devil. I am the same I was.

Joan. But I am changed.

Devil. Again I'll change thee to the same thou wert, quench to my lust; come forth by thunder led, my coadjutors in the spoil of mortals.

Thunder.　Enter Spirits.

Clasp in your ebon arms that prize of mine; mount her as high as palled Hecate,[36] and on this rock I'll stand to cast up fumes and darkness o'er the blue-faced firmament; from Britain, and from Merlin I'll remove her; they ne'er shall meet again.

Joan. Help me, some saving hand, if not too late; I cry let mercy come.

Enter MERLIN.

Mer. Stay you black slaves of night! let loose your hold! set her down safe, or by the infernal Styx, I'll bind you up with exorcisms so strong, that all the black pentagaron of hell shall ne'er release you; save yourselves and vanish.

[*Exit* Spirits.

Devil. Ha! what's he?

Mer. The child has found his father! do you not know me?

Devil. Merlin!

Joan. Oh, help me, gentle son.

Mer. Fear not, they shall not hurt you.

Devil. Relievest thou her to disobey thy father?

Mer. Obedience is no lesson in your school; nature and kind to her commands my duty; the part that you begot was against kind, so all I owe to you is to be unkind.

Devil. I'll blast thee, slave, to death, and on this rock stick thee an eternal monument.

Mer. Ha, ha! thy power's too weak; what art thou, devil, but an inferior lustful Incubus, taking advantage of the wanton flesh, wherewith thou dost beguile the ignorant? Put off the form of thy humanity, and crawl upon thy speckled belly, serpent, or I'll unclasp the jaws of Acheron,[37] and fix thee ever in the local fire.

Devil. Traitor, to hell! curse that I e'er begot thee.

Mer. Thou didst beget thy scourge; storm not nor stir, the power of Merlin's art is all confirmed in the Fates' decretals. I'll ransack hell, and make thy master bow unto my spells, thou first shall taste it. (*Thunder and Lightning in the Rock.*) *Tenebrarum precis, divitiarum, et inferorum, Deus, hunc Incubum in ignis eterni abiscum, accipite aut in hoc carcére tenebroso, in sempiternum astringere mando.*[38] (*The Rock encloses him.*) So there beget earthquakes, or some noisome damps, for never shall thou touch a woman more. How cheer you, mother?

Joan. Oh, now my son is my deliverer, yet I must name him with my deepest sorrow.

[*Alarum afar off.*

Mer. Take comfort now, past times are ne'er recalled; I did foresee your mischief and prevent it. Hark, how the sounds of war now call me hence to aid Pendragon, that in battle stands against the Saxons, from whose aid Merlin must not be absent. Leave this soil, and I'll conduct you to a place retired, which I by art have raised, called Merlin's Bower; there shall you dwell with solitary sighs, with groans and passions your companions, to weep away this flesh you have offended with, and leave all bare unto your aerial soul; and when you die, I will erect a monument upon the verdant plains of Salisbury;[39] no king shall have so high a sepulchre, with pendulous stones that I will hang by art, where neither lime nor mortar shall be used, a dark enigma to thy memory, for none shall have the power to number them, a place that I will hallow for your rest,

Where no night-hag shall walk, nor ware-wolf tread,

Where Merlin's mother shall be sepulchred.

[*Exeunt.*

SCENE II.—*The* British *Camp.*

Enter DONOBERT, GLOSTER, *and* Hermit.

Dono. Sincerely, Gloster, I have told you all. My daughters are both vowed to single life, and this day gone into the nunnery, though I begot them to another end, and fairly promised them in marriage,—one to earl Cador; t'other to your son, my worthy friend, the earl of Gloster. Those lost, I am lost: they are lost, all's lost. Answer me this, then,—is't a sin to marry?

Her. Oh, no, my lord!

Dono. Go to, then, I'll go no further with you. I persuade you to no ill: persuade you, then, that I persuade you well.

Glos. 'Twill be a good office in you, sir.

Enter CADOR *and* EDWIN.

Dono. Which, since they thus neglect, my memory shall lose them now for ever. See, see! the noble lords, their promised husbands! Had fate so pleased, you might have called me father.

Edwin. Those hopes are past, my lord, for ever: this minute we saw them both enter the monastery, secluded from the world and men for ever.

Cador. 'Tis both our griefs we cannot, sir; but, from the king, take you the time's joy from us. The Saxon king, Ostorius, slain, and Octa fled; that woman fury, queen Artesia, is fast in hold, and forced to re-deliver London and Winchester (which she had fortified) to princely Uter, lately styled Pendragon, who now triumphantly is marching hither to be invested wth the British crown.

Dono. The joy of this shall banish from my breast all thought that I was father to two children, two stubborn daughters, that have left me thus. Let my old arms embrace and call you sons; for by the honour of my father's house, I'll part my estate most equally betwixt you.

Edwin. }
Cador. } Sir, you are most noble.

Flourish of trumpets. Enter EDOL, *with Drum and Colours;* OSWOLD, *bearing the Standard;* TOCLIO, *the Shield, with the Red Dragon pictured on them; Two* Bishops, *with the Crown;* PRINCE UTER, MERLIN, ARTESIA, *bound;* Guards *and* CLOWN.

Prince. Set up our shield and standard, noble soldiers:
We have fair hope that though our dragon sleep,
Merlin will us and our fair kingdom keep.

Clown. As his uncle lives I warrant you.

Glos. Happy restorer of the Briton's fame: uprising sun, let us salute thy glory! Ride in a day perpetual about us, and no night be in thy throne's zodiac! Why do we stay to bind those princely brows with this imperial honour?

Prince. Stay, noble Gloster; that monster first must be expelled our eye, or else we take no joy in it.

Dono. If that be hindrance, give her quick judgment, and send her hence to death; she has long deserved it.

Edol. Let my sentence stand for all: Take her hence, and stake her carcase in the burning sun till it be parched and dry; and then flay off her wicked skin, and stuff the pelt with straw, to be shown up and down at fairs and markets. Twopence a-piece to see so foul a monster will be a fair monopoly.

Artes. Ha! ha! ha!

Edol. Dost laugh, Erictho? [40]

Artes. Yes, at thy poor invention; is there no better torture-monger?

Dono. Burn her to dust.

Artes. That's a phœnix-death, and glorious.

Edol. Ay, that's too good for her.

Prince. Alive she shall be buried, circled in a wall, thou murderess of a king; there starve to death.

Artes. Then I'll starve death when he comes for his prey; and i' the mean time I'll live upon your curses.

Edol. Ay, 'tis diet good enough; away with her.

Artes. With joy, my best of wishes is before;
Thy brother's poison'd, but I wanted more. [*Exit.*

Prince. Why does our prophet, Merlin, stand apart, sadly observing these our ceremonies, and not applaud our joys with thy hid knowledge? Let thy divining art now satisfy some part of my desires; for well I know 'tis in thy power to show the full event that shall both end our reign and chronicle. Speak, learned Merlin, and resolve my fears; whether by war we shall expel the Saxons, or govern what we hold with beauteous peace in Wales and Britain?

Mer. Long happiness attend Pendragon's reign; what heaven decrees, fate has no power to alter. The Saxons, sir, will keep the ground they have, and by supplying numbers still increase till Britain be no more. So please your grace I will, in visible apparitions, present you prophecies which shall concern
Succeeding princes, which my art shall raise,
Till men shall call these times the latter days.

Prince. Do it, my Merlin, and crown me with much joy and wonder. [MER. *strikes with his Wand.*

Hautboys. Enter a King *in Armour, his Shield quartered with thirteen Crowns. At the other Door enter divers* Princes *who present their Crowns to him at his Feet, and do him Homage; then enters* Death, *and strikes him; he growing sick, crowns* CONSTANTINE. [*Exeunt.*

Mer. This king, my lord, presents your royal son, who, in his prime of years, shall be so fortunate, that thirteen several princes shall present their several crowns to him, and all kings else shall so admire his fame and victories, that they shall all be glad, either through fear or love, to do him homage; but death (who favours neither the weak nor valiant) in the midst of all his glories, soon shall seize him, scarcely permitting him to appoint one in all his purchased kingdoms to succeed him.

Prince. Thanks to our prophet for this so wished-for satisfaction, and hereby now we learn that always fate must be observed whatever that decree,
All future times shall still record this story,
Of Merlin's learned worth, and Arthur's glory.

[*Exeunt omnes.*

NOTES TO THE BIRTH OF MERLIN; OR, THE CHILD HATH FOUND HIS FATHER.

[1] *The parling enemy.*

The talking enemy, the enemy who is desirous of a conference.

[2] *I'd be loth that any man should make a holy-day for me yet.*

The holy-days held in honour of the saints or heroes of those times were not attributed to them until after their death. Toclio, alluding to this custom, means he should be loth to die, and so give any occasion for a holy-day to his memory.

[3] *If ever I change my virgin name, by you it gains or loses.*

That is, if ever I marry, you shall be my husband; my name shall either gain or lose distinction by being changed to yours.

[4] *Argues desire of cure, but not knowledge of art.*

I have interpolated the word *knowledge*, which was wanting to complete the sense.

[5] *Shame take thy tongue.*

In the copy of 1662, the following speech also is given to Donobert:—"I have restored it to the king, who is evidently the speaker."

[6] *To deny so high and noble a proposal to my fame and country.*

The old copy reads:—"so high and noble to my fame and country." Some word seems to have been omitted: so high and noble what? I have hazarded the insertion of *a proposal.*

[7] *Marry a pagan, an idolater.*

The religion of the Saxons, before they were won to the acknowledgment of Christianity, was a very wild, imaginary, and savage idolatry: indeed, Odin or Woden, the father of the gods, was called "the terrible and severe god, the father of slaughter, the god that carries desolation and fire, *the active and roaring deity.*" His wife Frigga, or Frea, was the goddess of pleasure and sensuality: she was represented as an hermaphrodite. They had many children, who each presided over some portion of the world; thus Thor was the god of tempests, Balder of light, Kiord of the waters, Tyr of champions, Brage of orators and poets, while Heimdal was the door-keeper of heaven and the guardian of the rainbow. They had, besides, a long array of inferior deities and spirits, amongst which were the goddess Hela, the wolf Fenris, the great dragon, the giants, and the evil genii. To their devil, or the personification of evil, they gave

the name of Lok. Their heaven was called Valhalla where the spirits of the brave fought all day and feasted all night, their repast being the flesh of the great boar, Scrimner, which was eaten up every evening, but always renewed the next morning. Their hell was Niflheim, where the mean and cowardly dwelt with anguish and fed with famine. There was one great comfort in all this, it was not to last for ever: a terrible conflagration was, in the end, to destroy gods, men, and spirits, the earth, Valhalla, and Niflheim—when a purer God and a new and higher state of things was to arise out of the ruin. These rude ancestors of ours seem to have had good sense enough to suppose, that though their barbarous deities and sensual goblins did exist, that it was but for a time; they were not pure and good enough for eternity.

[8] *Be you ambassador unto our brother, the brother of our queen Artesia : tell him for such our entertainment looks him.*

The sense would be clearer if we read "tell him *as* such our entertainment looks *for* him;" that is, as a brother we expect him.

[9] *Speak as a man, and I shall hope to obey thee.*

That is, speak as one considering the passions and frailties of our race. Regard my affection for Artesia, not with the cold eyes of a saint, but with the yielding heart of a man.

[10] *Must let no joy beneath to move his eye.*

The old copy reads—

Must leave no joy beneath, to move his eye.

This expresses exactly the reverse of what the hermit evidently means. He is desiring Modestia to leave all joy on earth and fix her eyes on heaven.

[11] *Pygmalion, then I tasted thy sad fate.*

Pygmalion was a celebrated sculptor of Cyprus, who entertained an aversion to women on account of the extreme immorality of those of Amathus, to which he had been an unwilling witness. But nature was strong in the bosom of the sculptor, and he fell in love with a beautiful marble statue that he had made. The Prince means, that he, like Pygmalion, had fallen in love with a lifeless, unreal thing—with one who, as far he was concerned, might as well be a statue. But the sculptor was more fortunate than the Prince. At his earnest prayers, the goddess Venus changed his cold marble statue into a warm living woman, who was eventually married to the love-smitten artist.

[12] *She's a maid yet.*

Recollecting the interesting situation of the lady, I do

not see how this could be. Perhaps we should read—she's *scarce* a maid yet; but you, &c.

[13] *Tell me, woman, what sin have you committed worthy this?*

Joan's offence was apparent enough. I think we should read—what sin have *I* committed, &c.; i.e., what have I done that you should slander me with being the father of your child?

[14] *Beats her.*

This violence is not only unprincely, but unmanly and savage. Shakspere could not have written this: he never shocks at once our feelings and our sense of probability.

[15] *By the rood;* i.e. the cross.

[16] *Oh, the gods!*

Edol is lamenting the prevalence of idolaters and the depression of Christianity; but here and throughout the drama he not very consistently swears by the pagan deities.

[17] *Hector, our great ancestor.*

Alluding to the tradition that the Britons were descended from King Brute and the Trojans, who, upon the destruction of their city, fled, and eventually settled in this island. See note 4 to Locrine.

[18] *And she dares owe me still.*

That is, own me still—acknowledge me. The word *owe* is invariably used in this sense by Shakspere.

[19] *Vices are virtues, if so thought and seen.*

This is a very ambiguous line; but I suppose the author means that feelings which, unrestrained, hurry us into vicious excesses, are, when under the guidance of thought, productive of virtue. Thus, obstinacy is a vice, firmness a virtue; violent anger a sin, but anger upon justifiable occasions merely proper manly spirit. The poet Pope thus recognises this doctrine:

Lust through some certain strainers well refined,
Is gentle love, and charms all womankind.

[20] *Let her challenge any man, the child shall call him father.*

It is scarcely necessary to say that the introduction in the present drama of this mode of affiliating illegitimate children is a gross anachronism. Although women, among the ancient Britons, appear to have been much respected—for they assumed the prophetic office, commanded armies, and governed states—yet their customs respecting the intercourse of the sexes were, if not loose, at least very singular. A sort of promiscuous polygamy appears to have prevailed among them; and ten or twelve families are reported to have lived together under the same roof, the ladies bestowing their favours indifferently upon any of the husbands of this large domestic circle. A Roman historian reports a conversation supposed to have taken place upon this subject between the wife of a British chief and the Empress Julia, where the former lady,

being reproached with the immoral habits of her country-women, answered proudly that the British women did openly with their best men what the Roman ladies did secretly with their worst.

[21] *Marriage was blest, I know, with heaven's own hand.*

So, also, Milton, in his exquisite lines on the same subject, in the fourth book of *Paradise Lost*.

Whatever hypocrites austerely talk
Of purity, and place, and innocence;
Defaming as impure what God declares
Pure, and commands to some, leaves free to all.
Our Maker bids increase; who bids abstain
But our destroyer, foe to God and man? &c.

[22] *Enter Lucina and the three Fates.*

Lucina presided over the birth of children, and her presence was supposed to give an easy labour; this was in consequence of her mother Juno having brought her into the world without pain. The Fates or Parcæ presided over the birth and life of all the human race.

[23] *The Castle Camelot.*

This was the castle in which the old romances say King Arthur kept his court in the west. Thus Drayton:

Like Camelot, what place was ever yet renown'd,
Where, as at Carlion, oft he kept his table round?

[24] *A cast of Merlin's;* i.e. a trick of his.

[25] *A covey of cardecus.*

A *cardeeu* was a corruption of *un quart d'ecu*, the fourth part of a crown.

[26] *The bards, the Druids.*

The Bards of that period were a branch of the Druids, who were divided into three orders, called Druids, Vates, and Bards. The first were Druids proper, and the most eminent of the class: they were priests, moral teachers, lawgivers, astronomers, and professors of the occult art. They cultivated magic, with a number of mysterious and awful ceremonies, amongst which human sacrifices were sometimes included. In the Irish language, a magician is still called Drui, and the art of magic Druidheach. The Vates were poets and sacred musicians. The Latin word *vates* is generally used to signify a poet, and sometimes a poet of a divine or prophetic character. The office of the Bards appears to have been of a similar nature.

[27] *Still in our eye your message, Proximus, we keep to spur our speed.*

That is, we keep the information you brought us from Ostorius constantly in mind, to spur us to further activity. Vortiger had just been reading the letter Proximus had brought from the Saxons.

[28] *A tucket sounded;* i.e., a toccata, a flourish on a trumpet.

[29] *Calling themselves Hingest-men.*

That is, followers of Hengest, the great Saxon chief,

whom Vortiger, or rather Vortigern, invited to Britain to assist him against incursions of the Picts. Hengist and his brother Horsa, were supposed to be descended from their god Odin; indeed, they claimed to be the grandsons of that imaginary deity—a circumstance which added considerably to their influence over their rude countrymen.

30 *For Vortiger is dead.*

Vortigern has been differently painted by the pencil of history, some writers representing him to be an exceedingly vicious man, and others calling him merely weak and unfortunate. In a tract called *Merlin's Life and Prophecies* (1755), there is the following dark charge against him; but I am ignorant what authority it rests upon:—"These two brothers, Ambrosius Aurelius and Uter Pendragon, made their speedy expedition towards Wales; where Vortigern, the Usurper, was sorely besieged by them; and in his own castle they burned him and all his people alive. Such was the fall of the wicked Vortigern; for of him it was reported that he had carnal society with his own daughter, in hopes that kings should issue from them. Thus died he miserably, when he had reigned since his last inauguration (he had once been deposed), nine years and some months."

31 *Some mystic Python.*

I think it should be *Pythian.* Python was the name of the monstrous serpent that Apollo killed, for which he received the name of Pythias. The priestess of Apollo's oracle at Delphi was always called the Pythia; hence, probably, the term was applied to any one supposed to possess prophetic power.

32 *How swiftly mischief creeps.*

To creep swiftly is a contradiction, one of those errors which arose from a slip of the pen, and was rendered permanent by the author not having corrected the printed copy of his drama.

33 *Bi-formed;* i. e. composed of two forms or bodies.

34 *All after time shall fill their chronicles with fame of his renown.*

This famous son of Pendragon's was the celebrated King Arthur, glorious in nursery legends, and dear to the memory of every schoolboy. Among the fabulous acts attributed to him was a great victory over the Romans, in which he slew Prince Lucius and ten other kings, who invaded Britain with an immense army. On his death, he sent for his cousin, Constantine, and crowned him. His death and burial are supposed to have resembled those of the Hebrew prophet Moses, for he perished in solitude, and no man knows his grave.

Modern historians have conjectured that he was but a myth, invented by the bards to keep alive the valour of the Britons.

35 *To a Heptarchy.*

The Heptarchy was the seven Saxon kingdoms into which Britain was divided by its northern conquerors. The word is a derivation from the Greek, signifying *seven* and *chief.*

36 *As high as palled Hecate.*

Hecate appears to have been identical with the moon, for mythologists tell us she was called Luna in heaven, Diana on earth, and Hecate or Proserpine in hell. As *high* as Hecate, is, therefore, an appropriate direction. Perhaps we should read *pallid* for palled. Shakspere has been censured for introducing Hecate among the vulgar witches in Macbeth, and thus confounding ancient and modern superstitions.

37 *The jaws of Acheron;* i.e. the mouth of hell.

38 *Tenebrarum, precis divitiarum et inferorum, &c.*

This magic spell of Merlin's is in a Latin that Virgil never sung or Pliny wrote. It is very difficult to render into English at all; yet, as the curious but unlearned reader may wish to know the meaning of the words which had such power over the devil, I offer the following translation:—"Receive this incubus, this curse of darkness, riches, and the shades below. God, into eternal fire I commit him, to be shut up for ever in a darksome prison."

39 *I will erect a monument upon the verdant plains of Salisbury.*

In the tract I have already referred to in note 30, is another wonderful account, connecting the name of Merlin with the origin of Stonehenge:—"This Prince (Aurelius Ambrosius), by the help of Merlin, caused the great stones to be brought in a whirlwind, in one night, out of Ireland, and placed where they now stand on Salisbury Plain, in remembrance of the British lords there slain and after buried, in the time of the pretended treaty and communication between Vortigern and Hengist; but Polychronicon and some other writers ascribe their transportage to his brother Uter Pendragon, at whose request to Merlin that miraculous conveyance was performed."

40 *Erictho.*

The name of one of the Furies; also that of a Thessalonian woman, famous for her knowledge of poisons. Either of them forms an appropriate simile for the abandoned Artesia.

H. T.

First Part of
Sir John Oldcastle

Like *Thomas Lord Cromwell* and *Sir Thomas More,* in which Shakespeare had a hand, the play entitled *The First Part of the True and Honorable history of the life of Sir John Oldcastle, the good Lord Cobham,* falls within the rubric of biographical drama.

Shakespeare's gratification at the success of *1* and *2 Henry IV* was marred by an unfortunate accident. The name he originally gave to the character Falstaff was Sir John Oldcastle, taken over directly from *The Famous Victories of Henry V,* in which Oldcastle, familiarly called "Jockey," has a minor part among the boisterous followers of the Prince, with scarcely a suggestion of Falstaff's overflowing humor. Perhaps the most taking thing he says is a jocular comment on King Henry IV: "He is a good old man, God take him to his mercy sooner." Hardly a character in Shakespeare is, however, more entirely the creation of his own mind than Falstaff (who is a combination of two characters in the old play, Oldcastle and Derrick the clown). Sidney Lee says with simple justice, "Shakespeare touched the comic scenes of the old drama with a magic of his own, and summoned out of its dust and ashes the radiance of the inimitable Falstaff."

The more Shakespeare thought about Sir John Oldcastle, the clearer he became. There were, as Marchette Chute points out, a great many opportunities to observe old soldiers in London, since the city contained a fourth of the men in the entire kingdom, and Shakespeare knew the elaborate army graft schemes on which many an old captain had retired. He was familiar with the cheating and the lying and the cadging of these disreputable old fellows, which he combined with the Roman tradition of the *Miles Gloriosus,* or Braggart Soldier, and out of this material was born one of the greatest comedy creations in the history of drama.

As soon as Sir John Oldcastle appeared on the stage in the production by the Chamberlain's Men of *1 Henry IV,* a howl of unregenerate joy went up from the audiences who at once took the disgraceful old gentleman to their collective hearts. But the extraordinary notoriety of the character as portrayed by Shakespeare seems to have led to resentment by Henry Brooke, Lord Cobham, a lineal descendant of Sir John Oldcastle, who had been in real life a renowned soldier. Lord Cobham, we may suppose, complained to the Master of the Revels, who was responsible for licensing plays, or possibly to his near neighbor the Lord Chamberlain, who had general oversight of dramatic productions and who was the patron of the company performing the offending play. In view of this altogether unexpected complaint, Shakespeare agreed to change the name of his comic hero. Casting about in his mind for a new name, he stumbled upon Sir John Fastolfe (another respectable fifteenth-century soldier), who had figured as a coward in *1 Henry VI,* a play he was then engaged in revising:

> Here had the conquest fully been seal'd up
> If Sir John Fastolfe had not play'd the coward.
> He, being in the vaward, plac'd behind
> With purpose to relieve and follow them,
> Cowardly fled, not having struck one stroke.
>
> [I. i. 130–34]

Altering the name slightly, Shakespeare changed the cowardly Sir John Oldcastle's designation to Sir John Falstaff. Probably the alteration made it necessary to delete a few passages in *1 Henry IV,* but one was overlooked, in which Hal addresses Falstaff as "my old lad of the castle" (I. ii. 47–48). The pun had now, of course, entirely lost its point.

Shakespeare had done the best he could to right a wholly unintentional wrong against the Cobham family. Yet so indelibly had the "old lad of the castle" stamped his name upon the minds of the public during the short interval preceding the birth of Falstaff, that it could not be so easily erased. For many years afterwards writers continued to allude to Falstaff as Sir John Oldcastle, and the general public was even slower to accept their popular hero's change of name. Moreover, the reference to Falstaff as "my old lad of the castle" was not necessary to omit, since that was a common slang phrase for a roisterer. Gabriel Harvey, for instance, spoke of Robert Greene and his companions as "old lads of the castle." However, Shakespeare finally felt it incumbent to remind London audiences in an Epilogue attached to *2 Henry IV* that "Oldcastle died a martyr, and this is not the man." He went even further. Early in 1598 he gave *1 Henry IV* to the press (it was entered in the

Stationers' Register on February 25) in order to show that the fat knight was now called Sir John Falstaff. But all in vain. The name Oldcastle could not be expunged from the minds of the public. Thereupon Lord Cobham, in order to rectify the injury done, induced the Admiral's Men to produce a long two-part play (of which only the first part is extant) narrating the "true life" and martyrdom of the real Sir John Oldcastle. The task of composing the work was placed in the hands of Michael Drayton, Anthony Munday, Robert Wilson, and Richard Hathaway. In collaboration they wrote a tiresome but presumably veracious history of the old Lollard martyr, under the title *The True and Honorable History of the Life of Sir John Oldcastle, the Good Lord Cobham.*

In a Prologue, the authors say to the public, with an oblique jibe both at Shakespeare and Falstaff:

> It is no pamper'd glutton we present,
> Nor aged counsellor to youthful sin,
> But one, whose virtue shone above the rest,
> A valiant martyr, and a virtuous peer;
> In whose true faith and loyalty, express'd
> Unto his sovereign and his country's weal,
> We strive to pay that tribute of our love,
> Your favours merit. Let fair truth be grac'd,
> Since forg'd invention former time defac'd.

The play was acted by the Admiral's Men at the Rose in 1599, possibly to the loud applause of Lord Cobham and his friends. And shortly afterwards, in order to give it wider publicity and erase the bad impression Shakespeare's Oldcastle had created, it was printed and offered to the public at the bookstalls. In 1601, in yet another counterblast to Shakespeare's misrepresentation of the Cobham family's ancestor, John Weever issued a narrative poem entitled *The Mirror of Martyrs, or the Life and Death of That Thrice Valiant Captain and Most Godly Martyr, Sir John Oldcastle, Lord Cobham.*

But Lord Cobham and his friends, and even Shakespeare himself, were swimming against the stream. In spite of all their efforts, the name Oldcastle for Falstaff simply would not down. For instance, when on March 6, 1600, Shakespeare's company presented *Henry IV* at the Lord Chamberlain's house before Vereiken and the other ambassadors from the Spanish Low Countries, Rowland Whyte wrote in a letter to Sir Robert Sidney: "Thursday my Lord Chamberlain feasted him [Vereiken], and made him a very great and a delicate dinner; and there in the afternoon his players acted before Vereiken *Sir John Oldcastle*, to his great contentment."

And even so well-informed a man as Nathaniel Field, actor and playwright, in his *Amends for Ladies* (1618), writes:

> . . . Did you ever see
> The play where the fat Knight, high Oldcastle,
> Did tell you truly what his "honor" was?

By now Shakespeare probably was growing tired of Falstaff. At the end of 2 *Henry IV*, he represents him as having deteriorated in character and as being rejected by Hal, now crowned King of England. When Sir John thrusts himself forward, confident of being received by the new sovereign with open arms, the King frowns upon him, and says:

> I know thee not, old man. Fall to thy prayers.
> How ill white hairs become a fool and jester!
>   [V. v. 50–52]

And a few moments later we see him, thus humiliated, carried off to prison. But if Shakespeare, as J. Q. Adams (1) notes, hoped to get rid of him so easily, he reckoned without the public, and without Queen Elizabeth. Yielding to the popular demand, he promised in a late Epilogue to 2 *Henry IV* that "our humble author will continue the story, with Sir John in it, and make you merry with fair Katherine of France; where, for anything I know, Falstaff shall die of a sweat. . . ." From this announcement we may infer that the dramatist intended to amuse the public with one more—and the last—representation of Falstaff in his humors and, in order to get rid of him forever, planned to end his life in the sweat of some arduous exploit in France.

But before Shakespeare could carry out this promise, his intentions were interfered with by no less a person than Queen Elizabeth. As was her custom, she summoned the Lord Chamberlain's Men in the Christmas season of 1597–98 to amuse Her Majesty at Windsor with their latest plays. Naturally the actors would present before her the two parts of *Henry IV*, then new and the chief sensation of London. According to a well-founded tradition, she was so delighted with Falstaff that she called for the author and requested him to write especially for her a play in which Falstaff should be made to fall in love. A request from the Queen could not be ignored; and Shakespeare was compelled to lay aside his proposed *Henry V*, with its already announced plan of putting Sir John to death, and at once set to work on a comedy representing the hero in an amorous escapde. Tradition states that he completed the comedy within two weeks, for the Queen "was so eager to see it acted, that she commanded it to be finished in fourteen days"—possibly in order to have it acted before the end of the Christmas festivities then in progress at Windsor. It is likely that Shakespeare merely reworked an old manuscript, entitled *The Jealous Comedy*, which had been in the possession of his troupe since 1593.

In this fashion, we may believe, came into existence *The Merry Wives of Windsor.* Possibly, too, this explains why the setting of that play is Windsor, for Elizabeth's residence there would render this setting highly pleasing to her and her ladies. As Charles Gildon notes in his work *The Lives and Characters of the English Dramatic Poets:* "The fairies in the fifth act make a handsome compliment to the Queen and her palace at Windsor." The title page expressly states that the play had been presented "before Her Majesty," and tradition adds that she was "very well pleased at the representation." It was also, of course, acted before the public during the winter and spring of 1598. Gildon suggests that the form in which it was advertised in the players' bills posted throughout the city is possibly indicated by the title page of the edition that shortly appeared: "A Most pleasant and excellent conceited Comedy, of Sir John Falstaff, and the Merry Wives of Windsor. Intermixed with sundry variable and pleasing humors, of Sir Hugh, the Welsh Knight, Justice Shallow, and his wise Cousin M. Slender. With the swaggering vain of Ancient Pistol and Corporal Nym. By William Shakespeare." A playbill promising so many attractive features as this would surely fill the theatre to capacity.

After completing *The Merry Wives* for the Queen, Shakespeare turned his attention to *Henry V,* which he had already announced he was contemplating. But he did not carry out his promise of representing Falstaff once more in action. Indeed the Knight gets no nearer the stage than an adjoining room, where, we are told, he lies "shak'd of a burning quotidian tertian that it is most lamentable to behold" (II. i, 124–25). And from a comic figure he has been changed into an almost tragic one, for his illness was due to the King's harsh renunciation of him—"his heart is fracted" (II. i. 130). With this slight preparation, we are suddenly informed that he is dead and is gone to "Arthur's bosom" (II. iii. 10). The Hostess, in language at once amusing and pathetic, says:

> For after I saw him fumble with the sheets, and play with flowers, and smile upon his fingers' ends, I knew there was but one way; for his nose was as sharp as a pen, and 'a babbled of green fields. [II. iii. 14–18]

So the greatest comic creation of the drama "went away an it had been any christom child" (II. iii. 11–12).

Shakespeare's comic talent, manifest in Falstaff and in his progenitor Oldcastle, is equally wonderful, Schlegel believes, as that which he has shown in the pathetic and tragic. Not only has he delineated many kinds of folly, but even of sheer stupidity has he contrived to give a most diverting and entertaining picture. Schlegel points out that there is also in his plays a distinct species of the farcical, which apparently seems to be introduced more arbitrarily, but which is, however, founded on imitation of some actual custom. This is the introduction of the merrymaker, the fool with his cap and bells and motley dress, called more commonly a clown, who appears in several comedies, though not in all, but of the tragedies in King Lear alone, and who generally merely expresses his wit in conversation with the principal characters, though he is occasionally incorporated into the action.

In those times it was not only usual for princes and kings to have their court fools or clowns, but many distinguished families, among their retainers, kept such an exhilarating housemate as a good antidote against the insipidity and wearisomeness of ordinary life and as a welcome interruption of established formalities. Great statesmen, and even ecclesiastics, did not consider it beneath their dignity to recruit and solace themselves after important business with the conversation of their clowns; the celebrated Sir Thomas More had his fool painted with him in his portrait by Holbein. As Viola in *Twelfth Night* says:

> This fellow is wise enough to play the fool,
> And to do that well craves a kind of wit.
> He must observe their mood on whom he jests,
> The quality of persons, and the time;
> Not, like the haggard, check at every feather
> That comes before his eye. This is a practice
> As full of labour as a wise man's art;
> For folly that he wisely shows, is fit;
> But wise men, folly-fall'n, quite taint their wit.
>
> [III. i. 67–75]

Just as Sir Toby finds his station in *Twelfth Night,* so Andrew and even Malvolio there, in Andrew's case simply to display his own foolish inanity as do the witless in all sorts of comedy, and in Malvolio's to enter almost as Jonson gave his characters entry, for a more subtle but still classical kind of discomfiture. As Malvolio in *Twelfth Night*, so Jacques in *As You Like It*, another of the few attempts of Shakespeare to project what H. B. Charlton calls, "malcontentism for comic purposes" in *Shakespearean Comedy*. Besides these, traditional clowns may now also play their part, whether the English Shakespearean ones of the tribe of Bottom, such as Dogberry or Verges, or the more technical ones, Feste and Touchstone, grown now by contact with Costards into something more substantial and more homely than the mere traditional corrupters of words, and therefore playing not the part of an added funny interlude, but an essential role in the orientation of the idea of comedy. "Since the little wit that fools have was silenced, the little foolery that wise men have makes a great show" (*As You Like It* I. ii. 95–97). The true fool's return is restorative. A fool of his sort will use his folly like a stalking-horse, and under the presentation of that, will shoot his wit. Yet his range will necessarily be limited now. Only the crassest folly falls to such arrows, for those who have become expert in human traffickings can assume an easy indifference to simple and direct hits:

> He that a fool doth very wisely hit
> Doth very foolishly, although he smart,
> Not to seem senseless of the bob. If not,
> The wise man's folly is anatomiz'd
> Even by the squand'ring glances of the fool.
> [*As You Like It* II. vii. 53–57]

Thus the motley of romantic comedies is subtler than the slapdash skittle-knocking of the satire in classical comedy. Their reformatory way, too, is fundamentally different from the simple exposure of ludicrous abnormality, which had been the approved manner of older comedy. They entice to a richer wisdom by alluring the imagination into desire for larger delights. They are not mainly concerned to whip offenders into conventional propriety by scorn and by mockery. They persuade one to the better sense by presenting it in all its attractiveness: they depict a land of heart's desire, and, doing that, reveal the way of human and natural magic by which it is to be attained.

In fine, the true comic, be he clown or fool—as Shakespeare's Oldcastle or Falstaff, Jonson's Mosca or Morose, Cervantes' Sancho Panza—is, in Samuel Coleridge's happy phrase, "the blossom of the nettle."

PERSONS REPRESENTED.

KING HENRY THE FIFTH.
Appears, Act I. sc. 2. Act II. sc. 3. Act III. sc. 4. Act IV.
sc. 1; sc. 2. Act V. sc. 1.

SIR JOHN OLDCASTLE, *Lord* Cobham.
Appears, Act I. sc. 3. Act II. sc. 3. Act III. sc. 1. Act
IV. sc. 2; sc. 3; sc. 4. Act V. sc. 1; sc. 4; sc. 7; sc. 8;
sc. 9; sc. 11.

LORD HERBERT.
Appears, Act I. sc. 1.

LORD POWIS.
Appears, Act I. sc. 1; sc. 3. Act III. sc. 1. Act V. sc. 11.

DUKE OF SUFFOLK.
Appears, Act I. sc. 2. Act II. sc. 3. Act III. sc. 4. Act IV.
sc. 1; sc. 2. Act V. sc. 1.

EARL OF HUNTINGDON.
Appears, Act I. sc. 2. Act II. sc. 3. Act IV. sc. 1; sc. 2.

EARL OF CAMBRIDGE,
LORD SCROOPE,   } *Conspirators against the*
SIR THOMAS GREY,   *King.*

Appear, Act III. sc. 1. Act V. sc. 1.

SIR ROGER ACTON,
MASTER BOURN,
MASTER BEVERLEY,   } *Rebels.*
MURLEY, *a Brewer of* Dunstable,

Appear, Act II. sc. 2. Act III. sc. 2. Act IV. sc. 2.

BISHOP OF ROCHESTER.
Appears, Act I. sc. 2. Act II. sc. 3. Act IV. sc. 2; sc. 3;
sc. 4. Act V. sc. 10.

SIR RICHARD LEE.
Appears, Act V. sc. 9; sc. 11.

TWO JUDGES OF ASSIZE.
Appear, Act I. sc. 1. Act V. sc. 11.

LORD WARDEN OF THE CINQUE-PORTS.
Appears, Act IV. sc. 3.

BUTLER, *a Gentleman of the Privy-chamber.*
Appears, Act I. sc. 2; sc. 3. Act II. sc. 3. Act III. sc. 4.
Act IV. sc. 1.

CHARTRES, *a French Agent, in league with the*
Conspirators.
Appears, Act III. sc. 1.

CROMER, *Sheriff of* Kent.
Appears, Act IV. sc. 3.

MAYOR OF HEREFORD.
SHERIFF OF HEREFORDSHIRE.
Appear, Act I. sc. 1.

SIR JOHN, *the Parson of* Wrotham.
Appears, Act I. sc. 2. Act II. sc. 1. Act III. sc. 3; sc. 4.
Act IV. sc. 1; sc. 2. Act V. sc. 2; sc. 10; sc. 11.

LIEUTENANT OF THE TOWER.
Appears, Act IV. sc. 6.

MAYOR OF ST. ALBANS.
Appears, Act V. sc. 5; sc. 6; sc. 8; sc. 11.

A Kentish CONSTABLE *and an* ALE-MAN.
Appear, Act II. sc. 1.

DICK *and* TOM, *Servants to* Murley.
Appear, Act III. sc. 2.

MACK-SHANE, *an* Irish *Ruffian.*
Appears, Act V. sc. 2; sc. 3; sc. 6; sc. 10; sc. 11.

HARPOOL, *Servant to* Lord Cobham.
Appears, Act I. sc. 3. Act II. sc. 1. Act III. sc. 1. Act IV.
sc. 3; sc. 4. Act V. sc. 4; sc. 6; sc. 7; sc. 8; sc. 11.

GOUGH, *Servant to* Lord Herbert.
OWEN *and* DAVY, *Servants to* Lord Powis.
Appear, Act I. sc. 1.

CLUN, *Sumner to the* Bishop of Rochester.
Appears, Act II. sc. 1. Act IV. sc. 3.

LADY COBHAM.
Appears, Act III. sc. 1. Act IV. sc. 3. Act V. sc. 8; sc. 9;
sc. 11.

LADY POWIS.
Appears, Act III. sc. 1. Act V. sc. 11.

DOLL, *Concubine to the* Parson of Wrotham.
Appears, Act II. sc. 1. Act III. sc. 3; sc. 4. Act V. sc. 2;
sc. 10; sc. 11.

KATE, *the* Carrier's *Daughter.*
Appears, Act V. sc. 3; sc. 8.

An Host, Ostler, Carriers, Soldiers, Beggars, Con-
stables, Wardens of the Tower, Bailiffs, Messengers,
and other Attendants.

SCENE.--ENGLAND.

FIRST PART OF

Sir John Oldcastle.

PROLOGUE.

THE doubtful title, gentlemen, prefix'd
Upon the argument we have in hand,
May breed suspense, and wrongfully disturb
The peaceful quiet of your settled thoughts.
To stop which scruple, let this brief suffice:
It is no pamper'd glutton we present,
Nor aged counsellor to youthful sin,[1]

But one, whose virtue shone above the rest,
A valiant martyr, and a virtuous peer;
In whose true faith and loyalty, express'd
Unto his sovereign and his country's weal,
We strive to pay that tribute of our love
Your favours merit.   Let fair truth be grac'd,
Since forg'd invention former time defac'd.

ACT I.

SCENE I.—Hereford.   *A Street.*

Enter LORD HERBERT, LORD POWIS, OWEN,
GOUGH, DAVY, *and several other followers of the
lords* Herbert *and* Powis; *they fight.   Then
enter the* SHERIFF OF HEREFORDSHIRE *and a*
Bailiff.

Sher. My lords, I charge ye, in his highness'
   name,
To keep the peace; you and your followers.

Her. Good master sheriff, look unto yourself.

Pow. Do so, for we have other business.
   [*They attempt to fight again.*

Sher. Will ye disturb the judges, and the assize?
Hear the king's proclamation, ye were best.

Pow. Hold then; let's hear it.

Her. But be brief, ye were best.

Bail. O——-yes.

Davy. Cossone, make shorter O, or shall mar
   your yes.

Bail. O——-yes.

Owen. What, has hur nothing to say, but O yes?

Bail. O——-yes.

Davy. O nay; py coss plut,[2] down with hur,
down with hur.   A Powis, a Powis.

Gough. A Herbert, a Herbert, and down with
Powis.   [*They fight again.*

Sher. Hold in the king's name, hold.

Owen. Down with a' knave's name, down.
   [*The bailiff is knock'd down, and the sheriff
      runs away.*

Her. Powis, I think thy Welsh and thou do
   smart.

Pow. Herbert, I think my sword came near thy
   heart.

Her. Thy heart's best blood shall pay the loss
   of mine.

Gough. A Herbert, a Herbert.

Davy. A Powis, a Powis.

As they are fighting, Enter the MAYOR OF HERE-
FORD, *his* Officers *and* Townsmen, *with Clubs.*

May. My lords, as you are liegemen to the
   crown,
True noblemen, and subjects to the king,
Attend his highness' proclamation,
Commanded by the judges of assize,
For keeping peace at this assembly.

Her. Good master mayor of Hereford, be brief.

May. Serjeant, without the ceremonies of O yes,
Pronounce aloud the proclamation.

Ser. The king's justices, perceiving what public
mischief may ensue this private quarrel, in his
majesty's name do straitly charge and command

334

all persons, of what degree soever, to depart this
city of Hereford, except such as are bound to give
attendance at this assize, and that no man presume
to wear any weapon, especially Welsh-hooks, and
forest bills;—

Owen. Haw! No pill, nor Wells hoog? ha?

May. Peace, and hear the proclamation.

Ser. And that the lord Powis do presently disperse and discharge his retinue, and depart the
city in the king's peace, he and his followers, on
pain of imprisonment.

Davy. Haw? pud her lord Powis in prison? A
Powis, a Powis. Cossoon, hur will live and tye
with hur lord.

Gough. A Herbert, a Herbert.

[*They fight.* LORD HERBERT *is wounded, and
falls to the ground. The* Mayor *and his*
Attendants *interpose.* LORD POWIS *runs
away.*

Enter two Judges, *the* Sheriff, *and his* Bailiffs
before them.

1st Judge. Where's the lord Herbert? Is he
hurt or slain?

Sher. He's here, my lord.

2nd Judge. How fares his lordship, friends?

Gough. Mortally wounded, speechless; he cannot live.

1st Judge. Convey him hence, let not his wounds
take air;
And get him dress'd with expedition.
[*Exeunt* L. HERB. *and* GOUGH.
Master mayor of Hereford, master sheriff o'the
shire,
Commit lord Powis to safe custody,
To answer the disturbance of the peace,
Lord Herbert's peril, and his high contempt
Of us, and you the king's commissioners:
See it be done with care and diligence.

Sher. Please it your lordship, my lord Powis is
gone past all recovery.

2nd Judge. Yet let search be made,
To apprehend his followers that are left.

Sher. There are some of them: Sirs, lay hold of
them.

Owen. Of us? and why? what has hur done, I
pray you?

Sher. Disarm them, bailiffs.

May. Officers, assist.

Davy. Hear you, lord shudge, what resson is for
this?

Owen. Cossoon, pe 'puse for fighting for our
lord?

1st Judge. Away with them.

Davy. Harg you, my lord.

Owen. Gough, my lord Herbert's man, is a dirty
knave.[3]

Davy. Ice live and tye in good quarrel.

Owen. Pray you do shustice, let awl be prison.

Davy. Prison! no; lord shudge, I wool give you
pail, good surety.

2nd Judge. What bail? what sureties?

Davy. Hur cozen ap Rice, ap Evan, ap Morice,
ap Morgan, ap Lluellyn, ap Madoc, ap Meredith,
ap Griffin, ap Davy, ap Owen, ap Skinken, ap
Shones.

2nd Judge. Two of the most sufficient are enough.

Sher. An it please your lordship, these are all
but one.

1st Judge. To gaol with them, and the lord Her-
bert's men:
We'll talk with them, when the assize is done.
[*Exeunt* Bailiffs, OWEN, DAVY, *&c.*
Riotous, audacious, and unruly grooms,
Must we be forc'd to come from the bench,
To quiet brawls, which every constable
In other civil places can suppress?

2nd Judge. What was the quarrel that caus'd all
this stir?

Sher. About religion, as I heard, my lord.
Lord Powis detracted from the power of Rome,
Affirming Wickliff's doctrine to be true,
And Rome's erroneous: hot reply was made
By the lord Herbert; they were traitors all
That would maintain it. Powis answered,
They were as true, as noble, and as wise
As he; they would defend it with their lives;
He nam'd for instance sir John Oldcastle,
The lord Cobham: Herbert reply'd again,
He, thou, and all are traitors that so hold.
The lie was given, the several factions drawn,
And so enraged that we could not appease it.

1st Judge. This case concerns the king's prero-
gative,
And 'tis dangerous to the state and commonwealth.
Gentlemen, justices, master mayor, and master
sheriff,
It doth behove us all, and each of us,
In general and particular, to have care
For the suppressing of all mutinies,
And all assemblies, except soldiers' musters,
For the king's preparation into France.
We hear of secret conventicles made,
And there is doubt of some conspiracies,
Which may break out into rebellious arms,
When the king's gone, perchance before he go:

Note as an instance, this one perilous fray:
What factions might have grown on either part,
To the destruction of the king and realm?
Yet, in my conscience, sir John Oldcastle's
Innocent of it; only his name was us'd.
We therefore from his highness give this charge:
You, master mayor, look to your citizens;
You, master sheriff, unto your shire; and you
As justices, in every one's precinct
There be no meetings: when the vulgar sort
Sit on their ale-bench, with their cups and cans,
Matters of state be not their common talk,
Nor pure religion by their lips profan'd.
Let us return unto the bench again,
And there examine further of this fray.

Enter a Bailiff *and a* Serjeant.

Sher. Sirs, have ye taken the lord Powis yet?
Bail. No, nor heard of him.
Ser. No, he's gone far enough.
2nd Judge. They that are left behind, shall answer all. [*Exeunt.*

SCENE II.—Eltham. *An Antechamber in the Palace.*

Enter the DUKE OF SUFFOLK, BISHOP OF ROCHESTER, BUTLER, *and* SIR JOHN OF WROTHAM.

Suff. Now, my lord bishop, take free liberty
To speak your mind: what is your suit to us?
Roch. My noble lord, no more than what you
    know,
And have been oftentimes invested with.
Grievous complaints have pass'd between the lips
Of envious persons, to upbraid the clergy;
Some carping at the livings which we have,
And others spurning at the ceremonies
That are of ancient custom in the church:
Amongst the which, lord Cobham is a chief.
What inconvenience may proceed hereof,
Both to the king, and to the commonwealth,
May easily be discern'd, when, like a frenzy,
This innovation shall possess their minds.
These upstarts will have followers to uphold
Their damn'd opinion, more than Henry shall,
To undergo his quarrel 'gainst the French.
Suf. What proof is there against them to be had,
That what you say the law may justify?
Roch. They give themselves the name of Protestants,
And meet in fields and solitary groves.
S. John. Was ever heard, my lord, the like till
    now?

That thieves and rebels, s'blood, my lord, heretics,
Plain heretics, (I'll stand to 't to their teeth)
Should have, to colour their vile practices,
A title of such worth, as "Protestant?"

Enter a Messenger, *with a letter, which he gives to the* Duke of Suffolk.

Suf. O, but you must not swear; it ill becomes
One of your coat to rap out bloody oaths.
Roch. Pardon him, good my lord; it is his zeal.
An honest country prelate, who laments
To see such foul disorder in the church.
S. John. There's one, they call him sir John
    Oldcastle;
He has not his name for nought; for, like a castle,
Doth he encompass them within his walls:
But till that castle be subverted quite,
We ne'er shall be at quiet in the realm.
Roch. That is our suit, my lord; that he be ta'en,
And brought in question for his heresy.
Beside, two letters brought me out of Wales,
Wherein my lord of Hereford writes to me,
What tumult and sedition was begun,
About the lord Cobham, at the 'sizes there,
(For they had much ado to calm the rage)
And that the valiant Herbert is there slain.
Suf. A fire that must be quench'd. Well, say
    no more;
The king anon goes to the council chamber,
There to debate of matters touching France.
As he doth pass by, I'll inform his grace
Concerning your petition. Master Butler,
If I forget, do you remember me.
But. I will, my lord.
Roch. Not as a recompense,
But as a token of our love to you,
By me, my lords, the clergy doth present
This purse, and in it full a thousand angels,
Praying your lordship to accept their gift.
                    [*Offers the* Duke *a purse.*
Suf. I thank them, my lord bishop, for their love,
But will not take their money: if you please
To give it to this gentleman, you may.
Roch. Sir, then we crave your furtherance herein.
But. The best I can, my lord of Rochester.
Roch. Nay, pray you take it, trust me sir, you
    shall.
S. John. Were ye all three upon New-market
    heath,
You should not need strain curt'sy who should
    have it;
Sir John would quickly rid ye of that care. [*Aside.*
Suf. The king is coming. Fear ye not, my lord;

The very first thing I will break with him,
Shall be about your matter.

Enter KING HENRY *and the* EARL OF HUNTINGTON.

K. Henry. My lord of Suffolk,
Was it not said the clergy did refuse
To lend us money toward our wars in France?
   Suf. It was, my lord, but very wrongfully.
   K. Henry. I know it was: for Huntington here
     tells me
They have been very bountiful of late.
   Suf. And still they vow, my gracious lord, to
     be so,
Hoping your majesty will think on them
As of your loving subjects, and suppress
All such malicious errors as begin
To spot their calling, and disturb the church.
   K. Henry. God else forbid!—Why, Suffolk, is
     there
Any new rupture to disquiet them?
   Suf. No new, my lord; the old is great enough;
And so increasing, as, if not cut down,
Will breed a scandal to your royal state,
And set your kingdom quickly in an uproar.
The Kentish knight, lord Cobham, in despite
Of any law, or spiritual discipline,
Maintains this upstart new religion still;
And divers great assemblies, by his means,
And private quarrels, are commenc'd abroad,
As by this letter more at large, my liege,
Is made apparent.
   K. Henry. We do find it here,
There was in Wales a certain fray of late,
Between two noblemen.   But what of this?
Follows it straight, lord Cobham must be he
Did cause the same? I dare be sworn, good knight,
He never dream'd of any such contention.
   Roch. But in his name the quarrel did begin,
About the opinion which he held, my liege.
   K. Henry. What if it did? was either he in
     place
To take part with them, or abet them in it?
If brabbling fellows, whose enkindled blood
Seeths in their fiery veins, will needs go fight,
Making their quarrels of some words that pass'd
Either of you, or you, amongst their cups,
Is the fault yours? or are they guilty of it?
   Suf. With pardon of your highness, my dread
     lord,
Such little sparks, neglected, may in time
Grow to a mighty flame.   But that's not all;
He doth beside maintain a strange religion,
And will not be compell'd to come to mass.

   Roch. We do beseech you therefore, gracious
     prince,
Without offence unto your majesty,
We may be bold to use authority.
   K. Henry. As how?
   Roch. To summon him unto the arches,[4]
Where such offences have ther punishment.
   K. Henry. To answer personally? is that your
     meaning?
   Roch. It is, my lord.
   K. Henry. How, if he appeal?
   Roch. My lord, he cannot in such a case as this.
   Suf. Not where religion is the plea, my lord.
   K. Henry. I took it always, that ourself stood
     on 't
As a sufficient refuge, unto whom
Not any but might lawfully appeal:
But we'll not argue now upon that point.
For sir John Oldcastle, whom you accuse,
Let me entreat you to dispense a while
With your high title of pre-eminence.
Report did never yet condemn him so,
But he hath always been reputed loyal:
And, in my knowledge, I can say thus much,
That he is virtuous, wise, and honourable.
If any way his conscience be seduc'd
To waver in his faith, I'll send for him,
And school him privately: if that serve not,
Then afterward you may proceed against him.
Butler, be you the messenger for us,
And will him presently repair to court.
       [*Exeunt* K. HENRY, HUNT., SUF., *and* BUT.
   S. John. How now, my lord? why stand you
     discontent?
In sooth, methinks the king hath well decreed.
   Roch. Ay, ay, sir John, if he would keep his
     word:
But I perceive he favours him so much
As this will be to small effect, I fear.
   S. John. Why then I'll tell you what you're
     best to do:
If you suspect the king will be but cold
In reprehending him, send you a process too,
To serve upon him; so you may be sure
To make him answer it, howsoe'er it fall.
   Roch. And well remember'd; I will have it so;
A sumner[5] shall be sent about it straight. [*Exit.*
   S. John. Yea, do so. In the mean space this
     remains
For kind sir John of Wrotham, honest Jack.
Methinks the purse of gold the bishop gave
Made a good show, it had a tempting look:
Beshrew me, but my fingers' ends do itch

To be upon those golden ruddocks.[6] Well, 'tis
    thus ;
I am not as the world doth take me for :
If ever wolf were clothed in sheep's coat,
Then I am he ; old huddle and twang i'faith :
A priest in shew, but, in plain terms, a thief.
Yet let me tell you too, an honest thief ;
One that will take it where it may be spar'd,
And spend it freely in good fellowship.
I have as many shapes as Proteus had ;
That still when any villany is done,
There may be none suspect it was sir John.
Besides, to comfort me, (for what 's this life,
Except the crabbed bitterness thereof
Be sweeten'd now and then with lechery ?)
I have my Doll, my concubine as 'twere,
To frolic with ; a lusty bouncing girl.
But whilst I loiter here, the gold may 'scape,
And that must not be so : it is mine own.
Therefore I 'll meet him on his way to court,
And shrive him of it ;[7] there will be the sport.
                              [*Exit.*

SCENE III.—Kent. *An Outer Court before* Lord
  Cobham's *House. A public road leading to it ;
  and an Alehouse appearing at a little distance.*

      Enter two Old Men *and two* Soldiers.

1st Sold. God help, God help ! there 's law for
    punishing,
But there 's no law for our necessity :
There be more stocks to set poor soldiers in,
Than there be houses to relieve them at.

    1st Old M. Ay, house-keeping decays in every
    place,
Even as Saint Peter writ, still worse and worse.

    2nd Old M. Master mayor of Rochester has
given command, that none shall go abroad out of
the parish ; and has set down an order forsooth,
what every poor householder must give for our
relief ; where there be some 'sessed,[8] I may say to
you, had almost as much need to beg as we.

    1st Old M. It is a hard world the while.

    2nd Old M. If a poor man ask at door for God's
sake, they ask him for a licence, or a certificate
from a justice.

    1st Sold. Faith we have none, but what we bear
upon our bodies, our maim'd limbs, God help
us.

    2nd Sold. And yet as lame as I am, I 'll with
the king into France, if I can but crawl a ship-
board. I had rather be slain in France, than starve
in England.

    1st Old M. Ha, were I but as lusty as I was at
Shrewsbury battle, I would not do as I do :—but
we are now come to the good lord Cobham's, the
best man to the poor in all Kent.

    2nd Old M. God bless him ; there be but few
such.

        Enter Lord Cobham *and* Harpool.

    Cob. Thou peevish froward man, what wouldst
    thou have ?

    Har. This pride, this pride, brings all to beggary.
I serv'd your father, and your grandfather ;
Shew me such two men now : no, no ; your backs,
Your backs,[9] the devil and pride, has cut the throat
Of all good house-keeping ; they were the best
Yeomen's masters that ever were in England.

    Cob. Yea, except thou have a crew of filthy
    knaves
And sturdy rogues, still feeding at my gate,
There is no hospitality with thee.

    Har. They may sit at the gate well enough, but
the devil of anything you give them, except they'll
eat stones.

    Cob. 'Tis 'long then of such hungry knaves as
    you :
Yea, sir, here's your retinue ; your guests be come ;
They know their hours, I warrant you.

    1st Old M. God bless your honour ! God save
the good lord Cobham, and all his house !

    1st Sold. Good your honour, bestow your blessed
alms upon poor men.

    Cob. Now, sir, here be your alms-knights : now
    are you
As safe as the emperor.

    Har. My alms-knights ? Nay, they 're yours : it
is a shame for you, and I 'll stand to 't ; your foolish
alms maintains more vagabonds than all the noblemen in Kent beside. Out, you rogues, you knaves,
work for your livings. Alas, poor men, they may
beg their hearts out ; there's no more charity among
men than among so many mastiff dogs. [*Aside.*]
What make you here, you needy knaves ? Away,
away, you villains.

    2nd Sold. I beseech you, sir, be good to us.

    Cob. Nay, nay, they know thee well enough ; I
    think
That all the beggars in this land are thy
Acquaintance : go bestow your alms, none will
Control you, sir.

    Har. What should I give them ? you are grown
so beggarly that you can scarce give a bit of bread
at your door. You talk of your religion so long,
that you have banish'd charity from you. A man

may make a flax-shop in your kitchen chimneys,
for any fire there is stirring.

Cob. If thou wilt give them nothing, send them
    hence :
Let them not stand here starving in the cold.

Har. Who ! I drive them hence ? If I drive poor
men from the door, I 'll be hang'd : I know not
what I may come to myself. God help ye, poor
knaves, ye see the world. Well, you had a
mother ; O God be with thee, good lady, thy soul's
at rest : She gave more in shirts and smocks to
poor children, than you spend in your house ; and
yet you live a beggar too.   [*To* COB.

Cob. Even the worst deed that e'er my mother
    did,
Was in relieving such a fool as thou.

Har. Ay, I am a fool still : with all your wit
you 'll die a beggar ; go to.

Cob. Go, you old fool, give the poor people
    something.
Go in, poor men, into the inner court,
And take such alms as there is to be had.

Sold. God bless your honour !

Har. Hang you, rogues, hang you ; there 's
nothing but misery amongst you ; you fear no
law, you.

2nd Old M. God bless you good master Ralph,
God save your life ; you are good to the poor still.
        [*Exeunt* HAR., Old M., *and* Sold.

Enter LORD POWIS, *disguised*

Cob. What fellow's yonder comes along the
    grove ?
Few passengers there be that know this way.
Methinks, he stops, as though he staid for me,
And meant to shroud himself among the bushes.
I know, the clergy hates me to the death,
And my religion gets me many foes :
And this may be some desperate rogue, suborn'd
To work me mischief :—as it pleaseth God.
If he come toward me, sure I 'll stay his coming,
Be he but one man, whatsoe'er he be.
        [LORD POW. *advances.*
I have been well acquainted with that face.

Pow. Well met, my honourable lord and friend.

Cob. You are very welcome, sir, whate'er you be ;
But of this sudden, sir, I do not know you.

Pow. I am one that wisheth well unto your
    honour ;
My name is Powis, an old friend of yours.

Cob. My honourable lord, and worthy friend,
What makes your lordship thus alone in Kent ?
And thus disguised in this strange attire ?

Pow. My lord, an unexpected accident
Hath at this time enforc'd me to these parts,
And thus it happ'd. Not yet full five days since,
Now at the last assize at Hereford,
It chanc'd that the lord Herbert and myself,
'Mongst other things, discoursing at the table,
Did fall in speech about some certain points
Of Wickliff's doctrine, 'gainst the papacy
And the religion catholic maintain'd
Through the most part of Europe at this day.
This wilful testy lord stuck not to say,
That Wickliff was a knave, a schismatic,
His doctrine devilish, and heretical ;
And whatsoe'er he was, maintain'd the same,
Was traitor both to God, and to his country.
Being moved at his peremptory speech,
I told him, some maintained those opinions,
Men, and truer subjects than lord Herbert was :
And he replying in comparisons,
Your name was urg'd, my lord, against his chal-
    lenge,
To be a perfect favourer of the truth.
And, to be short, from words we fell to blows,
Our servants, and our tenants, taking parts ;—
Many on both sides hurt ; and for an hour
The broil by no means could be pacified ;
Until the judges, rising from the bench,
Were in their persons forc'd to part the fray.

Cob. I hope no man was violently slain.

Pow. 'Faith none, I trust, but the lord Herbert's
    self,
Who is in truth so dangerously hurt,
As it is doubted he can hardly scape.

Cob. I am sorry, my good lord, for these ill news.

Pow. This is the cause that drives me into Kent,
To shroud myself with you, so good a friend,
Until I hear how things do speed at home.

Cob. Your lordship is most welcome unto Cobham ;
But I am very sorry, my good lord,
My name was brought in question in this matter,
Considering I have many enemies,
That threaten malice, and do lie in wait
To take the vantage of the smallest thing.
But you are welcome ; and repose your lordship,
And keep yourself here secret in my house,
Until we hear how the lord Herbert speeds.

Enter HARPOOL.

Here comes my man : sirrah, what news ?

Har. Yonder's one Master Butler of the privy
chamber, is sent unto you from the king.

Pow. Pray God, that the lord Herbert be not
    dead,

And the king, hearing whither I am gone,
Hath sent for me.

Cob. Comfort yourself, my lord; I warrant you.

Har. Fellow, what ails thee? dost thou quake? dost thou shake? dost thou tremble? ha?

Cob. Peace, you old fool. Sirrah, convey this gentleman in the back way, and bring the other into the walk.

Har. Come, sir, you are welcome, if you love my lord.

Pow. Gramercy, gentle friend.

　　　　　　　　[*Exeunt* Pow. *and* HAR.

Cob. I thought as much, that it would not be long Before I heard of something from the king, About this matter.

　　　　Enter HARPOOL *and* BUTLER.

Har. Sir, yonder my lord walks, you see him; I'll have your men into the cellar the while.

Cob. Welcome, good master Butler.

But. Thanks, my good lord. His majesty doth commend his love unto your lordship, and wills you to repair unto the court.

Cob. God bless his highness, and confound his enemies!
I hope his majesty is well.

But. In good health, my lord.

Cob. God long continue it! Methinks you look As though you were not well: what ail ye, sir?

But. 'Faith I have had a foolish odd mischance,
That angers me. Coming o'er Shooter's Hill,
There came one to me like a sailor, and
Ask'd my money; and whilst I staid my horse,
To draw my purse, he takes the advantage of
A little bank, and leaps behind me, whips
My purse away, and with a sudden jerk,
I know not how, threw me at least three yards
Out of my saddle. I never was so robb'd
In all my life.

Cob. I am very sorry, sir, for your mischance;
We will send our warrant forth, to stay all such
Suspicious persons as shall be found:
Then Master Butler we'll attend on you.

But. I humbly thank your lordship, I'll attend
　　you　　　　　　　　　　　　　[*Exeunt.*

ACT II.

SCENE I.—*The Same.*

Enter a Sumner.

Sum. I have the law to warrant what I do; and though the lord Cobham be a nobleman, that dispenses not with law: I dare serve a process, were he five noblemen. Though we sumners make sometimes a mad slip in a corner with a pretty wench, a sumner must not go always by seeing: a man may be content to hide his eyes where he may feel his profit. Well, this is lord Cobham's house; if I cannot speak with him, I'll clap my citation upon his door; so my lord of Rochester bade me: but methinks here comes one of his men.

Enter HARPOOL.

Har. Welcome, good fellow, welcome; who would'st thou speak with?

Sum. With my lord Cobham I would speak, if thou be one of his men.

Har. Yes, I am one of his men: but thou canst not speak with my lord.

Sum. May I send to him then?

Har. I'll tell thee that, when I know thy errand.

Sum. I will not tell my errand to thee.

Har. Then keep it to thyself, and walk like a knave as thou cam'st.

Sum. I tell thee, my lord keeps no knaves, sirrah.

Har. Then thou servest him not, 'I believe. What lord is thy master?

Sum. My lord of Rochester.

Har. In good time: And what would'st thou have with my lord Cobham?

Sum. I come, by virtue of a process, to cite him to appear before my lord in the court at Rochester.

Har. [*Aside.*] Well, God grant me patience! I could eat this conger. My lord is not at home; therefore it were good, Sumner, you carried your process back.

Sum. Why, if he will not be spoken withal, then will I leave it here; and see that he take knowledge of it.　　　　[*Fixes a Citation on the Gate.*

Har. 'Zounds you slave, do you set up your bills here? Go to; take it down again. Dost thou know what thou dost? Dost thou know on whom thou servest a process?

Sum. Yes, marry do I; on sir John Oldcastle, lord Cobham.

Har. I am glad thou knowest him yet. And sirrah, dost thou not know that the lord Cobham is a brave lord, that keeps good beef and beer in his house, and every day feeds a hundred poor people at his gate, and keeps a hundred tall fellows?[10]

Sum. What's that to my process?

Har. Marry this, sir; is this process parchment?

Sum. Yes, marry is it.

Har. And this seal wax?

Sum. It is so.

Har. If this be parchment, and this wax, eat you this parchment and this wax, or I will make parchment of your skin, and beat your brains into wax. Sirrah, Sumner, dispatch; devour, sirrah, devour.

Sum. I am my lord of Rochester's sumner; I came to do my office, and thou shalt answer it.

Har. Sirrah, no railing, but betake yourself to your teeth. Thou shalt eat no worse than thou bring'st with thee. Thou bring'st it for my lord, and wilt thou bring my lord worse than thou wilt eat thyself?

Sum. Sir, I brought it not my lord to eat.

Har. O, do you "sir" me now? All's one for that; I'll make you eat it, for bringing it.

Sum. I cannot eat it.

Har. Can you not? 'sblood I'll beat you till you have a stomach. [*Beats him.*

Sum. O hold, hold, good master Servingman; I will eat it.

Har. Be champing, be chewing, sir, or I'll chew you, you rogue. Tough wax is the purest honey.

Sum. The purest of the honey!—O, Lord, sir! oh! oh! [*Eats.*

Har. Feed, feed; 'tis wholesome, rogue, wholesome. Cannot you, like an honest sumner, walk with the devil your brother, to fetch in your bailiff's rents, but you must come to a nobleman's house with process? If thy seal were as broad as the lead that covers Rochester church, thou should'st eat it.

Sum. O, I am almost chok'd, I am almost chok'd.

Har. Who's within there? will you shame my lord? is there no beer in the house? Butler, I say.

Enter BUTLER.

But. Here, here.

Har. Give him beer. There; tough old sheepskin's bare dry meat.[11] [*The* Sumner *drinks.*

Sum. O, sir, let me go no further; I'll eat my word.

Har. Yea marry, sir, I mean you shall eat more than your own word; for I'll make you eat all the words in the process. Why, you drab-monger, cannot the secrets of all the wenches in a shire serve your turn, but you must come hither with a citation, with a pox? I'll cite you.—A cup of sack for the sumner.

But. Here, sir, here.

Har. Here, slave, I drink to thee.

Sum. I thank you, sir.

Har. Now, if thou find'st thy stomach well, because thou shalt see my lord keeps meat in his house, if thou wilt go in, thou shalt have a piece of beef to thy breakfast.

Sum. No, I am very well, good master servingman, I thank you; very well, sir.

Har. I am glad on't: then be walking towards Rochester to keep your stomach warm. And, Sumner, if I do know you disturb a good wench within this diocese, if I do not make thee eat her petticoat, if there were four yards of Kentish cloth in it, I am a villain.

Sum. God be wi' you, master Servingman.
[*Exit* Sumner.

Har. Farewell, Sumner.

Enter Constable.

Con. Save you, master Harpool.

Har. Welcome constable, welcome constable; what news with thee?

Con. An't please you, master Harpool, I am to make hue and cry for a fellow with one eye, that has robb'd two clothiers; and am to crave your hindrance to search all suspected places; and they say there was a woman in the company.

Har. Hast thou been at the ale-house? hast thou sought there?

Con. I durst not search in my lord Cobham's liberty, except I had some of his servants for my warrant.

Har. An honest constable: call forth him that keeps the ale-house there.

Con. Ho, who's within there?

Enter Ale-man.

Ale-man. Who calls there? Oh, is't you, master constable, and master Harpool? you're welcome with all my heart. What make you here so early this morning?

Har. Sirrah, what strangers do you lodge? there is a robbery done this morning, and we are to search for all suspected persons.

Ale-man. Gods-bore, I am sorry for't. I'faith,

sir, I lodge nobody, but a good honest priest, call'd sir John a Wrotham, and a handsome woman that is his niece, that he says he has some suit in law for; and as they go up and down to London, sometimes they lie at my house.

Har. What, is she here in thy house now?

Ale-man. She is, sir; I promise you, sir, he is a quiet man, and because he will not trouble too many rooms, he makes the woman lie every night at his bed's feet.

Har. Bring her forth, constable; bring her forth: let's see her, let's see her.

Ale-man. Dorothy, you must come down to master constable.

Enter DOROTHY.

Doll. Anon forsooth.

Har. Welcome, sweet lass, welcome.

Doll. I thank you, good sir, and master constable also.

Har. A plump girl by the mass, a plump girl. Ha, Doll, ha! Wilt thou forsake the priest, and go with me, Doll?

Con. Ah! well said, master Harpool; you are a merry old man i'faith; you will never be old. Now by the mack, a pretty wench indeed!

Har. You old mad merry constable, art thou advis'd of that? Ha, well said Doll; fill some ale here.

Doll. Oh, if I wist this old priest would not stick to me, by Jove I would ingle this old serving-man.[12]   [*Aside.*

Har. O you old mad colt, i'faith I'll ferk you:[13] fill all the pots in the house there.

Con. Oh! well said, master Harpool; you are a heart of oak when all's done.

Har. Ha, Doll, thou hast a sweet pair of lips by the mass.

Doll. Truly you are a most sweet old man, as ever I saw; by my troth, you have a face able to make any woman in love with you.

Har. Fill, sweet Doll, I'll drink to thee.

Doll. I pledge you, sir, and thank you therefore, and I pray you let it come.[14]

Har. [*Embracing her.*] Doll, canst thou love me? A mad merry lass; would to God I had never seen thee!

Doll. I warrant you, you will not out of my thoughts this twelvemonth; truly you are as full of favour, as a man may be.[15] Ah, these sweet grey locks! by my troth they are most lovely.

Con. Cuds bores, master Harpool, I'll have one buss too.

Har. No licking for you, constable; hands off, hands off.

Con. By'r lady, I love kissing as well as you.

Doll. O, you are an old boy, you have a wanton eye of your own: Ah, you sweet sugar-lip'd wanton, you will win as many women's hearts as come in your company.

Enter SIR JOHN OF WROTHAM.

Sir John. Doll, come hither.

Har. Priest, she shall not.

Doll. I'll come anon, sweet love.

Sir John. Hands off, old fornicator.

Har. Vicar, I'll sit here in spite of thee. Is this fit stuff for a priest to carry up and down with him?

Sir John. Sirrah, dost thou not know that a good-fellow parson may have a chapel of ease, where his parish church is far off?

Har. You whorson-ston'd vicar.

Sir John. You old stale ruffian, you lion of Cotswold.[16]

Har. 'Zounds, vicar, I'll geld you.
                                    [*Flies upon him.*

Con. Keep the king's peace.

Doll. Murder, murder, murder!

Ale-man. Hold, as you are men, hold; for God's sake be quiet; put up your weapons, you draw not in my house.

Har. You whorson bawdy priest.

Sir John. You old mutton-monger.

Con. Hold, sir John, hold.

Doll. I pray thee, sweet heart, be quiet; I was but sitting to drink a pot of ale with him; even as kind a man as ever I met with.

Har. Thou art a thief, I warrant thee.

Sir John. Then I am but as thou hast been in thy days. Let's not be asham'd of our trade; the king has been a thief himself.

Doll. Come, be quiet. Hast thou sped?

Sir John. I have, wench; here be crowns i'faith.

Doll. Come, let's be all friends then.

Con. Well said, mistress Dorothy.

Har. Thou art the maddest priest that ever I met with.

Sir John. Give me thy hand, thou art as good a fellow. I am a singer, a drinker, a bencher,[17] a wencher; I can say a mass, and kiss a lass: 'faith, I have a parsonage, and because I would not be at too much charges, this wench serveth me for a sexton.

Har. Well said, mad priest; we'll in, and be friends.   [*Exeunt.*

SCENE II.—London.—*A Room in the Axe Inn, without Bishop-gate.*

Enter SIR ROGER ACTON, BOURN, BEVERLEY, *and* MURLEY.

Act. Now, master Murley, I am well assur'd
You know our errand, and do like the cause,
Being a man affected as we are.

Mur. Marry God dild ye,[18] dainty my dear: no
master, good sir Roger Acton, master Bourn, and
master Beverley, gentlemen and justices of the
peace; no master, I, but plain William Murley,
the brewer of Dunstable, your honest neighbour
and your friend, if ye be men of my profession.

Bev. Professed friends to Wickliff, foes to Rome.

Mur. Hold by me, lad; lean upon that staff,
good master Beverley; all of a house. Say your
mind, say your mind.

Act. You know, our faction now is grown so
            great
Throughout the realm, that it begins to smoke
Into the clergy's eyes, and the king's ears.
High time it is that we were drawn to head,
Our general and officers appointed;
And wars, you wot, will ask great store of coin.
Able to strength our action with your purse,
You are elected for a colonel
Over a regiment of fifteen bands.

Mur. Phew, paltry, paltry! in and out, to and
fro, be it more or less upon occasion. Lord have
mercy upon us, what a world is this! Sir Roger
Acton, I am but a Dunstable man, a plain brewer,
you know. Will lusty cavaliering captains, gentlemen, come at my calling, go at my bidding? dainty
my dear, they'll do a dog of wax, a horse of cheese,
a prick and a pudding. No, no; ye must appoint
some lord or knight at least, to that place.

Bourn. Why, master Murley, you shall be a
            knight.
Were you not in election to be sheriff?
Have you not pass'd all offices but that?
Have you not wealth to make your wife a lady?
I warrant you, my lord, our general,
Bestows that honour on you, at first sight.

Mur. Marry God dild ye, dainty my dear. But
tell me, who shall be our general. Where's the
lord Cobham, sir John Oldcastle, that noble alms-
giver, house-keeper, virtuous, religious gentleman?
Come to me there, boys; come to me there.

Act. Why, who but he shall be our general?

Mur. And shall he knight me, and make me
colonel?

Act. My word for that, sir William Murley knight.

Mur. Fellow, sir Roger Acton knight, all fellows,
I mean in arms, how strong are we? how many
partners? Our enemies beside the king are mighty:
be it more or less upon occasion, reckon our force.

Act. There are of us, our friends, and followers,
Three thousand and three hundred at the least;
Of northern lads four thousand, beside horse;
From Kent there comes, with sir John Oldcastle,
Seven thousand; then from London issue out,
Of masters, servants, strangers, 'prentices,
Forty odd thousand into Ficket field,
Where we appoint our special rendezvous.

Mur. Phew, paltry, paltry, in and out, to and
fro. Lord have mercy upon us, what a world is
this! Where's that Ficket field, sir Roger?

Act. Behind St. Giles's-in-the-field, near Holborn.

Mur. Newgate, up Holborn, St. Giles's-in-the-
Field, and to Tyburn; an old saw. For the day,
for the day?

Act. On Friday next, the fourteenth day of
            January.

Mur. Tilly vally,[19] trust me never, if I have any
liking of that day. Phew, paltry, paltry! Friday,
quoth-a, a dismal day: Childermas day this year
was Friday.

Bev. Nay, master Murley, if you observe such
            days,
We make some question of your constancy:
All days are alike to men resolved in right.

Mur. Say amen, and say no more, but say and
hold, master Beverley: Friday next, and Ficket field,
and William Murley and his merry men, shall be
all one. I have half a score jades that draw my
beer-carts; and every jade shall bear a knave, and
every knave shall wear a jack, and every jack shall
have a skull,[20] and every skull shall show a spear,
and every spear shall kill a foe at Ficket field, at
Ficket field. John and Tom, Dick and Hodge,
Ralph and Robin, William and George, and all
my knaves, shall fight like men at Ficket field,
on Friday next.

Bourn. What sum of money mean you to dis-
burse?

Mur. It may be, modestly, decently, and soberly,
and handsomely, I may bring five hundred pound.

Act. Five hundred, man? five thousand's not
            enough:
A hundred thousand will not pay our men
Two months together. Either come prepar'd
Like a brave knight and martial colonel,
In glittering gold, and gallant furniture,
Bringing in coin, a cart-load at the least,

And all your followers mounted on good horse,
Or never come disgraceful to us all.

Bev. Perchance you may be chosen treasurer;
Ten thousand pound's the least that you can bring.

Mur. Paltry, paltry, in and out, to and fro:
upon occasion I have ten thousand pound to spend,
and ten too. And rather than the bishop shall
have his will of me, for my conscience, it shall all
go. Flame and flax, flax and flame. It was got
with water and malt, and it shall fly with fire and
gunpowder. Sir Roger, a cart-load of money, till
the axletree crack; myself and my men in Ficket
field on Friday next; remember my knighthood
and my place: there's my hand, I'll be there.
[*Exit* Mur.

Act. See what ambition may persuade men to:
In hope of honour he will spend himself.

Bourn. I never thought a brewer half so rich.

Bev. Was never bankrupt brewer yet but one,
With using too much malt, too little water.

Act. That is no fault in brewers now-a-days:
Come, let's away about our business. [*Exeunt.*

SCENE III.—*An Audience-chamber in the Palace
at Eltham.*

Enter King Henry, *the* Duke of Suffolk,
Butler, *and* Lord Cobham. *He kneels to the*
King.

K. Henry. 'Tis not enough, lord Cobham, to
submit;
You must forsake your gross opinion.
The bishops find themselves much injured;
And though, for some good service you have done,
We for our part are pleas'd to pardon you,
Yet they will not so soon be satisfy'd.

Cob. My gracious lord, unto your majesty,
Next unto my God, I do owe my life;
And what is mine, either by nature's gift,
Or fortune's bounty, all is at your service.
But for obedience to the pope of Rome,
I owe him none; nor shall his shaveling priests
That are in England, alter my belief.
If out of Holy Scripture they can prove
That I am in an error, I will yield,
And gladly take instruction at their hands:
But otherwise, I do beseech your grace
My conscience may not be encroach'd upon.

K. Henry. We would be loth to press our sub-
jects' bodies,
Much less their souls, the dear redeemed part
Of him that is the ruler of us all:
Yet let me counsel you, that might command.

Do not presume to tempt them with ill words,
Nor suffer any meetings to be had
Within your house; but to the uttermost
Disperse the flocks of this new gathering sect.

Cob. My liege, if any breathe, that dares come
forth,
And say, my life in any of these points
Deserves the attainder of ignoble thoughts,
Here stand I, craving no remorse at all,[21]
But even the utmost rigour may be shown.

K. Henry. Let it suffice we know your loyalty.
What have you there?

Cob. A deed of clemency;
Your highness' pardon for lord Powis' life,
Which I did beg, and you, my noble lord,
Of gracious favour did vouchsafe to grant.

K. Henry. But yet it is not signed with our hand.

Cob. Not yet, my liege.

K. Henry. The fact you say was done
Not of pretensed malice,[22] but by chance.

Cob. Upon mine honour so, no otherwise.

K. Henry. There is his pardon; bid him make
amends, [*Signs the pardon.*
And cleanse his soul to God for his offence:
What we remit, is but the body's scourge.
How now, lord bishop?

Enter Bishop of Rochester.

Roch. Justice, dread sovereign:
As thou art king, so grant I may have justice.

K. Henry. What means this exclamation? let
us know.

Roch. Ah, my good lord, the state is much
abus'd,
And our decrees most shamefully profan'd.

K. Henry. How? or by whom?

Roch. Even by this heretic,
This Jew, this traitor to your majesty.

Cob. Prelate, thou ly'st, even in thy greasy
maw,[23]
Or whosoever twits me with the name
Of either traitor, or of heretic.

K. Henry. Forbear, I say: and bishop, shew the
cause
From whence this late abuse hath been deriv'd.

Roch. Thus, mighty king. By general consent
A messenger was sent to cite this lord
To make appearance in the consistory;
And coming to his house, a ruffian slave,
One of his daily followers, met the man;
Who, knowing him to be a paritor,[24]
Assaults him first, and after, in contempt
Of us and our proceedings, makes him eat

The written process, parchment, seal and all;
Whereby his master neither was brought forth,
Nor we but scorn'd for our authority.
   K. Henry. When was this done?
   Roch. At six o'clock this morning.
   K. Henry. And when came you to court?
   Cob. Last night, my liege.
   K. Henry. By this, it seems he is not guilty of it,
And you have done him wrong to accuse him so.
   Roch. But it was done, my lord, by his appointment;
Or else his man durst not have been so bold.
   K. Henry. Or else you durst not be bold to interrupt
And fill our ears with frivolous complaints.
Is this the duty you do bear to us?
Was't not sufficient we did pass our word
To send for him, but you, misdoubting it,
Or which is worse, intending to forestal
Our regal power, must likewise summon him?
This savours of ambition, not of zeal;
And rather proves you malice his estate,
Than any way that he offends the law.
Go to, we like it not; and he your officer
Had his desert for being insolent,
That was employ'd so much amiss herein.
So, Cobham, when you please, you may depart.
   Cob. I humbly bid farewell unto my liege.
                        [*Exit* COB.

          Enter HUNTINGTON.

   K. Henry. Farewell. What is the news by Huntington?
   Hun. Sir Roger Acton and a crew, my lord,

Of bold seditious rebels, are in arms,
Intending reformation of religion;[25]
And with their army they intend to pitch
In Ficket-field, unless they be repuls'd.
   K. Henry. So near our presence? Dare they be so bold?
And will proud war and eager thirst of blood,
Whom we had thought to entertain far off,
Press forth upon us in our native bounds?
Must we be forc'd to handsel our sharp blades
In England here, which we prepar'd for France?
Well, a God's name be it. What's their number, say,
Or who's the chief commander of this rout?
   Hun. Their number is not known as yet, my lord;
But 'tis reported, sir John Oldcastle
Is the chief man, on whom they do depend.
   K. Henry. How! the lord Cobham?
   Hun. Yes, my gracious lord.
   Roch. I could have told your majesty as much
Before he went, but that I saw your grace
Was too much blinded by his flattery.
   Suf. Send post, my lord, to fetch him back again.
   But. Traitor unto his country, how he smooth'd,
And seem'd as innocent as truth itself!
   K. Henry. I cannot think it yet he would be false;
But if he be, no matter;—let him go:
We'll meet both him and them unto their woe.
      [*Exeunt* K. HENRY, SUF., HUNT., *and* BUT.
   Roch. This falls out well; and at the last I hope
To see this heretic die in a rope.   [*Exit.*

ACT III.

SCENE I.—*An Avenue leading to* Lord Cobham's *House in Kent.*

Enter the EARL OF CAMBRIDGE, LORD SCROOPE, SIR THOMAS GREY, *and* CHARTRES.

   Scroope. Once more, my lord of Cambridge, make rehearsal
How you do stand entitled to the crown;
The deeper shall we print it in our minds,
And every man the better be resolv'd,
When he perceives his quarrel to be just.
   Cam. Then thus, lord Scroope, sir Thomas Grey, and you

Monsieur de Chartres, agent for the French:
This Lionel, duke of Clarence, (as I said)
Third son of Edward (England's king) the third,
Had issue, Philip, his sole daughter and heir;
Which Philip afterward was given in marriage
To Edmund Mortimer, the earl of March,
And by him had a son call'd Roger Mortimer;
Which Roger likewise had of his descent,
Edmund and Roger, Anne and Eleanor,
Two daughters and two sons; but of those, three
Dy'd without issue. Anne, that did survive,
And now was left her father's only heir,
My fortune was to marry; being too

By my grandfather, of king Edward's line:
So of his sur-name, I am called you know,
Richard Plantagenet: my father was
Edward the duke of York, and son and heir
To Edmund Langley, Edward the Third's fifth son.

    Scroope. So that it seems your claim comes by
        your wife,
As lawful heir to Roger Mortimer,
The son of Edmund, which did marry Philip,
Daughter and heir to Lionel duke of Clarence.

    Cam. True; for this Harry, and his father both,
Harry the Fourth, as plainly doth appear,
Are false intruders, and usurp the crown.
For when young Richard was at Pomfret slain,
In him the title of prince Edward died,
That was the eldest of king Edward's sons.
William of Hatfield, and their second brother,
Death in his nonage had before bereft:
So that my wife, deriv'd from Lionel,
Third son unto king Edward, ought proceed,
And take possession of the diadem,
Before this Harry, or his father king,
Who fetch their title but from Lancaster,
Fourth of that royal line.   And being thus
What reason is 't, but she should have her right?

    Scroop. I am resolv'd our enterprize is just.

    Grey. Harry shall die, or else resign his crown.

    Char. Perform but that, and Charles the king
        of France
Shall aid you, lords, not only with his men,
But send you money to maintain your wars.
Five hundred thousand crowns he made me proffer,
If you can stop but Harry's voyage for France.

    Scroope. We never had a fitter time than now,
The realm in such division as it is.

    Cam. Besides, you must persuade you, there is due
Vengeance for Richard's murther, which although
It be deferr'd, yet it will fall at last,
And now as likely as another time.
Sin hath had many years to ripen in;
And now the harvest cannot be far off,
Wherein the weeds of usurpation
Are to be cropp'd, and cast into the fire.

    Scroope. No more, earl Cambridge; here I plight
        my faith
To set up thee and thy renowned wife.

    Grey. Grey will perform the same, as he is
        knight.

    Char. And, to assist ye, as I said before,
Chartres doth gage the honour of his king.

    Scroope. We lack but now lord Cobham's fellow-
        ship,
And then our plot were absolute indeed.

    Cam. Doubt not of him, my lord; his life pur-
        su'd
By the incensed clergy, and of late
Brought in displeasure with the king, assures
He may be quickly won unto our faction.
Who hath the articles were drawn at large
Of our whole purpose?

    Grey. That have I, my lord.

    Cam. We should not now be far off from his
        house.
Our serious conference hath beguil'd the way;
See where his castle stands.   Give me the writing;
When we are come unto the speech of him,
Because we will not stand to make recount
Of that which hath been said, here he shall read
Our minds at large, and what we crave of him.

Enter LORD COBHAM.

    Scroope. A ready way.   Here comes the man
        himself,
Booted and spurr'd; it seems he hath been riding.

    Cam. Well met, lord Cobham.

    Cob. My lord of Cambridge!
Your honour is most welcome into Kent,
And all the rest of this fair company.
I am new come from London, gentle lords:
But will ye not take Cowling for your host,[26]
And see what entertainment it affords?

    Cam. We were intended to have been your
        guests:
But now this lucky meeting shall suffice
To end our business, and defer that kindness.

    Cob. Business, my lord? what business should
        let
You to be merry?[27] We have no delicates:
Yet this I 'll promise you; a piece of venison,
A cup of wine, and so forth, hunter's fare:
And if you please, we 'll strike the stag ourselves
Shall fill our dishes with his well-fed flesh.

    Scroope. That is indeed the thing we all desire.

    Cob. My lords, and you shall have your choice
        with me.

    Cam. Nay, but the stag which we desire to strike,
Lives not in Cowling: if you will consent,
And go with us, we 'll bring you to a forest
Where runs a lusty herd; among the which
There is a stag superior to the rest,
A stately beast, that, when his fellows run,
He leads the race, and beats the sullen earth,
As though he scorn'd it with his trampling hoofs;
Aloft he bears his head, and with his breast,
Like a huge bulwark, counter-checks the wind:
And, when he standeth still, he stretcheth forth

His proud ambitious neck, as if he meant
To wound the firmament with forked horns.

Cob. 'Tis pity such a goodly beast should die.

Cam. Not so, sir John; for he is tyrannous,
And gores the other deer, and will not keep
Within the limits are appointed him.
Of late he's broke into a several,[28]
Which doth belong to me, and there he spoils
Both corn and pasture.   Two of his wild race,
Alike for stealth and covetous encroaching,
Already are remov'd; if he were dead,
I should not only be secure from hurt,
But with his body make a royal feast.

Scroope. How say you then? will you first hunt
with us?

Cob. 'Faith, lords, I like the pastime: where's
the place?

Cam. Peruse this writing, it will show you all,
And what occasion we have for the sport.

[Presents a paper.

Cob. [*Reads.*] Call ye this hunting, my lords?
Is this the stag
You fain would chase, Harry, our most dread king?
So we may make a banquet for the devil;
And, in the stead of wholesome meat, prepare
A dish of poison to confound ourselves.

Cam. Why so, lord Cobham?   See you not our
claim?
And how imperiously he holds the crown?

Scroope. Besides, you know yourself is in dis-
grace,
Held as a recreant, and pursu'd to death.
This will defend you from your enemies,
And stablish your religion through the land.

Cob. Notorious treason! yet I will conceal
My secret thoughts, to sound the depth of it. [*Aside.*
My lord of Cambridge, I do see your claim,
And what good may redound unto the land,
By prosecuting of this enterprise.
But where are men? where's power and furniture
To order such an action?   We are weak;
Harry, you know, is a mighty potentate.

Cam. Tut, we are strong enough; you are be-
lov'd,
And many will be glad to follow you;
We are the like, and some will follow us:
Nay, there is hope from France: here's an am-
bassador
That promiseth both men and money too.
The commons likewise, as we hear, pretend
A sudden tumult; we will join with them.

Cob. Some likelihood, I must confess, to speed:
But how shall I believe this in plain truth?

You are, my lords, such men as live in court,
And have been highly favour'd of the king,
Especially lord Scroope, whom oftentimes
He maketh choice of for his bed-fellow.
And you, lord Grey, are of his privy-council:
Is not this a train laid to entrap my life?

Cam. Then perish may my soul! What, think
you so?

Scroope. We'll swear to you.

Grey. Or take the sacrament.

Cob. Nay, you are noblemen, and I imagine,
As you are honourable by birth, and blood,
So you will be in heart, in thought, in word.
I crave no other testimony but this:
That you would all subscribe, and set your hands
Unto this writing which you gave to me.

Cam. With all our hearts: Who hath any pen
and ink?

Scroope. My pocket should have one: O, here
it is.

Cam. Give it me, lord Scroope.   There is my
name.

Scroope. And there is my name.

Grey. And mine.

Cob. Sir, let me crave
That you would likewise write your name with
theirs,
For confirmation of your master's words,
The king of France.

Char. That will I, noble lord.

Cob. So, now this action is well knit together,
And I am for you: where's our meeting, lords?

Cam. Here, if you please, the tenth of July next.

Cob. In Kent? agreed.   Now let us in to supper,
I hope your honours will not away to-night.

Cam. Yes, presently, for I have far to ride,
About soliciting of other friends.

Scroope. And we would not be absent from the
court,
Lest thereby grow suspicion in the king.

Cob. Yet taste a cup of wine before ye go.

Cam. Not now, my lord, we thank you; so farewell.

[Exeunt SCROOPE, GREY, CAM., *and* CHAR.

Cob. Farewell, my noble lords.—-My noble lords!
My noble villains, base conspirators!
How can they look his highness in the face,
Whom they so closely study to betray?
But I'll not sleep until I make it known:
This head shall not be burthen'd with such thoughts,
Nor in this heart will I conceal a deed
Of such impiety against my king.
Madam, how now?

Enter Lady Cobham, Lord Powis, Lady Powis, *and* Harpool.

L. Cob. You're welcome home, my lord:
Why seem you so unquiet in your looks?
What hath befall'n you that disturbs your mind?

L. Pow. Bad news, I am afraid, touching my
 husband.

Cob. Madam, not so; there is your husband's
 pardon:
Long may ye live, each joy unto the other.

L. Pow. So great a kindness, as I know not how
To make reply;—my sense is quite confounded.

Cob. Let that alone; and, madam, stay me not,
For I must back unto the court again,
With all the speed I can: Harpool, my horse.

L. Cob. So soon my lord? what, will you ride
 all night?

Cob. All night or day; it must be so, sweet wife,
Urge me not why, or what my business is,
But get you in.—Lord Powis, bear with me;
And, madam, think your welcome ne'er the worse;
My house is at your use.   Harpool, away.

Har. Shall I attend your lordship to the court?

Cob. Yea, sir; your gelding mount you presently.   [*Exit* Cob.

L. Cob. I prithee, Harpool, look unto thy lord;
I do not like this sudden posting back. [*Exit* Har.

Pow. Some earnest business is a-foot belike;
Whate'er it be, pray God be his good guide.

L. Pow. Amen, that hath so highly us bestead.

L. Cob. Come, madam, and my lord, we'll hope
 the best;
You shall not into Wales till he return.

Pow. Though great occasion be we should depart,
Yet, madam, we will stay to be resolv'd
Of this unlook'd-for doubtful accident.   [*Exeunt.*

SCENE II.—*A Road near* Highgate.

Enter Murley *and his* Followers.

Mur. Come, my hearts of flint, modestly, decently, soberly, and handsomely; no man afore his
leader: follow your master, your captain, your
knight that shall be, for the honour of meal-men,
millers, and malt-men. Dun is the mouse.[29] Dick
and Tom, for the credit of Dunstable ding down
the enemy to-morrow. Ye shall not come into
the field like beggars. Where be Leonard and
Lawrence, my two loaders? Lord have mercy
upon us, what a world is this! I would give a
couple of shillings for a dozen of good feathers for
you, and forty pence for as many scarfs to set you

out withal. Frost and snow, a man has no heart
to fight till he be brave.

Dick. Master, we are no babes, our town foot-
balls can bear witness: this little 'parel we have,
shall off, and we'll fight naked before we run away.

Tom. Nay, I'm of Lawrence' mind for that, for
he means to leave his life behind him; he and
Leonard, your two loaders, are making their wills,
because they have wives; and we bachelors bid our
friends scramble for our goods, if we die. But,
master, pray ye let me ride upon Cut.

Mur. Meal and salt, wheat and malt, fire and
tow, frost and snow; why Tom thou shalt. Let
me see, here are you: William and George are
with my cart, and Robin and Hodge holding my
own two horses; proper men, handsome men, tall
men, true men.

Dick. But master, master; methinks you are
mad to hazard your own person, and a cart-load of
money too.

Tom. Yea, and master, there's a worse matter
in 't; if it be, as I heard say, we go to fight against
all the learned bishops, that should give us their
blessing: and if they curse us, we shall speed ne'er
the better.

Dick. Nay by 'r lady, some say the king takes
their part; and, master, dare you fight against the
king?

Mur. Fye, paltry, paltry, in and out, to and fro
upon occasion; if the king be so unwise to come
there, we'll fight with him too.

Tom. What, if you should kill the king?

Mur. Then we'll make another.

Dick. Is that all? do you not speak treason?

Mur. And if we do, who dare trip us? we come
to fight for our conscience, and for honour. Little
know you what is in my bosom; look here, mad
knaves, a pair of gilt spurs.

Tom. A pair of golden spurs? Why do you not
put them on your heels? Your bosom's no place
for spurs.

Mur. Be 't more or less upon occason, Lord
have mercy upon us. Tom thou 'rt a fool, and
thou speak'st treason to knighthood. Dare any
wear gold or silver spurs, till he be a knight? No,
I shall be knighted to-morrow, and then they shall
on. Sirs, was it ever read in the church-book of
Dunstable, that ever malt-man was made knight?

Tom. No, but you are more: you are meal-man,
malt-man, miller, corn-master, and all.

Dick. Yea, and half a brewer too, and the devil
and all for wealth: you bring more money with
you than all the rest.

Mur. The more's my honour; I shall be a knight to-morrow. Let me 'spose my men; Tom upon Cut, Dick upon Hob, Hodge upon Ball, Ralph upon Sorrel, and Robin upon the fore-horse.

Enter ACTON, BOURN, *and* BEVERLEY.

Tom. Stand; who comes there?

Act. All friends, good fellow.

Mur. Friends and fellows indeed, sir Roger.

Act. Why, thus you show yourself a gentle-
man,
To keep your day, and come so well prepar'd.
Your cart stands yonder guarded by your men,
Who tell me it is loaden well with coin.
What sum is there?

Mur. Ten thousand pound, sir Roger; and modestly, decently, soberly, and handsomely, see what
I have here against I be knighted.

Act. Gilt spurs? 'Tis well.

Mur. Where's our army, sir?

Act. Dispers'd in sundry villages about;
Some here with us in Highgate, some at Finch-
ley,
Tot'nam, Enfield, Edmonton, Newington,
Islington, Hogsdon, Pancras, Kensington;
Some nearer Thames, Ratcliff, Blackwall, and
Bow:
But our chief strength must be the Londoners,
Which, ere the sun to-morrow shine,[30]
Will be near fifty thousand in the field.

Mur. Marry, God dild ye, dainty my dear; but
upon occasion, sir Roger Acton, doth not the king
know of it, and gather his power against us?

Act. No, he's secure at Eltham.

Mur. What do the clergy?

Act. They fear extremely, yet prepare no force.

Mur. In and out, to and fro, bully my boykin,
we shall carry the world afore us. I vow, by my
worship, when I am knighted, we'll take the king
napping, if he stand on their part.

Act. This night we few in Highgate will repose;
With the first cock we'll rise and arm ourselves,
To be in Ficket field by break of day,
And there expect our general, sir John Oldcastle.

Mur. What if he comes not?

Bourn. Yet our action stands;
Sir Roger Acton may supply his place.

Mur. True, master Bourn; but who shall make
me knight?

Bev. He that hath power to be our general.

Act. Talk not of trifles; come let us away;
Our friends of London long till it be day.

[*Exeunt.*

SCENE III.—*A High-road in Kent.*

Enter SIR JOHN *and* DOLL.

Doll. By my troth, thou art as jealous a man as
lives.

Sir John. Canst thou blame me, Doll? thou art
my lands, my goods, my jewels, my wealth, my
purse: none walks within forty miles of London,
but a' plies thee as truly as the parish does the
poor man's box.

Doll. I am as true to thee as the stone is in the
wall; and thou know'st well enough I was in as
good doing when I came to thee, as any wench
need to be; and therefore thou hast tried me, that
thou hast: and I will not be kept as I have been,
that I will not.

Sir John. Doll, if this blade hold, there's not a
pedlar walks with a pack, but thou shalt as boldly
choose of his wares, as with thy ready money in a
merchant's shop: we'll have as good silver as the
king coins any.

Doll. What, is all the gold spent you took the
last day from the courtier?

Sir John. 'Tis gone, Doll, 'tis flown; merrily
come, merrily gone. He comes a horseback that
must pay for all; we'll have as good meat as
money can get, and as good gowns as can be bought
for gold: be merry wench, the malt-man comes on
Monday.

Doll. You might have left me at Cobham, until
you had been better provided for.

Sir John. No, sweet Doll, no; I like not that.
Yon old ruffian is not for the priest; I do not like
a new clerk should come in the old belfry.

Doll. Thou art a mad priest, i'faith.

Sir John. Come Doll, I'll see thee safe at some
alehouse here at Cray; and the next sheep that
comes shall leave behind his fleece.   [*Exeunt.*

SCENE IV.—Blackheath.

Enter KING HENRY, *disguised*, SUFFOLK, *and*
BUTLER.

K. Henry. My lord of Suffolk, post away for
life,
And let our forces of such horse and foot
As can be gathered up by any means,
Make speedy rendezvous in Tothill-fields.
It must be done this evening, my lord;
This night the rebels mean to draw to head
Near Islington; which if your speed prevent not,
If once they should unite their several forces,

Their power is almost thought invincible.
Away, my lord, I will be with you soon.

Suf. I go, my sovereign, with all happy speed.

K. Henry. Make haste, my lord of Suffolk, as
you love us. [*Exit* Suf.

Butler, post you to London with all speed:
Command the mayor and sheriffs, on their alle-
giance.
The city gates be presently shut up,
And guarded with a strong sufficient watch;
And not a man be suffered to pass
Without a special warrant from ourself.
Command the postern by the Tower be kept,
And proclamation, on the pain of death,
That not a citizen stir from his doors,
Except such as the mayor and shrives shall choose
For their own guard, and safety of their persons.
Butler away, have care unto my charge.

But. I go, my sovereign.

K. Henry. Butler.

But. My lord.

K. Henry. Go down by Greenwich, and command a boat
At the Friars-Bridge attend my coming down.

But. I will, my lord. [*Exit* But.

K. Henry. It's time, I think, to look unto re-
bellion,
When Acton doth expect unto his aid
No less than fifty thousand Londoners.
Well, I'll to Westminster in this disguise,
To hear what news is stirring in these brawls

Enter Sir John *and* Doll.

Sir John. Stand true man, says a thief.

K. Henry. Stand thief, says a true man: how if
a thief?

Sir John. Stand thief too.

K. Henry. Then thief or true man, I must stand,
I see. Howsoever the world wags, the trade of
thieving yet will never down. What art thou?

Sir John. A good fellow.

K. Henry. So I am too; I see thou dost know me.

Sir John. If thou be a good fellow, play the good
fellow's part; deliver thy purse without more ado.

K. Henry. I have no money.

Sir John. I must make you find some before we
part. If you have no money, you shall have ware;
as many sound blows as your skin can carry.

K. Henry. Is that the plain truth?

Sir John. Sirrah, no more ado; come, come, give
me the money you have. Dispatch, I cannot stand
all day.

K. Henry. Well, if thou needs will have it, there

it is. Just the proverb, one thief robs another.
Where the devil are all my old thieves? Falstaff,
that villain is so fat, he cannot get on his horse;[31]
but methinks Poins and Peto should be stirring
hereabouts.

Sir John. How much is there on 't, o' thy word?

K. Henry. A hundred pound in angels, on my
word.
The time has been I would have done as much
For thee, if thou hadst past this way, as I
Have now.

Sir John. Sirrah, what art thou? thou seem'st a
gentleman?

K. Henry. I am no less; yet a poor one now,
for thou hast all my money.

Sir John. From whence cam'st thou?

K. Henry. From the court at Eltham.

Sir John. Art thou one of the king's servants?

K. Henry. Yes, that I am, and one of his chamber.

Sir John. I am glad thou'rt no worse; thou
may'st the better spare thy money: And think
you thou might'st get a poor thief his pardon, if he
should have need?

K. Henry. Yes, that I can.

Sir John. Wilt thou do so much for me, when I
shall have occasion?

K. Henry. Yes 'faith will I, so it be for no
murder.

Sir John. Nay, I am a pitiful thief;[32] all the hurt
I do a man, I take but his purse: I'll kill no man.

K. Henry. Then, on my word I'll do 't.

Sir John. Give me thy hand on the same.

K. Henry. There 'tis.

Sir John. Methinks the king should be good to
thieves, because he has been a thief himself, although I think now he be turned a true man.

K. Henry. 'Faith, I have heard indeed he has
had an ill name that way in his youth; but how
canst thou tell that he has been a thief?

S. John. How? because he once robb'd me before I fell to the trade myself, when that foul villanous guts, that led him to all that roguery, was in
his company there, that Falstaff.

K. Henry. Well, if he did rob thee then, thou
art but even with him now, I'll be sworn. [*Aside.*]
Thou knowest not the king now, I think, if thou
sawest him?

Sir John. Not I, i'faith.

K. Henry. So it should seem. [*Aside.*

Sir John. Well, if old king Harry had liv'd, this
king that is now, had made thieving the best trade
in England.

K. Henry. Why so?

Sir John. Because he was the chief warden of our company. It's pity that e'er he should have been a king, he was so brave a thief. But sirrah, wilt remember my pardon if need be?

K. Henry. Yes, 'faith will I.

Sir John. Wilt thou? well then, because thou shalt go safe, for thou may'st hap (being so early) be met with again before thou come to Southwark, if any man, when he should bid thee good morrow, bid thee stand, say thou but "Sir John," and they will let thee pass.

K. Henry. Is that the word? then let me alone.

Sir John. Nay, sirrah, because I think indeed I shall have some occasion to use thee, and as thou com'st oft this way, I may light on thee another time, not knowing thee, here I'll break this angel: take thou half of it: this is a token betwixt thee and me.

K. Henry. God-a-mercy; farewell. [*Exit.*

Sir John. O my fine golden slaves! here's for thee, wench, i'faith. Now, Doll, we will revel in our bever;[33] this is a tithe pig of my vicarage. God-a-mercy, neighbour Shooter's-Hill, you ha' paid your tithe honestly. Well, I hear there is a company of rebels up against the king, got together in Ficket-field near Holborn; and, as it is thought here in Kent, the king will be there to-night in his own person. Well, I'll to the king's camp, and it shall go hard, if there be any doings, but I'll make some good boot among them.[34]

[*Exeunt* SIR JOHN *and* DOLL.

ACT IV.

SCENE I.—*A Field near* London. *King Henry's Camp.*

Enter KING HENRY *disguised,* SUFFOLK, HUNTINGTON, *and* Attendants *with Torches.*

K. Henry. My lords of Suffolk and of Huntington,
Who scouts it now? or who stand sentinels?
What men of worth, what lords, do walk the round?

Suf. May it please your highness—

K. Henry. Peace, no more of that:
The king's asleep; wake not his majesty
With terms, nor titles; he's at rest in bed.
Kings do not use to watch themselves; they sleep,
And let rebellion and conspiracy
Revel and havoc in the commonwealth.
Is London look'd unto?

Hunt. It is, my lord;
Your noble uncle Exeter is there,
Your brother Gloucester, and my lord of Warwick;
Who, with the mayor and the aldermen,
Do guard the gates, and keep good rule within.
The earl of Cambridge and sir Thomas Grey
Do walk the round; lord Scroope and Butler scout:
So, though it please your majesty to jest,
Were you in bed, well might you take your rest.

K. Henry. I thank ye lords; but you do know of old,
That I have been a perfect night-walker.
London, you say, is safely look'd unto,
(Alas, poor rebels, there your aid must fail;)
And the lord Cobham, sir John Oldcastle,
Quiet in Kent. Acton, you are deceiv'd;
Reckon again, you count without your host;
To-morrow you shall give account to us:
Till when, my friends, this long cold winter's night
How can we spend? King Harry is asleep,
And all his lords; these garments tell us so;
All friends at foot-ball, fellows all in field,
Harry, and Dick, and George. Bring us a drum,
Give us square dice; we'll keep this court of guard
For all good fellows' companies that come.
Where's that mad priest ye told me was in arms,
To fight as well as pray, if need requir'd?

Suf. He's in the camp, and if he knew of this,
I undertake he would not be long hence.

K. Henry. Trip Dick, trip George.

Hunt. I must have the dice: what do we play at?

Suf. Passage, if you please.[35]

Hunt. Set round then: so; at all.

K. Henry. George, you are out;
Give me the dice, I pass for twenty pound:
Here's to our lucky passage into France.

Hunt. Harry, you pass indeed, for you sweep all.

Suf. A sign king Harry shall sweep all in France.

Enter SIR JOHN.

Sir John. Edge ye, good fellows;[36] take a fresh gamester in.

K. Henry. Master parson, we play nothing but gold.

Sir John. And, fellow, I tell thee that the priest hath gold. Gold! what? ye are but beggarly soldiers to me; I think I have more gold than all you three.

Hunt. It may be so; but we believe it not.

K. Henry. Set, priest, set: I pass for all that gold.

Sir John. You pass indeed.

K. Henry. Priest, hast any more?

Sir John. More! what a question's that?
I tell thee I have more than all you three.
At these ten angels.

K. Henry. I wonder how thou com'st by all
    this gold.
How many benefices hast thou, priest?

Sir John. 'Faith, but one. Dost wonder how I come by gold? I wonder rather how poor soldiers should have gold. For I'll tell thee, good fellow; we have every day tithes, offerings, christenings, weddings, burials; and you poor snakes come seldom to a booty. I'll speak a proud word; I have but one parsonage, Wrotham; 'tis better than the bishoprick of Rochester: there's ne'er a hill, heath nor down, in all Kent, but 'tis in my parsh;—Barham-down, Cobham-down, Gads-hill, Wrotham-hill, Blackheath, Cocks-heath, Birchen wood, all pay me tithe. Gold quoath-a? ye pass not for that.

Suf. Harry, you are out: now parson, shake the dice.

Sir John. Set, set, I'll cover ye;—at all:—a plague on't, I am out. The devil, and dice, and a wench, who will trust them?

Suf. Say'st thou so, priest? set fair; at all for once.

K. Henry. Out, sir; pay all.

Sir John. Sir, pay me angel gold:
I'll none of your crack'd French crowns nor pistolets;
Pay me fair angel gold, as I pay you.

K. Henry. No crack'd French crowns! I hope to see more crack'd French crowns ere long.

Sir John. Thou mean'st of Frenchmen's crowns, when the king's in France.

Hun. Set round; at all.

Sir John. Pay all. This is some luck.

K. Henry. Give me the dice; 'tis I must shred
    the priest: [37]
At all, sir John.

Sir John. The devil and all is yours. At that.
'Sdeath, what casting's this?

Suf. Well thrown, Harry, i'faith.

K. Henry. I'll cast better yet.

Sir John. Then I'll be hang'd. Sirrah, hast thou not given thy soul to the devil for casting?

K. Henry. I pass for all.

Sir John. Thou passest all that e'er I play'd withal. Sirrah, dost thou not cog, nor foist, nor slur?

K. Henry. Set, parson, set; the dice die in my
    hand.
When, parson, when? [38] what, can you find no
    more?
Already dry? was't you bragg'd of your store?

Sir John. All's gone but that.

Hun. What? half a broken angel.

Sir John. Why, sir, 'tis gold.

K. Henry. Yea, and I'll cover it.

Sir John. The devil give ye good on't! I am
    blind:
You have blown me up!

K. Henry. Nay, tarry, priest; you shall not leave
    us yet:
Do not these pieces fit each other well?

Sir John. What if they do?

K. Henry. Thereby begins a tale,
There was a thief, in face much like sir John,
(But 'twas not he—that thief was all in green,)
Met me, last day, on Black-heath near the Park;
With him a woman. I was all alone
And weaponless; my boy had all my tools,
And was before, providing me a boat.
Short tale to make, sir John—the thief I mean—
Took a just hundred pound in gold from me.
I storm'd at it, and swore to be reveng'd,
If e'er we met. He, like a lusty thief,
Brake with his teeth this angel just in two,
To be a token at our meeting next;
Provided I should charge no officer
To apprehend him, but at weapon's point
Recover that and what he had beside.
Well met, sir John; betake you to your tools,
By torch-light; for, master parson you are he
That had my gold.

Sir John. 'Zounds I won it in play, in fair square play, of the keeper of Eltham-park; and that I will maintain with this poor whynniard. Be you two honest men, to stand and look upon us, and let us alone, and take neither part.

K. Henry. Agreed; I charge ye do not budge a
    foot:
Sir John, have at ye.

Sir John. Soldier, 'ware your sconce.

    [*As they are preparing to engage,* BUTLER
    enters, and draws his sword to part them.

But. Hold, villain, hold; my lords, what do ye
    mean,
To see a traitor draw against the king?

Sir John. The king? God's will, I am in a proper pickle.

K. Henry. Butler, what news? why dost thou trouble us?

But. Please your majesty, it is break of day;
And as I scouted near to Islington,
The grey-ey'd morning gave me glimmering
Of armed men coming down Highgate-hill,
Who by their course are coasting hitherward.

K. Henry. Let us withdraw, my lords; prepare our troops
To charge the rebels, if there be such cause.
For this lewd priest, this devilish hypocrite,
That is a thief, a gamester, and what not,
Let him be hang'd up for example sake.

Sir John. Not so, my gracious sovereign. I confess I am a frail man, flesh and blood as others are; but set my imperfections aside, you have not a taller man, nor a truer subject to the crown and state, than sir John of Wrotham is.

K. Henry. Will a true subject rob his king?

Sir John. Alas, 'twas ignorance and want, my gracious liege.

K. Henry. 'Twas want of grace. Why, you should be as salt
To season others with good document;
Your lives, as lamps to give the people light;
As shepherds, not as wolves to spoil the flock:
Go hang him, Butler. Didst thou not rob me?

Sir John. I must confess I saw some of your gold; but, my dread lord, I am in no humour for death. God wills that sinners live; do not you cause me to die. Once in their lives the best may go astray; and if the world say true, yourself, my liege, have been a thief.

K. Henry. I confess I have;
But I repent and have reclaim'd myself.

Sir John. So will I do, if you will give me time.

K. Henry. Wilt thou? my lords, will you be his sureties?

Hunt. That when he robs again he shall be hang'd.

Sir John. I ask no more.

K. Henry. And we will grant thee that.
Live and repent, and prove an honest man;
Which when I hear, and safe return from France,
I'll give thee living. Till when, take thy gold,
But spend it better than at cards, or wine;
For better virtues fit that coat of thine.

Sir John. Vivat rex, et currat lex. My liege, if ye have cause of battle, ye shall see sir John bestir himself in your quarrel.

[*Exeunt.*

SCENE II.—*A field of Battle near* London.

Alarum. Enter KING HENRY, SUFFOLK, HUNTINGTON, *and* SIR JOHN *bringing forth* ACTON, BEVERLEY, *and* MURLEY, *prisoners.*

K. Henry. Bring in those traitors, whose aspiring minds
Thought to have triumph'd in our overthrow:
But now ye see, base villains, what success
Attends ill actions wrongfully attempted.
Sir Roger Acton, thou retain'st the name
Of knight, and shouldst be more discreetly temper'd
Than join with peasants; gentry is divine,
But thou hast made it more than popular.[39]

Act. Pardon, my lord, my conscience urg'd me to it.

K. Henry. Thy conscience! then thy conscience is corrupt;
For in thy conscience thou art bound to us,
And in thy conscience thou shouldst love thy country:
Else what's the difference 'twixt a Christian,
And the uncivil manners of the Turk?

Bev. We meant no hurt unto your majesty,
But reformation of religion.

K. Henry. Reform religion? was it that you sought?
I pray, who gave you that authority?
Belike then we do hold the sceptre up,
And sit within the throne but for a cipher.
Time was, good subjects would make known their grief,
And pray amendment, not enforce the same,
Unless their king were tyrant; which I hope
You cannot justly say that Harry is.
What is that other?

Suf. A malt-man, my lord,
And dwelling in Dunstable, as he says.

K. Henry. Sirrah, what made you leave your barley-broth,
To come in armour thus against your king?

Mur. Fie, paltry, paltry, to and fro, in and out upon occasion, what a world is this! Knighthood, my liege, 'twas knighthood brought me hither: they told me I had wealth enough to make my wife a lady.

K. Henry. And so you brought those horses which we saw
Trapp'd all in costly furniture; and meant
To wear these spurs when you were knighted once.

Mur. In and out upon occasion, I did.

K. Henry. In and out upon occasion, therefore

You shall be hang'd, and in the stead of wearing
These spurs upon your heels, about your neck
They shall bewray your folly to the world.

Sir John. In and out upon occasion, that goes hard.

Mur. Fie, paltry, paltry, to and fro. Good my
liege, a pardon; I am sorry for my fault.

K. Henry. That comes too late. But tell me,
     went there none
Beside sir Roger Acton, upon whom
You did depend to be your governor?

Mur. None, my good lord, but sir John Old-
     castle.

K. Henry. Bears he a part in this conspiracy?

Act. We look'd, my lord, that he would meet us
     here.

K. Henry. But did he promise you that he
     would come?

Act. Such letters we received forth of Kent.

Enter the BISHOP OF ROCHESTER.

Roch. Where is my lord the king? Health to
     your grace.
Examining, my lord, some of these rebels,
It is a general voice among them all,
That they had never come into this place,
But to have met their valiant general,
The good lord Cobham, as they title him;
Whereby, my lord, your grace may now perceive,
His treason is apparent, which before
He sought to colour by his flattery.

K. Henry. Now, by my royalty I would have
     sworn,
But for his conscience, which I bear withal,
There had not liv'd a more true-hearted subject.

Roch. It is but counterfeit, my gracious lord;
And therefore may it please your majesty
To set your hand unto this precept here,
By which we'll cause him forthwith to appear,
And answer this by order of the law.

K. Henry. Not only that, but take commission
To search, attach, imprison, and condemn
This most notorious traitor as you please.

Roch. It shall be done, my lord, without delay.
So, now I hold, lord Cobham, in my hand,
That which shall finish thy disdained life. [*Aside.*

K. Henry. I think the iron age begins but now,
Which learned poets have so often taught;
Wherein there is no credit to be given
To either words, or looks, or solemn oaths:
For if there were, how often hath he sworn,
How gently tun'd the music of his tongue!
And with what amiable face beheld he me,
When all, God knows, was but hypocrisy!

Enter COBHAM.

Cob. Long life and prosperous reign unto my lord.

K. Henry. Ah villain! canst thou wish prosperity,
Whose heart includeth nought but treachery?
I do arrest thee here myself, false knight,
Of treason capital against the state.

Cob. Of treason, mighty prince? your grace
     mistakes;
I hope it is but in the way of mirth.

K. Henry. Thy neck shall feel it is in earnest
     shortly.
Dar'st thou intrude into our presence, knowing
How heinously thou hast offended us?
But this is thy accustomed deceit;
Now thou perceiv'st thy purpose is in vain,
With some excuse or other thou wilt come
To clear thyself of this rebellion.

Cob. Rebellion! good my lord, I know of none.

K. Henry. If you deny it, here is evidence.
See you these men? you never counselled,
Nor offer'd them assistance in their wars?

Cob. Speak, sirs, not one but all; I crave no
     favour;
Have ever I been conversant with you,
Or written letters to encourage you?
Or kindled but the least or smallest part
Of this your late unnatural rebellion?
Speak, for I dare the uttermost you can.

Mur. In and out upon occasion, I know you not.

K. Henry. No! didst thou not say, that Sir John
     Oldcastle
Was one with whom you purpos'd to have met?

Mur. True, I did say so; but in what respect?
Because I heard it was reported so.

K. Henry. Was there no other argument but
     that?

Act. To clear my conscience ere I die my lord,
I must confess we have no other ground
But only rumour, to accuse this lord;
Which now I see was merely fabulous.

K. Henry. The more pernicious you to taint him
     then,
Whom you know was not faulty, yea or no.

Cob. Let this, my lord, which I present your
     grace,
Speak for my loyalty; read these articles,
And then give sentence of my life or death.

K. Henry. Earl Cambridge, Scroope, and Grey,
     corrupted
With bribes from Charles of France, either to win
My crown from me, or secretly contrive
My death by treason! Is it possible?

Cob. There is the platform, and their hands, my lord,
Each severally subscribed to the same.

K. Henry. Oh never-heard-of, base ingratitude!
Even those I hug within my bosom most,
Are readiest evermore to sting my heart.
Pardon me, Cobham, I have done thee wrong;
Hereafter I will live to make amends.
Is then their time of meeting so near hand?
We'll meet with them, but little for their ease,
If God permit. Go take these rebels hence,
Let them have martial law: but as for thee,
Friend to thy king and country, still be free.

                   [*Exeunt* K. HENRY *and* COB.

Mur. Be it more or less, what a world is this?
Would I had continued still of the order of knaves,
And ne'er sought knighthood, since it costs so dear:
Sir Roger, I may thank you for all.

Act. Now 'tis too late to have it remedied,
I pr'ythee, Murley, do not urge me with it.

Hunt. Will you away, and make no more to do?

Mur. Fie, paltry, paltry, to and fro, as occasion
serves:
If you be so hasty, take my place.

Hunt. No, good sir knight, e'en take it yourself.

Mur. I could be glad to give my betters place.

                           [*Exeunt.*

SCENE III.—Kent. *Court before* Lord Cobham's
house.

Enter the BISHOP OF ROCHESTER, LORD WARDEN
OF THE CINQUE PORTS, CROMER, LADY COBHAM,
and Attendants.

Roch. I tell ye, lady, 'tis not possible
But you should know where he conveys himself;
And you have hid him in some secret place.

L. Cob. My lord, believe me, as I have a soul,
I know not where my lord my husband is.

Roch. Go to, go to; you are an heretic,
And will be forc'd by torture to confess,
If fair means will not serve to make you tell.

L. Cob. My husband is a noble gentleman,
And need not hide himself for any fact
That e'er I heard of; therefore wrong him not.

Roch. Your husband is a dangerous schismatic,
Traitor to God, the king, and commonwealth;
And therefore, master Cromer, shrieve of Kent,
I charge you take her to your custody,
And seize the goods of sir John Oldcastle,
To the king's use: let her go in no more,
To fetch so much as her apparel out:
There is your warrant from his majesty.

L. War. Good my lord bishop, pacify your wrath
Against the lady.

Roch. Then let her confess
Where Oldcastle her husband is conceal'd.

L. War. I dare engage mine honour and my life,
Poor gentlewoman, she is ignorant
And innocent of all his practices,
If any evil by him be practised.

Roch. If, my lord warden? Nay, then I charge
you,
That all cinque-ports, whereof you are chief,
Be laid forthwith;[40] that he escapes us not.
Show him his highness' warrant, master sheriff.

L. War. I am sorry for the noble gentleman.

Roch. Peace, he comes here; now do your office.

Enter COBHAM *and* HARPOOL.

Cob. Harpool, what business have we here in
hand?
What makes the bishop and the sheriff here?
I fear my coming home is dangerous;
I would I had not made such haste to Cobham.

Har. Be of good cheer, my lord: if they be foes,
we'll scramble shrewdly with them; if they be
friends, they are welcome.

Crom. Sir John Oldcastle, lord Cobham, in the
king's name, I arrest you of high treason.

Cob. Treason, master Cromer!

Har. Treason, master sheriff! what treason?

Cob. Harpool, I charge thee stir not, but be
quiet.
Do you arrest me of treason, master sheriff?

Roch. Yea, of high treason, traitor, heretic.

Cob. Defiance in his face that calls me so:
I am as true a loyal gentleman
Unto his highness, as my proudest enemy.
The king shall witness my late faithful service,
For safety of his sacred majesty.

Roch. What thou art, the king's hand shall tes-
tify:
Show him, lord Warden.

Cob. Jesu defend me!
Is't possible your cunning could so temper
The princely disposition of his mind,
To sign the damage of a loyal subject?
Well, the best is, it bears an antedate,
Procured by my absence and your malice.
But I, since that, have show'd myself as true
As any churchman that dare challenge me.
Let me be brought before his majesty;
If he acquit me not, then do your worst.

Roch. We are not bound to do kind offices
For any traitor, schismatic, nor heretic.

The king's hand is our warrant for our work,
Who is departed on his way for France,
And at Southampton doth repose this night.

Har. O that thou and I were within twenty
miles of it, on Salisbury plain! I would lose my
head if thou brought'st thy head hither again.

                                         [*Aside.*

Cob. My lord warden of the cinque-ports, and
lord of Rochester, ye are joint commissioners : favour me so much, on my expense, to bring me to
the king.

Roch. What, to Southampton ?

Cob. Thither, my good lord :
And if he do not clear me of all guilt,
And all suspicion of conspiracy,
Pawning his princely warrant for my truth,
I ask no favour, but extremest torture.
Bring me, or send me to him, good my lord ;
Good my lord warden, master shrieve, entreat.

                         [*They both entreat for him.*

Come hither, lady ;—nay sweet wife, forbear
To heap one sorrow on another's neck.
'Tis grief enough falsely to be accused,
And not permitted to acquit myself ;
Do not thou, with thy kind respective tears,
Torment thy husband's heart, that bleeds for thee,
But be of comfort. God hath help in store
For those that put assured trust in him.
Dear wife, if they commit me to the Tower,
Come up to London, to your sister's house ;
That, being near me, you may comfort me.
One solace find I settled in my soul,
That I am free from treason's very thought.
Only my conscience for the gospel's sake
Is cause of all the troubles I sustain.

L. Cob. O my dear lord, what shall betide of us?
You to the Tower, and I turn'd out of doors ;
Our substance seized unto his highness' use,
Even to the garments 'longing to our backs?

Har. Patience, good madam, things at worst will
    mend ;
And if they do not, yet our lives may end.

Roch. Urge it no more ; for if an angel spake,
I swear by sweet Saint Peter's blessed keys,
First goes he to the Tower, then to the stake.

Crom. But, by your leave, this warrant doth not
    stretch
To imprison her.

Roch. No ; turn her out of doors,
Even as she is, and lead him to the Tower,
With guard enough, for fear of rescuing.

L. Cob. O God requite thee, thou blood-thirsty
    man !

Cob. May it not be, my lord of Rochester ?
Wherein have I incurred your hate so far,
That my appeal unto the king's deny'd ?

Roch. No hate of mine, but power of holy
    church,
Forbids all favour to false heretics.

Cob. Your private malice, more than public
    power,
Strikes most at me ; but with my life it ends.

Har. O that I had the bishop in that fear
That once I had his sumner by ourselves ! [*Aside.*

Crom. My lord, yet grant one suit unto us all ;
That this same ancient servingman may wait
Upon my lord his master, in the Tower.

Roch. This old iniquity, this heretic,
That, in contempt of our church discipline,
Compell'd my sumner to devour his process !
Old ruffian past-grace, upstart schismatic,
Had not the king pray'd us to pardon you,
You had fry'd for 't, you grizzled heretic.

Har. 'Sblood, my lord bishop, you wrong me ; I
am neither heretic nor puritan, but of the old
church. I 'll swear, drink ale, kiss a wench, go to
mass, eat fish all Lent, and fast Fridays with cakes
and wine, fruit and spicery ; shrive me of my old
sins afore Easter, and begin new before Whitsun-
tide.

Crom. A merry mad conceited knave, my lord.

Har. That knave was simply put upon the bishop.

Roch. Well, God forgive him, and I pardon him :
Let him attend his master in the Tower,
For I in charity wish his soul no hurt.

Cob. God bless my soul from such cold charity !

Roch. To the Tower with him ; and when my
    leisure serves,
I will examine him of articles.
Look, my lord warden, as you have in charge,
The shrieve perform his office.

War. Ay, my lord.

           [*Exeunt* WAR., CROM., *and* COB.

Enter from Lord Cobham's *House,* Sumner, *with
Books.*

Roch. What bring'st thou there ? what, books
    of heresy ?

Sum. Yea, my lord, here 's not a Latin book, no
not so much as our Lady's Psalter. Here 's the
" Bible," the " Testament," the " Psalms " in metre,
" The Sick Man's Salve," the " Treasure of Gladness," all English ; no not so much but the Almanack's English.

Roch. Away with them, to the fire with them,
    Clun :

Now fye upon these upstart heretics.
All English! burn them, burn them quickly,
    Clun.
    Har. But do not, Sumner, as you'll answer it;
for I have there English books, my lord, that I'll
not part withal for your bishopric; "Bevis of
Hampton," "Owleglass," "The Friar and the
Boy," "Elinour Rumming," "Robin Hood,"[41] and
other such godly stories; which if ye burn, by this
flesh I'll make you drink their ashes in Saint
Margaret's ale.[42]

        [*Exeunt* ROCH., L. COB., HAR., *and* SUM.

SCENE IV.—*The entrance of the Tower.*

Enter the BISHOP OF ROCHESTER, *attended.*

1st Ser. Is it your honour's pleasure we shall
    stay,
Or come back in the afternoon to fetch you?
    Roch. Now you have brought me here into the
        Tower,
You may go back unto the porter's lodge,
Where, if I have occasion to employ you,
I'll send some officer to call you to me.
Into the city go not, I command you:
Perhaps I may have present need to use you.
    2nd Serv. We will attend your honour here
        without.
    3rd Serv. Come, we may have a quart of wine
at the "Rose" at Barking, and come back an hour
before he'll go.
    1st Serv. We must hie us then.
    3rd Serv. Let's away.   [*Exeunt.*
    Roch. Ho, master lieutenant.

Enter LIEUTENANT OF THE TOWER.

    Lieu. Who calls there?
    Roch. A friend of yours.
    Lieu. My lord of Rochester! your honour's wel-
        come.
    Roch. Sir, here is my warrant from the council,
For conference with sir John Oldcastle,
Upon some matter of great consequence.
    Lieu. Ho, sir John.
    Har. [*Within.*] Who calls there?
    Lieu. Harpool, tell sir John, that my lord of
        Rochester
Comes from the council to confer with him.
I think you may as safe without suspicion
As any man in England, as I hear,
For it was you most labour'd his commitment.
    Roch. I did, sir,
And nothing do repent it, I assure you.

Enter LORD COBHAM *and* HARPOOL.

Master lieutenant, I pray you give us leave
I must confer here with sir John a little.
    Lieu. With all my heart, my lord. [*Exit* LIEU.
    Har. My lord, be rul'd
By me; take this occasion while 'tis offer'd,
And on my life your lordship will escape. [*Aside.*
    Cob. No more I say; peace, lest he should sus-
        pect it.
    Roch. Sir John, I am come to you from the lords
        o' the council,
To know if yet you do recant your errors.
    Cob. My lord of Rochester, on good advice,
I see my error; but yet understand me;
I mean not error in the faith I hold,
But error in submitting to your pleasure.
Therefore your lordship, without more to do,
Must be a means to help me to escape.
    Roch. What means, thou heretic?
Dar'st thou but lift thy hand against my calling?
    Cob. No, not to hurt you, for a thousand pound.
    Har. Nothing but to borrow your upper gar-
ments a little: not a word more; peace for waking
the children. There; put them on; dispatch, my
lord; the window that goes out into the leads is
sure enough: as for you, I'll bind you surely in the
inner room.

    [*Carries the* BISHOP *into the Tower, and returns.*
    Cob. This is well begun; God send us happy
        speed:
Hard shift, you see, men make in time of need.
                    [*Puts on the* Bishop's *cloak.*

Re-enter the Bishop of Rochester's *Servants.*

    1st Ser. I marvel that my lord should stay so
long.
    2nd Ser. He hath sent to seek us, I dare lay my
life.
    3rd Ser. We come in good time; see where he is
coming.
    Har. I beseech you, good my lord of Rochester,
Be favourable to my lord and master.
    Cob. The inner rooms be very hot and close;
I do not like this air here in the Tower.
    Har. His case is hard, my lord. [*Aside.*] You
shall scarcely get out of the Tower, but I'll down
upon them: in which time get you away. Hard
under Islington wait you my coming; I will bring
my lady ready with horses to get hence.
    Cob. Fellow, go back again unto thy lord,
And counsel him.
    Har. Nay, my good lord of Rochester, I'll bring

you to St. Alban's, through the woods, I warrant
you.

Cob. Villain, away.

Har. Nay, since I am past the Tower's liberty,
You part not so.   [*He draws.*

Cob. Clubs, clubs, clubs.

1st Ser. Murder, murder, murder.

2nd Ser. Down with him.

Har. Out you cowardly rogues.   [*Cob. escapes.*

Enter LIEUTENANT OF THE TOWER *and* Warders.

Lieu. Who is so bold to dare to draw a sword
So near unto the entrance of the Tower?

1st Ser. This ruffian, servant to sir John Oldcastle,
Was like to have slain my lord.

Lieu. Lay hold on him.

Har. Stand off, if you love your puddings.

Roch. [*Within.*] Help, help, help, master lieutenant, help.

Lieu. Who's that within? some treason in the
Tower,
Upon my life.   Look in, who's that which calls?
                    [*Exit one of the* Warders.

Re-enter Warder *and the* BISHOP OF ROCHESTER
bound.

Lieu. Without your cloak, my lord of Rochester?

Har. There, now I see it works; then let me
speed,
For now's the fittest time to scape away. [*Exit* HAR.

Lieu. Why do you look so ghastly and affrighted?

Roch. Oldcastle that traitor, and his man,
When you had left me to confer with him,
Took, bound, and stripp'd me, as you see I am,
And left me lying in his inner chamber,
And so departed.

1st Ser. And I——

Lieu. And you now say that the lord Cobham's
man
Did here set on you like to murder you.

1st Ser. And so he did.

Roch. It was upon his master then he did,
That in the brawl the traitor might escape.

Lieu. Where is this Harpool?

2nd Ser. Here he was even now.

Lieu. Where fled, can you tell?—They are both
escap'd.
Since it so happens that he is escap'd,
I am glad you are a witness of the same:
It might have else been laid unto my charge,
That I had been consenting to the fact.

Roch. Come:
Search shall be made for him with expedition.
The haven's laid that he shall not escape;
And hue and cry continue throughout England,
To find this damned, dangerous heretic.   [*Exeunt.*

----◆----

ACT V.

SCENE I.—*A Room in* Lord Cobham's *House in*
Kent.

Enter CAMBRIDGE, SCROOPE, *and* GREY.   *They sit
down at a Table;* KING HENRY, SUFFOLK, COB-
HAM, *and other* Lords, *listening at the door.*

Cam. In mine opinion, Scroope hath well advis'd;
Poison will be the only aptest mean,
And fittest for our purpose to dispatch him.

Grey. But yet there may be doubt in the de-
livery:
Harry is wise; and therefore, earl of Cambridge,
I judge that way not so convenient.

Scroope. What think ye then of this?   I am his
bedfellow,
And unsuspected nightly sleep with him.
What if I venture, in those silent hours
When sleep hath sealed up all mortal eyes,
To murder him in bed? how like ye that?

Cam. Herein consists no safety for yourself:
And you disclos'd, what shall become of us?
But this day, as ye know, he will aboard,
(The wind's so fair) and set away for France:
If, as he goes, or entering in the ship,
It might be done, then were it excellent.

Grey. Why, any of these: or, if you will, I'll
cause
A present sitting o' the council, wherein
I will pretend some matter of such weight
As needs must have his royal company;
And so dispatch him in his council-chamber.

Cam. Tush, yet I hear not anything to pur-
pose.
I wonder that lord Cobham stays so long;
His counsel in this case would much avail us.
                    [*The* KING *and his* Lords *advance.*

Scroope. What, shall we rise thus, and determine
nothing?

K. Henry. That were a shame indeed : no, sit
     again,
And you shall have my counsel in this case.
If you can find no way to kill the king,
Then you shall see how I can furnish you.
Scroope's way by poison was indifferent :
But yet, being bed-fellow to the king,
And unsuspected sleeping in his bosom,
In mine opinion that 's the likelier way :
For such false friends are able to do much,
And silent night is treason's fittest friend.
Now, Cambridge, in his setting hence for France,
Or by the way, or as he goes aboard,
To do the deed, that was indifferent too,
But somewhat doubtful.
Marry, lord Grey came very near the point,
To have the king at council, and there murder him,
As Cæsar was, among his dearest friends.
Tell me, oh tell me, you, bright honour's stains,
For which of all my kindnesses to you,
Are ye become thus traitors to your king,
And France must have the spoil of Harry's life ?
     All. Oh pardon us, dread lord.
     K. Henry. How ! pardon you ? that were a sin
     indeed.
Drag them to death, which justly they deserve :
And France shall dearly buy this villany,
So soon as we set footing on her breast.
God have the praise for our deliverance !
And next our thanks, lord Cobham, is to thee,
True perfect mirror of nobility.   [*Exeunt.*

SCENE II.—*A high Road near St. Albans.*

Enter SIR JOHN *and* DOLL.

Sir John. Come Doll, come, be merry, wench.
Farewell Kent ; we are not for thee. Be lusty my
lass ; come, for Lancashire : we must nip the bung
for these crowns.[43]

Doll. Why is all the gold spent already, that
you had the other day ?

Sir John. Gone, Doll, gone ; flown, spent, vanish'd.
The devil, drink, and dice, has devoured all.

Doll. You might have left me in Kent, till you
had been better provided.

Sir John. No, Doll, no ; Kent's too hot, Doll,
Kent's too hot. The weathercock of Wrotham
will crow no longer ; we have pluck'd him, he has
lost his feathers ; I have prun'd him bare, left him
thrice ; he is moulted, he is moulted, wench.

Doll. I might have gone to service again ; old
master Harpool told me he would provide me a
mistress.

Sir John. Peace, Doll, peace. Come, mad wench,
I 'll make thee an honest woman ; we 'll into Lancashire to our friends : the troth is, I 'll marry thee.
We want but a little money, and money we will
have, I warrant thee. Stay ; who comes here ?
Some Irish villain methinks, that has slain a man,
and now is rifling of him. Stand close, Doll ; we 'll
see the end.

Enter an Irishman *with his dead Master. He lays*
him down, and rifles him.

Irishm. Alas poe master, sir Richard Lee ; be
Saint Patrick, Ise rob and cut thy trote, for de
shain, and dy mony, and dy gold ring. Be me
truly, Ise love de well, but now dow be kill, dow
be dirty knave.[44]

S. John. Stand, sirrah ; what art thou ?

Irishm. Be Saint Patrick, mester, Ise poor Irisman ; Ise a leufter.[45]

S. John. Sirrah, sirrah, you're a damn'd rogue ;
you have kill'd a man here, and rifled him of all
that he has. 'Sblood you rogue, deliver, or I 'll
not leave you so much as a hair above your shoulders, you whorson Irish dog.   [*Robs him.*

Irishm. We's me ! by saint Patrick, Ise kill my
mester for his shain and his ring ; and now Ise be
rob of all. Me's undo.

S. John. Avaunt, you rascal ; go sirrah, be walking. Come Doll, the devil laughs when one thief
robs another. Come, wench, we 'll to St. Albans,
and revel in our bower, my brave girl.

Doll. O, thou art old sir John, when all 's done,
i'faith.   [*Exeunt.*

SCENE III.— St. Albans. *The entrance of a*
Carrier's *Inn.*

Enter Host *and the* Irishman.

Irishm. Be me tro, mester, Ise poor Irisman, Ise
want ludging. Ise have no mony, Ise starve and
cold : good master give hur some meat ; Ise famise
and tye.

Host. 'Faith, fellow, I have no lodging, but what
I keep for my guests. As for meat, thou shalt have
as much as there is ; and if thou wilt lie in the
barn, there 's fair straw, and room enough.

Irishm. Ise tank my mester heartily.

Host. Ho, Robin.

Enter ROBIN.

Rob. Who calls ?

Host. Shew this poor Irishman to the barn ; go
sirrah.   [*Exeunt* ROB. *and* Irishm.

Enter Carrier *and* KATE.

Car. Who's within here? who looks to the horses? Uds heart, here's fine work; the hens in the maunger, and the hogs in the litter. A bots 'found you all; here's a house well look'd to, i'faith.

Kate. Mas gaff Club, Ise very cawd.

Car. Get in, Kate, get in to fire, and warm thee. John ostler.

Host. What, gaffer Club! Welcome to St. Albans. How does all our friends in Lancashire?

Enter Ostler.

Car. Well, God-a-mercy. John, how does Tom? where is he?

Ostl. Tom's gone from hence; he's at the three horse-loaves[46] at Stony-Stratford. How does old Dick Dun?

Car. Uds heart, old Dun has bin moyr'd in a slough in Brick-hill-lane. A plague 'found it! yonder's such abomination weather as was never seen.

Ostl. Uds heart! Thief! 'a shall have one half peck of pease and oats more for that, as I am John ostler; he has been ever as good a jade as ever travelled.

Car. 'Faith, well said, old Jack; thou art the old lad still.

Ostl. Come, gaffer Club, unload, unload, and get to supper.　　　　　　　　　　　　　[*Exeunt.*

SCENE IV.—*The Same. A Room in the* Carrier's *Inn.*

Enter Host, LORD COBHAM, *and* HARPOOL.

Host. Sir, you're welcome to this house, to such as is here with all my heart; but I fear your lodging will be the worst. I have but two beds, and they are both in a chamber; and the carrier and his daughter lies in the one, and you and your wife must lie in the other.

Cob. 'Faith, sir, for myself I do not greatly pass: My wife is weary, and would be at rest, For we have travell'd very far to day; We must be content with such as you have.

Host. But I cannot tell what to do with your man.

Har. What? hast thou never an empty room in thy house for me?

Host. Not a bed in troth. There came a poor Irishman, and I lodg'd him in the barn, where he has fair straw, although he have nothing else.

Har. Well, mine host, I pr'ythee help me to a pair of clean sheets, and I'll go lodge with him.

Host. By the mass that thou shalt, a good pair of hempen sheets were ne'er lain in: come.
　　　　　　　　　　　　　[*Exeunt.*

SCENE V.—*The Same. A Street.*

Enter Mayor, Constable, *and* Watch.

Mayor. What? have you search'd the town?

Con. All the town, sir; we have not left a house unsearch'd that uses to lodge.

Mayor. Surely my lord of Rochester was then deceiv'd,
Or ill inform'd of sir John Oldcastle;
Or if he came this way, he's past the town:
He could not else have scap'd you in the search.

Con. The privy watch hath been abroad all night;
And not a stranger lodgeth in the town
But he is known; only a lusty priest
We found in bed with a young pretty wench,
That says she is his wife, yonder at the Shears:
But we have charg'd the host with his forth-coming
To-morrow morning.

Mayor. What think you best to do?

Con. 'Faith, master mayor, here's a few straggling houses beyond the bridge, and a little inn where carriers use to lodge; although I think surely he would ne'er lodge there: but we'll go search, and the rather because there came notice to the town the last night of an Irishman, that had done a murder, whom we are to make search for.

Mayor. Come then, I pray you, and be circumspect.
　　　　　　　　　　　　　[*Exeunt* Mayor, Con., &c.

SCENE VI.—*The Same. Before the* Carrier's *Inn.*

Enter Watch.

1st Watch. First beset the house, before you begin to search.

2nd Watch. Content; every man take a several place.　　　　　　　　　　[*A noise within.*
"Keep, keep, strike him down there, down with him."

Enter, from the Inn, the Mayor *and* Constable, *with the* Irishman *in Harpool's apparel.*

Con. Come, you villanous heretic, tell us where your master is.

Irishm. Vat mester?

Mayor. Vat mester, you counterfeit rebel? This shall not serve your turn.

Irishm. Be Sent Patrick I ha' no mester.

Con. Where's the lord Cobham, sir John Oldcastle, that lately escaped out of the Tower?

Irishm. Vat lort Cobham?

Mayor. You counterfeit, this shall not serve
you: we'll torture you, we'll make you to confess where that arch-heretic is. Come, bind him
fast.

Irishm. Ahone, ahone, ahone, a cree.

Con. Ahone! you crafty rascal?   [*Exeunt.*

SCENE VII.—*The Same. The Yard of the Inn.*

Enter Lord Cobham *in his Night-gown.*

Cob. Harpool, Harpool, I hear a marvellous noise
About the house. God warrant us, I fear
We are pursued. What, Harpool?

Har. [*From the barn.*] Who calls there?

Cob. 'Tis I; dost thou not hear a noise about
the house?

Har. [*From the Barn.*] Yes, marry do I.
    'Zounds I cannot find
My hose. This Irish rascal, that lodg'd with me
All night, hath stolen my apparel, and
Has left me nothing but a lowsy mantle,
And a pair of brogues. Get up, get up, and, if
The carrier and his wench be yet asleep,
Change you with him, as he hath done with me,
And see if we can scape.   [*Exit* Cob.

SCENE VIII.—*The Same.*

A noise about the House for some time. Then Enter
  Harpool *in the* Irishman's *Apparel; the* Mayor,
  Constable, *and* Watch of St. Albans *meeting him.*

Con. Stand close, here comes the Irishman that
did the murder; by all tokens this is he.

Mayor. And perceiving the house beset, would
get away. Stand, sirrah.

Har. What art thou that bidd'st me stand?

Con. I am the officer: and am come to search
for an Irishman, such a villain as thyself, that hast
murder'd a man this last night by the highway.

Har. 'Sblood, constable, art thou mad? am I an
Irishman?

Mayor. Sirrah, we'll find you an Irishman before
    we part:
Lay hold upon him.

Con. Make him fast. O thou bloody rogue!

Enter Lord and Lady Cobham, *in the Apparel of*
  the Carrier *and his* Daughter.

Cob. What will these ostlers sleep all day? Good

morrow, good morrow. Come wench, come. Saddle,
saddle; now afore God two fair days, ha?

Con. Who goes there?

Mayor. O 'tis Lancashire carrier; let them pass.

Cob. What, will no body ope the gates here?
Come, let's in to stable, to look to our capons.
            [*Exeunt* Lord *and* L. Cob.

Car. [*Within.*] Host. Why ostler? Zooks here's
such abomination company of boys. A pox of this
pigstye at the house' end; it fills all the house full
of fleas. Ostler, ostler.

Enter Ostler.

Ostl. Who calls there? what would you have?

Car. [*Within.*] Zooks, do you rob your guests?
Do you lodge rogues, and slaves, and scoundrels, ha?
They ha' stolen our clothes here. Why ostler.

Ostl. A murrain choke you: what a bawling you
keep!

Enter Host.

Host. How now? what would the carrier have?
Look up there.

Ostl. They say that the man and the woman that
lay by them, have stolen their clothes.

Host. What, are the strange folks up, that came
in yesternight?

Con. What, mine host, up so early?

Host. What, master mayor, and master constable?

Mayor. We are come to seek for some suspected
    persons,
And such as here we found have apprehended.

Enter Carrier *and* Kate, *in* Lord *and* Lady
    Cobham's *Clothes.*

Con. Who comes here?

Car. Who comes here? a plague 'found 'em.
You bawl, quoth-a; ods-heart I'll forswear your
house; you lodg'd a fellow and his wife by us, that
ha' run away with our 'parel, and left us such gew-
gaws here:—Come Kate, come to me; thou's diz-
eard i'faith.[47]

Mayor. Mine host, know you this man?

Host. Yes, master mayor, I'll give my word for
him. Why neighbour Club, how comes this gear
about?

Kate. Now a foul on 't, I cannot make this gew-
gaw stand on my head.

Mayor. How came this man and woman thus
    attired?

Host. Here came a man and woman hither this
    last night,
Which I did take for substantial people,

And lodg'd all in one chamber by these folks;
Methinks they have been so bold to change apparel,
And gone away this morning ere they rose.

Mayor. That was that traitor Oldcastle that thus
Escap'd us. Make hue and cry yet after him;
Keep fast that traitorous rebel his servant there:
Farewell, mine host.   [*Exit* Mayor.

Car. Come Kate Owdham,[48] thou and I's trimly
dizard.

Kate. I'faith, neam Club, Ise wot ne'er what to
do, Ise be so flouted and so shouted at; but by the
mess Ise cry.   [*Exeunt* Car. *and his* Daughter,
                            Host, HAR., Constables, &c.

SCENE IX.—*A Wood near* St. Albans.

Enter LORD AND LADY COBHAM *disguised.*

Cob. Come, madam, happily escap'd. Here let
     us sit;
This place is far remote from any path;
And here a while our weary limbs may rest
To take refreshing, free from the pursuit
Of envious Rochester.

L. Cob. But where, my lord,
Shall we find rest for our disquiet minds?
There dwell untamed thoughts, that hardly stoop
To such abasement of disdained rags:
We were not wont to travel thus by night,
Especially on foot.

Cob. No matter, love;
Extremities admit no better choice,
And, were it not for thee, say froward time
Impos'd a greater task, I would esteem it
As lightly as the wind that blows upon us.
But in thy sufferance I am doubly task'd;
Thou wast not wont to have the earth thy stool,
Nor the moist dewy grass thy pillow, nor
Thy chamber to be the wide horizon.

L. Cob. How can it seem a trouble, having you
A partner with me in the worst I feel?
No, gentle lord, your presence would give ease
To death itself, should he now seize upon me.
     [*She produces some bread and cheese, and a bottle.*
Behold, what my foresight hath underta'en,
For fear we faint; they are but homely cates;
Yet sauc'd with hunger, they may seem as sweet
As greater dainties we were wont to taste.

Cob. Praise be to Him whose plenty sends both
     this
And all things else our mortal bodies need!
Nor scorn we this poor feeding, nor the state
We now are in; for what is it on earth,
Nay under heaven, continues at a stay?

Ebbs not the sea, when it hath overflow'd?
Follows not darkness when the day is gone?
And see we not sometimes the eye of heaven
Dimm'd with o'erflying clouds? There's not that
     work
Of careful nature, or of cunning art,
How strong, how beauteous, or how rich it be,
But falls in time to ruin. Here, gentle madam,
In this one draught I wash my sorrow down.
                     [*Drinks.*

L. Cob. And I, encourag'd with your cheerful
     speech,
Will do the like.

Cob. 'Pray God, poor Harpool come.
If he should fall into the bishop's hands,
Or not remember where we bade him meet us,
It were the thing of all things else, that now
Could breed revolt in this new peace of mind.

L. Cob. Fear not, my lord, he's witty to devise,
And strong to execute a present shift.

Cob. That power be still his guide, hath guided
     us!
My drowsy eyes wax heavy; early rising,
Together with the travel we have had,
Makes me that I could gladly take a nap,
Were I persuaded we might be secure.

L. Cob. Let that depend on me: whilst you do
     sleep,
I'll watch that no misfortune happen us.

Cob. I shall, dear wife, be too much trouble to
     thee.

L. Cob. Urge not that:
My duty binds me, and your love commands
I would I had the skill, with tuned voice
To draw on sleep with some sweet melody.
But imperfection, and unaptness too,
Are both repugnant: fear inserts the one;
The other nature hath denied me use.
But what talk I of means to purchase that
Is freely happen'd? Sleep with gentle hand
Hath shut his eye-lids. O victorious labour,
How soon thy power can charm the body's sense?
And now thou likewise climb'st unto my brain,
Making my heavy temples stoop to thee.
Great God of heaven from danger keep us free!
                     [*Falls asleep.*

Enter SIR RICHARD LEE, *and his* Servants.

Sir Rich. A murder closely done? and in my
     ground?
Search carefully; if any where it were,
This obscure thicket is the likeliest place.
                     [*Exit a* Serv.

Re-enter Servant *bearing a dead body.*

Ser. Sir, I have found the body stiff with cold,
And mangled cruelly with many wounds.
    Sir Rich. Look, if thou know'st him; turn his
        body up.
Alack, it is my son, my son and heir,
Whom two years since I sent to Ireland,
To practise there the discipline of war;
And coming home, (for so he wrote to me,)
Some savage heart, some bloody devilish hand,
Either in hate, or thirsting for his coin,
Hath here sluic'd out his blood.   Unhappy hour!
Accursed place! but most inconstant fate,
That hadst reserv'd him from the bullet's fire,
And suffer'd him to scape the wood-kerns' fury,[49]
Didst here ordain the treasure of his life,
Even here within the arms of tender peace,
To be consum'd by treason's wasteful hand!
And, which is most afflicting to my soul,
That this his death and murder should be wrought
Without the knowledge by whose means 'twas done.
    2nd Ser. Not so, sir; I have found the authors
        of it.
See where they sit; and in their bloody fists
The fatal instruments of death and sin.
    Sir Rich. Just judgment of that power, whose
        gracious eye,
Loathing the sight of such a heinous fact,
Dazzled their senses with benumbing sleep,
'Till their unhallow'd treachery was known.
Awake ye monsters, murderers awake;
Tremble for horror; blush, you cannot choose,
Beholding this inhuman deed of yours.
    Cob. What mean you, sir, to trouble weary souls,
And interrupt us of our quiet sleep?
    Sir Rich. O devilish! can you boast unto your-
       selves
Of quiet sleep, having within your hearts
The guilt of murder waking, that with cries
Deafs the loud thunder, and solicits heaven
With more than mandrakes' shrieks for your offence?
    L. Cob. What murder? You upbraid us wrong-
       fully.
    Sir Rich. Can you deny the fact? see you not here
The body of my son, by you misdone?[50]
Look on his wounds, look on his purple hue:
Do we not find you where the deed was done?
Were not your knives fast closed in your hands?
Is not this cloth an argument beside,
Thus stain'd and spotted with his innocent blood?
These speaking characters, were there nothing else
To plead against you, would convict you both.

To Hertford with them, where the 'sizes now
Are kept; their lives shall answer for my son's
Lost life.
    Cob. As we are innocent, so may we speed.
    Sir Rich. As I am wrong'd, so may the law pro-
       ceed.   [*Exeunt.*

SCENE X.—St. Albans.

Enter the BISHOP OF ROCHESTER, Constable *of*
St. Albans, *with* SIR JOHN *and* DOLL, *and the*
Irishman *in* Harpool's *Apparel.*

    Roch. What intricate confusion have we here?
Not two hours since we apprehended one
In habit Irish, but in speech not so;
And now you bring another, that in speech
Is Irish, but in habit English: yea,
And more than so, the servant of that heretic
Lord Cobham.
    Irishm. Fait me be no servant of de lort Cob-
ham; me be Mack-Shane of Ulster.
    Roch. Otherwise call'd Harpool of Kent; go to,
       sir,
You cannot blind us with your broken Irish.
    Sir John. Trust me, lord bishop, whether Irish
       or English,
Harpool or not Harpool, that I leave to the trial:
But sure I am, this man by face and speech,
Is he that murder'd young sir Richard Lee;
(I met him presently upon the fact)
And that he slew his master for that gold,
Those jewels, and that chain, I took from him.
    Roch. Well, our affairs do call us back to London,
So that we cannot prosecute the cause,
As we desire to do; therefore we leave
The charge with you, to see they be convey'd
                  [*To the* Constable.
To Hertford 'sizes: both this conterfeit,
And you, sir John of Wrotham, and your wench:
For you are culpable as well as they,
Though not for murder, yet for felony.
But since you are the means to bring to light
This graceless murder, you shall bear with you
Our letters to the judges of the bench,
To be your friends in what they lawful may.
    Sir John. I thank your lordship.   [*Exeunt.*

SCENE XI.—Hertford. *A Hall of Justice.*

Enter Gaoler *and his* Servant, *bringing forth* LORD
COBHAM *in Irons.*

    Gaol. Bring forth the prisoners, see the court
       prepar'd;

The justices are coming to the bench:
So, let him stand; away and fetch the rest.
[*Exit* Serv.

Cob. O, give me patience to endure this scourge,
Thou that art fountain of this virtuous stream;
And though contempt, false witness, and reproach
Hang on these iron gyves, to press my life
As low as earth, yet strengthen me with faith,
That I may mount in spirit above the clouds.

Re-enter Gaoler's Servant, *bringing in* LADY
COBHAM *and* HARPOOL.

Here comes my lady. Sorrow, 'tis for her
Thy wound is grievous; else I scoff at thee.
What, and poor Harpool, art thou i' the briars too?
Har. I'faith, my lord, I am in, get out how I can.
L. Cob. Say, gentle lord, (for now we are alone,
And may confer) shall we confess in brief
Of whence, and what we are, and so prevent
The accusation is commenc'd against us?
Cob. What will that help us? Being known,
        sweet love,
We shall for heresy be put to death,
For so they term the religion we profess.
No, if we die, let this our comfort be,
That of the guilt impos'd our souls are free.
Har. Ay, ay, my lord; Harpool is so resolv'd.
I reck of death the less, in that I die
Not by the sentence of that envious priest.
L. Cob. Well, be it then according as heaven
        please.

Enter the Judge of Assize, *and* Justices; *the* Mayor
of St. Albans, LORD *and* LADY POWIS, *and* SIR
RICHARD LEE. *The* Judge *and* Justices *take
their places on the Bench.*

Judge. Now, master mayor, what gentleman is
        that
You bring with you before us to the bench?
Mayor. The lord Powis, an if it like your honour,
And this his lady travelling toward Wales,
Who, for they lodg'd last night within my house,
And my lord bishop did lay wait for such,
Were very willing to come on with me,
Lest, for their sakes, suspicion we might wrong.
Judge. We cry your honour mercy; good my
        lord,
Will 't please you take your place. Madam, your
        ladyship
May here, or where you will, repose yourself,
Until this business now in hand be past.
L. Pow. I will withdraw into some other room,
So that your lordship and the rest be pleas'd.

Judge. With all our hearts: Attend the lady
        there.
Pow. Wife, I have ey'd yon prisoners all this
        while,
And my conceit doth tell me, 'tis our friend
The noble Cobham, and his virtuous lady. [*Aside.*
L. Pow. I think no less: are they suspected for
        this murder?
Pow. What it means
I cannot tell, but we shall know anon.
Mean time, as you pass by them, ask the question:
But do it secretly that you be not seen,
And make some sign, that I may know your mind.
        [*She passes over the Stage by them.*
L. Pow. My lord Cobham! Madam!
Cob. No Cobham now, nor madam, as you love us;
But John of Lancashire, and Joan his wife.
L. Pow. O tell, what is it that our love can do
To pleasure you, for we are bound to you?
Cob. Nothing but this, that you conceal our
        names;
So, gentle lady, pass; for being spied——
L. Pow. My heart I leave, to bear part of your
        grief.   [*Exit* L. Pow.
Judge. Call the prisoners to the bar. Sir Richard
        Lee,
What evidence can you bring against these people,
To prove them guilty of the murder done?
Sir Rich. This bloody towel, and these naked
        knives:
Beside, we found them sitting by the place
Where the dead body lay within a bush.
Judge. What answer you, why law should not
        proceed,
According to this evidence given in,
To tax you with the penalty of death?
Cob. That we are free from murder's very thought,
And know not how the gentleman was slain.
1st Just. How came this linen-cloth so bloody
        then?
L. Cob. My husband hot with travelling, my lord,
His nose gush'd out a bleeding; that was it.
2nd Just. But how came your sharp edged knives
        unsheath'd?
L. Cob. To cut such simple victual as we had.
Judge. Say we admit this answer to those ar-
        ticles,
What made you in so private a dark nook,
So far remote from any common path,
As was the thick,[51] where the dead corpse was
        thrown?
Cob. Journeying, my lord, from London, from
        the term,[52]

Down into Lancashire, where we do dwell,
And what with age and travel being faint,
We gladly sought a place where we might rest,
Free from resort of other passengers;
And so we stray'd into that secret corner.

   Judge. These are but ambages to drive off time;
And linger justice from her purpos'd end.

   Enter Constable, *with the* Irishman, Sir John,
       and Doll.

But who are these?

   Con. Stay judgment, and release those innocents;
For here is he whose hand hath done the deed
For which they stand indicted at the bar;
This savage villain, this rude Irish slave:
His tongue already hath confess'd the fact,
And here is witness to confirm as much.

   Sir John. Yes, my good lord; no sooner had he
     slain
His loving master for the wealth he had,
But I upon the instant met with him:
And what he purchas'd with the loss of blood,
With strokes I presently bereav'd him of:
Some of the which is spent; the rest remaining
I willingly surrender to the hands
Of old sir Richard Lee, as being his:
Beside, my lord judge, I do greet your honour
With letters from my lord of Rochester.

                     [Delivers a Letter.

   Sir Rich. Is this the wolf whose thirsty throat
     did drink
My dear son's blood? art thou the cursed snake
He cherish'd, yet with envious piercing sting
Assaild'st him mortally? Wer't not that the
     law
Stands ready to revenge thy cruelty,
Traitor to God, thy master, and to me,
These hands should be thy executioner.

   Judge. Patience, sir Richard Lee, you shall have
     justice.
The fact is odious; therefore take him hence,
And being hang'd until the wretch be dead,
His body after shall be hang'd in chains,
Near to the place where he did act the murder.

   Irishm. Prethee, lord shudge, let me have mine
own clothes, my strouces there;[53] and let me be

hang'd in a wyth[54] after my country, the Irish
fashion.

   Judge. Go to; away with him. And now, sir
     John.   *[Exeunt* Gaoler *and* Irishm.
Although by you this murder came to light,
Yet upright law will not hold you excus'd,
For you did rob the Irishman; by which
You stand attainted here of felony:
Beside, you have been lewd, and many years
Led a lascivious, unbeseeming life.

   Sir John. O but, my lord, sir John repents, and
     he will mend.

   Judge. In hope thereof, together with the favour
My lord of Rochester intreats for you,
We are contented that you shall be prov'd.

   Sir John. I thank your lordship.

   Judge. These other, falsely here
Accus'd, and brought in peril wrongfully,
We in like sort do set at liberty.

   Sir Rich. And for amends,
Touching the wrong unwittingly I have done,
I give these few crowns.

   Judge. Your kindness merits praise, sir Richard
     Lee;
So let us hence. *[Exeunt all except* Pow. *and* Cob.

   Pow. But Powis still must stay.
There yet remains a part of that true love
He owes his noble friend, unsatisfied
And unperform'd; which first of all doth bind me
To gratulate your lordship's safe delivery;
And then entreat, that since unlook'd-for thus
We here are met, your honour would vouchsafe
To ride with me to Wales, where, to my power,
Though not to quittance those great benefits
I have receiv'd of you, yet both my house,
My purse, my servants, and what else I have,
Are all at your command. Deny me not:
I know the bishop's hate pursues you so,
As there's no safety in abiding here.

   Cob.' Tis true, my lord, and God forgive him
     for it.

   Pow. Then let us hence. You shall be straight
     provided
Of lusty geldings: and once enter'd Wales,
Well may the bishop hunt; but, spite his face,
He never more shall have the game in chace.

                     [Exeunt.

NOTES TO SIR JOHN OLDCASTLE.

(PART THE FIRST.)

———◆———

¹ *It is no pamper'd glutton we present,*
Nor aged counsellor to youthful sin.

An allusion to Shakspere's character of Sir John Falstaff, supposed to have been originally called Sir John Oldcastle. See note 8 to *Henry the Fourth*, Part I.

² *Py coss plut.*

The Welshman's corruption of a very solemn oath—by God's blood.

³ *Is a dirty knave.*

I have substituted the word *dirty* for one of similar signification, but exceedingly offensive.

⁴ *To summon him unto the arches.*

The court of *arches*, so called because it was anciently held in the church of St. Mary-le-Bow, Sancta Maria, de *arcubus*.

⁵ *A sumner.*

An apparitor or messenger employed to summon persons to appear in the spiritual court.

⁶ *Those golden ruddocks.*

The *ruddock* is the robin-redbreast. The word is here used as a cant term for money. The vulgar still call our gold coins gold-finches.

⁷ *And shrive him of it.*

That is, rob or unburden him of it; to *shrive* a man was to ease him from the burden of his sins by receiving his confession.

⁸ *'Sessed,* i.e. assessed, taxed.

⁹ *Show me such two men now : no, no ; your backs,*
Your backs.

That is, such charitable men as your father and grandfather no longer exist; for the present generation spend in superfluous dressing that money which the last bestowed upon the poor. So in *King Henry the Eighth*—

—————— Many
Have broke their backs with laying manors on them
For this great journey.

¹⁰ *A hundred tall fellows.*

That is, stout fighting men.

¹¹ *There ; tough old sheep-skins bare dry meat.*

Perhaps we should read—tough old sheepskins *but* dry meat.

¹² *I would ingle this old serving-man.*

Probably *angle* him; throw out lures to win him. Steevens says—" Perhaps it means the same as *inveigle* him, and may be a contraction of that word."

¹³ *I'faith I'll ferk you.*

The word *ferk* or *firk* is used in various senses by the old writers, but its ordinary meaning appears to be *to*

chastise. Thus in *Henry the Fifth,* when Pistol learns that the name of his French prisoner is Fer, he threatens him as follows :—" Master Fer! I'll fer him, and *firk* him, and ferret him." Harpool is pretending to reprove the constable for his gaiety.

¹⁴ *I pledge you, sir, and thank you therefore, and I pray*
you let it come.

These words are conjectured to be part of some old ballad.

¹⁵ *Truly you are as full of favour as a man may be.*

That is, you are as handsome as a man may be.

¹⁶ *You lion of Cotswold.*

That is, you old ram. The *Cotswold* hills in Gloucestershire were famous on account of the number of sheep fed upon them. A Cotswold lion, therefore, meant a male Cotswold sheep; as an Essex lion is still the cant term for an Essex calf.

¹⁷ *I am a singer, a drinker, a bencher.*

A *bencher* was a tavern idler, a lounger upon the benches placed outside public houses for the accommodation of those who in fine weather liked to take their refreshment in the open air. Thus, Prince Hal says to Falstaff, " Thou art so fat-witted with drinking of old sack, and unbuttoning thee after supper, *and sleeping upon benches at noon*," &c.

¹⁸ *God dild ye.*

That is, yield ye, requite ye.

¹⁹ *Tilly vally.*

An interjection of contempt.

²⁰ *Every jack shall have a skull,* i.e. a helmet.

²¹ *Craving no remorse at all.*

No mercy or pity.

²² *Not of pretensed malice.*

Malice aforethought. Pretence in Shakspere commonly means design.

²³ *Prelate, thou ly'st, even in thy greasy maw.*

Cobham here sneers at sacerdotal luxury. You lie in your greasy over-fed throat.

²⁴ *Knowing him to be a paritor.*

That is, an *apparitor,* or summoner.

²⁵ *Intending reformation of religion.*

Intending and *pretending* were anciently considered as synonymous.

²⁶ *But will ye not take Cowling for your host?*

Cowling was the name of Lord Cobham's seat in Kent. It was a castle of such great strength that its builder, fearful of exciting the jealousy of his sovereign, had the following inscription engraved on a scroll, and fixed in front of the eastern tower, by the principal entrance :—

> Knoweth that beth and shall be
> That I am made in help of the contre ;
> In knowing of which thing,
> This is charter and witnessing.

27 ———— *What business should let You to be merry.*

To *let* is an obsolete expression for to hinder. Thus in *Hamlet*—

> By heaven, I 'll make a ghost of him that *lets* me.

28 *He 's broke into a several.*

That is, into an enclosed field appropriated to corn or meadow. Some one observed of a lord that was newly married, that he grew fat; "Yes," said Sir Walter Raleigh, "any beast will grow fat, if you take him from the *common* and graze him in the *several*." This word occurs in *Love's Labour's Lost*, and also in *The Rival Friends*, 1632—

> —— My sheep have quite disgrest
> Their bounds, and leap'd into the *several*.

29 *Dun is the mouse.*

A proverbial expression, probably signifying, keep a good heart, be courageous. See note 52 to the *London Prodigal*.

30 *Which, ere the sun to-morrow shine.*

The metre of this line is defective. Malone suggests that perhaps the author wrote—

> Which ere the sun to-morrow shine *upon us*.

31 *Where the devil are all my old thieves? Falstaff that villain is so fat, he cannot get on his horse.*

From this passage it is certain that *Sir John Oldcastle* was written after the first part of Shakspere's *Henry the Fourth*, or the author could not have alluded to Falstaff's thieving exploits; and *probable* that it was written before the appearance of the second part, or he would have known that king Henry had banished Falstaff, and condemned him to reformation.

32 *I am a pitiful thief*, i.e. a merciful one.

33 *We will revel in our bevor.*

Probably this is a corruption, for in a subsequent scene Sir John says to Doll—" We'll to St. Alban's, *and revel in our bower*, and the same word might have been intended here. But Mr. Steevens explains *bevor* to mean a luncheon before dinner; something eaten in order to drink with it.

34 *I'll make some good boot among them.*

Some gain or plunder; perhaps the author wrote *booty*.

35 *Passage if you please.*

Passage was the name of a game at tables.

36 *Edge ye, good fellows*, i.e. sit sideways; sit closer.

37 *'Tis I must shred the priest.*

Probably, *shrive* the priest, though *shred* will bear a meaning, i.e. strip him of everything he has.

38 *When, parson, when?*

An exclamation of impatience equivalent to,—when will you do it? how long must we wait?

39 ———— *Gentry is divine, But thou hast made it more than popular.*

Thou hast made it vulgar; by pandering to the passions of an ignorant people, thou hast degraded thyself to their level.

40 *Be laid forthwith.*

Be watched by persons directed to waylay and arrest all who attempt to leave the kingdom.

41 *Bevis of Hampton, Owleglass, the Friar and the Boy, Elinour Rumming, Robin Hood.*

These appear to have been exceedingly popular works in the time of Shakspere, and some of them are referred to in his undoubted works. *Bevis of Hampton*, or Southampton, is an extravagant story of knight-errantry ; *Owleglass* is a translation from the Dutch of *Uyle-Spegel*. In an old black-letter book without date, there is the following account of how " Howleglas was buried ."—" Thus as Howleglas was deade, then they brought him to be buryed. And as they put the coffyn into the pytte with II cordes, the corde at the fete brake, so that the fete of the coffyn fell into the botome of the pyt, and the coffyn stood bolt upryght in the middes of the grave. Then desired the people that stode about the grave that tyme, to let the coffyn to stand bolt upryght. For in his lyfe tyme he was a very marvelous man, and shall be buryed as marvailously ; and in this manner they left Howleglas." *The Friar and the Boy*, is a sample of our ancient ballad literature. It is bound up with twenty-five other curious tracts in the University Library at Cambridge, vol. D. 5.2. The commencement is as follows :—" Here begynneth a mery geste of the Frere and the Boye."

> God that dyed for us all,
> And dranke bothe eysell and gall,
> Brynge us out of bale !
> And gyve them good lyfe and longe,
> That lysteneth to my songe,
> Or tendeth to my tale.

The story itself is more comical than delicate. *Elinour Rumming* is a poem by Skelton, and the ballads concerning *Robin Hood* are still popular amongst us.

42 *I'll make you drink their ashes in Saint Margaret's ale.*

St. Margaret's ale is probably a cant name for water, that simple beverage being now sometimes called *Adam's ale*. The old copies read Saint *Marget's* ale, doubtless a corruption of Margaret's.

43 *We must nip the bung for these crowns.*

In the cant language of the thieves of our author's

time, to *nip a bung* was to cut a purse. It appears from Greene's *Art of Coney-catching*, that *cuttle* and *cuttle-boung* were the cant terms for the knife used by the sharpers of that age to cut the bottoms of purses, which were then worn hanging at the girdle: and in *Martin Mark-all's Apologie to the Bel-man of London*, 1610, it is said that " *Bung* is now used for a *pocket*, heretofore for a *purse*."

44 *Dow be dirty knave.*

I have here taken the same liberty with the text as that noticed in note 3; namely, the substitution of an inoffensive word for a very disgusting one of a similar signification.

45 *Ise u leufter*, i.e. a destitute vagrant.

46 *He's at the Three Horse-loaves.*

Dr. Percy informs us, on the authority of the Earl of Northumberland's *Household Book*, that horses were not so usually fed with corn loose in the manger, in the present manner, as with their provender made into loaves. Hence the sign of the house.

47 *Thou dizard i' faith.*

He means *dizzened*, gaudily dressed.

48 *Come Kate Owdham.*

Although Kate is called the carrier's daughter, she seems to have been intended for his niece. She calls him *neam* Club, a corruption of *eame* or uncle Club.

49 *The wood-kern's fury.*

The *kern* was the Irish light-armed soldier, but it appears also to be the name given to the wild Irish. From Spencer's *View of Ireland*, it appears that the mode of fighting generally adopted by the Irish kerns was to draw their enemies into an engagement in the thick woods with which their country abounded, or if they were obliged to fight in the open country, to fly for refuge, when defeated, to those almost impenetrable retreats. From this practice the epithet in question is probably derived.

50 *The body of my son, by you misdone.*

That is, destroyed; as to *do* is to make, so to *misdo* is to destroy. Thus misdeeds for criminal actions.

51 *The thick*, i.e. an abbreviation of thicket.

52 *Journeying, my lord, from London, from the term.*

Mr. Malone remarks, " The *law-terms* are mentioned in our ancient dramas as the great eras of business, pleasure, and profit. No one goes from any distant county to London till the term begins, or leaves the metropolis till the term ends. No book is published till the beginning of term. From that period shopkeepers hope for custom, and the players expect audiences. It should seem from the various passages of this kind in our old plays, that law-suits were more numerous formerly than at present."

53 *My strouces there.*

Strouces are trowsers, at that time a peculiarity of Irish costume.

54 *Let me be hanged in a with.*

That is, in a band made of twigs. Bacon says, " An Irish rebel put up a petition that he might be hanged in a *with*, and not in a halter, because it had been so used with former rebels."

H. T.

Bibliography

The following bibliography does not pretend to be exhaustive. It merely suggests a number of books, carefully selected, that may prove as useful and interesting to the reader as to the editor in connection with the material published in this collection of plays.

1. Adams, Joseph Q. *A Life of William Shakespeare*. Boston: Hougton Mifflin, 1927.
2. Arber, Edward, ed. *A Transcript of the Registers of the Company of Stationers of London, 1554–1640*. 5 vols. Gloucester, Mass.: Peter Smith.
3. Bradbrook, M. C. *Elizabethan Stage Conditions*. New York: Cambridge Univ. Press, 1932.
4. ———. *The Growth and Structure of Elizabethan Comedy*. New York: Hillary, 1955.
5. ———. *The Rise of the Common Player*. Cambridge, Mass.: Harvard Univ., 1962.
6. Bradley, A. C. *Shakespearean Tragedy*. New York: World, 1960.
7. Brandes, Georg. *William Shakespeare*. Havertown, Pa.: R. West, 1973.
8. Brooke, C. R. Tucker. *Shakespeare Apocrypha*. New York: Oxford Univ. Press, 1908.
9. Chambers, E. K. *The Elizabethan Stage*. 4 vols. New York: Oxford Univ. Press, 1923.
10. ———. *William Shakespeare: A Study of Facts and Problems*. 2 vols. New York: Oxford Univ. Press, 1930.
11. Chute, Marchette. *Shakespeare of London*. New York: Dutton, 1949.
12. Cowling, G. H. *Music on the Shakespearean Stage*. New York: Cambridge Univ. Press, 1913.

13. Doran, Madeleine. *Endeavors of Art*. Madison, Wis.: Univ. of Wisconsin Press, 1954.
14. Farnham, Willard. *The Medieval Heritage of Elizabethan Tragedy*. New York: Barnes & Noble, 1957.
15. Ford, Boris, ed. *The Age of Shakespeare*. New York: Penguin, 1962.
16. Gollancz, Israel, ed. *Studies in the First Folio*. London, 1924.
17. Gosson, Stephen. *The School of Abuse*. Edited by John P. Collier. New York: AMS Press, 1841.
18. Halliwell-Phillips, James O. *Outlines of the Life of Shakespeare*. 2 vols. New York: AMS Press, 1907.
19. Hamilton, A. C. *The Early Shakespeare*. San Marino, Calif.: Huntington Library, 1967.
20. Harbage, Alfred. *Shakespeare's Audience*. Gloucester, Mass.: Peter Smith.
21. Henslowe, Phillip. *Henslowe Papers*. Edited by Walter Wilson Greg. New York: AMS Press, 1907.
22. ————. *Henslowe's Diary*. Edited by Walter Wilson Greg. 2 vols. Folcroft, Pa.: Folcroft, 1904.
23. Herrick, Marvin T. *Tragicomedy*. Urbana, Ill.: Univ. of Illinois Press, 1962.
24. Holinshed, Raphael. *The Whole Volume of Chronicles*. London: 1587.
25. Jacob, Edward. *The History of the Town and Port of Feversham*. London: 1774.
26. Lerner, Laurence, ed. *Shakespearean Comedies*. London: Penguin Shakespeare Library, 1967.
27. Maxwell, Baldwin. *Studies in the Shakespeare Apocrypha*. New York: Greenwood Press, 1956.
28. Muir, Kenneth. *Shakespeare as Collaborator*. New York: Barnes & Noble, 1960.
29. Naylor, Edward W. *Shakespeare and Music*. Havertown, Pa.: R. West, 1973.
30. Onions, C. T. *A Shakespeare Glossary*. New York: Oxford Univ. Press, 1911.
31. Parrott, Thomas Marc. *William Shakespeare: A Handbook*. New York: Scribner, 1955.
32. Peterson, Douglas L. *Time, Tide and Tempest*. San Marino, Calif.: Huntington Library, 1972.
33. Pollard, A. W. *Shakespeare Folios and Quartos . . . 1594–1685*. New York: Cooper Square, 1970.
34. Quennell, Peter. *Shakespeare: A Biography*. New York: World, 1963.
35. Rose, E. "Shakespeare as an Adapter." *Macmillan's Magazine*, 1878.
36. Rossiter, Arthur P. *English Drama from Early Times to the Elizabethans*. New York: Barnes & Noble, 1962.
37. Rowse, A. L. *William Shakespeare: A Biography*. New York: Simon and Shuster, 1964.
38. Schelling, Felix E. *Elizabethan Playwrights*. New York: Benjamin Blom, 1925.
39. Schlegel, A. W. von, *Lectures on Dramatic Art and Literature*. London: George Bell & Sons, 1809–11.
40. Scott-Kilvert, Ian. *British Writers and Their Work*. Vol. 2. Lincoln, Nebr.: Univ. of Nebraska Press, 1966.
41. Simpson, Richard, ed. *School of Shakespeare*. 2 vols. New York: AMS Press, 1878.

42. Smith, Hallett. "Shakespeare's Romances," in *Huntington Library Quarterly* 27, 1964.

43. Swinburne, Algernon Charles. *A Study of Shakespeare*. Folcroft, Pa.: Folcroft, 1973.

44. Symonds, J. A. *Shakespeare's Predecessors in the English Drama*. Havertown, Pa.: R. West, 1973.

45. Thorndike, A. H. *Shakespeare's Theatre*. New York: Macmillan, 1928.

46. Tillyard, E. M. W. *Shakespeare's History Plays*. New York: Macmillan, 1962.

47. Tolman, Albert H. *Falstaff and Other Shakespearean Topics*. Havertown, Pa.: R. West, 1973.

48. Traversi, D. A. *An Approach to Shakespeare*. New York: Doubleday, 1969.